Ottemiller's Index to Plays in Collections

An author and title index to plays appearing in collections published between 1900 and early 1975

by

John M. Connor

and

Billie M. Connor

Sixth Edition
Revised and Enlarged

The Scarecrow Press, Inc.

Metuchen, N.J. 1976

Library of Congress Cataloging in Publication Data

Ottemiller, John Henry, 1916-1968.
Ottemiller's Index to plays in collections.

1. Drama--Bibliography. I. Connor, John M., 1908- II. Connor, Billie M., 1934- III. Title. IV. Title: Index to plays in collections.
Z5781.08 1976 [PN1655] 016.80882 71-166073
ISBN 0-8108-0919-2

Manufactured in the United States of America

A great while ago the world begun,
  With a hey, ho, the wind and the rain:
But that's all one, our play is done,
  And we'll strive to please you every day.

--Twelfth Night

CONTENTS

Preface to the Sixth Edition	vii
from the Introduction to the Fourth Edition	ix
Directions for Use	xii
Author Index	1
List of Collections Analyzed and Key to Symbols	205
Title Index	433

PREFACE TO THE SIXTH EDITION

This sixth edition of Ottemiller's Index to Plays in Collections now includes books published, in England and the United States, from 1900 through early 1975.

Play anthologies and collections of literature are indexed and identified following the criteria established in previous editions. These criteria are explained in the introduction to the fourth edition, immediately following this preface. A deviation from the selection criteria appears in this edition. In examining the over 685 titles representing potential collections (including English literature textbooks, college readers, etc.) there were several scholarly drama anthologies translated from the Chinese and Japanese. It was decided to include these because of the increasing importance of Oriental drama. We have encountered some contradictory authorities in the form of Oriental playwrights' names and it is hoped that the more responsible authorities have been selected.

To the fifth edition there have now been added 190 collections published from late 1970 through early 1975. This represents 293 new authors and 537 new plays. The work now indexes 10,351 copies of 3686 different plays by 1937 different authors. Collections analyzed total 1237.

Once again the compilers have had considerable difficulty in determining the accurate birth and death dates of authors and first performance dates of plays. As in the fifth edition, when no performance data is known, the date of completion or publication appears in parenthesis, and where such date is in doubt, it is given with a question mark. Considerable time and effort has been expended and some progress is evident in further verifying and completing the author and production dates information carried forward from the earlier editions.

Every effort has been made to guarantee complete accuracy of the contents of the new anthologies added. Every new collection has been located and examined. In case the compilers "fumbled or muffed their lines" please ask our publisher to "prompt" us, so the errors, and there are sure to be some in such a detailed undertaking, will not be perpetuated.

To many of our friends, colleagues and associates we owe much thanks: once again to the staff of the Literature Department of the Los Angeles Public Library, especially James Saunders and Roger Quimby; to Miss Elizabeth Betz at the Library of Congress; to Mrs. Linda Appel, Library School student at the University of California, Berkeley; and to the staff of the University of California, Los Angeles, Research Library.

The number of authors, collections and titles were added on a pocket computer and if this exercise is again undertaken; i.e., a seventh edition, the possibility of a computer printout will be explored. This will make possible a more simple coding of the collections, since present mnemonics are now in some instances cumbersome. More important, it will reduce the time interval between the deadline date for the inclusion of new collections, and the completion of the manuscript.

Los Angeles — John M. Connor
January 22, 1976 — Billie M. Connor

from the

INTRODUCTION TO THE FOURTH EDITION

Plays from the earliest times to the present day, from the Greeks to current Broadway and London successes, which have been published in play anthologies and collections of literature are indexed and identified in this volume. It is limited to books published in England and the United States from 1900 through 1962 [6th ed., early 1975].

The Index has been prepared for the following purposes: the location of plays which are not available locally in an author's works or in separate form; the location of duplicate copies of plays for class assignments, production groups, reading clubs, Little Theatre groups, amateur theatricals, and plays made current by revivals, the movies, or television; and the verification and identification of authors, dates, production dates, titles (English and foreign), partial titles, etc. The List of Collections Analyzed may serve as a buying guide both for filling in a library's book collection and for comparison in future buying.

A play anthology is defined as a collection of plays by three or more authors published in book form and usually cited by an editor's name or by title. Collections of general literature fall within that definition. Plays in foreign languages published in anthologies in England and the United States have been included. All editions of the same collection have been included when the contents of successive editions vary (see, for example, in the List of Collections Analyzed, entries under Moses, M. J.). If the contents do not vary, the earliest edition has been cited and indexed.

The index is further limited to dramatic literature, better defined as standard full length plays. Only complete texts of plays are indexed; partial or selected texts have been omitted. Children's

plays, amateur plays, one-act plays, radio and television plays, and holiday and anniversary plays and pageants have not been included. But--for the sake of completeness--such plays are indexed when they appear in books as defined above. Anthologies which contain only plays by William Shakespeare plus one-act plays, or fragments, or selections, have been excluded since Shakespeare's plays are so freely available. Anthologies of Chinese, Japanese, Burmese, Cretan, Tibetan and Turkish plays have been omitted because in the main they are selections and are generally of value only from a subject point of view. [Please note exceptions in Preface to the 6th Edition.]

An index to plays has two functions: (1) to identify plays indexed, and (2) to indicate their location in books. This Index is therefore arranged in three parts: (1) Author Index, (2) List of Collections Analyzed and Key to Symbols, and (3) Title Index.

For the purposes of identification, the following information is given in the Author Index: author's name and dates, title of the play, the date of first production, references from both original titles and variant translated titles, references from joint authors and any others who have some connection with the play either as supposed authors, attributed authors, or translators and adapters. Plays of unknown authorship are listed in the Author Index under the general heading Anonymous Plays. The translator is given for foreign plays translated into English. If an exact date cannot be determined, an approximate date is given and indicated by a question mark, e.g., 1891? This is particularly true of production dates. Authorities differ as to the first dates of production in many instances and anyone familiar with the circumstances of production will realize that errors cannot be totally avoided.

Plays in a foreign language are entered under the original title with references from translated titles. Foreign plays translated into English are entered under the English titles with references from translated titles. In all cases, foreign plays in English are to be distinguished by translator notes. If no translator appears, it is to be assumed that the play is in the original language.

The Title Index helps further to identify the plays. References have been made freely from all forms of the titles, especially

from variant titles, translated titles, and subtitles.

Each collection analyzed has been given a symbol which is used to refer from the Author Index to the List of Collections Analyzed and Key to Symbols; the List is arranged alphabetically by symbols. Under each book cited is a contents note of the plays in the volume, arranged alphabetically by authors. Numbers appended to the symbols in the Author Index (e.g., MOSS1) and to the titles of the plays in the contents notes are volume numbers and refer to the particular volume of a collection in which the play is printed. When volumes are better identified by year of issue, the year has been similarly used (e.g., BES41).

I wish to thank the many librarians who criticized the original plans for this work, the first, second, and third editions and who made the publication of this fourth edition, revised, enlarged and brought up to date, possible, by their enthusiasm and constructive suggestions.

John H. Ottemiller
1963

DIRECTIONS FOR USE

The main entry is the author entry in the Author Index. The following information is given: Author's name and dates, title of the play, the date of first production, and references from variant titles, e.g.,

Hodge, Merton, 1903-
    As it was in the beginning. See The Wind and the rain
    Grief goes over. 1935. FAMH
    The island. 1937. SIXP
    The wind and the rain. 1933. FAME
        Variant title: As it was in the beginning

Plays of unknown authorship are entered in the Author Index under the general heading, Anonymous plays, e.g.,

Anonymous plays
    A comedy called Misogonus. See Misogonus
    Common conditions. 1570? FARM
    The contract of marriage between wit and wisdom. 1579? FARM
        Variant titles: The marriage of wit and wisdom; Wit and wisdom
    The conversion of St. Paul (Digby). 15th cent. ADA, MAL, SWIT

Foreign plays translated into English are entered in the Author Index under the English titles with references from the original titles, e.g.,

Giacosa, Giuseppe, 1847-1906
    As the leaves fall. See Like falling leaves
    Come le foglie. See Like falling leaves
    Like falling leaves. 1900. Updegraff, E. and A., trs. MOSQ
        Variant titles: As the leaves fall; Come le foglie

Foreign plays in both the original language and in translation are entered in the Author Index under the original title with references from the translated titles. Foreign plays in English are to

be distinguished in all cases by translator notes. If no translator appears, it is to be assumed that the play is in the original language.

Destouches, Philippe Néricault, 1680-1754
The conceited count. See Le glorieux
Le glorieux. 1732. BRE
Aldington, R., tr. ALD
Variant title: The conceited count

Symbols (e.g., MOSS1) are used to refer from the Author Index to the List of Collections Analyzed and Key to Symbols, which are arranged alphabetically by symbols. Numbers appended to the symbols and to the titles of the plays in the contents notes are volume numbers and refer to the particular volume of a collection in which the play is printed. When volumes are better identified by year of issue, the year has been used similarly, (e.g., BES41).

In the Title Index reference is made from all titles, variant titles and subtitles to the author and title under which full information is to be found in the Author Index.

AUTHOR INDEX

ABBOTT, GEORGE, 1887- , and BISSELL, RICHARD
The pajama game (lyrics and music by Richard Adler and Jerry Ross; based on the novel, 7-1/2 cents, by Richard Bissell.) 1954. THEA54

-- and BRIDGERS, ANN PRESTON
Coquette. 1927. BES27

-- and GLEASON, JAMES
The fall guy. 1925. BES24

--See DUNNING, PHILIP; HOLM, JOHN CECIL; WEIDMAN, JEROME, jt. auths.

ABEL, LIONEL
Absalom. 1956. MACH
The death of Odysseus. 1953. PLAA

ABELL, KJELD, 1901-1961
Anna Sophie Hedvig. 1939.
Larsen, H., tr. SCAN2
Days on a cloud. 1947.
Roughton, A., and Bredsdorff, E., trs. SPR
Dronning gaar igen. See The queen on tour
The queen on tour. 1943.
Pearce, J., tr. CONT
Variant title: Dronning gaar igen

ABLEMAN, PAUL
Green Julia. 1972. BES72

ABSE, DANNIE, 1923-
House of cowards. 1960. DEAS, PLAN23

ACEVEDO HERNANDEZ, ANTONIO, 1886-
Cabrerita. 1927.
Bailey, W., tr. SSTE

ACHARD, MARCEL, 1889-1974
Auprès de ma blonde. See Behrman, Samuel Nathaniel. I know my love (adapted from)
Patate. See Rollo
Rollo (adapted by Felicity Douglas). 1956. PLAN20
Variant title: Patate

ACHESON, SAM HANNA, 1900-
We are besieged. 1941. THX

ACKLAND, RODNEY, 1908-
After October. 1936. FAMI
Before the party (based on a short story by W. Somerset Maugham). 1949. PLAN2
A dead secret. 1957. PLAN16
The diary of a scoundrel. See Ostrovsky, Alexander. The diary of a scoundrel (tr. and adapted by)
The old ladies. 1935. FAMG
Strange orchestra. 1932. FAMC

ADAM DE LA HALLE (Adam Le Boçus; Adam Le Bossu, pseuds.), ca. 1250-ca. 1306

Le jeu de la feuillée. 1275?
Axton, R., and Stevens, J., trs. AXT
Variant title: The play of the greensward
Le jeu de Robin et Marion. 1285?
Axton, R., and Stevens, J., trs. AXT
Mandel, O., tr. MAN
Variant title: The play of Robin and Marion
The play of Robin and Marion. See Le jeu de Robin et Marion
The play of the greensward. See Le jeu de la feuillée

ADAM LE BOÇUS. See Adam de la Halle

ADAM LE BOSSU. See Adam de la Halle

ADAMOV, ARTHUR, 1908-1970
All against all. 1952.
Gildea, D., tr. WELT
Variant title: Tous contre tous
Professor Toranne. 1953.
Bermel, A., tr. FOUF, TAUJ
Tous contre tous. See All against all

ADAMS, LEE, 1924-
Applause (lyrics by).
See Comden, Betty and Green, Adolph. Applause
"It's a bird, it's a plane, it's superman" (lyrics by).
See Newman, David and Benton, Robert. "It's a bird, it's a plane, it's superman."

ADDISON, JOSEPH, 1672-1719
Cato. 1713. DOB, EIGH, HAN, LIBR, MCM, MCMI, MOR, NET, STM, TAT, TAU, TUP, TUQ

ADE, GEORGE, 1866-1944
The college widow. 1904. COT
The county chairman. 1903. BES99

ADLER, RICHARD
The pajama game (lyrics and music by).
See Abbott, George and Bissell, Richard. The pajama game

A. E., pseud. See Russell, George William

AESCHYLUS, 525-456 B.C.
Agamemnon. 458 B.C.
Anon. tr. CHR, EVB1
Blackie, J., tr. BUCK, BUCL, BUCM
Campbell, L., tr. LAP
Cookson, G., tr. GRDB5
Hamilton, E., tr. EVC1, HAM, KRE, TREB, TREC1, TREE1, TREI1
Lattimore, R., tr. FIFT, GREP1, GRER1
Lucas, F., tr. LUCA, LUCAB, LUCAF
MacNeice, L., tr. ALLK, DEAP, DEAR, DEAS, FIFR, FREG, LIND, MACJ, MACL1, MACM1, MACN, MCKK1, SWA, VANV1, VON
Morshead, E., tr. HARC8, HOWE, HOWF, LOCM1, MAU, OAT1, OATE, OATH, ROBJA, THP, WARN1
Murray, G., tr. CAR, CARA, FEFT, TEN, TRE, TREA2
Plumptre, E., tr. HIB, HIBA, HIBB, HOUS, ROB, THOM, THON
Potter, R., tr. GREE
Robinson, C., tr. ROBK
Sylvester, W., tr. COOA
Thomson, G., tr. AUDE, DIZ, FIFV, HAPRL, ROBI, WEAV1
Vellacourt, P., tr. BENQ,

SOU, STY
Way, A., tr. PLAG
The choephori. See Choephoroe
Choephoroe. 458 B.C.
Arnott, D., tr. CLO, FOR
Cookson, G., tr. GRDB5
Lattimore, R., tr. GREP1, GRER2
Morshead, E., tr. HARC8, OAT1
Murray, G., tr. FEFT, TEN
Thomson, G., tr. AUDE, FIFV, ROBJ
Way, A., tr. PLAG
Variant titles: The choephori; The libation-bearers; The mourners
Eumenides. 458 B.C.
Cookson, G., tr. GRDB5
Lattimore, R., tr. GREP1, GRER3
Morshead, E., tr. HARC8, OAT1, OATE
Murray, G., tr. FEFT, TEN
Plumptre, E., tr. BAT1
Thomson, G., tr. AUDE, FIFT, FIFV, ROBJ
Way, A., tr. PLAG
Variant titles: The furies; The gracious ones
The furies. See Eumenides
The gracious ones. See Eumenides
Hepta epi Thebas. See The seven against Thebes
Hiketides. See The suppliants
The house of Atreus (trilogy: Agamemnon, Choephoroe, and Eumenides). See Agamemnon; Choephoroe; Eumenides; Oresteia
The libation-bearers. See Choephoroe
The mourners. See Choephoroe
Oresteia (trilogy: Agamemnon, Choephoroe, and Eumenides).
458 B.C.
ranged for the stage by A. V. Griffin). GRIF
See also Agamemnon; Choephoroe; Eumenides
The Persians, 472 B.C.
Anon. tr. WED
Bernadete, S., tr. GREP1
Cookson, G., tr. GRDB5
Potter, R., tr. OAT1
Prometheus bound. 478? B.C.
Anon. tr. ATT3
Blackie, J., tr. BUCK, BUCL, BUCM, CLF1, SEBO, SEBP
Browning, E., tr. CROS, DRA1, GREB2, GREE, MAST, MIK7, PLAB1
Cookson, G., tr. GRDB5
Dolin, E., and Sugg, A., trs. COOA
Grene, D., tr. GREN, GREP1, GRER1
Hamilton, E., tr. BURR, DOWN, FIFT, HAM, HARPL, MACM1
Havelock, E., tr. BARC
Lucas, F., tr. LUCA, LUCAB, LUCAF
McLeish, K., tr. MCKM
Mendell, C., tr. CLKW, ROBJ
More, P., tr. MURP, OAT1, OATE, OATH
Plumptre, E., tr. CROV, HARC8, SML
Walker, C., tr. BENSB1
Warner, R., tr. LIND
Whitelaw, R., tr. FEET
Variant titles: Prometheus desmotes; Prometheus vinctus
Prometheus desmotes. See Prometheus bound
Prometheus vinctus. See Prometheus bound
Septem contra Thebas. See The seven against Thebes
The seven against Thebes. 467 B.C.
Cookson, G., tr. GRDB5
Grene, D., tr. GREP1

Variant titles: Hepta epi Thebas; Septem contra Thebas
The suppliant maidens. See The suppliants
The suppliants. 492? B.C.
Bernadete, S., tr. GREP1
Cookson, G., tr. GRDB5
Morshead, E., tr. OAT1
Variant titles: Hiketides; The suppliant maidens

AFINOGENYEV, ALEKSANDR NIKOLAEVICH, 1904-1941
Distant point. See Far taiga
Far taiga. 1935. Bakshy, A., tr. BAKS
Variant titles: Distant point; Remote
Fear. 1931. Malamuth, C., tr. LYK
On the eve. 1942. Afinogenova, E., tr. SEVP
Remote. See Far taiga

AGEE, JAMES, 1909-1955
Abraham Lincoln, the early years. SHER
The bride comes to yellow sky (screen play; based on the story by Stephen Crane). 1971? SUT3
A death in the family. See Mosel, Tad. All the way home (based on)

AGENOUX, SOREN
Charles Dickens' Christmas carol. 1966. SLM

AIKEN, GEORGE L., 1820-1876
Life among the lowly. See Uncle Tom's cabin
Uncle Tom's cabin; or, Life among the lowly (based on the novel by Harriet Beecher Stowe). 1852. BLAI2, CEY, GARX, GATZA1, MONR, MOSS2

AIKINS, CARROLL
The god of gods. 1919. MAS2

AKINS, ZOE, 1886-1958
Declassee. 1919. BES19
The old maid. 1935. BES34

AKRITAS, LOUKIS, 1909-1965
Hostages.
Gianos, M., tr. GIA

ALARCON Y MENDOZA, JUAN RUIZ DE. See Ruiz de Alarcón y Mendoza, Juan

ALBEE, EDWARD, 1928-
The American dream. 1961. MAO, MCNB, REIO
A delicate balance. 1966. BES66
The sandbox. 1960. BARS, CORB, CUBH, PERT, PERU, SATI, SATJ, THOD
Tiny Alice. 1964. BES64, GARV
Who's afraid of Virginia Woolf? 1962. BES62, GARSA, GARZA4, REIL, TREJ
The zoo story. 1959. COK, FAM, GOLH, HOWP2, KERP, REIT, SCNT, SHR, WAIW

ALBERTI, RAFAEL, 1902-
Night and war in the Prado Museum. 1956.
Johnson, L., tr. BENA
Variant title: Noche de guerra en el Museo del Prado
Noche de guerra en el Museo del Prado. See Night and war in the Prado Museum

ALBERY, JAMES, 1838-1889
Two roses. 1870. ROWE

ALBERY, PETER
Anne Boleyn. 1956. PLAN14

ALDRIDGE, IRA, 1807-1867
The Black doctor. 1847. HARY

ALFIERI, VITTORIO, 1749-1803
Myrrha. 1788?
Bowring, E., tr. BAT5
Saul. 1784. BIN
Bowring, E., tr. CLF2

ALFRED, WILLIAM, 1922-
Hogan's goat. 1965. BES65, GARV

ALFRIEND, EDWARD M., 1843-? and WHEELER, ANDREW CARPENTER
The great diamond robbery. 1885. AMP8, CLA

ALI, AKHUND-ZATH FATH'. See Fath'Ali, Akhundzadah

ALLEN, JAY, 1922-
Forty carats. 1968. BES68

ALPERT, HOLLIS, (Robert Carroll, pseud.)
Heat lightning. BRNR

ALSINA, ARTURO, 1897-
La marca de fuego. 1926. ALPE

ALVAREZ QUINTERO, JOAQUIN, 1873-1944. See Alvarez Quintero, Serafín, jt. auth.

ALVAREZ QUINTERO, SERAFIN, 1871-1938, and ALVAREZ QUINTERO, JOAQUIN
An autumn morning. See A bright morning
A bright morning. 1905.
Castillo, C., and Overman, E., trs. DIK1
Floyd, L., tr. EDAD, WHF
Variant titles: An autumn morning; Mañana de sol; A sunny morning
The centenarian. See A hundred years old
Doña Clarines. 1909.
Granville-Barker, H., and H., trs. CHA, CHAN
A hundred years old. 1909.
Granville-Barker, H., and H., trs. PLAP3
Variant titles: The centenarian; Papá Juan: centenario
Malvaloca. 1912.
Fassett, J., tr. DIE
Mañana de sol. See A bright morning
Papá Juan: centenario. See A hundred years old
Pueblo de las mujeres. See The women's town
A sunny morning. See A bright morning
The women have their way. See The women's town
The women's town. 1912.
Turrell, C., tr. TUR
Variant titles: Pueblo de las mujeres; The women have their way

ALVARO, CORRADO, 1895-1956
The long night of Medea. 1949.
Friedman, E., tr. PLAC

ALYOSHIN, SAMUEL
Alone. 1956.
McLean, H., and Vickery, W., trs. MCKL
Variant title: Odna
Odna. See Alone

AMES, WINTHROP, 1871-1937
A kiss in Xanadu. 1932? LEV, LEVE

AMESCUA, ANTONIO MIRA DE. See Mira de Amescua, Antonio

ANCEY, GEORGES, pseud. See Curnieu, Georges de

ANDERSON, GARLAND, 1886-1939
Appearances. 1925. HARY

ANDERSON, MAXWELL, 1888-1959
Anne of the thousand days. 1948. BES48, GARW, OHL
The bad seed (based on the

novel by William March). 1954. BES54, RICI, THEA55
Barefoot in Athens. 1951. BARS, BES51
Both your houses. 1933. BES32, CORD, CORE, CORF, LOOA, LOOB
Candle in the wind. 1941. BES41
Elizabeth the queen. 1930. BES30, STEI, THO, TRE, TREA1, TREBA, TREC2, TREE3, TREI3, TREJ, WATC2, WATI, WHI
The eve of St. Mark. 1942. BES42
The feast of Ortolans. 1938. KIN, STAT
A girl from Lorraine. See Joan of Lorraine
Gypsy. 1929. BES28
High Tor. 1937. BES36, CLDP, CRIT, GARZA2, GAS, GAVE, GOW, GOWA, HAP, MERT
Joan of Lorraine. 1946. BES46
Variant title: A girl from Lorraine
Journey to Jerusalem. 1940. GALB
Key Largo. 1940. BES39, ROLF
Mary of Scotland. 1933. BES33, CLKW, THF
The masque of kings. 1936. MOSL
Saturday's children. 1927. BES26, GASB, TUCD
The star-wagon. 1937. BES37
Storm operation. 1944. BES43
Valley Forge. 1934. BES34, WARH
The wingless victory. 1936. LOR, SANM
Winterset. 1935. BES35, BROU, CALM, CALN2, CASS, CHAN, CHAP, COTE, COTH, CRIT, DAVI, DUR, GAS, GAVE, GRIF, HAT, HATA, HAVD, HAVE, HIL, HOLM, MOSH, NELS, QUIM, QUIN, RAVA, SIXC, WAIT, WALB

-- and HICKERSON, HAROLD
Gods of the lightning. 1928. GASB

-- and STALLINGS, LAWRENCE
What price glory? 1924. BES24, CHA, GASB, MACG, TRE, TREA1, TREBA, TREC2, TREE3, TREI3, VANM

-- and WEILL, KURT
Lost in the stars (based on the novel Cry, the beloved country by Alan Paton). 1949. BES49, HEWE

ANDERSON, ROBERT WOODRUFF, 1917-
I never sang for my father. 1968. BES67
Silent night, lonely night. 1959. GARSA
Tea and sympathy. 1953. BES53, FAM, GART, GARZA4, NEWV, THEA54
You know I can't hear you when the water's running. 1967. BES66, GARV

ANDERSON, SHERWOOD, 1876-1941
Textiles. 193-? ING

ANDREEV, LEONID NIKOLAEVICH, 1871-1919
He who gets slapped. 1915.
Guthrie, J., adapter. HOUG
MacAndrew, A., tr. GARZJ, MACE
Reeve, F. D., tr. REEV2
Zilboorg, G., tr. BES21, DIE, MOSG, MOSH, THF, TUCG, TUCM, TUCN, TUCO, WATI, WATL4
Variant titles: The knock about; The painted laugh
An incident.
Anon. tr. CHR

The knock about. See He who gets slapped
The life of man. 1906.
Meader, C., and Scott, F., trs. SML
Seltzer, T., tr. DIK2, MOSQ
The painted laugh. See He who gets slapped
Professor Storitsyn. 1912.
Minkoff, I., Noyes, G., and Kaun, A., trs. NOY

ANDREYEFF, LEONID NIKOLAEVICH. See Andreev, Leonid Nikolaevich

ANDREYEV, LEONID NIKOLAEVICH. See Andreev, Leonid Nikolaevich

ANDRIEU DE LA VIGNE. See La Vigne, Andrieu de

ANDRIEV, LEONID NIKOLAEVICH. See Andreev, Leonid Nikolaevich

ANGEL PEREZ DE SAAVEDRA, RIVAS. See Rivas, Angel Pérez de Saavedra

ANNUNZIO, GABRIELE D', 1863-1938
La città morta. See The dead city
The daughter of Jorio. 1904.
Porter, C., Isola, P., and Henry, A., trs. MOSQ
Variant title: La figlia di Jorio
The dead city. 1898.
Mantellini, G., tr. SAY
Variant title: La città morta
La figlia di Jorio. See The daughter of Jorio
Francesca da Rimini. 1902.
Symons, A., tr. DIK1, TUCG, TUCM, WATL3
Gioconda. 1898.
Symons, A., tr. DID, SMI

ANONYMOUS PLAYS
Abraham (Wakefield). 15th cent. DAVJ, TOWN
Abraham (York). 15th cent. DAVJ
Abraham and Isaac (Brome). 15th cent. ADA, BARD, BENY, CAWL, CHI, DAVJ, FRAN, FREF, GARZB, GREC1, HOPP, HUD, KINN, LIE, MAK, MAT, PAR, PARR, POLL, SCW, SNYD1, SWIT, TAT, TAU, TREA2, TREB, TREC1, TREE1, TREI1
Variant titles: The Brome Abraham and Isaac; The sacrifice of Isaac
Abraham and Isaac (Dublin). 15th cent. DAVJ
Abraham and Isaac (Ludus Coventriae). 15th cent. DAVJ
Abraham, Melchisedec and Isaac (Chester). 15th cent. ASH, CHES, DAVJ, EVER, KRE, POLL
Variant titles: Abraham, Melchizedek and Lot, with the sacrifice of Isaac; The histories of Lot and Abraham; Lot and Abraham; The sacrifice of Isaac
Abraham, Melchizedek and Lot, with the sacrifice of Isaac. See Abraham, Melchisedec and Isaac
Abstraction. 14th cent.?
Chamberlin, B., tr. CLF1, ORI2
Adam. 1150?
Axton, R., and Stevens, J., trs. AXT
Barrow, S., and Hulme, W., trs. CROV
Stone, E., tr. CLF1, KRE
Variant titles: Le jeu d'Adam; Le mystère d'Adam; The mystery of Adam; The play of Adam
Adam and Eve (Norwich, Text B, non-cycle mystery play).

12th cent. ? FRAN
The adoration of the kings. Anon. tr. RAV
The adoration of the kings (Chester). See The adoration of the magi (Chester)
The adoration of the magi (Chester). 15th cent. CHES
Variant title: The adoration of the kings
The adoration of the shepherds (Chester). 15th cent. CHES
Albion, knight. See A moral play of Albion, knight
All's one, or one of the foure plaies in one, called A York-Shire tragedy. See A Yorkshire tragedy
The annunciation (Ludus Coventriae). 15th cent. CAWL
The annunciation (Wakefield). 15th cent. LOOM, TOWN
Antichrist (Chester). 15th cent. CHES
Apius and Virginia (sometimes attributed to Richard Bower). 1563? FARM, HAO
Variant title: Appius and Virginia
The apostles at the tomb (Ludus Coventriae). 15th cent. DAVJ
Appearance to Cleopas and Luke (Ludus Coventriae). 15th cent. DAVJ
Appearance to Mary Magdalen (Ludus Coventriae). 15th cent. DAVJ
Appearance to Thomas (Ludus Coventriae). 15th cent. DAVJ
Appius and Virginia. See Apius and Virginia
Arden of Feversham (sometimes attributed to Thomas Arden; Thomas Kyd; William Shakespeare). 1586? BAS, BRO, GARZAE, MCJ, MIN1, MIO1, MONV, OLH, OLI1, SCH
Variant title: The lamentable and true tragedy of Master Arden of Feversham in Kent
Ascension (Ludus Coventriae). 15th cent. DAVJ
The ascension of the Lord (Wakefield). 15th cent. TOWN
Assumption (Ludus Coventriae). 15th cent. DAVJ
Attowell's jig (Francis' new jig) (sometimes attributed to George Attowell). 1595? BAS, NES
Variant titles: Francis' new jig; Mr. Attowell's jig
Banns (Ludus Coventriae). 15th cent. ADA, SCW
The battle of Brooklyn. 1776. AMPA, PHI
The beauty and good properties of women (commonly called Calisto and Melibaea). 1530? FARO
The Benediktbeuren play. 13th cent. Robinson, D., and Francke, K., trs. and adapters. ROBM
The betrayal (Wakefield). 15th cent. HEIL
The betrayal of Christ (Chester). 15th cent. CHES, GARZB
The betraying of Christ (Ludus Coventriae). 15th cent. ADA
The bilker bilk'd. 1742? HUGH
Bilsen play. See The star
The bird catcher in hell. See Esashi Jūō. The bird catcher in hell.
The birth of Jesus (York). 15th cent. ADA
The birth of Merlin; or, The child hath found his father (sometimes attributed to William Rowley; William Shakespeare). 1597? BRO
Birth of the Son (Ludus Coventriae). 15th cent. DAVJ

The blockheads; or, The affrighted officers (attributed to Mercy Otis Warren). 1776. PHI

The book of Job. See Job

The Brome Abraham and Isaac. See Abraham and Isaac

Brome plays. See Abraham and Isaac

The buffeting (Wakefield). 15th cent. TOWN

The buggbears. See Jeffere, John (supposed author)

The butterfly dream. 1368? SCX1
Variant title: Hu tieh meng

Caesar Augustus (Wakefield). 15th cent. TOWN

Cain and Abel. (Ludus Coventriae). 15th cent. CAWL, DAVJ, FRAN

Calisto and Melibaea. See The beauty and good properties of women

The castle of perseverance. 1425? ADA, BEV, HOPP, POLL, SCAT

Celestina. See Rojas, Fernando de. Celestina

The chalk circle. 13th cent. ? Van Der Meer, E., tr. CLF1, KRE

The Chantilly play. See Bourlet, Katherine. The nativity

Chester play of the deluge; The deluge

Chester plays. See Abraham, Melchisedec and Isaac; The adoration of the magi; The adoration of the shepherds; Antichrist; The betrayal of Christ; Christ's ascension; Christ's ministry; Christ's passion; Christ's resurrection; The creation of man; Adam and Eve; The death of Herod; The deluge; The fall of Lucifer; The last judgment; The magi's oblation; The nativity; The prophets; The resurrection, harrowing of hell, and the last judgment; The sacrifice of Isaac; Simon the leper; The slaying of the innocents

The chicken pie and the chocolate cake. 15th cent. Mandel, O., tr. MAN
Variant title: Le pâté et de la torte

A Christmas mumming: The play of Saint [Prince] George. 15th cent. GARZB
Variant titles: Christmas play of St. George; The play of St. George

Christmas play of St. George See A Christmas mumming: The play of Saint [Prince] George

Christ's ascension (Chester). 15th cent. CHES

Christ's ministry (Chester). 15th cent. ADA

Christ's passion (Chester). 15th cent. CHES

Christ's resurrection (Chester). 15th cent. CHES

Coliphizacio (Wakefield). 15th cent. CAWM

A comedy called Misogonus. See Misogonus

Common conditions. 1570? FARM

The conspiracy (Wakefield). 15th cent. TOWN

The contract of marriage between wit and wisdom. 1579? FARM
Variant titles: The marriage of wit and wisdom; Wit and wisdom

The conversion of St. Paul (Digby). 15th cent. ADA, MAL, SWIT

The Cornish mystery play of the three Maries. See The three Maries

Cornish plays. See The death of Pilate; The legend of the rood; The three Maries

Courtois d'Arras.

Axton, R., and Stevens, J., trs. AXT
Coventry plays. See Ludus Coventriae plays
The creation (Wakefield). 15th cent. TOWN
Creation and fall of Lucifer (Ludus Coventriae). See The fall of Lucifer (Ludus Coventriae)
The creation and fall of Lucifer (York). 15th cent. CAWL, GARZB, POLL
Creation and fall of man (Ludus Coventriae). 15th cent. DAVJ
The creation of Adam and Eve (York). 15th cent. CAWL
The creation of Eve, with the expelling of Adam and Eve out of Paradise. 15th cent. ADA
The creation of man: Adam and Eve (Chester). 15th cent. CHES
The crucifixion (Wakefield). 15th cent. EVER, GARZB, TOWN
The crucifixion (York). 15th cent. CAWL, HEIL
Le cuvier. See The washtub
The Daimyo.
Duran, L., tr. DUP
The dance of death. See Totentanz
The dead stone's banquet. See Don Juan and Don Pietro
The death of Herod (Chester). 15th cent. GARZB
The death of Pilate (Cornish). 15th cent. CAWL, GARZB, HAH, TREB
The death of stone.
Aston, W., tr. BAT3
The deceived. 1531.
Peacock, T., tr. BENSA
Variant title: Gl'ingannati
The deliverance of souls (Wakefield). 15th cent. TOWN
The deluge (Chester). 15th cent. ADA, BENY, CAWL, CHES, EVER, FRAN, HOPP, MAK, MIL, PARR, POLL, SNYD1, TAT, TAU, WEAT1
Variant titles: Chester play of the deluge; Noah's deluge; Noah's flood
The deluge (Wakefield). 15th cent. GARZB
Variant title: Noah and his sons
Depositio cornuti typographici. See The printer's apprentice
The destruction of Jerusalem. Anon. tr. RAV
The devil and his dame. See Grim the collier of Croydon
A dialogue, between a Southern delegate, and his spouse, on his return from the grand Continental Congress (attributed to Mary V. V.). 1774. PHI
Digby plays. See The conversion of St. Paul
The distracted emperor. BUL2
Le docteur amoureux. 1691? LAN
Dr. Kranichs sprechstunde. See Birmelin, John. Em Docktor Fogel sei offis schtunn (based on)
Don Juan and Don Pietro; or, The dead stone's banquet (a puppet play from Augsburg). Sonnenfeld, M., tr. MAN
Doomsday (Ludus Coventriae). 15th cent. DAVJ
The double Dutch act (Vaudeville skit). RAVA
The double Wop act (Vaudeville skit). RAVA
The dream of Vāsavadatta. See Bhāsa (supposed author)
Duk Moraud. 13th cent. ADA
An Easter resurrection play. 10th cent. GARZB
Edward III. See The reign of King Edward the third
The Elche mystery play.

See The mystery play of Elche
Elckerlijk. See Everyman
Everyman. 1529? ABC, ABRB1, ADA, ALL, ALT, ALTE, ASF, ASH, BAC, BALL, BARD, BAT4, BENP, BENY, BIER, BOW, BROJ, BROK, CALD, CAWL, CHI, CLF1, CLK1, COJ, DOWS, EVE, EVER, FARO, FIF, FREG, GARZAP, GARZB, GASS, GOOD, GREB1, GREC1, GRIF, HEIL, HOPP, HOUS, HUD, KER, KERN, KERO, KON, KRE, LEV, LEVE, LIE, LOOM, MACM1, MCA, MCNI, MOO, PAR, PERS, PERU, POLL, REIL, REIN, ROB, ROBE, ROHR, RUB, SCAT, SCW, SEN, SHAH1, SHAI1, SHAJ1, SHRO, SML, SNYD1, STA, STY, SWIT, TAT, TAU, TAV, TRE, TREA2, TREB, TREC1, TREE1, TREI1, WAIW, WEAT1, WELT, WHFM, WOOD1, WOOE1
Variant titles: Elckerlijk; The moral play of Everyman; The summoning of Everyman
The extraction of souls from hell (Wakefield). See The harrowing of hell
Fair Em. The miller's daughter of Manchester with the love of William the conqueror. 1590? BRO
The fall of Lucifer (Chester). 15th cent. CHES
The fall of Lucifer (Ludus Coventriae). 15th cent. ADA, DAVJ, SCW
The fall of man (York). 15th cent. CAWL
The famous victories of Henry the fifth (sometimes attributed to Richard Tarlton). 1585? ADA
Variant title: Henry the fifth
La farce de Maître Pathelin. See La farce de Maître Pierre Pathelin
La farce de Maître Pierre Pathelin. 1469? SCN, SET
Allen, J., tr. ALL
Holbrook, R., tr. THO
Jagendorf, M., tr. CAR, CLF1, LOND
Mandel, O., tr. MAN
Variant titles: La farce de Maître Pathelin; The farce of the worthy Master Pierre Patelin; The farce of the worthy master, Pierre Patelin; The farce of the worthy master, Pierre Patelin, the lawyer; Master Pierre Patelin; Peter Quill's shenanigans; Pierre Patelin
The farce of the worthy Master Pierre Patelin. See La farce de Maître Pierre Pathelin
The farce of the worthy master, Pierre Patelin, the lawyer. See La farce de Maître Pierre Pathelin
The fatal error.
McClatchie, T., tr. BAT21
Variant title: Kago-Sodo
Festa de Elche. See The mystery play of Elche
Fifteen strings of cash. 1627? SCX2
Variant title: Shih wu kuan
The final judgment.
McAfee, B. and Cornyn, J., trs. RAV
The first part of the reign of King Richard the second; or, Thomas of Woodstock. See Woodstock
The first part of the return from Parnassus. See The return from Parnassus; or, The scourge of Simony
The first shepherds' play (Wakefield). 15th cent. CAWM, TOWN
Variant title: Prima pas-

torum
The flight into Egypt (Wakefield). 15th cent. TOWN
Forsaken love.
Duran, L., tr. DUP
The four elements. See The nature of the four elements
Francis' new jig. See Attowell's jig
Gammer Gurton's needle. See Stevenson, William (supposed author)
Le garçon et l'aveugle.
Axton, R., and Stevens, J., trs. AXT
George a Greene, the pinner of Wakefield. See Greene, Robert (supposed author)
Godley Queen Hester. 1525? FARP
Variant title: An interlude of Godley Queen Hester
Grim the collier of Croydon; or, The devil and his dame (sometimes attributed to John Tatham). 1600? FARM
The hands in the box.
Duran, L., tr. DUP
The hanging of Judas (Wakefield). 15th cent. TOWN
The harrowing of hell (Chester). 15th cent. ADA, CAWL, POLL
The harrowing of hell; or, The extraction of souls from hell (Wakefield). 15th cent. EVER
Harrowing of hell II (Ludus Coventriae). 15th cent. DAVJ
Hegge plays. See Ludus Coventriae plays
Henry the fifth. See The famous victories of Henry the fifth
Herod (Ludus Coventriae). See The magi, Herod, and the slaughter of the innocents
Herod and the magi (Ludus Coventriae). See The magi, Herod, and the slaughter of the innocents
Herod and the three kings (Ludus Coventriae). See The magi, Herod, and the slaughter of the innocents
Herod the great (Wakefield). 15th cent. CAWL, TOWN
The Hessian Christmas play. 15th cent.
Robinson, D., tr. and adapter ROBM
Hickscorner. 1534? FARO
The histories of Lot and Abraham. See Abraham, Melchisedec and Isaac
The history of Jacob and Esau. See Jacob and Esau
The honor of Danzo.
Duran, L., tr. DUP
The horns.
Duran, L., tr. DUP
How the blessed Saint Helen found the holy cross.
McAfee, B., tr. RAV
Hu tieh meng. See The butterfly dream
Impatient poverty. 1560? FARN
Variant title: An interlude of impatient poverty
Gl'ingannati. See The deceived
An interlude of Godley Queen Hester. See Godley Queen Hester
An interlude of impatient poverty. See Impatient poverty
The interlude of John the evangelist. See John the evangelist
An interlude of wealth and health. See Wealth and health
The interlude of youth. See Youth
The iron crown.
Kato, E., tr. KEE
Variant title: Kanawa
Isaac (Wakefield). 15th cent. TOWN
Jack Juggler. 1553? FAR
Jacob (Wakefield). 15th cent.

TOWN
Jacob and Esau. 1558? FARP
Variant title: The history of Jacob and Esau
Jesse (Ludus Coventriae). 15th cent. DAVJ
Jesus and the doctors (Ludus Coventriae). 15th cent. DAVJ
Le jeu d'Adam. See Adam
Job. 400? B.C. BUCL, BUCM, DAVK, SML, TRE, TREA2
Variant title: The book of Job
John the Baptist (Wakefield). 15th cent. TOWN
John the evangelist. 1557? FARN
Variant titles: The interlude of John the evangelist; Saint John the evangelist
The judgment (Wakefield). 15th cent. TOWN
The judgment (York). See The judgment day
The judgment day (York). 15th cent. ADA, CAWL, SCW
Variant title: The judgment
Kaga-Sodo. See The fatal error
Kanawa. See The iron crown
The kept mistress. 1756. BEVI
The killing of Abel (Wakefield). 15th cent. ADA, TOWN
King Darius. 1565? FAR
King Edward the third. See The reign of King Edward the third
King Herod (Chester). 12th cent.? FRAN
The lamentable and true tragedy of Master Arden of Feversham in Kent. See Arden of Feversham
The lamentable tragedy of Locrine (sometimes attributed to George Peele; William Shakespeare). 1586? BRO
Variant title: Locrine
The last judgment (Chester). 15th cent. CHES
Lazarus (Wakefield). 15th cent. TOWN
The legend of the rood (Cornish). 15th cent. HAH
Leicestershire St. George play. 1863. ADA
The life and death of Lord Cromwell. See Thomas, Lord Cromwell
The little clay cart. See Shudraka, King (supposed author)
Locrine. See The lamentable tragedy of Locrine
The London prodigal (sometimes attributed to William Shakespeare). 1603? BRO
Longing for worldly pleasures. 1368? SCX2
Variant title: Ssu fan
Lot and Abraham. See Abraham, Melchisedec and Isaac
Ludus Coventriae plays. See Abraham and Isaac; The annunciation; The apostles at the tomb; Appearance to Cleopas and Luke; Appearance to Mary Magdalen; Appearance to Thomas; Ascension; Assumption; Banns; The betraying of Christ; Cain and Abel; Doomsday; The fall of Lucifer; Harrowing of hell II; Jesse; Jesus and the doctors; The magi, Herod, and the slaughter of the innocents; Matthias; Moses; Mother of Mercy; The mystery of the redemption; Noah; The pageant of the shearmen and tailors; Passion I; Passion II; Passion III; Pentecost; Presentation and purification; Raising of Lazarus; Resurrection and appearance to Mother; The salutation and conception; The shepherds'

play; Story of the watch; Three Marys at the tomb; The trial of Christ; Trial of Joseph and Mary; The woman taken in adultery
Variant cycle titles: Coventry plays; Hegge plays; N. Town plays

Ludus super iconia Sancti Nicolai. 15th cent. POLL

The Maastricht play (adapted from Paachspel). 14th cent.
Robinson, D., tr. and adapter ROBM

Macro Morals. See The castle of perseverance; Mankynd; and, Mind, will, and understanding

Mactacio Abel (Wakefield). 15th cent. CAWM, GARZB, ROBE
Variant title: The murder of Abel

The magi, Herod, and the slaughter of the innocents. (Ludus Coventriae). 15th cent. ADA, DAVJ, MAK
Variant titles: Herod; Herod and the magi; Herod and the three kings; The massacre of the innocents; The slaughter of the innocents

The magi's oblation (Chester). 15th cent. CHES

Magnus Herodes (Wakefield). 15th cent. CAWM

Mankind. See Mankynd

Mankynd. ca. 1465-1471. ADA, BEV, FARN
Variant title: Mankind

Manohra.
Bhukkanasut, U., tr. BRA

Man's disobedience and the fall of man (York). 15th cent. GARZB

The marriage of wit and science. 1569? FARM
Variant titles: Wit and science; Wyt and science

The marriage of wit and wisdom. See The contract of marriage between wit and wisdom

The martyr'd souldier. BUL1

The martyrdom of Ali.
Pelly, L., tr. BAT3
Variant title: Ta'ziya

Mary Magdalene. 15th cent. ADA, POLL

Mary Magdalene and the apostles. See The mystery of Mary Magdalene and the apostles

The massacre of the innocents. See The magi, Herod, and the slaughter of the innocents

Master Pierre Patelin. See La farce de Maître Pierre Pathelin

Matthias (Ludus Coventriae). 15th cent. DAVJ

The mayde's metamorphosis. BUL2

The merchant.
McAfee, B., tr. RAV

The merry devil of Edmonton (sometimes attributed to Michael Drayton). 1600? BRO, GAY2, MCI, OLH, OLI1

The miller's daughter of Manchester with the love of William the conqueror. See Fair Em

Mind, will, and understanding. ca. 1460-1463. BEV
Variant title: Wisdom; or, Mind, will, and understanding

Minstrel show. ca. 1850-ca. 1870. MONR

The miracle of Saint Nicholas and the school-boys. 15th cent. LOOM

The miracle of Saint Nicholas and the virgins. 15th cent. LOOM

Misogonus. 1560? BOND, FARP
Variant title: A comedy called Misogonus

Mr. Attowell's jig. See Attowell's jig

A moral play of Albion, knight. 1566? FARP
Variant title: Albion, knight
Moses (Ludus Coventriae). 15th cent. DAVJ
A most pleasant comedie of Mucedorus the kings sonne of Valentia and Amadine, the kings daughter of Arragon. See Mucedorus
Mother of Mercy (Ludus Coventriae). 15th cent. (Mother of Mercy: Conception; Parliament of Heaven and Annunciation; Joseph; Salutation). DAVJ
The motley assembly (attributed to Mercy Otis Warren). 1779. PHI
Mucedorus (sometimes attributed to Thomas Lodge; William Shakespeare). 1588? BAS, BRO, NES, WINN
Variant title: A most pleasant comedie of Mucedorus the kings sonne of Valentia and Amadine, the kings daughter of Arragon
Mundus et infans. See The world and the child
The murder of Abel (Wakefield). See Mactacio Abel (Wakefield)
Le mystère d'Adam. See Adam
Mysterium resurrectionis D. N. Jhesu Christi. 15th cent. POLL
The mystery of Adam. See Adam
The mystery of Mary Magdalene and the apostles. 15th cent. EVER
Variant title: Mary Magdalene and the apostles
The mystery of the redemption (Ludus Coventriae). 15th cent. LOOM
Variant title: The redemption
The mystery play of Elche. 13th cent. Starkie, W., tr. SSTW
Variant title: The Elche mystery play; Festa de Elche
N. Town plays. See Ludus Coventriae plays
The nativity (The Chantilly play). See Bourlet, Katherine. The nativity
The nativity (Chester). 15th cent. CHES
The nativity (Wakefield). See The second shepherds' play
The nativity (York). See The York nativity
Nativity play (Ludus Coventriae). See The pageant of the shearmen and tailors
The nature of the four elements (sometimes attributed to John Rastell). 1520. FARO, POLL
Variant title: The four elements
Nero. 1623? NERO
New custom. 1573? FAR
Nice wanton. 16th cent. CLKW
Variant title: A pretty interlude called Nice Wanton
Noah (Ludus Coventriae). 15th cent. DAVJ
Noah (Wakefield). 15th cent. ADA, HEIL, SCW, TOWN
Noah and his sons. See The deluge (Wakefield)
Noah's deluge. See The deluge (Chester)
Noah's flood. See The deluge
The noble souldier. BUL1
Nonomiya. See The shrine in the fields
Norwich play of Adam and Eve. See Adam and Eve
Oberufer plays. See The paradise play; The shepherds' play; The three kings' play
Octavia. See Seneca, Lucius Annaeus. Octavia
The offering of the magi (Wakefield). 15th cent. TOWN

The Orléans sepulcher. 13th cent. GARZB
The Oxfordshire St. George play. 18th cent. ADA, CHI, PAR
Paachspel. See The Maastricht play
The pageant of the shearmen and the tailors (Ludus Coventriae). 15th cent. ALL, EVER, FIF, GARZB
Brown, J., adapter. ROBM
Variant title: The nativity play
A pantomime for Easter day. GARZB
The paradise play (Oberufer). 16th cent.
Harwood, A., tr. HARW
Parnassus plays (1598-1601). See The pilgrimage to Parnassus; The return from Parnassus
Passion I (Ludus Coventriae). 15th cent.
(Passion I: Prologues; Council of Jews I; Entry into Jerusalem; Maundy I; Council of Jews II; Maundy II; Betrayal; Maundy III; Agony at Olivet; Taking of Jesus). DAVJ
Passion II (Ludus Coventriae). 15th cent.
(Passion II: Prologue; Jesus before Herod; Before Annas and Caiphas; Peter's denial; Before Pilate; Before Herod II; Dream of Pilate's wife; Before Pilate II; Way of the cross; Crucifixion; Harrowing of Hell I; Centurion; Longeus and burial; Setting of watch; Way of the cross). DAVJ
The passion play of Alsfeld.
Katzin, W., tr. SEVE
Le pâté et de la torte. See The chicken pie and the chocolate cake
Pentecost (Ludus Coventriae). 15th cent. DAVJ
Pharaoh (Wakefield). 15th cent. ADA, TOWN
Le philosophe dupé de l'amour. See The philosopher duped by love
The philosopher duped by love (sometimes attributed to François Dessandrais-Sebire). 17th cent.
Chambers, W., tr. BAT7
Variant title: Le philosophe dupé de l'amour
Pierre Patelin. See La farce de Maître Pierre Pathelin
Pilgrimage. See The pilgrimage to Parnassus
The pilgrimage to Parnassus. 16th cent. LEIS
Variant title: Pilgrimage
The pilgrims (Wakefield). 15th cent. TOWN
The play of Adam. See Adam
The play of St. George. See A Christmas mumming: The play of Saint [Prince] George
The play of St. George, version reconstructed from memory by Thomas Hardy. 13th cent. ? CLF1
The play of the doctors (Wakefield). 15th cent. TOWN
The play of the sacrament. 15th cent. ADA
Presentation and purification (Ludus Coventriae). 15th cent. DAVJ
A pretty interlude called Nice wanton. See Nice wanton
The price of wine.
Hung, J. BRA
Prima pastorum. See The first shepherds' play
The printer's apprentice. 1648?
Rist, J., tr. (from the German of William Blades). BAT4
Variant title: Depositio cornuti typographici
The procession of the prophets (Wakefield). 15th cent. TOWN

Processus noe cum filiis (Wakefield). 15th cent. CAWM

The prophets (Chester). 15th cent. ADA

The Provençal play. 13th cent.
Robinson, D., tr. and adapter. ROBM

The purification of Mary (Wakefield). 15th cent. TOWN

The puritan; or, The widow of Watling street (sometimes attributed to William Shakespeare). 1606? BRO
Variant title: The puritan widdow

The puritan widdow. See The puritan; or, The widow of Watling street

The quem quaeritis (trope). 9th cent. BARI, CHI, GARZB, HUD, PAR, SCW
Chambers, E., tr. BARH

Querolus. 15th cent.?
Duckworth, G., tr. DUC2

The raigne of King Edward the third. See The reign of King Edward the third

Raising of Lazarus (Ludus Coventriae). 15th cent. DAVJ

Red detachment of women. SNO

The redemption (Ludus Coventriae). See The mystery of the redemption

The reign of King Edward the third (sometimes attributed to Thomas Lodge; Christopher Marlowe; William Shakespeare). 1590? ARMS, BRO, WINN
Variant titles: Edward III; King Edward the third; The raigne of King Edward the third

Respublica (attributed to Nicholas Udall). 1553? FARN, HAO (extracts), SCAT

Resurrection (York). 15th cent. CAWL, SWIT

Resurrection and appearance to Mother (Ludus Coventriae). 15th cent. DAVJ

The resurrection, harrowing of hell, and the last judgment (synoptic version of Chester, Coventry, and Wakefield plays). 15th cent. GARZB

The resurrection of Christ (Wakefield). 15th cent. ADA, TOWN

The return from Parnassus; or, The scourge of Simony, pt. I (1601?). LEIS
pt. II (1602?) LEIS, SCH, SCI, SCJ
Variant titles: The first part of the return from Parnassus; The second part of the return from Parnassus

The Revesby sword play. 1779. ADA

Rip Van Winkle (as played by Joseph Jefferson; adapted by Dion Boucicault). 1865. CEY, LAW, MASW, QUIJ, QUIK, QUIL, QUIM, QUIN
--See also Burke, Charles. Rip Van Winkle

Robin Hood and the friar. 15th cent. ADA, CHI, PAR, SCW

Robin Hood and the knight. 15th cent. CHI

Robin Hood and the potter. 15th cent. CHI

Robin Hood and the sheriff of Nottingham. 15th cent. ADA

The sacrifice of Isaac.
McAfee, B. and Cornyn, J., trs. RAV

The sacrifice of Isaac. See also Abraham and Isaac; Abraham, Melchisedec and Isaac

St. George and the dragon. 19th cent. EVER, SCW

St. George plays. See Leicestershire St. George play;

The Oxfordshire St. George play; The play of St. George, version reconstructed from memory by Thomas Hardy; St. George and the dragon

Saint John the evangelist. See John the evangelist

Saint Nicholas and the three scholars. 12th cent. MAK
Variant title: Tres clerici

Saint Nicholas plays. See The miracle of Saint Nicholas and the school-boys; The miracle of Saint Nicholas and the virgins; Saint Nicholas and the three scholars

The salutation and conception (Ludus Coventriae). 15th cent. ADA, POLL

The salutation and conception (Ludus Coventriae). See also Mother of Mercy

The salutation of Elizabeth (Wakefield). 15th cent. TOWN

Le savetier calbain. 1500? BRN

The school act (Vaudeville skit). RAVA

The scourage of Simony. See The return from Parnassus

The scourging (Wakefield). 15th cent. TOWN

The second part of the return from Parnassus. See The return from Parnassus; or, The scourge of Simony

The second play of the shepherds. See The second shepherds' play

The second shepherds' pageant. See The second shepherds' play

The second shepherds' play (Wakefield). 15th cent. ABRB1, ADA, ALLK, BARD, BAUL, BENY, BRIX, CALD, CAWL, CAWM, CHI, CLF1, CLK1, CLKW, COL1, DAV1, DOV, EVE, EVER, FRAN, GARZB, HARW, HEIL, HOPP, HUD, KER, KRE, LIE, LIED1, LIEE1, LOOM, MAK, MAT, PAR, POLL, ROBE, RUB, SCW, SEN, SHAJ1, SPF1, STA, TAT, TAU, TAV, TOBI, TOWN, TREB, TREC1, TREE1, TREI1, WOO1, WOOD1, WOOE1
Variant titles: The nativity; The second play of the shepherds; The second shepherds' pageant; Secunda pastorum; The shepherds; A Wakefield nativity; The Wakefield second nativity play

Secunda pastorum. See The second shepherds' play

La seinte resureccion. 12th cent. ?
Axton, R., and Stevens, J., trs. AXT

Schachiapang. SNO

The shepherds. See The second shepherds' play

The shepherds' play (Ludus Coventriae). 15th cent. DAVJ, EVE, PARR

Shetland sword dance. 18th cent. ADA, PAR

Shih wu kuan. See Fifteen strings of cash

Shōkun.
Sesar, C., tr. KEE

The shrine in the fields.
Varley, H., tr. KEE

Simon the leper (Chester). 15th cent. CHES

Sir Gyles Goosecappe. 1606. BUL2

Sir John Oldcastle, pt. I (sometimes attributed to Michael Drayton; Richard Hathway; Anthony Munday; Robert Wilson). 1598? BRO
Variant title: The true and honorable historie of the life of Sir John Oldcastle, the good Lord Cobham

Sir Thomas More (An ill May-day) (sometimes attributed

to Anthony Munday). 1590? BRO, SCH, SCI, SCJ
The slaughter of the innocents (Ludus Coventriae). See The magi, Herod, and the slaughter of the innocents
The slaying of the innocents (Chester). 15th cent. CHES
The sorrows of Han.
Anon, tr. EDAD
Davis, J., tr. ORI4, TAV
Souls and testamentary executors.
McAfee, B. and Cornyn, J., trs. RAV
The Spanish play. See The wisemen
Ssu fan. See Longing for worldly pleasures
Ssu Lang t'an mu. See Ssu Lang visits his mother
Ssu Lang visits his mother. 1616. SCX1
Variant title: Ssu Lang t'an mu
The star (Bilsen play). 11th cent.
Robinson, D., tr. and adapter. ROBM
Story of the watch (Ludus Coventriae). 15th cent. DAVJ
The straight and the Jew (Vaudeville skit). RAVA
A stratagem of interlocking rings. LIU
The summoning of Everyman. See Everyman
Taking Tiger Mountain by strategy. SNO
The talents (Wakefield). 15th cent. TOWN
Tanikō. See The valley rite
Ta'ziya. See The martyrdom of Ali
Thersites. 1537? FARO, POLL
Thomas, Lord Cromwell. 1592? BRO
Variant titles: The life and death of Lord Cromwell; The true chronical history of the whole life and death of Thomas Lord Cromwell
Thomas of India (Wakefield). 15th cent. TOWN
Thomas of Woodstock. See Woodstock
The three cuckolds. 16th cent.
Katz, L., adapter. BENR1
Variant title: Li tre becchi
The three kings (York). 12th cent.? FRAN
The three kings' play (Oberufer). 16th cent. HARW
The three Maries (Cornish). 15th cent. EVER
Variant title: The Cornish mystery play of the three Maries
Three Marys at the tomb' (Ludus Coventriae). 15th cent. DAVJ
Tom Tyler and his wife. 1550? FARP
Totentanz. (tr. by Margaret Trinklein from the German text of Martin F. Schloss). 15th cent. SWIT
Variant title: The dance of death
The Towneley play. 15th cent.
Burrell, R., adapter. ROBM
Towneley plays. See Wakefield plays
Tragedy of Nero. BUL1
Li tre becchi. See The three cuckolds
Tres clerici. See Saint Nicholas and the three scholars
The trial of Atticus before Judge Beau, for a rape. 1771? AMPA
The trial of Christ (Ludus Coventriae). 15th cent. ADA
Trial of Joseph and Mary (Ludus Coventriae). 15th cent. DAVJ
Trial of treasure. 1565? FAR

The true and honorable historie of the life of Sir John Oldcastle, the good Lord Cobham. See Sir John Oldcastle, pt. I
The true chronicle history of the whole life and death of Thomas Lord Cromwell. See Thomas, Lord Cromwell
The tryall of chevalry. BUL2
The two noble kinsmen. See Fletcher, J., and Shakespeare, W.
The Umbrian play. 14th cent.
Robinson, D., tr. and adapter. ROBM
The valley rite.
Tyler, R., tr. KEE
Variant title: Tanikō
Wakefield plays. See Abraham; The annunciation; The ascension of the Lord; The betrayal; The buffeting; Caesar Augustus; Coliphizacio; The conspiracy; The creation; The crucifixion; The deliverance of souls; The deluge; The first shepherds' play; The flight into Egypt; The hanging of Judas; The harrowing of Hell; Herod the great; Isaac; Jacob; John the Baptist; The judgment; The killing of Abel; Lazarus; Magnus Herodes; Noah; The offering of the magi; Pharaoh; The pilgrims; The play of the doctors; The procession of the prophets; Processus noe cum filiis; The purification of Mary; The resurrection of Christ; The salutation of Elizabeth; The scourging; The second shepherds' play; The talents; Thomas of India
The Wakefield second nativity play. See The second shepherds' play
The washtub. 15th cent.
Mandel, O., tr. MAN
Variant title: Le cuvier
Wealth and health. 1557? FARN
Variant title: An interlude of wealth and health
The wept of the wish-ton-wish (based on the novel by James Fenimore Cooper.) 1834. BAT19
The Widow of Watling Street. See The puritan
The wisdom of Dr. Dodypoll. 1600. BUL2
Wisdom; or, Mind, will, and understanding. See Mind, will, and understanding
The wise virgins and the foolish virgins. 1150?
Hughes, B., and G., trs. CLF1
The wisemen (The Spanish play). 12th cent.
Robinson, D., tr. and adapter. ROBM
Wit and science. See The marriage of wit and science; Redford, John. The play of wit and science
Wit and wisdom. See The contract of marriage between wit and wisdom
The woman taken in adultery (Ludus Coventriae). 15th cent. CAWL, DAVJ
Woodstock. ca. 1591-ca. 1595. ARMS
Variant titles: The first part of the reign of King Richard the second; or, Thomas of Woodstock; Thomas of Woodstock
The world and the child. 1522? FARO, SCAT
Variant title: Mundus et infans
Wyt and science. See The marriage of wit and science; Redford, John. The play of wit and science
The York crucifixion. See The crucifixion (York)
The York nativity. 15th cent.
Baird, J., tr. LEV,

LEVE, MAK
Variant title: The nativity
York plays. See The birth of Jesus; The creation and the fall of Lucifer; The creation of Adam and Eve; The crucifixion; The fall of man; The judgment day; Resurrection; The three kings; The York nativity
A Yorkshire tragedy (sometimes attributed to William Shakespeare). 1605? BRO, OLH, OLI1, RUB
Variant title: All's one, or one of the four plaies in one, called a York-Shire tragedy
Youth. 1555? FARP, HAO, SCAT
Variant title: The interlude of youth

ANOUILH, JEAN, 1910-
L'alouette. See The lark
L'amour puni. See The rehearsal
Antigone. 1944. GRAF
Anon. tr. FOUA, PATP, SUT2
Galantière, L., tr. and adapter. ASF, BES45, BLOC, CASE, DOT, GORDP, JOHO, MCNA, MIJE, SSSU, ULAN, WATE, WISF
Variant titles: Antigone and the tyrant; Antigone et le tyrant
Antigone and the tyrant. See Antigone
Antigone et le tyrant. See Antigone
Ardèle. 1950.
Hill, L., tr. COTK
Variant titles: Ardèle; ou, la Marguerite; The cry of the peacock
Ardèle; ou, la Marguerite. See Ardèle
Le bal des voleurs. See Thieves' carnival
Becket; or, The honor of God. 1959.
Hill, L., tr. ALT, ALTE, BES60, CUBH, GOLH, MORV, MORX
Variant title: Becket; ou, L'honneur de Dieu
Becket; ou, L'honneur de Dieu. See Becket; or, The honor of God
Cecile; or, The school for fathers. 1953.
Klein, L., and A., trs. BENS3
Variant title: Cécile; ou, L'école de pères
Cécile; ou, L'école des pères. See Cecile; or, The school for fathers
The cry of the peacock. See Ardèle
Le dîner des têtes. See Poor Bitos
Episode de la vie d'un auteur. See Episode in the life of an author
Episode in the life of an author. 1948.
John, M., tr. RICK
Variant title: Episode de la vie d'un auteur
The ermine. 1932.
John, M., tr. PLAN13
Variant title: L'hermine
Euridice. See Eurydice
Eurydice. 1941.
Black, K., tr. COTKW, COTQ
Variant titles: Euridice; Legend of lovers; Point of departure
L'hermine. See The ermine
L'invitation au chateau. See Ring round the moon
The lark. 1955.
Fry, C., tr. BERM, CLO, WEAN
Hellman, L., adapter. BES55, GARZH, THEA56, TREBA, TREI3, TREJ
Variant title: L'alouette
Legend of lovers. See Eurydice
Léocadia. See Time remem-

bered
Madame de...
Whiting, J., tr. RICJ
Medea. 1948.
Klein, L., and A., trs. BENT5, SANM
Small, L., tr. PLAN15
Variant title: Médée
Médée. See Medea
The orchestra. 1962.
John, M., tr. RICJ
Variant title: L'orchestre
L'orchestre. See The orchestra
Pauvre Bitos. See Poor Bitos
Point of departure. See Eurydice
Poor Bitos. 1956.
Hill, L., tr. BES64
Variant titles: Le dîner des têtes; Pauvre Bitos
The rehearsal. 1950.
Johnson, P., and Black, K., adapters. BES63
Variant titles: L'amour puni; La répétition; ou, L'amour puni
La répétition; ou, L'amour puni. See The rehearsal
Ring round the moon. 1947.
Fry, C., tr. BROSA
Variant title: L'invitation au chateau
Thieves' carnival. 1932.
Anon. tr. ZIM
Hill, L., tr. BENT3, BLOC
Variant title: Le bal des voleurs
Time remembered. 1954.
Moyes, P., tr. and adapter. BES57
Variant title: Léocadia
La valse de toréadors. See The waltz of the toreadors
The waltz of the toreadors. 1952.
Hill, L., tr. and adapter. BES56, PLAN8
Variant title: La valse de toréadors

-- and AURENCHE, JEAN
Humulus le muet. See Humulus the mute
Humulus the mute. 1929.
Benedikt, M., tr. BEN
Variant title: Humulus le muet.

ANSKI, S. A., pseud. See Rappoport, Shloyme Zanvl

ANSKY, S. A., pseud. See Rappoport, Shloyme Zanvl

ANSPACHER, LOUIS KAUFMAN, 1878-1947
The unchastened woman. 1915. BAK, BES09, DIG

ANTHONY, C. L., pseud. See Smith, Dorothy Gladys

ANZENGRUBER, LUDWIG, 1839-1889
The farmer forsworn. 1872.
Busse, A., tr. FRA16
Variant title: Meineidbauer
The fourth commandment. See Das vierte gebot
Meineidbauer. See The farmer forsworn
Das vierte gebot. 1877. CAM
Variant title: The fourth commandment

APOLINAR, DANNY, 1934-
Your own thing (music and lyrics by). See Driver, Donald. Your own thing

APOLLINAIRE, GUILLAUME, pseud. See Kostrowisky, Guillaume Apollinaire de

APPLEGATE, JAMES EARL. See ADV Adventures in world literature

ARAGON, LOUIS, 1897-
L'armoire â glace un beau soir. See The mirror-wardrobe one fine evening
The mirror-wardrobe one fine evening. 1923.

Benedikt, M., tr. BEN
Variant title: L'armoire à glace un beau soir

ARBUZOV, ALEXEI
It happened in Irkutsk. 1959?
Prokofieva, R., tr. THY, WEIM

ARCE, GASPAR NUNEZ DE.
See Núñez de Arce, Gaspar

ARCHER, WILLIAM, 1856-1924
The green goddess. 1921. BES20, CAR, CEU, LAW, LOV

ARCHIBALD, WILLIAM, 1919-
The innocents (based on the novel The turn of the screw by Henry James). 1950. BES49

ARCIPRESTE DE HITA. See Ruiz, Juan

ARDEN, JANE
The party. 1958. PLAN18

ARDEN, JOHN, 1930-
Live like pigs. 1958. NEWE3
Serjeant Musgrave's dance. 1959. POP
Soldier, soldier. 1960. CONB

-- and D'ARCY, MARGRETTA
The happy haven. 1960. NEWE4

ARDEN, THOMAS, d. 1551
Arden of Feversham (sometimes attributed to). See Anonymous plays. Arden of Feversham

ARDREY, ROBERT, 1908-
The murderers. See Stone and star
Shadow of heroes. See Stone and star
Stone and star. 1958. BES61
Variant titles: The murderers; Shadow of heroes
Thunder rock. 1939. FIR

ARENT, ARTHUR, 1905?-
One-third of a nation (edited by). 1938. FEE, NAGE
Power, a living newspaper. 1937. FEF

ARIOSTO, LUDOVICO, 1474-1544
I suppositi. See Gascoigne, George. Supposes (adapted from)

ARISTOPHANES, 446?-385? B.C.
The Acharnians. 425 B.C.
Anon. tr. OAT2
Casson, L., tr. CASU
Frere, J., tr. KRE
Rogers, B., tr. GRDB5
Aves. See The birds
The birds. 414 B.C.
Anon. tr. FIFV, OAT2, WED
Fitts, D., tr. BARJ, FEFL, FIFR
Frere, J., tr. CROV, HOUS
Kerr, W., tr. WHFM
MacGregor, M., tr. CLKW
Rogers, B., tr. FEFT, GRDB5
Variant title: Aves
The clouds. 423 B.C.
Anon. tr. BAT2, MURP, OAT2, PLAG
Cumberland, R., tr. HOWE, HOWF
Hickie, W., tr. GREE
Lucas, F., tr. LUCA, LUCAB, LUCAF
Mitchell, T., tr. CLF1
Rogers, B., tr. BARB, FEFT, GRDB5, MIK7, ROBJ, WARN1
Variant title: Nubes
The council of women. See The ecclesiazusae
The ecclesiazusae. 392 B.C.
Anon. tr. BAT21, OAT2
Rogers, B., tr. GRDB5
Variant title: The council of women

Equites. See The knights
The frogs. 405 B.C.
Anon. tr. PLAG
Fitts, D., tr. SHRO
Frere, J., tr. BUCK, BUCL, BUCM, HIB, HIBA, HIBB, LAP, MAU, SEBO, SEBP, SMR, TAV, TEN, THOM, THON
Hawthorne, J., tr. MCKK1
McLeish, K., tr. MCLM
Murray, G., tr. HOWF, OAT2, OATH
Rogers, B., tr. FEFT, GRDB5, HARC8, ROB, ROBJ, TREB, TREC1, TREE1, TREI1
Variant title: Ranae
The god of riches. See Plutus
The knights. 424 B.C.
Anon. tr. OAT2
Frere, J., tr. DRA1, PLAB1
Rogers, B., tr. GRDB5
Variant title: Equites
Lysistrata. 411 B.C.
Anon. tr. DAVM, GOU1, OAT2, PLAG, WORP
Fitts, D., tr. SAFF, VANV1, WELT
Murphy, C., tr. ALLK, BOW, HOLP, JOHN, LIND, LOCM1, MACM1, OATE, ROBI, SOU, VON
Oates, W., and Murphy, C., trs. EVC1, MACN
Roby, D., tr. MESS
Rogers, B., tr. GRDB5
Seldes, G., tr. TRE, TREA2
Smolin, D., tr. and adapter. PLAH
Sutherland, D., tr. COTKC, COTKI, HAPRL
Wilbur, R., tr. WEIS, WEIW
Nubes. See The clouds
Pax. See Peace
Peace. 421 B.C.
Anon. tr. OAT2
Rogers, B., tr. GRDB5
Variant title: Pax
Plutus, the god of riches. 388 B.C.
Anon. tr. OAT2
Hickie, W., tr. GREE
Rogers, B., tr. GRDB5
Sanford, D., tr. TEN
Variant title: Wealth
Ranae. See The frogs
Thesmophoriazusae. 411 B.C.
Anon. tr. OAT2
Rogers, B., tr. GRDB5
Variant title: The women celebrating the Thesmophoria
Vespae. See The wasps
The wasps. 422 B.C.
Anon. tr. OAT2
Rogers, B., tr. GRDB5
Variant title: Vespae
Wealth. See Plutus
The women celebrating the Thesmophoria. See Thesmophoriazusae

ARLEN, MICHAEL, 1895-1956
The green hat. 1925. BES25

ARMSTRONG, ANTHONY, pseud. See Willis, Anthony Armstrong

ARNO, OWEN G.
The other player. BRNB

ARNOLD, MATTHEW, 1822-1888
Empedocles on Etna. 1852. KAU, PRAT2
The strayed reveler. 1849. PRAT2

AROUT, GABRIEL, 1909-
Beware of the dog (adapted from short stories of Chekhov). 1967.
Mitchell, Y., tr. PLAN33

ARRABAL, FERNANDO, 1932-
First communion. 1962.
Benedikt, M., tr. BENA
Picnic on the battlefield. 1959.
Anon. tr. HOGI, OHL
Hewitt, J., tr. COX, KERO
Wright, B., tr. BARO
Variant title: Pique-nique

en campagne
Pique-nique en campagne.
See Picnic on the battlefield

ARTAUD, ANTONIN, 1896-1948
Le jet de sang. See The jet of blood
The jet of blood. 1925.
Cohn, R., tr. TREJ
Wellwarth, G., tr. BEN
Variant titles: Le jet de sang; The spurt of blood
The spurt of blood. See The jet of blood

ASCH, SHOLEM, 1880-1957
God of vengeance.
Landis, J., tr. LAO, LAOG

ASHBERY, JOHN
The heroes. 1953. MACH

ASHTON, WINIFRED (CLEMENCE DANE, pseud.), d. 1965
A bill of divorcement. 1921.
BES21, COT, MAP, MOSO
Granite. 1926. MYB, TUCD
Moonlight is silver. 1934.
SEV
Wild Decembers. 1932.
BARV, SIXH

ASPENSTROM, WERNER, 1918-
The apes shall inherit the earth. 1959.
Sjöberg, L., and Goodman, R., trs. GOOR
Variant title: Det eviga
Det eviga. See The apes shall inherit the earth

ATHAS, DAPHNE SPENCER.
See Campbell, Marion Gurney, jt. auth.

ATLAS, LEOPOLD LAWRENCE, 1907-
"L." 1928. LEV, LEVE
Wednesday's child. 1934.
BES33

ATTOWELL, GEORGE, fl. 1599
Attowell's jig (sometimes attributed to). See Anonymous plays. Attowell's jig

AUBIGNY, D', pseud. See Baudouin, Jean Marie Théodore

AUDEN, WYSTAN HUGH, 1907- and ISHERWOOD, CHRISTOPHER
The ascent of F6. 1937.
TUCN
The dog beneath the skin.
1935. KOZ, KRE

AUGIER, EMILE, 1820-1889
Le mariage d'Olympe. 1855.
BOR
Clark, B., tr. SSTG
Variant title: Olympe's marriage
Olympe's marriage. See Le mariage d'Olympe

-- and SANDEAU, JULES
Le gendre de M. Poirier.
1854. BOR, GRA, SEA
Clark, B., tr. CLF2, MAU
Variant titles: M. Poirier's son-in-law; The son-in-law of M. Poirier
M. Poirier's son-in-law.
See Le gendre de M. Poirier
The son-in-law of M. Poirier.
See Le gendre de M. Poirier

AULETTA, ROBERT
Stops. 1972. BALLE10

AURENCHE, JEAN. See Anouilh, Jean, jt. auth.

AURTHUR, ROBERT ALAN
A very special baby. 1956.
BES56

AUSTEN, JANE, 1775-1817
Pride and prejudice. See Jerome, Mrs. Helen (Burton).

Pride and prejudice (based on the novel by)

AXELROD, GEORGE, 1923-
The seven year itch. 1952. GART, GARZA4, NEWV, THEA53

AYALA, ADELARDO LOPEZ DE. See López de Ayala, Adelardo

AYME, MARCEL, 1902-1967
Clérambard. 1950.
Denny, N., tr. FOUF
Variant title: The Count of Clerambard
The Count of Clerambard. See Clérambard

B

BABEL, ISAAC, 1894-1941
Marya. 1967.
Glenny, M., tr. GLE
Glenny, M., and Shukman, H., trs. PLAN35

BABO, JOSEPH MARIUS, 1756-1822
Dagobert, der franken König. See Dagobert, king of the Franks
Dagobert, king of the Franks. 1779.
Thompson, B., tr. BAT12
Variant title: Dagobert, der franken König

BACHER, WILLIAM A.
The snow goose. See Gallico, Paul. The snow goose (adapted by)

BACON, FRANK, 1864-1922.
See Smith, Winchell, jt. auth.

BAGNOLD, ENID, 1889-
Call me Jacky. 1968. PLAN34
The chalk garden. 1955. BES55, COTKH, THEA56
National velvet. 1946. EMB2

BAHR, HERMANN, 1863-1934
The concert. 1909.
Morgan, B., tr. DID
Variant title: Das konzert
Das konzert. See The Concert

BAKER, E. IRENE, and DRUMMOND, ALEXANDER MAGNUS
A day in the vineyard. DRU

BAKER, ELIZABETH, 1879-
Chains. 1909. DIG, PLAP1

BALDERSTON, JOHN LLOYD, 1889-1954
Berkeley square. 1926. BES29, GASB

BALDWIN, JAMES, 1924-
The amen corner. 1964. HARY, PATR
Blues for Mister Charlie. 1964. GARV, OLIV

-- and HUMPHREY, HUBERT H.
My childhood. BAYM

BALE, JOHN, 1495-1563
God's promises. 1538? EVER
Variant title: A tragedy or interlude manifesting the chief promises of God unto man
King John. 1539? ARMS, CRE, POLL
Variant title: Kynge Johan
Kynge Johan. See King John
A tragedy or interlude manifesting the chief promises of God unto man. See God's promises

BALL, DAVID.
Assassin. BALLE7

BALLESTEROS, ANTONIO M.
The best of all possible worlds. 1966?
Salerno, H., and Gross, S., trs. WELL, WELT

The hero.
Blue, R., tr. WELL

BALZAC, HONORE DE, 1799-1850
Mercadet. 1851. BOR

BARAKA, IMAMU AMIRI, pseud. See Jones, LeRoi

BARBA, PRESTON ALBERT, 1883-
An der lumpa parti. 1933. BUFF
Dié verrechelte rechler (adapted from the novel by Charles C. More). 1933. BUFF

BARBER, PHILIP WILLSON, 1903-
I, Elizabeth Otis, being of sound mind. 1964. BALLE3

BARCA, PEDRO CALDERON DE LA. See Calderón de la Barca, Pedro

BARING, MAURICE, 1874-1945
The rehearsal. 1911? WEB

BARKENTIN, MARJORIE
Ulysses in Nighttown (adapted from the novel Ulysses by James Joyce). 1958. COTK

BARKER, GEORGE, 1913-
Rococo. WEAN

BARKER, HARLEY GRANVILLE. See Granville-Barker, Harley Granville

BARKER, JAMES NELSON, 1784-1858
The Indian princess; or, La belle sauvage. 1808. MOSS1
Superstition. 1824. GARX, HAL, QUIJ, QUIK, QUIL, QUIM, QUIN

BARLACH, ERNST, 1870-1938
Squire Blue Boll. 1926?
Ritchie, J., and Garten, H., trs. RITS

BARLOW, ANNA MARIE
Mr. Biggs. NEWA1

BARNARD, CHARLES, 1838-1920. See De Mille, Henry Churchill, jt. auth.

BARRAS, CHARLES M., 1826-1873
The black crook. 1866. MASW

BARRIE, SIR JAMES MATTHEW, 1860-1937
The admirable Crichton. 1903. CHAR, CLKW, COTH, DUR, RED, REDM, SALE, SPER, TREBA, TREC2, TREE3, TREI3, WARI
Dear Brutus. 1917. BROW, COTKR, WATF2, WATI
The little minister. 1897. BES94
Mary Rose. 1920. BES20
The old lady shows her medals. 1921. INGG, INGH
Shall we join the ladies? 1928. WORL4
The twelve pound look. 1910. BOGO, CONP, DAVI, MCNA, WEAT2
A well-remembered voice. 1918. FULT
What every woman knows. 1908. CEU, WATF1, WATI, WATO
The will. 1914. MILL

BARRY, PHILIP, 1896-1949
The animal kingdom. 1932. BES31, GAS
Foolish notion. 1945. BES44
God bless our home. See The youngest
Here come the clowns. 1938. BES38, GARU
Holiday. 1928. BES28, KEY,

MACG, MERW, MOSK, MOSL
Hotel Universe. 1930. LEV, LEVE, THF, WATC2, WATI, WHI
In a garden. 1925. TUCD, TUCM
The joyous season. 1934. CATH, DAVI
Paris bound. 1927. BES27, GASB, QUIL, QUIM, QUIN
Variant title: The wedding
The Philadelphia story. 1939. BES38, BROU, GARZ, GARZA2, WAIT, WAIU
Second threshold (revised by Robert E. Sherwood). 1951. BES50
Tomorrow and tomorrow. 1931. BES30
The wedding. See Paris bound
You and I. 1923. BES22, HAL
The youngest. 1924. BES24
Variant title: God bless our home

BART-WILLIAMS, GASTON
The drug. PIET

BASS, KINGSLEY B.
We righteous bombers. 1968. TUQT

BASSHE, EMANUEL JO, 1900-1939
Doomsday circus. See The dream of the dollar
The dream of the dollar. 1933. AME5
Variant title: Doomsday circus

BATEMAN, MRS. SIDNEY FRANCES (COWELL), 1823-1881
Self. 1857. MOSS2

BATES, ESTHER WILLARD, 1884-
The two thieves. 1925? FED2

BAUDOIN, JEAN MARIE THEODORE (D'AUBIGNY, pseud.). See Caigniez, Louis Charles, jt. auth.

BAUM, VICKI, 1888-1960
Grand Hotel. 1930.
Drake, W., tr. BES30, CEW
Variant title: Menschen im hotel
Menschen im hotel. See Grand hotel

BAUS, MANUEL TAMAYO Y. See Tamayo y Baus, Manuel

BAX, CLIFFORD, 1886-1962
The rose without a thorn. 1932. FAMB, PLAD
Socrates. 1929. SIXD
The Venetian. 1930. MYB

BAYARD, J. F. A. See Scribe, Augustin Eugène, jt. auth.

BAYON HERRERA, LUIS
Santos Vega. 1913.
Fassett, J., tr. BIES

BEACH, LEWIS, 1891-
The clod. 1914. BUR, GASB
The goose hangs high. 1924. BES23, KEY

BEAUMARCHAIS, PIERRE AUGUSTIN CARON DE, 1732-1799
The barber of Seville. See Le barbier de Seville
Le barbier de Seville; ou, La précaution inutile. 1775. BOV, BOVE, BRN, STJ1, ZDA
Bermel, A., tr. BERM
Fowlie, W., tr. FOWL
Myrick, A., tr. MAU
Taylor, W., tr. CLF2
Variant title: The barber of Seville
Figaro's marriage; or, One mad day. See Le mariage de Figaro
Le mariage de Figaro. 1784. BRE, SEA
Barzun, J., tr. BENR4
Variant titles: Figaro's marriage; or, One mad day; The marriage of Figaro

The marriage of Figaro. See Le mariage de Figaro

BEAUMONT, FRANCIS, 1584-1616, and FLETCHER, JOHN
A king or no king. 1611. WALL
The knight of the burning pestle. 1610. ANG, BALD, BAS, BAT14, BENY, BROC, HOW, NEI, OLH, OLI2, ORNC, SCI, SCJ, SPE, WHE, WINE
The maid's tragedy. 1611. BAS, BROC, CLF1, CLKW, DUN, MCK, NEI, OLH, OLI2, RUB, SCH, SCI, SCJ, SPE
Philaster; or, Love lies a-bleeding. 1609. BAS, BROC, HARC47, HOW, HUD, LIE, MAT, NEI, OLH, OLI2, PAR, SCH, SCI, SCJ, SPE, TAT, TAU, THA, WAT, WHE, WINE
--See Fletcher, John, jt. auth.

BECKETT, SAMUEL, 1906-
Act without words. 1957. ALLJ, ALLK, HAVH
All that fall. 1957. ALLJ, ALLK, CALD, CLO, SCNO, WEIM, WEIS
Les beaux jours. See Happy days
Embers. 1959. COK
En attendant Godot. See Waiting for Godot
Endgame. 1957.
Beckett, S., tr. BLOC, COTQ
Variant title: Fin de partie
Fin de partie. See Endgame
Happy days; ou, Les beaux jours. 1961. GOLD
Variant titles: Les beaux jours; Ou les beaux jours
Ou les beaux jours. See Happy days.
Waiting for Godot. 1952. BES55
Beckett, S., tr. SEVD
Variant title: En attendant Godot

BECQUE, HENRI, 1837-1899
Les corbeaux. 1882. BOR, GRA, SEA, STJ2
Tilden, F., tr. MOSQ, TREBA, TREC2, TREE2, TREI2, TREJ, WATL1
Variant titles: The crows; The ravens; The vultures
The crows. See Les corbeaux
The Parisian woman. See La Parisienne
La Parisienne. 1882.
Barzun, J., tr. BENS1, BENT1
Vaughn, E., tr. COTKW
Variant titles: The Parisian woman; The woman of Paris
The ravens. See Les corbeaux
The vultures. See Les corbeaux
The woman of Paris. See La Parisienne

BEECHER, CLARE. See Kummer, Mrs. Clare (Beecher)

BEECHER, HARRIET ELIZABETH. See Stowe, Mrs. Harriet (Beecher)

BEERBOHM, MAX, 1872-1956
A social success. 1913. BENT6

BEHAN, BRENDAN, 1923-1964
The hostage. 1958. BES60, POP
The new house. 1958. RICJ
The quare fellow. 1954. SEVD

BEHN, MRS. APHRA (AMIS), 1640-1689
The emperor of the moon. 1687. HUGH

BEHRMAN, SAMUEL NATHANIEL, 1893-1973
Amphitryon 38 (adapted from

Amphitryon 38, by Jean Giraudoux). 1937. BES37, CEW, THH
Biography. 1932. BES32, BROU, CET, GARU, MIJY, WAIT, WARH, WARL, WHI
Brief moment. 1931. BES31
The cold wind and the warm. 1958. BES58
End of summer. 1936. BES35, CLUR, GAS, WATS
I know my love (adapted from Auprès de ma blonde by Marcel Achard). 1949. BES49
Jacobowsky and the Colonel (adapted from the play by Franz Werfel). 1944. BES43, GARZH
Jane (from the story by W. Somerset Maugham). 1952. BES51
No time for comedy. 1939. BES38, CER, SIXL
Rain from heaven. 1934. CHAN, CHAP, THF
The second man. 1927. CAR, CARA, GASB, MOSK, MOSL

-- and LOGAN, JOSHUA
Fanny (based on the trilogy Marius, Fanny and César by Marcel Pagnol) (music and lyrics by Harold Rome). 1954. THEA55

BEITH, JOHN HAY, 1876-1952. See Hay, Ian, pseud.

BELASCO, DAVID, 1859-1931
La belle Russe. 1881. AMP18
The girl of the golden west. 1905. MOSJ, MOSK, MOSL
The heart of Maryland. 1895. AMP18, BES94, CLA
Naughty Anthony. 1899. AMP18
The return of Peter Grimm. 1911. BAK, MIL, MOSS3
The stranglers of Paris. 1881. AMP18

-- and DE MILLE, HENRY CHURCHILL
The charity ball. 1889. AMP17
Lord Chumley. 1888. AMP17
Men and women. 1890. AMP17
The wife. 1887. AMP17

-- and FYLES, FRANKLIN
The girl I left behind me. 1893. AMP18

-- and LONG, JOHN LUTHER
The darling of the gods. 1902. BES99
Madame Butterfly. 1900. QUIG, QUIJ, QUIK, QUIL, QUIM, QUIN, QUIO2

BELLIDO, JOSE-MARIA, 1922-
Bread and rice or geometry in yellow. Lima, R., tr. WELL
Variant title: El pan y el arroz o geometría en amarillo
Football. 1963. Turner, D., tr. BENA
El pan y el arroz o geometría en amarillo. See Bread and rice or geometry in yellow
Train to H... 1968? Flores, R., tr. WELL
Variant title: Tren a F...
Tren a F... See Train to H...

BELLOW, SAUL, 1915-
The last analysis. 1964. COTKI, GARV, SSTY
Orange souffle. 1965. RICK, SANK
The wrecker. 1954? NEWW6

BELLVIS, GUILLEM DE CASTRO Y. See Castro y Bellvis, Guillem

BENAVENTE Y MARTINEZ, JACINTO, 1866-1954

The bias of the world. See The bonds of interest
The bonds of interest. 1907.
Underhill, J., tr. DID, FLOS, MOSQ, WHI
Variant titles: The bias of the world; Los intereses creados; Interests created; Vested interests
Las brujas del domingo. See The witches' sabbath
His widow's husband. 1908?
Underhill, J., tr. MCCP
Variant title: El marido de su viuda
Los intereses creados. See The bonds of interest
Interests created. See The bonds of interest
La malquerida. See The passion flower
El marido de su viuda. See His widow's husband
The nest of another. See El nido ajeno
El nido ajeno. 1895. BRET
Variant title: The nest of another
No fumadores. See No smoking
No smoking. 1904.
Underhill, J., tr. INGW
Variant title: No fumadores
The passion flower. 1913.
Underhill, J., tr. GARZH, TUCG, TUCM, TUCN, TUCO, WATI, WATL3
Variant title: La malquerida
Vested interests. See The bonds of interest
The witches' sabbath. 1903.
Oliver, W., tr. COTP
Variant title: Las brujas del domingo

BENEDICTO, JOAQUIN DICENTA Y. See Dicenta y Benedicto, Joaquín

BENEDIX, RODERICH, 1811-1873
Eigensinn. See Obstinacy
Obstinacy. 1864.
Chambers, W., tr. BAT11
Variant title: Eigensinn

BENELLI, SEM, 1877-1949
L'amore dei tre re. See The love of the three kings
La cena delle beffe. See The jest
A Florentine wager. See The jest
A fool there was. See The jest
The jest. 1919.
Sheldon, E., tr. and adapter. BES19
Variant titles: La cena delle beffe; A Florentine wager; A fool there was; The jesters' supper; The love feast; The love thief; The supper of pranks
The jesters' supper. See The jest
The love feast. See The jest
The love of the three kings. 1910.
Jones, H., tr. DIE
Variant title: L'amore dei tre re
The love thief. See The jest
The supper of pranks. See The jest

BENET, STEPHEN VINCENT, 1898-1943
The devil and Daniel Webster. 1939. BART, HEI

BENGAL, BEN
Plant in the sun. 1937? KOZ

BENNETT, ARNOLD, 1867-1931
Flora. 1933. FIT
The great adventure. 1913. CHU, COT
-- and KNOBLOCK, EDWARD
Milestones. 1912. CEU, COD, DID, MAP, MOD, PEN, TUCJ, WAGC4

BENNETT, CLARENCE
A royal slave. 1898? AMP8

BENNETT, RICHARD R.

The mines of sulphur, an opera (music by). See Cross, Beverley. The mines of sulphur, an opera.

BENRIMO, JOSEPH HENRY 1871-1942. See Hazleton, George Cochrane, jt. auth.

BENSON, ROBERT HUGH, 1871-1914
The upper room. 191-? PRON

BENSON, MRS. SALLY, 1900-1972
Junior miss (based on the book by). See Fields, Joseph and Chodorov, Jerome. Junior miss

BENTLEY, ERIC RUSSELL, 1916-
Are you now or have you ever been: The investigation of show business by the Un-American Activities Committee, 1947-48. (1972) RICK
Celestina; or, The tragicomedy of Calisto and Melibea. See Rojas, Fernando de. Celestina; or, The tragi-comedy of Calisto and Melibea (adapted by)
Larry Parks' day in court. See Are you now or have you ever been... (excerpt)
Mary Stuart. See Schiller, Johann. Mary Stuart (adapted by)

BENTON, ROBERT, 1932-
See Newman, David, jt. auth.

BEOLCO, ANGELO (called Ruzzante), 1502-1542
Bilora. 1527?
Hughes, B., and G., trs. CLF2
Il reduce. See Ruzzante returns from the wars
Ruzzante returns from the wars. 1522?
Ingold, A., and Hoffman, T., trs. BENR1
Variant title: Il reduce

BERCOVICI, ERIC
The heart of age. 195-? NEWW4

BERG, GERTRUDE, 1900-1966
Me and Molly. 1948. BES47

BERGMAN, HJALMAR, 1883-1931
Herr Sleeman kommer. See Mr. Sleeman is coming
Mr. Sleeman is coming. 1917.
Alexander, H., tr. SCAN1
Variant title: Herr Sleeman kommer
The swedenhielms. 1925.
Alexander, H., and Jones, L., trs. SCAN3

BERGMAN, INGMAR, 1918-
The seventh seal. 1972?
Anon. tr. KNO
Malstrom, L., and Rushner, D. ABC

BERKELEY, REGINALD CHEYNE, 1890-1935
The lady with a lamp. 1929. FAO, PLAD
The white chateau. 1927. MAP

BERKEY, RALPH. See Denker, Henry, jt. auth.

BERMANGE, BARRY, 1933-
No quarter. 1962. NEWE12
Scenes from family life. 1969. MESS

BERNARD, JEAN-JACQUES, 1888-1972
Arver's secret. See Le secret d'Arvers
Glamour. 1924.
Boyd, E., tr. DIK2
Katzin, W., tr. KAT
Variant titles: L'Invitation au voyage; The years between
L'invitation au voyage. See Glamour

Martine. 1922. RHO
Katzin, W., tr. KAT
Le secret d'Arvers. 1926. GRAF
Variant title: Arver's secret
The years between. See Glamour

BERNARD, KENNETH
The unknown Chinaman. 1971. BALLE10
BERNARD, LAWRENCE J.
Lars killed his son. 1935? TOD
BERNARD, PAUL. See Bernard, Tristan, pseud.

BERNARD, TRISTAN (pseud. of Paul Bernard), 1866-1947
L'anglais tel qu'on le parle. 1899. SET
Variant titles: English as it is spoken; French without a master
English as it is spoken. See L'anglais tel qu'on le parle
French without a master. See L'anglais tel qu'on le parle

BERNEY, WILLIAM. See Richardson, Howard, jt. auth.

BERNHARD, EMIL (pseud. of Emil Cohn), 1881-
The Marranos. 1935?
Meyer, B., and Arlet, V., trs. RUA

BERNSTEIN, HENRY, 1876-1953
Le secret. 1913. HARV

BERNSTEIN, LEONARD, 1918-
Candide. See Hellman, Lillian. Candide (music by)
Wonderful town. See Fields, Joseph and Chodorov, Jerome. Wonderful town (music by)

BERRIGAN, DANIEL J., S.J., 1921-
The trial of the Catonsville nine. 1971. BES70

BESIER, RUDOLF, 1878-1942
The Barretts of Wimpole Street. 1930. BES30, CEU, FAMA, GARZAP, GASS, GOW, GOWA, INGH, KNIE, PLAD, PLAL2, SPER, THO
The virgin goddess. 1906. MAP
BETTI, UGO, 1892-1953
Corruption in the palace of justice. 1949.
Reed, H., tr. CONO, COTR, FREG, KERP
Satin, J., tr. SATI
Variant title: Corruzione al palazzo di giustizia
Corruzione al palazzo di giustizia. See Corruption in the palace of justice
Crime on Goat Island. 1950.
Reed, H., tr. COTN
Variant titles: Delitto all' Isola delle Capre; Island of Goats
Delitto all' Isola delle Capre. See Crime on Goat Island
Island of Goats. See Crime on Goat Island
The queen and the rebels. 1951.
Reed, H., tr. BROSA, COTQ, ULAN
Variant title: La regina e gli insorti
Le regine e gli insorti. See The queen and the rebels

BEYNON, RICHARD
The shifting heart. 1957. OBSE
BEZE, THEODORE DE, 1519-1605
Abraham sacrifiant. FOUR

BHASA, 4th cent. B.C.-1st cent. A.D.
The dream of Vāsavadatta (supposed author). 4th cent. B.C.-1st cent. A.D.
Irwin, V., tr. IRW

Lal, P., tr. LAL
Woolner, A., and Sarup, L., trs. WEL
Variant title: The vision of Vāsavadatta
The vision of Vāsavadatta. See The dream of Vāsavadatta

BHAVABHUTI, 8th cent.
The later story of Rama. 8th cent.
Josl, C., tr. WEL
Lal, P., tr. LAL
Variant title: Rama's later history
Rama's later history. See The later story of Rama

BIBIENA, BERNARDO CARDINAL DOVIZI DA. See Dovizi da Biblena, Bernardo Cardinal

BIGGERS, EARL DERR, 1884-1933
Seven keys to Baldpate. See Cohan, George M. Seven keys to Baldpate (based on the novel by)

BILLETDOUX, FRANÇOIS, 1927-
Tchin-Tchin. See Michaels, Sydney. Tchin-Tchin (based on the play by)

BINGHAM, J. See MacBeth, George

BIRD, ROBERT MONTGOMERY, 1806-1854
The broker of Bogota. 1834. QUIJ, QUIK, QUIL, QUIM, QUIN
Caridorf; or, The avenger. 1827? AMP12
The cowled lover. 1827? AMP12
The gladiator. 1831. HAL, MONR
News of the night; or, A trip to Niagara. 1829. AMP12
'Twas all for the best; or, 'Tis all a notion. 1827? AMP12

BIRMELIN, JOHN, 1873-1950
Der gnopp (based on the play Ein knopf by Julius Rosen). 1935. BUFF
Em Docktor Fogel sei offis schtunn (based on the farce Dr. Kranichs, sprechstunde) 1935? BUFF

BIRMISA, GEORGE, 1924-
Georgie porgie. 1968. SME

BISSELL, RICHARD PIKE. See Abbott, George, jt. auth.

BIZET, GEORGES, 1838-1875
Carmencita and the soldier (based on the opera Carmen). See Lipskeroff, Konstantin. Carmencita and the soldier

BJØRNSON, BJØRNSTJERNE, 1832-1910
Between the battles. 1858.
Weingarten, J., tr. MCCP
Variant title: Mellem slagene
Beyond human might. See Beyond our power
Beyond human power. See Beyond our power
Beyond our power. 1883.
Björkman, E., tr. TUCG
Hollander, L., tr. DIC
Variant titles: Beyond human might; Beyond human power; Over evne; Pastor song
A gauntlet. 1883.
Edwards, O., tr. BAT17
Variant titles: A glove; En hanske
A glove. See A gauntlet
En hanske. See A gauntlet
Mellem slagene. See Between the battles
Over evne. See Beyond our power
Pastor song. See Beyond our power

BLADES, WILLIAM, 1824-1890

The printer's apprentice (tr. from Latin into German by). See Anonymous plays. The printer's apprentice

BLITZSTEIN, MARC, 1905-
Another part of the forest (music by). See Hellman, Lillian. Another part of the forest.
The cradle will rock. 1937. KOZ

BLOCK, TONI
You must stay to tea. 1948? RUA

BLOK, ALEKSANDR ALEKSANDROVICH, 1880-1921
The puppet show. 1906.
Reeve, F., tr. REEV2

BOCK, JERRY, 1928-
The apple tree (jt. auth. and music by). See Harnick, Sheldon. The apple tree
Fiddler on the roof (music by). See Stein, Joseph. Fiddler on the roof
Fiorello! (music by). See Weisman, Jerome and Abbott, George. Fiorello!
She loves me (music by). See Masteroff, Joe. She loves me

BODEL, JEAN. See Bodel, Jehan

BODEL, JEHAN, ca. 1167-ca. 1210
Le jeu de Saint Nicolas. See The play of Saint Nicholas
The play of Saint Nicholas. ca. 1200.
Axton, R., and Stevens, J., trs. AXT
Mandel, O., tr. MAN
Variant title: Le jeu de Saint Nicolas

BOIS ROBERT, FRANÇOIS. See Bois-Robert, François Le Métel de

BOIS-ROBERT, FRANÇOIS LE METEL DE, 1592-1662
L'amant ridicule. 1655. LAN

BOKER, GEORGE HENRY, 1823-1890
The bankrupt. 1855. AMP3
Francesca da Rimini. 1855. ELLI1, HAL, MASW, MCDO, MONR, MOSS3, QUIJ, QUIK, QUIL, QUIM, QUIN, QUIO1
Glacus. 1886. AMP3
The world a mask. 1851. AMP3

BOLAND, BRIDGET
Cockpit. 1948. PLAN1
Gordon. 1961. PLAN25
The prisoner. 1954. PLAN10
The return. 1953. PLAN9

BOLITHO, WILLIAM, pseud. See Ryall, William Bolitho

BOLT, ROBERT, 1924-
A man for all seasons. 1960. BES61, CEQA, COTKH, COTR, NEWE6
Vivat! Vivat Regina! 1972. BES71

BOLTON, GUY REGINALD, 1884-1961
Anastasia. See Maurette, Marcelle. Anastasia (adapted by)
Chicken feed. 1923. BES23
Variant title: Wages for wives
Don't listen ladies! See Guitry, Sacha. Don't listen ladies! (adapted by)
Wages for wives. See Chicken feed

-- and MIDDLETON, GEORGE
Adam and Eva. 1919. BES19

BONNER, MARITA, 1905-
The purple flower. 1928. HARY

BONTEMPS, ARNA, 1903-1973 and CULLEN, COUNTEE

The St. Louis woman. 1946. PATR

BOOTHE, CLARE, (married name Clare Boothe Luce), 1903-
Kiss the boys good-bye. 1938. BES38
Margin for error. 1939. BES39, CER, FIR
The women. 1936. BES36, CET, FAMK, GAS, SUB

BORCHERT, WOLFGANG, 1921-1947
Draussen vor der Tür. See The outsider
The man outside. See The outsider
The outsider. 1947. Benedikt, M., tr. BENB
Variant titles: Draussen vor der Tür; The man outside

BORETZ, NICK
Shelter area. 1964. BALLE2

BORSOOK, HENRY
Three weddings of a hunchback. 1924. MAS1

BOSAKOWSKI, PHILIP A.
Bierce takes on the railroad. 1972. BALLE11

BOTTOMLEY, GORDON, 1874-1948
Gruach. 1923. KRE

BOUCICAULT, DION, 1822-1890
After dark. 1868. BAI
Belle Lamar. 1874. LEV, LEVE
Boursiquot. See The Colleen Bawn
The Colleen Bawn; or, The brides of Garryowen. 1860. ROWE
Variant title: Boursiquot
The Corsican brothers. 1852. BOOA2
Dot (adapted from The cricket on the hearth, by Charles Dickens). 1859. AMP1
Flying scud; or, A four-legged fortune. 1866. AMP1, CLA
Forbidden fruit. 1876. AMP1
London assurance. 1841. ASG, BAI, BAT22, BENY, COTKF, MAT, MOSN, MOSO
Louis XI. 1855. AMP1
Mercy Dodd; or, Presumptive evidence. 1869. AMP1
The octoroon; or, Life in Louisiana. 1859. COY, GARX, MASW, QUIJ, QUIK, QUIL, QUIM, QUIN
Rip Van Winkle (adapted by). See Anonymous plays. Rip Van Winkle (as played by Joseph Jefferson)
Robert Emmet. 1884. AMP1
The Shaughraun. 1874. BOOA2

BOURLET, KATHERINE, 15th cent.
The nativity (The Chantilly play). 15th cent. Sanchez, E., and Robinson, D., trs. and adapters. ROBM

BOVASSO, JULIE, 1930-
Schubert's last serenade. 1971. OWE

BOWEN, JOHN GRIFFITH, 1924-
After the rain. 1967. BES67
The waiting room. 1970. RICK

BOWEN, MARGARET ELIZABETH
Crude and unrefined. 194-? PROG

BOWER, RICHARD, fl. 1570
Apius and Virginia (sometimes attributed to). See Anonymous plays. Apius and Virginia

BOWLES, JANE AUER, 1917-
In the summer house. 1953. BES53

BOX, MURIEL, 1905-
Angels of war. 1935? FIN

BOX, SYDNEY, 1907-
The woman and the walnut tree. 1935? FIN

BOYER, CLAUDE, 1618-1698
Le faux Tonaxare. See Oropastes
Oropaste; ou, Le faux Tonaxare. See Oropastes
Oropastes. 1662.
Lockert, L., tr. LOCU
Variant titles: Le faux Tonaxare; Oropaste

BRACCO, ROBERTO, 1862-1943
I fantasmi. See Phantasms
Phantasms. 1906.
St. Cyr, D., tr. TUCG
Variant title: I fantasmi

BRACKENRIDGE, HUGH HENRY, 1748-1816
The battle of Bunkers-hill. 1776? MOSS1
The death of General Montgomery, in storming the City of Quebec. 1777. PHI

BRADDON, MARY ELIZABETH, 1837-1915
Lady Audley's secret. See Hazlewood, Colin Hazlewood. Lady Audley's secret (from the novel by)

BRADDON, RUSSELL
Naked island. 1960. PLAN22

BRADFORD, ROARK, 1896-1948
Ol' man Adam and his chillun. See Connelly, Marc. The green pastures (based on the novel by)

BRANCH, WILLIAM, 1927-
In splendid error. 1954. HARY, PATR
A medal for Willie. 1951. KINN

BRAND, MILLEN, 1906-
The outward room. See Kingsley, Sidney. The world we make (based on the novel by)

BRANNER, H. C., 1903-1966
The judge. 1951.
Roughton, A., tr. CONT
Variant title: Søskende
Søskende. See The judge

BRECHT, BERTOLT, 1898-1956
Die ausnahme und die regel. See The exception and the rule
Baal. 1922.
Bentley, E., and Esslin, M., trs. SOK
The Caucasian chalk circle. 1954.
Anon. tr. BLON, CLN
Bentley, E., tr. ALLJ, BAUL, BENSB2, BES62, COTQ, DEAS, DIT, ESS, FEL, GOU2, HAVH, JOHO, MACM2, MIJB, REIL, REIO, REIT, SMA
Bentley, E., and Apelman, M., trs. COTL, WEIS, WEIW
Variant title: Der kaukasische Kreidekreis
Dreigroschenoper. See The threepenny opera
The exception and the rule. 1930?
Bentley, E., tr. NEW55
Variant title: Die ausnahme und die regel
Fear and misery of the Third Reich. See The private life of the master race
Furcht und Elend des Dritten Reiches. See The private life of the master race
Galileo. 1947.
Laughton, C., tr. BENS2, HILP, RAI, TREJ, TRIA
Variant title: Das Leben des Galilei
The good woman of Setzuan. 1943.

Bentley, E., tr. AUG, BLOC, BRIX, BUR, DOT, GOLD, REIN, REIP, SHRO, TREJ, VANV2, WEIM
Variant title: Der gute mensch von Sezuan
Der gute mensch von Sezuan. See The good woman of Setzuan
Herr Puntila und sein knecht matti. See Puntila and his hired man
Der kaukasische Kreiderkreis. See The Caucasian chalk circle
Das Leben des Galilei. See Galileo
Die massnahme. See The measures taken
The measures taken. 1930.
Bentley, E., tr. BENT6
Variant title: Die massnahme
Mother Courage. 1941.
Bentley, E., tr. BENSB2, BENT2, BES62, BLOC, BONC, CLO, COTS, GOLD, JOHN, KERN, KERO, KERP, WAIW
Hays, H., tr. NEW41
Variant titles: Mother Courage and her children; Mutter Courage und ihre kinder
Mother Courage and her children. See Mother Courage
Mutter Courage und ihre kinder. See Mother Courage
A penny for the poor. See The threepenny opera
The private life of the master race. 1938.
Bentley, E., tr. KERO, TREBA, TREC2, TREE2, TREI2
Variant titles: Fear and misery of the Third Reich; Furcht und Elend des Dritten Reiches
Puntila and his hired man. 1940.
Nellhaus, G., tr. COTKI
Variant title: Herr Puntila und sein knecht matti
Saint Joan of the stockyards. 1932?
Jones, F., tr. BENS3
The seven deadly sins of the lower middle classes. 1933.
Auden, W., and Kullman, C., trs. GOOR
Variant title: Die sieben todsunden der kleinbürger
Die sieben todsunden der kleinbürger. See The seven deadly sins of the lower middle classes
The threepenny opera (music by Kurt Weill). 1928.
Bentley, E., tr. ASF
Vesey, D., and Bentley, E., trs. BENS1, BENT1
Variant titles: Dreigroschenoper; A penny for the poor
Das verhor des Lukullus. 1939? FEFH2

BREEN, RICHARD, and SCHNIBBE, HARRY
"Who ride on white horses," the story of Edmund Campion. 1940. THEC

BREIT, HARVEY, 1913- . See Schulberg, Budd, jt. author

BRENDLE, THOMAS ROYCE, 1889-
Die hoffning. 19-? BUFF
Die mutter. 1934. BUFF

BRETON, ANDRE, 1896-1966, and SOUPAULT, PHILIPPE
If you please. 1920.
Wellwarth, G., tr. BEN
Variant title: S'il vous plaît
S'il vous plaît. See If you please

BRETON DE LOS HERREROS, MANUEL, 1796-1873
Muérete ¡y verás! 1837. BRET

BRICUSSE, LESLIE, 1931- , and NEWLEY, ANTHONY
Stop the world--I want to get off (book, lyrics and music by). 1962. BES62

BRIDGERS, ANN PRESTON. See Abbott, George, jt. auth.

BRIDIE, JAMES, pseud. See Mavor, Osborne Henry

BRIEUX, EUGENE, 1858-1932
The aim of the law. See La robe rouge
False gods. 1909.
Fagan, J., tr. TUCG
Variant title: La foi
La foi. See False gods
The letter of the law. See La robe rouge
The red robe. See La robe rouge
La robe rouge. 1900. GRA
Reed, F., tr. DIC, DIK2, WHI
Variant titles: The aim of the law; The letter of the law; The red robe
The three daughters of M. Dupont. See Les trois filles de M. Dupont
Les trois filles de M. Dupont. 1897. BER, BOR
Variant title: The three daughters of M. Dupont

BRIGHOUSE, HAROLD, 1882-1958
Hobson's choice. 1916. MAP, TUCD

BRITTON, KENNETH PHILLIPS and HARGRAVE, ROY
Houseparty. 1928? LEV, LEVE

BROCH, HERMANN, 1886-1951
The atonement. 1934.
Wellwarth, G., and Rotherman, H., trs. WELG

BROME, RICHARD, d. 1652?
The antipodes. 1638. GAY3, KNOW
A jovial crew. 1641. LAWS, OLH, OLI2
A mad couple well matched. 1653? KNOW, WALL

BRONTË, CHARLOTTE, 1816-1855
Jane Eyre. See Jerome, Mrs. Helen (Burton). Jane Eyre (based on the novel by)

BROOKS, HARRY, 1876-
See Malleson, Miles, jt. auth.

BROPHY, BRIGID, 1929-
The waste disposal unit. 1964. RICJ

BROUGH, WILLIAM, and HALLIDAY, ANDREW
The area belle. 1864. BOOA4

BROUGHAM, JOHN, 1810-1880
The duke's motto; or, I am here! 1862. AMP14
Po-ca-hon-tas. See Pocahontas; or, The gentle savage
Pocahontas; or, The gentle savage. 1855. AMPA, BAT20, MONR
Variant title: Po-ca-hon-tas

BROWER, BROCK, 1931-
A little to the left. 1959. PAJ

BROWN, DAVID PAUL, 1795-1875
Sertorius; or, The Roman patriot. 1830. MOSS2

BROWN, WILLIAM WELLS, 1814-1884
The escape; or, A leap to freedom. 1858. HARY, RAVA

BROWNE, MAURICE, 1881-1955
See Nichols, Robert Malise Boyer, jt. auth.

BROWNE, PORTER EMERSON, 1879-1934
The bad man. 1920. BES20

BROWNE, ROBERT F. GORE. See Gore-Browne, Robert F.

BROWNE, THEODORE, 1910-
Natural man. 1937. HARY

BROWNE, WYNYARD, 1911-
The holly and the ivy. 1950. PLAN3

BROWNING, ROBERT, 1812-1889
A blot in the 'scutcheon. 1843. ASH, GRE, HARC18, MOSN, MOSO, TAT
In a balcony. 1884. GREC2
King Victor and King Charles. KAU
Pippa passes. 1841. BAI

BRUCE, RICHARD, 1905-
Sahdji, an African ballet. 1927. LOC

BRUNO, GIORDANO, 1548-1600
Il candelaio. See The candle bearer
The candle bearer. 16th cent.
Hale, J., tr. BENSA
Variant title: Il candelaio

BRUNSON, BEVERLY
A bastard of the blood. 19-? NEWW10

BRUST, ALFRED, 1891-
Die Wölff. See The wolves
The wolves. 1922.
Ritchie, J., and Garten, H., trs. RITS
Variant title: Die Wölff

BRYDEN, BILL
Willie Rough. 1973. PLAN43

BUCHANAN, GEORGE, 1506-1582
Jephté; ou, Le voeu. 1552? FOUR
Variant title: Le voeu
Le voeu. See Jephté

BUCHNER, GEORG, 1813-1837
Danton's death. 1836.
Holmstrom, J., tr. BENT5
Lustig, T., tr. LUST
Spender, S., and Rees, G., trs. BENS1, TREB, TREC1, TREE1, TREI1
Variant title: Dantons tod
Dantons tod. See Danton's death
Leonce and Lena. 1911.
Bentley, E., tr. BENS3, ESS
Woyzeck. 1879.
Hoffman, T., tr. BENT1
Mueller, C., tr. COTKIR, COTL, COTQ
Sorell, W., tr. ASF
Schnitzler, H., and Ulman, S., trs. NEW50
Wellwarth, G., tr. WELT
Variant title: Wozzeck
Wozzeck. See Woyzeck

BUCK, PEARL S., 1892-1973
Will this earth hold? INGA

BUCKHURST, LORD. See Sackville, Thomas

BUCKINGHAM, GEORGE VILLIERS, 1628-1687
The rehearsal. 1671. FAL, LEV, LEVE, MCM, MCMI, MOSE1, NET, REST, STM

BUCKSTONE, JOHN BALDWIN, 1802-1879
Luke the labourer; or, The lost son. 1826. BAI, MOR

BUECHNER, GEORG. See Büchner, Georg

BUENAVENTURA, ENRIQUE
In the right hand of God the father. 1960.
Oliver, W., tr. OLIW

BUERO VALLEJO, ANTONIO, 1916-

The concert at Saint Ovide. 1962.
Anderson, F., tr. HOLT
Variant title: El concierto de San Ovidio
El concierto de San Ovidio. See The concert at Saint Ovide
The dream weaver. 1952.
Oliver, W., tr. COTP
Variant title: La tejedora de sueños
La tejedora de sueños. See The dream weaver

BULGAKOV, MIKHAIL ALFANASEVICH, 1891-1940
Days of the Turbins. 1926.
Lyons, E., tr. LYK
Reeve, F., tr. REEV2
Variant title: Last of the Turbins
Last of the Turbins. See Days of the Turbins

BULKLEY, A. M.
The crown of light. 1934. SEVE

BULLINS, ED, 1935-
The corner. 1972. KINH
Dialect determinism. 1965. OWE
The electronic nigger. 1968. HOGI, NEWA3
The fabulous Miss Marie. 1971. NEWL
Gentleman caller. 1970. BLA, OLIV
Goin' a Buffalo. 1966. HARY
How do you do. 1969. JON
In the wine time. 1968. PATR
A son, come home. 1968. BAIC, BAIE, CLN

BULWER-LYTTON, EDWARD GEORGE EARLE LYTTON, 1803-1873
The conspiracy. See Richelieu
The lady of Lyons; or, Love and pride. 1838. ASG, STA, TAT, TAU
Variant title: Love and pride
Love and pride. See The lady of Lyons
Money. 1840. BAT16, BOOA3, ROWE
Richelieu; or, The conspiracy. 1839. BAI, BOOA1, CROS, DUR, MAT, MOSN, MOSO
Variant title: The conspiracy

BUNCE, OLIVER BELL, 1828-1890
Love in '76. 1857. MOSS3

BURGESS, JOHN, and MAROWITZ, CHARLES
The Chicago conspiracy (based on a script by Jonathan Cross). 1972. MAOC

BURK, JOHN DALY, ?-1808
Bunker-Hill; or, The death of General Warren. 1797. MONR
Variant title: The death of General Warren
The death of General Warren. See Bunker-Hill

BURKE, CHARLES ST. THOMAS, 1822-1854
Rip Van Winkle. 1850. BAT19, MOSS3
See also Anonymous plays. Rip Van Winkle (as played by Joseph Jefferson)

BURNHAM, BARBARA, 1900-
Children in uniform (tr. and adapted by). See Winsloe, Christa. Children in uniform

BURNS, ALAN, and MAROWITZ, CHARLES
Palach. 1970. MAOC

BURRILL, MARY BURRILL
They that sit in darkness. 1919. HARY

BURROWS, ABE. See Burrows,

Abram S.

BURROWS, ABRAM S., 1910-
Cactus flower. 1965. BES65

-- WEINSTOCK, JACK and GILBERT, WILLIE
How to succeed in business without really trying (based on the book by Shepherd Mead) (music by Frank Loesser). 1961. BES61

-- See also Swerling, Jo, jt. auth.

BURTON, HELEN. See Jerome, Mrs. Helen (Burton)

BUSH, JOSEF, 1933-
French gray. 1966. NEWA2

BUTLER, RACHEL BARTON
Mamma's affair. 1920. BES19

BYRNE, MRS. DOLLY. See Varesi, Gilda, jt. auth.

BYRNE, MURIEL ST. CLARE. See Sayers, Dorothy Leigh, jt. auth.

BYRNE, SEAMUS, 1904-
Design for a headstone. 1950. HOGE

BYRON, GEORGE GORDON, 1788-1824
Cain. 1821. BARG, KOH2
Heaven and earth. 1821? KOH2
Manfred. 1817. BERN, GREB2, HAPT2, HARC18, KAU, SML

C

CABANA, AUGUSTIN MORETO Y. See Moreto y Cavaña, Augustin

CAIGNIEZ, LOUIS CHARLES, 1762-1842, and BAUDOUIN, JEAN MARIE THEODORE (d'Aubigny, pseud.)
La pie voleuse; ou, La servante de Palaiseau. See Payne, John Howard. Trial without jury (adapted from)

CALDERON DE LA BARCA, PEDRO, 1600-1681
El alcalde de Zalamea. See The mayor of Zalamea
Amar después de la muerte. See Love after death
Belshazzar's feast. 1632. MacCarthy, D., tr. BAT4
Variant title: La cena de Baltasar
La cena de Baltasar. See Belshazzar's feast
The constant prince. 1629? MacCarthy, D., tr. CLF2, STA
Variant title: El príncipe constante
El gran teatro del mundo. See The great theater of the world
Elvira. See No siempre lo peor es cierto
The great theater of the world. 1642. Singleton, M., tr. FLOR
Variant title: El gran teatro del mundo
Guárdate del agua mansa. See Keep your own secret
Keep your own secret. 1649. Fitzgerald, E., tr. ROB
Variant title: Guárdate del agua mansa
Life a dream. See La vida es sueño
Life is a dream. See La vida es sueño
Love after death. 1651? Campbell, R., tr. BENR3
Variant title: Amar después de la muerte
El mágico prodigioso. See The wonder-working magician
The mayor of Zalamea. 1651. Starkie, W., tr. SSTW

Variant title: El alcalde de Zalamea
No siempre lo peor es cierto. 1648? HILL
Variant titles: Elvira; The worst not always true
El postrer duelo de España. See Payne, John Howard. The last duel in Spain (adapted from)
El príncipe constante. See The constant prince
Such stuff as dreams are made of. See La vida es sueño
La vida es sueño. 1635. ALP
Campbell, R., tr. BENR3, BENSB1, MACM1, MACN1
Fitzgerald, E., tr. DRA1, HARC26, PLAB1
Huberman, E., and E., trs. FLOS, HOUE, TREB
MacCarthy, D., tr. ALPF, MAU, TAV
Variant titles: Life a dream; Life is a dream; Such stuff as dreams are made of
The wonder-working magician. 1637?
Shelley, P., tr. BENR3
Variant title: El mágico prodigioso
The worst not always true. See No siempre lo peor es cierto

CALDWELL, BEN, 1937-
All white caste. (1971) KINH
The devil and Otis Redding. See The king of soul
The first militant minister. See Prayer meeting
The king of soul; or, The devil and Otis Redding. (1969) RAVA
Prayer meeting; or, The first militant minister. (1969) BLA, JON

CALDWELL, ERSKINE, 1903-
See Kirkland, Jack, jt. auth.

CAMERON, KENNETH, 1931-
The hundred and first. 1963? NEWA1
Papp. 1969? SCV

CAMPBELL, BARTLEY, 1843-1888
Fairfax. 1879. AMP19
The galley slave. 1879. AMP19
My partner. 1879. AMP19, CLA
The Virginian. 1873. AMP19
The white slave. 1882. AMP19

CAMPBELL, MARION GURNEY and ATHAS, DAPHNE SPENCER
Sit on the earth. 19-? OBSE

CAMPBELL, WILLIAM EDWARD MARCH. See March, William (pseud.)

CAMPISTRON, JEAN GALBERT DE, 1656-1723
Andronic. See Andronicus
Andronicus. 1685.
Lockert, L., tr. LOCR
Variant title: Andronic
Tiridate. 1691.
Lockert, L., tr. LOCU

CAMPTON, DAVID, 1924-
Soldier from the wars returning. 1963. PLAJ1
Then... 1960. THOD

CAMUS, ALBERT, 1913-1960
Caligula. 1945
Anon. tr. FOUA
Gilbert, S., tr. BLOC, MORW, RAI, TAUJ
O'Brien, J., tr. and adapter. BES59
Le malentendu. 1944. PUCC

CAPEK, JOSEF, 1887-1927.
See Capek, Karel, jt. auth.

CAPEK, KAREL, 1890-1939
R. U. R. (Rossum's universal robots). 1923.
Anon. tr. BART, BROU, STAU

Selver, P., tr. BES22, BROF, BROG, BRR3, CALN1, COTH, DIE, DIK1, HAV, HAVD, HAVE, HORN, HUDT, MCD, NAGE, PROX, TREBA, TREI2, TUCG, TUCM, TUCN, TUCO, WATI, WATL4, WATO
Selver, P., and Playfair, N., trs. CEW, CONG, COTKJ, TREC2, TREE2

-- and CAPEK, JOSEF
Adam stvoritel. See Adam the creator
Adam the creator. 1927.
Round, D., tr. MOSG, MOSH
Variant title: Adam stvoritel
And so ad infinitum. 1921.
Davis, O., tr. and adapter GARZH
Selver, P., tr. CHA, CHAN, CLKW, INTE, SSTF
Variant titles: The insect comedy; The insect play; The life of the insects; The world we live in; Ze zivota honyzu
The insect comedy. See And so ad infinitum
The insect play. See And so ad infinitum
The life of the insects. See And so ad infinitum
The world we live in. See And so ad infinitum
Ze zivota honyzu. See And so ad infinitum

CAPOTE, TRUMAN, 1924-
The grass harp. 1952. WISF

CARBALLIDO, EMILIO, 1925-
The day the lions got loose. See The day they let the lions loose
The day they let the lions loose. 1963.
Oliver, W., tr. OLIW
Variant titles: The day the lions got loose; El día que se soltaron los leones
El día que se soltaron los leones. See The day they let the lions loose
I also speak of the rose. See I too speak of roses
I too speak of roses. 1966.
Oliver, W., tr. WOOG
Variant titles: I also speak of the rose; Yo también hablo de la rosa
Yo también hablo de la rosa. See I too speak of roses

CARRETTE, LOUIS, 1913-
See Marceau, Félicien, pseud.

CARROLL, PAUL VINCENT, 1900-
Shadow and substance. 1937. BES37, CALM, CEW, DUR, FIG, MOSH
The strings, my Lord, are false. 1943? NEWR1
The white steed. 1939. BES38

CARROLL, ROBERT, pseud.
See Alpert, Hollis

CARY, FALKLAND L., 1897-
See King, Philip, jt. auth.

CASALIS, JEANNE DE. See De Casalis, Jeanne

CASELLA, ALBERTO, 1891-
Death takes a holiday. 1929.
Ferris, W., tr. and adapter. BES29
Variant title: La morte in vacanze
La morte in vacanze. See Death takes a holiday

CASINO, JESUS. See Sicam, Gerónimo D., jt. auth.

CASONA, ALEJANDRO, pseud.
See Rodríguez Alvarez, Alejandro

CASTRO Y BELLVIS, GUILLEM DE, 1569-1631
Exploits of the Cid. See

Las mocedades del Cid
Las mocedades del Cid. 1621. ALP
Anon. tr. BENR4
Variant title: Exploits of the Cid; The youthful adventures of El Cid
The youthful adventures of El Cid. See Las mocedades del Cid

CAVAN, ROMILLY
All my own work. 1958. OBSE

CAVANA, AUGUSTIN MORETO Y. See Moreto y Cavaña, Augustín

CAVERHILL, ALAN, 1910-
See Melville, Alan, pseud.

CAYZER, CHARLES WILLIAM, 1869-?
David and Bathshua. 1911? KOH2

CERVANTES SAAVEDRA, MIGUEL DE, 1547-1616
The cave of Salamanca. 1615?
Honig, E., tr. TREB
Jagendorf, M., tr. CLF2
Variant title: La cueva de Salamanca
La cueva de Salamanca. See The cave of Salamanca
La guarda cuidadosa. See The vigilant sentinel
The jealous old man. 1611.
Starkie, W., tr. SSTW
Variant title: El viejo celoso
La Numance. See La Numancia
La Numancia. 1585. ALP
Campbell, R., tr. BENR3
Variant titles: La Numance; The siege of Numantia
Pedro de Urdemalas. See Pedro, the artful dodger
Pedro, the artful dodger. 1615.
Starkie, W., tr. SSTW
Variant title: Pedro de Urdemalas
The siege of Numantia. See La Numancia
El viejo celoso. See The jealous old man
The vigilant sentinel. 158-?
Flores, A., and Liss, J., trs. FLOS
Variant title: La guarda cuidadosa

CHAMBERS, CHARLES HADDON, 1860-1921
The tyranny of tears. 1899. BOOA3

CHANCEL, LA GRANGE. See La Grange-Chancel

CHANDEZON, LEOPOLD (Léopold, pseud.) and CUVELIER DE TYRE, JEAN GUILLAUME ANTOINE
Mazeppa; ou, Le cheval Tartare. See Payne, John Howard. Mazeppa; or, The wild horse of Tartary (adapted from)

CHAPIN, HAROLD, 1886-1915
Augustus in search of a father. 1910. WEB
The new morality. 1920. MAP

CHAPMAN, GEORGE, 1559?-1634
Bussy D'Ambois. 1604. BAS, BROC, HAPRA1, HAPRB1, MCK, NEI, NES, ORNT, RYL, SPE
The revenge of Bussy D'Ambois. 1610? WALL

-- JONSON, BEN, and MARSTON, JOHN
Eastward ho! 1605. BROC, GAY2, OLI1, RUB, SCH, SCI, SCJ, SPE, WALL
Variant title: Eastward hoe
Eastward hoe. See Eastward ho!

CHAPMAN, JOHN, 1927-
Simple spymen. 1958. PLAJ2

CHAPMAN, ROBERT HARRIS, 1919- . See Coxe, Louis O., jt. auth.

CHARLES, MARTIE
Black cycle. KINH
Job security. 1970. HARY

CHASE, MARY COYLE, 1912-
Bernardine. 1952. BES52, THEA53
Harvey. 1944. BES44, CORB, GARU, GARZA3, MIJY
Mr. Thing. See Mrs. McThing
Mrs. McThing. 1952. BES51
Variant title: Mr. Thing

CHAUSSEE, PIERRE CLAUDE NIVELLE DE LA. See La Chaussée, Pierre Claude Nivelle de

CHAYEFSKY, PADDY, 1923- [given name: SIDNEY]
The dybbuk from Woodhaven. See The tenth man
Gideon. 1961. BES61, GARS
The latent heterosexual. 1966. SANK
Marty. 1953? BLAH, BLOC, DAVM, DOD, HEI, MCNA, SHER
The passion of Josef D. 1964. BES63
The tenth man. 1959. BES59, CEQ, CES
Variant title: The dybbuk from Woodhaven

CHEKHOV, ANTON PAVLOVICH, 1860-1904
The anniversary. See The jubilee
The bear. See The boor
The boor. 1888.
Anon. tr. BART, KNIE
Banknage, H., tr. KNIC, KNID, PATM
Bentley, E., tr. PERS, PERT, PERU
Clark, B., and Banknage, H., trs. HUD
Variant titles: The bear; The brute
The brute. See The boor
The cherry orchard. 1904.
Anon. tr. BARR, DIZ, DUH, EDAD, FOUK, SILM, WORP, ZIM
Ashley, L., tr. ASF
Calderon, G., tr. DIC, HAV, HAVD, MOSG, MOSH, SSST, THOM, THON, TUCG, TUCM, TUCN, TUCO
Corrigan, R., tr. CLO, COTKI, COTO, COTQ, DIT
Covan, J., tr. CAR, CARA, DEAP, DEAR, DEAS, DOV, HIG, MOS, SCNN, SCNO, SCNP, WHI
Daniels, C., and Noyes, G., trs. NOY
Garnett, C., tr. ALLI, ALLJ, ALLK, ALT, ALTE, CUBE, CUBG, DIK1, GARZ, GOLD, HOUG, KERN, KERO, KERP, KON, LID, ROET, SMA, TRE, TREA1, TREBA, TREC2, TREE2, TREI2, WEIM, WHK
Guthrie, T., and Kipnis, L., trs. BOW, WHFM
O'Dell, B., tr. BONB, BONC
Skariatina, I., tr. HIBB, WEAV2
Szogyi, A., tr. SOU
West, J., tr. CALD, STE, WATI, WATL4, WATR
Yarmolinsky, A., tr. BAUL, BLAH, CUBH, MACN
Young, S., tr. BLOC, REIO, REIT, SEN, VOLI
-- See also Logan, Joshua. The Wisteria trees (adapted from)
The harmful effects of smoking. See Gassner, John. Then and now (adapted from)

-- See also Ginsbury, Norman.
The safety match (based on)
Ivanoff. 1887.
Fell, M., tr. MOSA
Winer, E., tr. ULAN
A joke in one act. See A wedding
The jubilee. 1903.
Roberts, C., tr. ROE
Variant title: The anniversary
A marriage proposal. 1889.
Anon. tr. SUT1
Chambers, W., tr. BAT18
Hoffman, T., tr. ROSS
Variant title: The proposal
-- See also Gassner, John.
Then and now (adapted from)
The proposal. See A marriage proposal
The sea-gull. 1896.
Anon. tr. SHR
Calderon, G., tr. MOSQ
Fell, M., tr. WALT3
Corrigan, R., tr. HOUP
Garnett, C., tr. BROK, BUR, CEW, CLKW, WAIW
Goodman, R., tr. GOOR
Nagarshack, D., tr. WARL
Reeve, F., tr. REEV2
Young, S., tr. BLOC, DOWN, GARZH, GRIF, WALJ
Svadba. See A wedding
The swan song. 1888.
Fell, M., tr. BLAG, BLAH
The three sisters. 1901.
Anon. tr. BLON
Corrigan, R., tr. DOT, TRI, TRIA
Covan, J., tr. MOS
Fen, E., tr. CAPU, GOLH, HOGA, REIN, REIP, SANE, SIXB
Garnett, C., tr. BAIC, BAIE, BLOO, DOWS, LEG
Guerney, B., tr. GUE
MacAndrew, A., tr. GARZB, MACE
Magershak, D., tr. BENSB2
Young, S., tr. FREG, REIL, SCNR
Uncle Vanya. 1897.
Anon. tr. CLN, MESS, SILN, SILQ
Corrigan, R., tr. COTKC, COTO, COTQ
Covan, J., tr. MOS
Fell, M., tr. BARB, BENQ, HARB, MIL, SATI, SATJ, WATA, WATI, WATL2
Garnett, C., tr. WEIS, WEIW
Garrett, C., tr. HAPO
Hampton, C., tr. PLAN39
Magarshack, D., tr. MAGA
Young, S., tr. CLM
Variant title: The wood demon
A wedding; a joke in one act. 1890.
Bentley, E., tr. ALLE, FEFL
Roberts, C., tr. ROE
Variant titles: A joke in one act; Svadba; The wedding
The wedding. See A wedding
The wood demon. See Uncle Vanya

CHEN-CHIN HSIUNG. See Hsiung, Cheng-chin

CHENG TEH-HUI
The soul of Ch'ien-nu leaves her body.
Liu, J., tr. LIU

CHETHAM-STRODE, WARREN, 1897-
Background. 1950. PLAN4
Sometimes even now. 1933. FAMD

CHI, CHUN-HSIANG
The orphan of Chao.
Liu, J., tr. LIU

CHIA AH. See Ou-hung, Wong, jt. auth.

CHIARELLI, LUIGI, 1884-1947
La maschera ed il volto.
See The mask and the face

The mask and the face. 1916.
Vic Beamish, N., tr. INTE
Variant title: La maschera ed il volto

CHI-HUANG, LI. See Seh, Sha, jt. auth.

CHIH-YUAN, MA. See Ma, Chih-Yüan

CHIKAMATSU MONZAEMON. See Chikamatsu (Sugimori Nobumori)

CHIKAMATSU (SUGIMORI NOBUMORI), 1652-1724
The courier for hell. 1711.
Keene, D., tr. ANDF
Variant title: Meido No Hikyaku
Fair ladies at a game of poem-cards. 1705.
Miyamora, A., and Nichols, R., trs. CLF1
Meido No Hikyaku. See The courier for hell

CHILDRESS, ALICE, 1920-
Trouble in mind. 1955. PATR
Wine in the wilderness. 1969. HARY, SUB

CHLUMBERG, HANS, 1897-1930
The miracle at Verdun. 1931.
Crankshaw, E., tr. FAMC
Leigh, J., tr. CHA, CHAN
Variant title: Wunder um Verdun
Wunder um Verdun. See The miracle at Verdun

CHODOROV, EDWARD, 1904-
Decision. 1944. BES43
Kind lady (adapted from a story by Hugh Walpole). 1935. CART, FREE
Oh, men! oh, women! 1953. THEA54

CHODOROV, JEROME, 1911- See Fields, Joseph, jt. auth.

CHORELL, WALENTIN, 1912-
The sisters. 1955.
Morduch, T., tr. FIL
Variant title: Systrarna
Systarna. See The sisters

CHRISTIE, AGATHA (MILLER) 1891-1976
Witness for the prosecution. 1953. BES54, FAMO, RICI, THEA55

CHRISTIE, CAMPBELL, 1893-1963 See Christie, Dorothy, jt. auth.

CHRISTIE, DOROTHY, 1896- and CHRISTIE, CAMPBELL
Carrington, V. C. 1953. FAMO
His excellency. 1950. PLAN4

CHUN-HSIANG, CHI. See Chi, Chün-hsiang

CHURCH, MRS. VIRGINIA WOODSON (FRAME), 1880-
What men live by. 1924? CHU, LAW, SRYG

CHURCHILL, CARYL
The ants. 1962. NEWE12

CIBBER, COLLEY, 1671-1757
The careless husband. 1704. MOSE1, NET
Hob; or, The country wake (sometimes attributed to). See Dogget, Thomas. Hob; or, The country wake
Love's last shift; or, The fool in fashion. 1695? MCM, MCMI, TUQ
The provoked husband; or, A journey to London (from an unfinished play by John Vanbrugh). 1727? BAT15, TICK

CIBBER, THEOPHILUS, 1703-1758. See Jevons, Thomas, jt. auth.

CLARK, JOHN PEPPER, 1935-
Song of a goat. (1964) LITT

CLARK, MRS. MABEL MARGARET (COWIE). See Storm, Lesley, pseud.

CLARKE, WILLIAM KENDALL
The ghost patrol (based on a story by Sinclair Lewis). 195-? INGB

CLAUDEL, PAUL, 1868-1955
L'annonce faite à Marie. 1912. HARV, RHO
Sill, L., tr. DIK1, HAV, TREBA, TREI3, TREJ, TUCG
Variant title: The tidings brought to Mary
L'histoire de Tobie et de Sara. See Tobias and Sara
The satin slipper; or, The worst is not the worst. 1919?
O'Connor, J., tr. HIBB
Variant title: Le soulier de satin; ou, Le père n'est pas toujours sûr
The tidings brought to Mary. See L'annonce faite à Marie
Tobias and Sara. 1942?
Fiske, A., tr. HAYE
Variant title: L'histoire de Tobie et de Sara

CLAUSEN, SVEN, 1893-
The bird of contention. 1933?
Thornton, P., and A., trs. CONT
Variant title: Kivflugen
Kivflugen. See The bird of contention

CLEMENS, SAMUEL LANGHORNE, 1835-1910
The king and the duke. See Fergusson, Francis. The king and the duke (based on the novel Huckleberry Finn by)

CLEMENTS, COLIN CAMPBELL, 1894-1948
Columbine. 1922? SHAY
The siege. 1922? SHAY
--See Ryerson, Florence, jt. auth.

CLINCH, CHARLES POWELL, 1797-1880
The spy, a tale of the neutral ground. 1822. AMP14

COCTEAU, JEAN, 1891-1963
Antigone. See Sophocles. Antigone (adapted by)
The Eiffel Tower wedding party. See Les mariés de la Tour Eiffel
The infernal machine. See La machine infernale
Intimate relations. 1938.
Frank, C., tr. BENS3
Variant titles: Les parents terribles; The storm within
La machine infernale. 1934. PUCC
Anon. tr. SANO
Wildman, C., tr. BENS1, BOY, INTE, LOCL, LOCLA, LOCLB, TUCN, TUCO
Variant title: The infernal machine
Les mariés de la Tour Eiffel. 1921.
Benedikt, M., tr. BEN
Fitts, D., tr. MIJE, NEW37
Variant titles: The Eiffel Tower wedding party; The wedding on the Eiffel Tower
Les parents terrible. See Intimate relations
Orphée. 1926.
Wildman, C., tr. BLOC
The storm within. See Intimate relations
The wedding on the Eiffel Tower. See Les mariés de la Tour Eiffel

COFFEE, LENORE (MRS. W. J. COWEN), and COWEN, WILLIAM JOYCE

Family portrait. 1939. BES38, PLAN1

COFFEY, CHARLES, d. 1745.
See Jevon, Thomas, jt. auth.

COHAN, GEORGE MICHAEL, 1878-1942
Pigeons and people. 1933. BES32, WAGC3
Seven keys to Baldpate (based on the novel by Earl Derr Biggers). 1913. BES09, CART, CONG

COHN, EMIL, 1881-1948
See Bernhard, Emil, pseud.

COKAIN, SIR ASTON, 1608-1684
Trappolin suppos'd a prince. See Tate, Nahum. A duke or no duke (adapted from)

COKAYNE, SIR ASTON. See Cokain, Sir Aston

COLERIDGE, SAMUEL TAYLOR, 1820-1894
Remorse. 1813. KAU

COLETTE, SIDONIE GABRIELLE, 1873-1954
Gigi. See Loos, Anita. Gigi (from the novel by)

COLLINGS, PIERRE. See Gibney, Sheridan, jt. auth.

COLLINS, MARGARET
Love is a daisy. COLI
3 filosofers in a fire-tower. COLI

COLMAN, GEORGE, 1732-1794
The jealous wife. 1761. NET, NIC
Polly Honeycombe. 1760. BEVI

-- and GARRICK, DAVID
The Clandestine marriage. 1766. BAT15, HAN, MCM, MCMI, MOR, MOSE2, TWE

COLMAN, GEORGE, the younger, 1762-1836
The iron chest. 1796. BOO
John Bull. 1803. BOOA3

COLTON, JOHN, 1889-1946, and RANDOLPH, CLEMENCE
Rain (based on the story, Miss Thompson, by W. Somerset Maugham). 1922. BES22, GARU, GARZA1, TUCD

COLUM, PADRAIC, 1881-1972
The land. 1905. CAP
Thomas Muskerry. 1910. MOSN

COMDEN, BETTY, 1919- , and GREEN, ADOLPH
Applause (music by Charles Strouse; lyrics by Lee Adams). 1970. BES69
Wonderful town (lyrics by). See Fields, Joseph and Chodorov, Jerome. Wonderful town

COMPANY THEATRE ENSEMBLE. See Opper, Don Keith (script by)

CONGREVE, WILLIAM, 1670-1729
Love for love. 1695. BENY, CAR, CARA, KRM, MIL, SALR, STM, TWE
The way of the world. 1700. ALLK, ARB1, ASH, BARG, BENY, BLON, BROJ, BROK, COL1, COTKIR, DEAP, DEAR, FAL, FOUB, GAY4, GOS, GOSA, GREB1, GREC1, KER, KRM, KRON, LIE, MAT, MCM, MCMI, MCMS, MEN, MOR, MORR, MOSE1, NET, REST, ROET, RUB, SHAI1, SMO, SPF1, STM, TAT, TAU, TRE, TREA2, TREB, TREC1, TREE1, TREI1, TUP, TUQ, TWE,

WALJ, WILS, WOOE,
WRIR

CONKLE, ELLSWORTH PROUTY, 1899-
Minnie Field. 1928. GASB
Prologue to glory. 1938. BES37, FEE, SWI

CONNELLY, MARCUS COOK, 1890-
The green pastures (based on the novel, Ol' man Adam and his chillun, by Roark Bradford). 1930. BES29, CET, CHA, CHAN, CHAP, CONN, CORD, CORE, CORF, COTE, DUR, FUL, GARZA1, GAS, GRD, KNIC, KNID, KNIE, LOOA, LOOB, LOOC, LOOD, LOOE, MCD4, MOSK, MOSL, PROI, SIM, SIXD, TRE, TREA1, TREBA, TREC2, TREE3, TREI3, WATE
The wisdom tooth. 1926. BES25
--See also Elser, Frank Ball; Kaufman, George S., jt. auths.

CONRAD, JOSEPH, 1857-1924
One day more. 1905. BENT3

CONRAD, ROBERT TAYLOR, 1810-1858
Jack Cade, the captain of the commons. 1835. MOSS2

CONWAY, HIRAM J.
The battle of Stillwater; or, The maniac. 1840. AMP14

COOKE, BRITTON, d. 1923
The translation of John Snaith. 1923. MAS1

COOPER, GILES, 1918-1966
Everything in the garden. 1962. NEWE7
Happy family. 1966. NEWE11
The object. 1964. NEWE12
Out of the crocodile. 1963. PLAN27
Unman, Wittering, and Zigo. 1950. ENG

COOPER, JAMES FENIMORE, 1789-1851
The wept of the wish-ton-wish (based on the novel by). See Anonymous plays. The wept of the wish-ton-wish

COPEAU, JACQUES, 1879-1949
The little poor man. 1925?
Thurman, B., tr. HAYE
Variant title: Le petit pauvre
Le petit pauvre. See The little poor man

COPPEE, FRANÇOIS EDOUARD JOACHIM, 1842-1908
Le luthier de Crémone. See The violin maker of Cremona
The violin maker of Cremona. 1877.
Jerome, J., tr. BEAC
Lord, I., tr. COOK1
Variant title: Le luthier de Crémone

COPPEL, ALEC
I killed the count. 1939. SIXP

CORLETT, WILLIAM
Tinker's curse. 1968. PLAN34

CORMACK, BARTLETT
The racket. 1927. BES27

CORMON, EUGENE, 1811-1903.
See D'Ennery, Adolphe, jt. auth.

CORNEAU, PERRY BOYER
Masks. 1922? LAW

CORNEILLE, PIERRE, 1606-1684
Le cid. 1636. LYO, SCN, SER, SERD, STJ1
Anonymous tr. GAUB
Cooper, F., tr. CLF2,

CROV, GREA, MAU, SMN, TAV
Fowlie, W., tr. FOWL, TREB
Schevill, J., tr. HOUE
Schevill, J., Goldsby, R., and A., trs. BENR4
Variant title: The cid
The cid. See Le cid
Cinna; or, The mercy of Augustus. 1639.
Landis, P., tr. KRE
Horace. 1639. SER
The liar. See Le menteur
Le menteur. 1642. LYO
Variant title: The liar
Polyeucte. 1640. LYO, SER
Constable, T., tr. HARC26, LOGG, STA

CORNEILLE, THOMAS, 1625-1709
Ariadne. 1672.
Lockert, L., tr. LOCU
Variant title: Ariane
Ariane. See Ariadne
Le comte d'Essex. See The earl of Essex
The earl of Essex. 1678.
Lockert, L., tr. LOCR
Variant title: Le comte d'Essex
Laodice. 1668.
Lockert, L., tr. LOCR
Maximian. 1662.
Lockert, L., tr. LOCU
Timocrate. See Timocrates
Timocrates. 1656.
Lockert, L., tr. LOCU
Variant title: Timocrate

CORNISH, ROGER
Open twenty-four hours. 1968. HAVL, WELT

COURTELINE, GEORGES (pseud. of Georges Moinaux), 1860-1929
Les boulingrin. See These cornfields
La commissionaire est bon enfant. See The commissioner
The commissioner. 1899?
Bermel, A., tr. FOUF
Variant title: La commissionaire est bon enfant
These cornfields. 1898.
Bentley, E., tr. BENSC
Variant title: Les boulingrin

CORWIN, NORMAN LEWIS, 1910-
Ann Rutledge. 1942? LOVR
El capitan and the corporal. 1942? NAGE
Good heavens. 1941. BRS, LOOD
My client Curley. 1942. WATS
The odyssey of Runyon Jones. 1942? PROD
Radio primer. 1942. WATS
They fly through the air. 1939? PROC
We hold these truths. 1941. BROU

COTTER, JOSEPH S., SR., 1861-1949
Caleb the degenerate. 1903. HARY

COWARD, NOEL PIERCE, 1899-1973
Blithe spirit. 1941. BES41, FULT, KRM, TREBA, TREC2, TREE3, TREI3, WALB, WARI
Brief encounter. 1946. GRED
Cavalcade. 1931. CEU, VOAD
Come into the garden Maud. 1966. RICJ
Conversation piece. 1934. SEV
Design for living. 1932. BES32, SIXH
Easy virtue. 1925. MOSO
Fumed oak. 1936. ANDE, COOP
Hay fever. 1925. MOD, MYB
Noel Coward in two keys. 1974. BES73
Point Valaine. 1934. SIXP
Private lives. 1930. CHA, CHAN, CHAR, COTKH,

LON, PLAL2
A song at twilight. 1966. RICK
The vortex. 1924. TUCD, TUCM
Ways and means. 1935. WATE
The young idea. 1923. MAP

COWEN, MRS. LENORE (COFFEE). See Coffee, Lenore

COWEN, RON, 1944-
Summertime. 1967. HOLP

COWEN, WILLIAM JOYCE. See Coffee, Lenore, jt. auth.

COWIE, MABEL MARGARET, 1903- . See Storm, Lesley, pseud.

COWLEY, ABRAHAM, 1618-1677
Cutter of Coleman-street. 1661. GAY4

COWLEY, MRS. HANNAH (PARKHOUSE), 1743-1809
The belle's stratagem. 1780. BAT15

COXE, LOUIS O., 1918- and CHAPMAN, ROBERT HARRIS
Billy Budd (based on the novel by Herman Melville). 1949. BES50, COTX, DAVI, GARW, HAVG, SSST, SSSU
Variant title: Uniform of flesh
Uniform of flesh. See Billy Budd

COYNE, J. STIRLING, 1803-1868
How to settle accounts with your laundress. 1847. BOOA4

CRANE, STEPHEN, 1871-1900
The bride comes to yellow sky. See Agee, James. The bride comes to yellow sky (based on)

CRAVEN, FRANK, 1880-1945
The first year. 1920. BES20

CREBILLON, PROSPER JOLYOT DE, 1674-1762
Rhadamiste et Zénobie. 1711. BRE
Lockert, L., tr. LOCR
Variant title: Rhadamistus and Zenobia
Rhadamistus and Zenobia. See Rhadamiste et Zénobie

CREGAN, DAVID, 1931-
Transcending. 1966. CONB

CREIGHTON, ANTHONY, 1920- . See Osborne, John, jt. auth.

CROCKER, CHARLES TEMPLETON
The land of happiness. 1917. BOH3

CROPPER, MARGARET
Two sides of the door. 1925. FED2

CROSS, BEVERLEY, 1931-
The mines of sulphur, an opera (music by Richard R. Bennett). 1965. PLAN30

CROSS, JONATHAN
The Chicago conspiracy. See Burgess, John, and Marowitz, Charles. The Chicago conspiracy (based on a script by)

CROTHERS, RACHEL, 1871-1958
As husbands go. 1931. BES30, CHA
Expressing Willie. 1924. COT
He and she. 1911. QUIG, QUIJ, QUIK, QUIL, QUIM, QUIN
Variant title: The Herfords
The Herfords. See He and she
Let us be gay. 1929. BES28
Mary the third. 1923. BES22, DIG, TUCD, TUCJ, TUCM

Nice people. 1921. BES20, MOSJ, MOSK, MOSL, QUI
Susan and God. 1937. BES37
When ladies meet. 1932. BES32

CROUSE, RUSSEL, 1893-1966.
See Lindsay, Howard, jt. auth.

CROWLEY, MART, 1935-
The boys in the band. 1968. BES67

CROWNE, JOHN, 1640?-1712
The destruction of Jerusalem, pt. 2. 1677. DOA
Sir Courtly Nice; or, It cannot be. 1685. SUM

CULBERTSON, ERNEST HOWARD
Rackey. 1919. LOC

CULLEN, COUNTEE PORTER, 1903-1946. See Bontemps, Arna, jt. auth.

CUMBERLAND, RICHARD, 1732-1811
The fashionable lover. 1772. MOSE2
The West Indian. 1771. BENY, HAN, MCM, MCMI, MIL, MOR, NET

CUMMINGS, EDWARD ESTLIN, 1894-1962
him. 1928. BENS2

CUREL, FRANÇOIS DE, 1854-1928
L'envers d'une sainte. 1892. BOR
Variant title: The other side of a saint
The fossils. 1892.
Clark, B., tr. CLD, WATI, WATL1
The lion's share. See Le repas du lion
The other side of a saint. See L'envers d'une sainte
Le repas du lion. 1897. RHO
Variant title: The lion's share

CURNIEU, GEORGES DE (Georges Ancey, pseud.), 1860-1917
The dupe. 1891.
Clark, B., tr. CLD

CURRIE, CARLETON H.
Whither goest thou? 1926. FED2

CUSTIS, GEORGE WASHINGTON PARKE, 1781-1857
Pocahontas; or, The settlers of Virginia. 1830. QUIJ, QUIK, QUIL, QUIM, QUIN

CUVELIER DE TRYE, JEAN GUILLAUME ANTOINE, 1766-1824. See Chandezon, Léopold, jt. auth.

D

DA BIBIENA, BERNARDO CARDINAL DOVIZI. See Dovizi da Bibiena, Bernardo Cardinal

DAGERMAN, STIG, 1923-1954
The condemned. 1947.
Alexander, H., and Jones, L., trs. SCAN3
Variant title: Den dödsdömde
Den dödsdömde. See The condemned

DALY, AUGUSTIN, 1838-1899
The big bonanza (adapted from Ultimo, by Gustav von Moser). 1875. AMP20
Divorce. 1871. AMP20
Horizon. 1871. HAL
Man and wife. 1870. AMP20
Needles and pins (adapted from Starke mitteln, by Julius Rosen). 1880. AMP20
Pique. 1875. AMP20
Under the gaslight. 1867. BOOB

DAMEL, CARLOS S. See Darthes, Juan Fernando, jt. auth.

DANCHENKO, VLADIMIR IVANOVICH NEMIROVICH. See Nemirovich-Danchenko, Vladimir Ivanovich

DANCOURT, FLORENT CARTON, 1661-1725
Les bourgeoises de qualité. See Woman's craze for titles
Le chevalier à la mode. 1687. BRE
Woman's craze for titles. 1700.
Chambers, W., tr. BAT8
Variant title: Les bourgeoises de qualité

DANE, CLEMENCE, pseud. See Ashton, Winifred

DANIEL, SAMUEL, 1562-1619
The vision of the twelve goddesses. 1604. PAR

DANJURO, I.
Narukami. 1684.
Irwin, V., tr. IRW

D'ANNUNZIO, GABRIELE. See Annunzio, Gabriele d'

DA PONTE, LORENZO. See Ponte, Lorenzo Da

D'ARCY, MARGRETTA. See Arden, John, jt. auth.

DARION, JOSEPH, 1917-
Man of La Mancha (lyrics by). See Wasserman, Dale. Man of La Mancha

DARTHES, JUAN FERNANDO CAMILO, and DAMEL, CARLOS S.
La hermana Josefina. See The quack doctor
The quack doctor. 1938.
Jones, W., tr. JONA
Variant title: La hermana Josefina

DAUMAL, RENE, 1908-1944
En gggarrrde! 1924.
Benedikt, M., tr. BEN

D'AVENANT, SIR WILLIAM, 1606-1668
Love and honor. 1934. WALL
The siege of Rhodes, pt. I. 1661. MCM, MCMI
The wits. 1635. KNOW

-- and DRYDEN, JOHN
The tempest; or, The enchanted island. 1667. SUMB

DAVENANT, WILLIAM. See D'Avenant, Sir William

DAVENPORT, ROBERT, 1600?-1651?
The city night-cap. 1624? BUL4
A crowne for a conquerour. 1623? BUL4
King John and Matilda. 1655? ARMS, BUL4
A new trick to cheat the divell. 1639? BUL4
A survey of the sciences. BUL4
Too late to call backe yesterday. 1623? BUL4

DAVIDSON, ROBERT, 1808-1876
Elijah. 1860? KOH2

DAVIES, HUBERT HENRY, 1865-1917
The mollusc. 1907. DIG, ROWC

DAVIES, MARY CAROLYN
The slave with two faces. 1918? PEN

DAVIOT, GORDON, pseud. See MacKintosh, Elizabeth

DAVIS, ANDRE
Four men. 1938? OBSE

DAVIS, DONALD, 1907- . See Davis, Owen, jt. auth.

DAVIS, MRS. IRVING KAYE. See Shelley, Elsa (Mrs. Irving Kaye Davis)

DAVIS, OSSIE, 1917-
Purlie victorious. 1961. ALLK, BRAS, DIZ, OLIV, PATR, TUGT

DAVIS, OWEN, 1874-1956
And so ad infinitum. See Capek, Karel and Capek, Josef. And so ad infinitum (adapted by)
The detour. 1921. MOSJ, MOSK, MOSL
Icebound. 1923. BES22, CORD, CORE, CORF, DIG, HAL
Mr. and Mrs. North (based on the novel, The Norths meet murder, by Frances and Richard Lockridge). 1941. BES40

-- and DAVIS, DONALD
Ethan Frome (based on the novel by Edith Wharton). 1936. BES35, GARU, GARZA2

DAY, CLARENCE, 1874-1935
Life with father. See Lindsay, Howard and Crouse, Russel. Life with father (based on the book by)
Life with mother. See Lindsay, Howard and Crouse, Russel. Life with mother (based on the book by)

DAY, JOHN, 1574-1640?
Humour out of breath. 1608? NER
The parliament of bees. 1641? NER

DAYTON, KATHARINE and KAUFMAN, GEORGE S.
First lady. 1935. BES35

DE AMESCUA, ANTONIO MIRA. See Mira de Amescua, Antonio

DEAN, ALEXANDER, 1893-1939
Just neighborly. 1921. LAW

DEAN, PHILIP H.
The owl killer. (1972) KINH

DE ANDA, PETER
Ladies in waiting. 1971. BES70, KINH

DEANE, HAMILTON, and WARBURTON, H. L.
Dracula. 1927. RICI

DEBENHAM, ARTHUR HENRY, 1881-
Good will toward men. 1934. SEVE
The prince of peace. 1934. SEVE

DE CASALIS, JEANNE, 1897-1966. See Sherriff, Robert Cedric, jt. auth.

DECOUR, CHARLES HERBERT and THEODORE, ANNE
Le coq de village. See Smith, Richard Penn (adapted from). The last man

DE CUREL, FRANÇOIS. See Curel, François de

DE CURNIEU, GEORGES. See Curnieu, Georges de

DEEVY, TERESA
Kati Roche. 1936. FAMI

DE FILIPPO, EDUARDO. See Filippo, Eduardo de

DE GHELDERODE, MICHEL. See Ghelderode, Michel de

DEKKER, THOMAS, 1507?-1641?
The gentle craft. See The

shoemakers' holiday
A pleasant comedy of a gentle craft. See The shoemakers' holiday
The pleasant comedy of Old Fortunatus. 1599. SCH, SCI
The shoemakers' holiday; or, The gentle craft. 1599. BALD, BAS, BENY, BLOO, BROC, CLKW, COF, DUN, FOUD, GARZAE, GAY3, GREC1, HARC47, HAY, HOW, LAWR, MCCL, MCI, MONV, NEI, NES, ORNC, PAR, RUB, SCI, SCJ, SCW, SHAJ1, SPE, SPF1, TAT, TAU, TAV, WHE, WINE, WOO1, WRIH
Variant titles: The gentle craft; A pleasant comedy of a gentle craft
--See Ford, John, jt. auth.

-- and MIDDLETON, THOMAS
The honest whore, pt. I. 1604. BAS, NEI, NES, SPE, WALL
The honest whore, pt. II. 1605. NEI, OLH, OLI1, SPE

DE KOCK, CHARLES PAUL. See Kock, Charles Paul de

DE KRUIF, PAUL HENRY, 1890-1971. See Howard, Sidney Coe, jt. auth.

DE LA BARCA, PEDRO CALDERON. See Calderón de la Barca, Pedro

DELACOUR, ALFRED CHARLEMAGNE LARTIGNE, known as, 1817-1883. See Labiche, Eugène Marin, jt. auth.

DELAFIELD, E. M., pseud. See De La Pasture, Edmée Elizabeth Monica

DELANEY, SHELAGH, 1939-
A taste of honey. 1958. BES60, POP, SEVC

DE LA PASTURE, EDMEE ELIZABETH MONICA (E. M. Delafield, pseud.), 1890-1943
To see ourselves. 1930. FAMA, PLAD

DE LA TAILLE, JEAN. See Taille, Jean de La

DELAVIGNE, CASIMIR. See Delavigne, Jean François Casimir

DELAVIGNE, JEAN FRANÇOIS CASIMIR, 1793-1843
Marino Faliero. 1829. BOR

DELDERFIELD, RONALD FREDERICK, 1912-
Peace comes to Peckham. 1947. EMB3
Worm's eye view. 1945. EMB1

DELL, FLOYD, 1887-1969, and MITCHELL, THOMAS
Little accident. 1928. BES28

DELL, JEFFREY, 1899-
Payment deferred (based on the novel by Cecil Forester). 1934? CART

DEL VALLE-INCLAN, RAMON MARIA. See Valle-Inclán, Ramón María del

DE MAUPASSANT, GUY. See Maupassant, Guy de

DE MILLE, HENRY CHURCHILL, 1850-1893, and BARNARD, CHARLES
The main line; or, Rawson's Y. 1886. AMP17
--See Belasco, David, jt. auth.

DE MILLE, WILLIAM CHURCHILL, 1878-1955
The Warrens of Virginia.

1907. AMP16

DE MONTHERLANT, HENRY.
See Montherlant, Henry Marie Joseph Millon de

DENISON, MERRILL, 1893-
Balm. 1923. MAS1
Brothers in arms. 1921. MAS1
The weather breeder. 1924. MAS1

DENKER, HENRY
A far country. 1961. BES60

-- and BERKEY, RALPH
Breaking point. See Time limit!
Time limit! 1956. THEA56
Variant title: Breaking point

D'ENNERY, ADOLPHE, 1811-1899, and CORMON, EUGENE
Les deux orphelines. See The two orphans
Orphans of the storm. See The two orphans
The two orphans (adapted by N. Hart Jackson). 1874. CEY
Variant titles: Les deux orphelines; Orphans of the storm

DENNEY, REUEL
September lemonade. 1955? NEWW7

DENNIS, NIGEL FORBES, 1912-
August for the people. 1961. RHE
Cards to identify. 1956. WELT

DESNOS, ROBERT, 1900-1945
La Place de l'Etoile. (1944)
Benedikt, M., tr. BEN

DESSANDRAIS-SEBIRE, FRANÇOIS
The philosopher duped by love (sometimes attributed to). See Anonymous plays. The philosopher duped by love

DESTOUCHES, PHILLIPPE NERICAULT, 1680-1754
The conceited count. See La glorieux
Le glorieux. 1732. BRE
Aldington, R., tr. ALD
Variant title: The conceited count

DEVAL, JACQUES, 1893-
Tovarich. 1936.
Sherwood, R., tr. and adapted. BES36, CEW

DE VISE, JEAN DONNEAU.
See Donneau de Visé, Jean

DEWHURST, KEITH
Rafferty's chant. 1967. PLAN33

DEY, JAMES PAUL, 1930-
Passacaglia. 1965. NEWA2

DIAMANT-BERGER, MAURICE (André Gillois, pseud.)
Paddle your own canoe. See Regnier, Max. A. M. (based on)

DIAZ, JORGE, 1930-
El lugar donde mueren los mamíferos. See The place where the mammals die
The mammals' graveyard. See The place where the mammals die
The place where the mammals die. 1963.
Nelson, N., tr. WOOG
Variant titles: El lugar donde mueren los mamíferos; The mammals' graveyard

DICENTA Y BENEDICTO, JOAQUIN, 1860-1917
Juan José. 1895.
Skidmore, M., tr. TUR

DICKENS, CHARLES, 1812-1870

A Christmas carol. See Shay, Frank. A Christmas carol (adapted from the story by)
The cricket on the hearth. See Smith, Albert Richard. The cricket on the hearth (adapted from the story by)
Dot. See Boucicault, Dion. Dot (adapted from The cricket on the hearth)
Pickwick Papers. See Young, Stanley. Mr. Pickwick (based on)

DIDEROT, DENIS, 1713-1784
The father. See Le père de famille
La père de famille. 1761. BRE
Variant title: The father

DIGHTON, JOHN, 1909-
The happiest days of your life. 1948. PLAN1
Who goes there! 1951. PLAN6

DINNER, WILLIAM, and MORUM, WILLIAM
The late Edwina Black. 1949. PLAN2

DIZENZO, CHARLES JOHN, 1938-
The drapes come. 1965. OFF
An evening for Merlin Finch. 1968. OFF

DOBIE, LAURENCE, and SLOMAN, ROBERT
The tinker. 1960. PLAN24

DODD, LEE WILSON, 1879-1933
The changelings. 1923. BES23

DODSON, OWEN, 1914-
Bayou legend. 1946. TUQT
Divine comedy. 1938. HARY

DOGGET, THOMAS, d. 1721
Flora; or, Hob in the well. See Hob; or, The country wake
Hob; or, The country wake (sometimes attributed to Colley Cibber). 1711. HUGH
Variant titles: Flora; or, Hob in the well; The opera of Flora; or, Hob in the well
The opera of Flora; or, Hob in the well. See Hob; or, The country wake

DOHERTY, BRIAN
Father Malachy's miracle (adapted from the novel by Bruce Marshall). 1945. EMBI

DOLAN, HARRY
Losers weepers. (1967) DOD

DONLEAVY, JAMES PATRICK, 1926-
The interview. THOD

DONNAY, MAURICE CHARLES, 1859-1945
Les amants. See The lovers
L'autre danger. See The other danger
The lovers. 1895.
Clark, B., tr. MOSQ
Steeves, H., tr. STE
Variant title: Les amants
The other danger. 1902.
David, C., tr. THR
Variant title: L'autre danger

DONNEAU DE VISE, JEAN, 1638?-1710?
Le gentilhomme guespin. 1670? LAN

DORSET, THOMAS SACKVILLE, 1st earl of. See Sackville, Thomas

DORST, TANKRED, 1925-
The curve. 1960.
Rosenberg, J., tr. COTT
Variant title: Die Kurve
Freedom for Clemens. 1960.
Wellwarth, G., tr. BENB
Variant titles: Freedom

for Clement; Freiheit für Clemens
Freedom for Clement. See Freedom for Clemens
Freiheit für Clemens. See Freedom for Clemens
Die Kurve. See The curve

DOSTOEVSKII, FEDOR MIKHAILOVICH, 1821-1881
The brothers Karamazoff (based on the novel by). See Nemīrovich-Danchenko, Vladīmīr. The brothers Karamazoff

DOSTOIEVSKY, FEDOR. See Dostoevskiĭ, Fedor Mikhaĭlovich

DOUGLAS, FELICITY. Rollo. See Achard, Marcel. Rollo (adapted by)

DOUGLAS, GEORGIA. See Johnson, Mrs. Georgia (Douglas)

DOUGLAS, JAMES, 1929-
The ice goddess. 1964. HOGE

DOVIZI DA BIBIENA, BERNARDO CARDINAL, 1470-1520
La Calandria. See The follies of Calandro
The follies of Calandro. Early 16th cent.
Evans, O., tr. BENSA
Variant title: La Calandria

DOWLING, JENNETTE and LETTON, FRANCIS
Before the throne. See The young Elizabeth
Princess Elizabeth. See The young Elizabeth
The young Elizabeth. 1951. PLAN7
Variant titles: Before the throne; Princess Elizabeth

DOWN, OLIPHANT, 1885-1917
The maker of dreams. 1912. BEAC12

DOWSON, ERNEST CHRISTOPHER, 1867-1900
The Pierrot of the minute. 1902. BENP, SECK

DOYLE, SIR ARTHUR CONAN, 1859-1930
Sherlock Holmes. See Gillette, William Hooker. Sherlock Holmes (based on the stories by)

DRAGUN, OSVALDO, 1929-
And they told us we were immortal. 1963.
Green, A., tr. WOOG
Variant title: Y nos dijeron que éramos inmortales
Y nos dijeron que éramos inmortales. See And they told us we were immortal

DRAKE, WILLIAM A., 1899-1965
Grand hotel (tr. and adapted by). See Baum, Vicki. Grand hotel

DRANSFIELD, JANE, 1875-1975
The lost pleiad. 1910. SHAY

DRAYTON, MICHAEL, 1563-1631
The merry devil of Edmonton (sometimes attributed to). See Anonymous plays. The merry devil of Edmonton
Sir John Oldcastle, pt. I (sometimes attributed to). See Anonymous plays. Sir John Oldcastle, pt. I

DRAYTON, RONALD
Notes from a strange God. (1968) JON

DRINKWATER, JOHN, 1882-1937
Abraham Lincoln. 1918. BES19, DID, PLAP1, SWI
Cophetua. 1911. PEN

Oliver Cromwell. 1923. DIG

DRIVER, DONALD, 1922-
Your own thing (music and lyrics by Hal Hester and Danny Apolinar). 1968. BES67

DRUMMOND, ALEXANDER MAGNUS
The lake guns of Seneca and Cayuga. DRU
--See Baker, E. Irene, jt. auth.

DRUTEN, JOHN VAN. See Van Druten, John

DRYDEN, JOHN, 1631-1700
All for love; or, The world well lost. 1677. BAUG, BENY, CLK1, COTX, DOB, FREG, GOS, GOSA, HARC18, KET, LIE, LIED1, LIEE1, MAL, MAT, MCCL, MCM, MCMI, MIL, MOO, MOR, NET, REST, SHAH1, SHAJ1, SMN, SNYD1, STM, TUP, TUQ, TWE, WILS, WOOE1, WRIR
Almanzor and Almahide; or, The conquest of Granada by the Spaniards. 1670. MOR, NET, TAT, TAU, TUP, TUQ
Variant titles: The conquest of Granada; The conquest of Granada by the Spaniards, pt. I
Aureng-zebe. 1675. DOA, MEN, STM, TICK
The conquest of Granada. See Almanzor and Almahide
The conquest of Granada by The Spaniards, pt. I. See Almanzor and Almahide
Marriage a la mode. 1572. DAVR
The secular masque. 1700. ABRA, HAPT1
The Spanish fryar; or, The double discovery. 1679. GAY4, MOSE1
--See D'Avenant, William, jt. auth.
-- and HOWARD, SIR ROBERT
The Indian queen. 1663. BENY, MCM, MCMI

DUBERMAN, MARTIN B., 1930-
In white America. 1963. LAM, GARV

DUBOIS, WILLIAM EDWARD BURGHARDT, 1868-1963
Haiti. 1938. FEE

DUCANGE, VICTOR HENRY JOSEPH BRAHAIN, 1783-1833. See Goubaux, Prosper Parfait, jt. auth.

DUERRENMATT, FRIEDRICH, 1921-
Abendstunde im Spätherbst. See Incident at twilight
Der besuch der alten dame. See The visit
Incident at twilight. 1959. Wellwarth, G., tr. BENB, WELT
Variant title: Abendstunde im Spätherbst
The old lady's visit. See The visit
The physicists. 1962. Kirkup, J., tr. BES64
Variant title: Die Physiker
Die Physiker. See The physicists
Time and again. See The visit
Trapps. See Yaffe, James. The deadly game (adapted from)
The visit. 1956. Bowles, P., tr. COTQ
Valency, M., tr. and adapter. BAUL, BES57, BLOC, BOW, CALD, CASE, GOOD
Variant titles: Der besuch der alten dame; La visite de la vieille dame; The old lady's visit; Time and again

La visite de la vieille dame. See The visit

DUFFET, THOMAS, fl. 1678
The mock-tempest; or, The enchanted castle. 1674. SUMB

DUFFIELD, BRAINERD
The lottery (from the story by Shirley Jackson). 1953? LOVR

DUFFY, MAUREEN, 1933-
Rites. 1969. SUB

DUKES, ASHLEY, 1885-1959
The man with a load of mischief. 1925. MAP, PLAP3
The mask of virtue (tr. and adapted by). See Sternheim, Carl. The mask of virtue
Such men are dangerous (adapted from The patriot, by Alfred Neumann). 1928. FAO

DUMAS, ALEXANDRE, père, 1802-1870
Antony. 1831. BOR, COM
The Count of Monte Cristo. See Fechter, Charles Albert. Monte Cristo (based on the novel, The Count of Monte Cristo, by)
Henry III et sa cour. 1829. BOR, GRA

DUMAS, ALEXANDRE, fils, 1824-1895
Camilla; or, The fate of a coquette. See La dame aux camélias
Camille. See La dame aux camélias
La dame aux camélias. 1852. BOR, GRA
Ashley, L., tr. ASF
Reynolds, E., and Playfair, N., trs. SSTG
Variant titles: Camilla; or, The fate of a coquette; Camille; The lady of the camelias; The queen of the camelias
Le demi-monde. See The outer edge of society
The ideas of Madame Aubray. See Les idées de Madame Aubray
Les idées de Madame Aubray. 1867. BOR
Variant title: The ideas of Madame Aubray
The lady of the camelias. See La dame aux camélias
The outer edge of society. 1855.
Clark, B., tr. MAU
Harper, H., tr. CLF2
Varient title: Le demimonde
The queen of the camelias. See La dame aux camélias

DUNBAR-NELSON, ALICE, 1875-1935
Mine eyes have seen. 1918. HARY

DUNCAN, RONALD FREDERICK, 1914-
The death of Satan. 1954. LOR, SATA
The gift. 1968. RICK

DUNCAN, THELMA
The death dance. 1923. LOC

DUNLAP, WILLIAM, 1766-1839
André. 1798. COY, HAL, MOSS1, QUIJ, QUIK, QUIL, QUIM, QUIN
Darby's return. 1789. AMPA
False shame; or, The American orphan in Germany (adapted from Falsche scham, by August Kotzebue). 1799. AMP2
The glory of Columbia: Her yeomancy! 1803. MONR
Thirty years; or, The gambler's fate (adapted from Trente ans, by Prosper Goubaux and Victor Ducange). 1828. AMP2
A trip to Niagara; or, Travellers in America. 1828. MONR

DUNNING, PHILIP HART, 1892- , and ABBOTT, GEORGE
Broadway. 1926. BES26, CART, GASB

DUNSANY, EDWARD JOHN MORETON, 1878-1957
The glittering gate. 1909. WATF1, WATI
The gods of the mountain. 1911. MOSN, MOSO
If. 1921. HAU
King Argimenes and the unknown warrior. 1911. DID
The lost silk hat. 1921. CHU, PROM, PRON, SCWI
A night at an inn. 1916. BEAC11, BLAG, BLAH, COOK3, GARZAP, GASS, HUD, PEN, PROB
The queen's enemies. 1916. AND

DURAS, MARGUERITE, 1914-
Department of forestry. See The rivers and forests
Les eaux et forêts. See The rivers and forests
The rivers and forests. 1965. Brae, B., tr. MIJE
Variant titles: Department of forestry; Les eaux et forêts

DURRENMATT, FRIEDRICH. See Duerrenmatt, Friedrich

DU RYER, PIERRE, 1600?-1658
Esther. 1642? Lockert, L., tr. LOCU
Saul. 1640. Lockert, L., tr. LOCR
Scaevola. 1644? Lockert, L., tr. LOCR

D'USSEAU, ARNAUD, 1916- . See Gow, James Ellis, jt. auth.

DUVAL, ALEXANDRE VINCENT, 1767-1842
La jeunesse de Henri V. See Payne, John Howard. Charles the second (adapted from)
Shakespeare amoureux; ou, La pièce á l'étude. See Smith, Richard Penn. Shakespeare in love (adapted from)

DYER, CHARLES, 1926-
Rattle of a simple man. 1961. BES62, PLAN26
Staircase. 1966. BES67

E

E., A., pseud. See Russell, George William

EBB, FRED, 1932-
Cabaret (lyrics by). See Masteroff, Joe. Cabaret

EBERHART, RICHARD, 1904-
The visionary forms. 1952. NEWW3

ECHEGARAY Y EIZAGUIRRE, JOSE, 1832-1916
La esposa del vengador. See The street singer
El gran Galeoto. 1891. BRET
Bontecou, E., tr. CLDM, DIK2
Lynch, H., tr. FLOS
Nirdlinger, C., tr. and adapter. MOSQ
Variant titles: The great Galeoto; Slander; The world and his wife
The great Galeoto. See El gran Galeoto
Slander. See El gran Galeoto
The street singer. 1874. Underhill, J., tr. MCCP
Variant title: La esposa del vengador
The world and his wife. See El gran Galeoto

EDMONDS, RANDOLPH, 1900-
Bad man. 1934. HARY
Earth and stars. 1946. TUQT

EDWARD, H. F. V., 1898-

1973
Job hunters. 1931. HARY

EDWARDS, RICHARD, 1523?-1566
Damon and Pithias. 1564? ADA

EDWARDS, SHERMAN, 1919-
1776 (music and lyrics by). See Stone, Peter H. 1776

EGAN, MICHAEL, 1895-1956
The dominant sex. 1934. FAMG
To love and to cherish. 1938. FAML

EICHELBAUM, SAMUEL, 1894-
Divorcio nupcial. 1941. ALPE

EISENSTEIN, MARK
The fighter. 1958. GARZAL

EIZAGUIRRE, JOSE ECHEGARAY Y. See Echegaray y Eizaguirre, José

ELDER, LONNE, III, 1931-
Ceremonies in dark old men. 1969. PATR
Charades on East Fourth Street. 1967. KINH

ELIOT, THOMAS STEARNS, 1888-1965
The cocktail party. 1949. BES49, FEL
The confidential clerk. 1954. BES53, THEA54
The family reunion. 1939. BROS
Murder in the cathedral. 1935. BALL, BROH, COK, CONP, COTQ, CUBH, DEAP, DEAR, HAVG, LEVJ, MACM2, TAUJ, TUCO, WARI, WATA
Sweeney Agonistes. 1926. BENS1

ELLIOTT, SUMNER LOCKE. See Locke-Elliott, Sumner

ELSER, FRANK BALL, 1885-1935, and CONNELLY, MARCUS COOK
The farmer takes a wife. See Low bridge
Low bridge. 1934. BES34, LEV
Variant title: The farmer takes a wife

EMERY, GILBERT, pseud. See Pottle, Emery Bemsley

EMIG, EVELYN (MELLON), 1895-
The china pig. 1920? SHAY

ENAMAI NO SAYEMON, fl. 1400
The cormorant fisher. 15th cent.
Waley, A., tr. TAV

ENGLAND, BARRY, 1934-
Conduct unbecoming. 1970. BES70

ENNERY, ADOLPHE D'. See D'Ennery, Adolphe

ENRICO, ROBERT
On Owl Creek. 1961. HAVL

ERCKMANN-CHATRIAN (pseud. of Erckmann, Emile, 1822-1899, and Chatrain, Alexandre, 1826-1890, collaborators)
The Polish Jew. See Lewis, Leopold David. The bells (adapted from Le juif polonais by)

ERVINE, ST. JOHN GREER, 1883-1971
The first Mrs. Fraser. 1929. BES29
Jane Clegg. 1913. BES19, PALP1
John Ferguson. 1915. BES09, CHA, CHAN, CHAR, DUR, THF, TUCD, TUCM, TUCN, TUCO
Mixed marriage. 1911. DID

ESASHI JUO
The bird catcher in hell.
Waley, A., tr. INGW, TAV

ESTABROOK, HOWARD
The human comedy (screen play based on the book by William Saroyan). 1943. NAGE

ESTRIN, MARC
An American playground sampler. (1970) NEWA3

ETHEREGE, SIR GEORGE, 1635?-1691
The man of mode; or, Sir Fopling Flutter. 1675. CLKW, GOSA, KRM, LID, MCM, MCMI, MCMS, MOR, MOSE1, NET, REIL, REST, SALR, STM, TUQ, WILS
She would if she could. 1668. DAVR

ETIENNE, CHARLES GUILLAUME, 1777-1845
Les deux gendres. See Payne, John Howard. The two sons-in-law (adapted from)

EUBA, FEMI
Abiko. PIET

EURIPIDES, 480?-406? B.C.
Alcestis. 438 B.C.
Aldington, R., tr. ALLI, LIND, LOCK, OAT1, OATH
Browning, R., tr. MAST
Coleridge, E., tr. GRDB5
Fitts, D., and Fitzgerald, R., trs. FEL, FIFR, FIFT
Lattimore, R., tr. GREP3, GRER3, WEAN
Murray, G., tr. CLKW
Potter, R., tr. CLF1
Way, A., tr. GREE, HOWE, HOWF, THOM, THON
Andromache. 431? B.C.
Coleridge, E., tr. GRDB5, OAT1
Johnson, V., tr. FIFV
LeRue, J., tr. COOA
Lind, L., tr. LIND
Nims, J., tr. GREP3
The bacchae. 405 B.C.
Anon. tr. ALLK
Arrowsmith, W., tr. GREP4, GRER3, TREB
Birkhead, H., tr. LIND
Boer, C., tr. COOA
Cavender, K., tr. COTX
Coleridge, E., tr. GRDB5
Curry, N., tr. BENSB1
Kerr, A., tr. DOWS
Lucas, F., tr. LUCA, LUCAB, LUCAF
Milman, H., tr. ROBJ, VON
Murray, G., tr. HARC8, OAT2, OATE
Vellacott, M., tr. BAIC
Vellacott, P., tr. ALLJ, BAIE, SANE, WEIS, WELT
Volanakis, M., tr. HAPRL
Variant title: The bacchantes
The bacchantes. See The bacchae
The children of Heracles. See The Heracleidae
The cyclops. 5th cent. B.C.
Arrowsmith, W., tr. GREP3
Coleridge, E., tr. GRDB5, OAT2
Green, R., tr. RUSV
Shelley, P., tr. PLAG
Smith, G., tr. BAT1
Electra. 413? B.C.
Coleridge, E., tr. GRDB5, OAT2
Murray, G., tr. FEFT, TEN, TRE, TREA2
Vellacott, P., tr. FOR
Vermeule, E., tr. GREP4, GRER2
Way, A., tr. WEAV1
Hecuba. 425? B.C.
Arrowsmith, W., tr. GREP3
Coleridge, E., tr. GRDB5, OAT1
Helen. 412 B.C.
Coleridge, E., tr. GRDB5, OAT2
Lattimore, R., tr. GREP3
The Heracleidae. 431? B.C.
Coleridge, E., tr. GRDB5, OAT1

Gladstone, R., tr. GREP3
Variant title: The children of Heracles
Heracles. 420? B.C.
Arrowsmith, W., tr. GREP3
Coleridge, E., tr. GRDB5, OAT1
Variant titles: Heracles mad; The madness of Heracles
Heracles mad. See Heracles
Hiketides. See The suppliants
Hippolytus. 428 B.C.
Coleridge, E., tr. GRDB5, OAT1, THP, WARN1
Grene, G., tr. FIFT, GREN, GREP3, GRER1
Lucas, F., tr. BARC, LUCA, LUCAB, LUCAF
Murray, G., tr. FEFT, HARC8, MIL, MURP, OATE
Vellacott, P., tr. GOLH, SANP
Warner, R., tr. VANV1
Way, A., tr. ATT2, HOUS, ROBI
Ion. 5th cent. B.C.
Coleridge, E., tr. GRDB5
Doolittle, H., tr. KRE
Potter, R., tr. OAT1
Willetts, R., tr. GREP4
Iphigenia among the Tauri. See Iphigenia in Tauris
Iphigenia at Aulis. 405 B.C.
Coleridge, E., tr. GRDB5
Potter, R., tr. CROS, ROB
Stawell, F., tr. OAT2
Walker, C., tr. GREP4
Way, A., tr. BUCK, BUCL, BUCM
Variant title: Iphigenia in Aulis
Iphigenia in Aulis. See Iphigenia at Aulis
Iphigenia in Tauris. 420? B.C.
Anon. tr. WED
Bynner, W., tr. GREP3, GRER2
Coleridge, E., tr. GRDB5
Murray, G., tr. FEFT, TEN
Potter, R., tr. OAT1, PLAG
Variant title: Iphigenia among the Tauri
The madness of Heracles. See Heracles
Medea. 431 B.C.
Anon. tr. EVB1, SSTF
Agard, W., tr. MCKK1
Coleridge, E., tr. EDAD, GRDB5, LOCM1, OAT1, OATH
Jeffers, R., tr. and adapter. GARW, GARZA3, KIN, LOR, SANM
McLeish, K., tr. MCKM
Murray, G., tr. FEFT, MAU, ROET, SEBO, SEBP, SMP, TEN
Prokosh, F., tr. FIFT, FREG, GOOD, TAUJ
Robinson, C., tr. ROBK
Taylor, J., tr. TAV
Trevelyan, R., tr. ROBI
Vellacott, P., tr. HAPRL, SANM
Warner, R., tr. GREP3, MACJ, MACL1, MACM1, MACN
Way, A., tr. ATT2, BUCL, BUCM, GREE, HOWE, HOWF, LAP, PROW, ROBJA
Wodhull, M., tr. DRA1, EVA1, EVC1, HIB, HIBB, MIK7, PLAB1
Orestes. 408 B.C.
Arrowsmith, W., tr. GREP4
Coleridge, E., tr. GRDB5, OAT2
Kirn, H., tr. TAUJ
The Phoenician Maidens. See The Phoenissae
The Phoenician women. See The Phoenissae
The Phoenissae. 413? B.C.
Coleridge, E., tr. GRDB5, OAT2
Wyckoff, E., tr. GREP4
Variant titles: The Phoenician maidens; The Phoenician women
Rhesus. 5th cent. B.C.

Coleridge, E., tr. GRDB5
Lattimore, R., tr. GREP4
Murray, G., tr. OAT2
The suppliants. 424 B.C.
Coleridge, E., tr. GRDB5, OAT1
Jones, F., tr. GREP4
Lind, L., tr. LIND
Variant titles: Hiketides; The suppliant women
The suppliant women. See The suppliants
Troades. See The Trojan women
The Trojan women. 415 B.C.
Coleridge, E., tr. GRDB5
Doria, C., tr. COOA
Hamilton, E., tr. CLO, HAM, MACM1, SCNR
Lattimore, R., tr. FIFT, GREP3, GRER2, TREB, TREC1, TREE1, TREI1
Murray, G., tr. CAR, CARA, OAT1, STA
Potter, R., tr. ROBJA
Raubitschek, I., and A., trs. (assisted by A. Mc-Cabe) ROBJ
Variant title: Troades

EVREINOV, NIKOLAI NIKOLAEVICH, 1879-
The back stage of the soul. See The theatre of the soul
The beautiful despot. 1906.
Roberts, C., tr. ROE
Behind the curtain of the soul. See The theatre of the soul
A merry death, a harlequinade. 1914.
Collins, M., tr. COLI
Roberts, C., tr. ROE
Styopic and Manya.
Collins, M., tr. COLI
The theatre of the soul. 1912.
Potapenko, M., and St. John, C., trs. DIE, HIB, HIBA
Variant titles: The back stage of the soul; Behind the curtain of the soul

EWING, THOMAS, 1862-1942
Jonathan. 1902? KOH2

EXTON, CLIVE, 1930-
Have you any dirty washing, mother dear. 1969. PLAN37

EYEN, TOM, 1940-
Grand tenement and November 22. 1967. SME
The white whore and the bit player. 1964. NEWA2

F

FAGAN, JAMES BERNARD, 1873-1933
The improper duchess. 1931. FAMA, PLAD

FAIRCHILD, WILLIAM
The sound of murder. 1959. PLAN20

FALKLAND, SAMUEL. See Heijermans, Herman (pseud. of)

FARIGOULE, LOUIS HENRI JEAN. See Romains, Jules

FARJEON, ELEANOR, 1881-1965
The plane-tree. 1950. OULD
-- and FARJEON, HERBERT
The two bouquets. 1936. FAMJ

FARJEON, HERBERT, 1887-1945. See Farjeon, Eleanor, jt. auth.

FARQUHAR, GEORGE, 1678-1707
The beaux' stratagem. 1707. BAT22, BLOO, CLF1, CLK1, GOS, GOSA, HUD, MAT, MCM, MCMI, MOR, MOSE2, NET, REST, STM, TAY, TICK, TUP, TUQ, TWE, UHL, WEAT1, WILS, WRIR
The recruiting officer. 1706. GAY4, RUB

FATH'ALI, AKHUND-ZADAH, 1812-1878

The alchemist. 186-?
Le Strange, G., tr. BAT3
The magistrates. 186-?
Wilson, E., tr. TUQH

FATH ALI, MIRZA. See Fath'-Ali, Akhund-zadah

FAUCHOIS, RENE, 1882-
The late Christopher Bean. 1933.
Howard, S., tr. and adapter. BES32, GARZAP, GARZH, GASS, SPES, WARH
Williams, E., tr. and adapter. FAMD
Variant titles: Muse of all work; Prenez garde à la peinture.
Muse of all work. See The late Christopher Bean
Prenez garde à la peinture. See The late Christopher Bean

FAULKNER, WILLIAM, 1897-1962. See Ford, Ruth, jt. auth.

FECHTER, CHARLES ALBERT, 1824-1879
Monte Cristo (based on the novel, The Count of Monte Cristo, by Alexandre Dumas, père). 1883. AMP16, CLA, GARX, SAFM

FEELY, TERENCE
Don't let summer come. 1964. PLAN29

FEIFFER, JULES, 1929-
Crawling Arnold. 1961. RICJ
Little murders. 1966. LIEF
The White House murder case. 1970. BES69

FELTHAUS-WEBER, MARY
The world tipped over and laying on its side. 1966. BALLE4

FERBER, EDNA, 1887-1968. See Kaufman, George S., jt. auth.

FERDINAND, VAL, 1947-
Blk love song #1. 1969. HARY

FERGUSSON, FRANCIS
The king and the duke (based on Huckleberry Finn, by Samuel Clemens). 1939? BENS2

FERLINGHETTI, LAWRENCE, 1919-
Our little trip. FREF

FERNANDEZ DE MORATIN, LEANDRO. See Moratín, Leandro Fernández de

FERRIS, WALTER, 1882-
Death takes a holiday (tr. and adapted by). See Casella, Alberto. Death takes a holiday

FETH-ALI, AKHOUD ZAIDE MIRZA. See Fath'Ali, Akhund-zadah

FEYDEAU, GEORGES LEON JULES MARIE, 1862-1921
Breakfast in bed. See Keep an eye on Amélie!
Get out of my hair.
Davies, F., tr. LAB
Keep an eye on Amélie! 1908.
Duffield, B., tr. BENSC
Variant titles: Breakfast in bed; Occupe-toi d'Amélie; Oh, Amelia
Occupe-toi d'Amélie. See Keep an eye on Amélie!
Oh, Amelia. See Keep an eye on Amélie!

FIELD, CHARLES KELLOGG, 1873-
The cave man. 1910. BOH2
The man in the forest. 1902. BOH1
The owl and cave. 1906. BOH1

FIELD, EDWARD SALISBURY, 1876-1936
Wedding bells. 1919. BES19

FIELD, JOSEPH M., 1810-1856
Job and his children. 1852. AMP14
FIELD, NATHANIEL, 1587-1633
Amends for ladies. 1611. NER
Woman is a weathercock. 1609. NER

FIELD, RACHEL, 1894-1942
The patchwork quilt. 193-? COOK2
FIELDING, HENRY (H. Scriblerus Secundus, pseud.), 1707-1754
The historical register for year 1736. 1737. BEVI
The tragedy of tragedies; or, The life and death of Tom Thumb the great. 1731. EIGH, HAN, NET, STM, TAT, TAU, TAY, TUP, TUQ

FIELDS, JOSEPH, 1895-
The doughgirls. 1942. BES42

-- and CHODOROV, JEROME
Junior miss (based on the book by Mrs. Sally Benson). 1941. BES41, GOW, GOWA
My sister Eileen (based on the stories by Ruth McKenney). 1940. BES40
The ponder heart (adapted from the story by Eudora Welty). 1956. BES55, THEA56
Wonderful town (based on the play My sister Eileen; music by Leonard Bernstein; lyrics by Betty Comden and Adolph Green). 1953. BES52, THEA53

FIGUEROA, JOHN, 1912-
Everybody's a Jew. RAVA

FILIPPO, EDUARDO DE, 1900-
Filumena Marturano. 1946. Bentley, E., tr. BENSA, COTN
Variant title: A mother's a mother
A mother's a mother. See Filumena Marturano

FINK, EDITH ROMIG
Nooschens duhn viel. See Noshions duhn
Noshions duhn. 1950? BUFF
Variant title: Nooschens duhn viel

FINLEY, IAN HAMILTON, 1925-
The estate hunters. NEWE14
Walking through seaweed. 1962. NEWE14

FISCHER, LECK, 1904-
The mystery tour. 1949. Pearce, J., tr. CONT
Variant title: Selskabsrejsen
Selskabsrejsen. See The mystery tour

FITCH, CLYDE, 1865-1909
Barbara Frietchie. 1899. BES99
Beau Brummell. 1890. COH
Captain Jinks of the horse marines. 1901. BENT4
The city. 1909. MONR, MOSJ, MOSK, MOSL
The climbers. 1901. BES99, COT
The girl with the green eyes. 1902. QUIL, QUIM, QUIN, SHA2
Her great match. 1905. QUIG, QUIJ, QUIK
The moth and the flame. 1898. MOSS3
Nathan Hale. 1898. COOK2, PROF, PROG, PROH, SCWE
A trip abroad. See Labiche, Eugène Marin and Martin, Edouard. Le voyage de Monsieur Perrichon
The truth. 1907. DIC, GARX, STA

FITCH, WILLIAM CLYDE.

See Fitch, Clyde

FITZMAURICE, GEORGE
The dandy dolls. 1914? CAP

FLAVIN, MARTIN, 1883-1967
Amaco. 1932? TOD
The criminal code. 1929. BES29

FLEMING, Mrs. DOROTHY (SAYERS). See Sayers, Dorothy

FLETCHER, JOHN, 1579-1625
The chances. 1616. RUB
Buckingham, Duke of, adapter. PLAN25
An equal match. See Rule a wife and have a wife
The faithful shepherdess. 1609. BAS, GRE, NEI, SCI, SCJ
The island princess; or, The generous Portugal. 1621. BROC
Rule a wife and have a wife. 1624. GAY3, SCH, SCI
Variant title: An equal match
The wild-goose chase. 1609? BENY, NEI, SPE, TAT, TAU, WALL
--See Beaumont, Francis, jt. auth.

-- MASSINGER, PHILIP [and BEAUMONT, FRANCIS]
Beggars' bush. 1609. BROC

-- and SHAKESPEARE, WILLIAM
The two noble kinsmen. 1613. BRO, PAR, THA

FLETCHER, LUCILLE
Sorry, wrong number. 1948. HEI, WHF

FONTAINE, ROBERT
The happy time. See Taylor, Samuel. The happy time (based on the novel by)

FONVIZIN, DINIS IVANOVICH, 1744-1792
The choice of a tutor. 1792.
Roberts, C., tr. ROE
The infant.
Cooper, J., tr. COOPA
The minor. 1782.
Reeve, F., tr. REEV1
The young hopeful. 1782.
Patrick, G., and Noyes, G., trs. NOY

FOOTE, SAMUEL, 1720-1777
The commissary. 1765. BEVI
The mayor of Garret. 1764. MOR

FORBES, JAMES, 1871-1938
The famous Mrs. Fair. 1919. BES19, MOSJ, MOSK, MOSL

FORBES, KATHRYN
Mama's bank account. See Van Druten, John. I remember mama (based on the book by)

FORD, HARRIET, 1868-1949
Youth must be served. 1926? TOD

FORD, JOHN, 1586-1640?
The broken heart. 1629? BALD, BAS, BROC, HAPRA2, HAPRB2, NEI, OLH, OLI2, ORNT, SCI, SCJ, SPE, WINE
The chronicle history of Perkin Warbeck. 1633? ARMS, BAS, SCH
Variant title: Perkin Warbeck
Perkin Warbeck. See The chronicle history of Perkin Warbeck
'Tis a pity she's a whore. 1628? BENY, DUN, HUST, MCK, PAR, RUB, RYL, WALL

-- DEKKER, THOMAS and ROWLEY, WILLIAM
The witch of Edmonton. 1623? BAS, LAWS

FORD, RUTH, and FAULKNER,

WILLIAM
Requiem for a nun (adapted from the novel by William Faulkner). 1956? BES58

FOREST, LOUIS, 1872-1933
Par un jour de pluie. 192-? SET

FORESTER, CECIL SCOTT, 1899-1966
Payment deferred. See Dell, Jeffrey. Payment deferred (based on the novel by)

FORNES, MARIA IRENE, 1931-
Dr. Kheal. 1968. SLM
The successful life of 3. 1965. BALLE2, ORZ
Tango palace. 1965. BALLE2

FORSSELL, LARS, 1928-
Söndags promenaden. See The Sunday promenade
The Sunday promenade. (1963) Carlson, H., tr. COTT
Variant title: Söndags promenaden

FORSYTH, JAMES, 1913-
Héloise. 1931. COTK

FORTUNE, MRS. JAN ISABELLE, 1892-
The cavalier from France. 194-? PROG

FOSTER, PAUL, 1931-
Balls. 1964. ORZ

FOX, STEPHEN
Never come Monday. See Knight, Eric. Never come Monday (adapted by)

FRAME, VIRGINIA. See Church, Mrs. Virginia Woodson (Frame)

FRANCE, ANATOLE, 1844-1924
La comédie de celui qui épousa une femme muette. 1913. SET
Jackson, W., and E., trs. SMR
Page, C., tr. LEV, LEVE
Variant title: The man who married a dumb wife
The man who married a dumb wife. See La comédie de celui qui épousa une femme muette

FRANCIS, ANN
The song of songs which is Solomon's. 1781? KOH2

FRANCIS, WILLIAM
Portrait of a queen. 1965. PLAN30

FRANK, ANNE, 1929-1945
Diary of a young girl. See Goodrich, Frances and Hackett, Albert. The diary of Anne Frank (based on the book by)

FRANK, MAUDE MORRISON, 1870-
A mistake at the manor. 1915? WEB

FRANK, MIGUEL
El hombre del siglo. See The man of the century
The man of the century. 1958.
Jones, W., tr. JONA
Variant title: El hombre del siglo

FRANK, WALDO DAVID, 1889-1967
New Year's eve. 1928? AME2

FRANKEN, MRS. ROSE D. (Lewin), 1895-
Another language. 1932. BES31
Claudia. 1940. BES40, CALN1
Outrageous fortune. 1943. BES43
Soldier's wife. 1944. BES44

FRATTI, MARIO, 1927-
The academy. (1962)

Rosenthal, R., tr. COTN, RICJ
Variant title: L'accademia
L'accademia. See The academy
The bridge. 1969.
Anon. tr. DIZ
Variant title: Il ponte
The cage. (1961)
Carra, M., and Warner, L., trs. COTS
Variant title: La gabbia
La gabbia. See The cage
Il ponte. See The bridge
The return. (1960)
Corrigan, R., and Fratti, M., trs. COTN
Variant title: Il ritorno
Il ritorno. See The return
The suicide. (1959)
Carra, M., and Warner, L., trs. COTS
Variant title: Il suicidio
Il suicidio. See Fratti, M. The suicide

FREDERICKS, CLAUDE, 1923-
A summer ghost. 1961. NEWA1

FREEMAN, CAROL, 1941-
The suicide. (1968). JON

FREEMAN, DAVID E., 1945-
Creeps. 1973. BES73

FREYTAG, GUSTAV, 1816-1895
The journalists. 1853?
Henderson, E., tr. FRA12
Variant title: Die journalisten
Die journalisten. See The journalists

FRIEDMAN, BRUCE JAY, 1930-
Scuba duba. 1967. BES67
Steambath. 1970. BES70

FRIEL, BRIAN, 1929-
Lovers. 1968. BES68
Philadelphia, here I come! 1966. BES65

FRINGS, KETTI (HARTLEY), 1916-
Look homeward, angel (based on the novel by Thomas Wolfe). 1957. BES57, GARS, GARZA4, WATA

FRISBY, TERENCE
There's a girl in my soup. 1966. PLAN32

FRISCH, MAX, 1911-
Andorra. 1961.
Bullock, M., tr. BES62
Biedermann and the firebugs. 1958.
Gorelik, M., tr. BLOC, JOHO, KNO, RICJ, STY
Variant titles: Biedermann und die brandstifter; The fire raisers; The firebugs
Biedermann und die brandstifter. See Biedermann and the firebugs
The Chinese wall. 1946.
Rosenberg, J., tr. COTQ
Variant title: Die chinesische Mauer
Die chinesische Mauer. See The Chinese wall
The fire raisers. See Biedermann and the firebugs
The firebugs. See Biedermann and the firebugs
The great fury of Philip Hotz. 1958.
Benedikt, M., tr. BENB
Variant titles: The great rage of Philip Hotz; Die grosse Wut des Philipp Hotz; Philip Hotz's fury
The great rage of Philip Hotz. See The great fury of Philip Hotz
Die grosse Wut des Philipp Hotz. See The great fury of Philip Hotz
Philip Hotz's fury. See The great fury of Philip Hotz

FROST, REX
Small hotel. 1955. PLAN13

FROST, ROBERT, 1875-1963
A masque of reason. 1945. KNID

FRY, CHRISTOPHER, 1907-
The boy with a cart. 1938. POOL
The dark is light enough. 1954. BES54
Duel of angels. See Giraudoux, Jean. Duel of angels (adapted by)
A phoenix too frequent. 1946. BAC, BLAH, BROS, FEFL, WARI, WARL
A sleep of prisoners. 1951. COTQ
Tiger at the gates. See Giraudoux, Jean. Tiger at the gates (tr. and adapted by)
Venus observed. 1950. BES51, HAVG, WATE

FUGARD, ATHOL, 1932-
The blood knot. 1960. NEWE13, WELT
Boesman and Lena. 1970. BES70

FULDA, LUDWIG, 1862-1939
Beneath four eyes. See Tête-à-tête
By ourselves. See Tête-à-tête
Tête-à-tête. 1886. Townsend, E., tr. FRA17
Variant titles: Beneath four eyes; By ourselves; Unter vier augen
Unter vier augen. See Tête-à-tête

FULWELL, ULPIAN, fl. 1586
Like will to like. 1568. HAO

FUNT, JULIAN
Child of Grace. See The magic and the loss
The magic and the loss. 1954. BES53
Variant title: Child of Grace

FURTH, GEORGE, 1932-
Company (music and lyrics by Stephen Sondheim). 1970. BES69

FYLES, FRANKLIN, 1847-1911.
See Belasco, David, jt. auth.

G

GAGLIANO, FRANK, 1931-
Father Uxbridge wants to marry. 1967. LAH

GAINES, FREDERICK
The new Chautauqua. 1968. BALLE5

GAINES, J. E.
What if it had never turned up heads. 1972. NEWL

GAINES-SHELTON, RUTH, 1873-
The church fight. 1925. HARY

GALANTIERE, LEWIS, 1893-
Antigone. See Anouilh, Jean. Antigone (adapted by)

GALDOS, BENITO PEREZ
See Pérez Galdós, Benito

GALE, ZONA, 1874-1938
Miss Lulu Bett. 1920. CORD, CORE, CORF

GALLARATI-SCOTTI, TOMMASO, 1878-1966
Cosi sia. See Thy will be done
Thy will be done. 1923. Petri, V., tr.
Variant title: Cosi sia

GALLICO, PAUL, 1897-
The snow goose (adapted for radio by William A. Bacher and Malcolm Meacham). 195-? INGA, INGB

GALSWORTHY, JOHN, 1867-1933
Escape. 1926. BES27, TRE, TREA1, TREBA, TREC2, TREE3, TREI3
Justice. 1910. BROW, HAU, HAVD, HAVE, ROWC, WATF1, WATI, WATO,

WATR
Loyalties. 1922. ANDE, BES22, BROX, CEU, COTKH, COTKR, LEWI, PEN, SNYD2, SPER, WARI, WATF2, WATI
The pigeon. 1912. HARB
The silver box. 1906. CHAR, CLKW, COTH, CROS, MOSN, MOSO, SALE, STAT, TOD
The skin game. 1920. BES20
Strife. 1909. DIC, DUR, INGE, INGG, MAP, MCCB, MCCD, MCCF, MCCG, STET, WATS, WHI, WHK, WOO2

GAMBARO, GRISELDA
The camp. 1967.
Oliver, W., tr. OLIW

GARCIA GUTIERREZ, ANTONIO, 1813-1884
Juan Lorenzo. 1865. BRET
El trovador. 1835. TRES

GARCIA LORCA, FEDERICO, 1899-1936
Amor de don Perlimplin. See The love of don Perlimplin and Belisa in the garden
El amor de don Perlimplin con Belisa en su jardin. See The love of don Perlimplin and Belisa in the garden
Bitter oleander. See Blood wedding
Blood wedding. 1933.
Neiman, G., tr. NEW39
O'Connell, R., and Graham-Luján, J., trs. ALT, ALTE, BIER, BLOC, FLOX, KERP, LOCLB, PERS, PERT, PERU, TREBA, TREC2, TREE2, TREI2, TREJ, WATA
Variant titles: Bitter oleander; Bodas de sangre
Bodas de sangre. See Blood wedding
La casa de Bernarda Alba. See The house of Bernarda Alba
The house of Bernarda Alba. 1945. PARV
Anon. tr. CLN
Graham-Luján, J., and O'Connell, R., trs. ALLI, ALLJ, ALLK, CLM, CLO, DOT, HOGA, SEN, WEIM
Variant title: La casa de Bernarda Alba
In the frame of don Cristobal. 193-?
Honig, E., tr. NEW44
The king of Harlem.
Morison, W., tr. VANV2
Lament for Ignacio Sánchez Mejías.
Spender, S., and Gill, J., trs. VANV2
Variant titles: Lament for the death of a bullfighter; Llanto por Ignacio Sánchez Mejías
Lament for the death of a bullfighter. See Lament for Ignacio Sánchez Mejías
Llanto por Ignacio Sánchez Mejías. See Lament for Ignacio Sánchez Mejías
The love of don Perlimplin and Belisa in the garden. 1931.
O'Connell, R., and Graham-Luján, J., trs. BENS1, COTP
Variant titles: Amor de don Perlimplin; El amor de don Perlimplin con Belisa en su jardin
The shoemaker's prodigious wife. 1930.
O'Connell, R., and Graham-Luján, J., trs. BENA
Variant title: La zapatera prodigiosa
The tragi-comedy of Don Cristobita and Doña Rosita. 1937.
Oliver, W., tr. NEWW8
Yerma. 1934.
Graham-Luján, J., and

O'Connell, R., trs. COTQ, FREG, ULAN
La zapatera prodigiosa. See The shoemaker's prodigious wife

GARCIA VILLA, JOSE. See Villa, José García

GARD, ROBERT E., 1910-
Let's get on with the marrin'. DRU
Mixing up the rent. DRU
Raisin' the devil. DRU

GARDEL, JULIO SANCHEZ. See Sánchez Gardel, Julio

GARDINER, WREY
The last refuge. 1943? NEWR1

GARDNER, MRS. DOROTHY (Butts)
Eastward in Eden. 1947. BES47

GARDNER, HERB, 1934-
A thousand clowns. 1962. BES61, GARS, HOLP

GARNETT, PORTER, 1871-1950
The green knight. 1911. BOH2

GARRETT, JIMMY
We own the night. 1968. JON

GARRICK, DAVID, 1717-1779
The lying valet. 1741. NET
Miss in her teens. 1747. BEVI
--See Colman, George, jt. auth.

GASCOIGNE, GEORGE, 1525?-1577
Supposes (adapted from I suppositi, by Ludovico Ariosto). 1566. ADA, BAS, BOA, BON, NES, ORNC

-- and KINWELMERSH, FRANCIS
Jocasta. 1566. CUN

GASCOYGNE, GEORGE. See Gascoigne, George

GASSNER, JOHN, 1903-1967
Les précieuses ridicules. See Molière, Jean Baptiste Poquelin. Les précieuses ridicules (tr. and adapted by)
Then and now (adapted from The marriage proposal and The harmful effects of smoking, by Anton Chekhov). 19-? GARZAP, GASS

GAY, DELPHINE. See Girardin, Delphine (Gay) de

GAY, JOHN, 1685-1732
The beggar's opera. 1728. ASH, BARB, CLKJ, EIGH, FEL, HAN, KER, KRO, MACK, MCM, MCMI, MOR, MOSE2, NET, SMR, STJM, STM, TAY, TREB, TUP, TUQ, TWE, UHL, WILE

GAZUL, CLARA, pseud. See Mérimée, Prosper

GAZZO, MICHAEL VINCENTE
A hatful of rain. 1956. FAM, GART, THEA56

GEAR, BRIAN
The sky is green. 1963. PLAN27

GEDDES, VIRGIL, 1897-
The stable and the grove. 1933. AME4

GELBER, JACK, 1932-
The connection. 1959. SEVD

GENET, JEAN, 1910-
Le balcon. See The balcony
The balcony. 1960. Frechtman, B., tr. SEVD
Variant title: Le balcon
Les bonnes. See The maids
Deathwatch. 1949. Frechtman, B., tr.

COTQ
Variant title: Haute surveillance
Haute surveillance. See Deathwatch
The maids. 1947.
Frechtman, B., tr. TREBA, TREI3
Variant title: Les bonnes
The screens. 1971.
Volanakis, M., tr. BES71

GEORGE, ERNEST, pseud. See Wise, Ernest George

GEORGE, GRACE, 1883-
The nest (tr. and adapted by). See Geraldy, Paul. The nest

GERALDY, PAUL, 1885-
The nest. 1922.
George, G., tr. and adapter. BES21
Variant titles: Les noces d'argent; Silver weddings
Les noces d'argent. See The nest
Silver weddings. See The nest

GERSHE, LEONARD
Butterflies are free. 1969. BES69
GERSHWIN, GEORGE, 1899-1937
Of thee I sing (music by). See Kaufman, George S. and Ryskind, Morris. Of thee I sing

GERSHWIN, IRA, 1896- . See Kaufman, George S., jt. auth.

GERSTENBERG, ALICE
Ever young. 1920? SHAY
Overtones. 1915. HUD, SUB
A patroness. 1917? SHAY

GESNER, CLARK, 1942-
You're a good man, Charlie Brown (book, music and lyrics by). 1967. BES66

GHELDERODE, MICHEL DE, 1898-1962
Christophe Colomb. 1927. PRO
Hauger, G., tr. COTKW
Valency, M., tr. CASE
Variant title: Christopher Columbus
Christopher Columbus. See Christophe Colomb
The chronicles of hell.
Hauger, G., tr. REIT
Escurial. 1929.
Abel, L., tr. BENT5
Pantagleize. 1930.
Haugher, G., tr. COTR

GIACOSA, GIUSEPPE, 1847-1908
As the leaves fall. See Like falling leaves
Come le foglie. See Like falling leaves
Like falling leaves. 1900.
Updegraff, E., and A., trs. MOSQ
Variant titles: As the leaves fall; Come le foglie

GIBBS, WOLCOTT, 1902-1958
Season in the sun. 1950. BES50
GIBNEY, SHERIDAN and COLLINGS, PIERRE
The story of Louis Pasteur. 195-? STAT, STAU

GIBSON, PAULINE, 1908- . See Gilsdorf, Frederic, jt. auth.

GIBSON, WILFRID WILSON
The family's pride. 1914. RICH
GIBSON, WILLIAM, 1914-
The miracle worker. 1960. SUT1, WHFA
Two for the seesaw. 1958. GARS, GARZA4

GIDE, ANDRE PAUL GUILLAUME, 1869-1951
The immoralist. See Goetz, Ruth and Goetz, Augustus. The immoralist (based on

the novel by)
Oedipus.
Russell, J., tr. SANO

GIELGUD, VAL HENRY, 1900-
Away from it all. 1946. EMB3
Chinese white. 1928. FIT

GIL Y ZARATE, ANTONIO, 1793-1861
Guzmán el Bueno. 185-? BRET

GILBERT, MICHAEL FRANCIS, 1912-
The bargain. 1961. PLAN23
A clean kill. 1959. PLAN21

GILBERT, WILLIAM SCHWENCK, 1836-1911, [and SULLIVAN, SIR ARTHUR SEYMOUR, composer]
Engaged. 1877. BAI, BOOA3
H. M. S. Pinafore; or, The lass that loved a sailor. 1878. ASG, COOP, MOSN, MOSO
--See also Moss, Alfred Charles. H. M. S. Pinafore; oder, Das maedle und ihr sailor kerl (based on)
Iolanthe; or, The peer and the peri. 1882. BOWY, HUD, LAW
The mikado; or, The town of Titipu. 1885. MIJ2, PROD
Patience; or, Bunthorne's bride. 1881. COTKF, SMR
Pygmalion and Galatea. 1871. MAP, MAT
Sweethearts. 1874. BAT16, COT, WEB
Tom Cobb. 1875. BOOA4

GILBERT, WILLIE. See Burrows, Abram S., and Weinstock, Jack, jt. auths.

GILBERT-LECOMTE, ROGER, 1907-1943
L'odyssée d'Ulysse le palmipède. See The odyssey of Ulysses the palmiped
The odyssey of Ulysses the palmiped. 1924.
Wellwarth, G., tr. BEN
Variant title: L'odyssée d'Ulysse le palmipède

GILLETTE, WILLIAM HOOKER, 1855-1937
Secret service. 1896. BES94, GARX, QUIG, QUIJ, QUIK, QUIL, QUIM, QUIN
Sherlock Holmes (based on the stories by Sir Arthur Conant Doyle). 1899. CART

GILLIAT, SIDNEY. See Launder, Frank, jt. auth.

GILLMAN, JONATHAN
The marriage test. 1968. BALLE6

GILLOIS, ANDRE, pseud. See Diamond-Berger, Maurice

GILROY, FRANK D., 1925-
The subject was roses. 1964. BES64, GARV

GILSDORF, FREDERICH, 1903- , and GIBSON, PAULINE
The ghost of Benjamin Sweet. 1956? WAGC1

GINSBURY, NORMAN, 1903-
The advertisement. 1968. SUB
The first gentleman. 1935. FIR
John Gabriel Borkman. See Ibsen, Henrik. John Gabriel Borkman (adapted by)
The safety match (based on a short story by Anton Pavlovich Chekhov) RICK
Viceroy Sarah. 1934. FAMG

GIRARDIN, DELPHINE (Gay) de ("Mme. Emile de Girardin"), 1804-1855
La joie fait peur. 1854. BENZ
Variant titles: Sunshine follows rain; Sunshine through the clouds

Sunshine follows rain. See La joie fait peur
Sunshine through the clouds. See La joie fait peur

"GIRARDIN, MME. EMILE DE." See Girardin, Delphine (Gay) de

GIRAUDOUX, JEAN, 1882-1944
Amphitryon 38. See Behrman, Samuel Nathaniel. Amphitryon 38 (adapted from)
The Apollo of Bellac. 1942.
Valency, M., adapter. COX, GARZAP, GASS, MIJE
Variant titles: L'Apollon de Bellac; L'Apollon de Marsac
L'Apollon de Bellac. See The Apollo of Bellac
L'Apollon de Marsac. See The Apollo of Bellac
Cantique des cantiques. See Song of songs
Duel of angels. 1953.
Fry, C., tr. and adapter. BES59
Variant title: Pour Lucrece
Electra. 1937.
Smith, W., tr. BENS2, BENT1, BLOC, COTKW, COTQ, FOR, LOR
Variant title: Electre
Electre. See Electra
The enchanted (adapted by Maurice Valency). 1950. BES49
Variant title: Intermezzo
La folle de Chaillot. See The madwoman of Chaillot
La guerre de Troie n'aura pas lieu. See Tiger at the gates
Intermezzo. See The enchanted
Judith. 1931.
Savacool, J., tr. BENT3
The madwoman of Chaillot (adapted by Maurice Valency). 1948. ALLI, ALLK, BES48, BLOC, BROX, COTKI, FOUA, GARZH, GRIF, HAVG, SCAR, TREJ, WATE
Variant title: La folle de Chaillot
Ondine. 1954? (from the novel Undine by Baron de la Motte Fouque; adapted by Maurice Valency). CLM, CLN, GARZH, THEA54, WEIM
Pour Lucrece. See Duel of angels
Siegfried. 1928. GRAF
Sodom and Gomorrah. 1943.
Anon. tr. SANK
Briffault, H., tr. ULAN
Valency, M., tr. ALLJ, BROY, JOHN, TREBA, TREI3
Song of songs. 1938?
Briffault, H., tr. ULAN
Raikes, J., tr. BERM
Variant title: Cantique des cantiques
Tiger at the gates. 1955. CLOU, PUCC
Fry, C., tr. BES55, CLO, DOT, DOWS, GARZH, KERO, ROET, SATJ, SCNR, THEA56, WAIU
Variant title: La guerre de Troie n'aura pas lieu

GLASPELL, SUSAN, 1882-1948
Alison's house. 1930. BES30, CORD, CORE, CORF, SIXD
Trifles. 1916. BEAC11, CARM, FREI, GASB, HUD, PEN, PROD, PROF, PROG, STAT, STAU, STAV

GLEASON, JAMES, 1885-1959. See Abbott, George, jt. auth.

GLEBOV, ANATOLE GLEBOVITCH, 1899-
Inga. 1928.
Malamuth, C., tr. LYK

GLOVER, HALCOTT, 1877-
The king's jewry. 1928. TUCD

GODFREY, THOMAS, 1736-1763
The prince of Parthia. 1767? MOSS1, QUIJ, QUIK, QUIL, QUIM, QUIN

GOERING, REINHARD, 1887-
Naval encounter. 1917.
Ritchie, J., and Stowell, J., trs. RITV
Variant titles: Sea fight; Seeschlacht
Sea fight. See Naval encounter
Seeschlacht. See Naval encounter

GOETHE, JOHANN WOLFGANG VON, 1749-1832
Egmont. 1791.
Hamburger, M., tr. BENR2
Lamport, F., tr. LAMP
Lustig, T., tr. LUST
Swanwick, A., tr. CLF3, HARC19
Faust, pt. I. 1829. EVB2
Anon. tr. DRA2, PLAB2
MacIntyre, C., tr. TREB, TREC1, TREE1, TREI1, VANV2
MacNeice, L., tr. MACJ, MACL2, MACM2, MACN
Priest, G., tr. EVC2, GRDB47, HOUK
Raphael, A., tr. GOUZ
Swanwick, A., tr. BUCK, BUCL, BUCM, CROV, ESS, EVA2, FRA1, HARC19, ROB, THOM, THON, WEAV2
Taylor, B., tr. HIB, HIBA, HIBB, LOCM2, TRE, TREA2, VON, WORP
Faust, pt. II. 1829.
MacNeice, L., tr. MACJ, MACL2
Priest, G., tr. GRDB47
Swanwick, A., tr. BUCM, FRA1
Goetz von Berlichingen. 1774.
Scott, W., tr. MAU
Iphigenia in Tauris. 1802.
Swanwick, A., tr. BAT11, FRA1
Variant titles: Iphigenia of Tauris; Iphigenie auf Tauris
Iphigenia of Tauris. See Iphigenia in Tauris
Iphigenie auf Tauris. See Iphigenia in Tauris
Stella. 1776.
Thompson, B., tr. BAT12
Torquato Tasso. 1807.
Swanwick, A., tr. KRE

GOETZ, AUGUSTUS. See Goetz, Ruth Goodman, jt. auth.

GOETZ, RUTH GOODMAN, and GOETZ, AUGUSTUS
The doctor's daughter. See The heiress
The heiress (based on the novel, Washington Square, by Henry James, Jr.). 1947. BES47
Variant titles: The doctor's daughter; Washington Square
The immoralist (based on the novel by André Gide). 1954. BES53
Washington Square. See The heiress

GOGOL, NIKOLAI VASILEVICH, 1809-1852
Gamblers. 1833.
Bentley, E., tr. BENT3
The government inspector. See The inspector
The inspector. 1836.
Anon. tr. COUR
Cooper, J., tr. COOPA
Davies, T., tr. BAT18
Guerney, B., tr. GUE, HOUG
MacAndrew, A., tr. GARZE, MACD
Magarshack, D., tr. MAGA
Reeve, F., tr. REEV1
Saffron, R., tr. SAFF
Seymour, J., and Noyes, G., trs. NOY, TREB,

TREC1, TREE1, TREI1
Sykes, A., tr. CLKW, COUS
Variant titles: The government inspector; The inspector general; Revisor
The inspector general. See The inspector
The marriage. 1842.
Bentley, E., tr. BENT4
Revisor. See The inspector

GOHEI, NAMIKI, III. See Namiki Gohei III

GOLD, MICHAEL, 1894-1967
Hoboken blues; or, The black Rip Van Winkle. 1927? AME1

GOLDING, WILLIAM GERALD, 1911-
The brass butterfly. 1958. BARG

GOLDMAN, JAMES, 1927-
Follies (music and lyrics by Stephen Sondheim). 1971. BES70
The lion in winter. 1966. BES65, GARV

GOLDONI, CARLO, 1707-1793
Un curioso accidente. 1757. BIN
Zimmern, H., tr. CROV
Variant titles: A curious mishap; A curious misunderstanding
A curious mishap. See Un curioso accidente
A curious misunderstanding. See Un curioso accidente
The fan. 1763.
Fuller, H., tr. CLF2
Variant title: Il ventaglio
La locandiera. See The mistress of the inn
Mirandolina. See The mistress of the inn
The mistress of the inn. 1753.
Gregory, I., tr. BENR1
Lohmann, H., tr. LEG
Pierson, M., tr. MAU, MOSA
Variant titles: La locandiera; Mirandolina
L'osteria della posta. See The post-inn
The post-inn. 1761.
Chambers, W., tr. BAT5
Variant title: L'osteria della posta
The servant of two masters. 1743?
Dent, E., tr. BENR1, SMA
Lopworth, P., tr. PLAN36
Variant title: Il servitore di due padroni
Il servitore di due padroni. See The servant of two masters
Il ventaglio. See The fan

GOLDSMITH, CLIFFORD, 1900-1971
What a life. 1938. BES37

GOLDSMITH, OLIVER, 1728-1774
The good-natured man. 1768. STM
She stoops to conquer; or, The mistakes of a night. 1773. BARG, BARU, BEAC11, BENN, BENY, CLF1, COL1, DAI, DEM, DOWS, DRA1, DUH, EIGH, FOUB, GOU2, HARC18, HUD, JAFF, KEY, KRM, MAT, MCM, MCMI, MOO, MOR, MORR, MOSE2, NET, PLAB1, POOL, PROM, RUB, SHAH1, SMO, SRY, SRYG, STA, STM, TAT, TAU, TAY, TUP, TUQ, TWE, UHL, WILE

GOLL, IWAN, 1891-1950
The eternal bourgeois. See Methusalem
Der ewige Bürger. See Methusalem
The immortal one. (1920)
Sokel, W., and J., trs. SOK

Methusalem; oder, Der ewige Bürger. See Methusalem; or, The eternal bourgeois
Methusalem; or, The eternal bourgeois. 1922.
Ritchie, J., and Garten, H., trs. RITS
Wensinger, A., and Atkinson, C., tr. PLAC

GOLL, YVAN. See Goll, Iwan

GOMES, ALFREDO DIAS, 1922-
O pagador de promesas. See Payment as pledged
Payment as pledged. 1960.
Fernández, O., tr. WOOG
Variant title: O pagador de promesas

GONDINET, EDMOND. See Labiche, Eugène Marin, jt. auth.

GONNE, FRANCIS
In the city of David. 1934. SEVE

GOODHART, WILLIAM
Generation. 1965. BES65

GOODMAN, KENNETH SAWYER
Dust of the road. 1912? FED1

-- and HECHT, BEN
The hand of Siva. 192-? STAT, STAU

GOODMAN, PAUL, 1911-
The towel of Babel. 1940. NEW40

GOODRICH, FRANCES, and HACKETT, ALBERT
The diary of Anne Frank (based on the book by Anne Frank). 1955. BES55, CARM, GARU, GARZA4, THEA56, WHFA

GOOLD, MARSHALL NEWTON, 1881-1935
The quest divine. 1925? FED2
St. Claudia. 1924? FED2
The shepherds. 192-? FED2

GORDON, GEORGE, 1788-1824. See Byron, George Gordon

GORDON, RUTH (MRS. GARSON KANIN), 1896-
Over 21. 1943. BES43
Years ago. 1946. BES46, WAGC1, WAGE

GORDONE, CHARLES, 1925-
The breakout. KINH
No place to be somebody. 1969. BES68, OLIV, PATR

GORE-BROWNE, ROBERT F., 1893- . See Harwood, Harold Marsh, jt. auth.

GORKI, MAXIM (pseud. of Alekseĭ Maksimovich Pîeskov), 1868-1936
At the bottom. See The lower depths
Dans les fonds. See The lower depths
Down and out. See The lower depths
From the depths. See The lower depths
In the depths. See The lower depths
The lower depths. 1902.
Anon. Tr. SMA
Bakshy, A., tr. BLOC, FOUM
Burke, H., tr. COTO, COTQ
Chambers, W., tr. BAT18
Covan, J., tr. CEW, DIK2, HAV, HOUG, MOS, TRE, TREA1, TREBA, TREC2, TREE2, TREI2, TREJ, TUCN, TUCO, WHI
Guerney, B., tr. GUE
Hopkins, E., tr. DID, MOSG, MOSH, SMP, TUCG, WATI, WATL3
MacAndrew, W., tr. GARZJ, MACE
Magarshack, D., tr. MAGA

Noyes, G., and Kaun, A., trs. NOY
Reeve, F., tr. REEV2
Variant titles: At the bottom; Dans les fonds; Down and out; From the depths; In the depths; A night shelter; Night's lodging; Submerged

A night shelter. See The lower depths

Night's lodging. See The lower depths

Submerged. See The lower depths

Yegor Bulichov and others. 1932.
Bakshy, A., tr. HOGA
Wixley, A., tr. FOUS

GORKY, MAXIM. See Gorki, Maxim

GOSS, CLAY, 1946-
On being hit. 1970. NEWL

GOUBAUX, PROSPER PARFAIT, 1795-1859, and DUCANGE VICTOR HENRY JOSEPH BRAHAIN
Trente ans; ou, La vie d'un joueur. See Dunlap, William. Thirty years; or, The gambler's fate (adapted from)

GOULDING, EDMUND, 1891-1959. See Selwyn, Edgar, jt. auth.

GOW, JAMES ELLIS, 1907-1952 and D'USSEAU, ARNAUD
Deep are the roots. 1945. BES45
Tomorrow the world. 1942. BES42, GARZ

GOW, ROGER, 1899- , and GREENWOOD, WALTER
Love on the dole. 1934. PLAL

GOW, RONALD, 1897-
Ann Veronica (adapted from the novel by H. G. Wells). 1949. PLAN2
The Edwardians (adapted from the novel by Victoria Mary Sackville-West). 1959. PLAN20
Variant title: Weekend in May

Weekend in May. See The Edwardians

GOZZI, CARLO, conte, 1722-1806
The king stag. 1762?
Wildman, C., tr. BENR1
Turandot. 1761.
Levy, J., tr. BENSA

GRABBE, CHRISTIAN DIETRICH, 1801-1836
Don Juan and Faust. (1829)
Edwards, E., tr. MANO
Variant title: Don Juan und Faust

Don Juan und Faust. See Don Juan and Faust

Jest, satire, irony, and deeper significance. 1827?
Edwards, M., tr. BENS2

GRANGE, CHANCEL LA. See La Grange-Chancel

GRANT, DAVID
The king cat. FRO

GRANVILLE-BARKER, HARLEY GRANVILLE, 1877-1946
Deburau (tr. and adapted by). See Guitry, Sacha. Deburau

The Madras house. 1910. DIC, MOSN, MOSO, WEAL

The Voysey inheritance. 1905. DIG, PLAP1, ROWC

Waste. 1909. TUCD
--See Houseman, Laurence, jt. auth.

GRASS, GUNTER, 1927-
Beritten hin und zurück. See Rocking back and forth

Die bösen Köche. See The wicked cooks

Rocking back and forth. 1960. Benedikt, M., and Goradza, J., trs. BENB
Variant title: Beritten hin und zurück
The wicked cooks. 1961. Rosenberg, J., tr. COTS
Variant title: Die bösen Köche

GRAVES, RUSSELL, 1922-
The battle of the carnival and Lent. 1967. PAJ

GRAY, SIMON
Butley. 1972. BES72

GREAVES, DONALD, 1943-
The marriage. (1971) KINH

GRECCO, STEPHEN
The Orientals. BALLE7

GREEN, ADOLPH, 1915- .
See Comden, Betty, jt. auth.

GREEN, ERMA, 1894- .
See Green, Paul, jt. auth.

GREEN, JANET, 1913-
Murder mistaken. 1952. PLAN8

GREEN, JULIEN, 1900-
South. 1953. Anon. tr. PLAN12
Variant title: Sud
Sud. See South

GREEN, PAUL, 1894-
The field god. 1927. HAL, TUCD, TUCM, TUCN
The house of Connelly. 1931. BES31, GARU
Hymn to the rising sun. 1936. KOZ
In Abraham's bosom. 1927. BES26, CORD, CORE, CORF, DIE, LOC, TOD, WHI
Johnny Johnson (music by Kurt Weill). 1937. AND, ANDE, BES36, GAS
The Lord's will. 1925. LEV, LEVE
The man who died at twelve o'clock. 1925. CHU
The no'count boy. 1924. LOC
Potter's field. See Roll sweet chariot
Roll sweet chariot. 1934. CLKW
Variant title: Potter's field
Supper for the dead. 1926? AME1
Tread the green grass. 1928. AME3
Unto such glory. 1926? FLAN, HUDS2
White dresses. 1920. GASB, LOC
--See Wright, Richard, jt. auth.

-- and GREEN, ERMA
Fixin's: the tragedy of a tenant farm woman. 1934. RAVA
Variant title: The renewal
The renewal. See Fixin's: the tragedy of a tenant farm woman

GREENBERG, DANIEL. See Levine, Mark L., jt. auth.

GREENE, GRAHAM, 1904-
The complaisant lover. 1959. BES61
The living room. 1952. BES54
The potting shed. 1957. BES56

GREENE, PATTERSON
Papa is all. 1942. GALB

GREENE, ROBERT, 1558-1592
Friar Bacon and Friar Bungay. See The honorable history of Friar Bacon and Friar Bungay
George a Greene, The pinner of Wakefield (supposed author). 1588? ADA, BAS,

NES, SCH
Variant title: A pleasant conceited comedy of [George a Greene] the pinner of Wakefield
The honorable history of Friar Bacon and Friar Bungay. 1589? ASH, BAS, BENY, BROC, GARZAE, GAY1, HEIL, HOW, MCI, MIN2, MIO2, NEI, NES, OLH, OLI1, ORNC, PAR, SCI, SCJ, SCW, SPE, TICO
Variant title: Friar Bacon and Friar Bungay
James the fourth. 1591? MIN2, MIO2
A pleasant conceited comedy of [George a Greene] the pinner of Wakefield. See George a Greene, the pinner of Wakefield

GREENWOOD, WALTER, 1903- .
See Gow, Roger, jt. auth.

GREGORY, ISABELLA AUGUSTA (Persse), lady, 1859-1932
The Canavans. 1906. BARF
The dragon. 1917. WEB
Hyacinth Halvey. 1906. CAP, MIL, WATF1, WATI, WATT2
The rising of the moon. 1907. BEAC12, DIC, PROB, SHAR, SSTA
Spreading the news. 1904. BEAC8, FIG, PEN, PROC, WATS
The workhouse ward. 1908. COD, MOSN, MOSO, TOD, TREBA, TREC2, TREE2, TREI3

GRESSET, JEAN BAPTISTE LOUIS, 1709-1777
Le méchant. 1747. BRE

GRIBOIEDOV, ALEXANDR SERGIEEVICH, 1795-1829
Chatsky; or, The misery of having a mind. 1823.
Cooper, J., tr. COOPA
Intelligence comes to grief. See Wit works woe
The misery of having a mind. See Chatsky
The misfortune of being clever. See Wit works woe
The trouble with reason. 1824?
Reeve, F., tr. REEV1
Wit works woe. 1831.
Pares, B., tr. NOY
Variant titles: Intelligence comes to grief; The misfortune of being clever; Woe from wit
Woe from wit. See Wit works woe

GRIBOYEDOV, ALEXSANDER.
See Griboîedov, Alexandr Sergîeevîch

GRIEG, NORDAHL, 1902-1943
The defeat: a play about the Paris Commune. 1936.
Watkins, J., tr. SCAN2
Variant title: Nederlaget
Nederlaget. See The defeat
Our power and our glory.
Gathorne-Hardy, G., tr. FIL

GRIFFIN, ALICE VENEZKY, 1921-
Oresteia. See Aeschylus. Oresteia (arranged for the stage by)

GRIFFITH, HUBERT FREELING, 1896-1953
Youth at the helm (tr. and adapted by). See Vulpius, Paul. Youth at the helm

GRILLPARZER, FRANZ, 1791-1872
The fortunes and death of King Ottokar. See König Ottokars glück und ende
The Jewess of Toledo. 1873.
Danton, G., and A., trs. FRA6
Variant title: Die jüdin von Toledo

Die jüdin von Toledo. See
The Jewess of Toledo
König Ottokars glück und
ende. 1825. CAM
Variant title: The fortunes
and death of King Ottokar
Medea. 1821.
Lamport, F., tr. LAMP
Miller, T., tr. FRA6
Sappho. 1818. CAM
Frothingham, E., tr. SMN
Der traum ein leben. 1834.
FEFH1

GRIMKE, ANGELINA WELD,
1880-1958
Rachel. 1916. HARY

GROVER, LEONARD
Our boarding house. 1877.
AMP4

GRUMBINE, EZRA LIGHT, 1845-
1880
Die inschurens bissness. See
Die insurance business
Die insurance business. 1880?
BUFF
Variant title: Die inschurens
bissness

GRUNDY, SYDNEY, 1848-1914
A pair of spectacles (adapted
from Les petits oiseaux by
Eugène Labiche and Dela-
cour). 1890. ROWE

GUARE, JOHN, 1938-
Cop-out. 1968. OFF
The house of blue leaves.
1971. BES70
Muzeeka. 1967. LAH, OFF

GUERDON, DAVID
The laundry. 1962.
Richardson, H., tr. COTT

GUERRERO, WILFRIDO MARIA,
1917-
Forever. 1947. EDAD

GUIMERA, ANGEL, 1847-1924
Daniela. 1902.
Underhill, J., tr. CLDM
Variant titles: La pecadora;
The sinner
La pecadora. See Daniela
The sinner. See Daniela

GUINON, ALBERT, 1863-1923,
and MARNIERE, JEANNE
MARIE FRANÇOISE
Le joug. See The yoke
The yoke. 1902.
Anon. tr. BAT21
Variant title: Le joug

GUITRY, SACHA, 1885-1957
Deburau. 1920.
Granville-Barker, H., tr.
and adapter. BES20
Don't listen, ladies! (adapted
by Stephen Powys and Guy
Bolton). 1948. PLAN1
Pasteur. 1919.
Brown, I., tr. DID

GURNEY, A. R., JR.
The golden fleece. 1968.
BAYM

GUTHRIE, J.
He who gets slapped. See
Andreev, Leonid Nikolae-
vich. He who gets slapped
(adapted by)

GUTHRIE, TYRONE, 1900-1971
Top of the ladder. 1950.
PLAN3

GUTIERREZ, ANTONIO GARCIA.
See García Gutiérrez, Antonio

GUTZKOW, KARL FERDINAND,
1811-1878
Pigtail and sword. See
Sword and queue
Sword and queue. 1843.
Colbron, G., tr. FRA7
Variant titles: Pigtail and
sword; Zopf und schwert
Zopf und schwert. See
Sword and queue

H

HACKETT, ALBERT, 1900- .
See Goodrich, Frances, jt. auth.

HACKETT, WALTER, 1876-1944.
See Megrue, Roi Cooper, jt. auth.

HADLER, WILLIAM
Flite cage. 1969. SME

HAGAN, JAMES, d. 1947.
One Sunday afternoon. 1933. BES32

HAILEY, ARTHUR
Flight into danger. 1956. BRNB
Shadow of suspicion. GREG

HAILEY, OLIVER, 1932-
Hey you, light man! 1961. GASY
Who's happy now? 1967. LAH

HAINES, JOHN THOMAS, 1799?-1843
My Poll and my partner Joe. 1835. BOOB

HAINES, WILLIAM WISTER, 1908-
Command decision. 1947. BES47, CLDP, MIJY, QUIN, TUCN

HALBE, MAX, 1865-1944
Mother earth. 1897. Grummann, P., tr. FRA20
Variant title: Mutter erde
Mutter erde. See Mother earth

HALE, JOHN, 1926-
The black swan winter. 1969. PLAN37
Spithead. 1969. PLAN38

HALL, HOLWORTHY, 1887-1936, and MIDDLEMASS, ROBERT M.
The valiant. 1921. BEAC10

HALL, WILLIS, 1929-
The long and the short and the tall. 1959. NEWE3
--See Waterhouse, Keith, jt. auth.

HALLE, ADAM DE LA. See Adam de la Halle

HALLIDAY, ANDREW. See Brough, William, jt. auth.

HALPER, LEIVICK (H. Leivick, pseud.), 1888-1962
The golem. 1920. Landis, J., tr. LAO, LAOG

HAMILTON, PATRICK, 1904-
Angel street. 1941. BES41, CART, RICI, SAFM
Variant title: Gaslight
Gaslight. See Angel street

HAMLIN, MARY P.
The rock. 1921? FED1

HAMMERSTEIN II, OSCAR, 1695-1960
Allegro (music by Richard Rodgers). 1947. BES47
The king and I (music by Richard Rodgers). 1951. CORB
Oklahoma! (based on Green grown the lilacs by Lynn Riggs; music by Richard Rodgers). 1943. BES42, CEY

-- and LOGAN, JOSHUA
South Pacific (based on Tales of the South Pacific by James A. Michener; music by Richard Rodgers). 1949. QUIN

HAMPTON, CHRISTOPHER, 1946-
The philanthropist. 1971. BES70

HAN-CH'ING, KUAN. See Kuan Han-ch'ing

HANKIN, ST. JOHN EMILE CLAVERING, 1869-1909
The Cassilis engagement. 1907. DIG, MOSN, MOSO,

ROWC
The last of the De Mullins. 1908. CHA, CHAN, CHAR
The return of the prodigal. 1905. MAP, WEAL

HANLEY, JAMES, 1901-
Say nothing. 1962. PLAN27

HANLEY, WILLIAM, 1931-
Slow dance on the killing ground. 1964. BES64, GARV

HANSBERRY, LORRAINE, 1930-1965
The drinking gourd. 1960. HARY
A raisin in the sun. 1959. ALS, BARO, BES58, CEQ, CEQA, CES, DIT, DIV, FORD (act. 1 only), GARV, HAPO, HEI, KIN, LAV, MONA, OLIV, PATR, PERU, SCNP, WHFM
The sign in Sidney Brustein's window. 1964. THT

HANSHEW, THOMAS W., 1857-1914
The forty-niners. 1879. BAT20

HAO-KU, LI. See Li Hao-Ku

HARBURG, EDGAR Y., 1896- and SAIDY, FRED
Finian's rainbow. 1947. HUDE

HARDT, ERNST, 1876-1947
Tantris the fool. See Tristram the jester
Tristram the jester. 1907. Heard, J., tr. FRA20
Variant title: Tantris the fool

HARDY, ALEXANDRE, 1575?-1631?
Mariamne. 1605-1615? Lockert, L., tr. LOCU

HARDY, THOMAS, 1840-1928
The day after the fair. See Harvey, Frank. The day after the fair (based on a story by)
The play of St. George (reconstructed from memory by). See Anonymous plays. The play of St. George

HARGRAVE, ROY. See Britton, Kenneth Phillips, jt. auth.

HARLAN, WALTER, 1867-1931
The Nüremberg egg. 1913. Katzin, W., tr. KAT
Variant title: Das Nürnburgisch ei
Das Nürnburgisch ei. See The Nüremberg egg

HARNICK, SHELDON, 1924-
The apple tree (jt. auth. and music by Jerry Bock). 1966. BES66
Fiddler on the roof (lyrics by). See Stein, Joseph. Fiddler on the roof
Fiorello! (lyrics by). See Weidman, Jerome and Abbott, George. Fiorello!
She loves me (lyrics by). See Masteroff, Joe. She loves me

HARNWELL, MRS. ANNA JANE (WILCOX), 1872- , and MEAKER, MRS. ISABELLE (JACKSON)
The alabaster box. 1940. FED2

HARRIGAN, EDWARD, 1845-1911
The Mulligan guard ball. 1879. MONR

HARRIS, TOM, 1930-
Always with love. 1967. NEWA3

HARRISON, JOHN, 1937-
Knight in four acts. PLAN38
Unaccompanied cello. 1970. PLAN40

HARSHA, SON OF HIRA, 12th century

Nagananda. 12th century.
Boyd, P., tr. WEL
The necklace. See Retnavali
Ratnavali. See Retnavali
Retnavali; or, The necklace. 12th century.
Lal, P., tr. LAL
Wilson, H., tr. BAT3
Variant titles: The necklace; Ratnavali

HART, MOSS, 1904-1961
Christopher Blake. 1946. BES46
The climate of Eden (based on the novel Shadows move among them by Edgar Mittelhölzer). 1952. BES52, THEA53
Lady in the dark. 1941. BES40
Light up the sky. 1948. BES48
Winged victory (music by David Rose). 1943. BES43
--See Kaufman, George S., jt. auth.

HARTOG, JAN DE, 1914-
The fourposter. 1951. BES51, GART, GARZA4
Skipper next to God. 1945. BES47, EMB2

HARTZENBUSCH, JUAN EUGENIO, 1806-1880
Los amantes de Teruel. 1837. BRET
Variant title: The lovers of Teruel
The lovers of Teruel. See Los amantes de Teruel

HARVEY, FRANK
The day after the fair (based on a story by Thomas Hardy). 1972. PLAN43

HARWOOD, HAROLD MARSH, 1874-1959
Old folks at home. 1933. FAMF
-- and GORE-BROWN, ROBERT F.
Cynara. 1930. BES31

HASENCLEVER, WALTER, 1890-1940
Antigone. 1917.
Ritchie, J., and Stowell, J., trs. RITV
Humanity. 1918.
Sokel, W., and J., trs. SOK
Variant title: Die Menschen
Die Menschen. See Humanity

-- and TUCHOLSKY, KARL
Christopher Columbus. 1932.
Spalter, M. and Wellwarth, G., trs. WELG

HASTINGS, BASIL MACDONALD, 1881-1928
The new sin. 1912. PLAP2

HASTINGS, CHARLOTTE
Bonaventure. 1949. PLAN3
Variant titles: Mary Bonaventure; Sister Cecilia
Mary Bonaventure. See Bonaventure
Sister Cecilia. See Bonaventure
Uncertain joy. 1953. PLAN12

HASTINGS, HUGH, 1917-
Seagulls over Sorrento. 1950. PLAN4

HASTINGS, MICHAEL
Yes, and after. 1957. NEWE4

HATCH, JAMES V., 1928- . See Jackson, C. Bernard, jt. auth.

HATHWAY, RICHARD, fl. 1602
Sir John Oldcastle, pt. I (sometimes attributed to). See Anonymous plays. Sir John Oldcastle, pt. I

HAUPTMANN, CARL FERDINAND MAXIMILIAN, 1858-1921

Kreig, ein Te Deum. See War, A Te Deum
War, a Te Deum. 1913?
Ritchie, J., and Stowell, J., trs. RITV
Variant title: Kreig, ein Te Deum

HAUPTMANN, GERHART, 1862-1946
The assumption of Hannele. See Hannele
The beaver coat. 1893.
Lewisohn, L., tr. STE, WATI, WATL1
Variant title: Der biberpelz, eine diebs komödie
Der biberpelz, eine diebs komödie. See The beaver coat
The coming of peace. See Das friedensfest
Einsame menschen. 1891. CAM
Variant title: Lonely lives
The festival of peace. See Das friedensfest
Das friedensfest. 1890. STI1
Variant titles: The coming of peace; The festival of peace; The reconciliation
Hannele. 1893.
Archer, W., tr. BAT12
Frenz, H., and Waggoner, M., trs. ULAN
Meltzer, C., tr. HAV, HUD, INTE
Variant titles: The assumption of Hannele; Hannele's assumption; Hanneles himmelfahrt; The journey to heaven of Hannele
Hannele's assumption. See Hannele
Hanneles himmelfahrt. See Hannele
The journey to heaven of Hannele. See Hannele
Lonely lives. See Einsame menschen
Michael Kramer. 1900. FEFH2
Lewisohn, L., tr. FRA18
The rats. 1911.
Lewisohn, L., tr. TUCG, TUCM, TUCN, TUCO
Variant title: Die ratten
Die ratten. See The rats
The reconciliation. See Das friedensfest
The sunken bell. 1896.
Meltzer, C., tr. BUCK, BUCL, BUCM, FRA18, MCCP, MOSQ, WHK
Variant title: Die versunkene glocke
Die versunkene glocke. See The sunken bell
The weavers. 1892.
Frenz, H., and Waggoner, M., trs. BLOC, HOUP
Huebsch, B., tr. THON
Morison, M., tr. CEW, DIC, DIK1, FRA18, SMP, TRE, TREA1, TREBA, TREC2, TREE2, TREI2, TREJ, WHI
Mueller, C., tr. COTL, COTQ
Variant title: Die weber
Die weber. See The weavers
Der weisse heiland. See The white saviour
The white redeemer. See The white saviour
The white saviour. 1920.
Muir, W., and E., trs. KRE
Variant titles: Der weisse heiland; The white redeemer

HAUTEROCHE, NOEL LEBRETON, 1617-1707
Crispin médecin. See Ravenscroft, Edward and Motteux, P. A. The sham doctor (based on)

HAVEL, VACLAV, 1936-
The memorandum.
Blackwell, V., tr. THOR

HAWKES, JACQUETTA (HOPKINS), 1910- . See Priestley, John Boynton, jt. auth.

HAWKES, JOHN, 1925-
The wax museum. 1966. PLAC

HAWTHORNE, RUTH (WARREN).
See Kennedy, Mary, jt. auth.

HAY, IAN (pseud. of John Hay Beith), 1876-1952
"Let my people go!" 1948. EMB3

HAY, JULIUS, 1900-
The horse. 1964.
Hay, P., tr. THOR

HAYDEN, JOHN
Lost horizons. 1935. BES34

HAYES, ALFRED, 1911-
Act of love. See The girl on the Via Flaminia
The girl on the Via Flaminia. 1954. BES53, COTK
Variant title: Act of love

HAYES, JOSEPH, 1918-
The desperate hours. 1955. BES54, BIER, THEA55

HAZELTON, GEORGE COCHRANE, JR., 1868-1921
Mistress Nell. 1900. AMP16

-- and BENRIMO, JOSEPH HENRY
The yellow jacket. 1912. DID

HAZELWOOD, COLIN HAZELWOOD, 1820-1875
Lady Audley's secret (from the novel by Mary Elizabeth Braddon). 1863. ROWE

HEALEY, FRANCES
The copper pot. 1919? WEB

HEBBEL, CHRISTIAN FRIEDRICH, 1813-1863
Agnes Bernauer. 1852. CAM
Pattee, L., tr. SMK
Herodes und Mariamne. 1849. CAM
Maria Magdalena. See Maria Magdalene
Maria Magdalene. 1844. CAM
Fairley, B., tr. BUCK, BUCL, BUCM, FEFH1, TREA2, TREB, TREC1, TREE1, TREI1
Green, P., tr. CLKW, GRIF
Mueller, C., tr. COTL, COTQ
Thomas, P., tr. FRA9, SMI
Variant title: Maria Magdalena
Siegfried's death. 1862.
Royce, K., tr. FRA9

HECHT, BEN, 1893-1964.
See Goodman, Kenneth S., jt. auth.

-- and MacARTHUR, CHARLES
The front page. 1928. BES28, CET, GARZA1, GASB

HEGGEN, THOMAS, 1918-1949, and LOGAN, JOSHUA
Mister Roberts. 1948. BES47, CEQA, GARW, GARZA3, HATA, SIXC

HEIBERG, GUNNAR EDWARD RODE, 1857-1929
Kjaerlighedens tragedie. See The tragedy of love
The tragedy of love. 1904.
Björkman, E., tr. DID
Variant title: Kjaerlighedens tragedie

HEIDE, ROBERT
At war with the Mongols. 1970. NEWA4
Moon. 1967. SLM

HEIJERMANS, HERMAN (Samuel Falkland, pseud.), 1864-1924
The good hope. 1900?
Saunders, L., and Heijermans-Houwink, C., trs. GARZH
Variant title: Op hoop van

zegen
Op hoop van zegen. See The good hope

HELLMAN, LILLIAN, 1905-
Another part of the forest (music by Marc Blitzstein). 1946. BES46, WATE
The autumn garden. 1951. BES50, CLM, FAM, GARW
Candide (based on Candide by Voltaire; music by Leonard Bernstein; lyrics by Richard Wilbur, John Latouche and Dorothy Parker). 1956. BES56
The children's hour. 1934. BES34, FIP, GARZA2, GAS, PLAN5, SUB
The lark. See Anouilh, Jean. The lark (tr. and adapted by)
The little foxes. 1939. BARS, BES38, BLOO, CET, CORB, COTE, COTH, COTQ, DOT, HARB, HAVE, HILP, MIJY, SIXC, SIXL, TREBA, TREC2, TREE3, TREI3, TREJ
Variant title: Regina
Regina. See The little foxes
The searching wind. 1944. BES43
Toys in the attic. 1960. BES59, CEQ, CES
Watch on the Rhine. 1941. BES40, CALN2, CALP, CALQ, CASS, CRIT, CUBE, GARZ, GAVE, HAVD, NAGE

HEMRO.
Poor ostrich. 1948? RUA

HENSHAW, JAMES ENE, 1924-
The jewels of the shrine. 1952? LITT

HERBERT, FREDERICK HUGH, 1897-1958
Kiss and tell. 1943. BES42
The moon is blue. 1951. GARW

HERBERT, JOHN
Fortune and men's eyes. 1968. MAOC

HERMAN, HENRY. See Jones, Henry Arthur, jt. auth.

HERMAN, JERRY, 1932-
Hello, Dolly! (music and lyrics by). See Stewart, Michael. Hello, Dolly!

HERMITE, l'TRISTAN, 1601-1655
The death of Seneca. 1643? Lockert, L., tr. LOCU
Variant title: La mort de Seneque
Mariamne. 1636. Lockert, L., tr. LOCR
Variant title: La Mariane
La Mariane. See Mariamne
La mort de Seneque. See The death of Seneca
La mort du grand Osman. See Osman
Osman. 1646-1647? Lockert, L., tr. LOCU
Variant title: La mort du grand Osman

HERNANDEZ, ANTONIO ACEVEDO. See Acevedo Hernández Antonio

HERNANDEZ, LOUISA JOSEFINA
Mullato's orgy. 1966? Oliver, W., tr. OLIW

HERNDON, VENABLE
Until the monkey comes. 1966. NEWA2

HERNE, JAMES A., 1839-1901
Drifting apart. 1888. AMP7
Variant title: The fisherman's child
The fisherman's child. See Drifting apart
Margaret Fleming. 1890. COY, MASW, QUIL, QUIM, QUIN
The minute men of 1774-1775.

1886. AMP7
The Reverend Griffith Davenport, Act. IV. 1899. AMP7
Shore acres. 1892. DOWM, MONR
Within an inch of his life. 1879. AMP7

HERRERA, LUIS BAYON. See Bayón Herrera, Luis

HERREROS, MANUEL BRETON DE LOS. See Bretón de los Herreros, Manuel

HERSEY, JOHN, 1914-
A bell for Adano. See Osborn, Paul. A bell for Adano (based on the novel by)

HERSHADEVA, SRI. See Harsha, son of Hira

HERVERA, LUIS BAYON. See Bayón Herrera, Luis

HERVIEU, PAUL ERNEST, 1857-1915
Connais-toi. See Know thyself
La course du flambeau. 1901. BER
Variant titles: The passing of the torch; The torch race; The trail of the torch
Know thyself. 1909.
Cerf, B., tr. DIC
Variant title: Connais-toi
The passing of the torch. See La course du flambeau
The torch race. See La course du flambeau
The trail of the torch. See La course du flambeau

HESTER, HAL, 1933-
Your own thing (music and lyrics by). See Driver, Donald. Your own thing

HEYWARD, MRS. DOROTHY HARTZELL (KUHNS), d. 1961, and HEYWARD, DuBOSE
Porgy. 1927. BES27, GARZA1, GASB, MACG, MIJY, THF

HEYWARD, DuBOSE, 1885-1940. See Heyward, Mrs. Dorothy Hartzell (Kuhns), jt. auth.

HEYWOOD, JOHN, 1497?-1580?
The four pp. 1569? ADA, BOA, GARZB, HOPP, PARR, TAV, TICO
Variant titles: The four p's; The playe called The foure pp
The four p's. See The four pp
Johan Johan. See John, Tyb and Sir John
Johan Johan, the husbande. See John, Tyb and Sir John
Johan, Tyb his wife, and Sir Jhan the preest. See John, Tyb and Sir John
John, Tyb and Sir John. 1533. ADA, CRE, GAY1, HOPP, LOOM, PAR, RUB
Variant titles: Johan Johan; Johan Johan, the husbande; Johan, Tyb his wife and Sir Jhan the preest; John, Tyb and the curate; A merry play; A mery play betweene Johan Johan, the husbande, Tyb his wyfe, and Syr Jhan, the preest; A mery play betweene Johan Johan, Tyb, his wyfe and Syr Jhan, the preest
John, Tyb and the curate. See John, Tyb and Sir John
A merry play. See John, Tyb and Sir John
A mery play betweene Johan Johan, the husbande, Tyb his wyfe, and Syr Jhan, the preest. See John, Tyb and Sir John

A mery play betweene Johan Johan, Tyb, his wyfe and Syr Jhan, the preest. See John, Tyb and Sir John
A mery playe betwene the pardoner and the frere, the curate and neybour Pratte. See The pardoner and the friar
The pardoner and the friar. 1521? LOOM, POLL
Variant title: A mery playe betwene the pardoner and the frere, the curate and neybour Pratte
The play of the wether. 1515. ADA, HAO, GAY1, PARR
The playe called the foure pp. See The four pp

HEYWOOD, THOMAS, 1574?-1641
The fair maid of the west. 1631. MAL
A woman killed with kindness. 1603. ASH, BAS, BROC, CLF1, DUN, GARZAE, LAWR, MAT, MCJ, NEI, NES, OLH, OLI1, PAR, RYL, SCH, SCI, SCJ, SMI, SPE, TAT, TAU, WALL

HICKERSON, HAROLD. See Anderson, Maxwell, jt. auth.

HIERHOLZER, ALEXANDER
Grace and George and God. 1970. BALLE7

HILARIUS, 12th century
Ludus super iconia Sancti Nicolai. See The statue of Saint Nicholas
The miracle of Saint Nicholas and the image. 12th cent. LOOM
The statue of Saint Nicholas. 12th cent. MAK
Variant title: Ludus super iconia Sancti Nicolai

HILDESHEIMER, WOLFGANG, 1916-
Nachtstück. See Nightpiece
Nightpiece. 1962. Hildesheimer, W., tr. BENB
Variant title: Nachtstück

HILL, ABRAHAM, 1911-
Walk hard. 1944. HARY

HILL, ERROL, 1921-
Man better man. 1960. GASY
Strictly matrimony. 1959. KINH

HILL, FREDERIC STANHOPE, 1805-1851
The six degrees of crime. 1834. SATI

HILL, LUCIENNE
Paddle your own canoe. See Regnier, Max Albert Marie. Paddle your own canoe (tr. and adapted by)
The waltz of the toreadors. See Anouilh, Jean. The waltz of the toreadors (tr. and adapted by)

HINES, LEONARD JOHN
Simon. 1934. SEVE

HIRSHBEIN, PERETZ, 1880-1948
Green fields. 1917. Landis, J., tr. LAO, LAOG

HITE, BARBARA
Birdwatchers. COLI
Sandcastle. COLI

HIVNOR, ROBERT
The assault upon Charles Sumner. 1966. PLAC
The ticklish acrobat. 1954. PLAA

HIYOSHI, SA-AMI-YASUKIYO, 1383?-1458
Benkei on the bridge. 15th cent. Waley, A., tr. ANDF
Variant title: Hashi-Benki

Hashi-Benki. See Benkei on the bridge

HOADLY, BENJAMIN, 1706-1757
The suspicious husband. 1747. MOR

HOARE, PRINCE, 1755-1834
No song no supper (music by Stephen Storace). 1790. HUGH

HOCHHUTH, ROLF, 1931-
The deputy. 1963.
Winston, R., and C., trs. BES63
Variant titles: The representative; Der Stellvertreter
The representative. See The deputy
Der Stellvertreter. See The deputy

HOCHWÄLDER, FRITZ, 1911-
Das heilige experiment. See The strong are lonely
The holy experiment. See The strong are lonely
Der öffentliche ankläger. See The public prosecutor
The public prosecutor. 1947.
Black, K., tr. PLAN16
Variant title: Der öffentliche ankläger
The strong are lonely. 1942.
LeGallienne, E., tr. PLAN14
Wellwarth, G., tr. WELT
Variant titles: Das heilige experiment; The holy experiment

HODGE, MERTON, 1903-
As it was in the beginning. See The wind and the rain
Grief goes over. 1935. FAMH
The island. 1937. SIXP
The wind and the rain. 1933. FAME
Variant title: As it was in the beginning

HODSON, JAMES LANSDALE, 1891-
Harvest in the north. 1939. FAML
Red night. 1936. FAMI

HOFFE, MONCKTON, 1880-1951
Many waters. 1926. FAO, PLAD

HOFFMAN, BYRD
The king of Spain. 1969. NEWA3

HOFFMAN, WILLIAM M., 1939-
A quick nut bread to make your mouth water. 1970. OWE
Thank you, Miss Victoria. 1965. NEWA3
X X X X X. 1969. SME

HOFMANNSTAHL, HUGO HOFMANN VON, 1874-1929
Death and the fool. See Der tor und der tod
The death of Titian. 1892.
Heard, J., tr. FRA17
Variant title: Der tod des Tizian
Electra. 1904.
Mueller, C., tr. COTKJ, COTQ
Symons, A., tr. DIE
Die hochzeit der Sobeide. See The marriage of Sobeide
The marriage of Sobeide. 1899.
Morgan, B., tr. FRA20
Variant title: Die hochzeit der Sobeide
Das Salzburger grosse weltheater. 1920. FEFH2
Der tod des Tizian. See The death of Titian
Der tor und der tod. 1893. STI1
Hamburger, M., tr. BLOC
Heard, J., tr. FRA17
Variant title: Death and the fool

HOGAN, R., and MOLIN, S. E.
The silent woman. See Jonson, Ben. The silent woman (adapted by)

HOLBERG, LUDWIG, 1684-1754
Erasmus Montanus. See Rasmus Montanus
Jeppe of the hill. 1722.
Campbell, O., tr. SPR
Jagendorf, M., tr. CLF2
Variant title: Jeppe paa bjerget
Jeppe paa bjerget. See Jeppe of the hill
The loquacious barber. 1723.
Chambers, W., tr. BAT17
Variant title: Mester Gert Westphaler eller den meget talende barbeer
Mester Gert Westphaler eller den meget talende barbeer. See The loquacious barber
Rasmus Montanus. 1747.
Campbell, O., and Schenck, F., trs. MAU
Variant title: Erasmus Montanus

HOLCROFT, THOMAS, 1745-1809
A tale of mystery. 1802. BAI

HOLM, JOHN CECIL, 1906- , and ABBOTT, GEORGE
Three men on a horse. 1935. GAS

HOLME, CONSTANCE
"I want!" 1933. FIT

HOLT, BRIAN
Noah's ark. 1963. FRO

HOME, JOHN, 1722-1808
Douglas. 1756. BAT14, BOO, MCM, MCMI, MOR, MOSE2, NET, STM

HOME, WILLIAM DOUGLAS, 1912-
The jockey club stakes. 1970. PLAN40
Lloyd George knew my father. 1972. PLAN42
The queen's highland servant. 1968. PLAN35
The secretary bird. 1963. PLAN36
The thistle and the rose. 1949. PLAN4

HOOTE, HORTON
The dancers. 1954? WAGC2

HOPKINS, ARTHUR MELANCTHON, 1878-
Moonshine. 1921. PROF, PROG, PROH, PROI, TOD
--See Watters, George Manker, jt. auth.

HOPKINS, JOHN, 1931-
Find your way home. 1974. BES73

HOPKINSON, FRANCIS, 1737-1791
A dialogue and ode. 1762. MONR
Variant title: An exercise containing a dialogue and ode on the accession of His present gracious Majesty George III
An exercise containing a dialogue and ode on the accession of His present gracious Majesty George III. See A dialogue and ode

HOPWOOD, AVERY, 1882-1928. See Rinehart, Mary Roberts, jt. auth.

HORACE. See Horatius Flaccus, Quintus

HORATIUS FLACCUS, QUINTUS, 65-8 B.C.
Ars poetica.
DeWitt, N., tr. COTU
The bore; a dramatic version of Horace (Satires I, 9)
Ullman, B., tr. HOWK

HORNE, KENNETH, 1900-

Trial and error. 1953. PLAN9

HOROVITZ, ISRAEL, 1939-
The Indian wants the Bronx. 1968. LAN, OFF1
It's called the sugar plum. 1967. OFF1, RICK

HOUGHTON, STANLEY, 1881-1913
Fanny Hawthorne. See Hindle wakes
Hindle wakes. 1912. DIG, PLAP1, ROWC, TUCD
Variant title: Fanny Hawthorne

HOUSMAN, LAURENCE, 1865-1959
A good lesson! (from Victoria Regina). 1934. COOP
Victoria Regina. 1935. BES35, CEU
-- and GRANVILLE-BARKER, HARLEY GRANVILLE
Prunella; or, Love in a Dutch garden. 1906. PLAP2

HOWARD, BRONSON CROCKER, 1842-1908
The banker's daughter. 1873. AMP10, CLA
Baron Rudolph. 1881. AMP10
The Henrietta. 1887. HAL
Hurricanes. 1878. AMP10
Old love letters. 1878. AMP10
One of our girls. 1885. AMP10
Shenandoah. 1888. COY, MASW, MONR, MOSS3, QUIG, QUIJ, QUIK, QUIL, QUIM, QUIN

--See Young, Sir Charles Lawrence, jt. auth.

HOWARD, SIR ROBERT, 1626-1698. See Dryden, John, jt. auth.

HOWARD, SIDNEY COE, 1891-1939
Alien corn. 1933. BES32, FAMD
Dodsworth (based on the novel by Sinclair Lewis). 1934. BES33, HAT
The late Christopher Bean (tr. and adapted by). See Fauchois, René. The late Christopher Bean
Lucky Sam McCarver. 1925. MOSK, MOSL
Madam, will you walk. 1939. THEA54
Ned McCobb's daughter. 1926. MIL
Pi-Pa-Ki. See Lute song
The silver cord. 1926. BES26, BROW, BROX, CHAN, CHAP, COTE, DIE, FUL, JORG, MOSG, MOSH, QUIL, QUIM, QUIN, THF, TUCD, TUCM, TUCN, TUCO, WATC1, WATI, WATO, WHI
They knew what they wanted. 1924. BES24, CET, CORD, CORE, CORF, GASB, MACG, MCD, MERW
--See also Loesser, Frank. The most happy fella (based on the play by)

-- and De KRUIF, PAUL HENRY
Yellow jack. 1934. GARU, MERV, NAGE, SCWI

-- and IRWIN, WILLIAM HENRY
Lute song (adapted from the Chinese classic Pi-Pa-Ki by Kao-Tong-Kia or Tse-Tching). 1946. BES45
Variant title: Pi-Pa-Ki

HOWARTH, DONALD, 1931-
A lily in little India. 1965. NEWE9
Three months gone. 1970. PLAN39

HOWE, MRS. JULIA (WARD), 1819-1910
Hippolytus. 1911. AMP16

Leonora; or, The world's own. 1857. QUIJ, QUIK

HOWELLS, WILLIAM DEAN, 1837-1920
A letter of introduction. 1892. MONR
The mouse trap. 1889? GARX
The unexpected guests. 1893? QUIO2

HOYT, CHARLES HALE, 1860-1900
A bunch of keys; or, The hotel. 1883. AMP9
A midnight bell. 1889. AMP9
A milk white flag. 1894. AMP9
A temperance town. 1893. AMP9, MONR
A Texas steer; or, "Money makes the mare go." 1890. MOSJ, MOSK, MOSL
A trip to Chinatown; or, Idyl of San Francisco. 1891. AMP9, CLA

HROSWITHA. See Hrotsvit, of Gandersheim

HROTSVIT, OF GANDERSHEIM, 935?-1000?
Dulcitius. 10th cent.
Butler, M., tr. GARZB
Taylor, J., tr. TAV
Paphnutius. 10th cent.
Butler, M., tr. GARZB, TREB

HROTSVITHA. See Hrotsvit, of Gandersheim

HSIUNG, CHEN-CHIN
The thrice promised bride. WEB

HSUN, LU
The passer-by.
Hsein-yi, Y., and Yang, G., trs. MESE

HUGHES, HATCHER, 1883-1945
Hell-bent fer heaven. 1924. BES23, CORD, CORE, CORF, COT, MCD, TUCJ

HUGHES, JAMES LANGSTON. See Hughes, Langston

HUGHES, LANGSTON, 1902-1967
Don't you want to be free? 1937. HARY
Emperor of Haiti. 1938. TUQR
Limitations of life. 1938. HARY
Little ham. 1935. HARY
Mother and child. 1973. KINH
Mulatto. 1963. BRAS, TIIT
Simply heaven. 1957. PATR
Soul gone home. 1937. RAVA

HUGHES, RICHARD ARTHUR WARREN, 1900-
A high wind in Jamaica. See Osborn, Paul. The innocent voyage (based on the novel by)
The sister's tragedy. 1922. MORT, SUTL

HUGHES, THOMAS, fl. 1587
The misfortunes of Arthur. 1588. CUN

HUGO, VICTOR MARIE, 1802-1885
Hernani. 1830. BOR, COM, GRA, SEA
Asher, L., tr. BERM, HOUK, TREB
Crosland, Mrs. N., tr. CAR, CLF2, MAU
Ruy Blas. 1838. COM, GRA, SCN, STJ2
Crosland, Mrs. N., tr. GREA

HUMPHREY, HUBERT H. See Baldwin, James, jt. auth.

HUNTER, G. K.
Androboros. AMPA

HUNTER, NORMAN C., 1908-
A day by the sea. 1953. FAMO
Waters of the moon. 1951. FAOS

HURLBUT, WILLIAM JAMES, 1883-
The bride of the lamb. 1926. BES25

HUSSON, ALBERT
La cuisine des anges. See Spewack, Bella and Spewack, Samuel. My 3 angels (adapted from)

HUSTON, JOHN. See Koch, Howard, jt. auth.

HUTCHINS, MRS. MAUDE (PHELPS)
Aunt Julia's Caesar. 195-? SPC
The case of Astrolable. 1944? NEW44
A play about Joseph Smith, jr. 1944? NEW44
The wandering Jew. 1951? NEW51

HUTCHINSON, ALFRED, 1924-
The rain-killers. LITT

HUTTON, JOSEPH, 1787-1828
Fashionable follies. 1809. MOSS2

HYDE, DOUGLAS, 1860-1949
The twisting of the rope. 1901. CAP

HYMAN, MAC, 1923-
No time for sergeants. See Levin, Ira. No time for sergeants (adapted from the novel by)

I

IBSEN, HENRIK, 1828-1906
Bygmester solness. See The master builder
The child wife. See A doll's house
A doll's house. 1879.
Archer, W., tr. CLF2, COJ, DRA2, EDAD, HOUS, HUD, KNIC, KNID, MAU, MCD, PLAB2, PROW, THOM, THON, WATI, WATL1, WHT
Le Gallienne, E., tr. AUG
Meyer, M., tr. BARI, SCNP
Variant titles: The child wife; Et dukkehjem; Nora
Et dukkehjem. See A doll's house
An enemy of society. See An enemy of the people
An enemy of the people. 1882.
Anon. tr. BUCK, BUCL, BUCM, DEAR, EVB2, GARZAP, GASS, HARB, JOHO, KNIE, KON, LAM, MCA, MESS, OHL, PERS, PERT, ROGE, SAND, ZIM
Farquhorson, R., tr. BONB, BONC
Le Gallienne, E., tr. PATM
Mark-Aveling, E., tr. FREF, HOLM, MOSA, WALJ, WHK
Myer, M., tr. CASE
Miller, A., adapter. BUR, HAVH, HOUP, MERV
Sharp, R., tr. ABC, BONA, COD, DOV, DUR, EVA2, GOLK, INGW, STA, THO
Variant titles: An enemy of society; En folkefiende
En folkefiende. See An enemy of the people
Fruen fra havet. See The lady from the sea
Gengangere. See Ghosts
Ghosts. 1881.
Anon. tr. DOWN, SILM, SILN, SILQ
Archer, W., tr. ALT, ALTE, BARC, BAT17, BOY, CROV, DEAS, FEL, FREG, GLO, KERP, MIL, ROB, SAY, SEBO, SEBP, SHR, SMP, STE, TREBA, TREC2, TREE2, TREI2, TREJ
Le Gallienne, E., tr. BENU, BLOC, LEVI

Meyer, M., tr. BARO, BOW, CLO, COTKIR
Sharp, R., tr. ADV, WEIS, WEIW, WHFM
Variant titles: Gengangere; When we dead awaken
Hedda Gabler. 1890.
Anon. tr. BLON, HAVL, LOCL, LOR
Ellis-Fermor, U., tr. GOLH, SIN, SOM, SOMA, TAUJ
Goodman, R., tr. GOOR
Gosse, E., tr. GPA
Gosse, E., and Archer, W., trs. ALLI, ALLJ, ALLK, BLAG, BLOO, BROF, BROG, BROH, CAR, CARA, CLKW, COOP, FOUK, FOUM, GLO, GOU2, GRIF, HAV, HAVD, HAVE, KERN, KERO, SMI, TRE, TREA1, TREBA, TREC2, TREE2, TREI2, TREJ, WALB, WATA, WATI, WATL2, WATR
Le Gallienne, E., tr. LOCLA, LOCLB
Legallienne, J., and Leysac, P., trs. LEG
Meyer, M., tr. VANV2
Paulson, A., tr. WAIW
Reinert, O., tr. ALS, BARJ, BAUL, COTQ, KNO, REIO
John Gabriel Borkman. 1897.
Archer, W., tr. ULAN
Ginsbury, N., adapter PLAN23
Kongsemnerna. See The pretenders
The lady from the sea. 1888.
Archer, W., tr. SAY
Variant title: Fruen fra havet
Lille Eyolf. See Little Eyolf
Little Eyolf. 1894.
Archer, W., tr. LID
Variant title: Lille Eyolf
The master builder. 1892.
Amble, K., tr. COTX
Anon. tr. BONB, BRIT, CROS, GUTH, GUTL, HIB, HIBA, HIBB, SIXB
Archer, W., tr. DOWS, VON
Fjelde, R., tr. SPR
Gosse, E., and Archer, W., trs. WARL, WORP
McFarlane, J., tr. SANE
Perone, E., tr. CALD
Variant titles: Bygmester solness; Solness, the master builder
Nora. See A doll's house
Peer Gynt. 1876.
Ginsbury, N., tr. BLOC
Pillars of society. 1877.
Le Gallienne, E., tr. MACF
Variant title: Samfundets støtter
The pretenders. 1864.
Archer, W., tr. SMK
Variant title: Kongsemnerna
Rosmersholm. 1886.
Anon. tr. BROJ, BROK, LOCM2
Archer, W., tr. BENQ, TUCN, TUCO
Jellicoe, A., tr. CUBH, FOUM
Le Gallienne, E., tr. JOHN, ROET
McFarlane, J., tr. CLKJ
Meyer, M., tr. BENSB2
Samfundets støtter. See Pillars of society
Solness, the master builder. See The master builder
Vildanden. See The wild duck
When we dead awaken. See Ghosts
The wild duck. 1885.
Anon. tr. CEW, CLN, SSST, SSSU
Archer, F., tr. ASF, BIER, DLM, CUBE, CUBG, DEAP, GOLD, LEV, LEVE, MACJ, MACL2, MACM2, MOSQ, SPR, WEAN, WEAV2, WHI
Archer, W., tr. BRIX

Ellis-Fermor, U., tr. LEVJ
Faber, M., tr. WEIM
Fjelde, R., tr. TRI, TRIA
LeGallienne, E., tr. DOT, VOLI
McFarlane, J., tr. CAPU, SEN
Meyer, M., tr. BENSB2, SEN
Reinert, O., tr. COTQ, DIT, REIL, REIN, REIP, REIT
Sharp, R., tr. BARR
Variant title: Vildanden

IDZUMO, TAKEDA, 1688-1756
Bushido. 1746.
Eliot, S., tr. LAW

IFFLAND, AUGUST WILHELM, 1759-1814
Conscience. 1800?
Thompson, B., tr. BAT11
Variant title: Das gewissen
Das gewissen. See Conscience

IJIMERE, OBOTUNDE, 1930-
Born with the fire on his head. THTN

ILYENKOV, VASSILY PAVLOVICH
Campo dei fiori. See The square of flowers
The square of flowers. 1944.
Bakshy, A., tr. BAKS
Variant title: Campo dei fiori

INCHBALD, MRS. ELIZABETH (SIMPSON), 1753-1821
Adventures of a shawl. See Appearance is against them
Appearance is against them. 1785. HUGH
Variant titles: Adventure of a shawl; Mistake upon mistake; or, Appearance is against them
Everyone has his fault. 1793. NIC
Mistake upon mistake; or, Appearance is against them. See Appearance is against them

INGE, WILLIAM, 1913-1973
Bus stop. 1955. BES54, GART, HOGA, THEA55
Come back, little Sheba. 1950. BES49, CEQA, CUBG, GARW, GARZA4, NEWV, WATA
The dark at the top of the stairs. 1957. BES57, CES, GARS, HUDE
Variant title: Farther off from heaven
The disposal. 1972. RICJ
Farther off from heaven. See The dark at the top of the stairs
Margaret's bed. RICK
Picnic. 1953. BESS52, GART, GAVE, THEA53

INGHAM, ROBERT E., 1934-
A simple life. 1964. GARZAL

IOBST, CLARENCE F., 1894-
Die Calline browierts. 1930. BUFF
Es Heller's Chrischtdag (based on the story Es wasch Heller's Chrischtdag's zug by Charles C. More). 1931. BUFF

IONESCO, EUGENE, 1912-
The bald prima donna. See The bald soprano
The bald soprano. 1950.
Allen, D., tr. AUG, BLOC, NEWW9, ULAN, WEIM
Variant title: The bald prima donna; La cantatrice chauve
La cantatrice chauve. See The bald soprano
The chairs. See Les chaises
Les chaises. 1952. PRO
Allen, D., tr. ALT, ALTE, COTQ, JOHN, KERP, TREBA, TREI3

Variant title: The chairs
The gap.
Lamont, R., tr. BARI, HOLP
L'impromptu de l'alma. See Improvisation
Improvisation; or, The shepherd's chameleon.
Watson, D., tr. COTKW, SCNO
Variant title: L'impromptu de l'alma; The shepherd's chameleon
La jeune fille a marier. See Maid to marry
The leader. 1953.
Prouse, D., tr. HAVN, RAI
Variant title: Le maître
La leçon. See The lesson
The lesson. 1951.
Allen, D., tr. REIN, REIP
Variant title: La leçon
Maid to marry. 1953.
Calder, J., tr. LID
Variant title: La jeune fille a marier
Le maître. See The leader
The new tenant. 1955.
Watson, D., tr. COTKC, THOD
Variant title: Le nouveau locataire
Le nouveau locataire. See The new tenant
The painting. 1954.
Watson, D., tr. DIV
Wellwarth, G., tr. BEN
Variant titles: The picture; Le tableau
The picture. See The painting
Rhinoceros. 1959.
Prouse, D., tr. BES60, SEVD
Variant title: Les rhinocéros
Les rhinocéros. See Rhinoceros
The shepherd's chameleon. See Improvisation
Le tableau. See The painting

IRELAND, WILLIAM HENRY, 1777-1835
Vortigern. 1796. BAT22

IRVING, WASHINGTON, 1783-1859
Rip Van Winkle. See Rauch, Edward H. Rip Van Winkle (based on the book by)

--See Payne, John Howard, jt. auth.

IRWIN, WILL. See Irwin, William Henry

IRWIN, WILLIAM HENRY, 1873-1948
The Hamadryads. 1804. BOH1
--See Howard, Sidney, jt. auth.

ISHERWOOD, CHRISTOPHER, 1904-
The Berlin stories. See Van Druten, John. I am a camera (adapted from the stories by)

--See Auden, Wystan Hugh, jt. auth.

ITALLIE, JEAN-CLAUDE VAN. See Van Itallie, Jean-Claude

J

JACKMAN, MARVIN E.
Flowers for the trashman. JON

JACKSON, C. BERNARD, 1927- and HATCH, JAMES V.
Fly blackbird. 1960. HARY

JACKSON, ELAINE
Toe jam. (1971) KINH

JACKSON, ISABELLE. See Meaker, Mrs. Isabelle (Jackson)

JACKSON, N. HART
The two orphans. See D'Ennery, Adolphe Phillippe and Cormon, Eugène. The two orphans (adapted by)

JACKSON, SHIRLEY, 1920-
The lottery. See Duffield, Brainerd. The lottery (from a story by)

JACOBS, WILLIAM WYMARK, 1863-1943
A love passage. 1897? PEN

JAMES, DAN, 1911-
Winter soldiers. 1942. BES42

JAMES, HENRY, 1843-1916
The American. 1891. HOGA
The turn of the screw. See Archibald, William. The innocents (based on the novel by)
Washington Square. See Goetz, Ruth Goodman and Goetz, Augustus. The heiress (based on the novel by)

JAMESON, STORM (née Margaret Storm Jameson), 1897-
William the defeated. 194-? OULD

JARRY, ALFRED, 1873-1907
King Ubu. 1896.
Bagley, D., tr. TREJ
Benedict, M., and Wellwarth, G., trs. BEN, WELT
Gans, M., and Ashley, L., trs. ASF
Variant titles: Ubu Roi; Ubu the king
Ubu Roi. See King Ubu
Ubu the King. See King Ubu

JASUDOWICZ, DENNIS
Blood money. 1965? NEWA1

JEANS, RONALD, 1887-1973
Count your blessings. 1951. PLAN5
Young wives' tale. 1949. PLAN3

JEFFERE, JOHN
The buggbears (supposed author). 1561? BOND

JEFFERS, ROBINSON, 1887-1962
The Cretan woman. 1951. BENS3
Medea. See Euripides. Medea (tr. and adapted by)

JEFFERSON, JOSEPH, 1829-1905
Rip Van Winkle. See Anonymous plays. Rip Van Winkle (as played by); see also Burke, Charles. Rip Van Winkle

JELLICOE, ANNE, 1927-
The knack. 1961. COTKH, COTKIR
The sport of my mad mother. (1957) OBSE

JENNINGS, GERTRUDE E., d. 1958
Family affairs. 1934. FAMF

JENNINGS, TALBOT
No more frontier. 1929. TOD

JEROME, MRS. HELEN (BURTON), 1883-
Charlotte Corday. 1939. FIP
Jane Eyre (based on the novel by Charlotte Brontë). 1936. FOUP, THH
Pride and prejudice (based on the novel by Jane Austen). 1935. BES35, FOUP, THH, VOAD

JERROLD, DOUGLAS WILLIAM, 1803-1857
All in the downs. See Black ey'd Susan
Black ey'd Susan; or, All in the downs. 1829. ASG, BOOA1, MOSN, MOSO, ROWE

Variant title: All in the downs
Mr. Paul Pry. 1826. BOOA4
The rent-day. 1832. BAI

JESSOP, GEORGE HENRY, d. 1915
Sam'l of Posen; or, The commercial drummer. 1881. AMP4

JEVON, THOMAS, 1652-1688
Devil of a wife. See The devil to pay; or, The wives metamorphos'd (adapted from)

-- and COFFEY, CHARLES; MOTTLEY, JOHN; CIBBER, THEOPHILUS
The devil to pay; or, The wives metamorphos'd (adapted from Devil of a wife by Thomas Jevon). 1731. HUGH

JOAQUIN, NICK
A portrait of the artist as Filipino. 1952. EDAD

JOB, THOMAS, d. 1947
Uncle Harry. 1942. BES41

JODELLE, ETIENNE, 1532-1573
Didon se sacrifiant. 1560? FOUR

JOHN, ERROL
Moon on a rainbow shawl. 195-? OBSE

JOHNSON, B. S., 1933-
You're human like the rest of them. 1967. NEWE14

JOHNSON, CHARLES, 1679-1748
The cobler of Preston. 1716. HUGH

JOHNSON, ELIZABETH
A bad play for an old lady. 1964. BALLE1

JOHNSON, MRS. GEORGIA (DOUGLAS), 1886-1966
Plumes. 1927? LOC
A Sunday morning in the south. 1925? HARY

JOHNSON, PAMELA HANSFORD
The duchess at sunset. 1948. OULD

JOHNSON, PHILIP, 1900-
Lovers' leap. 1934. FAMG

JOHNSON, SAMUEL, 1709-1784
Irene. 1749. BOO

JOHNSTON, DENIS, 1901-
The moon in the Yellow river. 1931. BROT
The old lady says "No!" 1929. CAN

JONES, EDITH NEWBOLD. See Wharton, Mrs. Edith Newbold (Jones)

JONES, HENRY ARTHUR, 1851-1929
The case of rebellious Susan. 1894. BES94
The dancing girl. 1891. MAL
Dolly reforming herself. 1908. CHA, CHAN, CHAR
The goal. 1898. HUD, PEN
Judah. 1894. RUB
The liars. 1897. DUR, MAP, MAT, ROWC, SALE
The masqueraders. 1894. BAI, MOSN, MOSO
Michael and his lost angel. 1896. ASG, BOWY, DIC
Mrs. Dane's defence. 1900. BOOA2, COT

-- and HERMAN, HENRY
The silver king. 1882. BAI

JONES, JACK, 1895-1970
Rhondda roundabout. 1939. SIXL

JONES, JOSEPH STEVENS, 1809-1877
The people's lawyer. See Solon Shingle
Solon Shingle. 1839. BAT20,

MOSS2
Variant title: The people's lawyer
The usurper; or, Americans in Tripoli. 1841? AMP14

JONES, LEROI (IMAMU AMIRI BARAKA, pseud.), 1934-
Ba-ra-ka. OWE
Bloodrites. (1971) KINH
Dutchman. 1964. DOV, HOLP, HOWP2, KNO, OLIV, PATR, REIL, SCNT, TREJ
Great goodness of life. (1967) BLA, RAVA, RICJ
Junkies are full of (SHHH...). KINH
Madheart. 1967. JON
The slave. 1964. HARY, TAUJ, THT
The toilet. 1964. ALLK, BES64, GARV

JONES, PAUL, d. 1966
Birthday honours. 1953. PLAN9
JONES, PETER, 1920- , and JOWETT, JOHN
The party spirit. 1954. PLAN11
JONES, TOM, 1928-
Celebration (music by Harvey Schmidt). 1969. BES68
The fantasticks. 1960. GARV

JONSON, BEN, 1572-1637
The alchemist. 1610. ASH, BAS, BENY, BROC, CASE, DEAS, GAY2, GRE, HARC47, HOW, KRM, LIE, LIEE1, NEI, OLH, OLI2, ORNC, REIO, ROET, SPE, TAT, TAU, THA
Bartholomew Fair. 1614. OLH, OLI2, SPE
Epicoene; or, The silent woman. 1609. BALD, BROC, CLKW, GAY2, RUB, STA
Hogan, R., and Molin, S., adapters HOGA
Everyman in his humour. 1598. ANG, BAS, BAT14, BROC, CLF1, CLK1, GARZAE, GAY2, HAPRA1, HAPRB1, MAT, NEI, ORNC, PAR, SCI, SCJ, SCW, SPE, WAT
The gipsies metamorphosed. 1621. BROC
The hue and cry after cupid. 1608. BAS, SCH, SCI, SCJ
The masque of blackness. 1605. WINE
Oberon, the fairy prince. 1611. PAR
The sad shepherd; or, A tale of Robin Hood. 1641? BAS, SCH
Sejanus, his fall. 1603. BAS, NEI, PAR
The silent woman. See Epicoene
The vision of delight. 1617. ABRA, ABRB1, TREB
Volpone; or, The fox. 1606. ALLI, ALLJ, ALLK, BAC, BARD, BAS, BENSB1, BROC, COTKI, DEAO, DEAP, DEAR, DUN, FOU, FOUD, HUD, HUST, KRE, KRM, LIED1, MORR, NEI, OLH, OLI1, PAR, PARR, SCH, SCI, SCJ, SEN, SPE, SUL, TRE, TREA2, TREB, TREC1, TREE1, TREI1, WAIW, WALL, WINE, WRIH

--See also Zweig, Stefan. Volpone (adapted by)
--See Chapman, George, jt. auth.

JOSEPH, ALLEN
Anniversary on weedy hill. (1970) BALLE8

JOSEPHSON, RAGNAR, 1891-
Kanske en diktare. See Perhaps a poet
Perhaps a poet. 1932. Lundbergh, H., tr. SCAN1

Variant title: Kanske en diktare

JOWETT, JOHN. See Jones, Peter, jt. auth.

JOYCE, JAMES, 1882-1941. See Barkentin, Marjorie
Ulysses in Nighttown (based on the novel by)
--See Leonard, Hugh.
Stephen D (based on Portrait of the artist as a young man, and Stephen Hero)

JULLIEN, JEAN, 1854-1919
The serenade. 1887.
Clark, B., tr. CLD

JUO, ESASHI. See Esashi Jūō

JUPP, KENNETH
The socialites. 1961? SATA

K

KAFKA, FRANZ, 1883-1924
The guardian of the tomb. 1916?
Ritchie, J., and Garten, H., trs. RITS

KAISER, GEORGE, 1878-1945
Alkibiades saved. 1920?
Morgan, B., tr. SOK
Variant title: Der gerettete Alkibiades
Der brand im opernhaus. See The fire in the opera house
The conflagration of the opera house. See The fire in the opera house
The coral. 1917.
Katzin, W., tr. DIK2, TUCG, TUCM, TUCN, TUCO
Variant title: Die koralle
The fire in the opera house. 1916.
Katzin, W., tr. KAT
Variant titles: Der brand im opernhaus; The conflagration of the opera house
Das Floss der Medusa. See The raft of the Medusa
From morn to midnight. 1916.
Dukes, A., tr. BLOC, DIE, GARZH, MOSG, MOSH, ROET
Weisstein, U., tr. BRIX
Variant title: Von morgens bis mitternachts
Gas I. 1918. STI2
Scheffauer, H., tr. TUCG, TUCM, TUCN, TUCO
Gas II. 1920. FEFH2
Katzin, W., tr. TUCG, TUCM, TUCN, TUCO
Der gerettete Alkibiades. See Alkibiades saved
Die koralle. See The coral
Der Protagonist. See The protagonist
The protagonist. 1922.
Ritchie, J., and Garten, H., trs. RITS
Variant title: Der Protagonist
The raft of the Medusa. 1943.
Wellwarth, G., tr. BENB, ENG
Variant title: Das Floss der Medusa
Von morgens bis mitternachts. See From morn to midnight

KALCHEIM, LEE H.
...and the boy who came to leave. 1965. BALLE2

KALIDASA. 4th century
Abhijnanashakuntala. See Shakuntalā
The fatal ring. See Shakuntalā
The hero and the nymph. See Vikramorvacie
Sakoontalā. See Shakuntalā
Shakuntalā. 4th cent.
Edgren, A., tr. WEL

Jones, W., tr. TAV
Lal, P., tr. LAL
Monier-Williams, M., tr. ANDF, BUCK, BUCL, BUCM, CLF1, EDAD, ORI3, TRE, TREA2, TREB, TREC1, TREE1, TREI1, YOHA
Ryder, A., tr. WARN1
Variant titles: Abhijnanashakuntala; The fatal ring; Sakoontalā; Shakuntala and the ring of recognition; Shakuntala recognized by a ring-token

Shakuntala and the ring of recognition. See Shakuntalā

Shakuntala recognized by a ring-token. See Shakuntalā

Urvashi won by valour. See Vikramorvacie

Vikramorvacie; or, The hero and the nymph. 4th cent.
Aurobindo, S., tr. WEL
Variant tites: The hero and the nymph; Urvashi won by valour; Vikramorvashiya

Vikramorvashiya. See Vikramorvacie

KAMARCK, EDWARD
Chenango crone. DRU

KAN'AMI, KANZE KIYOTSUGU. See Kanze Kiyotsugu Kan'ami

KAN-AMI KIYOTSUGU. See Kanze Kiyotsugu Kan'ami

KANDER, JOHN, 1927-
Cabaret (music by). See Masteroff, Joe. Cabaret

K'ANG CHIN-CHIH, fl. 1279?
Li K'uei carries thorns.
Anon. tr. BIR1
Variant title: Li K'uei fu ching

Li K'uei fu ching. See Li K'uei carries thorns

KANIN, FAY (MITCHELL) (Michael Kanin), 1917-
Goodbye, my fancy. 1948. BES48
Variant title: Most likely to succeed

Most likely to succeed. See Goodbye, my fancy

KANIN, GARSON, 1912-
Born yesterday. 1946. BES45, GARZ, GARZA3

KANIN, MRS. GARSON. See Gordon, Ruth

KANIN, MICHAEL. See Kanin, Fay (Mitchell)

KANZE KIYOTSUGU KAN'AMI, 1333-1384
Kayoi Komachi. See Komachi and the hundred nights

Komachi and the hundred nights. 14th cent.
Kato, E., tr. KEE
Variant title: Kayoi Komachi

Matsukase. 14th cent.
Tyler, R., tr. KEE

Motomezuka. See The sought-for grave

Sotoba Komachi. 14th cent.
Waley, A., tr. TRE, TREB, TREC1, TREE1, TREI1

The sought-for grave. 14th cent.
Jackman, B., tr. KEE
Variant title: Motomezuka

KANZE KOJIRO NOBUMITSU, 1435-1516
Dōjōji (attributed to).
Keene, D., tr. KEE

The priest and the willow.
Beichman, J., tr. KEE
Variant title: Yugyō Yanagi

Yugyō Yanagi. See The priest and the willow

KANZE MOTOKIYO ZEAMI.
See Seami, Motokiyo

KAO, TONG KIA
Pi-Pa-Ki. See Howard, Sidney and Irwin, William Henry. Lute song (adapted from)

KATAEV, VALENTIN PETROVICH, 1897-
Squaring the circle. 1928. Malamuth, C., and Lyons, E., trs. HAV, HAVE, LYK

KATAYEV, VALENTIN PETROVICH. See Kataev, Valentin Petrovich

KATZ, L.
The three cuckolds. See Anonymous plays. The three cuckolds (converted by)

KAUFMAN, GEORGE S., 1889-1961
The butter and egg man. 1925. BES25, LEV, LEVE

--See Dayton, Katharine; Lardner, Ring; Marquand, John P.; Teichmann, Howard, jt. auths.

-- and CONNELLY, MARCUS COOK
Beggar on horseback. 1923. BES23, CAR, CARA, CHAN, CHAP, COT, GASB, WARH, WATC1, WATI
Dulcy. 1921. BES21, COH, CONG, MOSJ, MOSK, MOSL
Merton of the movies (based on the novel by Harry L. Wilson). 1922. BEAC12, BESS22, PEN
To the ladies! 1922. QUI, TUCD

-- and FERBER, EDNA
Dinner at eight. 1932. BES32, SIXH
Minich. 1924. BES24
The royal family. 1927. BES27
Stage door. 1936. BES36, CLDP, GAS

-- and HART, MOSS
The American way. 1939. BES38, PROC
George Washington slept here. 1940. BES40
The man who came to dinner. 1939. BES39, CET, DAVK, GARZ, GARZA2, SIXC
Merrily we roll along. 1934. BES34
Once in a lifetime. 1930. BES30, FAMB
You can't take it with you. 1936. BES36, CLDP, CORE, CORF, GARZA2, GAS, LAM, LOOC, LOOD, LOOE, LOOF, MERS, SPES

-- RYSKIND, MORRIE and GERSHWIN, IRA
Of thee I sing (music by George Gershwin). 1931. BES31, CORD, CORE, CORF, DUR, FAMD, HIL, ROLF, TRE, VAN

-- and TEICHMANN, HOWARD
The solid gold cadillac. 1953. GART

KAY, KWESI
Laughter and hubbub in the house. PIET

KEANE, JOHN B., 1928-
Many young men of twenty. 1961. HOGE
Sharon's grave. 1960. HOGE

KEATS, JOHN, 1795-1821
Otho the Great. 1950? KAU

KELLY, GEORGE EDWARD, 1887-1974
Behold the bridegroom. 1927. BES27
Craig's wife. 1925. BES25, CORD, CORE, CORF, GASB, HARB, MERW, MOSG, MOSH
Daisy Mayme. 1926. BES26
The fatal weakness. 1946. BES46
Finders-keepers. 1916? WAGC3
Variant title: The lesson
The lesson. See Finders-keepers
Poor Aubrey. 1925. GASB, PROH, SCWG, THO
The show-off. 1924. BES23, KRM, MOSJ, MOSK, MOSL

KELLY, HUGH, 1739-1777
False delicacy. 1768. MCM, MCMI

KEMP, R.
The satire of the three estates. See Lindsay, Sir David. The satire of the three estates (modernized by)

KENNAWAY, JAMES PEBLES EWING, 1928-
Country dance. 1967. PLAN33

KENNEDY, ADRIENNE, 1931-
Funnyhouse of a negro. 1964. BRAS, OLIV
The owl answers. 1965. ASF, HARY, NEWA2
A rat's mass. 1966. SME
Sun. (1972) OWE

-- LENNON, JOHN, and SPINETTI, VICTOR
The Lennon play: in his own write. (1972). RICK

KENNEDY, MARGARET, 1896-1967
Escape me never! 1933. SEV

KENNEDY, MARY and HAWTHORNE, RUTH (WARREN)
Mrs. Partridge presents. 1925. BES24

KENNEY, JAMES
Raising the wind. 1803. BOOA4

KENYON, CHARLES, 1880-
Kindling. 1911. DIG

KERR, JEAN (COLLINS), 1923-
Finishing touches. 1973. BES72
Mary, Mary. 1961. BES60, GARS

KESSELRING, JOSEPH, 1902-1967
Arsenic and old lace. 1941. BES40, CEY, CORB, FREE, GARZ, GARZA3, RICI
Variant title: Bodies in our cellar
Bodies in our cellar. See Arsenic and old lace

KIA, KAO TONG. See Kao, Tong Kia

KIELLAND, TRYGVE, 1897-
Dronningen og hennes menn. See Queen Margaret of Norway
Queen Margaret of Norway. 1950.
Malleson, C., tr. MODS

KILLIGREW, THOMAS, 1612-1683
The parson's wedding. 1640. KNOW, SUM

KIMBALL, ROSAMOND
The resurrection. 191-? FED1

KIMMEL, HAROLD
The cell. PIET

KIMMINS, ANTHONY, 1901-1964
The amorous prawn. 1959. PLAN21

KING, NORMAN
The shadow of doubt. 1955. PLAN12

KING, PHILIP, 1904-
Serious charge. 1953. PLAN11

-- and CARY, FALKLAND L.
Sailor, beware! 1955. PLAN12
Watch it, sailor! 1960. PLAN22

KINGSLEY, SIDNEY, 1906-
Darkness at noon (based on the novel by Arthur Koestler). 1951. BES50, GARW, GAVE, WISD
Dead end. 1935. BES35, FREE, CET, GAS, JAFF
Detective story. 1949. BES48, GARW, HAVG
Lunatics and lovers. 1954. THEA55
Men in white. 1934. BES33, CORD, CORE, CORF, FAMF, GARU, GARZA1, MERV
Thomas Jefferson. See The patriots
The patriots. 1943. BES42, CRIT, GARZ, GAVE
Variant title: Thomas Jefferson
The world we make (based on the novel The outward room by Millen Brand). 1939. BES39

KINOSHITA, JUNJI, 1914-
Twilight crane. 1949.
Scott, A., tr. PLAA
Variant title: Yûzuru
Yûzuru. See Twilight crane

KINWELMERSH, FRANCIS, fl. 1570. See Gascoigne, George, jt. auth.

KIPPHARDT, HEINAR, 1922-
In der Sache J. Robert Oppenheimer. See In the matter of J. Robert Oppenheimer
In the matter of J. Robert Oppenheimer. 1964.
Speirs, R., tr. BES68
Variant title: In der Sache J. Robert Oppenheimer

KIRKLAND, JACK, 1904-1969, and CALDWELL, ERSKINE
Tobacco road. 1933. CEY, GARZA1, GAS

KIRSHON, VLADIMIR MIKHAILOVICH, 1902-
Bread. 1931.
Volochora, S., tr. LYK

KIYOTSUGU, KWANAMI. See Kanze Kiyotsugu Kan'ami

KLEB, WILLIAM, 1939-
Honeymoon in Haiti. 1965. GARZAL

KLEIST, HEINRICH BERNT WILHELM VON, 1777-1811
The broken jug. See Der zerbrochene krug
Kaethchen of Heilbronn; or, The test of fire. 1810.
Pierce, F., tr. PIE
Variant title: Das Käthchen von Heilbronn; oder, Die feuerprobe
Das Käthchen von Heilbronn; oder, Die feuerprobe. See Kaethchen of Heilbronn; or, The test of fire
Penthesilea. 1876.
Lamport, F., tr. LAMP
Trevelyan, H., tr. BENR2
Prince Frederick of Homburg. See Prinz Friedrich von Homburg
The Prince of Homburg. See Prinz Friedrich von Homburg
Prinz Friedrich von Homburg. 1821. CAM
Anon. tr. PLAN36
Esselin, M., tr. ESS
Hagedorn, H., tr. FRA4, SMK
Kirkup, J., tr. BENR2, WEIS
Lustig, T., tr. LUST
Scheurer, L., tr. BENSB1

Variant titles: Prince Frederick of Homburg; The Prince of Homburg
Der zerbrochene krug. 1808. CAM
Wilson, L., tr. ALLE
Variant title: The broken jug

KNIGHT, ERIC MOWBRAY, 1897-1943
Never come Monday (adapted by Stephen Fox). 1939? PROC

KNIGHT, VICK
Cartwheel. 194-? PROC

KNOBLOCK, EDWARD, 1874-1945. See Bennett, Arnold, jt. auth.

KNOTT, FREDERICK, 1919-
Dial "M" for murder. 1952. BES52, FAOS, FICI, THEA53

KNOWLES, JAMES SHERIDAN, 1784-1862
The love-chase. 1837. MAL
Virginius. 1820. BOOA1, MOSN, MOSO

KNOX, FLORENCE CLAY
For distinguished service. 1918. SHAY

KOBER, ARTHUR, 1900-1975
"Having wonderful time." 1937. CET
Wish you were here (based on "Having wonderful time;" music and lyrics by Harold Rome). 1953. THEA53

KOCH, HOWARD and HUSTON, JOHN
In time to come. 1941. BES41

KOCH, KENNETH, 1925-
The academic murders. 1966. GLI

KOCHERGA, IVAN, 1885-
Masters of time. 1934.
Wixley, A., tr. FOUS
Variant title: Watchmaker and the hen
Watchmaker and the hen. See Masters of time

KOCK, CHARLES PAUL DE, 1794-1871
A happy day. 184-?
Chambers, W., tr. BAT9
Variant title: Une journée de bonheur
Un journée de bonheur. See A happy day

KOEBNICK, SARAH MONSON
Fair beckoning one. 1967. BALLE5

KOESTLER, ARTHUR, 1905-
Darkness at noon. See Kingsley, Sidney. Darkness at noon (based on the novel by)

KOKOSCHKA, OSKAR, 1886-
Hiob. See Job
Job. 1917.
Benedikt, M., tr. WELG
Sokol, W., and J., trs. SOK
Variant title: Hiob
Mörder, Haffnung der Frauen. See Murderer hope of womankind
Murderer hope of womankind. 1907.
Hamburger, M., tr. SOK
Ritchie, J., and Garten, H., trs. RITS
Variant titles: Mörder, Haffnung der Frauen; Murderer the women's hope.
Murderer the women's hope. See Murderer hope of womankind

KOMPARU-ZENCHIKU, 1405-1468
The queen mother of the West (attributed to). 15th cent.

Sesar, C., tr. KEE
Variant title: Seiōbo
Seiōbo. See The queen mother of the West
Yōkihi. 15th cent.
Sesar, C., tr. KEE

KONGO YAGORO. 16th cent?
The bird-scaring boat (attributed to). 16th cent.?
Tyler, R., tr. KEE
Variant title: Torioibune
Torioibune. See The bird-scaring boat

KOPIT, ARTHUR L., 1937-
Indians. 1969. BES69
Oh dad, poor dad, mamma's hung you in the closet and I'm feelin' so sad. 1960.
BES61, FREF, GARS, GARZA4, OFF, SMA, WHFM

KOPS, BERNARD, 1926-
Enter Solly Gold. 1961?
COTKR, SATA
The hamlet of Stepney Green. 1958. NEWE1

KORNEICHUK, ALEKSANDR EVDOKONOVICH, 1905-1972
The front. 1942.
Anon. tr. FOUT
Kotem, B., and Voynow, Z., trs. SEVP
Guerillas of the Ukrainian Steppes. 1942.
Anon. tr. FOUT
Variant title: Partisans on the steppes of the Ukraine; Partizany v stepakh Ukrainy
Partisans on the steppes of the Ukraine. See Guerillas on the Ukrainian Steppes
Partizany v stepakh Ukrainy. See Guerillas on the steppes of the Ukraine
Platon Krechet. 1935?
Prokofieva, R., tr. THY

KORNEICHUK, ALEXANDER EVDOKONOVICH. See Korneichuk, Aleksandr Evdokonovich

KORR, DAVID
Encore. 1970. BALLE9

KOSACH, LARISA PETROVNA (Lesya Ukrainka, pseud.)
The Babylonian captivity. 19th cent.
Volska, S., tr. ROE

KOSTROWISKY, GUILLAUME APOLLINAIRE DE (GUILLAUME APOLLINAIRE, pseud.), 1880-1918
The breasts of Tiresias. 1917.
Simpson, L., tr. BEN
Variant title: Les mamelles de Tirésias
Les mamelles de Tirésias. See The breasts of Tiresias

KOSTROWITZKI, WILHELM. See Kostrowisky, Guillaume Apollinaire de

KOTZEBUE, AUGUST FRIEDRICH FERDINAND VON, 1761-1819
Der egoist und kritikus. See Egotist and pseudo-critic Herr Gottlieb Merks
Egotist and pseudo-critic Herr Gottlieb Merks. 179-?
Chambers, W., tr. BAT11
Variant title: Der egoist und kritikus
Falsche scham. See Dunlap, William. False shame (adapted from)
Das kind der liebe. See Lovers' vows
Lovers' vows; or, The natural son. 1798?
Thompson, B., tr. BAT21
Variant title: Das kind der liebe
Menschenhass und reue. See

The stranger
Pharaoh's daughter. 179-?
Beebe, B., tr. WEB
Variant title: Die tochter Pharaonis
The stranger. 1789.
Thompson, B., tr. MCM, MCMI
Variant title: Menschenhass une reue
Die tochter Pharaonis. See Pharaoh's daughter

KOUTOUKAS, H. M.
Kill, kaleidoscope, kill. See Tidy passions
Tidy passions; or, Kill, kaleidoscope, kill. 1972. SME
Variant title: Kill, kaleidoscope, kill

KOZLENKO, WILLIAM, 1908-
This earth is ours. 1937? KOZ

KRAMM, JOSEPH, 1907-
The shrike. 1952. BES51

KRANES, DAVID
Drive-in. BALLE7

KRASNA, NORMAN, 1909-
Dear Ruth. 1944. BES44
John loves Mary. 1947. BES46

KRAUS, KARL, 1874-1936
The last days of mankind, (excerpt). 1919-1922.
Spalter, M., tr. WELG
Variant title: Die letzten tage der menschheit
Die letzten tage der menschheit. See The last days of mankind

KREYMBORG, ALFRED, 1883-1966
The dead are free. 1935. AME5
Hole in the wall. 192-? KRE
Lima beans. 1925? LEV, LEVE
Manikin and Minikin. 1918. SHAY
Rocking chairs. 1921? SHAY

KROG, HELGE, 1889-
Konkylien. See The sounding shell
The sounding shell. 1929.
Campbell, R., tr. SCAN2
Variant title: Konkylien

KUAN HAN-CH'ING
The injustice done to Tou Ngo.
Liu, J., tr. LIU
Snow in mid-summer.
Hsien-yi, Y., and Yang, G., trs. MESE

KUHNS, DOROTHY HARTZELL. See Heyward, Mrs. Dorothy Hartzell (Kuhns)

KUMMER, MRS. CLARE (BEECHER)
Good gracious Annabelle. 1916. BES09
Her master's voice. 1933. BES33

KURNITZ, HARRY, 1909-1968
Reclining figure. 1954. THEA55

KVARES, DONALD
Mushrooms. 1967. SLM

KWANAMI KIYOTSUGU. See Kiyotsugu, Kwanami

KWANZE KOJIRO NOBUMITSU. See Kanze Kojiro Nobumitsu

KYD, THOMAS, 1558-1594
Arden of Feversham (sometimes attributed to). See Anonymous plays. Arden of Feversham
The Spanish tragedy; or, Hieronimo is mad again. 1589? BAS, BROC, GARZAE, HEIL, HOW, HUST, MAT, MCJ, MINI, MIO1, NEI, NES, OLH, OLI1, ORNT, PAR, RUB, SCI, SCJ, SCW, SPE, TICO

L

LABICHE, EUGENE MARIN, 1815-1888, and LEVEAUX, ALPHONSE
La grammaire. 1867. BENZ, STOC

--See Legouvé, Ernest, jt. auth.

-- and DELACOUR, ALFRED CHARLEMAGNE LARTIGNE
La cagnolte. See Pots of money
Célimare. 1863.
Hoffman, L., and T., and Bentley, E., trs. BENSB
Variant title: Célimare le bien-aimé
Célimare le bien-aimé. See Célimare
Les petits oiseaux. See Grundy, Sydney. A pair of spectacles (adapted from)
Pots of money. 1864?
Bermel, A., tr. BERM
Variant title: La cagnolte

-- and GONDINET, EDMOND
The happiest of the three.
Davies, F., tr. LAB

-- and MARTIN, EDOUARD
Bluffers. See La poudre aux yeux
Cousin Billy. See Le voyage Monsieur Perrichon
Dust in the eyes. See La poudre aux yeux
Perrichon's voyage. See Le voyage de Monsieur Perrichon
La poudre aux yeux. 1861. SCN
Variant titles: Bluffers; Dust in the eyes
The 37 sous of M. Montaudoin. See Les trente-sept sous de M. Montaudoin
Les trente-sept sous de M. Montaudoin. 1862. BRN
Variant title: The 37 sous of M. Montaudoin
A trip abroad. See Le voyage de Monsieur Perrichon
Le voyage de Monsieur Perrichon. 1860. MCL
Ward, R., tr. BENSC
Variant titles: Cousin Billy; Perrichon's voyage; A trip abroad

-- and MICHEL, MARC ANTOINE AMEDEE
Haste to the wedding. See An Italian straw hat
An Italian straw hat. 1851.
Hoffman, L., and T., trs. BENT3, COTKIR
Variant titles: Haste to the wedding; The wedding march
The wedding march. See An Italian straw hat

LA CHAUSSEE, PIERRE CLAUDE NIVELLE DE, 1692-1754
Fashionable prejudice. See Le préjugé à la mode
Le préjugé à la mode. 1735. BRE
Variant title: Fashionable prejudice

LADIPO, DURO
Moremi.
Beier, U., tr. THTN

LA FARGE, W. E. R.
Escape by balloon. 1972. BALLE10

LA FOSSE, ANTOINE DE, sieur d'Aubigny, 1653-1708
Manlius Capitolinus. 1698.
Lockert, L., tr. LOCR

LAGERKVIST, PAR, 1891-1974
The difficult hour, I-III. 1918.
Buckman, T., tr. SPR
Variant title: Den svåra stunden, I-III
Låt människan leva. See Let man live

Let man live. 1949.
Alexander, H., and Jones, L., trs. SCAN3
Gustafsson, W., tr. FIL
Variant titles: Låt människan leva; The man who lived his life over
The man without a soul. 1936.
Kökeritz, H., tr. SCAN1
Variant title: Mannen utan själ
Mannen utan själ. See The man without a soul
Den svåra stunden, I-III. See The difficult hour, I-III

LA GRANGE-CHANCEL, 1677-1758
Ino and Melicertes. 1713.
Lockert, L., tr. LOCU
Variant title: Ino et Mélicerte
Ino et Mélicerte. See Ino and Melicertes

LAMB, MYRNA, 1931-
But what have you done for me lately? See Scyklon Z: But what have you done for me lately?; or, Pure polemic
Pure polemic. See Scyklon Z: But what have you done for me lately?; or, Pure polemic.
Scyklon Z: But what have you done for me lately? or, Pure polemic. 1969. BAYM, RAVA
Variant titles: Pure polemic; But what have you done for me lately

LANGLEY, NOEL, 1911- .
See Morley, Robert, jt. auth.

LARDNER, RING WILMER, 1885-1933
Thompson's vacation. CARL
-- and KAUFMAN, GEORGE S.
June moon. 1929. BES29

LASZLO, CARL
The Chinese icebox. 1956.
Wellwarth, G., tr. BENB
Variant title: Der Chinesische Kühlschrank
Der Chinesische Kühlschrank. See The Chinese icebox
Essen wir Haare. See Let's eat hair!
Let's eat hair! 1956.
Wellwarth, G., tr. BENB
Variant title: Essen wir Haare

LASZLO, MIKLOS, 1904-1973
She loves me. See Masteroff, Joe. She loves me (based on a play by)

LA TAILLE, JEAN DE. See Taille, Jean de La

LATOUCHE, JOHN TREVILLE, 1917-1956
Candide. See Hellman, Lillian. Candide (lyrics by)
The golden apple (music by Jerome Moross). 1954. BES53, THEA54

LAUCKNER, ROLF T., 1887-1954
Cry in the street. 1922.
Edwards, M., and Reich, V., trs. SOK
Variant title: Schrei aus der Strasse
Schrei aus der Strasse. See Cry in the street

LAUNDER, FRANK, and GILLIAT, SIDNEY
The body was well nourished. See Meet a body
Meet a body. 1940. PLAN10
Variant title: The body was well nourished

LAURENTS, ARTHUR, 1918-
A clearing in the woods. 1957. BES56
Home of the brave. 1945. BES45, GARZ, HEWE

The time of the cuckoo. 1952. BES52, THEA53

LAVEDAN, HENRI LEON EMILE, 1859-1940
The prince d'Aurec. 1892. Clark, B., tr. THR

LAVERY, EMMET, 1902-
The magnificent Yankee. 1946. BES45, MERT, SPES

-- and MURPHY, GRACE
Kamiano, the story of Damien. 1938. THEC

LA VIGNE, ANDRIEU DE, 15th century
The miracle of the blind man and the cripple. 15th cent. LOOM

LAW, WARNER
Indomitable blacksmith. 195-? LOVR

LAWLER, RAY, 1922-
Summer of the 17th doll. 1955. BES57

LAWRENCE, JEROME, 1915- , and LEE, ROBERT E.
Inherit the wind. 1955. BES54, GART, SHER, THEA55

LAWSON, JOHN HOWARD, 1895-
Processional. 1925. WATC1, WATI
Roger Bloomer. 1923. FULT
Success story. 1932. LOO

LAYA, JEAN LOUIS, 1761-1833
L'ami des lois. 1793. BRE

LEACOCK, JOHN
The fall of British tyranny; or, American liberty triumphant. 1776. MOSS1, PHI

LEAMON, DOROTHY
Barabas. 20th cent. FED2

LEAVITT, JOHN McDOWELL, 1824-190?
The Jewish captives. 1876? KOH2

LECOCQ, ALEXANDRE CHARLES, 1832-1918
The daughter of Madame Angot. 1872. Seldes, G., and G., trs. PLAH
Variant title: La fille de Madame Angot
La fille de Madame Angot. See The daughter of Madame Angot

LEE, JAMES HENRY
Career. 1956. COTK

LEE, JEANNIE
On the corner of Cherry and elsewhere. COLI

LEE, LANCE
Fox, hound and huntress. 1971. BALLE10

LEE, NATHANIEL, 1653?-1692
The rival queens; or, The death of Alexander the great. 1677. MCM, MCMI
Sophonisba. 1675. DOA

LEE, ROBERT E. See Lawrence, Jerome, jt. auth.

LEGOUVE, ERNEST, 1807-1903, and LABICHE, EUGENE MARIN
La cigale chez les fourmis. 188-? BOVE
Variant title: The grasshopper at the home of the ants
The grasshopper at the home of the ants. See La cigale chez les fourmis

LEICHMAN, SEYMOUR
Freddie the pigeon. BALLE7

LEIGH, MITCH, 1928-
Man of La Mancha (music by). See Wasserman, Dale.

Man of La Mancha

LEIVICK, H., pseud. See Halper, Leivick

LEMAITRE, JULES, 1853-1914
Forgiveness. See The pardon
Le pardon. See The pardon
The pardon. 1895.
Clark, B., tr. THR
Variant titles: Forgiveness; Le pardon

LENNON, JOHN, 1940- .
See Kennedy, Adrienne, jt. auth.

LENNOX, GILBERT
Close quarters. See Somin, W. O. Close quarters (tr. and adapted by)

LENORMAND, HENRI RENE, 1882-1938
The coward. 1925.
Orna, D., tr. CHA, CHAN
Variant title: La lâche
Crépuscle du théâtre. See In Theatre street
The devourer of dreams. See The dream doctor
The dream doctor. 1922.
Orna, D., tr. MOSG, MOSH
Variant titles: The devourer of dreams; Le mangeur de rêves
L'homme et ses fantômes. 1924. RHO
Variant title: Man and his phantoms
In Theatre street. 1936.
Dukes, A., tr. FAMK
Variant title: Crépuscle du théâtre
Le lâche. See The coward
Man and his phantoms. See L'homme et ses fantômes
Le mangeur de rêves. See The dream doctor
Simoom. See Le simoun
Le Simoun. 1920. HARV
Variant title: Simoom
Le temps est un songe. See Time is a dream
Time is a dream. 1919.
Katzin, W., tr. DIE, HAV
Variant title: Le temps est un songe

LEONARD, HUGH, 1926-
The Patrick Pearse motel. 1971. PLAN41
The poker session. 1964. PLAN28
Stephen D (based on James Joyce's Portrait of the artist as a young man, and Stephen Hero). 1962. ENG

LEONOV, LEONID MAXIMOVICH, 1899-
Invasion. 1943.
Anon. tr. FOUT
The orchards of Polovchansk. 1938.
Robbins, J., tr. SEVP

LEOPOLD, pseud. See Chandezon, Léopold

LERNER, ALAN JAY, 1918-
Brigadoon (music by Frederick Loewe). 1947. BES46
My fair lady (adapted from Bernard Shaw's Pygmalion; music by Frederick Loewe). 1956. BES55

LE SAGE, ALAIN RENE, 1668-1747
Crispin, rival de son maître. See Crispin, rival of his master
Crispin, rival of his master. 1707.
Chambers, W., tr. BAT8
Variant title: Crispin, rival de son maître
The financier. See Turcaret
Turcaret. 1709. BRE, ZDA
Aldington, R., tr. ALD
Merwin, W., tr. BENR4
Variant titles: The financier; Turcaret; or, The financier

Turcaret; or, The financier. See Turcaret

LESSING, DORIS MAE, 1919-
Each his own wilderness. 1958. NEWE1
Play with a tiger. 1962. SUB, PLAJ1

LESSING, GOTTHOLD EPHRAIM, 1729-1781
Emilia Galotti. 1772.
Lamport, F., tr. LAMP
Lewes, C., tr. ESS
Minna von Barnhelm; or, The soldier's fortune. 1767.
Bell, E., tr. BAT10, CROV, GREA, HARC26, MAU
Miss Sara Sampson. 1753.
Bell, E., tr. CLF2
Nathan der weise. See Nathan the wise
Nathan the wise. 1783.
Frothingham, E., tr. KOH2
Lustig, T., tr. LUST
Variant title: Nathan der weise

LETHBRIDGE, NEMONE
The Portsmouth defence. 1966. PLAN32

LETTON, FRANCIS. See Dowling, Jennette, jt. auth.

LEVEAUX, ALPHONSE, b. 1810. See Labiche, Eugène Marin, jt. auth.

LEVIN, IRA
No time for sergeants (adapted from the novel by Mac Hyman). 1955. BES55, GART, THEA56

LEVINE, MARK L.; McNAMEE, GEORGE C., and GREENBERG, DANIEL
The tales of Hoffman - a series of excerpts from the "Chicago conspiracy" trial. RAVA

LEVINSON, ALFRED
Socrates wounded. 1959? NEWA1

LEVITT, SAUL, 1911-
The Andersonville trial. 1959. BES59, CEQ

LEVY, BENN WOLF, 1900-1973
Clutterbuck. 1949. BES49
The devil passes. 1932. BES31
The member for Gaza. 1966. PLAN32
Mrs. Moonlight. 1928. FAO
Springtime for Henry. 1931. LEV, LEVE

LEWIN, JOHN
Five easy payments. 1966. BALLE3

LEWIN, ROSE D. See Franken, Mrs. Rose D. (Lewin)

LEWIS, LEOPOLD DAVID, 1828-1890
The bells (adapted from Le juif Polonais by Erckmann-Chatrian). 1871. ASG, BOOB, COTKF, ROWE
Variant title: The Polish Jew
The Polish Jew. See The bells

LEWIS, SAUNDERS, 1893-
King's daughter. See Siwan
Siwan. 1954.
Humphreys, E., tr. PLAN21
Variant title: King's daughter

LEWIS, SINCLAIR, 1885-1951
Dodsworth. See Howard, Sidney. Dodsworth (based on the novel by)
The ghost patrol. See Clarke, William Kendall. The ghost patrol (based on the story by)

LI HAO-KU
Chang boils the sea.
Liu, J., tr. LIU

LILLO, GEORGE, 1693-1739
The London merchant; or, The history of George Barnwell. 1731. BENY, BOO, BROJ, BROK, EIGH, HAN, MCM, MCM1, MOR, NET, SMI, STM, TAU, TREB, TUQ, WILE

LINARES RIVAS, MANUEL, 1866-
The claws. 1914.
Turrell, C., tr. TUR
Variant title: La garra
La garra. See The claws

LINDSAY, SIR DAVID, 1490-1555
The satire of the three estates. 1540
Kemp, R., modernizer ROET

LINDSAY, HOWARD, 1889-1968, and CROUSE, RUSSEL
Life with father (based on the book by Clarence Day). 1939. BES39, CASS, CET, CEY, COOP, GARZ, GARZA2, LOVR, MERS, SPER, STRB
Life with mother (based on the book by Clarence Day). 1948. BES48
Remains to be seen. 1951. BES51
State of the union. 1945. BES45, GARW, GARZA3

LIPSCOMB, WILLIAM PERCY, 1887- , and MINNEY, RUBEIGH J.
Clive of India. 1934. FAME

LIPSKEROFF, KONSTANTIN, 1899-
Carmencita and the soldier (based on the opera Carmen by Georges Bizet; libretto by Prosper Mérimée.) 1923.
Seldes, G., and G., trs. PLAH

LIVING NEWSPAPER. See Staff of the Living Newspaper

LIVINGS, HENRY, 1930-
Nil carborundum. 1962. NEWE6
Stop it, whoever you are. 1961. NEWE5
There's no room for you here for a start. 1963. CONB

LIVINGSTON, MYRTLE SMITH, 1901-
For unborn children. 1901. HARY

LOCHER, JENS, 1889-1952
Tea for three. 1943.
Anon. trs. (revised by Furbank, P., and Bredsdorff, E.) CONT
Variant title: Tre maa man vaere
Tre maa man vaere. See Tea for three

LOCKE-ELLIOTT, SUMNER
Rusty bugles. 1948. HANG

LOCKRIDGE, FRANCES (MRS. RICHARD LOCKRIDGE), d. 1963, and LOCKRIDGE, RICHARD
The Norths meet murder. See Davis, Owen. Mr. and Mrs. North (based on the novel by)

LOCKRIDGE, RICHARD, 1898-
See Lockridge, Frances, jt. auth.

LODGE, THOMAS, 1558?-1625
Mucedorus (sometimes attributed to). See Anonymous plays. Mucedorus
The reign of King Edward the third (sometimes attributed to). See Anonymous plays. The reign of King Edward the third

LOESSER, FRANK, 1910-
Guys and dolls. See Swerling, Jo, and Burrows, Abe. Guys and dolls (music and lyrics by)
How to succeed in business

without really trying. See Burrows, Abram S. How to succeed in business without really trying (music and lyrics by)
The most happy fella (based on Sidney Howard's play They knew what they wanted). 1956. THEA56

LOEWE, FREDERICK, 1901-
Brigadoon. See Lerner, Alan Jay. Brigadoon (music by)
My fair lady. See Lerner, Jay. My fair lady (music by)

LOGAN, JOSHUA, 1908-
The wisteria trees (based on the Cherry orchard by Anton Chekhov). 1950. BES49

--See Behrman, Samuel Nathaniel; Hammerstein II, Oscar; Heggen, Thomas; Kober, Arthur, jt. auths.

LONG, JOHN LUTHER, 1861-1927. See Belasco, David, jt. auth.

LONGFELLOW, HENRY WADSWORTH, 1807-1882
The Spanish student. 1843? BAT19

LONGFORD, CHRISTINE
Mr. Jiggins of Jigginstown. 1933. CAN

LONGFORD, EDWARD ARTHUR HENRY, 1902-
Yahoo. 1933. CAN

LONSDALE, FREDERICK, 1881-1954
Aren't we all? 1923. SEV
Half a loaf. See Let them eat cake
The last of Mrs. Cheyney. 1925. BES25
Let them eat cake. 1959. PLAN19
Variant titles: Half a loaf; Once is enough
Once is enough. See Let them eat cake

LOOS, ANITA, 1893-
Gigi (from the novel by Colette). 1951. BES51

LOPE DE RUEDA. See Rueda, Lope de

LOPE DE VEGA. See Vega Carpio, Lope Félix de

LOPEZ, SABATINO, 1867-1951
Il passero. See The sparrow
The sparrow. 1918. Goldberg, I., tr. GOL
Variant title: Il passero

LOPEZ DE AYALA, ADELARDO, 1828-1879
Consuelo. 1878. BRET

LOPEZ RUBIO, JOSE, 1903-
The blindfold. (1954) Holt, M., tr. HOLT
Variant title: La venda en los ojos
La venda en los ojos. See The blindfold

LORCA, FEDERICO GARCIA. See García Lorca, Federico

LOS HERREROS, MANUEL BRETON DE. See Bretón de los Herreros, Manuel

LOW, SAMUEL, b. 1765
The politician out-witted. 1789. MOSS1

LOWELL, ROBERT, 1917-
Beneto Cereno. 1964. ABC, BROTA, BUR, DOV, GARV, RICJ, TREJ, VON
Variant title: Old glory; Beneto Cereno
My kinsman, Major Molineux. 1964. ALS, CASE, DOD, SCNR
Old glory: Beneto Cereno.

See Beneto Cereno

LUCE, CLARE BOOTHE. See Boothe, Clare

LUDLAM, CHARLES
Bluebeard. 1970. SME

LUDWIG, OTTO, 1813-1865
Der erbförster. 1850. CAM
Remy, A., tr. FRA9
Variant title: The hereditary forester
The hereditary forester. See Der erbförster

LUKE, PETER, 1919-
Hadrian VII. 1967. BES68, PLAN33

LUPTON, THOMAS, fl. 1588
All for money. 1577. SCAT

LYLY, JOHN, 1554?-1606
Alexander and Campaspe. See Campaspe
Campaspe. 1584. ADA, GAY1, MCI, OLH, OLI1
Variant title: Alexander and Campaspe
Endimion. See Endymion, the man in the moon
Endymion, the man in the moon. 1588. BAS, BROC, MIN2, MIO2, NEI, NES, ORNC, PAR, SCH, SCI, SCJ, SCW, SPE
Variant title: Endimion
Midas. 1589. WINN
Mother Bombie. 1589? TAT, TAU

LYNCH, HAL
Three miles to Poley. 1971. BALLE10

LYNDON, BARRE, 1896-
The amazing Dr. Clitterhouse. 1936. FOUP, THH
The man in Half moon street. 1939. SIXL
They came by night. 1937. FIP

LYNNE, JAMES BROOM
The trigon. 1963. NEWE8

LYTTON, EDWARD GEORGE BULWER. See Bulwer-Lytton, Edward George Earle Lytton

M

MA CHIH-YUAN, fl. 1251
Autumn in Han Palace. See Autumn in the Palace of Han
Autumn in the Palace of Han. 13th cent.
Liu, J., tr. BIR1, LIU
Variant titles: Autumn in Han Palace; Han Kung Ch'in
Han Kung Ch'in. See Autumn in the Palace of Han

MacARTHUR, CHARLES, 1895-1956. See Hecht, Ben, jt. auth.

MACAULEY, PAULINE
The creeper. 1964. PLAN29
Monica. RICJ

MacBETH, GEORGE, 1932- and BINGHAM, J.
The doomsday show. 1964. NEWE14

McCARTHY, JUSTIN HUNTLEY, 1861-1936
If I were king. 1901. BES99
Variant title: The vagabond king
The vagabond king. See If I were king

McCAULEY, CLARICE VALLETTE
The conflict. 1920. SHAY
The seeker. 1919. FED1

McCLOSKEY, JAMES J., 1825-1913
Across the continent; or, Scenes from New York life and the Pacific railroad. 1870. AMP4, MONR

McCRACKEN, MRS. ESTHER (ARMSTRONG), 1902-
Quiet wedding. 1938. SIXL

McCULLERS, MRS. CARSON (SMITH), 1917-1967
The member of the wedding. 1950. BES49, GARW, GARZA3, GAVE, HEWE, MIJY, PATM, PATP

McDANIEL, CHARLES A.
The ends of justice. 1968. BRNB

MacDONAGH, DONAGH, 1912-
Happy as Larry. 1947. BROS, NEWW6
Step-in-the-hollow. 1957. BROT

McDONALD, CATHERINE and MASON, WILTON
Spring for sure. 1950. PAJ

MacDOUGALL, ROGER, 1910-
The gentle gunman. 1950. PLAN5
To Dorothy, a son. 1950. PLAN4

McENROE, ROBERT EDWARD, 1916-
Oliver Erwenter. See The silver whistle
The silver whistle. 1948. BES48
Variant title: Oliver Erwenter

McEVOY, CHARLES, 1879-1829
The likes of her. 1923. MAP

McGEEHAN, MRS. SOPHIE (TREADWELL). See Treadwell, Sophie

McGOUGH, ROGER
The puny little life show. 1970. MAOC

McGUIRE, WILLIAM ANTHONY, 1885-1940
Six cylinder love. 1921. BES21

McHARDY, AIMEE. See Stuart, Mrs. Aimée (McHardy)

MACHIAVELLI, NICCOLO, 1469-1527
La mandragola. See Mandragola
Mandragola. 1525?
Hale, J., tr. BARB
May, F., and Bentley, E., trs. BENR1
Young, S., tr. HAYD
Variant titles: La mandragola; The mandrake
The mandrake. See Mandragola

McILWRAITH, BILL
The anniversary. 1966. PLAN31

MACKAY, CONSTANCE D'ARCY, d. 1966
Benjamin Franklin, journeyman. 1912? LAW
Counsel retained. 1915? PEN
The prince of court painters. 1915? WEB

MACKAY, MRS. ISABEL (MACPHERSON) ECCLESTONE, 1875-1928
The second life. 1921. MAS1

MACKAY, L. A.
The freedom of Jean Guichet. 1925. MAS2

MacKAYE, PERCY WALLACE, 1875-1956
Napoleon crossing the Rockies. 1924. CHU
The pilgrim and the book. 1920. FED1
Sam Average. 1911. BEAC11
The scarecrow. 1909. DIC, FLAN, GARX, GARZAP, GASS, MOSJ, MOSK, MOSL, QUIG, QUIJ, QUIK, QUIL, QUIM, QUIN

MacKAYE, STEELE, 1842-1894

An arrant knave. 1889. AMP11
Hazel Kirke. 1880. QUIG, QUIJ, QUIK, QUIL, QUIM, QUIN
In spite of all. 1885. AMP11
Paul Kauvar; or, Anarchy. 1890. MOSS3
Rose Michel. 1875. AMP11
Won at last. 1877. AMP11

McKENNEY, RUTH, 1911-
My sister Eileen (based on the stories by). See Fields, Joseph and Chodorov, Jerome. My sister Eileen
Wonderful town. See Fields, Joseph and Chodorov, Jerome. Wonderful town (based on the stories My sister Eileen by)

MacKENZIE, RONALD, 1903-1932
The Maitlands. 1934. FAMF
Musical chairs. 1931. FAMB, PLAD

MACKEY, WILLIAM W.
Requiem for Brother X. KINH

MACKIE, PHILIP
The big killing. 1962. PLAN25
The whole truth. 1955. PLAN13

McKINNEY, JACK
The well. 1960. HANG

MacKINTOSH, ELIZABETH (Gordon Daviot, pseud.), d. 1952.
The laughing woman. 1934. FAME
The pen of my aunt. 1954. BRNB
Queen of Scots. 1934. FAMF
Richard of Bordeaux. 1933. FAMD, PLAL1

MACKLIN, CHARLES
A will and no will. 1746. BEVI

MacLEISH, ARCHIBALD, 1892-
Air raid. 1938. MCCF
The fall of the city. 1937. BROU, BRR3, GAS, KERN, KRE, LOOB, LOOC, LOOD, LOOE, NELS, VOAD, WAIT
J. B. 1958. BES58, COTX, GARS, HILP, SCNP
The music crept by me upon the waters. 1953? SUL
The Trojan horse. 1952. WHF

McLELLAN, C. M. S. (Hugh Morton, pseud.), 1865-1916
Leah Kleschna. 1904. BES99

MacMAHON, BRYAN, 1909-
Song of the anvil. 1916. HOGE

MacMILLAN, DOUGALD, 1897-
Off Nags head; or, The bell buoy. 1922? LAW

MACMILLAN, MARY LOUISE
The pioneers. 1917? LAW

McNALLY, TERRENCE, 1930-
And things that go bump in the night. 1964. BALLE1
Bad habits. 1974. BES73
Botticelli. 1969. OFF
Next. 1969. BES68
Sweet eros. 1968. OFF
Tour. 1968. GLI
Where has Tommy Flowers gone? 1971. BES71

McNAMEE, GEORGE C. See Levine, Mark L., jt. auth.

MACNEICE, LOUIS, 1907-
The dark tower. 1946. ANDE, BENS2

MacOWAN, NORMAN, 1877-
Glorious morning. 1938. FAML

MACPHERSON, ISABEL. See Mackay, Mrs. Isabel (Macpherson) Ecclestone

MACRAE, ARTHUR, 1908-
Both ends meet. 1954. PLAN10

MAETERLINCK, MAURICE, 1862-1949
The death of Tintagiles. 1899.

Sutro, A., tr. BAT21, SHAY
Variant title: La mort de Tintagiles
Home. See Interior
L'intérieur. See Interior
Interior. 1894.
Archer, W., tr. MCCP, MIL
Variant titles: Home; L'intérieur
The intruder. 1890.
Anon. tr. PATM, TREBA, TREI2, TREJ
Block, H., tr. BLOC
Hovey, R., tr. BENP, CAR, CARA, HUD, TREC2, TREE2
Variant title: L'intruse
L'intruse. See The intruder
Monna Vanna. 1903.
Sutro, A., tr. MOSQ
La mort de Tintagiles. See The death of Tintagiles
Pelléas and Mélisande. See Pelléas et Mélisande
Pelléas et Mélisande. 1892. RHO
Hovey, R., tr. AUG, DIC, DIK1, HAV, SMN, TUCG, TUCM, TUCN, TUCO, WATI, WATL2, WATR, WHI
Variant title: Pelléas and Mélisande

MAGGI, CARLOS
The library. 1959.
Oliver, W., tr. OLIW

MAGNUSON, JIM
African Medea. 1968. NEWA4

MAIRET, JEAN DE, 1604-1686
Sophonisba. 1634.
Lockert, L., tr. LOCR

MALJEAN, JEAN RAYMOND
A message from cougar. 1967. NEWA2

MALLESON, MILES, 1888-1969
La malade imaginaire. See Molière, Jean Baptiste Poquelin. Le malade imaginaire (tr. and adapted by)
The misanthrope. See Molière, Jean Baptiste Poquelin. Le misanthrope (tr. and adapted by)
The miser. See Moliere, Jean Baptiste Poquelin. The miser (tr. and adapted by)
The prodigious snob. See Molière, Jean Baptiste Poquelin. Le bourgeois gentilhomme (tr. and adapted by)
School for wives. See Molière, Jean Baptiste Poquelin. L'école des femmes (tr. and adapted by)
Sganarelle. See Molière, Jean Baptiste Poquelin. Sganarelle (tr. and adapted by)
Tartuffe. See Molière, Jean Baptiste Poquelin. Tartuffe (tr. and adapted by)

-- and BROOKS, HARRY
Six men of Dorset. 1938. FAML

MALTZ, ALBERT, 1908-
Private Hicks. 1935? KOZ

MANCO, SILVERIO
Juan Moreira. 1886.
Fassett, J., tr. BIE

MANHOFF, BILL
The owl and the pussycat. 1964. GARV

MANKOWITZ, WOLF, 1924-
It should happen to a dog. THOD

MANN, HEINRICH, 1871-1950
Madame Legros. 1914.
Katzin, W., tr. KAT

MANNERS, JOHN HARTLEY, 1870-1928
Peg o' my heart. 1912. CEY

MANNING, MARY
Youth's the season...? 1931. CAN

MARASCO, ROBERT, 1936-
Child's play. 1970. BES69, RICI

MARCEAU, FELICIEN (pseud. of Louis Carrette), 1913-
The egg. 1957?
Schlitt, R., tr. and adapter BES61
Variant title: L'oeuf
L'oeuf. See The egg

MARCEL, GABRIEL, 1887-1973
Ariadne. 1936?
Heywood, R., tr. ULAN
Variant title: Le chemin de Crête
Le chemin de Crête. See Ariadne

MARCH, WILLIAM (pseud. of William Edward March Campbell), 1894-1954
The bad seed. See Anderson, Maxwell. The bad seed (based on the novel by)

MARC-MICHEL (pseud. of Marc Antoine Amédee Michel), 1812-1868. See Labiche, Eugène, jt. auth.

MARCUS, FRANK, 1928-
Formation dancers. 1964. PLAN28
The killing of Sister George. 1965. BES66, PLAN31
Mrs. Mouse are you within? 1968. PLAN35
Notes on a love affair. 1972. PLAN42
The window. RICJ

MARIVAUX, PIERRE CARLET DE CHAMBLAIN DE, 1688-1763
The false confessions. 1737.
Merwin, W., tr. BENR4
Variant title: Les fausses confidences
Les fausses confidences. See The false confessions
The game of love and chance. See Le jeu de l'amour et du hazard
Le jeu de l'amour et du hazard. 1730. BRE, SEA, STJ1, ZDA
Aldington, R., tr. ALD
Fowlie, W., tr. FOWL
Variant title: The game of love and chance

MARKS, MRS. L. S. See Peabody, Josephine Preston

MARLOWE, CHRISTOPHER, 1564-1593
Doctor Faustus. See The tragical history of Doctor Faustus
Edward II. See The troublesome reign and lamentable death of Edward the second
Faustus. See The tragical history of Doctor Faustus
The Jew of Malta. 1589? BROC, NEI, PAR, SPE, THA
The reign of King Edward the third (sometimes attributed to). See Anonymous plays. The reign of King Edward the third
Tamburlaine the great. 1587? BROC, HOW, HUST, SCW
Tamburlaine the great, pt. I. 1587? BALD, BAS, KRE, NEI, RYL, SCI, SCJ, SPE, TICO
The tragical history of Doctor Faustus. 1588? ABRB1, ASF, BALL, BARD, BAS, BAUG, BENY, BROC, BROK, CLF1, CLK1, COF, COJ, COL1, CONO, COTX, DEAN, DEAO, DOWN, DUN, FOUD, FREG, GARZAE, GREB1, GREC1, GRIF, HARC19, HAY, HEIL, HOW, HUD, KER, LIE, LIED1, LIEE1, LOCK,

LOCL, MACF, MACM1, MACN, MCA, MCNI, MIL, MONV, MOO, NEI, NES, OLH, OLI1, ORNT, PAR, RUB, SCH, SCI, SCJ, SCW, SHAH1, SHAHI1, SHAJ1, SMI, SNYD1, SPE, SPF1, STA, SWA, TOBI, TREB, TREC1, TREE1, TREI1, WAT, WEAT1, WINE, WOO1, WOOD1, WOOE1, WRIH
Variant titles: Doctor Faustus; The tragical history of the life and death of Doctor Faustus
The tragical history of the life and death of Doctor Faustus. See The tragical history of Doctor Faustus
The troublesome reign and lamentable death of Edward the second. 1592? ASH, BAS, BROC, CLKW, GARZAE, GRE, HARC46, MAT, NEI, OLH, OLI1, PAR, RUB, SCH, SCI, SCJ, SPE, TAT, TAU
Variant title: Edward II

MARNI, JEANNE, pseud. See Marnière, Jeanne Marie Françoise

MARNIERE, JEANNE MARIE FRANÇOIS (Jeanne Marni, pseud.), 1854-1910. See Guinon, Albert, jt. auth.

MAROWITZ, CHARLES
An Othello. 1972. MAOC

--See Burgess, John, jt. auth.

--See Burns, Alan, jt. auth.

MARQUAND, JOHN PHILLIPS, 1894-1960, and KAUFMAN, GEORGE S.
The late George Apley. 1944. BES44, COTE, COTH
Point of no return. See Osborn, Paul. Point of no return (adapted from the novel by)

MARQUES, RENE, 1919-
The fanlights. 1958.
Wiezell, R., tr. WOOG
Los soles truncos. See The fanlights
Variant title: Los soles truncos

MARQUINA, EDUARDO, 1879-
Cuando florezcan las rosales. See When the roses bloom again
When the roses bloom again. 1913.
Turrell, C., tr. TUR
Variant title: Cuando florezcan las rosales

MARQUIS, DON. See Marquis, Donald Robert Perry

MARQUIS, DONALD ROBERT PERRY, 1878-1937
The old soak. 1922. BES22

MARSHAK, SAMUIL IAKOLEVICH, 1887-1964
Twelve months. 1943?
Bakshy, A., tr. BAKS

MARSHALL, BRUCE, 1899-
Father Malachy's miracle. See Doherty, Brian. Father Malachy's miracle (based on the novel by)

MARSTON, JOHN, 1576-1634
The Dutch courtesan. 1603. WALL
The malcontent. 1604. BAS, BROC, GOM, HAPRA1, HAPRB1, LAWR, NEI, NES, SPE

MARSTON, JOHN WESTLAND, 1819-1890
The patrician's daughter. 1842. BAI

MARTENS, ANNE COULTER
Blue beads. 1938? LOVR

MARTIN, EDOUARD, 1828-1866. See Labiche, Eugène Marin, jt. auth.

MARTINEZ, JACINTO BENAVENTE Y. See Benavente y Martínez, Jacinto

MARTINEZ SIERRA, GREGORIO, 1881-1947, and MARTINEZ SIERRA, MARIA
Canción de cuna. See The cradle song
The cradle song. 1911. Underhill, J., tr. BES26, CEW, COTP, HAV
Variant title: Canción de cuna
The kingdom of God. 1916. Granville-Barker, H., and H., trs. BES28
Variant title: El reino de Dios
A lily among thorns. 1911. Granville-Barker, H., and H., trs. DIE
Variant title: Lirio entre espinas
Lirio entre espinas. See A lily among thorns
Los pastores. See The two shepherds
El reino de Dios. See The kingdom of God
The two shepherds. 1913. Granville-Barker, H., and H., trs. LEV, LEVE
Variant title: Los pastores

MARTINEZ SIERRA, MARIA, 1880-1947. See Martínez Sierra, Gregorio, jt. auth.

MARTYN, EDWARD, 1859-1923
Maeve. 1900. CAP

MARY, V. V.
A dialogue between a southern delegate, and his spouse, on his return from the grand Continental Congress (attributed to). See Anonymous plays. A dialogue, between a southern delegate, and his spouse, on his return from the grand Continental Congress

MASEFIELD, JOHN, 1878-1967
The tragedy of Pompey the great. 1910. MOSN, PLAP2

MASON, CLIFFORD
Gabriel. KINH

MASON, HARRY SILVERNALE
At the gate beautiful. 1925? FED2

MASON, WILTON. See McConald, Catherine, jt. auth.

MASSEY, EDWARD, 1893-1942
Plots and playwrights. 1917? BAK

MASSINGER, PHILIP, 1583-1640
The bondman. 1623. RUB
The city madam. 1632. PLAN28
The maid of honor. 1621? BAS
A new way to pay old debts. 1632. ANG, BAS, BAT13, BROC, DUN, GAY3, HARC47, HOW, KRE, LAWR, MAT, NEI, OLH, OLI2, ORNC, PAR, RUB, SCH, SCI, SCJ, SMO, SPE, TAV, WALL, WHE
The Roman actor. 1626. MCK
--See Fletcher, John, jt. auth.

MASTEROFF, JOE, 1919-
Cabaret (music by John Kander, lyrics by Fred Ebb). 1967. BES66
She loves me (based on a play by Miklos Laszlo; music by Jerry Bock, lyrics by Sheldon Harnick). 1963. BES62

MATHEUS, JOHN, 1887-
'Cruiter. 1926. LOC, HARY

MATHEW, RAY, 1929-
We find the bunyip. 1955. HANG

MATHEWS, CHARLES
Patter versus clatter. 1938. BOOA4

MATTO, JOSE MARIA RIVAROLA
The fate of Chipí Gonzálezo 1954.
Jones, W., tr. JONA
Variant title: El fin de Chipí Gonzáles
El fin de Chipí Gonzáles. See The fate of Chipí González

MATURIN, CHARLES ROBERT, 1780-1824
Bertram; or, The castle of St. Aldobrand. 1816. BAI

MAUGHAM, ROBIN, 1916-
Enemy. 1969. PLAN39

MAUGHAM, WILLIAM SOMERSET, 1874-1965
Before the party. See Ackland, Rodney. Before the party (based on a short story by)
The breadwinner. 1930. CHA, CHAN, CHAR
The circle. 1921. BES21, BROH, CEU, CLM, COT, COTH, DIG, DUR, HAVE, KRM, MAP, MCD, MOSG, MOSH, MYB, TREBA, TREC2, TREE2, TREI3, TREJ, TUCD, TUCM, WALB, WATF2, WATI, WATO, WEE
The colonel's lady. See Sherriff, Robert Cedric. The colonel's lady (based on the story by)
The constant wife. 1927. BES26, HAU, LOR, WARI, WARL
For services rendered. 1932. MOD
Jane. See Behrman, Samuel Nathaniel. Jane (based on the story by)
The letter. 1927. RICI, SAFM
Loaves and fishes. 1911. WEAL
Miss Thompson. See Colton, John and Randolph, Clemence. Rain (based on the story by)
Our betters. 1917. DID, MOSO, SALE, SMO, WHI
Sheppey. 1933. SIXH

MAUPASSANT, GUY DE, 1850-1893
The household peace. 1893. Chambers, W., tr. BAT9
Variant title: La paix du ménage
La paix du ménage. See The household peace

MAURETTE, MARCELLE
Anastasia. 1953?
Bolton, G., adapter. PLAN9, THEA55

MAUREY, MAX, 1868-1947
Rosalie. 1900. SET

MAURIAC, FRANÇOIS, 1885-1970
Asmodée. 1938.
Thurman, B., tr. HAYE

MAVOR, OSBORNE HENRY (JAMES BRIDIE, pseud.), 1888-1951
Tobias and the angel. 1930. PLAL1

MAY, ELAINE, 1932-
Adaptation. 1969. BES68

MAY, VAL
Sixty thousand nights (script and research by George Rowell, music by Julian Slade, lyrics by Julian Slade and George Rowell). 1966. PLAN31

MAYAKOVSKY, VLADIMIR VLADIMIROVICH, 1894-1930
The bathhouse. 1929?
MacAndrew, A., tr. GARZJ, MACE
The bedbug. 1929.
Hayward, M., tr. COTO, GLE, RUSV
Reeve, F., tr. REEV2
Mystery-bouffe. (Second variant). 1921.
Noyes, G., and Kaun, A., trs. NOY

MAYER, EDWIN JUSTUS, 1897-1960
Children of darkness. 1930. GARU, KRM
The firebrand. 1924. BES24

MAYNE, RUTHERFORD, pseud. See Waddell, Samuel

MAYOR, BEATRICE, 1886-1971
The pleasure garden. 1924. PLAP3

MEACHAM, MALCOLM
The snow goose. See Gallico, Paul. The snow goose (adapted by)

MEAD, SHEPHERD, 1914-
How to succeed in business without really trying. See Burrows, Abram S. How to succeed in business without really trying (based on the book by)

MEAKER, MRS. ISABELLA (JACKSON), 1874- . See Harnwell, Mrs. Anna Jane (Wilcox), jt. auth.

MEDNICK, MURRAY, 1939-
Willie the germ. 1968. SME

MEDOFF, MARK, 1940-
When you comin' back, Red Ryder? 1973. BES73

MEDWALL, HENRY, fl. 1486-1500?
Fulgens and Lucrece. See Fulgens and Lucres
Fulgens and Lucres. 1497? BOA, CRE, HAO (extracts)
Variant title: Fulgens and Lucrece
Nature. 1495? FARN

MEE, CHARLES L., JR.
Constantinople Smith. 1959? NEWA1

MEGRUE, ROI COOPER, 1883-1927
Under cover. 1914. CART

-- and HACKETT, WALTER
It pays to advertise. 1914. MOSJ, MOSK, MOSL

MELDON, MAURICE
Purple path to the poppy field. 1953. NEWW5

MELFI, LEONARD, 1935-
Birdbath. 1967. RICJ
Cinque. 1972. OWE

MELL, MAX, 1882-
The apostle play. 1934.
White, M., tr. SEVE

MELLON, EVELYN EMIG. See Emig, Evelyn

MELVILLE, ALAN (pseud. of Alan Caverhill), 1910-
Castle in the air. 1949. PLAN3
Dear Charles. 1952. PLAN8
Simon and Laura. 1954. PLAN11

MELVILLE, HERMAN, 1819-1891
Billy Budd. See Coxe, Louis O., and Chapman, Robert. Billy Budd (based on the novel by)

MENANDER, OF ATHENS, 342?-292? B.C.
The arbitration. 4th cent. B.C.
Allinson, F., tr. HOWE, HOWF

Casson, L., tr. CASU
Post, L., tr. OAT2, OATE
Variant title: Epitrepontes
Dyskolos. See The grouch
Epitrepontes. See The arbitration
The girl from Samos. 4th cent. B.C.
Casson, L., tr. CASU
Post, L., tr. OAT2
Variant titles: Samia; The woman of Samos
The grouch. 317 B.C.
Casson, L., tr. CASU
Variant title: Dyskolos
The perikeiromene. See The shearing of Glycera
Samia. See The girl from Samos
The shearing of Glycera. 4th cent. B.C.
Casson, L., tr. CASU
Post, L., tr. OAT2
Variant titles: The perikeiromene; She who was shorn
She who was shorn. See The shearing of Glycera
The woman of Samos. See The girl from Samos

MENDOZA, JUAN RUIZ DE ALARCON. See Ruiz de Alarcón y Mendoza, Juan

MENOTTI, GIAN-CARLO, 1911-
The saint of Bleecker Street. 1954. THEA55

MERCER, DAVID, 1928-
The governor's lady. 1965. RICJ

MERCIER, MARY
Johnny no-trump. 1967. SSTY

MERIMEE, PROSPER (Clara Gazul, pseud.), 1803-1870
Carmencita and the soldier (based on the opera Carmen, by Georges Bizet). See Lipskeroff, Konstantin. Carmencita and the soldier
Inez Mendo; or, The triumph of prejudice. 1825. BAT21

MERRILL, JAMES, 1926-
The bait. 1953. MACH
The immortal husband. 1955. PLAA

MESSAGER, CHARLES. See Vildrac, Charles, pseud.

METASTASIO, PIETRO ANTONIO DOMENICO BUONAVENTURA (pseud. of Pietro Trepassi), 1698-1782
Achilles in Scyros. 1800?
Hoole, J., tr. JOH
Attilo Rigolo. 1740. BIN
The dream of Scipio. 1800?
Hoole, J., tr. BAT5
Variant title: Il sogno di Scipione
Il sogno di Scipione. See The dream of Scipio

MICHAELS, SIDNEY, 1927-
Dylan. 1964. BES63
Tchin-Tchin (based on the play, Chin-Chin, by François Billetdoux). 1962. BES62

MICHEL, MARC ANTOINE AMEDEE. See Labiche, Eugène, jt. auth.

MICHENER, JAMES, 1907-
Tales of the South Pacific. See Hammerstein II, Oscar and Logan, Joshua. South Pacific (adapted from)

MICK, HETTIE LOUISE
The maid who wouldn't be proper. 1921? LAW

MIDDLEMASS, ROBERT M., 1883- . See Hall, Holworthy, jt. auth.

MIDDLETON, GEORGE, 1880-1967. See Bolton, Guy Reginald, jt. auth.

MIDDLETON, THOMAS, 1580-1627
A chaste maid in Cheapside. 1612? WALL

A game at chess. 1624. BROC
Michaelmas term. 1606? SCI, SCJ
A trick to catch the old one. 1608. BAS, LAWS, NEI, SPE
Women beware women. 1622. GOM, OLH, OLI2
--See Dekker, Thomas, jt. auth.

-- and ROWLEY, WILLIAM
The changeling. 1622. BAS, BROC, GOM, HAPRA2, HAPRB2, HUST, LAWR, NEI, OLH, OLI2, ORNT, SALG, SCH, SCI, SCJ, SPE, TAT, TAU, TAUJ, WINE
A fair quarrel. 1617? OLH, OLI2
The Spanish gipsie. 1623. GAY3

MIHURA, MIGUEL, 1906-
Three top hats. 1932. Wellwarth, G., tr. BENA
Variant title: Tres sombreros de copa
Tres sombreros de copa. See Three top hats

MILLAR, RONALD, 1919-
Abelard and Heloise. 1970. PLAN39
The affair. 1961. PLAJ2
Waiting for Gillian. 1954. PLAN10

MILLAY, EDNA ST. VINCENT, 1892-1950
Aria da capo. 1919. CHU, GASB, KRE
The king's henchman. 1927. TUCD
The lamp and the bell. 1921. SHAY

MILLER, ARTHUR, 1915-
After the fall. 1964. BES63
All my sons. 1947. BARO, BES46, BROH, CLKJ, GARW, GAVE, HATA, HEWE, MACF, MCA, SIXB, WEAN
The creation of the world and other business. 1972. BES72
The crucible. 1953. BAUL, BES52, COOP, DOT, GART, GARZA4, GARZF, GOLK, GUTH, GUTL, LOR, MIJY, MORV, MORW, MORX, SUL, TAUJ, TREA53, WATA
Variant title: Those familiar spirits
Death of a salesman. 1949. ALLK, AUG, BENU, BES48, BIER, BLOC, BRIX, BROX, BROY, CALQ, CEQA, COTX, FOUM, GARW, GARZA3, GAVE, HAVL, HUNT, MCNA, MCNB, NEWV, PERS, PERT, PERU, STEI, STJM, STJN, TREBA, TREC2, TREE3, TREI3, TREJ, TUCO, WARH, WARN, WATE, WISE, WISF
An enemy of the people. See Ibsen, Henrik. An enemy of the people (adapted by)
Incident at Vichy. 1964. BES64, MAO
The man who had all the luck. 1943. CROZ1
A memory of two Mondays. 1955. LIEF, SSTF
The price. 1968. BES67
Pussycat and the expert plumber who was a man. 194-? PROX
Those familiar spirits. See The crucible
A view from the bridge. 1956. BAIC, BES55, BRIT, CLM, CLN, COTKIR, COTQ, CUBH, DIT, DOWS, GART, HILP, HOGI, MOL, REIN, THEA56, ULAN

MILLER, CINCINNATUS HEINE, 1831-1913. See Miller, Joaquin, pseud.

MILLER, DANIEL, 1843-1909?
En gespräch zwischer zweb demokrate über politiks. 18-? BUFF
Noch eppes vom Peter seim handwerk. BUFF
Der Peter soil en handwerk lernen. 18-? BUFF

MILLER, JASON, 1952-
Lou Gehrig did not die of cancer. RICK
That champion season. 1972. BES71

MILLER, JOAQUIN (pseud. of Cincinnatus Hiner (or Heine) Miller), 1841-1913
The Danites in the Sierras. 1877. HAL, RAVA

MILLER, MAY
Graven images. 1929. HARY

MILLER, SIGMUND STEPHEN
One bright day. 1956. PLAN14

MILLS, HUGH
The little glass clock. 1954. PLAN11
The house by the lake. 1956. PLAN14

MILMAN, HENRY HART, 1791-1868
Belshazzar. 1822? KOH2
The fall of Jerusalem. 1820. KOH2

MILNE, ALAN ALEXANDER, 1882-1956
The boy comes home. 1918. SRY, SRYG
The Dover road. 1922. BES21, DIE, MOD, WATT2
The great Broxopp. 1923. CHU
The ivory door. 1927. TUCJ
Michael and Mary. 1929. BES29
Mr. Pim passes by. 1919. CALM, CEU, MCD, THF, WATF2, WATI
Success. 1923. COT, MYB
The truth about Blayds. 1921. MOSG, MOSH, TUCD, TUCM
The ugly duckling. (1941) BART

MILNER, ROGER, 1925-
How's the world treating you? 1965. PLAN30

MILNER, RONALD, 1938-
The warning--a theme for Linda. 1969. BLA
Who's got his own. 1966. KINH

MILTON, JOHN, 1608-1674
Comus. 1634. CLK1, HARC4, OLH, OLI2, PAR, RICH
Samson Agonistes. 1670? BARD, FREG, GREB1, GREC1, GRED, HAPT2, HARC4, KOH2, SML

MINNEY, RUBEIGH J., 1895- . See Lipscomb, William Percy, jt. auth.

MIRA DE AMESCUA, ANTONIO, fl. 1600
El esclavo del demonio. 1612. ALP

MIRBEAU, OCTAVE, 1850-1917
Les affaires sont les affaires. 1903. BER
Variant title: Business is business
Business is business. See Les affaires sont les affaires
The epidemic. 1898? Barzun, J., tr. BENS2
Variant title: L'epidémie
L'epidémie. See The epidemic

MIRZA FATH-ALI. See Fath'-Alī, Akhund-zadah

MIRZA FETH-ALI AKHOUD ZAIDE. See Fath'Alī, Akhund-zadah

"MR. PUNCH," pseud.

A dramatic sequel to Hamlet; or, The new wing at Elsinor. 19th cent. BAT22
A dramatic sequel to The lady of Lyons; or, In the Lyons den. 19th cent. BAT22
Omar and oh my! 19th cent. BAT21

"MR. S. MR. OF ART," pseud. See Stevenson, William

MITCHELL, JULIAN, 1935-
A heritage and its history. 1965. PLAN30

MITCHELL, LANGDON ELWYN, 1862-1935
Becky Sharp. 1899. AMP16
The New York idea. 1906. BENT4, BLAI2, GARX, HAL, MONR, MOSS3, QUIG, QUIJ, QUIK, QUIM, QUIN, WATC1

MITCHELL, LOFTEN, 1919-
Star of the morning. 1964. HARY, KINH

MITCHELL, THOMAS. See Dell, Floyd, jt. auth.

MITCHELL, YVONNE, 1925-
Here choose I. See The same sky
The same sky. 1951. PLAN6
Variant title: Here choose I

MITSON, RONALD
Beyond the bourn; or, The night time stood still. 1966? FRO
Variant title: The night time stood still
The night time stood still. See Beyond the bourn

MITTELHOLZER, EDGAR
Shadows move among them. See Hart, Moss. The climate of Eden (based on the novel by)

MIYAMASU, 16th century?
Eboshi-ori. See The hatmaker
The hatmaker. 16th cent. ?
Waley, A., tr. ANDF
Variant title: Eboshi-ori

MOELLER, PHILIP, 1880-1958
Helena's husband. 1915. BEAC12
Madame Sand. 1917. HAL, TUCD

MOINAUX, GEORGES, 1861-1929. See Courteline, George (pseud. of)

MOLIERE, JEAN BAPTISTE POQUELIN, 1622-1673
The affected young ladies. See Les précieuses ridicules
L'amour médecin. See Love is the best doctor
L'avare. See The miser
Le bourgeois gentilhomme. 1670. SCN
Anon. tr. GAUB
Baker, H., and Miller, J., trs. CLF2, MACL2, MACJ
Bishop, M., tr. BAUL
Malleson, M., tr. and adapter PLAN6
Porter, M., tr. LOCLA
Taylor, H., tr. SAFF
Wood, J., tr. WELT
Variant titles: The bourgeois gentleman; The cit turned gentleman; The prodigious snob; The would-be gentleman
The bourgeois gentleman. See Le bourgeois gentilhomme
The cit turned gentleman. See Le bourgeois gentilhomme
The doctor in spite of himself. 1666.
Anon. tr. COPB, INGW, KNIE, SHAR
Clark, B., tr. LEV,

LEVE
Van Laun, H., tr. SATI, WEAV2
Wall, C., tr. SMR
Variant titles: Le médecin malgré lui; The physician in spite of himself
Doctor's delight. See Le malade imaginaire
Dom Juan, ou les festin de Pierre. See Don Juan
Don John; or, The libertine. See Don Juan
Don Juan. 1665.
Calder, J., tr. LID
Frame, D., tr. BENSB1
Ozell, J., tr. and Mandel, O., adapter. MAN
Variant titles: Dom Juan, ou le festin de Pierre; Don John; or, The libertine; Don Juan; or, The stone guest; The libertine
Don Juan; or, The stone guest. See Don Juan
L'école de maris. 1661.
Anon. tr. BAT7
Variant title: School for husbands
L'école des femmes. 1662.
Malleson, M., tr. and adapter. PLAN10
Variant title: School for wives
Les femmes savantes. See The intellectual ladies
The forced marriage. 1664.
Bermel, A., tr. MIJE
Variant title: Le mariage forcé
Les fourberies de Scapin. See Scapin
The gay invalid. See Le malade imaginaire
The high-brow ladies. See Les précieuses ridicules
The hypochrondriac. See Le malade imaginaire
The hypocrite. See Le Tartuffe
The imaginary invalid. See La malade imaginaire
The imposter. See Le Tartuffe
The intellectual ladies. 1672.
Fowlie W., tr. FOWL
Variant title: Les femmes savantes
The libertine. See Don Juan
Love as a doctor. See Love is the best doctor
Love is the best doctor. 1665.
Van Laun, H., tr. RUSV
Variant titles: L'amour médecin; Love as a doctor
Le malade imaginaire. 1673.
Baker, H., and Miller, J., trs. LOGG
Bishop, M., tr. DEAR
Jackson, B., tr. and adapter. PLAN5
Malleson, M., tr. and adapter. PLAN19
Marmur, M., tr. BERM
Variant titles: Doctor's delight; The gay invalid; The hypochrondriac; The imaginary invalid; The robust invalid; The would-be invalid
Le mariage forcé. See The forced marriage
Le médecin malgré lui. See The doctor in spite of himself
Le misanthrope. 1666.
LYO, SER, STJ1
Anon. tr. BLON, CAR, CARA, CROV, EDAD, GRIF, HOUS
Baker, H., and Miller, J., trs. ROB
Bentley, G., tr. MIL
Bishop, M., tr. BUR, DOWS
Grebanier, D., tr. GREC1
Guth, H., tr. GUTH
Malleson, M., tr. and adapter. PLAN11
Page, C., tr. KRE, WALJ
Van Laun, H., tr. BUCK, BUCL, BUCM, DEAP, HIB, HIBA, HIBB, LOCM2,

TRE, TREA2, TREB, TREC1, TREE1, TREI1
Wall, C., tr. DRA1, PLAB1
Wilbur, R., tr. ABC, ADV, ALTE, BAIC, BARI, BARJ, BENR4, BENSB1, CONO, DIT, DOV, FEFL, GOLD, GOOD, HOUE, KERN, KERO, PERS, PERT, PERU, REIO, ROET, VON, WAIW, WEIS, WEIW
Variant title: The misanthrope

The misanthrope. See Le misanthrope

The miser. 1668.
Anon. tr. ASF, CROS, THO
Baker, H., and Miller, J., trs. ALT, BARU
Barnet, S., Berman M., and Burto, W., trs. BARB
Malleson, M., tr. and adapter. PLAN1
Parks, L., tr. ALLI, ALLJ, ALLK, BENU, HAVH, SOU
Sutherland, D., tr. COTKIR
Van Laun, H., tr. THOM, THON
Wall, C., tr. CLKW
Wood, J., tr. GOLH
Wormeley, K., tr. STA
Variant title: L'avare

The physician in spite of himself. See The doctor in spite of himself

Les précieuses ridicules. 1659. LYO, SER, SERD
Anon. tr. COOP, SEBO, SEBP
Gassner, J., tr. and adapter. GARZAP, GASS
Variant titles: The affected young ladies; The high-brow ladies; The pretentious ladies; The ridiculous précieuses

The pretentious ladies. See Les précieuses ridicules

The prodigious snob. See Le bourgeois gentilhomme

The ridiculous précieuses. See Les précieuses ridicules

The robust invalid. See Le malade imaginaire

Scapin. 1671.
Roth, M., tr. CASE
Variant title: Les fourberies de Scapin

School for husbands. See L'école de maris

School for wives. See L'école des femmes

Sganarelle. 1660.
Malleson, M., tr. and adapter. PLAN11
Sweetkind, M., tr. HOBI

Le Tartuffe; ou, L'imposteur. 1669. LYO, SER
Anon. tr. EVB2, SMO
Bishop, M., tr. VOLI
Brown, C., tr. EVC2
Hartle, R., tr. DOWN
Hogan, R., and Molin, S., trs. HOGA
Malleson, M., tr. and adapter. PLAN3
Page, C., tr. HARC26, HUD, MAU
Rosenberg, J., tr. CALD, COTKC, COTKI, SMA
Van Laun, H., tr. BUCK, BUCL, BUCM, EVA2, WEAV2
Waldinger, R., tr. REIN, SANE
Wall, C., tr. BLAG, GREA
Wilbur, R., tr. DEAS, HILP, JOHO, KINN, MACM2, MACN, REIL, SHRO, VANV2, WHFM
Wood, J., tr. BRIX
Variant titles: The hypocrite; The imposter; Tartuffe

Tartuffe. See Le Tartuffe

The would-be gentleman. See Le bourgeois gentilhomme

The would-be invalid. See Le malade imaginaire

MOLIN, S. E. See Hogan, R., jt. auth.

MOLINA, TIRSO DE, pseud. See Téllez, Gabriel

MOLINARO, URSELE
The abstract wife. 1961. NEWA2

MOLLOY, MICHAEL JOSEPH, 1917-
The king of Friday's men. 1948. PLAN2
The visiting house. 1946. HOGE

MOLNAR, FERENC, 1878-1952
Csendélet. See Still life
The daisy. See Liliom
Liliom. 1909.
Glazer, B., tr. BES20, CEW, DIE, DIK1, HAV, LEV, LEVE, MOSG, MOSH, STE, THF, TRE, TREA1, TREBA, TREC2, TREE2, TREI2, TUCG, TUCM, TUCN, TUCO, WHI
Variant titles: The daisy; The lily
The lily. See Liliom
The play in the castle. See The play's the thing
The play's the thing. 1926.
Wodehouse, P., tr. and adapter. BES26, COTKJ, GARZH
Variant title: The play in the castle
Still life. 1937.
Anon. tr. CHR
Variant title: Csendélet
The swan. 1914.
Baker, M., tr. BES23
Glazer, B., tr. CHA, CHAN

MONCRIEFF, WILLIAM THOMAS, 1794-1857
Giovanni in London; or, The libertine reclaimed. 1828. MAN
Variant title: The libertine reclaimed
The libertine reclaimed. See Giovanni in London

MONKHOUSE, ALLAN NOBLE, 1858-1936
The conquering hero. 1924. HAU
First blood. 1926. MOSO
The grand cham's diamond. 1924. BEAC10, COOK2, PROB
Variant title: The grand cham's necklace
The grand cham's necklace. See The grand cham's diamond
Mary Broome. 1911. PLAP2

MONSON, WILLIAM N.
The nihilist. 1971. BALLE8

MONTANO, SEVERINO
Sabina. 195-? EDAD

MONTELLANO, BERNARDO ORTIZ DE. See Ortiz de Montellano, Bernardo

MONTENOY, CHARLES PALISSOT DE. See Palissot de Montenoy, Charles

MONTHERLANT, HENRY MARIE JOSEPH MILLON DE, 1896-1972
Le cardinal d'Espagne. See The cardinal of Spain
The cardinal of Spain. 1969.
Griffin, J., tr. PLAN37
Variant title: Le cardinal d'Espagne
Le maître de Santiago. See The master of Santiago
The master of Santiago. 1947.
Griffin, J., tr. ULAN
Variant title: La maître de Santiago
Port-Royal. 1954.
Griffin, J., tr. HAYE
The queen after death. See La reine morte
La reine morte. 1942. PUCC
Griffin, J., tr. COTKW

Variant title: The queen after death

MONZAEMON CHIKAMATSU. See Chikamatsu

MOOCK, ARMANDO. See Moock Bousquet, Armando

MOOCK BOUSQUET, ARMANDO, 1894-1942
La serpeinte. 1920. ALPE

MOODY, WILLIAM VAUGHN, 1869-1910
The death of Eve. 1912? KRE
The faith healer. 1909. QUIG, QUIJ, QUIK, QUIL, QUIN
The great divide. 1906. BES99, DIC, DOWN, GARX, MONR
Variant title: A Sabine woman
A Sabine woman. See The great divide

MOORE, EDWARD, 1712-1757
The gamester. 1753. BOO

MOORE, EDWARD J., 1935-
The sea horse. 1974. BES73

MOORE, ELVIE A., 1942-
Angela is happening. 1971. RAVA

MORAL, JOSE ZORILLA Y. See Zorrilla y Moral, José

MORATIN, LEANDRO FERNANDEZ DE, 1760-1828
The girls acquiescence. See El sí de las niñas
El sí de las niñas. 1805. BRET
Davis, W., tr. FLOS
Variant titles: The girls' acquiescence; When a girl says yes
When a girl says yes. See El sí de las niñas

MORE, CHARLES C.
Die verrechelte rechler. See Barba, Preston Albert. Die verrechelte rechler (adapted from the novel by)
Es wasch Heller's Chrischtdag's zug. See Iobst, Clarence F. Es Heller's Chrischtdag (based on the story by)

MORE, HANNAH, 1745-1833
Belshazzar. 1782? KOH2
Daniel. 1782? KOH2
David and Goliath. 1782? KOH2
Moses in the bulrushes. 1782? KOH2

MORETO Y CABANA, AGUSTIN. See Moreto y Cavana, Agustín

MORETO Y CAVANA, AGUSTIN, 1618-1669
El desdén con el desdén. 1654. ALP
Variant titles: Donna Diana; Love's victory; or, The school for pride
Donna Diana. See El desdén con el desdén
Love's victory; or, The school for pride. See El desdén con el desdén

MORGAN, DIANA, 1913-
A house in the square. 1940. FIR

MORLEY, CHRISTOPHER DARLINGTON, 1890-1957
Good theatre. 1926? CHU
Really, my dear... 1928? WEE
Rehearsal. 1922? SHAY
Thursday evening. 1922? PEN
Wagon-lits. 1928? WEE

MORLEY, ROBERT, 1908- , and LANGLEY, NOEL
Edward, my son. 1948. BES48

MOROSS, JEROME, 1913-
The golden apple. See Latouche, John. The golden apple (music by)

MORRIS, MRS. ELIZABETH (WOODBRIDGE), 1870-
The crusade of the children. 1923? FED1

MORRIS, LLOYD, 1893-1954. See Van Druten, John, jt. auth.

MORSELLI, ERCOLE LUIGI, 1882-1921
Acqua sul fuoco. See Water upon fire
Il domatore Gastone. See Gastone the animal tamer
Gastone the animal tamer. 1923.
Goldberg, I., tr. GOL
Variant title: Il domatore Gastone
Water upon fire. 1920.
Goldberg, I., tr. GOL
Variant title: Aqua sul fuoco

MORTIMER, JOHN CLIFFORD, 1923-
Bermondsey. 1970. RICK
David and broccoli. 1960. CONB
The dock brief. 1957. LONG, PLAN17
What shall we tell Caroline? 1958. PLAN17

MORTIMER, LILLIAN, d. 1946
No mother to guide her. 1905. AMP8

MORTON, HUGH, pseud. See McClellan, C. M. S.

MORTON, JOHN MADDISON, 1811-1891
Box and Cox. 1847. BOOA4, THO

MORTON, THOMAS, 1764?-1838
Speed the plough. 1800. MOR, NIC

MORUM, WILLIAM. See Dinner, William, jt. auth.

MOSEL, TAD, 1922-
All the way home (based on A death in the family by James Agee). 1960. BES60, GARS

MOSER, GUSTAV VON, 1825-1903
Ultimo. See Daly, Augustin. The big bonanza (adapted from)

MOSS, ALFRED CHARLES and NEWHARD, ELWOOD L.
H. M. S. Pinafore; oder, Das maedle und ihr sailor kerl (based on the opera by W. S. Gilbert and Sir A. S. Sullivan). 1882. BUFF

MOSS, HOWARD
No strings attached. 1944? NEW44

MOTOKIYO, SEAMI. See Seami, Motokiyo

MOTOYASU, ZEMBO. See Zembō, Motoyasu

MOTTE FOUQUE, HENRI AUGUSTE, BARON DE LA, 1698-1774
Undine. See Giraudoux, Jean. Ondine. (from the novel by)

MOTTEUX, PETER ANTHONY, 1663-1718. See Ravenscroft, Edward, jt. auth.

MOTTLEY, JOHN, 1692-1750. See Jevon, Thomas, jt. auth.

MOWATT, MRS. ANNA CORA (OGDEN) RITCHIE. See Ritchie, Mrs. Anna Cora (Ogden) Mowatt

MOYES, P.
Time remembered. See Anouilh, Jean. Time re-

membered (tr. and adapted by)

MROZEK, SLAVOMIR, 1930-
The police. 1958.
Bethell, N., tr. SCNP
Variant title: Policja
Policja. See The police

MUKERJI, DHAN GOPEL, 1890-1936
The judgment of Indra. (1920) PATM, PATP

MULLER, ROMEO
The great git-away. 1966. BALLE3

MULVAY, TIMOTHY J.
Letter to Tuffy. 194-? PROI

MUNDAY, ANTHONY, 1553-1633
Sir John Oldcastle, pt. I (sometimes attributed to). See Anonymous plays. Sir John Oldcastle, pt. I
Sir Thomas More (sometimes attributed to). See Anonymous plays. Sir Thomas More

MUNFORD, ROBERT (COLONEL), 1730?-1784
The candidates; or, The humours of a Virginia election. (1798) MONR
Variant title: The humours of a Virginia election
The humours of a Virginia election. See The candidates
The patriots. 1778. PHI

MUNK, KAJ, 1898-1944
Egelykke. 1939.
Jones, L., tr. MODS
Herod the king. 1933.
Keigwin, R., tr. CONT
Variant title: En idealist
En idealist. See Herod the king
Niels Ebbesen. 1942.
Larsen, H., tr. SCAN2

MUNRO, CHARLES KIRKPATRICK, 1889-1973
At Mrs. Beam's. 1923. MAP, MOSO, PLAP3
The rumour. 1922. MYB

MURDOCH, FRANK HITCHCOCK, 1843-1872
Davy Crockett; or, Be sure you're right, then go ahead. 1872. AMP4, CLA

MURDOCH, IRIS, 1919- , and PRIESTLEY, JOHN BOYNTON
A severed head. 1963. PLAJ2.

MURPHY, ARTHUR, 1727-1805
All in the wrong. 1761. MOR
The upholsterer. 1758. BEVI
The way to keep him. 1760. BEVI, NIC

MURPHY, GRACE. See Lavery, Emmet, jt. auth.

MURRAY, ROBERT BRUCE
The good lieutenant. (1965) GARZAL

MURRAY, THOMAS C., 1873-1959
Birthright. 1910. CAP

MURRAY, WILLIAM
Diamond cut diamond. 1838. BOOA4

MUSSET, ALFRED DE, 1810-1857
Camille and Perdican.
Meyer, P., tr. WEAN
Les caprices de Marianne. 1851. BOR
Variant title: The follies of Marianne
The chandelier. 1847.
Chambers, W., tr. BAT9
A door should be either open or shut. 1848.
Barzun, J., tr. BENS3
Variant title: Il faut qu'une porte soit ouverte ou fermée
Fantasio. 1834.

Baring, M., tr. BENS1, BENT2, CLOU
The follies of Marianne. See Les caprices de Marianne
Il faut qu'une porte soit ouverte ou fermée. See A door should be either open or shut
Lorenzaccio. 1896.
Bruce, R., tr. BENT6
No trifling with love. See On ne badine pas avec l'amour
On ne badine pas avec l'amour. 1861. COM, GRA
Pellissier, R., tr. TREB, TREC1, TREE1, TREI1
Variant title: No trifling with love

MYGATT, TRACY DICKINSON
The sword of the Samurai. 1925? FED2

MYRTLE, FREDERICK S.
Gold. 1916. BOH3

N

NABBES, THOMAS, 1605-1646
Covent Garden. 1632-3? BUL3
Hannibal and Scipio. 1635. BUL3
Tottenham Court. 1633. BUL3

NAGLE, URBAN, BROTHER, 1905-1965
Savonarola, the flame of Florence. 1941. THEC

NAHARRO, BARTHOLOME TORRES DE. See Torres de Naharro, Bartholomé de

NAJAC, EMILE DE, 1828-1889. See Sardou, Victorien, jt. auth.

NAMIKI GOHEI III, 1789-1855
Kanjinchō. See The subscription list
The subscription list. 1840.
Scott, A., tr. ANDF, ASF
Variant titles: Kanjinchō; The subscription scroll
The subscription scroll. See The subscription list

NASH, N. RICHARD, 1916-
The rainmaker. 1954. CORB

NEILSON, KEITH
The end of the world; or, Fragments from a work in progress. 1968. BALLE6
Variant title: Fragments From a work in progress
Fragments from a work in progress. See The end of the world

NEMIROVICH-DANCHENKO, VLADIMIR IVANOVICH, 1848-1936
The brothers Karamazoff (based on the novel by Fedor Dostoevskii). 1922?
Covan, J., tr. MOSA
Love and death, featuring "Aleko," by Rachmaninoff (based on the story by Aleksandr Pushkin). 1891.
Seldes, G. and G., trs. PLAH

NEUMANN, ALFRED, 1895-1952
The patriot. See Dukes, Ashley. Such men are dangerous (adapted from)

NEVEUX, GEORGES, 1900-
Juliett ou la clé des songes. (1930) PRO

NEWHARD, ELWOOD L. See Moss, Alfred Charles, jt. auth.

NEWLEY, ANTHONY, 1931- . See Bricusse, Leslie, jt. auth.

NEWMAN, DAVID, 1937- , and BENTON, ROBERT
"It's a bird, it's a plane, it's superman" (music by Charles Strouse, lyrics by Lee Adams). 1966. BES65

NEWSPAPER, STAFF OF THE

LIVING. See Staff of the Living Newspaper

NICCODEMI, DARIO, 1877-1934
The poet.
Rietty, R., tr. ALLE
Variant title: Il poeta
Il poeta. See The poet

NICHOLS, ANNE, 1891-1966
Abie's Irish rose. 1922. CEY

NICHOLS, DUDLEY
The informer. See O'Flaherty, Liam. The informer (adapted by)

NICHOLS, PETER, 1927-
A day in the death of Joe Egg. 1968. BES67

NICHOLS, ROBERT MALISE BOYER, 1893-1944, and BROWNE, MAURICE
Wings over Europe. 1928. BES28, CHU, MCCG, MOSG, MOSH

NIGGLI, JOSEFINA, 1909?-
Singing valley. 1936. PAJ
The ring of General Macías. BRNB
This bull ate nutmeg. 1937? GALB

NIRDLINGER, CHARLES FREDERIC, 1863-1940
The world and his life. See Echegaray y Eizaguirre, José. The great Galeoto (tr. and adapted by)

NIVELLE DE LA CHAUSSEE, PIERRE CLAUDE. See La Chaussée, Pierre Claude Nivelle de

NIVOIX, PAUL. See Pagnol, Marcel, jt. auth.

NKOSI, LEWIS, 1936-
The rhythm of violence. (1964) GREJ, LITT, WELT

NOAH, MORDECAI MANUEL, 1785-1851
She would be a soldier; or, The plains of Chippewa. 1819. MONR, MOSS1

NOBUMITSU, KANZE KOJIRO. See Kanze Kojiro Nobumitsu

NOBUMORI, SUGIMORI. See Chikamatsu

NORTON, THOMAS, 1532-1584. See Sackville, Thomas, jt. auth.

NO SAYEMON, ENAMAI. See Enamai No Sayemon

NUGENT, ELLIOTT, 1900-1965. See Thurber, James, jt. auth.

NUNEZ DE ARCE, GASPAR, 1834-1903
The face of wood. See El haz de leña
El haz de leña. 1872. BRET
Variant title: The face of wood

O

OBEY, ANDRE, 1892-
Noah. 1931.
Wilmurt, A., tr. and adapter. GARZH
Venus and Adonis. 1932?
Becker, W., tr. BENS2

O'BRIEN, EDNA
A cheap bunch of nice flowers. 1962. PLAN26

O'BRIEN, J.
Caligula. See Camus, Albert. Caligula (adapted by).

O'BRIEN, LIAM
The remarkable Mr. Pennypacker. 1953. THEA54

O'CASEY, SEAN, 1884-1964
Bedtime story. 1951. BRIU

Cock-a-doodle dandy. 1949. BENT5, BLOC, COTM
The end of the beginning. 1939. FREI, STAV, SUT4
Hall of healing. THOD
Juno and the paycock. 1925. ALLI, ALLJ, ALLK, BARR, BLOC, CAP, CLM, CLN, COT, CUBE, CUBG, DIE, DUR, FIG, HAVG, KRM, SNYD2, WARI, WARL, WATF2, WATI, WHI
Nannie's night out. 1924. RICJ
The plough and the stars. 1926. BES27, BARU, COTQ, HOGA, TREBA, TREC2, TREE3, TREI3, TREJ, TUCN, TUCO, WORP
Purple dust. 1953. BARF, COTK, ULAN, WATA
Red roses for me. 1943. MORT, SIXB
The shadow of a gunman. 1923. MERC
The silver tassie. 1929. COTM

O'CONNELL, LOUISE
Donalds O'Rourk. DRU

O'CONNOR, FRANK. See O'Donovan, Michael (pseud. of)

O'CONOR, JOSEPH, 1916-
The iron harp. 1955. BES56, BROT

ODETS, CLIFFORD, 1906-1963
Awake and sing. 1935. BES34, BLOC, CER, CLOR, COK, FAMI, GARU, GARZA2, GRIF, HAT, MOSL, TREA1
The big knife. 1954. FAMO
The country girl. 1950. BES50, CLM, CLN
Variant title: A winter journey
The flowering peach. 1954. BES54
Golden boy. 1937. BES37, FAML, GARZA2, GAS, MERT, MOSH, TREBA, TREC2, TREE3, TREI3
Rocket to the moon. 1938. BES38
Till the day I die. 1935. FAMJ
Waiting for Lefty. 1935. CASS, CET, DUR, GREG, HIL, KOZ, SUTL, WARH
A winter journey. See The country girl

O'DONOVAN, JOHN, 1921-
Copperfaced Jack. 1963. HOGE

O'DONOVAN, MICHAEL (Frank O'Connor, pseud.), 1903-
In the train. 1937. BARF

OFFENBACH, JACQUES, 1819-1880
La périchole. 1868. Seldes, G. and G., trs. PLAM
Variant title: Singing birds
Singing birds. See La périchole

O'FLAHERTY, LIAM, 1897-
The informer (adapted by Dudley Nichols). 1935. HAU, HAVD

OGDEN, ANNA CORA. See Ritchie, Mrs. Anna Cora (Ogden) Mowatt

OGUNYEMI, WALE, 1939-
The scheme. THTN

O'HARA, FRANK, 1926-1966
The general returns from one place to another. 1964. ORZ
Try! Try! 1953. MACH

OHNET, GEORGES, 1848-1918
The forge master. See The iron manufacturer
The iron manufacturer. 1883. Leslie, G., tr. BAT9
Variant titles: The forge

master; The iron master; Le maître de forges
The iron master. See The iron manufacturer
Le maître de forges. See The iron manufacturer

O'KEEFE, JOHN
Chamber piece. 1972. BALLE11

OLDENBURG, CLAES, 1929-
Fotodeath. 1961. HILP

OLESHA, YURI, 1899-1960
A list of assets. 1931? MacAndrew, A., tr. GARZJ, MACE

OLIANSKY, JOEL, 1935-
Here comes Santa Claus! 1962. GASY

OLMO, LAURO
The news item. 1963. Wellwarth, M., tr. BENA

O'MORRISON, KEVIN
The long war. 1966. BALLE4

O'NEILL, EUGENE GLADSTONE, 1888-1953
Ah, wilderness! 1933. BES33, CET, DAVK, HAVG, HIL, HOLM, JAFF, WATA
All God's chillun got wings. 1925. RAVA
Anna Christie. 1921. ASH, BES21, BLAG, CASS, CHAN, CHAP, CORD, CORE, CORF, COTE, COTH, CUBG, RICL2, TRE, TREA1, TREBA, TREC2, TREE3, TREI3
Before breakfast. 1916. SHAY
Beyond the horizon. 1920. BES19, CORB, CORD, CORE, CORF, FULT, GORDP, HAPD, HAT, HAVD, HAVE, LOOA, LOOB, LOOC, LOOD, LOOE, LOOF, MILL, QUIG, QUIK, QUIL, QUIM, QUIN, ROB, WHK
Bound east for Cardiff. 1916. BLAH, CONP, GPA, NELS, SAND
Desire under the elms. 1924. ALLK, ALT, ALTE, BAC, BARC, BES24, BONB, BONC, BOW, CAPU, COTQ, CUBH, FREG, GARZA1, GASB, GOOR, HAVH, HOWP2, LIEF, MCCP, MIJY, MOSG, MOSH, RAY2, SANP, SCNT, SEN, SSSF, VOLI, VOLP, WALJ, WARL, WEIM, WEIS, WHFM
Diff'rent. 1920. COT
The dreamy kid. 1919. LOC
The Emperor Jones. 1920. BES20, BLOC, BROX, CHU, CLK2, COJ, CUBE, DEAP, DIE, DOWN, ELLK, FOUK, FOUM, HARB, HAVL, HATA, HUBA2, HUD, HUTC, LOC, LOCK, MCCA, MCCB, MCCD, MCCF, MCCG, MCD, MIJA1, MOSJ, MOSK, MOSL, QUI, REIL, SCWG, SIXC, TUCJ, UNTE2, WAR, WATC1, WATI, WORP
The great god Brown. 1926. BES25, DUR, HAL, POCH2, STE, STEI, TAUJ, TUCD, TUCM, TUCN, TUCO
The hairy ape. 1922. AND, ANDE, BLAI2, BLAJ, BLON, BLOO, BROU, CLDP, CLKW, DAV1, DIG, DOWM, FUL, GARZA1, GASB, HARA, HIB, HIBA, HIBB, LEVI, MIL, RAI, SHA2, STL4, TREBA, TREC2, TREE3, TREI3, TREJ, WAIT, WAIU, WALB, WATC2, WATO, WHI
Hughie. 1958. CASE, GARV, GOLH
The iceman cometh. 1946. BES46, BLOC, CEQA, COK, GARW, MIKE2
"Ile." 1916. BEC12, GASB,

KNIC, KNID, KNIE, PEN, SUT3
In the zone. 1917. BROW, BUR, CARL, GRED, HAP, MIJB, THO, WAGC2
Lazarus laughed. 1928. NELS, OXF, QUIO2
Long day's journey into night. 1956. BES56
The long voyage home. 1919. ASF, CARA, COOP, LOCL, LOCLA, LOCLB, RAY2, ULAN
Marco millions. 1928. CHA, HUB, HUDS2, HUDT
A moon for the misbegotten. 1947. BES56, GART, LOR, TREJ
The moon of the Caribbees. 1918. LEV, LEVE, LOO, MACG
Mourning becomes Electra. 1931. BES31, WARH
The rope. 1919. ELLI2
Strange interlude. 1928. BES27, CORD, CORE, CORF, THF
A touch of the poet. 1957. BES58, COX, GARS
Where the cross is made. 1918. BENP, COD, ING, INGA, PROW, SCWE, TOD

OPPENHEIMER, JOEL, 1930-
The great American desert. 1961. ORZ

OPPER, DON KEITH, and The COMPANY THEATRE ENSEMBLE
Children of the kingdom (script by Don Keith Opper). 1970. BALLE9

ORRERY, ROGER BOYLE, 1st earl of, 1621-1679
The tragedy of Mustapha, the son of Solyman the magnificent. 1665. DOA

ORTIZ DE MONTELLANO, BERNARDO, 1899-
Salome's head. 1944? Mallan, L., tr. NEW44

ORTON, JOE, 1933-1967
Entertaining Mr. Sloane. 1964. CALD, NEWE8
Loot. 1966. NEWE13
What the butler saw. 1970. BES69

OSBORN, PAUL, 1901-
A bell for Adano (based on the novel by John Hersey). 1944. BES44
The innocent voyage (based on the novel A high wind in Jamaica by Richard Hughes). 1943. BES43
Morning's at seven. 1939. BES39, GARU, KRM
On borrowed time (based on the novel by Lawrence E. Watkin). 1938. BES37, GARU, GARZA2, GOW, GOWA
Point of no return (adapted from the novel by John P. Marquand). 1950. BES51, WAGC3

OSBORNE, JOHN, 1929-
The entertainer. 1957. BES44, TAUJ
Inadmissable evidence. 1964. BES65, COTT
Look back in anger. 1956. BES57, BLOC, CEQA, COK
Luther. 1961. BES63, DIT
A subject of scandal and concern. 1960. BARU, RICJ

-- and CREIGHTON, ANTHONY
Epitaph for George Dillon. 1958. BES58, NEWE2, TREJ

OSBORNE, MARIAN
The point of view. 1923. MAS1

OSGOOD, PHILLIPS ENDECOTT, 1882-1956
A sinner beloved. 192-? FED1

OSTROVSKII, ALEKSANDR NIKOLAEVICH, 1823-1886

The diary of a scoundrel. 1868.
Ackland, R., tr. BENT2
Kasherman, P., tr. MOSA
Variant titles: Enough stupidity in every wise man; Even a wise man stumbles
A domestic picture. 18-?
Voynich, E., tr. COUR
Easy money. 1870?
Magarshack, D., tr. BENS2
Variant title: Fairy gold
Enough stupidity in every wise man. See The diary of a scoundrel
Even a wise man stumbles. See The diary of a scoundrel
Fairy gold. See Easy money
The poor bride. 1852.
Seymour, J., and Noyes, G., trs. NOY
The storm. See The thunderstorm
Thunder. See The thunderstorm
The thunderstorm. 1880.
Cooper, J., tr. COOPA
MacAndrew, A., tr. GARZE, MACD, TREB
Magarshack, D., tr. MAGA
Reeve, F., tr. REEV1
Whyte, F., and Noyes, G., trs. CLF2
Variant titles: The storm; Thunder

OSTROVSKY, ALEKSANDER. See Ostrovskiĭ, Akelsandr Nikolaevich

OTIS, MERCY. See Warren, Mrs. Mercy (Otis)

OTWAY, THOMAS, 1652-1685
Venice preserv'd; or, A plot discover'd. 1682. DOB, GOS, GOSA, MAT, MCM, MCMI, MEN, MOR, MOSE1, NET, REST, RUB, STM, TAT, TAU, TICK, TUP, TUQ, TWE, WILS

OU-HUNG, WONG, and CHIA AH
The red lantern.
Hsein-yi and Yang, G., tr. MESE
Snow, L., tr. SNO

OULESS, E. U.
Our pageant. 1926? THU

OULTON, BRIAN, 1908-
Mr. Sydney Smith coming upstairs. 1972. PLAN42

OWEN, ALUN DAVIES, 1926-
Male of the species. 1969. RICK
Progress to the park. 1961. NEWE5

OWENS, ROCHELLE, 1936-
Futz. 1967. NEWA2
He wants shih. (1972) OWE

OYAMO
His first step. 1972. NEWL

OYONO, FERDINAND
Houseboy. PIET

P

PAGNOL, MARCEL, 1899-1974
Marius, Fanny and César. See Behrman, Samuel Nathaniel and Logan, Joshua. Fanny (based on the trilogy by)

-- and NIVOIX, PAUL
Les marchands de gloire. 1925. GRAF

PAILLERON, EDOUARD JULES HENRI, 1834-1899
The art of being bored. See Le mond où l'on s'ennuie
The cult of boredom. See Le monde où l'on s'ennuie
Le monde où l'on s'ennuie. 1881. BOR, BOV
Variant titles: The art of being bored; The cult of

boredom; This bored world; The world of boredom
This bored world. See Le monde où l'on s'ennuie
The world of boredom. See Le monde où l'on s'ennuie

PAKINGTON, MARY AUGUSTA, 1878-
The queen of hearts. 1926? THU

PALARCA, JULIA
Other tomorrows. 195-? EDAD

PALISSOT DE MONTENOY, CHARLES, 1730-1814
Les philosophes. 1760. BRE

PALMER, T. A.
East Lynne. 1874. ASG

PARKER, DOROTHY (ROTHSCHILD), 1893-1967
Candide. See Hellman, Lillian. Candide (lyrics by)

PARKER, LOUIS NAPOLEON, 1852-1944
Disraeli. 1911. BES09
A minuet. 1915. CAR

PARKHOUSE, HANNAH. See Cowley, Mrs. Hannah (Parkhouse)

PASSEUR, STEVE, 1899-1966
L'acheteuse. See A measure of cruelty
A measure of cruelty. 1930. Mitchell, Y., tr. PLAN29
Variant title: L'acheteuse

PATON, ALAN, 1903-
Cry, the beloved country. See Anderson, Maxwell and Weill, Kurt. Lost in the stars (based on the novel by)

PATRICK, JOHN, 1907-
The hasty heart. 1945. BES44, GARZ
The story of Mary Surratt. 1947. BES46
Variant title: This gentle ghost
The teahouse of the August moon (based on the novel by Vern Sneider). 1953. BES53, CORB, GARU, GARZA4, GAVE, THEA54
This gentle ghost. See The story of Mary Surratt

PATRICK, ROBERT, 1937-
The golden circle. 1969. NEWA3

PATTERSON, CHARLES, 1941-
Black ice. (1968) JON

PAU-HUA, CHANG, and YI-PING, C.
Yesterday. Shapiro, S., tr. MESE

PAUL, MRS. CLIFFORD
The fugitive king. 1926? THU

PAULDING, JAMES KIRKE, 1778-1860
The bucktails; or, Americans in England. 1947. HAL

PAWLEY, THOMAS, 1917-
The tumult and the shouting. 1969. HARY

PAYNE, JOHN HOWARD, 1791-1852
The black man; or, The spleen. 181-? AMP6
The boarding schools; or, Life among the little folks. 1841? AMP5
Brutus; or, The fall of Tarquin. 1818. GRE, MOSS
The Italian bride. 1832? AMP6
The last duel in Spain (adapted from El postrer duelo de España, by Calderón de la Barca). 1822? AMP6
Mazeppa; or, The wild horse of Tartary (adapted from Mazeppa, by Léopold Chandezon and Jean Cuvilier de

Trye). 1825? AMP5
Mount Savage (adapted from Le mont sauvage, by René Pixérécourt). 1822. AMP5
Romulus, the shepherd king. 1839? AMP6
The Spanish husband; or, First and last love. 1830. AMP5
Thérèse, the orphan of Geneva. 1821. BAT19
Trial without jury; or, The magpie and the maid (adapted from La pie voleuse, by Louis Caigniez and Jean Marie Théodore Baudoin). 1815? AMP5
The two sons-in-law (adapted from Les deux gendres, by Charles Etienne). 1824? AMP5
Woman's revenge. 1832. AMP6

-- and IRVING, WASHINGTON
Charles the second; or, The merry monarch (adapted from the book, La jeunesse de Henri V, by Alexandre Duval). 1824. GARX, QUIJ, QUIK, QUIL, QUIM, QUIN, TAFT

PEABODY, JOSEPHINE PRESTON (MRS. L. S. MARKS), 1874-1922
The piper. 1910. BRIK, DID, MOSJ, MOSK, MOSL

PEACOCK, MRS. BARBARA (BURNHAM). See Burnham, Barbara

PEACOCK, JOHN
Children of the wolf. 1971. PLAN40

PEACOCK, THOMAS LOVE, 1785-1866
Nightmare abbey. See Sharp, Anthony. Nightmare abbey (adapted from the frolic by)

PEARSE, PADRIAC, 1880-1916
The singer. 1915. CAP

PECHANTRE, 1638?-1709
Geta. 1687.
Lockert, L., tr. LOCU

PECHANTRES. See Péchantré

PEELE, GEORGE, 1558?-1597?
The arraignment of Paris. 1584? BAS, BROC, NES
David and Bethsabe. 1593. MIN1, MIO1
The lamentable tragedy of Locrine (sometimes attributed to). See Anonymous plays. The lamentable tragedy of Locrine
The old wives' tale. 1593? BAS, BROC, GAY1, MCI, MIN2, MIO2, NEI, NES, OLH, OLI1, PAR, PARR, RUB, SCI, SCJ, SCW

PELUSO, EMANUEL
Good day. 1965. OFF
Little fears. 1967? OFF
Moby tick. 1970. NEWA4

PERELMAN, SIDNEY JOSEPH, 1904-
The beauty part. 1962. SSTY

PEREZ DE SAAVEDRA RIVAS, ANGEL. See Rivas, Angel Pérez de Saavedra

PEREZ GALDOS, BENITO, 1845-1920
La de San Quintín. 1894. BRET
Hayden, P., tr. CLDM
Variant title: The duchess of San Quentin
The duchess of San Quentin. See La de San Quintín
Electra. 1901.
Anon. tr. BUCK
Turrell, C., tr. TUCG, TUR
Variant title: The nun and the barbarian
The nun and the barbarian. See Electra

PERTWEE, MICHAEL. See Pertwee, Roland, jt. auth.

PERTWEE, ROLAND, 1885-1963
Heat wave. 1929. FIT

-- and PERTWEE, MICHAEL
The paragon. 1948. PLAN1

PERYALIS, NOTIS
Masks of angels. 195-?
Finer, L., tr. COTR

PESHKEV, ALEXEI MAXIMOVITCH. See Pîeskov, Aleksîeĭ Maksimovich

PETERS, PAUL
Nat Turner. 1940. CROZ1

PETERSON, LOUIS STAMFORD, 1922-
Take a giant step. 1953.
BES53, FORD, HARY, PATR, TUQT

PHILLIPS, STEPHEN, 1868-1915
Paolo and Francesca. 1902.
DIG, SMN

PHILLIPS, WATTS, 1825-1874
Lost in London. 1867? BOOB

PICARD, LOUIS BENOIT, 1769-1828
The rebound. See Les ricochets
Les ricochets. 1807. BOR
Variant title: The rebound

PICASSO, PABLO, 1881-1974
Le désir attrapé par la queue. See Desire trapped by the tail
Desire trapped by the tail. 195-?
Briffault, H., tr. NEWW2
Variant title: Le désir attrapé la queue

PIESHKOV, ALEXEI. See Pîeskov, Aleksîeĭ Maksimovich

PIESKOV, ALEKSIEI MAKSIMOVICH, 1868-1926. See Gorki, Maxim, pseud.

PIETRO TREPASSI. See Metastasio, Pietro Antonio Domenico Buonaventura, pseud.

PILLOT, EUGENE
My lady dreams. 1922?
SHAY
Two crooks and a lady.
1917. COOK3

PILLOT, JOSEPH EUGENE. See Pillot, Eugene

PINERO, SIR ARTHUR WING, 1865-1934
The gay Lord Quex. 1899.
MOSN, MOSO, SMO
Iris. 1901. COT
The magistrate. 1885.
BENS3, BOOA4, PLAN38, SMR
Mid-channel. 1909. HAU, SMI, WATF1, WATI, WEAL, WHI
The notorious Mrs. Ebbsmith. 1895. BAI
The second Mrs. Tanqueray.
1893. ASG, BENY, BOOA2, BOWY, CEU, CLK2, COF, COTKF, DIC, DUR, FULT, HUD, MAT, ROWC, SALE, STE, TAU, WATT2
The thunder-bolt. 1908.
CHA, CHAN, CHAR, TUCD, TUCM, TUCN, TUCO
Trelawny of the "Wells."
1898. BES94, MAP
--See also Woods, Aubrey... Trelawny (based on)

PIÑERO, MIGUEL, 1946-
Short eyes. 1974. BES73

PINGET, ROBERT, 1919-
Architruc. 1961.
Benedikt, M., tr. BEN
La manivelle. See The old

tune
The old tune. 1962.
Beckett, S., tr. GOOR
Variant title: La manivelle

PINNER, DAVID, 1940-
Dickon. 1966. NEWE10
The drums of snow. NEWE13, PLAN42

PINSKI, DAVID, 1872-1959
King David and his wives. 1923.
Landis, J., tr. LAO, LAOG

PINTER, HAROLD, 1930-
The birthday party. 1958. SEVD
The black and white. THOD
The caretaker. 1960. BES61, POP
The collection. 1962. BES62
The dumbwaiter. 1960. COK, NEWE3, SOU
The homecoming. 1965. BES66
Last to go. THOD
A night out. 1960. CONB
A slight ache. 1961. TREJ
Trouble in the works. 1959. GLI

PIRANDELLO, LUIGI, 1867-1936
And that's the truth. See Right you are! If you think so
As you desire me. 1931.
Alba, M., tr. GARZH
Putnam, S., tr. HAV
Variant title: Come tu mi vuoi
Bellavita.
Murray, W., tr. RICJ
Ciascuno a suo modo. See Each in his own way
Come tu mi vuoi. See As you desire me
Cosi è se vi pare! See Right you are! If you think so
Each in his own way. 1924.
Livingston, A., tr. CHA, CHAN
Variant title: Ciascuno a suo modo
The emperor. See Henry IV
Enrico IV. See Henry IV
La giara. See The jar
Henry IV. 1922.
Bentley, E., tr. BENSA, COTQ
Caputi, A., tr. CAPU
Storer, E., tr. BARJ, BLOC, DOT, DOV, FREG, JOHN, MACN, SANE, ULAN, WATA, WATI, WATL4, WELT
Variant titles: The emperor; Enrico IV; The living mask; The mock emperor
The jar. 1917.
Anon. tr. CHR
Livingston, A., tr. HIBB
May, F., tr. ALLE
Variant title: La giara
The living mask. See Henry IV
Lumie di Sicilia. See Sicilian limes
The mock emperor. See Henry IV
Naked. 1922.
Livingston, A., tr. CLKW, DIE
Variant title: Vestire gl'ignudi
Our lord of the ships. 1925.
Anon. tr. MCCP
Variant title: La sagra del signore della nave
Il placere dell'onestà. See The pleasure of honesty
The pleasure of honesty. 1917.
Murray, W., tr. COTN
Variant title: Il placere dell'onestà
Questa sera si recita a soggetto. See Tonight we improvise
Right you are! If you think so. 1918.
Bentley, E., tr. BENSB2
Livingston, A., tr. ALT, ALTE, MOSG, MOSH
Variant titles: And that's the truth; Cosi è se vi

pare!; It is so (if you think so)
La sagra del signore della nave. See Our lord of the ships
Sei personaggi in cerca d'autore. See Six characters in search of an author
Sicilian limes. 1910.
Goldberg, I., tr. GOL
Variant title: Lumie di Sicilia
Six characters in search of an author. 1921.
Anon. tr. ALLK, MCNB
Bentley, E., tr. BENSB2
May, F., tr. STY
Mayer, P., tr. COTN, COTQ
Storer, E., tr. ASF, AUG, BAIC, BAIE, BARR, CEW, DEAS, DIK2, DIT, DIV, DOWS, GOLD, HAVL, KERP, KINN, REIO, REIP, REIT, SEN, TRE, TREA1, TREBA, TREC2, TREE2, TREI2, TREJ, TRI, TRIA, VON, WAIW, WEIM, WEIS, WEIW, WHFM, WHI
Variant title: Sei personaggi in cerca d'autore
Such is life. (1925)
Duplaix, L., tr. VANV2
Variant title: La vita che ti diedi
Tonight we improvise. 1930.
Abba, M., tr. WEAN
Variant title: Questa sera si recita a soggetto
Vestire gl'ignudi. See Naked
La vita che ti diedi. See Such is life

PISEMSKII, ALEKSIEI FEOFILAKTOVICH, 1820-1881
A bitter fate. 1859.
Kagan, A., and Noyes, G., trs. NOY
Variant titles: Cruel fate; A hard fate
Cruel fate. See A bitter fate
A hard fate. See A bitter fate

PITCHER, OLIVER, 1924?-
The one. (1971) KINH

PIXERECOURT, RENE CHARLES GUILBERT DE, 1773-1844
Coelina; ou, L'enfant du mystère. 1800. BOR
Le mont sauvage; ou, Le solitaire. See Payne, John Howard. Mount Savage (adapted from)

PIXLEY, FRANK, 1865-1919
Apollo. 1915. BOH3

PLAUTIUS, TITUS MACCIUS, 254?-184? B.C.
Amphitryon. 186? B.C.
Anon. tr. BAT21
Alison, R., tr. DUC1
Cassoon, L., tr. ALTE
Sugden, E., tr. LOCM1
Variant title: Jupiter in disguise
Asinaria. See The comedy of asses
Aulularia. 194? B.C.
Alison, R., tr. DUC1
Bennett, C., tr. CLKW
Nixon, P., tr. ASF
Riley, H., tr. BUCM
Rogers, H., tr. SEBO
Sugden, E., tr. STA
Variant titles: The crock of gold; the pot of gold
The braggart captain. See Miles gloriosus
The braggart soldier. See Miles gloriosus
The braggart warrior. See Miles gloriosus
The captives. 2d cent. B.C.
Anon. tr. CROV
Alison, R., tr. DUC1
Lieberman, S., tr. LIC
Riley, H., tr. MIK8
Sugden, E., tr. CLF1, HOUS, MAU, ROB, THOM, THON
Variant titles: Captivi; Prisoners of war
Captivi. See The captives
The Carthaginian. 2d cent.

B.C.
Duckworth, G., tr. DUC1
Variant title: The poenulus
Casina. 185? B.C.
Duckworth, G., tr. DUC1
The casket. 2d cent. B.C.
Duckworth, G., tr. DUC1
Variant title: Cistellaria
The churl. See Truculentus
Cistellaria. See The casket
The comedy of asses. 2d cent. B.C.
Sugden, E., tr. DUC1
Variant title: Asinaria
The crock of gold. See Aulularia
Curculio. 194? B.C.
Duckworth, G., tr. DUC1
Variant title: The weevil
Epidicus. 2d cent. B.C.
Duckworth, G., tr. DUC1
The girl from Persia. 2d cent. B.C.
Murphy, C., tr. DUC1
Variant title: The Persa
The haunted house. 2d cent. B.C.
Anon. tr. MCKK2
Bassett, E., Jarcho, L., and Murphy, C., trs.
Casson, L., tr. CASU
Copley, F., tr. ROM
Downer, S., tr. DOWS
Mitchell, L., tr. DUC1, GRIF
Nixon, P., tr. MIL
Variant titles: The little ghost; Mostellaria
Jupiter in disguise. See Amphitryon
The little ghost. See The haunted house
The Menaechmi. 2d cent. B.C.
Anon. tr. HOWJ, TREA2, TREB, TREC1, TREE1, TREI1
Bovie, P., tr. COTKIR, COTU
Copley, F., tr. ROM
Hyde, R., and Wiest, E., trs. BRIX, BROJ, BROK, DUC1, EDAD, GUI, GUIN, HAPV
Lieberman, S., tr. LIC
Nixon, P., tr. HUD
Riley, H., tr. CROS, MIK8, SEBP
Taylor, J., tr. TAV
Thornton, B., and Warner, R., trs. SMR
Variant titles: Menaechmi twins; The twin brothers; The twin Menaechmi
Menaechmi twins. See Menaechmi
Mercator. See The merchant
The merchant. 2d cent. B.C.
Murphy, C., tr. DUC1
Wilmurt, A., tr. COTU
Variant title: Mercator
Miles gloriosus. 205? B.C.
Anon. tr. PAR
Duckworth, G., tr. DUC1, ROET
Riley, H., tr. MIK8
Suskin, A., tr. HOWK
Variant titles: The braggart captain; The braggart soldier; The braggart warrior
Mostellaria. See The haunted house
The Persa. See The girl from Persia
The poenulus. See The Carthaginian
The pot of gold. See Aulularia
Prisoners of war. See The captives
Pseudolus. 2d cent. B.C.
Murphy, C., tr. DUC1
Variant title: The trickster
The rope. 2d cent. B.C.
Casson, L., tr. CASU
Chase, C., tr. DUC1, GUI, GUIN, HAPV
Copley, F., tr. ROM
Lieberman, S., tr. LIC
Variant titles: The rudens; The slipknot
The rudens. See The rope
The slipknot. See The rope
Stichus. 200 B.C.

Workman, J., tr. DUC2
The three penny day. 2d cent. B.C.
Duckworth, G., tr. DUC2
Variant titles: The three pieces of money; Trinummus
The three pieces of money. See The three penny day
The trickster. See Pseudolus
Trinummus. See The three penny day
Truculentus. 2d cent. B.C.
Duckworth, G., tr. DUC2
Variant title: The churl
The twin brothers. See The Menaechmi
The twin Menaechmi. See The Menaechmi
The two bacchides. 189? B.C.
Sugden, E., tr. DUC1
The weevil. See Curculio

POCOCK, ISAAC, 1782-1835
The miller and his men. 1813. BOOA1, BOOB

POGODIN, NIKOLAI FEDEROVICH, 1900-1962 (pseud. of Stukalov, N. F.)
Aristocrats. 1935.
Wixley, A., and Carr, R., trs. FOUS
Variant title: Aristokraty
Aristokraty. See Aristocrats
The chimes of the Kremlin. 1941.
Bakshy, A., tr. BAKS
Shoett, A., tr. THY
Variant titles: Kremlin chimes; Kremlevskie kuranty
Kremlin chimes. See The chimes of the Kremlin
Kremlevskie kuranty. See The chimes of the Kremlin
Temp. See Tempo
Tempo. 1930.
Talmadg, I., tr. LYK
Variant title: Temp

POLLOCK, CHANNING, 1880-1946
The enemy. 1925. BES25
The fool. 1922. BES22

POLLOCK, RICHARD
Zoo in Silesia. 1945. EMB1

PONTE, LORENZO DA, 1749-1838
Don Giovanni. See The punished libertine
The punished libertine; or, Don Giovanni. 1787.
Schizzano, A., and Mandel, O., trs. MAN

POPPLE, WILLIAM, 1701-1764?
Cure for jealousy. See The double deceit
The double deceit. 1735. PLAN26
Variant title: Cure for jealousy

POPPLEWELL, JACK
Dead on nine. 1955. PLAN13
Dear delinquent. 1957. PLAN16

POPPLEWELL, OLIVE M.
This bondage. 1935. FIN

PORTER, HAL, 1911-
The tower. 1963. THOP

PORTER, HENRY, fl. 1589-1599
The pleasant history of the two angry women of Abington. 1598? GAY1, NER, OLH, OLI1
Variant title: The two angry women of Abington
The two angry women of Abington. See The pleasant history of the two angry women of Abington

PORTO-RICHE, GEORGES DE, 1849-1930
Amoureuse. 1891. RHO
Crawford, J., tr. DID
Variant titles: Cupid's rival; The impassioned wife; A loving wife; The

tyranny of love
La chance de Françoise. See Françoise' luck
Cupid's rival. See Amoureuse
Françoise' luck. 1888.
Clark, B., tr. CLD
Variant title: La chance de Françoise
The impassioned wife. See Amoureuse
A loving wife. See Amoureuse
The tyranny of love. See Amoureuse

POTTLE, EMERY BEMSLEY (GILBERT EMERY, pseud.), 1875-
The hero. 1921. BES21, QUI, TUCD
Tarnish. 1923. BES23

POWELL, ARNOLD
The death of everymom. SHRO
The strangler. 1966. BALLE4

POWYS, STEPHEN (MRS. GUY BOLTON) (née Virginia de Lanty). See Guitry, Sacha. Don't listen, ladies! (Adapted by)

PRAGA, MARCO, 1862-1929
The closed door. 1913.
MacDonald, A., tr. SAY
Variant title: La porta chiusa
La porta chiusa. See The closed door

PRATT, WILLIAM W.
Ten nights in a bar-room. 1858. BOOB

PRESTON, JOHN
The brave Irishman (sometimes attributed). See Sheridan, Thomas. The brave Irishman

PRESTON, THOMAS, 1537-1598
Cambises, King of Persia. 1569. ADA, BAS, CRE, MIO1, NES
Variant titles: Cambyses; The life of Cambises, King of Percia
Cambyses. See Cambises, King of Persia
The life of Cambises, King of Percia. See Cambises, King of Persia

PREVELAKIS, PANDELIS, 1909-
The last tournament. 1966.
Gianos, M., tr. GIA

PREVERT, JACQUES, 1900-
La famille tuyare de poile; ou, Une famille bien unie. See A united family
A united family. 1955?
Allen, J., tr. BENSC
Variant title: La famille tuyare de poile; ou, Une famille bien unie

PRIESTLEY, JOHN BOYNTON, 1894-
Cornelius. 1935. SIXP
Dangerous corner. 1932. CEU, RICI, SIXH
An inspector calls. 1945. BES47, HUDE
Laburnum grove. 1933. SEV
They came to the city. 1943. BARV
-- and HAWKES, JACQUETTA
Dragon's mouth. 1952. COTK, FAOS
--See Murdoch, Iris, jt. auth.

PRITCHARD, BARRY
Captain Fantastic meets the ectomorph. 1965. SCAR
Visions of sugar plums. 1966. BALLE4

PRYCE, RICHARD, 1864-1942
Frolic wind. 1935. FAMG

PULMAN, JACK
The happy apple. 1967. PLAN34

"PUNCH." See "Mr. Punch," pseud.

PUSHKIN, ALEKSANDR SERGIE-

EVICH, 1799-1837
Boris Godunov. 1870.
Reeve, F., tr. REEV1
Love and death featuring "Aleko," by Rachmaninoff (based on the story by). See Nemirovich-Danchenko, Vladīmīr Īvanovīch. Love and death
The stone guest. 1847.
MacAndrew, A., tr. MACD, GARZE

Q

QUINAULT, PHILIPPE, 1635-1688
Astrate. See Astrates
Astrates. 1664-1665.
Lockert, L., tr. LOCU
Variant title: Astrate

QUINTANA, EDUARDO DE ZAMACOIS Y. See Zamacois, Eduardo

QUINTERO, JOAQUIN ALVAREZ. See Alvarez Quintero, Joaquín

QUINTERO, SERAFIN ALVAREZ. See Alvarez Quintero, Serafín

R

RABE, DAVID
Sticks and bones. 1971. BES71

RABINDRANATH TAGORE. See Tagore, Rabindranath

RACHMANINOFF, SERGEI, 1873-1943
Aleko. See Nemirovich-Danchenko, Vladīmīr Īvanovīch. Love and death featuring "Aleko," by Rachmaninoff

RACINE, JEAN BAPTISTE, 1639-1699
Andromache. See Andromaque
Andromaque. 1667. LYO, SCN, SER, SERD, STJ1
Abel, L., tr. BERM
Boswell, R., tr. CLKW
Variant title: Andromache
Athaliah. 1691.
Anon. tr. GAUB, HOUS
Boswell, R., tr. BUCK, BUCL, BUCM, GREA, KOH2, KRE
Bérénice. 1670.
Boswell, R., tr. CLF2
Masefield, J., tr. STA
Esther. 1689. SER
Phaedra. See Phèdre
Phèdre. 1677. LYO, SER
Anon. tr. GAUB, EVB2
Boswell, R., tr. CAR, CARA, DRA1, HARC26, LOCM2, LOGG, MACJ, MACL2, MAU, MIL, PLAB1, ROB, SEBO, SEBP, SMP
Fowlie, W., tr. DOV, FOWL
Goddard, W., tr. CALD, WEIS
Henderson, R., tr. EVA2, EVC2, HIB, HIBB, THOM, THON, TRE, TREA2, TREB, TREC1, TREE1, TREI1, WALJ
Lockert, L., tr. WEAV2
Lowell, R., tr. ALLK, BENR4, BENSB1, BOW, COTX, FREG, HOUE, MACM2, MACN, SANP, VANV2
Muir, K., tr. GOUZ, ROET
Variant titles: Phaedra; Phèdre and Hippolyte
Phèdre and Hippolyte. See Phèdre
Les plaideurs. 1668.
Browne, I., tr. BAT7
Variant title: The suitors
The suitors. See Les plaideurs

RADIGUET, RAYMOND, 1903-1923
Les pélican. See The pelicans

The pelicans. 1921.
Benedikt, M., tr. BEN
Variant title: Les pèlican

RAISIN, JACQUES, 1653?-1702
Merlin gascon. 1690. LAN

RANDALL, BOB
6 rms riv vu. 1972. BES72

RANDOLPH, CLEMENCE. See Colton, John, jt. auth.

RAPHAELSON, SAMSON, 1896-
Accent on youth. 1934. BES34, FAMH
Jason. 1942. BES41
Skylark. 1939. BES39

RAPPOPORT, SHLOYME ZANVL (A. S. ANSKY, pseud.), 1863-1920
Between two worlds. See The dybbuk
The dybbuk. 1920.
Alsberg, H., and Katzin, W., trs. BES25, CEW, DIE, GARZH
Landis, J., tr. LAO, LAOG
Variant title: Between two worlds

RAPPOPORT, SOLOMON. See Rappoport, Shloyme Zanvl

RASTELL, JOHN, d. 1536
The nature of the four elements (sometimes attributed to). See Anonymous plays. The nature of the four elements

RATTIGAN, SIR TERENCE MERVYN. See RATTIGAN, TERENCE

RATTIGAN, TERENCE, 1911-
After the dance. 1939. SIXL
The Browning version. 1949. HAMI
The deep blue sea. 1952. FAOS
French without tears. 1936. FIP, PLAL2, THH
Love in idleness. See O mistress mine
O mistress mine. 1946. BES45
Variant title: Love in idleness
Ross. 1960. PLAJ1
Separate tables. 1954. BES56
(2 one-act plays: Table by the window: Table number seven)
Table number seven (part of Separate tables). 1956. BENPB
The Winslow boy. 1946. BES47, BOGO, LOND, RED, REDM, SPER, WAGC2

RAUCH, EDWARD H. (PIT SCHWEFFELBRENNER, pseud.), 1826-1902
Rip Van Winkle; oder, Die shpooks fun Blowa Barrick (based on the book by Washington Irving). 18-? BUFF

RAVENSCROFT, EDWARD, fl. 1671-1697
The London cuckolds. 1681. SUM
-- and MOTTEUX, PETER ANTHONY
The anatomist; or, The sham doctor ... with the loves of Mars and Venus (based upon Crispin médecin, by Hautroche). 1696. HUGH

RAYFIEL, DAVID, 1923-
P. S. 193. 1962. BES62

RAYNAL, PAUL, 1890-
The tomb beneath the Arc de triomphe. See Le tombeau sous l'Arc de triomphe
Le tombeau sous l'Arc de triomphe. 1924. RHO
Variant titles: The tomb beneath the Arc de tri-

omphe; The unknown warrior
The unknown warrior. See Le tombeau sous l'Arc de triomphe

READE, CHARLES, 1814-1884.
See Taylor, Tom, jt. auth.

RECKORD, BARRY
Skyvers. 1963. NEWE9

REDDING, JOSEPH DEIGHN, 1859-1932
The attonement of Pan. 1912. BOH2

REDFORD, JOHN, fl. 1535
The play of wit and science. 1541? ADA, FARN, HAO, SCAT
Variant titles: Wit and science; Wyt and science
Wit and science. See The play of wit and science
Wyt and science. See The play of wit and science
--See also Anonymous plays. The marriage of wit and science

REED, MARK WHITE, 1893-
Yes, my darling daughter. 1937. BES36, GAS

REELY, MARY KATHERINE, 1881-1959
Flittermouse. 1927. GALB

REGNARD, JEAN FRANÇOIS, 1655-1709
Le légataire universel. 1708. BRE
Aldington, R., tr. ALD
Variant title: The residuary légatee
The residuary légatee. See Le légataire universel

REGNIER, MAX ALBERT MARIE, 1908-
The headshrinkers. See Paddle your own canoe
Paddle your own canoe (based on the scenario by André Gillois). 1957?
Hill, L., tr. and adapter. PLAN17
Variant title: The headshrinkers

REID, ARTHUR
People in love. 1937. FAMK

REID, BEN
The fourth room. 1944? NEW44

REID, LESLIE
Trespassers. 1923. MAS2

REIZENSTEIN, ELMER. See Rice, Elmer L.

REXROTH, KENNETH, 1905-
Iphigenia at Aulis. 1944? NEW44
Phaedra. 1944? NEW44

REYNOLDS, FREDERIC, 1764-1841
The dramatist; or, Stop him who can! 1789. MOR, NIC

RIBMAN, RONALD, 1932-
Fingernails blue as flowers. 1971. SCV

RICARDO DE LA VEGA. See Vega, Ricardo de la

RICE, ELMER L. (formerly Elmer Reizenstein), 1892-1967
The adding machine. 1923. DAV1, DIG, DUR, GARU, HAT, HATA, JORG, MOSJ, MOSK, MOSL, RAVA, SCNN, SMA, SSSF, THF
Counsellor-at-law. 1931. FAMC
Dream girl. 1945. BES45, GARZ, GARZA3
Flight to the west. 1940. BES40
Judgment day. 1934. FAMK
The left bank. 1931. BES31

On trial. 1914. BES09, CART
See Naples and die. 1929. FAMB
Street scene. 1929. BES28, CER, CHA, CHAN, CHAP, CLDP, CORD, CORE, CORF, COTE, COTH, FULT, GARZA1, GASB, GRIF, MACG, MERU, SIXD, WATC2, WATI, WATO
We, the people. 1933. BES32

RICHARDS, IVOR ARMSTRONG, 1893-
A leak in the universe. 1954. PLAA

RICHARDS, STANLEY, 1918-
District of Columbia. 1945. HARY

RICHARDSON, HOWARD, 1917- and BERNEY, WILLIAM
Barbara Allen. See Dark of the moon
Dark of the moon. 1945. PLAN2
Variant title: Barbara Allen

RICHARDSON, JACK CARTER, 1935-
Gallows humor. 1961. DOD, MAO, WELT
The prodigal. 1960. FOR
Xmas in Las Vegas. 1965. SSTY

RICHARDSON, WILLIS, 1889-
The broken banjo. 1925. LOC
The chip woman's fortune. 1923. TUQT
The flight of the natives. 1927. HARY, LOC
The idle head. 1927. HARY

RICHE, GEORGES DE PORTO. See Porto-Riche, Georges de

RICHMAN, ARTHUR, 1886-1944
Ambush. 1921. BES21

RICHMOND, SAMUEL S.
Career for Ralph. 1949? LOVR

RICKERT, VAN DUSEN, JR.
The bishop's candlesticks. 1945? GALB

RIGGS, LYNN, 1899-1954
Green grow the lilacs. 1931. BES30, CLDP, GARU, LEV, LEVE, SIM
--See also Hammerstein II, Oscar. Oklahoma! (based on).
Knives from Syria. 1927. BENP, TOD
Roadside. 1930. TUCN, TUCO

RINEHART, MRS. MARY (ROBERTS), 1876-1958, and HOPWOOD, AVERY
The bat. 1920. CART, CEY
Variant title: The circular staircase
The circular staircase. See The bat

RITCHIE, MRS. ANNA CORA (OGDEN) MOWATT, 1819-1870
Fashion; or, Life in New York. 1845. COY, GARX, HAL, MASW, MONR, MOSS2, QUIJ, QUIK, QUIL, QUIM, QUIN

RIVAS, ANGEL PEREZ DE SAAVEDRA, 1791-1865
Don Alvaro; ó la fuerza del sino. 1835. BRET, PATT, TRES
Variant title: Don Alvaro; or, The force of destiny; La forza del destino
Don Alvaro; or, The force of destiny. See Don Alvaro ó la fuerza del sino
La forza del destino. See Don Alvaro

RIVAS, MANUEL LINARES. See Linares Rivas, Manuel

RIVES, AMELIE. See Troubetskoy, Amélie (Rives) Chanler

ROBERT, FRANÇOIS LE METEL

DE BOIS. See Bois-Robert, François Le Métel de

ROBERTS, CYRIL, 1892-
Tails up. 1935? GALB

ROBERTSON, LOUIS ALEXANDER, 1856-1910
Montezuma. 1903. BOH1

ROBERTSON, THOMAS WILLIAM, 1829-1871
Caste. 1867. ASG, BAI, BOWY, COD, COT, DUR, MAP, MAT, MOSN, MOSO, ROWE, TAU
Society. 1865. BAT16, RUB

ROBINSON, LENNOX, 1886-1958
The bighouse. 1926. CAP
Church street. 1934. CAN
The far-off hills. 1928. CHA, CHAN, CHAR
The whiteheaded boy. 1916. MYB, PLAP3

RODRIGUEZ ALVAREZ, ALEJANDRO (ALEJANDRO CASONA, pseud.), 1903-1965
La barca sin pescador. See The boat without the fisherman
The boat without the fisherman. 1945.
Damar, R., tr. HOLT
Variant title: La barca sin pescador
Prohibido suicidarse en primavera. See Suicide prohibited in springtime
Suicide prohibited in springtime. 1937.
Horvath, A., tr. BENA
Variant title: Prohibido suicidarse en primavera

ROEMER, MICHAEL, and YOUNG, ROBERT
Nothing but a man. 1963. MESS

ROGERS, JOHN WILLIAM, JR., 1894-1965
Judge Lynch. 1924. LOC, PROG
Where the dear antelope play. 1941. THX

ROGERS, RICHARD, 1902-
Allegro (music by). See Hammerstein II, Oscar. Allegro
The king and I (music by). See Hammerstein II, Oscar. The king and I
Oklahoma! (music by). See Hammerstein II, Oscar. Oklahoma!
South Pacific (music by). See Hammerstein II, Oscar. South Pacific

ROGERS, ROBERT, 1731-1795
Ponteach; or, The savages of America. 1766? MOSS1

ROJAS, FERNANDO DE, d. 1541
Celestina; or, The tragicomedy of Calisto and Melibea (attributed to). (1499)
Mabbe, J., tr. and Bentley, E., adapter. BENR3
Variant titles: La Celestina; Comedia de Calisto y Melibea; Tragicomedia de Calixto y Melibea
La Celestina. See Celestina
Comedia de Calisto y Melibea. See Celestina
Tragicomedia de Calixto y Melibea. See Celestina

ROJAS, RICARDO, 1882-
Ollántay. 1938. ALPE

ROJAS ZORRILLA, FRANCISCO DE, 1607-1648
Del rey abajo, ninguno. 1650. ALP
Goldberg, I., tr. ALPF
Variant title: None beneath the king
None beneath the king. See Del rey abajo, ninguno

ROKK, VSEVOLOD

Engineer Sergeyev. 1941.
Moss, H., tr. SEVP

ROMAINS, JULES (formerly Louis Henri Jean Farigoule), 1885-1972
Cromedeyre-le-vieil. 1920. RHO
Dr. Knock. 1923.
Granville-Barker, H., tr. BENS3

ROME, HAROLD JACOB, 1908-
Fanny. See Behrman, Samuel Nathaniel and Logan, Joshua. Fanny (music and lyrics by)
Wish you were here. See Kober, Arthur and Logan, Joshua. Wish you were here (music and lyrics by)

RONDER, JACK
This year, next year. 1960. PLAN22
Variant title: Wedding day
Wedding day. See This year, next year

ROSE, DAVID, 1910-
Winged victory (music by). See Hart, Moss. Winged victory

ROSE, REGINALD, 1920-
Thunder on Sycamore Street. BRNB
Twelve angry men. 1957. CARL

ROSEN, JULIUS, 1833-1892
Ein knopf. See Birmelin, John. Der gnopp (based on the play by)
Starke mitteln. See Daly, Augustin. Needles and pins (adapted from)

ROSENBERG, JAMES L.
The death and life of Sneaky Fitch. NEWA1

ROSENBERG, JEROLD. See Ross, Jerry (pseud.)

ROSENTHAL, ANDREW
Third person. 1951. PLAN7

ROSS, GEORGE, 1907- , and SINGER, CAMPBELL
Any other business. 1957. PLAN18
Difference of opinion. 1965. PLAN27
Guilty party. 1960. PLAN24
Variant title: Refer to drawer
Refer to drawer. See Guilty party
The sacking of Norman Banks. 1969. PLAN37

ROSS, JERRY (pseud. of JEROLD ROSENBERG), 1926-1955
The pajama game. See Abbott, George and Bissell, Richard. The pajama game (lyrics and music by)

ROSSO DI SAN SECONDO, PIERMARIA, 1889-1958
La scale. See The stairs
The stairs. 1925.
Katzin, W., tr. KAT
Variant title: La scala

ROSTAND, EDMOND, 1868-1918
Cyrano de Bergerac. 1897. BOR, GRA, SEA
Anon. tr. LAM, WISD, ZIM
Dole, H., tr. SMN, STRB
Hall, G., tr. COTH, DID, DIK2, HAV, HUDS2, MCCD, MCCF, MCCG, MOSQ, TUCG, TUCM, TUCN, TUCO, WATI, WATL2, WATO, WATR, WHI, WHK
Henderson, D., tr. HUD
Hooker, B., tr. BLOO, CARA, CEW, GARZF, GOLK, HILP, KNIC, TREBA, TREC2, TREE2, TREI2, TREJ, WALJ, WISE
Kingsbury, H., tr. BLOD1,

COJ, HOUK, KON, LEV, LEVE, SHRO, TREA1
Thomas, G., and Guillemard, M., trs. MIL
Whitehall, H., tr. WORP
Wolfe, H., tr. BENU, FOUM
La dernière nuit de Don Juan. See The last night of Don Juan
Don Juan's last night. See The last night of Don Juan
The fantasticks. See The romancers
The last night of Don Juan. 1922.
Bagley, D., tr. MAN
Riggs, T., tr. KRE
Variant titles: La dernière nuit de Don Juan; Don Juan; Don Juan's last night
The romancers. 1894.
Anon. tr. COOK2
Clark, B., tr. BERM, PATM
Hendee, M., tr. COD
Variant titles: The fantasticks; The romantics; Les romanesques
Les romanesques. See The romancers
The romantics. See The romancers

ROSTEN, NORMAN, 1914-
Mister Johnson. 1955. THEA56

ROSWITHA VON GANDERSHEIM. See Hrotsvit, of Gandersheim

ROSZKOWSKI, DAVID
Canvas. 1972. BALLE11

ROTROU, JEAN DE, 1609-1650
Chosroes. 1648.
Lockert, L., tr. LOCR
Variant title: Cosroés
Cosroés. See Chosroes
Le feint véritable. See Saint Genesius
Saint Genesius. 1646?
Lockert, L., tr. LOCU
Variant titles: Le feint véritable; Saint Genest; Le véritable Saint Genest
Saint Genest. See Saint Genesius
Venceslas. See Wenceshaus
Le véritable Saint Genest. See Saint Genesius
Wenceshaus. 1647.
Lockert, L., tr. LOCR
Variant title: Venceslas

ROTTER, FRITZ, and VINCENT, ALLEN
Letters to Lucerne. 1941. BES41
ROWE, NICHOLAS, 1674-1718
The fair penitent. 1703. DOB, MCM, MCMI, WILE
The tragedy of Jane Shore. 1713. EIGH, HAN, MOSE2, NET, STM, TUQ

ROWELL, GEORGE
Sixty thousand nights (script, research and lyrics by). See May, Val. Sixty thousand nights

--See Woods, Aubrey, jt. auth.

ROWLEY, WILLIAM, 1585?-1642?
The birth of Merlin (sometimes attributed to). See Anonymous plays. The birth of Merlin
--See Ford, John; Middleton, Thomas, jt. auths.

ROYLE, EDWIN MILTON, 1862-1942
The squaw man. 1905. BES99
RUBENSTEIN, KEN
Icarus. NEWA4
RUDKIN, DAVID
Afore night come. (1963) NEWE7
RUEDA, LOPE DE, 1506-1565
Las aceitunas. See The olives

La carátula. See The mask
The mask. 1551?
Starkie, W., tr. SSTW
Variant title: La carátula
The olives. 1560?
Flores, A., tr. FLOS
Variant titles: Las aceitunas; El paso de las olivas
El paso de las olivas. See The olives
Paso séptimo. See The seventh farce
The seventh farce. 16th cent.
Chambers, W., tr. BAT6, PATT
Variant title: Paso séptimo

RUIBAL, JOSE
El asno. See The jackass
The jackass.
Seward, T., tr. WELL
Variant title: El asno
El hombre y la mosca. See The man and the fly
The man and the fly. 1968.
Zelonis, J., tr. WELL, WELT
Variant title: El hombre y la mosca

RUIZ, JUAN (ARCIPRESTE DE HITA), 1283?-1351?
Dialogue between Don Melón Ortiz and Doña Endrina. See The gallant, the bawd and the fair lady
The gallant, the bawd and the fair lady (adapted from El libro de buen amor). 1343?
Starkie, W., tr. and adapter. SSTW
Variant title: Dialogue between Don Melón Ortiz and Doña Endrina
El libro de buen amor (The book of good love). See The gallant, the bawd and the fair lady (adapted from El libro de buen amor)

RUIZ DE ALARCON Y MENDOZA, JUAN, 1581?-1639
No hay mal que por bien no venga (Don Domingo de Don Blas). 161-? HILL
Las paredes oyen. 161-? PATT
The suspecting truth. See La verdad sospechosa
The truth suspected. See La verdad sospechosa
La verdad sospechosa. 1619. ALP
Ryan, R., tr. FLOS
Variant titles: The suspecting truth; The truth suspected

RUNYON, DAMON, 1884-1946
Idyll of Miss Sarah Brown. See Swerling, Jo and Burrows, Abe. Guys and dolls (based on the story by)

RUSSELL, CHARLES L., 1932-
Five fingers on the black hand side. 1969? SCV

RUSSELL, GEORGE WILLIAM (A. E., pseud.), 1867-1935
Deirdre. 1902. CAP

RUSTEBUEF. See Rutebeuf

RUTEBEUF, fl. 1248-1277
Le miracle de Theophile. 13th cent. AXT

RUTEBUEF. See Rutebeuf

RUZZANTE. See Beolco, Angelo

RYALL, WILLIAM BOLITHO (William Bolitho, pseud.), 1890-1930
Overture. 1930. BES30

RYE, ELIZABETH
The three-fold path. 1935. FIN

RYERSON, FLORENCE, 1894- (MRS. COLIN CLEMENTS), and

CLEMENTS, COLIN CAMPBELL
Harriet. 1943. BES42

RYSKIND, MORRIE, 1895- .
See Kaufman, George S., jt. auth.

RYTON, ROYCE
Crown matrimonial. 1972. PLAN43

S

"S., MR., MR. OF ART," See Stevenson, William

SA-AMI-YASUKIYO, HIYOSHI. See Hiyoshi, Sa-Ami-Yasukiyo

SAAVEDRA, GUADALUPE DE
Justice. ASF

SAAVEDRA, MIGUEL DE CERVANTES. See Cervantes Saavedra, Miguel

SAAVEDRA RIVAS, ANGEL PEREZ DE. See Rivas, Angel Pérez de Saavedra

SACHS, HANS, 1494-1576
Der fahrende schüler im Paradies. See The wandering scholar from Paradise
Der fahrende schüller mit dem teufelbanner. See Raising the devil
The horse thief. 1553.
Leighton, W., tr. INGW
Raising the devil. 155-?
Chambers, W., tr. BAT10
Variant titles: Der fahrende schüller mit dem teufelbanner; The wandering scholar and exorcist
The wandering scholar and exorcist. See Raising the devil
The wandering scholar from Paradise. 1550.
Eliot, S., tr. CLF1, KRE, PROW
Variant title: Der fahrende schüller im Paradies

SACKLER, HOWARD, 1929-
The great white hope. 1968. BES68

SACKVILLE, THOMAS (LORD BUCKHURST, 1st Earl of Dorset), 1536-1608, and NORTON, THOMAS
Gorboduc; or, Ferrex and Porrex. 1561. ADA, BAS, CRE, CUN, GARZB, MCJ, MIN1, MIO1, NES, SCW, TAV
Variant title: The tragidie of [Gorboduc; or of] Ferrex and Porrex
The tragidie of [Gorboduc; or of] Ferrex and Porrex. See Gorboduc; or, Ferrex and Porrex

SACKVILLE, WEST, VICTORIA MARY, 1892-1962
The Edwardians. See Gow, Ronald. The Edwardians (adapted from)

SAIDY, FRED. See Harburg, Edgar Y., jt. auth.

SAINER, ARTHUR
The thing itself. 1967. BALLE6

ST. JOSEPH, ELLIS
A passenger to Bali. 1940. HAT

SALACROU, ARMAND, 1899-
A circus story. 1922.
Benedikt, M., tr. BEN
Variant title: L'histoire du cirque
L'histoire du cirque. See A circus story
Marguerite. 1944.
Voysey, M., tr. RICK
Variant title: La Marguerite
La Marguerite. See Marguerite

SAN SECONDO, PIERMARIA

ROSSO DI. See Rosso di San Secondo, Piermaria

SANCHEZ, FLORENCIO, 1875-1910
Los derechos de la salud. 1907. ALPE
The foreign girl. See La gringa
La gringa. 1904.
Coester, A., tr. SSTE
Variant title: The foreign girl

SANCHEZ, SONIA, 1934-
Uh, uh, but how do it free us? (1973) NEWL

SANCHEZ GARDEL, JULIO, d. 1937
La montaña de las brujas. See The witches' mountain
The witches' mountain. 1912?
Fassett, J., tr. BIE
Variant title: La montaña de las brujas

SANDEAU, JULES, 1811-1883. See Augier, Emile, jt. auth.

SANFORD, JEREMY
The whelks and the cromium. 1958. NEWE12

SAPINSLEY, ALVIN, 1921-
Even the weariest river. 1957? GRED

SARDOU, VICTORIEN, 1831-1908
Fatherland. See Patrie!
Patrie! 1869.
Clark, B., tr. LEV, LEVE
Variant title: Fatherland
Les pattes de mouche. 1860.
Gilmour, L., tr. DRA2, PLAB2, SSTG
Variant title: A scrap of paper
A scrap of paper. See Les pattes de mouche

-- and NAJAC, EMILE DE
Divorçons. See Let's get a divorce!
Let's get a divorce! 1880.
Davies, F., tr. LAB
Goldsby, A., and R., trs. BENSC, PLAN31
Variant title: Divorçons

SARMENT, JEAN, 1897-
The most beautiful eyes in the world. See Les plus beaux yeux du monde
Le pêcheur d'ombres. 1921. HARV
Variant title: The shadow fisher
Les plus beaux yeux du monde. 1925. RHO
Variant title: The most beautiful eyes in the world
The shadow fisher. See Le pêcheur d'ombres

SAROYAN, WILLIAM, 1908-
The cave dwellers. 1956. GARS
Hello out there. 1942. HOLP, WATE
The human comedy. See Estabrook, Howard. The human comedy (screen play based on the book by)
The man with the heart in the Highlands. See My heart's in the highlands
My heart's in the highlands. 1939. BART, BENT4, TREBA, TREC2, TREE3, TREI3, TREJ, VOAD
Variant title: The man with the heart in the highlands
The oyster and the pearl. 1953. THOD
The people with light coming out of them. 1942. GALB
The time of your life. 1939. BES39, BIER, BLOC, CET, CLUR, COTQ, CRIT, DAVM, GARZ, GARZA3, GAVE, HATA, KERN, LAV, MERU, SCAR, STEI

SARTRE, JEAN-PAUL, 1905-

Crime passionel. See Les mains sales
Dirty hands. See Les mains sales
The flies. 1943.
Gilbert, S., tr. TREBA, TREC2, TREE2, TREJ
Variant title: Les mouches
Huis clos. 1944. CLOU
Anon. tr. FOUA
Gilbert, S., tr. BROSA, CLKJ, MACM2, MACN, TREI2
Stuart, S., tr. BLOC, GARZH, HAMI
Variant titles: In camera; No exit
In camera. See Huis clos
Les mains sales. 1948. PUCC
Variant titles: Crime passionel; Dirty hands; Red gloves
Les mouches. See The flies
Men without shadows. See The victors
Morts sans sépulture. See The victors
No exit. See Huis clos
Red gloves. See Les mains sales
The victors. 1946.
Abel, L., tr. COTQ
Variant titles: Men without shadows; Morts sans sépulture

SASTRE, ALFONSO, 1926-
Ana Kleiber. See Anna Kleiber
Anna Kleiber. 1961.
Pronko, L., tr. COTQ, COTR
Variant title: Ana Kleiber
Condemned squad. See Death squad
Death squad. 1953.
Pronko, L., tr. HOLT
Variant titles: Condemned squad; Escuadra hacia la muerte
Death thrust. 1961.
Pronko, L., tr. COTP
Escuadra hacia la muerte. See Death squad
Guillermo Tell tiene los ojos tristes. See Sad are the eyes of William Tell
Sad are the eyes of William Tell.
Pronko, L., tr. WELL
Variant titles: Guillermo Tell tiene los ojos tristes; William Tell has sad eyes
William Tell has sad eyes. See Sad are the eyes of William Tell

SAUNDERS, JAMES, 1925-
Next time I'll sing to you. 1962. BES63

SAUNDERS, LOUISE
The knave of hearts. BEAC7, COOK1

SAVORY, GERALD, 1909-
George and Margaret. 1937. FIP, THH

SAVOY(!), GERALD. See Savory, Gerald

SAYEMON, ENAMAI NO. See Enamai No Sayemon

SAYERS, DOROTHY LEIGH (MRS. DOROTHY FLEMING), 1893-1957
The zeal of thy house. 1937. FAML
-- and BYRNE, MURIEL ST. CLARE
Busman's honeymoon. 1936. FAMK

SCALA, FLAMINO, fl. 1620
The faithful friend. 17th cent.?
Chambers, W., tr. BAT5
Variant title: Il fido amico
Il fido amico. See The faithful friend
The portrait. 1575?
Leverton, G., tr. TREB
Van Der Meer, E., tr. CLF2, LEV, LEVE

Variant title: Il rittrato
Il rittrato. See The portrait

SCHARY, DORE, 1905-
The devil's advocate (based on the novel by Morris L. West). 1961. BES60
Sunrise at Campobello. 1958. BES57, CES

SCHAUFFLER, MRS. ELSIE (TOUGH), 1888-1935
Parnell. 1936. FAMJ

SCHEFFAUER, HERMAN GEORGE, 1878-1927
The sons of Baldur. 1908. BOH1

SCHEHADE, GEORGES, 1910-
Histoire de Vasco. See Vasco
The history of Vasco. See Vasco
Vasco. 1956.
Victor, L., tr. and adapter. COTS
Variant titles: Histoire de Vasco; The history of Vasco

SCHEVILL, JAMES ERWIN, 1920-
American power. See The master; The space fan (cover title of two unrelated 1-act plays)
The master. 1964. BALLE1
The space fan. 1964. BALLE1

SCHILDT, RUNAR, 1888-1925
Galgamannen; en midvintersaga. See The gallows man: a midwinter story
The gallows man; a midwinter story. 1922.
Alexander, H., tr. SCAN1
Variant title: Galgamannen: en midvintersaga

SCHILLER, JOHANN CHRISTOPH FRIEDRICH VON, 1759-1805
The camp of Wallenstein. 1798.
Churchill, J., tr. BAT10
Variant titles: Das lager; Wallenstein; Wallensteins lager
The death of Wallenstein. 1799.
Coleridge, S., tr. ESS, FRA3, KRE
Variant titles: Wallenstein; Wallensteins tod
Don Carlos. 1787.
Kirkup, J., tr. BENR2
The homage of the arts. 1804.
Coleman, A., tr. FRA3
Variant title: Die huldigung des künste
Die huldigung des künste. See The homage of the arts
Das lager. See The camp of Wallenstein
Mary Stuart. 1801.
Goldstone, J., and Reich, J., trs. HOUK
Lamport, F., tr. LAMP
Lustig, T., tr. LUST, TREB
Mellish, J., tr., and Bentley, E., adapter. BENR2, DRA2, PLAB2
Wallenstein (trilogy). See The camp of Wallenstein; The death of Wallenstein
Wallensteins lager. See The camp of Wallenstein
Wallensteins tod. See The death of Wallenstein
Wilhelm Tell. See William Tell
William Tell. 1804.
Martin, T., tr. CLF2, FRA3, GREA, HARC26, MAU, SMK, STA, WEAV2
Variant title: Wilhelm Tell

SCHISGAL, MURRAY, 1926-
The Chinese. 1970. RICK
Luv. 1963. BES64, CEQA
The typists. 1960. MAO

SCHLITT, R.

The egg. See Marceau, Felicien. The egg (tr. and adapted by)

SCHLOSS, MARTIN F.
Totentanz. See Anonymous plays. Totentanz (from the German text of)

SCHLUTER, KARL, 1883-
Afsporet. See Off the rails
Off the rails. 1932.
Born, A., tr. CONT
Variant title: Afsporet

SCHMIDT, HARVEY, 1929-
Celebration (music by). See Jones, Tom. Celebration

SCHNEEMAN, CAROLEE
Meat joy. ASF

SCHNIBBE, HARRY. See Breen, Richard, jt. auth.

SCHNITZLER, ARTHUR, 1862-1931
The affairs of Anatol. See Anatol
Anatol. 1893.
Colbron, G., tr. CEW
Granville-Barker, H., tr. BENS3
Variant title: The affairs of Anatol
--See also A farewell supper (from Anatol)
The duke and the actress. See The green cockatoo
Der einsame weg. See The lonely way
A farewell supper (from Anatol). 1893.
Granville-Barker, H., tr. MILL
Flirtation. See Light-o'-love
Die frage an das schicksal. See Questioning the irrevocable
The game of love. See Light-o'-love
The green cockatoo. See Der gruene kakadu
Der gruene kakadu. 1899. FEFH2
Samuel, H., tr. FRA20
Van Der Meer, E., tr. LEV, LEVE
Variant titles: The duke and the actress; The green cockatoo
Hands around. See Round dance
Intermezzo. 1905.
Björkman, E., tr. STE
Variant title: Zwischenspiel
Lebendige stunden. 1902. STI1
Colbron, G., tr. DID
Variant title: Living hours
Liebelei. See Light-o'-love
Light-o'-love. 1895.
Morgan, B., tr. DIK1, TUCG, TUCM, TUCN, TUCO, WATI, WATL1
Mueller, C., tr. COTKJ
Variant titles: Flirtation; The game of love; Liebelei; Playing with love; The reckoning
Literatur. See Literature
Literature. 1902.
Coleman, A., tr. FRA20
Variant title: Literatur
Living hours. See Lebendige stunden
The lonely way. 1904.
Björkman, E., tr. MOSQ
Leigh, J., tr. WHI
Variant title: Der einsame weg
Merry go round. See Round dance
Playing with love. See Light-o'-love
Professor Bernhardi. 1912.
Borell, L., and Adam, R., trs. FAMJ
Questioning the irrevocable. 1893.
Chambers, W., tr. BAT12
Variant title: Die frage an das schicksal

The reckoning. See Light-o'-love
Reigen. See Round dance
La ronde. See Round dance
Round dance. 1897.
Bentley, E., tr. BENT2, WELT
Mueller, C., tr. COTKJ, COTQ
Wallis, K., tr. BENS1
Weigert, H., and Newhall, P., trs. BLOC
Variant titles: Hands around; Merry go round; Reigen; La ronde
Zwischenspiel. See Intermezzo

SCHONHERR, KARL, 1869-1943
Faith and fireside. 1910.
Mach, E., tr. FRA16
Variant title: Glaube und heimat
Glaube und heimat. See Faith and fireside

SCHROCK, GLADDEN
Madam Popov. 1970. BALLE9

SCHULBERG, BUDD, 1914- , and BREIT, HARVEY
The disenchanted (adapted from the novel by Budd Schulberg). 1958. BES58

SCHWARTZ, DELMORE, 1914-
Choosing company. 1936? AME5
Paris and Helen. 1941? NEW41
Shenandoah. 1941? KRE

SCHWARTZ, JOEL
Psalms for two Davids. 1971. BALLE9

SCHWARTZ, YEVGENY, 1897-
The dragon. 1944.
Hayward, M., and Shukman, H., trs. GLE

SCHWEFFELBRENNER, PIT. See Rauch, Edward H. (pseud. of)

SCOTT, DUNCAN CAMPBELL, 1862-1947
Pierre. 1921. MAS1

SCOTT, PAUL
Pillars of salt. 1947? RUA

SCOTTI, TOMMASO GALLARATI. See Gallarati-Scotti, Tommaso

SCRIBE, AUGUSTIN EUGENE, 1791-1861
Les doigts de fée. 1858. BENZ
Variant titles: Frocks and thrills; Lady Margaret
Frocks and thrills. See Les doigts de fée
A glass of water. See Le verre d'eau
Lady Margaret. See Les doigts de fée
Le verre d'eau. 1840. BOR
Bodee, D., tr. SSTG
Variant title: A glass of water

-- and BAYARD, J. F. A.
La frontière de savoie. See A peculiar position
A peculiar position. 1837.
Planche, J., tr. SSTG
Variant title: La frontière de savoie

SCRIBE, EUGENE. See Scribe, Augustin Eugène

SCRIBLERUS SECUNDUS, pseud. See Fielding, Henry

SEAMI, MOTOKIYO, 1363-1444
Aoi no Uye (sometimes attributed to). See Zenchiku, Ujinobu. Aoi no Uye
Ashikara. See The reed cutter
Atsumori. 14th cent.
Waley, A., tr. TAV, YOHA
The brocade tree.

French, C., tr. KEE
Variant title: Nishikigi
The deserted crone.
Jones, S., tr. KEE
Variant title: Obasute
The dwarf trees.
Waley, A., tr. PATM, PATP
Variant title: Hachi no ki
Hachi no ki. See The dwarf trees
Haku Rakuten. 14th cent.
Waley, A., tr. ANDF
Hanjo. See Lady Han
The imperial visit to Ohara (attributed to).
Hochstedler, C., tr. KEE
Variant title: Ohara gokō
Kanehira (attributed to).
Jones, S., tr. KEE
Komachi at Sekidera.
Brazell, K., tr. KEE
Variant title: Sekidera Komachi
Lady Han.
Tyler, R., tr. KEE
Variant title: Hanjo
Nakamitsu. 15th cent.
Chamberlain, B., tr. CLF1, KRE, ORI2
Nishikigi. See The brocade tree
Obasute. See The deserted crone
Ohara gokō. See The imperial visit to Ohara
The reed cutter.
O'Brien, J., tr. KEE
Variant title: Ashikara
Sekidera Komachi. See Komachi at Sekidera
Semimaru.
Matisoff, C., tr. KEE

SEBIRE, FRANÇOIS DESSANDRAIS. See Dessandrais-Sebire, François

SEBREE, CHARLES, 1914-
The dry August. 1949. HARY

SECOND, LOUIS, pseud.
Apollinaris. 1942? NEW42

SECONDO, PIERMARIA ROSSO DI SAN. See Rossi di San Secondo, Piermaria

SECUNDUS, H. SCRIBLERUS, pseud. See Fielding, Henry

SEDAINE, MICHEL JEAN, 1719-1797
Le philosophe sans le savoir. 1765. BRE, ZDA

SEDLEY, SIR CHARLES, 1639-1701
The mulberry garden. 1668. DAVR

SEGURA, MANUEL ASCENSIO, 1805-1871
Na Catita. 1856. ALPE

SEH, SHA; TO, FU; YUNG, MA; and CHI-HUANG, LI
Letters from the south.
Shapiro, S., tr. MESE

SEJOUR, VICTOR, 1817-1874
The brown overcoat. 1858. HARY

SELWYN, EDGAR, 1875-1944, and GOULDING, EDMUND
Dancing mothers. 1924. BES24

SENECA, LUCIUS ANNAEUS, 4? B.C.-65 A.D.
Agamemnon. 1st cent.
Miller, F., tr. DUC2
Hercules furens. See Mad Hercules
Hercules Oetaeus. See Hercules on Oeta
Hercules on Oeta. 1st cent.
Harris, E., tr. DUC2
Variant title: Hercules Oetaeus
Mad Hercules. 1st cent.
Miller, F., tr. DUC2
Variant title: Hercules furens
Medea. 1st cent.
Anon. tr. MCKK2
Hadas, M., tr. COTU, ROM
Harris, E., tr. CROS,

CROV, GUIN, HAPV
Miller, F., tr. CLF1, DUC2, LIC, SANM
Taylor, J., tr. TAV
Octavia. 1st cent.
Miller, F., tr. DUC2, HOWJ, HOWK
Oedipus. 1st cent.
Hadas, M., tr. ROM
Mendell, C., tr. LEVI
Miller, F., tr. DUC2, LIC, SANO
Phaedra. 1st cent.
Bradshaw, W., tr. MIK8
Harris, E., tr. HAPV
Miller, F., tr. DUC2, LIC, SANP
The Phoenician women. 1st cent.
Harris, E., tr. DUC2
Variant title: Phoenissae
Phoenissae. See The Phoenician women
Thyestes. 1st cent.
Hadas, M., tr. ROM
Harris, E., tr. DUC2, HAPV, PAR
Harris, E., tr., and Gassner, J., adapter. TREB
Heywood, L., tr. MCJ
Troades. See The Trojan women
The Trojan women. 1st cent.
Miller, F., tr. DUC2
Variant title: Troades

SERLING, ROD, 1924-1975
Patterns. 1955. HUNT
Requiem for a heavyweight. 1957. CORB, SUT3
The shelter. SUT2

SETTLE, ELKANAH, 1648-1724
The Empress of Morocco. 1673. DOA

SEYMOUR, ALAN
The one day of the year. 1962. THOP

SHADWELL, THOMAS, 1642?-1692
Bury fair. 1689? MOR, STM
The Lancashire witches and Tegue O. Divelly, the Irish priest. 1681? BAT22
The libertine. 1676. MAN
The squire of Alsatia. 1688. MCM, MCMI

SHAFFER, ANTHONY, 1926-
Sleuth. 1970. BES70, RICI

SHAFFER, PETER LEVIN, 1926-
Black comedy. 1967. BES66, HAVL
Five finger exercise. 1958. BES59, NEWE4
The private ear. 1962. ENG
The royal hunt of the sun. 1964. BES65, PLAJ1
White liars. See White lies
White lies. 1967. RICJ
Variant title: White liars

SHAIRP, MORDAUNT, 1887-1939
The green bay tree. 1933. BES33, CEU

SHAKESPEARE, WILLIAM, 1564-1616
All's well that ends well. 1595? GRDB27
Antony and Cleopatra. 1606? BROJ, BROH, BUR, CROS, DIT, DOWN, ELK, EVC2, GOLH, GRDB27, GUTH, GUTL, LID, MIL, OLI2, SHR, WELT, WOOE1
Variant title: The tragedy of Antony and Cleopatra
Arden of Feversham (sometimes attributed to). See Anonymous plays. Arden of Feversham
As you like it. 1599? BARJ, BRIK, GRDB26, HOUS, OLI1, SCW1, SOU
The birth of Merlin (sometimes attributed to). See Anonymous plays. The birth of Merlin
The comedy of errors. 1592? GRDB26, TAV

Coriolanus. 1607? GRDB27, LEVJ, OLI2

Cymbeline. 1609. GRDB27, OLI2

Hamlet. 1600? ALTE, BAC, BAIC, BAIE, BARI, CLO, DAVK, GORE, GRDB27, HAPD, HAPS1, HAPT1, HARC26, HAVH, HIG, JOHO, JORH, KERN, KERO, LOCM1, MACL1, MACM2, MACN, MCA, MONA, OLI1, REIL, RICH, ROGE, SHRO, SMA, STA, THOM, THON, TRE, TREA2, TREB, TREC1, TREE1, TREI1, WALJ, WARN2, WHFM
Variant title: The tragedy of Hamlet, Prince of Denmark

Henry IV. See King Henry the fourth

Julius Caesar. 1599? BEAC11, BENP, CARM, COOK3, GRDB26, KET, OLI1, RED, REDM, SUT2, WORL2

King Henry the eighth. 1613? GRDB27

King Henry the fifth. 1598? GRDB26, WHF, WHFA

King Henry the fourth, pt. I. 1597? ABRA, ABRB1, BEAL, BEAM, BOGO, BOY, BROJ, BROK, CALD, CASE, COL1, DAV1, DEAN, DEAS, GARZF, GRDB26, HAPS1, HAPT1, KERN, OLI1, PRAT1, SMK, STJM, STJN
Variant title: Henry IV

King Henry the fourth, pt. II. 1596? GRDB26, STJN

King Henry VI, pt. I. 1591? GRDB26

King Henry VI, pt. II. 1591? GRDB26

King Henry VI, pt. III. 1591? GRDB26

King John. 1596? GRDB26

King Lear. 1605? BARC, BENQ, BENSB1, BONB, BONC, BRIX, BROK, BROTA, COTX, CRAF, DEAN, DEAO, FOU, GOLD, GRDB27, GRED, HARC46, HIB, HIBA, HIBB, HOGA, HOUS, JOHN, KINN, OLI1, PRAT1, ROB, RUSS, SOU, STY, TRI, TRIA, WAIW
Variant title: The tragedy of King Lear

King Richard II. 1595? DUH, GRDB26
Variant titles: Richard II; The tragedy of King Richard II

King Richard III. 1592? CONG, GRDB26
Variant title: The tragedy of King Richard III

The lamentable tragedy of Locrine (sometimes attributed to). See Anonymous plays. The lamentable tragedy of Locrine

The London prodigal (sometimes attributed to). See Anonymous plays. The London prodigal

Love's labour's lost. 1594? GRDB26

Macbeth. 1605? BARD, BARU, BEAC12, BENN, BRIG, CALD, CARN, CLKJ, COTKC, DAI, GOOD, GRDB27, HARC46, HOGI, INGE, INGG, KIN, KNID, KNIE, MIJ2, MIJA2, NEVI, OLI2, PATM, PATP, POOL, PROM, PRON, REIN, ROHR, ROSS, SANK, SEN, SHAR, SHAV, SRY, SRYG, SUT4, WAGC4, WORL4
Variant title: The tragedy of Macbeth

Measure for measure. 1604? GRDB27, KRE, SIN

Merchant of Venice. 1596? BEAC10, GRDB26, GREJ, OLI1

The merry wives of Windsor.

1600? GRDB27

A midsummer night's dream. 1595? ALS, BART, BEAC9, BONA, BONB, GRDB26, HUDE, OLI1, SEN

Mucedorus (sometimes attributed to). See Anonymous plays. Mucedorus

Much ado about nothing. 1598? GRDB26

Othello, The Moor of Venice. 1604? BARJ, BEAR, BENU, BIER, BLON, BLOO, BOW, COOP, COTKIR, DOV, FREG, GLO, GRDB27, GREC1, HAVL, JAFF, LEVI, MESS, MOL, MON, OLI1, PERS, PERT, PERU, REIO, SCNN, SCNO, SCNP, SIN, SMP, SUTL, TAUJ, VOLI, VOLP, VON
Variant title: The tragedy of Othello

Pericles, Prince of Tyre. 1609? GRDB27

The puritan; or, The widow of Watling street (sometimes attributed to). See Anonymous plays. The puritan; or, The widow of Watling street

The reign of King Edward the third (sometimes attributed to). See Anonymous plays. The reign of King Edward the third

Richard II. See King Richard II

Romeo and Juliet. 1594? BARO, BLAH, EDAD, EVA2, EVB2, GARZAP, GASS, GLO, GPA, GRDB26, GRIF, HOLP, JORG, OLI1, SHAW, SMN, SOM, SOMA, THO

The taming of the shrew. 1593? GRDB26, SMR

The tempest. 1611? ADV, CALD, CONN, FEL, GRDB27, HAPS1, HAPT1, HARC46, KER, SSST, SSSU

Timon of Athens. 1607? GRDB27

Titus Andronicus. 1593? GRDB26

The tragedy of Antony and Cleopatra. See Antony and Cleopatra

The tragedy of Hamlet, Prince of Denmark. See Hamlet

The tragedy of King Lear. See King Lear

The tragedy of King Richard II. See King Richard II

The tragedy of King Richard III. See King Richard III

The tragedy of Macbeth. See Macbeth

The tragedy of Othello. See Othello, the Moor of Venice

Troilus and Cressida. 1602? BENSB1, GRDB27, WEAN

Twelfth night; or, What you will. 1599. BARB, BENU, BIER, COTKI, FEFL, GOLD, GRDB27, HILP, JOHO, MIL, OLI1, STY, WALJ

The two gentlemen of Verona. 1594? GRDB26

The winter's tale. 1610. GRDB27, OLI2, PRAT1

A Yorkshire tragedy (sometimes attributed to). See Anonymous plays. A Yorkshire tragedy

--See Fletcher, John, jt. auth.

SHARP, ALAN

The long-distance piano player. 1962. NEWE12

SHARP, ANTHONY

Nightmare abbey (adapted from the frolic by Thomas Love Peacock). 1952. PLAN7

SHAW, GEORGE BERNARD, 1856-1950

Androcles and the lion. 1913. CARN, KRM, SAND, STRB, WISF

Arms and the man. 1894.

ABRA, ABRB2, BAC, BARB, BARU, BARV, BEAL, BEAM, BEAR, BLON, BOWY, CALD, CASE, COTKF, COTKIR, CUBG, DOD, GARZAP, GASS, GOLD, HAVI, JORG, JORH, KERP, KNIE, LOOF, MIJB, REIN, REIP, SATJ, SCAR, SCNN, SCNO, SCNP, SHAX, WEAN, WHFM
Caesar and Cleopatra. 1899. BAIC, BIER, DIT, DIV, FREI, GAED, GOLH, JOHN, KET, KON, LOR, MORT, REIL, REIO, REIT, WEIS, WEIW
Candida. 1895. BARR, BONA, BONB, COOP, HAVG, KNIC, KNID, LOCLB, PERT, PERU, STEI, TRE, TREA1, TREBA, TREC2, TREE3, TREI3, TREJ
The devil's disciple. 1897. BAUL, BOY, CAPU, CLM, CLN, CUBH, FREF, KIN, LOCLA, SUL
The doctor's dilemma. 1906. LID, TRI, TRIA, WARI, WARL
Don Juan in hell (from Man and superman). 1907. BALL
Getting married. 1909. ULAN, WEAL
Heartbreak house. 1920. BONB, BONC, COTKH, DOT, SEN, TREJ
How he lied to her husband. 1904. HOGI
John Bull's other island. 1904. BARF, GREJ (act I, only)
Major Barbara. 1905. ABC, BAIC, BAIE, BARG, BARJ, BENSB2, BLOC, BOW, BUR, COK, COTKR, COTQ, GORE, LIEF, RAI, SALE, WAIU, WAIW, WEIM
Man and superman. 1903. AUG, BLOC, HAPS2, HAPT2, ROET, WATA
The man of destiny. 1897. ALTE, DANI, FEFL, STEI
Misalliance. 1919. COTKI
Mrs. Warren's profession. 1902. SIXB, WELT
Passion, poison and petrifaction; or, The fatal gazogene. 1905. THOD
Pygmalion. 1912. BROY, COX, DAI, DEAR, EAVE, FOUK, FOUM, GOLK, GOOR, HEI, KRM, ROHR, SHAV, SHAW, SIN, SOU, WATE, WISE
--See Lerner, Alan Jay. My fair lady (adapted from)
Saint Joan. 1923. ALLK, BENSB2, CLO, COTX, DOV, HIG, KER, MACN, SWA, THF, WAGC4
The shewing up of Blanco Posnet. 1909. BARH
The six of Calais. 1934. HOGA
Widowers' houses. 1892. BAI

SHAW, IRWIN, 1912-
Bury the dead. 1936. AND, BENSPB, EDAD, FAMJ, GARZA2, GAS, KOZ

SHAW, ROBERT, 1927-
The man in the glass booth. 1968. BES68, PLAN34

SHAY, FRANK, 1888-1954
A Christmas carol (adapted from the story by Charles Dickens). 1929? LEV, LEVE

SHEH, LU
Dragon beard ditch. Hung-ying, L., tr. MESE

SHEINEN, LEV ROMANOVICH, 1905- . See Tur, Leonid Davidovich, jt. auth.

SHELDON, EDWARD BREWSTER, 1886-1946

The boss. 1911. QUIG, QUIJ, QUIK, QUIL, QUIM, QUIN
The jest. See Benelli, Sem. The jest (tr. and adapted by)
"Man's extremity is God's opportunity." See Salvation Nell
Romance. 1913. BAK, BES09
Salvation Nell. 1908. GARX, GARZA1
Variant title: "Man's extremity is God's opportunity"

SHELLEY, ELSA (MRS. IRVING KAYE DAVIS)
Pick-up girl. 1944. BES43

SHELLEY, PERCY BYSSHE, 1792-1822
The Cenci. 1886. ASG, HARC18, KAU, KRE, MOSE2, SMP, TAT, TAU, TRE
Prometheus unbound. 1820. BERN, GREB2, HAPT2, PRAT2, SML

SHEPARD, SAM, 1943-
Chicago. 1965. ORZ
Forensic and the navigators. 1967. SLM
The holy ghostly. 1972. OFF
Red cross. 1968. OFF

SHEPP, ARCHIE
Junebug graduates tonight. KINH

SHERIDAN, RICHARD BRINSLEY BUTLER, 1751-1816
The critic; or, A tragedy rehearsed. 1779. ASH, COP, COPC1, FEFL, NET, STM
The duenna. 1775. STM
The rivals. 1775. ALLI, ALLJ, ALLK, BENP, CLK1, DEM, DRA2, EIGH, HIG, HOUS, KEY, MOR, NET, PLAB2, REIO, ROB, SCAR, SHAI2, SHAJ2, SNYD1, STM, TUP, TUQ, TWE, UHL, WEAT1, WOO1
The school for scandal. 1777. ABRB1, ALT, ALTE, BAC, BAUG, BENY, BONC, BRIG, BRIX, BROJ, BROK, CLF1, CLKW, COF, COJ, CONP, COTKI, DAV1, DEM, FOUB, GARZAP, GASS, GRE, GREB1, GREC1, HARC18, HAVH, HUD, KRM, KRO, LIE, LIED1, LIEE1, MAT, MCCL, MCM, MCMI, MCMS, MON, MOO, MORR, MOSE2, NET, RUB, RUSS, SHRO, SMO, SPF1, STA, STM, TAT, TAU, THO, TREB, TREC1, TREE1, TREI1, TUP, TUQ, TWE, UHL, WATT2, WILE, WOOD1, WOOE1

SHERIDAN, THOMAS, 1719-1788
The brave Irishman; or, Captain O'Blunder (sometimes attributed to John Preston). 1746. HUGH
Variant title: Captain O'-Blunder; or, The brave Irishman
Captain O'Blunder; or, The brave Irishman. See The brave Irishman

SHERRIFF, ROBERT CEDRIC, 1896-
Badger's green. 1930. SIXD
The colonel's lady (screenplay based on the story by W. Somerset Maugham). JORG
Home at seven. 1950. BARV
Journey's end. 1928. BES28, CEU, CHA, CHAN, CHAR, FAO, FREI, FUL, HUDS2, LOV, MOD, PLAD, STAT, STAU, STAV, TRE, TREA1, TREBA, TREC2, TREE3, TREI3
The long sunset. 1955. PLAN12
A shred of evidence. 1960. PLAN22

The telescope. 1957. PLAN15

-- and DE CASALIS, JEANNE
St. Helena. 1935. BES36, FAMI

SHERWOOD, ROBERT EMMET, 1896-1955
Abe Lincoln in Illinois. 1938. BES38, BIER, BROX, CALG, CALP, CASS, CLDP, COOJ, CORF, COTE, COTH, GARZ, GARZA2, GOW, GOWA, HAT, HATA, HAVD, HAVE, NAGE, PROD, ROLF, WAT1, WATO
Idiot's delight. 1936. BES35, CLUR, CORE, CORF, GAS, HIL, MERU, MOSH, SIXP
The petrified forest. 1935. BES34, CET, DOWM, MOSL, WATC2
Reunion in Vienna. 1931. BES31, FAME, THF
The road to Rome. 1926. BES26, GASB
The rugged path. 1945. BES45
Second threshold. See Barry, Philip. Second threshold (revised by)
There shall be no night. 1940. BES39, CORB, DUR
Tovarich. See Deval, Jacques. Tovarich (tr. and adapted by)

SHIELS, GEORGE, 1886-1949
The new gossoon. 1930. CAN

SHIELS, JOHN WILSON, 1871-1929
Nec-natama. 1914. BOH3

SHIKO, OKAMURA
The Zen substitute. 1963. Brendon, J., tr. and Niwa, T., trs. BRA

SHINE, TED, 1931-
Contribution. 1969. BRAS
Herbert III. 1974. HARY

SHIRLEY, JAMES, 1596-1666
The cardinal. 1641. BAS, BROC, NEI, PAR, WALL
The lady of pleasure. 1635. BAS, HAPRA2, HAPRB2, KNOW, NEI, SCH, SCI, SCJ, SPE
The royall master. 1638. GAY3
The traitor. 1631. OLH, OLI2, TAV
The wedding. 1626. KNOW

SHKVARKIN, VASILII VASIL'-EVICH, 1893-
Father unknown. 1933. Bakshy, H., tr. BAKS

SHUDRAKA (KING), 1st cent. B.C.-1st cent. A.D.?
The little clay cart (attributed to). 1st cent. B.C.-1st cent. A.D.?
Lal, P., tr. BRA, LAL
Oliver, R., tr. WEL, PLAN29
Ryder, A., tr. ANDF
Wilson, H., tr. DOWS
Variant title: The toy cart
The toy cart. See The little clay cart

SHULMAN, MAX, 1919- , and SMITH, ROBERT PAUL
The tender trap. 1954. THEA55

SHVARTS, EVGENII L'VOVICH, 1897-1958
The shadow. 1940. Reeve, F., tr. REEV2

SICAM, GERONIMO D., and CASINO, JESUS
Mir-i-nisa (based on the story by José García Villa). 195-? EDAD

SIDNEY, SIR PHILIP, 1554-1586
The lady of May. 1579? PAR

SIERRA, GREGORIO MARTINEZ.

See Martínez Sierra, Gregorio

SIERRA, MARIA MARTINEZ. See Martínez Sierra, María

SIEVEKING, LANCELOT DE GIBERNE, 1896-
The strange case of Dr. Jekyll and Mr. Hyde (adapted from the novel by Robert Louis Stevenson). 1956. PLAN15

SIFTON, CLAIRE, 1897- , and SIFTON, PAUL
Give all thy terrors to the wind. 1936? KOZ

SIFTON, PAUL. See Sifton, Claire, jt. auth.

SIGURJONSSON, JOHANN, 1880-1919
Bjaerg-Ejvind og hans hustru. See Eyvind of the hills
Eyvind of the hills. 1911. Schanche, H., tr. DIE
Variant title: Bjaerg-Ejvind og hans hustru
Galtra-Loftur. See The wish
Loftur the magician. See The wish
Ønsket. See The wish
The wish. 1914. Haugen, E., tr. HAVHA
Variant titles: Galtra-Loftur; Loftur the magician; Ønsket

SIMON, [MARVIN] NEIL, 1927-
Barefoot in the park. 1963. BES63
The gingerbread lady. 1970. BES70
The good doctor. 1973. BES73
Last of the red hot lovers. 1969. BES69
The odd couple. 1965. BES64, GARV, GARZA4
Plaza suite. 1968. BES67
(3 one-act plays: Visitor from Forest Hills; Visitor from Hollywood; Visitor from Mamaroneck)
The prisoner of Second Avenue. 1971. BES71
The sunshine boys. 1972. BES72
Visitor from Forest Hills (part of Plaza Suite). 1968. RICK

SIMONOV, KONSTANTIN MIKHAILOVICH, 1915-
The Russian people. See The Russians
The Russians. 1942. Odets, C., tr. SEVP
Shelley, G., and Guthrie, T., trs. FOUT
Variant titles: The Russian people; Russkie lyndie
Russkie lyndie. See The Russians

SIMPSON, ELIZABETH. See Inchbald, Mrs. Elizabeth (Simpson)

SIMPSON, NORMAN FREDERICK, 1919-
One way pendulum. 1959. POP
A resounding tinkle. 1957. NEWE2, OBSE

SINGER, CAMPBELL. See Ross, George, jt. auth.

SISSON, ROSEMARY ANNE
The queen and the Welshman. 1957. PLAN18
The splendid outcasts. 1959. PLAN19

SKELTON, JOHN, 1460-1529
Magnyfycence. 1516? POLL

SKINNER, CORNELIA OTIS, 1901- . See Taylor, Samuel, jt. auth.

SLADE, JULIAN, 1930-
Sixty thousand nights (music and lyrics by). See May,

Val. Sixty thousand nights
Trelawny, a musical play (music by). See Woods, Aubrey, and Rowell, George. Trelawny, a musical play

SLAWOMIR, MROZEK, 1930-
Tango. 1964. Bethell, N., and Stoppard, T., trs. THOR

SLOMAN, ROBERT. See Dobie, Laurence, jt. auth.

SMEE, LILLIAN
No thoroughfare. 1935. FIN

SMITH, ALBERT RICHARD, 1816-1860
The cricket on the hearth (adapted from the story by Charles Dickens). 1859. CAR

SMITH, BETTY, 1904-1972
Fun after supper. 1940. GALB

SMITH, DODIE, pseud. See Smith, Dorothy Gladys

SMITH, DOROTHY GLADYS (Dodie Smith; C. L. Anthony, pseuds.), 1896-
Autumn crocus. 1931. FAMA, PLAD, PLAL2
Call it a day. 1935. BES35, FAMI
Dear octopus. 1938. PLAL1
Service. 1932. FAMC
Touch wood. 1934. FAMF

SMITH, HARRY JAMES, 1880-1918
Mrs. Bumpstead-Leigh. 1911. BES09, MOSJ, MOSK, MOSL

SMITH, HOWARD FORMAN
Blackberryin'. 1922? SHAY

SMITH, JOHN, 1752-1809
A dialogue between an Englishman and an Indian. 1781? MONR
A little teatable chitchat, alamode; or an ancient discovery reduced to modern practice;--Being a dialogue, and a dish of tea. 1781? MONR

SMITH, MICHAEL, 1935-
Captain Jack's revenge. 1970. NEWA4
The next thing. 1966. SLM

SMITH, RICHARD PENN, 1799-1854
The bombardment of Algiers. 1829? AMP13
The last man; or, The cock of the village (adapted from Le coq de village, by Charles Décour and Anne Théodore). 1822. AMP13
The sentinels; or, The two sergeants. 1829. AMP13
Shakespeare in love (adapted from Shakespeare amoureux, by Alexandre Duval). 1804. AMP13
The triumph at Plattsburg. 1830. QUIJ, QUIK
A wife at a venture. 1829. AMP13
William Penn. 1829. AMP13

SMITH, ROBERT PAUL, 1915- See Shulman, Max, jt. auth.

SMITH, WILLIAM HENRY, 1806-1872
The drunkard; or, The fallen saved. 1844. MONR

SMITH, WINCHELL, 1871-1933, and BACON, FRANK
Lightnin'. 1918. CEY

SMOLIN, DMITRY
Lysistrata. See Aristophanes. Lysistrata (tr. and adapted by)

SNEIDER, VERN
The teahouse of the August

moon. See Patrick, John. The teahouse of the August moon (adapted from the novel by)

SOLOVEV, VLADIMIR ALEKSANDROVICH, 1907-
Field Marshal Kutuzov. 1939.
Robbins, J., tr. SEVP

SOLOVYOV, VLADIMIR A. See Solovev, Vladimir Aleksandrovich

SOMIN, WILLI OSCAR, 1898-
Attentat. See Close quarters
Close quarters. 1935.
Lennox, G., tr. and adapter. FAMH
Variant title: Attentat

SØNDERBY, KNUD, 1909-
En kvinde er overflødig. See A woman too many
A woman too many. 1942.
Roughton, A., tr. CONT
Variant title: En kvinde er overflødig

SONDHEIM, STEPHEN, 1930-
Company (music and lyrics by). See Furth, George. Company
Follies (music and lyrics by). See Goldman, James. Follies

SOPHOCLES, 496-406 B.C.
Ajax. 5th cent. B.C.
Jebb, R., tr. GRDB5
Moore, J., tr. GREP2
Trevelyan, R., tr. OAT1
Antigone. 441 B.C.
Anon. tr. BLON, BRIT, CARN, EVB1
Arnott, P., tr. HAVH
Banks, T., tr. MACM1, MACN, SOM, SOMA, VON
Cocteau, J., adapter, and Wildman, C., tr. BENU, CLM
Fitts, D., and Fitzgerald, R., trs. ABC, ADV, ALT, ALTE, BARI, BARU, BAUL, BEAR, BONA, BONB, BONC, CONG, CONP, COOP, COX, CRAF, DIT, DOV, DOWS, FIFT, GOLD, GOLH, GUTH, GUTL, HIG, HOGA, HOLP, JOHO, KERN, KERO, LEVJ, MON, MONA, MORT, MORV, MORW, MORX, PERU, REIO, ROHR, SCNP, SIN, SSST, SSSU, SUL, TAUJ
Francklin, T., tr. MIK7
Gassner, J., tr. GARZAP, GASS
Jebb, R., tr. GLO, GRDB5, GREE, HUD, KNID, KNIE, OAT1, OATE, OATH, SHAV, SHAX, THO, TRE, TREA2
Lucas, F., tr. LUCA, LUCAB, LUCAF
Neufeld, M., tr. MCKK1
O'Sheel, S., tr. FREF, LIND
Plumptre, E., tr. BAT1, BUCK, BUCL, BUCM, EVA1, HARC8, HAVI, HIB, HIBB, HOUS, HUDS2, HUDT, INGW, MAST, THOM, THON
Robinson, C., tr. ROBK
Roche, P., tr. BARH
Townsend, M., tr. CASE, COTKC, COTKIR, SUTL
Watling, E., tr. BLOO, KON, PATM, PATP
Way, A., tr. STA
Whitelaw, R., tr. ATTI, CLM, FEFT, ROBI, ROBJA, TEN
Wyckoff, E., tr. GREP2, GRER1
Young, G., tr. CLF1, CROS, PLAG, SEBO, SEBP
Electra. 5th cent.
Anon. tr. HAPD, WED
Campbell, L., tr. FEFT
Ferguson, F., tr. FIFT, FOR

Grene, D., tr. GREP2, GRER2
Jebb, R., tr. GRDB5, OAT1
Kitto, H., tr. CLO
Plumptre, E., tr. CLKW
Whitelaw, R., tr. ATT3
Young, G., tr. PLAG
King Oedipus. See Oedipus the king
Oedipus at Colonus. 401 B.C.
Anon. tr. GRER3
Campbell, L., tr. FEFT, ROBJA
Fitzgerald, R., tr. FIFT, GREP2, MACM1
Jebb, R., tr. GRDB5, OAT1
Moebius, W., tr. COOA
Plumptre, E., tr. ROBJ
Young, G., tr. KRE
Variant title: Oedipus coloneus
Oedipus coloneus. See Oedipus at Colonus
Oedipus, King of Thebes. See Oedipus the king
Oedipus rex. See Oedipus the king
Oedipus the king. 5th cent.
Anon. tr. EVB1, MCA, SANK, SATJ, SCNN
Arnott, P., tr. HAPRL, MOL
Banks, T., tr. BOY, MACM1
Berkowitz, L., tr. BAIC, MACN
Bywater, I., tr. SCNO
Cavender, K., tr. GOU1, SMA, WEIS, WEIW
Cook, A., tr. COOA, DAVK, HAPO, LIND
Fitts, D., and Fitzgerald, R., trs. ALLI, ALLJ, ALLK, ALS, BARI, BARJ, BEAM, BIER, BOW, BRIX, BUR, CALD, CLKJ, CONO, DEAR, DEAS, DIT, DIV, DOV, DOWN, DUH, ELK, FIFR, FREG, GOLD, GORE, HOGI, JAFF, JOHN, KINN, KNO, LEVI, LID, MACF, PERS, PERT, REIL, REIN, SEN, SIN, STY, TRI, TRIA, VANV1, VOLI, VOLP, WAIW
Francklin, T., tr. GREE
Gassner, J., tr. TREB, TREC1, TREE1, TREI1
Glasser, J., tr. HILP
Grene, D., tr. BEAL, BLAG, BLAH, GPA, GREN, GREP2, GRER1, LOCL, LOCLA, LOCLB, ROBI
Jebb, R., tr. BROK, GARZF, GRDB5, GREC1, LOCM1, MAU, MURP, OAT1, OATE, OATH, THP, WARN1
Knox, B., tr. GORDP
Lucas, F., tr. LUCA, LUCAB, LUCAF
Mendell, C., tr. ROBJA, WALJ
Murray, G., tr. CAR, CARA, COJ, FEFT, MIL, TEN
Plumptre, E., tr. BUCK, BUCL, BUCM, DRA1, EVA1, EVC1, HARC8, PLAB1, SMP
Roach, P., tr. JORH
Sheppard, J., tr. BARC, GLO, WEAV1
Starr, F., tr. LAP
Watling, E., tr. BENQ, BROTA, SANO
Whitelaw, R., tr. ATT1, HOWE, HOWF
Yeats, W., tr. DEAP, FIFT, MACJ, MACL1, MIJB, ROET, SHR, SHRO, WHFM
Young, G., tr. PLAG
Variant titles: King Oedipus; Oedipus, King of Thebes; Oedipus rex; Oedipus tyrannus; Oedipus turannos
Oedipus turannos. See Oedipus the king
Oedipus tyrannus. See Oedipus the king

Philoctetes. 409 B.C.
Cavender, K., tr. HAPRL
Chase, A., tr. FIFV
Dolin, E., and Sugg, A., trs. COOA
Francklin, T., tr. OAT1
Freeman, K., tr. LIND
Grene, D., tr. GREP2, GRER3
Jebb, R., tr. GRDB5
Workman, J., tr. ROBJ
The searching satyrs. 5th cent. B.C.
Green, R., tr. TREB
The trachiniae. 5th cent. B.C.
Jameson, M., tr. GREP2
Jebb, R., tr. GRDB5, OAT1
Variant title: The women of Trachis
The women of Trachis. See The trachiniae

SORGE, REINHARD JOHANNES, 1895-1944
The beggar. (1912)
Sokel, W., and J., trs. SOK
Variant title: Die Bettler
Die Bettler. See The beggar

SOUPAULT, PHILIPPE. See Breton, André, jt. auth.

SOUTHERNE, THOMAS, 1660-1746
Oroonoko. 1696. DOB

SOWERBY, KATHERINE GITHA
Rutherford and son. 1912. DIG, PLAP2

SOYA, C. E., 1896-
Lion with corset.
Knudson, B., tr. FIL
To traade. See Two threads
Two threads. 1943.
Anon. tr. (revised by P. N. Furbank) CONT
Variant title: To traade

SPARK, MURIEL SARAH, 1918-
Doctors of philosophy. 1962. RHE

SPENCE, EULALIE, 1894-
The starter. 1927. LOC
Undertow. 1928. HARY

SPEWACK, MRS. BELLA (COHEN), 1899- , and SPEWACK, SAMUEL
Boy meets girl. 1935. BES35, CET, FAMJ, GAS, SAFF
My 3 angels (adapted from La cuisine des anges, by Albert Husson). 1953. BES52, GARZH, THEA53

SPEWACK, SAMUEL, 1899-1971
Two blind mice. 1949. BES49
Under the sycamore tree. 1952. PLAN7
--See Spewack, Mrs. Bella (Cohen), jt. auth.

SPINETTI, VICTOR. See Kennedy, Adrienne, jt. auth.

SRI-HARSHADEVA. See Harsha, son of Hira

STAFF OF THE LIVING NEWSPAPER
Triple-A plowed under. 1936. FEF

STALLINGS, LAURENCE, 1894-1968. See Anderson, Maxwell, jt. auth.

STARKWEATHER, DAVID
The poet's papers. (1970) NEWA3

STEELE, SIR RICHARD, 1672-1729
The conscious lovers. 1722. COF, EIGH, MCM, MCMI, MCMS, MOR, MOSE1, NET, STM, TAT, TAU, TAY, TUP, TUQ, WILE

STEELE, RUFUS, 1877-1935
The fall of Ug. 1913. BOH3

STEELE, SILAS SEXTON
The crock of gold; or, The toiler's trials. 1845. AMP14

STEELE, WILBUR DANIEL, 1886-1970
The giant's stair. 1924? THO

STEFFANSSON, DAVID JOHANN, 1895-1964
The golden gate. 1941. Gathorne-Hardy, G., tr. FIL, HAVHA
Variant title: Gullna hlidid
Gullna hlidid. See The golden gate

STEIN, GERTRUDE, 1874-1946
Daniel Webster eighteen in America. 1937? NEW37, SPC

STEIN, JOSEPH, 1912-
Fiddler on the roof (music by Jerry Bock, lyrics by Sheldon Harnick). 1964. BES64, GARV, GARZA4

STEINBECK, JOHN, 1902-1968
The moon is down. 1942. BES41
Of mice and men. 1937. BENPB, BES37, CLUR, CRIT, GAS, GAVE, SATI

STEPHENS, HENRY MORSE, 1857-1919
St. Patrick at Tara. 1909. BOH2

STERNHEIM, CARL, 1878-1942
Die Kassette. See The strongbox
Die marquise von Arcis. See The mask of virtue
The mask of virtue. 1920. Dukes, A., tr. and adapter FAMH
Variant title: Die marquise von Arcis
A pair of drawers. See The underpants
A place in the world. 1913. Bentley, E., tr. BENS1
Clark, B., and Katzin, W., trs. KAT
Variant title: Der snob; The snob
Der snob. See A place in the world
The snob. See A place in the world
The strongbox. 1912. Edwards, M., and Reich, V., trs. SOK
Variant title: Die Kassette
The underpants. 1911. Bentley, E., tr. BENT6
Variant title: A pair of drawers

STEVENSON, ROBERT LOUIS, 1850-1894
The strange case of Jekyll and Mr. Hyde. See Sieveking, Lance. The strange case of Dr. Jekyll and Mr. Hyde (adapted from)

STEVENSON, WILLIAM ("MR. S. MR. of ART." pseud.), fl. 1551-1561
Gammer Gurton's nedle. See Gammer Gurton's needle
Gammer Gurton's needle (supposed author). 1552? ADA, BAS, BOA, CRE, FAR, GARZB, GAY1, HEIL, LEV, LEVE, MAL, NES, WATT2
Variant title: Gammer Gurton's nedle

STEWART, DONALD OGDEN, 1894-
Rebound. 1930. BES29

STEWART, DOUGLAS, 1913-
Ned Kelly. 1943? THOP

STEWART, MICHAEL, 1924-
Hello, Dolly! (music and lyrics by Jerry Herman;

based on The matchmaker, by Thornton Wilder). 1964. BES63

STIRLING, GEORGE
The triumph of Bohemia. 1906. BOH1

STONE, JOHN AUGUSTUS, 1800-1834
Metamora; or, The last of the Wampanoags. 1829. AMP14, CLA, COY, MONR
Tancred, King of Sicily; or, The archives of Palermo. 1831. AMP14

STONE, PETER H., 1930-
1776 (music and lyrics by Sherman Edwards). 1969. BES67

STOPPARD, TOM, 1937-
Jumpers. 1974. BES73
Rosencrantz and Guildenstern are dead. 1966. BES68

STORACE, STEPHEN
No song no supper. See Hoare, Prince. No song no supper (music by)

STOREY, DAVID MALCOLM, 1933-
The changing room. 1973. BES72
The contractor. 1969. BES73, PLAN40
Home. 1970. BES70, PLAN40
In celebration. 1969. PLAN38
The restoration of Arnold Middleton. 1967. PLAN35

STOREY, ROBERT
Touch it light. 1957. PLAN18

STORM, LESLEY (pseud. of Mrs. Mabel Margaret (Cowie) Clark), 1903-1971
Black chiffon. 1949. PLAN2

STOWE, MRS. HARRIET ELIZABETH (BEECHER), 1811-1896
Uncle Tom's cabin. See Aiken, George L. Uncle Tom's Cabin (based on the novel by)

STRAMM, AUGUST, 1874-1915
Awakening. 1915?
Ritchie, J., and Garten, H., trs. RITS

STRANACK, JOHN
With malice aforethought. 1966. BALLE3

STRINDBERG, AUGUST, 1849-1912
Brott och brott. See There are crimes and crimes
Comrades. 1888.
Oland, E., and W., trs. TUCG, TUCM, TUCN, TUCO
Variant title: Kamraterna; Marodörer
Countess Julie. See Miss Julia
Creditors. 1889.
Sprigge, E., tr. PLAN21
Variant title: Fordringsägare
Crimes and crimes. See There are crimes and crimes
The dance of death. 1901?
Ginsberg, N., tr. PLAN32
Locock, C., tr. ROET
A dream play. 1902.
Björkman, E., tr. WALJ, WATA, WATI, WATL3
Goodman, R., tr. GOOR
Locock, C., tr. DIK2
Paulson, A., tr. TREBA, TREI3, TREJ
Sprigge, E., tr. AUG, BAUL, CAPU, ROHR, WEIS
Variant titles: The dream play; Ett drömspel
The dream play. See A dream play
Ett drömspel. See The dream play
Fadren. See The father
The father. 1887.
Erichsen, M., tr. DIC,

SMI
Oland, E., and W., trs. TRE, TREA1, TREBA, TREC2, TREE2, TREI2, TREJ, WHI
Sprigge, E., tr. FREG, GLO, KERP
Variant title: Fadren
Fordringsägare. See Creditors
Fröken Julie. See Miss Julia
The ghost sonata. 1907.
Anon. tr. REIP
Palmstierna, E., and Fagan, J., trs. HAV
Sprigge, E., tr. BENY, BLOC, KERP, REIL, REIN, REIT, SEN
Sprichorn, E., tr. ALLK, COTQ, WAIW
Variant titles: Spogelsessonaten; The spook sonata
The great highway. 1910.
Paulson, A., tr. MODS
Variant title: Stora landsvägen
Kamraterna. See Comrades
Lady Julie. See Miss Julia
Marodörer. See Comrades
Miss Julia. 1888.
Anon. tr. BLON, CLN
Björkman, E., tr. CAR, HAV, WARL
Locock, C., tr. BARK, INTE SATI
Sprigge, E., tr. AUG, BLOC, CLM, COTX, DOV, GLO, REIO, SILN, SILQ, STY, WEIM
Sprinchorn, E., tr. BONC, COTKC, COTQ, DOT, HAVH, HOUP
Variant titles: Countess Julie; Fröken Julie; Lady Julie; Miss Julie
Miss Julie. See Miss Julia
Moderskärlek. See Motherly love
Motherly love. 1893.
Ziegler, F., tr. SHAY
Variant title: Moderskärlek
Spogelses-sonaten. See The ghost sonata
The spook sonata. See The ghost sonata
Stora landsvägen. See The great highway
The stronger. See The stronger woman
The stronger woman. 1890.
Anon. tr. PERS, PERT, PERU, SHAY
Oras, A., tr. MORT, MORV, MORW
Sprigge, E., tr. BUR, KERN, KERO
Variant title: The stronger
There are crimes and crimes. 1899.
Björkman, E., tr. MOSG, MOSH, TREBA, TREC2, TREE2, TREI2
Sprinchorn, E., tr. SPR
Variant titles: Brott och brott; Crimes and crimes
To Damascus, part 1. 1900.
Paulson, A., tr. ULAN
Sprinchorn, E., tr. SPR

STRODE, WARREN CHETHAM. See Chetham-Strode, Warren

STRONG, AUSTIN, 1881-1952
The drume of Oude. 1906. LEV, LEVE, MIL

STROUSE, CHARLES, 1928-
Applause (music by). See Comden, Betty and Green, Adolph. Applause
"It's a bird, it's a plane, it's superman" (music by). See Newman, David and Benton, Robert. "It's a bird, it's a plane, it's superman"

STUART, MRS. AIMEE (McHARDY), 1890-
Jeannie. 1940. FIR
Lace on her petticoat. 1950. PLAN5
Sixteen. 1934. FAME

STUKALOV, N. F. See

Pogodin, Nokolai Federovich, pseud.

STURGES, PRESTON, 1898-1959
Strictly dishonorable. 1929. BES29, GASB

SUDERMANN, HERMANN, 1857-1928
Casa paterna. See Magda
The fires of St. John. 1900.
Swickard, C., tr. MOSQ
Variant title: Johannisfeuer
Das glück im winkel. See The vale of content
Happiness in a nook. See The vale of content
Heimat. See Magda
Home. See Magda
Johannes. See John the Baptist
Johannisfeuer. See The fires of St. John
John the Baptist. 1898.
Marshall, B., tr. FRA17
Variant title: Johannes
Magda. 1893.
Winslow, C., tr. WATI, WATL2
Variant titles: Casa paterna; Heimat; Home
The vale of content. 1895.
Leonard, W., tr. DIC
Variant titles: Das glück im winkel; Happiness in a nook

SUDRAKA (KING). See Shudraka (King)

SUGIMORI NOBUMORI. See Chikamatsu

SULLIVAN, SIR ARTHUR SEYMOUR, 1842-1900 (composer). See Gilbert, William Schwenck

SUNDGAARD, ARNOLD
Spirochete. 1938. FEF

SUNDUKIANTS, GAVRILL NIKITOVICH, 1825-1911
The ruined family. 1888.
Collins, F., tr. ARM
Variant title: Die ruinerte Familie
Die ruinerte Familie. See The ruined family

SUTHERLAND, EFUA THEODORA, 1924-
Edufa. 1964. LITT

SUTRO, ALFRED, 1863-1933
John Glayde's honour. 1907. DIG
A marriage has been arranged. 1902. PEN
The walls of Jericho. 1904. MAP

SVEINBJORNSSON, TRYGGI, 1891-
Bishop Jón Arason. 1950.
Hollander, L., tr. MODS

SWERLING, JOSEPH, 1897- ; BURROWS, ABRAM, and LOESSER, FRANK
Guys and dolls (based on the story, Idyll of Miss Sarah Brown, by Damon Runyan). 1950. BENT4, BES50

SWINBURNE, ALGERNON CHARLES, 1837-1909
Atlanta in Calydon. (1865) KAU

SYLVAINE, VERNON
As long as they're happy. 1953. PLAN9

SYLVANUS, ERWIN, 1917-
Dr. Korczak and the children. 1957.
Wellwarth, G., tr. BENB
Variant title: Korczak und die Kinder
Korczak und die Kinder. See Dr. Korczak and the children

SYNGE, JOHN MILLINGTON, 1871-1909
Deirdre of the sorrows. 1910. BARF
In the shadow of the glen. 1903. BALL, LOCLA,

MERC
The playboy of the western world. 1907. AUG, BAC, BENSB2, BLOC, CEW, CLKW, COK, COL2, COTKI, COTM, COTQ, CUBE, CUBG, DOT, DUR, FIG, FOU, GREC2, GRED, HAU, KRM, LIED2, LIEE2, MACL2, MORV, MORW, MORX, REIO, REIT, SALE, SOM, SOMA, STEI, TREJ, WALJ, WEIM
Riders to the sea. 1904. ALLI, ALLJ, ALLK, ALT, ALTE, BARI, BLOC, BONC, BRIG, BRIU, CAP, CAR, CARA, CLO, COD, CONN, COTKC, COTM, COTQ, DAI, DAV1, DIC, FIG, GREG, HAVI, HOGI, HUD, INGE, INGG, INGH, KERO, LOOA, LOOB, LOOC, LOOD, LOOE, LOOF, MCCA, MCCB, MILL, MOSN, MOSO, PATM (1 act only), PATP, PROW, REIL, SANK, SEN, SILN, SILQ, SSTA, STEI, STJN (1 act only), TAUJ, TOBI, TRE, TREA1, TREBA, TREC2, TREE3, TREI3, TREJ, TUCN, TUCO, WARI, WARL, WATA, WATF1, WATI, WATT2, WEAT2, WHI, WHK, WOOD2, WOOE2
The shadow of the glen. 1903. STY
The well of the saints. 1905. ULAN

T

TABORI, GEORGE, 1914-
The cannibals. 1967? SCV
The emperor's clothes. 1953. BES52

TAGORE, RABINDRANATH, 1861-1941
The post office. 1914. BART

TAILLE, JEAN DE LA, 1533?-1608?
Saul le furieux. 1572? FOUR

TAKEDA IDZUMO. See Idzumo, Takeda

TALLMAN, ROBERT
The man who liked Dickens (television version by). See Waugh, Evelyn. The man who liked Dickens

TAMAYO Y BAUS, MANUEL, 1829-1898
Un drama nuevo. 1967. BRET

T'ANG HSIEN-TSU, 1550-1617
Huan hun chi. See Peony pavilion
Mu-tan t'ing. See Peony pavilion
Peony pavilion (scenes 7, 10, 14, 20) 1598?
Anon. tr. BIR2
Variant titles: Huan hun chi; Mu-tan chi; The soul's revenge
The soul's revenge. See Peony pavilion

TANKRED-DORST. See Dorst, Tankred

TARDIEU, JEAN, 1902-
One way for another. 1951.
Wellwarth, G., tr. BEN
Variant title: Un geste pour un autre
Un geste pour un autre. See One way for another

TARKINGTON, BOOTH, 1869-1946
Clarence. 1919. BES19, GARU
The intimate strangers. 1921. COH
Monsieur Beaucaire. 1901. PEN, PROB
The trysting-place. 1923? SCWE, SCWG

-- and WILSON, HARRY LEON
The Gibson upright. 1919. WEB
The man from home. 1908. BES99, CEY

TARLTON, RICHARD, d. 1588
The famous victories of Henry the fifth (sometimes attributed to). See Anonymous plays. The famous victories of Henry the fifth

TASSO, TORQUATO, 1544-1595
Aminta. 1573.
Hunt, L., tr. BENSA
Oldmixon, J., tr. HAYD
Variant title: Amyntas
Amyntas. See Aminta

TATE, NAHUM, 1652-1715
A duke and no duke; or, Trapolin's vagaries (adapted from Trappolin suppos'd a prince, by Sir Aston Cokain). 1684. HUGH
The history of King Lear. 1681? SUMB

TATHAM, JOHN, fl. 1600
Grim the collier of Croydon; or, The devil and his dame (sometimes attributed to). See Anonymous plays. Grim the collier of Croydon; or, The devil and his dame

TAVEL, RONALD, 1941-
Gorilla queen. 1967. SLM

TAYLEURE, CLIFTON W.
Horse-shoe Robinson. 1856. MOSS2

TAYLOR, CECIL P.
Bread and butter. 1966. NEWE10
Happy days are here again. 1967. NEWE12

TAYLOR, CHARLES A., 1864-1942
From rags to riches. 1903. AMP8

TAYLOR, CHRISTOPHER
The wings of the dove (based on the novel by Henry James). 1963. PLAN28

TAYLOR, SAMUEL, 1912-
The happy time (based on the novel by Robert Fontaine). 1950. BES49
Sabrina fair. 1953. THEA54

-- and SKINNER, CORNELIA OTIS
The pleasure of his company. 1958. BES58

TAYLOR, TOM, 1817-1880
Our American cousin. 1858. BAI
New men and old acres. 1869. BOOA3
The ticket-of-leave man. 1863. BOOA2, MOSN, MOSO, ROWE

-- and READE, CHARLES
Masks and faces; or, Before and behind the curtain. 1852. ROWE

TCHEKOFF, ANTON. See Chekhov, Anton Pavlovich

TCHING, TSE. See Kao, Tong Kia

TEH-HUI, CHENG. See Chêng Teh-hui

TEH-YAO, JEN
Magic aster.
White, W., tr. MESE

TEICHMANN, HOWARD, and KAUFMANN, GEORGE S.
The solid gold Cadillac. 1953. GART, THEA54

TEJADA, LUIS VARGAS. See Vargas Tejada, Luis

TELLEZ, GABRIEL (TIRSO DE MOLINA, pseud.), 1570?-1648

El burlador de Sevilla. 1630. ALP, HILL
Campbell, R., tr. BENR3, FLOR, MACM1
O'Brien, R., tr. FLOS
Schizzano, A., and Mandel, O., trs. MAN
Starkie, W., tr. SSTW
Variant titles: The love-rogue; The playboy of Seville; or, Supper with a statue; The rogue of Seville; The trickster of Seville; The trickster of Seville and his guest of stone
The love-rogue. See El burlador de Sevilla
The playboy of Seville; or, Supper with a statue. See El burlador de Sevilla
The rogue of Seville. See El burlador de Sevilla
The trickster of Seville. See El burlador de Sevilla
The trickster of Seville and his guest of stone. See El burlador de Sevilla

TEMPLE, JOAN, d. 1965
No room at the inn. 1945. EMB2

TENNYSON, ALFRED, 1809-1892
Becket. 1893. KAU, MOSN, SMK

TERENCE. See Terentius Afer, Publius

TERENTIUS AFER, PUBLIUS, 195?-159 B.C.
Adelphi. 160 B.C.
Anon. tr. DUC2, TREB, TREC1, TREE1, TREI1
Casson, L., tr. CASU
Copley, F., tr. ROM
Held, W., tr. COTU
Lieberman, S., tr. LIC
Oldfather, W., tr. GUI, GUIN, HAPV
Riley, H., tr. MIK8
Suskin, A., tr. HOWK
Variant title: The brothers
The Andria. See The woman of Andros
Andria, the fair Andrian. See The woman of Andros
The brothers. See Adelphi
The eunuch. 161 B.C.
Anon. tr. DUC2
Colman, G., tr. BAT2
Variant title: Eunuchus
Eunuchus. See The eunuch
Heautontimorumenos. 163 B.C.
Anon. tr. DUC2
Riley, H., tr. MIK8
Variant titles: The self avenger; The self-tormentors
Hecyra. See The mother-in-law
The mother-in-law. 165 B.C.
Anon. tr. DUC2
Variant title: Hecyra
Phormio. 161 B.C.
Anon. tr. CLF1, HOWJ
Casson, L., tr. CASU, COTU
Clark, B., tr. DUC2, WEAV1
Copley, F., tr. ROM
Lieberman, S., tr. LIC
Morgan, M., tr. CLKW, MAU
Oldfather, W., tr. GUI, GUIN, HAPV
The self-avenger. See Heautontimorumenos
The self-tormentors. See Heautontimorumenos
The woman of Andros. 166 B.C.
Anon. tr. DUC2, MCKK2
Copley, F., tr. ROM
Lieberman, S., tr. LIC
Riley, H., tr. CROS, SEBO, SEBP
Variant titles: The Andria; Andria, the fair Andrian

TERKEL, LOUIS "STUDS," 1912-
Monologues from "Division Street, USA" - a series of dramatic interviews of

disinherited Americans. (1967) RAVA

TERRY, MEGAN, 1932-
Calm down, Mother. 1965. BAYM, SUB
Ex-Miss Cooper Queen on a set of pills. (1966) BALLE1
The gloaming, oh my darling. 1965. BAIC, BAIE
The magic realists. 1968. DIZ
Sanibel and Captiva. OWE

TERSON, PETER, 1932-
The mighty reservoy. 1964. NEWE14
A night to make the angels weep. 1964. NEWE11

TESICH, STEVE, 1942-
The carpenters. 1970. SCV

THARP, NEWTON J.
The quest of the Gorgon. 1905. BOH1

THEODORE, ANNE. See Décour, Charles Hébert, jt. auth.

THEOTOKAS, GEORGE, 1906-1966
The game of folly vs. wisdom.
Gianos, M., tr. GIA

THOMA, LUDWIG, 1867-1921
Champions of morality. See Moral
Moral. 1908.
Recht, C., tr. DID
Variant title: Champions of morality

THOMAS, ALBERT ELLSWORTH, 1872-1947
No more ladies. 1934. BES33

THOMAS, AUGUSTUS, 1857-1934
As a man thinks. 1911. BAK
The copperhead. 1918. COH
In Mizzoura. 1893. MOSS3
The witching hour. 1907. BES99, DIC, GARX, MOSJ, MOSK, MOSL, QUIG, QUIJ, QUIK, QUIL, QUIM, QUIN

THOMAS, DYLAN, 1914-1953
The doctor and the devils. 1959. BEAR
Under milk wood. 1953. BES57

THOMAS, GWYN, 1913-
Jackie the jumper. 1963. PLAN26
The keep. 1961. PLAN24

THOMPSON, DENMAN, 1833-1911
Joshua Whitcomb. See The old homestead
The old homestead. 1875. CEY
Variant title: Joshua Whitcomb

THORDARSON, AGNAR, 1917-
Atoms and madams. 1955.
Haugen, E., tr. HAVHA
Variant title: Kjarnorka og kvenkylli
Kjarnorka og kvenkylli. See Atoms and madams

THURBER, JAMES, 1894-1961
A Thurber carnival. 1960. BES59
-- and NUGENT, ELIOT
The male animal. 1940. BES39, BLOO, GARZ, HARB, KRM, LOCK, MIJY, ROLF, WISD

THURSTON, ELLA L.
Family cooperative. DRU

TIECK, JOHANN LUDWIG, 1773-1853
Der gestiefelte kater. 1844. CAM
Winter, L., tr. FRA4
Variant title: Puss in boots

Puss in boots. See Der gestiefelte kater

TIRSO DE MOLINA, pseud. See Téllez, Gabriel

TO, FU. See Seh, Sha, jt. auth.

TOBIN, JOHN, 1770-1804
The honeymoon, 1805. BAT16

TOLLER, ERNST, 1893-1939
Hinkelmann. 1922?
Ritchie, J., and Stowell, J., trs. RITV
Hoppla! See Hoppla! Such is life!
Hoppla! Such is life! 1927?
Ould, H., tr. ULAN
Variant titles: Hoppla!; Hoppla, wir leben
Hoppla, wir leben. See Hoppla! Such is life
The machine-wreckers. 1922.
Dukes, A., tr. MOSG, MOSH
Variant title: Die maschinen-stuermer
Man and the masses. See Masse mensch
Die maschinen-stuermer. See The machine-wreckers
Masse mensch. 1921. STI2
Untermeyer, L., tr. WATI, WATL4
Variant title: Man and the masses
Nie wieder friede. See No more peace!
No more peace! 1937.
Crankshaw, E., and Auden, W., trs. CALM, WELG
Variant title: Nie wieder friede
Transfiguration. 1919.
Crankshaw, E., tr. HAV
Variant titles: Transformation; Wandlung
Transformation. See Transfiguration
Wandlung. See Transfiguration

TOLSTOI, ALEKSIEI KONSTANTINOVICH, 1817-1875
The death of Iván the terrible. 1867.
Noyes, G., tr. NOY
Tsar Fyodor Ivanovitch. 1868?
Covan, J., tr. MOS

TOLSTOI, LEV NICHOLAEVICH, 1828-1910
Condemnation. 18-?
Maude, L., and Aylmer, trs. COUR
The dominion of darkness. See The power of darkness
The live corpse. 1911.
Anon. tr. GARZH
Maude, L., and A., trs. CHA, CHAN
Variant titles: The living corpse; The man who was dead; Redemption
The living corpse. See The live corpse
The man who was dead. See The live corpse
The power of darkness; or, If a claw is caught the bird is lost. 1895.
Anon. tr. DIK1
MacAndrew, A., tr. GARZE, MACD
Magarshack, D., tr. MAGA
Noyes, G., and Patrick, G., trs. HOUG, NOY, TREBA, TREC2, TREE2, TREI2, TREJ
Reeve, F., tr. REEV1
Variant title: The dominion of darkness
Redemption. See The live corpse
Taxes. 18-?
Maude, L., and Aylmer, trs. COUR

TOLSTOY. See Tolstoi

TOMPKINS, FRANK GEROW, 1879-
Sham. 1920? MIJA1

TONG KIA, KAO. See Kao, Tong Kia

TOOMER, JEAN, 1894-1967
Balo. 1924. HARY, LOC

TORRENCE, FREDERICK RIDGELY, 1875-1950
The danse Calinda. 1922. LOC
Granny Maumee. 1917. LOC
The rider of dreams. 1917. LOC

TORRES NAHARRO, BARTOLOME DE, fl. 1517
Comedia Himenea. See Hymen
Hymen. 1517?
Chambers, W., tr. BAT6
Variant title: Comedia Himenea

TOTHEROH, DAN, 1894-
Wild birds. 1925. BES24

TOUGH, ELSIE. See Schauffler, Mrs. Elsie (Tough)

TOURNEUR, CYRIL, 1575?-1626
The atheist's tragedy. 1610? GOM
The revenger's tragedy. 1606? GOM, HAPRA2, HARPB2, HUST, OLH, OLI2, RYL, SALG

TOWNLEY, JAMES, 1714-1778
High life below stairs. 1759. BAT16, MOR

TREADWELL, SOPHIE (MRS. SOPHIE McGEEHAN), 1891-1970
Hope for a harvest. 1941. BES41
Machinal. 1928. BES28, GASB

TRENEV, KONSTANTIN FEDOROVICH, 1900-
Lyubov Yarovaya. 1926.
Bakshy, A., tr. BAKS

TRENYOV, KONSTANTIN FYODOROVICH. See Trenev, Konstantin Fedorovich

TREPASSI, PIETRO. See Metastasio, Pietro Antonio Domenico Buonaventura, pseud.

TRIANA, JOSE, 1931-
The criminals. 1964.
Fernandez, P., and Kustow, M., trs. WOOG
Variant title: La noche de los asesinos
La noche de los asesinos. See The criminals

TROUBETSKOY, AMELIE (RIVES) CHANLER, 1863-1945
Herod and Mariamne. 1888? KOH2

TRUMBO, DALTON, 1905-
Opening sequence. 1969. BAYM

TRYE, JEAN GUILLAUME ANTOINE CUVELIER DE. See Cuvelier de Trye, Jean Guillaume Antoine

TSE-TCHING. See Kao, Tong Kia

TUCHOLSKY, KARL. See Hasenclever, Walter, jt. auth.

TUR, LEONID DAVIDOVICH, 1905- ; TUR, PETR DAVIDOVICH, and SHEININ, LEV ROMANOVICH
Smoke of the fatherland. 1942.
Feinberg, A., tr. SEVP

TUR, PETR DAVIDOVICH, 1907- See Tur, Leonid Davidovich, jt. auth.

TURGENEV, IVAN SERGIEEVICH, 1818-1883
A month in the country. 1872.
MacAndrew, A., tr. GARZE, MACD
Mandell, M., tr. FAMK
Newnham, R., tr. COTO
Noyes, G., tr. NOY,

TREB, TREC1, TREE1, TREI1
Williams, E., adapter. GARZH, HOUG

TURNEY, CATHARINE
Bitter harvest. 1936. FOUP

TURNEY, ROBERT, 1900-
Daughter of Atreus. 1936. BES36

TURQUE, MICHAEL, 1933-
Shoptalk. 19-? GRED

TYLER, ROYALL, 1757-1826
The contrast. 1787. BLAI1, CADY, DOWM, ELLI1, GARX, GARZA1, HAL, HOWP1, MONR, MOSS1, QUIJ, QUIK, QUIL, QUIM, QUIN, QUIO1, SPI, STL1
The island of Barrataria. 18th cent. AMP15
Joseph and his brethren. 18th cent. AMP15
The judgment of Solomon. 18th cent. AMP15
The origin of the feast of Purim; or, The destinies of Haman and Mordecai. 18th cent. AMP15

TZARA, TRISTAN, 1896-1963
Le coeur à gaz. See The gas heart
The gas heart. 1920. Benedikt, M., tr. BEN
Variant title: Le coeur à gaz

U

UDALL, NICHOLAS, 1505-1556
Ralph Roister Doister. 1566? ADA, BAS, BAT13, BOA, CRE, GARZB, GAY1, MAT, MIN2, MIO2, NES, PAR, SCW, TAV
Variant titles: Roister Doister; Royster Doyster
Respublica (attributed to). See Anonymous plays
Roister Doister. See Ralph Roister Doister
Royster Doyster. See Ralph Roister Doister

UDOFF, YALE M.
A guy play. 1971. BALLE8

UJINOBU, ZENCHIKU. See Zenchiku, Ujinobu

UKRAINKA, LESYA, pseud. See Kosach, Larisa Petrovna

UNRUH, FRITZ VON, 1885-1970
Heinrich aus Andernach. 1925. STI2

UPSON, WILLIAM HAZLETT, 1891-1975
The master salesman. 1924. GALB

USSEAU, ARNAUD D'. See D'Usseau, Arnaud

USTINOV, PETER, 1921-
The love of four colonels. 1951. BES52, THEA53
The unknown soldier and his wife. 1968. PLAN36

V

VALENCY, MAURICE JACQUES, 1903-
The Apollo of Bellac. See Giraudoux, Jean. The Apollo of Bellac (adapted by)
The enchanted. See Giraudoux, Jean. The enchanted (adapted by)
The madwoman of Chaillot. See Giraudoux, Jean. The madwoman of Chaillot (adapted by)
Ondine. See Giraudoux, Jean. Ondine (adapted by)
The visit. See Duerrenmatt, Friedrich. The visit (tr. and adapted by)

VALLE-INCLAN, RAMON MARIA DEL, 1870-1936
Divinas palabras. See Divine words
Divine words. 1933. Williams, E., tr. BENA
Variant title: Divinas palabras

VALLEJO, ANTONIO BUERO. See Buero Vallejo, Antonio

VANBRUGH, SIR JOHN, 1664-1726
The confederacy. 1705. KRM
A journey to London (ms. completed by C. Cibber). 1728. BAT15, TICK
Variant title: The provoked husband
The provoked husband. See A journey to London
The provok'd wife. 1697. GAY4, GOS, GOSA, MAT, MOSE1, RUB, TWE
The relapse; or, Virtue in danger. 1696. DAVR, MCM, MCMI, MOR, NET, REST, TUQ

VAN DOREN, MARK, 1894-1972
The last days of Lincoln. 1961. SWI

VAN DRUTEN, JOHN, 1902-1957
After all. 1929. FAMA, MYB, PLAD
Behold we live. 1932. FAMC
Bell, book and candle. 1950 BES50, GARW
The distaff side. 1933. BES34, FAME
Flowers of the forest. 1934. FAMG
I am a camera (adapted from the Berlin stories by Christopher Isherwood). 1951. BES51, FAMO, GART, GAVE
Variant title: Sally Bowles
I remember mama (based on the book Mama's bank account by Kathryn Forbes). 1944. BES44, DAVI, GARZ, MERS, REDM, SPES, STAV
London wall. 1931. FAMA
Sally Bowles. See I am a camera
Somebody knows. 1932. FAMB
There's always Juliet. 1931. FAMB
The voice of the turtle. 1943. BES43, GARZ, KRM
Young Woodley. 1925. BES25, FAO, PLAD

-- and MORRIS, LLOYD
The damask cheek. 1942. BES42

VAN ITALLIE, JEAN-CLAUDE, 1936-
America hurrah. 1966. BES66, CLN, ORZ, SANE
Interview. 1966. BAIC, GLI
Variant title: Pavane produced. . .
A masque for three dolls. See Motel
Motel; a masque for three dolls (part of America hurrah). 1965. HAVL, RAVA
Pavane produced. . . . See Interview
The serpent: a ceremony. 1970. BES69
Where is de queen? 1966. BALLE3

VANE, SUTTON, 1888-1943
Outward bound. 1923. BES23, CEU, MAP

VARESI, GILDA, 1887- , and BYRNE, MRS. DOLLY
Enter madame. 1920. BES20

VARGAS TEJADA, LUIS, 1802-1829
Las convulsiones. 1828. Bailey, W., tr. SSTE
Variant title: My poor nerves
My poor nerves. See Las convulsiones

VEGA, RICARDO DE LA, 1829-1910
Pepa la frescachona. 190-? BRET

VEGA, VENTURA DE LA, 1807-1865
El hombre de mundo. 1845. BRET
Variant title: A man of the world
A man of the world. See El hombre de mundo

VEGA CARPIO, LOPE FELIX DE, 1562-1635
The dog in the manger. 1613?
Chambers, W., tr. BAT6
Variant titles: The gardener's dog; El perro del hortelano
La estrella de Sevilla. 1617? ALP
Hayden, P., tr. CLKW, CROV, MAU
Variant title: The star of Seville
Fuente ovejuna. 1619. ALP
Campbell, R., tr. BENR3, BENSB1
Flores, A., and Kittel, M., trs. FLOR, FLOS, HOUE, TREB, TREC1, TREE1, TREI1
Underhill, J., tr. ALPF, DOWN, KRE, WARN2
Variant title: The sheep well
The gardener's dog. See The dog in the manger
The king, the greatest Alcalde. 1620?
Underhill, J., tr. CLF2, LOCM1, WEAV1
Variant title: El mejor Alcalde el rey
El mejor Alcalde el rey. See The king, the greatest Alcalde
Peribanez and the commander of Ocana. See Peribáñez y el comendador de Ocaña
Peribáñez y el comendador de Ocaña. 1610? HILL
Starkie, W., tr. SSTW
Variant title: Peribanez and the commander of Ocana
El perro del hortelano. See The dog in the manger
The sheep well. See Fuenteovejuna
The star of Seville. See La estrella de Sevilla

VEILLER, BAYARD, 1869-1916
The thirteenth chair. 1916. CART
Within the law. 1912. CART

VENTURA DE LA VEGA. See Vega, Ventura de la

VERGA, GIOVANNI, 1840-1922
La caccia al lupo. See The wolf-hunt
Cavalleria rusticana. 1880?
Bentley, E., tr. BENT1
The wolf-hunt. 1901.
Goldberg, I., tr. GOL
Variant title: La caccia al lupo

VERHAEREN, EMILE, 1855-1916
Les aubes. See The dawn
The dawn. 1898.
Symons, A., tr. MOSQ
Variant title: Les aubes

VERNEUIL, LOUIS, 1893-1952
Affairs of state. 1950. BES50, PLAN8
Variant title: Irene
Irene. See Affairs of state

VIAN, BORIS, 1920-1959
Les bâtisseurs d'empire. See The empire builders
The empire builders. 1959.
Taylor, S., tr. PLAN25
Variant titles: Les bâtisseurs d'empire; Le Schmürz
L'équarrissage pour tous. See Knackery for all
The knacker's ABC. See

Knackery for all
Knackery for all. 1944.
Estrin, M., tr. PLAC
Variant titles: L'équarrissage pour tous; The knacker's ABC
Le Schmürz. See The empire builders

VIDAL, GORE, 1925-
The best man. 1960. BES59, GARS
Visit to a small planet. 1957. BES56, KIN, OHL

VIGNE, ANDRIEU DE LA. See La Vigne, Andrieu de

VIGNY, ALFRED VICTOR DE, 1797-1863
Chatterton. 1835. BOR, COM, GRA

VILDRAC, CHARLES (pseud. of CHARLES MESSAGER), 1882-
Michel Auclair. 1922.
Howard, S., tr. LEV, LEVE
Le paquebot Tenacity. 1920. HART, HARV
Howard, S., tr. TUCG, TUCM
Newberry, J., tr. DIE
Variant titles: S. S. Tenacity; The steamer Tenacity; The steamship Tenacity
S. S. Tenacity. See Le paquebot Tenacity
The steamer Tenacity. See Le paquebot Tenacity
The steamship Tenacity. See Le paquebot Tenacity

VILLA, JOSE GARCIA
Mir-i-nisa. See Sicam, Geronimo D., and Casiño, Jesús. Mir-i-nisa (based on the story by)

VILLA, LILIA A.
Educating Josefina. 195-? EDAD

VILLIERS, CLAUDE DESCHAMPS, 1600?-1681
L'apoticaire devalisé. 1658? LAN

VILLIERS, GEORGE. See Buckingham, George Villiers

VINCENT, ALLEN. See Rotter, Fritz, jt. auth.

VISE, JEAN DONNEAU DE. See Donneau de Visé, Jean

VISHAKADATTA. 9th cent.
The signet ring of Rakshasa. 9th cent.
Lal, P., tr. LAL

VISHNEVSKII, VSEVOLOD VITALEVICH, 1900-1951
Optimicheskaya tragediya. See An optimistic tragedy
An optimistic tragedy. 1933.
Scott, H., and Carr, R., trs. FOUS
Variant title: Optimicheskaya tragediya

VITRAC, ROGER, 1899-1952
Les mystères de l'amour. See The mysteries of love
The mysteries of love. 1927.
Goldstone, R., tr. BEN
Variant title: Les mystères de l'amour

VIZIN, DENIS VON. See Fonvizin, Dinís Ivanovich

VODAHOVIC, SERGIO VINA
Three beach plays. 1964.
Oliver, W., tr. OLIW

VOLLMER, LULA, 1898-1955
Sun-up. 1923. BES23, LOW, QUIG, QUIK, QUIL, QUIM, QUIN, TUCD, TUCM

VOLLMOLLER, KARL GUSTAV, 1878-1948
Uncle's been dreaming.

192-?
Katzin, W., tr. KAT

VOLTAIRE, FRANÇOIS MARIE AROUET DE, 1694-1778
Candide. See Hellman, Lillian. Candide (based on)
Mahomet. 1741.
Leigh, O., tr. BAT8
Nanine. 1749. BRE
Oedipe. See Oedipus
Oedipus. 1718.
Smollett, T., tr. SANO
Variant title: Oedipe
Socrates. 1759.
Leigh, O., tr. BAT8
Zaire. 1732. BRE, LOCR, SEA

VULPIUS, PAUL
Youth at the helm. 1934.
Griffith, H., tr. and adapter. FAMH

W

WADDELL, SAMUEL (RUTHERFORD MAYNE, pseud.), 1878-1967
Bridge head. 1934. CAN

WAGER, WILLIAM, fl. 1566
Enough is as good as a feast. ca. 1560-1570. SCAT

WALKER, JOHN
The factory lad. 19th cent. BOOA1

WALKER, JOSEPH A., 1935-
Ododo. 1970. KINH
The River Niger. 1973. BES72

WALKER, STUART, 1880-1941
The medicine show. 1917. BEAC11

WALLACK, LESTER, 1820-1888
Rosedale; or, The rifle ball. 1863. AMP4

WALPOLE, SIR HUGH, 1884-1941
Kind lady. See Chodorov, Edward. Kind lady (adapted from a story by)

WALTER, EUGENE, 1874-1941
The easiest way. 1908. BESO9, DID, GARX, MOSS3

WALTER, NANCY
Rags. BALLE7

WANG SHIH-FU, 13th cent.
The west chamber. 13th cent.
Irwin, V., tr. IRW

WAPUL, GEORGE. See Wapull, George

WAPULL, GEORGE, fl. 1576
The tide tarrieth no man. 1576. SCAT

WARBURTON, H. L. See Deane, Hamilton, jt. auth.

WARD, DOUGLAS TURNER, 1930-
Brotherhood. 1970. KINH
Day of absence. 1965. BAC, BRAS, HARY, OLIV, RAI, RICK
Happy ending. 1965. BARI, BRAS, HOLP, OLIV

WARD, Julia. See Howe, Mrs. Julia (Ward)

WARD, THEODORE, 1902-
Big white fog. 1938. HARY
Our lan'. 1946. TUQT

WARREN, MRS. MERCY (OTIS), 1728-1814
The blockheads; or, The affrighted officers (attributed to). See Anonymous plays. The blockheads; or, The affrighted officers
The group. 1775? MOSS1
The motley assembly (attributed to). See Anonymous plays. The motley assembly

WARREN, RUTH. See Hawthorne, Ruth (Warren)

WASHBURN, DERIC
Ginger Anne. (1961) NEWA1

WASSERMAN, DALE, 1917-
Man of La Mancha (music by Mitch Leigh, lyrics by Joe Darion). 1965. BES65

WATERHOUSE, KEITH, 1929- , and HALL, WILLIS
Billy liar. 1960. PLAJ1

WATKIN, LAWRENCE EDWARD, 1901-
On borrowed time. See Osborn, Paul. On borrowed time (based on the novel by)

WATKINS, ARTHUR THOMAS LEVY. See Watkyn, Arthur, pseud.

WATKINS, MAURINE
Chicago. 1926. BES26

WATKYN, ARTHUR (pseud. of Arthur Thomas Levy Watkins), d. 1965
Not in the book. 1958. PLAN17
For better, for worse. 1952. PLAN8

WATSON, HARMON C., 1943-
Those golden gates fall down. (1971) FORD

WATSON, MARJORIE R.
The dogs of war. BRNB

WATTERS, GEORGE MANKER, 1891-1943, and HOPKINS, ARTHUR MELANCTHON
Burlesque. 1927. BES27

WAUGH, EVELYN, 1903-1966
The man who liked Dickens (television version by Robert Tallman). SUT1

WEBBER, CECIL EDWIN
Be good, sweet maid. 1957. PLAN15

WEBBER, JAMES PLAISTED, 1878-1930
Frances and Francis. 1923. WEB

WEBER, MARY FELTHAUS. See Felthaus-Weber, Mary

WEBSTER, JOHN, 1580?-1625?
The Duchess of Malfi. 1613. ALLK, BALD, BAS, BAUL, BENQ, BROC, COTKIR, DEAN, DEAO, DOWS, DUN, FOUD, HARC47, HOW, HUST, MAT, MCK, NEI, OLH, OLI2, ROET, SCH, SCI, SCJ, SEN, SPF1, TAT, TAU, THA, TRE, TREA2, TREB, TREC1, TREE1, TREI1, WATT2, WHE, WINE, WRIH
Variant title: The tragedy of the Duchess of Malfi
The tragedy of the Duchess of Malfi. See The Duchess of Malfi
The white devil; or, Vittoria Corombona. 1612? BENY, HAPRA1, HAPRB1, KRE, OLH, OLI2, ORNT, PAR, RUB, RYL, SALG, SPE, WALL, WHE

WEDEKIND, FRANK, 1864-1918
The court singer. See Der kammersänger
The earth-spirit. See Erdgeist
The epicurean. See The Marquis of Keith
Erdegeist. 1895.
Eliot, S., tr. DIK2
Variant title: The earth-spirit
Frühlingserwachen. See Spring's awakening
Der kammersänger. 1899. STI1
Boesche, A., tr. FRA20
Tridon, A., tr. HUDE, TREBA, TREC2, TREE2,

TREI2, TREJ
Variant titles: The court singer; The tenor
King Nicolo. See Such is life
König Nikolo. See Such is life
The Marquis of Keith. 1900?
Gottlieb, B., tr. BENS2, BLOC
Mueller, C., tr. COTL, COTQ
Variant title: The epicurean
So ist das leben. See Such is life
Spring's awakening. 1906.
Bentley, E., tr. BENT6
Variant title: Frühlingserwachen
Such is life. 1902.
Esslin, M., tr. ESS
Ziegler, F., tr. DIE, TUCG
Variant titles: King Nicolo; König Nikolo; So ist das leben
The tenor. See Der kammersänger

WEIDMAN, JEROME, 1913- , and ABBOTT, GEORGE
Fiorello! (music by Jerry Bock; lyrics by Sheldon Harnick). 1959. BES59

WEILL, KURT, 1900-1950
Johnny Johnson. See Green, Paul. Johnny Johnson (music by)
Lost in the stars. See Anderson, Maxwell, jt. auth.
The threepenny opera. See Brecht, Bertolt. The threepenny opera (music by)

WEINSTOCK, JACK. See Burrows, Abram S., jt. auth.

WEISS, PETER, 1916-
Marat/Sade. See The persecution and assassination of Jean Paul Marat...
The persecution and assassination of Jean Paul Marat as performed by the inmates of the Asylum of Charenton under the direction of the Marquis de Sade. 1964.
Skelton, G., tr. and adapter, and Mitchell, A., verse adapter. BES65, REIL
Variant titles: Marat/Sade; The persecution and assassination of Marat...; Die Verfolgung und Ermordung Jean Paul Marats, dargestellt durch die Schauspielgruppe des Hospizes zu Charenton unter Antleitung des Herrn de Sade
The persecution and assassination of Marat... See The persecution and assassination of Jean Paul Marat...
The tower. (1948)
Anon. tr. RICJ
Benedikt, M., and Heine, M., trs. BENB
Variant title: Der Turm
Der Turm. See The tower
Die Verfolgung und Ermordung Jean Paul Marats, dargestellt durch die Schauspielgruppe des Hospizes zu Charenton unter Anleitung des Herrn de Sade. See The persecution and assassination of Jean Paul Marat...

WEITZENKORN, LOUIS, 1893-1943
Five star final. 1930. BES30

WELLER, MIKE, 1942-
The bodybuilder. 1969. OFF
Moonchildren. 1972. BES71
Now there's just the three of us. 1969. OFF

WELLS, HERBERT GEORGE, 1866-1946
Ann Veronica. See Gow, Ronald. Ann Veronica (adapted from the novel by)

WELTY, EUDORA, 1909-
The ponder heart. See Fields, Joseph and Chodorov, Jerome. The ponder heart (adapted from the novel by)

WERFEL, FRANZ, 1890-1945
Bockgesang. See Goat song
Goat song. 1921.
Langner, R., tr. THF
Variant title: Bockgesang
Jacobowsky and the Colonel. See Behrman, Samuel Nathaniel. Jacobowsky and the Colonel (adapted from the play by)

WERNER, FRIEDRICH LUDWIG ZACHARIAS, 1768-1823
The twenty-fourth of February. See Der vierundzwanzigste Februar
Der vierundzwanzigste Februar. 1809. CAM
Chambers, W., tr. BAT10
Variant title: The twenty-fourth of February

WESKER, ARNOLD, 1932-
Chicken soup with barley. 1958. NEWE1
Chips with everything. 1962? BES63, NEWE7
The four seasons. 1965. NEWE9
The kitchen. 1959. CONB, NEWE2
Roots. 1959. POP
Their very own and golden city. 1966. NEWE10

WESLEY, RICHARD, 1945-
Black terror. 1972. NEWL

WEXLEY, JOHN, 1902-
The last mile. 1930. BES29
Running dogs. 1938? KOZ
They shall not die. 1934. BES33

WHARTON, MRS. EDITH NEWBOLD (JONES), 1862-1937
Ethan Frome. See Davis, Owen and Davis, Donald. Ethan Frome (based on the novel by)

WHEELER, ANDREW CARPENTER, 1835-1903. See Alfriend, Edward, M., jt. auth.

WHEELER, HUGH CALLINGHAM, 1912-
Big fish, little fish. 1961. BES60
A little night music. 1973. BES72
Look: we've come through. 1961. SSTY

WHITE, JOSEPH, 1933-
The leader. 1969. JON

WHITE, LUCY
The bird child. 1922. LOC

WHITING, JOHN, 1917-1963
The devils. 1961. NEWE6
Marching song. 1954. NEWE3
Saint's day. 1951. PLAN6

WHITTINGTON, ROBERT, 1912-
The death of García Lorca. 1940. CROZ1

WIEAND, PAUL R.
Die huchzich um kreitz waig? 18-? BUFF
Der parra kumpt. 18-? BUFF
Tzu forwitsich. 18-? BUFF

WIECHERT, ERNST EMIL, 1887-1950
Das spiel vom deutschen bettelmann. 1933. STI2

WIED, GUSTAV JOHANNES, 1858-1914
Ranke viljer. See 2 x 2 = 5

2 x 2 = 5. 1906.
Boyd, E., and Koppel, H., trs. LEG
Variant title: Ranke viljer

WILBRANDT, ADOLF VON, 1837-1911
The master of Palmyra. 1889.
Stork, C., tr. FRA16
Variant title: Der meister von Palmyra
Der meister von Palmyra.
See The master of Palmyra

WILBUR, RICHARD, 1921-
Candide. See Hellman, Lillian. Candide (lyrics by)

WILCOX, ANNA JANE. See Harnwell, Mrs. Anna Jane (Wilcox)

WILDE, OSCAR, 1854-1900
An ideal husband. 1895. JAFF
The importance of being earnest. 1895. ASG, ASH, BARB, BARG, BARR, BENSB2, BENU, BOWY, BROG, CAR, CARA, CEU, COTKC, COTKF, COTKI, COTKR, CRAF, CRAN2, EDAD, FEFL, FOUM, GREB2, GREC2, HILP, HOUS, KER, KRM, LOO, LOOA, MON, MOSN, MOSO, NEV1, SAFF, SALE, SATI, SHAJ2, SMR, STE, STEI, STJN, STRB, STY, THOM, THON, TRE, TREA1, TREBA, TREC2, TREE3, TREI3, TREJ, TUCD, TUCM, TUCN, ,TUCO, WATA, WHI, WHFM, WOO2, WOOD2, WOOE2
Lady Windermere's fan. 1892. BAUG, BENY, BROJ, BROK, DAV1, DIC, HUD, LIE, LIED2, LIEE2, MAT, MCCL, MOO, RUB, SMO, TAT, TAU
A woman of no importance. 1893. COT

WILDE, PERCIVAL, 1887-1953
Blood of the martyrs. 191-? STAU
Confessional. 1916. BENP, PEN
The traitor. 191-? RICH

WILDENBRUCH, ERNST VON, 1845-1909
Heinrich und Heinrich's geschlecht. See King Henry
Henry IV of Germany, pt. I. See King Henry
King Henry. 1896.
Wernaer, R., tr. FRA17
Variant titles: Heinrich und Heinrich's geschlecht; Henry IV of Germany, pt. I

WILDER, THORNTON NIVEN, 1897-1975
The angel on the ship. 1928? CHU
The happy journey to Trenton and Camden. 1931. COOP, GALB, WATE
The long Christmas dinner. 1931. DOWM, MILL, SHAW, SHAX
The matchmaker. 1955. BARJ, BARS, BES55, BLOC, CASE, GART, GARZA2, GOLH, SHRO, THEA56, WEAN
Variant title: The merchant of Yonkers
--See Stewart, Michael. Hello, Dolly! (adapted from)
The merchant of Yonkers. See The matchmaker
Our town. 1938. BES37, BLOD1, BONB, BONC, BRR1, BRS, CARL, CATH, CET, COK, COOJ, CORB, CORF, CROX, EDAD, FULT, GOLK, HAT, ING, INGA, INGB, LAM, MCDL, NAGE, ROGE, SIM, SUT3, TREBA, TREC2, TREE3, TREI3, TREJ, WORL3
Pullman car Hiawatha. 1931?

BENT4, MCNB
The skin of our teeth. 1942. BES42, COTQ, CUBE, CUBG, CUBH, DOWS, HEWE, HOWP2, JOHO, JORH, KERO, LIEF, SCNO, SCNT, WATA

WILKINS, JOHN H., 1836?-1853
Signor Marc. 1854. AMP14

WILLARD, JOHN, 1885-1942
The cat and the canary. 1922. CART

WILLCOX, HELEN LIDA, 1883-
Larola. 1917? FED1

WILLIAMS, ARTHUR
The poor little watch girl. 1968. SME

WILLIAMS, CHARLES, 1886-1945
Thomas Cranmer of Canterbury. 1936. BROS

WILLIAMS, EMLYN, 1905-
The corn is green. 1938. BES40, CEU, EDAD, GREC2, PROX
The late Christopher Bean. See Fauchois, René. The late Christopher Bean (tr. and adapted by)
A month in the country. See Turgenev, Ivan. A month in the country (adapted by)
Night must fall. 1935. CART, FAMH

WILLIAMS, HUGH, 1904-1969, and WILLIAMS, MARGARET (VYNER)
By accident. 1959. PLAN21
Variant title: Special providence
Double yolk. 1960. PLAN21
The grass is greener. 1958. PLAN19
The happy man. 1957. PLAN17
The irregular verb to love. 1961. PLAN23
Plaintiff in a pretty hat. 1956. PLAN15
A sparrow falls. See With intent
Special providence. See By accident
With intent. 1959. PLAN21
Variant title: A sparrow falls

WILLIAMS, JESSE LYNCH, 1871-1929
And so they were married. See Why marry?
Why marry? 1917. BES09, CORD, CORE, CORF, QUI
Variant title: And so they were married
Why not? 1922. BES22

WILLIAMS, LAUREN
Over fourteen: and single. DRU

WILLIAMS, MARGARET (VYNER). See Williams, Hugh, jt. auth.

WILLIAMS, NORMAN
The mountain. GREG

WILLIAMS, TENNESSEE (b. Thomas Lanier Williams), 1914-
Camino real. 1953. CES, FAM, MIJY, SANK, ULAN
Cat on a hot tin roof. 1955. BES54, GART, GAVE, THEA55
The confessional. (1966) RICK
Dos ranchos; or, The purification. 1944? NEW44
The glass menagerie. 1944. BARI, BARS, BES44, BLOC, BLON, BONA, BONB, BONC, BROY, CLDP, COK, COOP, CORB, COTQ, CUBE, CUBG, CUBH, DEAS, DIT, DOWM, ELK, GARZ, GARZA3, GARZAP, GASS, GAVE, HAPO, HATA, HAVH, HAVI, KNIC, KNID, LAV, MCA, MCNA, MCNB,

MON, MONA, PERS, PERT, REIP, REIT, ROHR, SHRO, SILN, SILQ, SIXB, SIXC, SOM, SOMA, SOU, SPES, SSSF, STEI, STY, TREBA, TREC2, TREE3, TREI3, TREJ, WAIT, WAIU, WALB, WARH, WARL, WATE, WEIM, WEIS, WEIW
Hello from Bertha. RAVA
I rise in flame, cried the Phoenix. (1951) NEWW1
The last of my gold watches. 1947. BUR
The milk train doesn't stop here anymore. 1962. BES62
The night of the iguana. 1961. BES61, GARS
Orpheus descending. 1957. BES56, GARS, GORE
Period of adjustment. 1960. BES60
The rose tattoo. 1951. BES50, CLM, CLN, COTKC, GART, GRED
Small craft warnings. 1972. BES71
Something unspoken. 1953? SUL
A streetcar named desire. 1947. BARJ, BES47, CEQA, CLO, GARW, GARZA3, GAVE, GOOD, NEWV, TUCO
Suddenly last summer. 1958. LIEF, MESS
Summer and smoke. 1948. GARW, GOLH, HAVG, TAUJ
Sweet bird of youth. 1959. BES58
Talk to me like the rain and let me listen. 1970. RAVA
27 Wagons full of cotton. 1955. HALU, SPC

WILLIAMS, THOMAS LANIER. See Williams, Tennessee

WILLIAMS, WILLIAM CARLOS, 1883-1963
The first president. 1936? AME5
Trial horse no. 1: Many loves. 1942? NEW42

WILLIAMSON, HAROLD
Peggy. 1919. HUD

WILLIAMSON, HUGH ROSS, 1901-
Diamond cut diamond. 1952. PLAN7
Gunpowder, treason and plot. 1951. PLAN6
Heart of Bruce. 1959. PLAN20
A question of obedience. See Teresa of Avila
Teresa of Avila. 1961. PLAN24
Variant title: A question of obedience

WILLIS, ANTHONY ARMSTRONG (ANTHONY ARMSTRONG, pseud.), 1897-1976
Ten minute alibi. 1933. FAMD

WILLIS, NATHANIEL PARKER, 1806-1867
Bianca Visconti; or, The heart overtasked. 1837. HAL
Tortesa, the usurer. 1839. MOSS2, QUIJ, QUIK, QUIL, QUIM, QUIN

WILMOT, ROBERT, fl. 1568-1608
Tancred and Gismund; or, Gismond of Salerne. 1591? CUN

WILMURT, ARTHUR. See Obey, André. Noah (tr. and adapted by)

WILSON, ANGUS FRANK JOHNSTONE, 1913-
The mulberry bush. 1955. RHE

WILSON, FRANK H., 1886-1956
Sugar cane. 1925. LOC

WILSON, HARRY LEON, 1867-1939 -

Merton of the movies. See Kaufman, George S., and Connelly, Marc. Merton of the movies (based on the novel by)

--See Tarkington, Booth, jt. auth.

WILSON, JOHN, 1921-
Hamp. 1966. BES66

WILSON, LANGFORD, 1938-
The hot l Baltimore. 1973. BES72
The madness of Lady Bright. 1964. ORZ

WILSON, ROBERT, d. 1600
Sir John Oldcastle, pt. I (sometimes attributed to). See Anonymous plays. Sir John Oldcastle, pt. I.

WILSON, SANDY, 1924-
The boyfriend. 1953. BES54

WILSON, THEODORA WILSON
Champion north. 1933. FIT

WINCELBERG, SHIMON
The enemy. See Kataki
Kataki. 1959. BES58
Variant title: The enemy

WINSLOE, CHRISTA
Children in uniform. 1932. Burnham, B., tr. and adapter FAMC
Variant titles: Gestern und heute; Girls in uniform; Maedchen in uniform
Gestern und heute. See Children in uniform
Girls in uniform. See Children in uniform
Maedchen in uniform. See Children in uniform

WINTER, JOHN KEITH, 1906-
The rats of Norway. 1933. SIXH
The shining hour. 1934. BES33, SEV

WISE, ERNEST GEORGE (ERNEST GEORGE, pseud.), 1894-
Down our street. 1930. SIXD

WISHENGRAD, MORTON
The rope dancers. 1957. BES57, GARS

WITHERSPOON, KATHLEEN
Jute. 1930. THX

WITKIEWICZ, STANISLAW IGAACY, 1885-1939
The cuttlefish. 1922. Gerould, D., and Gerould, E., trs. TREJ

WODEHOUSE, PELLHAM GRENVILLE, 1881-1975
The play's the thing. See Molnár, Ferenc. The play's the thing (adapted by)

WOLFE, HUMBERT, 1885-1940
The silent knight. 1939. SIXP

WOLFE, THOMAS, 1900-1938
Look homeward, angel. See Frings, Ketti. Look homeward, angel (based on the novel by)

WOLFSON, VICTOR
Excursion. 1937. BES36

WOLLENWEBER, LUDWIG AUGUST, 1807-1888
Ein gesprach. 18-? BUFF
Das lied von der union. 18-? BUFF
Die Margareth und die Lea. 18-? BUFF
Eb Refschneider un Susu Leimbach. 18-? BUFF
Die Sara und die Bets. 18-? BUFF

WOOD, CHARLES, 1932-
Cockade. 1963. NEWE8
Fill the stage with happy hours. 1966. NEWE11

WOOD, MRS. HENRY, 1813-1887

East Lynne. 1963. BAI, CEY
Variant title: The marriage bells; or, The cottage on the cliff
The marriage bells; or, The cottage on the cliff. See East Lynne

WOODBRIDGE, ELIZABETH. See Morris, Elizabeth (Woodbridge)

WOODES, NATHANIEL, fl. 1580?
The conflict of conscience. 1581. SCAT

WOODS, AUBREY, and ROWELL, GEORGE
Trelawny, a musical play (based on Trelawny of the "Wells" by Sir Arthur Wing Pinero; music and lyrics by Julian Slade). 1972. PLAN41

WOODS, WALTER
Billy the kid. 1906. AMP8

WOODWORTH, SAMUEL, 1785-1842
The forest rose. 1825. MONR

WOOLF, BENJAMIN EDWARD, 1836-1901
The almighty dollar. See The mighty dollar
The mighty dollar. 1875. CLA
Variant title: The almighty dollar

WOOLL, EDWARD, 1878-
Libel! 1934? SEV

WORDSWORTH, WILLIAM, 1770-1850
The borderers. 1797. KAU

WOUK, HERMAN, 1915-
The Caine mutiny court-martial. 1953. BES53, GART, NEWV, RED, THEA54

WRIGHT, RICHARD, 1908-1960, and GREEN, PAUL
Native son. 1941. BES40, HARY

WUCHTER, ASTOR CLINTON
An der lumpa parti. See Barba, Preston Albert (based on the poem by)

WYCHERLEY, WILLIAM, 1640?-1716
The country wife. 1674? ALLK, BAUL, DAVR, FAL, FOUB, GOS, GOSA, HAVL, KRM, MCMS, REST, SALR, SEN, TAUJ, TUQ, TWE, WEAN, WILS, WRIR
The plain-dealer. 1676. GAY4, MAT, MCMI, MOR, MOSE1, NET

X

XENOPOULOS, GREGORIUS, 1867-1951
Divine dream.
Gianos, M., tr. GIA

Y

YAFFE, JAMES, 1927-
The deadly game (adapted from the novel Trapps by Friedrich Deurrenmatt). 1960. BES59

YAGORO, KONGO. See Kongō Yagorō

YANKOWITZ, SUSAN
Boxes. (1972) BALLE11
Slaughterhouse. 1971? NEWA4

YAO HSIN-NUNG, 1905-
Ch'ing kung yüan. See The malice of empire
The malice of empire (act I, scene 1). 1941?
Anon. tr. BIR2
Variant title: Ch'ing kung yüan

YASUKIYO, HYOSHI SA-AMI. See Hiyoshi, Sa-Ami-Yasukiyo

YEATS, JACK BUTLER, 1871-1957
La la noo. 1942. BARF

YEATS, WILLIAM BUTLER, 1865-1939
At the hawk's well. 1916? BLOC
Variant title: The well of immortality
Cathleen ni Houlihan. 1902. DUR, MERC, MILL, MOSN, MOSO
The Countess Cathleen. 1892. ASG, BOWY, COTM, SECK
Deirdre. 1906. SALE, SSTA
The dreaming of the bones. 1931. STEI
A full moon in March. 1935. BENS1
The hour-glass. 1903. DIC, REIT
The king's threshold. 1903. KRE
The land of heart's desire. 1894. BURR, DOV, HUD, MCCP, WATT2
On Baile's strand. 1904. AUG, BARC, CAP, COTQ, ULAN
The only jealousy of Emer. 1921? CAP, COK
Purgatory. 1939? ALT, BARH, BEAM, BENT2, CALD, REIN, REIP, TAUJ, TRI, TRIA, TREJ, ULAN
The resurrection. 1934. MERC
The well of immortality. See At the hawk's well.
The words upon the window-pane. 1935. ALT, BARF, CAN, SHR

YERBY, LOREES, 1930-
The golden bull of boredom. NEWA1

YEVREINOV, NIKOLAI. See Evreinov, Nikolaĭ

YI-PING, C. See Pau-hua, Chang, jt. auth.

YORDAN, PHILIP, 1914-
Anna Lucasta. 1944. BES44

YOUNG, SIR CHARLES LAWRENCE, 1839-1887, and HOWARD, BRONSON CROCKER
Knave and queen. 1882? AMP10

YOUNG, ROBERT. See Roemer, Michael, jt. auth.

YOUNG, STANLEY, 1906-
Mr. Pickwick (based on Charles Dickens' Pickwick papers). 1952. THEA53

YU, SUN
The women's representative. Sheng, T., tr. MESE

YUNG, MA. See Seh, Sha, jt. auth.

Z

ZAMACOIS, EDUARDO (EDUARDO DE ZAMACOIS Y QUINTANA), 1873-
The passing of the magi. 1912. Turrell, C., tr. TUR
Variant title: Los reyes pasan
Los reyes pasan. See The passing of the magi

ZAMACOIS Y QUINTANA, EDUARDO DE. See Zamacois, Eduardo

ZARATE, ANTONIO GIL Y. See Gil y Zárate, Antonio

ZEAMI. See Seami, Motokiyo

ZEAMI MOTOKIYO. See Seami, Motokiyo

ZEMBO, MOTOYASU, 1453-1532

Atsumori at Ikuta.
Waley, A., tr. ANDF
Variant titles: Ikuta; Ikuta Atsumori
Early snow.
Waley, A., tr. ANDF, KINN
Variant title: Hatsuyuki
Hatsuyuki. See Early snow
Ikkaku sennin. 1524.
Hoff, F., tr. BRA
Irwin, V., tr. IRW
Ikuta. See Atsumori at Ikuta
Ikuta Atsumori. See Atsumori at Ikuta

ZENCHIKU, KOMPARU-. See Komparu-Zenchiku

ZENCHIKU, UJINOBU, 1414-1499?
Aoi no Uye (sometimes attributed to Seami Motokiyo; adapted from Genji Monogatari (Romance of Genji or Tale of Genji), by Lady Murasaki Shikubu, 1004 A.D.). 15th cent.
Waley, A., tr. ANDF
Variant titles: Lady Aoi; Princess Hollyhock
Lady Aoi. See Aoi no Uye
Princess Hollyhock. See Aoi no Uye

ZINDEL, PAUL, 1936-
The effect of gamma rays on man-in-the-moon marigolds. 1970. BES69, HAVL

ZOLA, EMILE, 1840-1902
Thérèse Raquin. 1873.
Boutall, K., tr. BENS3, HOUP

ZORRILLA, FRANCISCO DE ROJAS. See Rojas Zorrilla, Francisco de

ZORRILLA Y MORAL, JOSE, 1817-1893
Don Juan Tenorio. 1844. BRET, TRES
Oliver, W., tr. MAN

ZUBER, RON
Three X love. KINH

ZUCKMAYER, CARL, 1896-
The Captain from Koepenick. See The Captain of Köpenick. 1931.
Mueller, C., tr. WELG
Variant titles: The Captain from Koepenick; Der Hauptmann von Koepenick
The devil's general. 1946.
Gilbert, I., and W., trs. BLOC
Variant title: Des Teufels General
Der Hauptmann von Koepenick. See The Captain of Köpenick
Des Teufels General. See The devil's general

ZWEIG, STEFAN, 1881-1942
Volpone (adapted from the play by Ben Jonson).
Langner, R., tr. GARZH

LIST OF COLLECTIONS ANALYZED AND KEY TO SYMBOLS

ABC Abcarian, Richard, and Klotz, Marvin, eds. Literature: the human experience. New York, St. Martins, 1973. 971p
- Bergman, I. The seventh seal
- Everyman
- Ibsen, H. An enemy of the people
- Lowell, R. Benito Cereno
- Molière, J. The misanthrope
- Shakespeare, W. Othello
- Shaw, G. Major Barbara
- Sophocles. Antigone

ABRA Abrams, Meyer Howard; Donaldson, E. Talbot; Smith, Hallett; Adams, Robert M.; Monk, Samuel Holt; Ford, George H. and Daiches, David, eds. The Norton anthology of English literature... New York, W. W. Norton [c1962] 2024p
- Dryden, J. The secular masque
- Jonson, B. The vision of delight
- Shakespeare, W. King Henry the fourth, pt. I
- Shaw, G. Arms and the man

ABRB Abrams, Meyer Howard; Donaldson, E. Talbot; Smith, Hallett; Adams, Robert M.; Monk, Samuel Holt; Ford, George H. and Daiches, David, eds. The Norton anthology of English literature... New York, W. W. Norton [c1962] 2v
- Congreve, W. The way of the world 1
- Everyman 1
- Jonson, B. The vision of delight 1
- Marlowe, C. The tragical history of the life and death of Doctor Faustus 1
- The second shepherds' play 1
- Shakespeare, W. King Henry the fourth, pt. I 1
- Shaw, G. Arms and the man 2
- Sheridan, R. The school for scandal 1

ADA Adams, Joseph Quincy, ed. Chief pre-Shakespearean dramas... Boston, Houghton Mifflin [c1924] 712p
- Banns
- The betraying of Christ
- The birth of Jesus
- The castle of perseverance
- Christ's ministry
- The conversion of St. Paul
- The creation of Eve, with the expelling of Adam and Eve out of Paradise
- The deluge
- Duk Moraud
- Edwards, R. Damon and Pithias
- Everyman
- The fall of Lucifer
- The famous victories of Henry

ADA (cont.)
the fifth
Gammer Gurton's nedle
Gascoygne, G. Supposes
George a Greene, the pinner of Wakefield
The harrowing of hell
Heywood, J. A mery play betwene Johan Johan, the husband, Tyb his wife and Syr Johan the preest
Heywood, J. The playe called the four pp
Heywood, J. The play of the wether
The judgment day
The killing of Abel
Leicestershire St. George play
Lyly, J. Campaspe
The magi, Herod, and the slaughter of the innocents
Mankind
Mary Magdalene
Noah
Norton, T., and Sackville, T. Gorboduc; or, Ferrex and Porrex
Oxfordshire St. George play
Pharaoh
The play of the sacrament
Preston, T. Cambises, king of Persia
The prophets
The resurrection of Christ
The Revesby sword play
Robin Hood and the friar
Robin Hood and the sheriff of Nottingham
The sacrifice of Isaac
The salutation and conception
The shepherds
Shetland sword dance
The trial of Christ
Udall, N. Roister Doister
Wyt and science

ADV Adventures in world literature, [by] James Earl Applegate, [and others] classic ed. New York, Harcourt, Brace, Jovanovich, 1970. 1046p
Ibsen, H. An enemy of the people
Molière, J. The misanthrope
Shakespeare, W. The tempest
Sophocles. Antigone

ALD Aldington, Richard, ed. French comedies of the XVIIIth century... London, Routledge [1923] 347p
Destouches, P. The conceited count
Le Sage, A. Turcaret; or, The financier
Marivaux, P. The game of love and chance
Regnard, J. The residuary légatee

ALL Allen, John, ed. Three medieval plays... London ...Heineman [c1953] 54p
The farce of Master Pierre Pathelin
The pageant of the shearmen and taylors
The summoning of Everyman

ALLE Allen, John, ed. Four continental plays. London, Heinemann [1964] 149p
Chekhov, A. A wedding
Kleist, H. The broken jug
Niccodemi, D. The poet
Pirandello, L. The jar

ALLI Allison, Alexander W.; Carr, Arthur J., and Eastman, Arthur M., eds. Masterpieces of the drama ...New York, Macmillan [c1957] 693p
Chekhov, A. The cherry orchard
Euripides. Alcestis
García Lorca, F. The house of Bernarda Alba
Giraudoux, J. The madwoman of Chaillot
Ibsen, H. Hedda Gabler
Jonson, B. Volpone; or, The fox

Molière, J. The miser
O'Casey, S. Juno and the paycock
Sheridan, R. The rivals
Sophocles. Oedipus rex
Synge, J. Riders to the sea

ALLJ Allison, Alexander Ward; Carr, Arthur J. and Eastman, Arthur M., eds. Masterpieces of the drama. 2d ed...New York, Macmillan [1966] 814p
Beckett, S. Act without words
Beckett, S. All that fall
Brecht, B. The Caucasian chalk circle
Chekhov, A. The cherry orchard
Euripides. The bacchae
García Lorca, F. The house of Bernarda Alba
Giraudoux, J. The madwoman of Chaillot
Ibsen, H. Hedda Gabler
Jonson, B. Volpone; or, The fox
Molière, J. The miser
O'Casey, S. Juno and the paycock
Sheridan, R. The rivals
Sophocles. Oedipus
Synge, J. Riders to the sea

ALLK Allison, Alexander Ward; Carr, Arthur J. and Eastman, Arthur M., eds. Masterpieces of the drama. 3d ed...New York, Macmillan, 1974. 937p
Aeschylus. Agamemnon
Aristophanes. Lysistrata
Beckett, S. Act without words
Beckett, S. All that fall
Brecht, B. Good woman of Setzuan
Chekhov, A. The cherry orchard
Congreve, W. The way of the world
Davis, O. Purlie victorious
Euripides. The Bacchae
García Lorca, F. The house of Bernarda Alba
Giraudoux, J. The madwoman of Chaillot
Ibsen, H. Hedda Gabler
Jones, L. The toilet
Jonson, B. Volpone; or, The fox
Miller, A. Death of a salesman
Molière, J. The miser
O'Casey, S. Juno and the paycock
O'Neill, E. Desire under the elms
Pirandello, L. Six characters in search of an author
Racine, J. Phaedra
The second shepherd play
Shaw, G. Saint Joan
Sheridan, R. The rivals
Sophocles. Oedipus rex
Strindberg, A. The ghost sonata
Synge, J. Riders to the sea
Webster, J. The Duchess of Malfi
Wycherley, W. The country wife

ALP Alpern, Hymen and Martel, José, eds. Diez comedias del siglo de oro... New York, Harper [c1939] 859p
Calderón de la Barca, P. La vida es sueño
Castro y Bellvis, G. Las mocedades del Cid
Cervantes Saavedra, M. La Numancia
Mira de Amescua, A. El esclavo del demonio
Moreto y Cabaña, A. El desdén con el desdén
Rojas Zorilla, F. Del rey abajo, ninguno
Ruiz de Alarcón y Mendoza, J. La verdad sospechosa
Téllez, G. El burlador de Sevilla
Vega Carpio, L. La estrella de Sevilla
Vega Carpio, L. Fuenteovejuna

ALPE Alpern, Hymen and Martel, José, eds. Teatro hispanoamericano..[1st ed.] New York, Odyssey Press [c1956] 412p
Alsina, A. La marca de fuego
Eichelbaum, S. Divorcio nupcial
Moock Bousquet, A. La serpiente
Rojas, R. Olläntay
Sánchez, F. Los derechos de la salud
Segura, M. Na Catita

ALPF Alpern, Hymen, ed. Three classic Spanish plays. New York, Washington Square Press [1963] 229p (The ANTA Series of Distinguished Plays)
Calderón de la Barca, P. Life is a dream
Rojas Zorilla, F. None beneath the king
Vega Carpio, L. The sheep

ALS Altenbernd, Lynn, ed. Exploring literature; fiction, poetry, drama, criticism. New York, Macmillan, 1970. 702p
Hansberry, L. A raisin in the sun
Ibsen, H. Hedda Gabler
Lowell, R. My kinsman, Major Molineux
Shakespeare, W. A midsummer night's dream
Sophocles. Oedipus Rex

ALT Altenbernd, Lynn and Lewis, Leslie L., eds. Introduction to literature: plays. New York, Macmillan, 1963. 440p
Anouilh, J. Becket; or, The honor of God
Chekhov, A. The cherry orchard
Everyman
García Lorca, F. Blood wedding
Ibsen, H. Ghosts
Ionesco, E. The chairs
Molière, J. The miser
O'Neill, E. Desire under the elms
Pirandello, L. It is so (if you think so)
Sheridan, R. The school for scandal
Sophocles. Antigone
Synge, J. Riders to the sea
Yeats, W. Purgatory
Yeats, W. The words upon the window-pane

ALTE Altenbernd, Lynn and Lewis, L. L., eds. Introduction to literature: plays. 2d ed. New York, Macmillan, 1969. 546p
Anouilh, J. Becket; or, The honor of God
Chekhov, A. The cherry orchard
Everyman
García Lorca, F. Blood wedding
Ibsen, H. Ghosts
Ionesco, E. The chairs
Molière, J. The misanthrope
O'Neill, E. Desire under the elms
Pirandello, L. It is so (if you think so)
Plautus, T. Amphitryon
Shakespeare, W. The tragedy of Hamlet, Prince of Denmark
Shaw, G. The man of destiny
Sheridan, R. The school for scandal
Sophocles. Antigone
Synge, A. Riders to the sea

AME American caravan, a yearbook of American literature ...Edited by Van Wyck Brooks, Alfred Kreymborg, Lewis Mumford and Paul Rosenfeld. New York, Macaulay [c1927-c1936] 5v Title varies: 1927, The American caravan; 1928,

The second American Caravan; 1929, The new American caravan; 1931, American caravan IV; 1936, The new caravan
Basshe, E. The dream of the dollar 5
Frank, W. New Year's eve 2
Geddes, V. The stable and the grove 4
Gold, M. Hoboken blues 1
Green, P. Supper for the dead 1
Green, P. Tread the green grass 3
Kreymborg, A. The dead are free 5
Schwartz, D. Choosing company 5
Williams, W. The first president 5

AMERICAN LITERATURE: a period anthology; Oscar Cargill, general editor. See
MCDO McDowell, Tremaine, ed. The romantic triumph...
NELS Nelson, John Herbert and Cargill, Oscar, eds. Contemporary trends.
SPI Spiller, Robert Ernest, ed. The roots of national culture...

AMERICAN PROFILE. See
CATH Catholic university of America. Committee for the revision of English curricula

AMP America's lost plays... Barrett H. Clark, general editor. Princeton, N.J., Princeton university press, 1940-41. 20v
Alfriend, E., and Wheeler, A. The great diamond robbery 8
Belasco, D. La belle russe 18
Belasco, D. The heart of Maryland 18
Belasco, D. Naughty Anthony 18
Belasco, D. The stranglers of Paris 18
Belasco, D. and De Mille, H. The charity ball 17
Belasco, D., and De Mille, H. The wife 17
Belasco, D., and Fyles, F. The girl I left behind me 18
Bennett, C. A royal slave 8
Bird, R. Caridorf; or, The avenger 12
Bird, R. The cowled lover 12
Bird, R. News of the night; or, A trip to Niagara 12
Bird, R. 'Twas all for the best; or, 'Tis all a notion 12
Boker, G. The bankrupt 3
Boker, G. Glaucus 3
Boker, G. The world a mask 3
Boucicault, D. Dot 1
Boucicault, D. Flying scud 1
Boucicault, D. Forbidden fruit 1
Boucicault, D. Louis XI 1
Boucicault, D. Mercy Dodd 1
Boucicault, D. Robert Emmet 1
Brougham, J. The duke's motto: or, I am here! 14
Campbell, B. Fairfax 19
Campbell, B. The galley slave 19
Campbell, B. My partner 19
Campbell, B. The Virginian 19
Campbell, B. The white slave 19
Clinch, D. The spy: or, A tale of the neutral ground 14
Conway, H. The battle of Stillwater; or, The maniac 14
Daly, A. The big bonanza 20

AMP (cont.)
Daly, A. Divorce 20
Daly, A. Man and wife 20
Daly, A. Needles and pins 20
Daly, A. Pique 20
De Mille, W. The Warrens of Virginia 16
De Mille, H., and Barnard, C. The main line 17
De Mille, H., and Belasco, D. Lord Chumley 17
De Mille, H., and Belasco, D. Men and women 17
Dunlap, W. False shame; or, The American orphan in Germany 2
Dunlap, W. Thirty years; or, The gambler's fate 2
Fechter, C. Monte Cristo 16
Field, J. Job and his children 14
Grover, L. Our boarding house 4
Hazelton, G. Mistress Nell 16
Herne, J. Drifting apart 7
Herne, J. "The minute men" of 1774-1775 7
Herne, J. The Reverend Griffith Davenport, Act IV 7
Herne, J. Within an inch of his life 7
Howard, B. The banker's daughter 10
Howard, B. Baron Rudolph 10
Howard, B. Hurricanes 10
Howard, B. Old love letters 10
Howard, B. One of our girls 10
Howe, J. Hippolytus 16
Hoyt, C. A bunch of keys 9
Hoyt, C. A midnight bell 9
Hoyt, C. A milk white flag 9
Hoyt, C. A temperance town 9
Hoyt, C. A trip to Chinatown 9
Jessop, G. Sam'l of Posen; or, The commercial drummer 4
Jones, J. The usurper; or, Americans in Tripoli 14
McCloskey, J. Across the continent; or, Scenes from New York life and the Pacific railroad 4
MacKaye, S. An arrant knave 11
MacKaye, S. In spite of all 11
MacKaye, S. Rose Michel 11
MacKaye, S. Won at last 11
Mitchell, L. Becky Sharp 16
Mortimer, L. No mother to guide her 8
Murdock, F. Davy Crockett; or, Be sure you're right, then go ahead 4
Payne, J. The black man; or, The spleen 6
Payne, J. The boarding schools; or, Life among the little folk 5
Payne, J. The Italian bride 6
Payne, J. The last duel in Spain 6
Payne, J. Mazeppa; or, The wild horse of Tartary 5
Payne, J. Mount Savage 5
Payne, J. Romulus, the shepherd king 6
Payne, J. The Spanish husband; or, First and last love 5
Payne, J. Trial without jury; or, The magpie and the maid 5
Payne, J. The two sons-in-law 5
Payne, J. Woman's revenge 6
Smith, R. The bombardment of Algiers 13
Smith, R. The last man; or, The cock of the village 13
Smith, R. The sentinels; or, The two sergeants 13
Smith, R. Shakespeare in love 13
Smith, R. A wife at a venture 13
Smith, R. William Penn 13

Steele, S. The crock of gold; or, The toiler's trials 14
Stone, J. Metamora; or, The last of the Wampanoags 14
Stone, J. Tancred, King of Sicily; or, The archives of Palermo 14
Taylor, C. From rags to riches 8
Tyler, R. The island of Barrataria 15
Tyler, R. Joseph and his brethren 15
Tyler, R. The judgment of Solomon 15
Tyler, R. The origin of the feast of Purim; or, The destinies of Haman & Mordecai 15
Wallach, L. Rosedale; or, The rifle ball 4
Wilkins, J. Signor Marc 14
Woods, W. Billy the Kid 8
Young, C., and Howard, B. Knave and queen 10

AMPA America's lost plays. v21. Satiric comedies; Meserve, Walter J. and Reardon, William R., eds. Bloomington, Ind., Indiana University Press, 1969. 158p
The battle of Brooklyn
Brougham, J. Po-ca-hon-tas
Dunlap, W. Darby's return
Hunter, G. Androboros
The trial of Atticus before Judge Beau, for a rape

AND Anderson, George Kumler and Walton, Edna Lou, eds. This generation... Chicago, Scott, Foresman [c1939] 975p
Dunsany, E. The queen's enemies
Green, P. Johnny Johnson
O'Neill, E. The hairy ape
Shaw, L. Bury the dead

ANDE Anderson, George Kumler and Walton, Edna Lou, eds. This generation. Revised edition... Chicago, Scott, Foresman [c1949] 1065p
Coward, N. Fumed oak
Galsworthy, J. Loyalties
Green, P. Johnny Johnson
MacNeice, L. The dark tower
O'Neill, E. The hairy ape

ANDF Anderson, George Lincoln, ed. The genius of the Oriental theatre. New York, New American Library [1966] 416p
Chikamatsu, M. The courier for hell
Hiyoshi, S. Benkei on the bridge
Kālidāsa. Shakuntalā and the ring of recognition
Miyamasu. The hatmaker
Namiki, G. The subscription list
Shudraka. The little clay cart
Zeami. Haku Rakuten
Zembō, M. Atsumori at Ikuta
Zembō, M. Early snow
Zenchiku, U. Aoi no Uye

ANG Andrews, John Douglass and Smith, Albert Reginald Wilson, eds. Three Elizabethan plays... London, Nelson [1929] 287p
Beaumont, F., and Fletcher, J. The knight of the burning pestle
Jonson, B. Everyman in his humour
Massinger, P. A new way to pay old debts

ANSORGE, ELIZABETH FRANCES. See PROC Prose and poetry for appreciation...

ARM Armenian literature comprising poetry, drama,

ARM (cont.)
folklore and classic traditions... introduction by Robert Arnot... Rev. ed. New York, Colonial press [c1901] 142p (The world's great classics)
Sundukianz, G. The ruined family

ARMS Armstrong, William A., ed. Elizabethan history plays... New York, Oxford University Press, 1965. 428p
Bale, J. King John
Davenport, R. King John and Matilda
Edward the third
Ford, J. Perkin Warbeck
Woodstock

ARNOT, ROBERT. See ARM Armenian literature...

ASF Ashley, Leonard R. N., comp. Mirrors for man: 26 plays of world drama. Cambridge, Mass., Winthrop Pubs., 1974. 967p
Anouilh, J. Antigone
Brecht, B. The three penny opera
Büchner, G. Woyzeck
Chekhov, A. The cherry orchard
Dumas, A., fils. Lady of the camellias
Everyman
Ibsen, H. The wild duck
Jarry, A. Ubu the King
Kennedy, A. The owl answers
Marlowe, C. The tragical history of Doctor Faustus
Molière, J. The miser
Namiki Gohei III. The subscription scroll
O'Neill, E. The long voyage home
Pirandello, L. Six characters in search of an author
Plautus. Pot of gold
Saavedra, G. Justice
Schneeman, C. Meat joy
Shakespeare, W. Macbeth
Shaw, G. Mrs. Warren's profession
Sheridan, R. The School for scandal
Sophocles. Antigone
Strindberg, A. Miss Julie
Synge, J. Riders to the sea
Van Itallie, J. America Hurrah
Williams, T. The glass menagerie
Wycherley, W. The country wife

ASG Ashley, Leonard R. N., comp. Nineteenth-century British drama... [Glenview, Ill.] Scott, Foresman [1967] 700p
Boucicault, D. London assurance
Bulwer-Lytton, E. The lady of Lyons
Gilbert, W. H. M. S. Pinafore
Jerrold, D. Black-ey'd Susan
Jones, H. Michael and his lost angel
Lewis, L. The bells
Palmer, T. East Lynne
Pinero, A. The second Mrs. Tanqueray
Robertson, T. Caste
Shelley, P. The Cenci
Wilde, O. The importance of being earnest
Yeats, W. The Countess Cathleen

ASH Ashton, John William, ed. Types of English drama... New York, Macmillan, 1940. 750p
Abraham and Melchizedek and Lot, with the sacrifice of Isaac
Browning, R. A blot in the 'scutcheon
Congreve, W. The way of

the world
Everyman
Gay, J. The beggar's opera
Greene, R. Friar Bacon and Friar Bungay
Heywood, T. A woman killed with kindness
Jonson, B. The alchemist
Marlowe, C. Edward II
O'Neill, E. Anna Christie
Sheridan, R. The critic
Wilde, O. The importance of being earnest

ATKINSON, BROOKS. See FOUB Four great comedies of the restoration and 18th century; NEWV New voices in the American theatre...

ATT Attic tragedies.. Boston, Bibliophile society, 1927. 3v

Aeschylus.	Prometheus bound	3
Euripides.	Hippolytus	2
Euripides.	Medea	2
Sophocles.	Antigone	1
Sophocles.	Electra	3
Sophocles.	Oedypus the king	1

AUDE Auden, Wystan Hugh, ed. The portable Greek reader ...New York, Viking, 1948. 726p
Aeschylus. Agamemnon
Aeschylus. Choephoroe
Aeschylus. Eumenides

AUG Aughtry, Charles Edward, ed. Landmarks in modern drama, from Ibsen to Ionesco. Boston, Houghton Mifflin [c1963] 726p
Brecht, B. The good woman of Setzuan
Ibsen, H. A doll's house
Ionesco, E. The bald soprano
Maeterlinck, M. Pelléas and Mélisande
Miller, A. Death of a salesman
Pirandello, L. Six characters in search of an author
Shaw, G. Man and superman
Strindberg, A. A dream play
Strindberg, A. Miss Julie
Synge, J. The playboy of the western world
Yeats, W. On Baile's strand

AXT Axton, Richard, and Stevens, John, comps. and trs. Medieval French plays. Oxford, Blackwell, 1971. 313p
Adam de la Halle. Le jeu de la feuillée
Adam de la Halle. Le jeu de Robin et de Marion
Bodel, J. Le jeu de Saint Nicolas
Courtois d'Arras
Le garçon et l'aveugle
Le jeu d'Adam: Adam and Eve; Cain and Abel
Rutebeuf. Le miracle de Théophile
La seinte resureccion

AYLIFF, H. K. See MAL Malvern festival plays...

B

BAC Bach, Bert C. and Browning, Gordon, comps. Drama for composition. Glenview, Ill., Scott, Foresman, 1973. 507p
Everyman
Fry, C. A phoenix too frequent
Jonson, B. Volpone; or, the fox
O'Neill, E. Desire under the elms
Shakespeare, W. Hamlet
Shaw, G. Arms and the man
Sheridan, R. The school for scandal

BAC (cont.)
Synge, J. The playboy of the western world
Ward, D. Day of absence

BAI Bailey, James Osler, ed. British plays of the nineteenth century...New York, Odyssey Press [1966] 535p
Boucicault, D. After dark
Boucicault, D. London assurance
Browning, R. Pippa passes
Buckstone, J. Luke the labourer; or, The lost son
Bulwer-Lytton, E. Richelieu; or, The conspiracy
Gilbert, W. Engaged
Holcroft, T. A tale of mystery
Jerrold, D. The rent-day
Jones, H. The masqueraders
Jones, H. The silver king
Marston, J. The patrician's daughter
Maturin, C. Bertram; or, The castle of St. Aldobrand
Pinero, A. The notorious Mrs. Ebbsmith
Robertson, T. Caste
Shaw, G. Widowers' houses
Taylor, T. Our American cousin
Wood, H. East Lynne

BAIC Bain, Carl E., ed. Drama. New York, Norton, 1973. 592p
Bullins, E. A son, come home
Chekhov, A. The three sisters
Euripides. The bacchae
Ibsen, H. The wild duck
Miller, A. A view from the bridge
Molière, A. The misanthrope
Pirandello, L. Six characters in search of an author
Shakespeare, W. Hamlet
Shaw, G. Caesar and Cleopatra
Shaw, G. Major Barbara
Sophocles. Oedipus tyrannis
Terry, M. The gloaming, oh my darling
Van Itallie, C. Interview

BAIE Bain, Carl E., and others, comps. The Norton introduction to literature ...New York, Norton, 1973. 1191p
Bullins, E. A son, come home
Chekhov, A. The three sisters
Euripides. The bacchae
Ibsen, H. The wild duck
Pirandello, L. Six characters in search of an author
Shakespeare, W. Hamlet
Shaw, G. Major Barbara
Terry, M. The gloaming, oh my darling

BAK Baker, George Pierce, comp. Modern American plays...New York, Harcourt, Brace and Howe, 1920. 544p
Anspacher, L. The unchastened woman
Belasco, D. The return of Peter Grimm
Massey, E. Plots and playwrights
Sheldon, E. Romance
Thomas, A. As a man thinks

BAKS Bakshy, Alexander, comp. and tr. Soviet scene; six plays of Russian life...New Haven, Yale university press, 1946. 348p
Afinogenov, A. Far taiga
Ilyenkov, V. The square of flowers
Marshak, S. Twelve months
Pogodin, N. The chimes of the Kremlin
Shkvarkin, V. Father un-

known
Trenyov, K. Lyubov Yarovaya

BALD Bald, Robert Cecil, ed. Six Elizabethan plays... Boston, Houghton Mifflin [c1963]
Beaumont, F., and Fletcher, J. The knight of the burning pestle
Dekker, T. The shoemakers' holiday
Ford, J. The broken heart
Jonson, B. Epicoene; or, The silent woman
Marlowe, C. Tamburlaine the great (Part 1)
Webster, J. The duchess of Malfi

BALL Ball, John, ed. From Beowulf to modern British writers. Based on Robert Shafer's From Beowulf to Thomas Hardy. [One-volume ed.] New York, Odyssey Press [1959] 1364p
Eliot, T. Murder in the cathedral
Everyman
Marlowe, C. The tragical history of Doctor Faustus
Shaw, G. Don Juan in hell
Synge, J. In the shadow of the glen

BALLE Ballet, Arthur Harold, ed. Playwrights for tomorrow; a collection of plays. Minneapolis, University of Minnesota Press, c1966-1973. 11v
Auletta, R. Stops 10
Ball, D. Assassin 7
Barber, P. I, Elizabeth Otis, being of sound mind 3
Bernard, K. The unknown Chinaman 10
Boretz, N. Shelter area 2
Bosakowski, P. Bierce takes on the railroad 11
Feldhaus-Weber, M. The world tipped over, and laying on its side 4
Fornes, M. The successful life of three 2
Fornes, M. Tango palace 2
Gaines, F. The new Chautauqua 5
Gillman, J. The marriage test 6
Grecco, S. The Orientals 7
Hierholzer, A. Grace and George and God 7
Johnson, E. A bad play for an old lady 1
Joseph, A. Anniversary on weedy hill 8
Kalcheim, L. ...and the boy who came to leave 3
Koebnick, S. Fair beckoning one 5
Korr, D. Encore 9
Kranes, D. Drive-in 7
LaFarge, W. Escape by balloon 10
Lee, L. Fox, hound and huntress 10
Leichman, S. Freddie the pigeon 7
Lewin, J. Five easy payments 3
Lynch, H. Three miles to Poley 10
McNally, T. And things that go bump in the night 1
Monson, W. The nihilist 8
Muller, R. The great git-away 3
Neilson, K. The end of the world; or, Fragments from a work in progress 6
O'Keefe, J. Chamber piece 11
O'Morrison, K. The long war 4
Opper, D. Children of the kingdom 9
Powell, A. The strangler 4
Pritchard, B. Visions of sugar plums 4
Roszkowski, D. Canvas 11
Sainer, A. The thing itself 6
Schevill, J. American

BALLE (cont.)
power: The master 1
Schevill, J. American power: The space fan 1
Schrock, G. Madam Popov 9
Schwartz, J. Psalms for two Davids 9
Stranack, J. With malice aforethought 3
Terry, M. Ex-Miss Copper Queen on a set of pills 1
Udoff, Y. A gun play 8
Van Itallie, J. Where is de queen? 3
Walter, N. Rags 7
Yankowitz, S. Boxes 11

BARB Barnet, Sylvan; Berman, Morton and Burto, William, eds. Eight great comedies [New York] New American Library [c1958] 472p
Aristophanes. The clouds
Chekhov, A. Uncle Vanya
Gay, J. The beggar's opera
Machiavelli, N. Mandragola
Molière, J. The miser
Shakespeare, W. Twelfth night; or, What you will
Shaw, G. Arms and the man
Wilde, O. The importance of being earnest

BARC Barnet, Sylvan; Berman, Morton and Burto, William, eds. Eight great tragedies ...[New York] New American Library [1957] 443p
Aeschylus. Prometheus bound
Euripides. Hippolytus
Ibsen, H. Ghosts
O'Neill, E. Desire under the elms
Shakespeare, W. King Lear
Sophocles. Oedipus the king
Strindberg, A. Miss Julie
Yeats, W. On Baile's strand

BARD Barnet, Sylvan; Berman, Morton and Burto, William, eds. The genius of the early English theatre..[New York] New American Library [c1962] 453p
Abraham and Isaac
Everyman
Jonson, B. Volpone
Marlowe, C. Doctor Faustus
Milton, J. Samson Agonistes
The second shepherds' play
Shakespeare, W. Macbeth

BARF Barnet, Sylvan; Berman, Morton and Burto, William, eds. The genius of the Irish theater...[New York] New American Library [c1960] 366p
Gregory, I. The Canavans
O'Casey, S. Purple dust
O'Donovan, M. In the train
Shaw, G. John Bull's other island
Synge, J. Deirdre of the sorrows
Yeats, J. La la noo
Yeats, W. The words upon the windowpane

BARG Barnet, Sylvan; Berman, Morton and Burto, William eds. The genius of the later English theater... [New York] New American Library [c1962] 536p
Byron, G. Cain
Congreve, W. The way of the world
Golding, W. The brass butterfly
Goldsmith, O. She stoops to conquer; or, The mistakes of a night
Shaw, G. Major Barbara
Wilde, O. The importance of being earnest

BARH Barnet, Sylvan; Berman, Morton and Burto, William, eds. An introduction to literature... Boston, Little, Brown [c1961] 491p
Quem quaeritis
Sophocles. Antigone
Shaw, G. The shewing up of Blanco Posnet

Yeats, W. Purgatory

BARI Barnet, Sylvan, [and others] comps. An introduction to literature... 4th ed. Boston, Little, Brown, 1971. 961p
Ibsen, H. A doll's house
Ionesco, E. The gap
Molière, J. The misanthrope
Quem quaeritis
Shakespeare, W. The tragedy of Hamlet: Prince of Denmark
Sophocles. Antigone
Sophocles. Oedipus Rex
Synge, J. Riders to the sea
Ward, D. Happy ending
Williams, T. The glass menagerie

BARJ Barnet, Sylvan; Berman, Morton and Burto, William, eds. Tragedy and comedy ... Boston, Little, Brown [1967] 764p
Aristophanes. The birds
Ibsen, H. Hedda Gabler
Molière, J. The misanthrope
Pirandello, L. Henry IV
Shakespeare, W. As you like it
Shakespeare, W. The tragedy of Othello
Shaw, G. Major Barbara
Sophocles. Oedipus the king
Wilder, T. The matchmaker
Williams, T. A streetcar named desire

BARNES, JOHN R. See PROW Prose and poetry of the world...

BARO Barranger, Milly Slater and Dodson, Daniel B. New York, Harcourt, Brace, Jovanovich, 1971. 431p
Arrabal, F. Picnic on the battlefield
Hansberry, L. A raisin in the sun
Ibsen, H. Ghosts
Miller, A. All my sons
Molière, J. The miser
Shakespeare, W. Romeo and Juliet
Sophocles. Antigone

BARR Barrows, Herbert; Heffner, Hubert; Ciardi, John and Douglas, Wallace, eds. An introduction to literature... Boston, Houghton Mifflin [c1959] 1331p
Chekhov, A. The cherry orchard
Ibsen, H. The wild duck
O'Casey, S. Juno and the paycock
Pirandello, L. Six characters in search of an author
Shaw, G. Candida
Wilde, O. The importance of being earnest

BARS Barrows, Marjorie Wescott, and others, eds. The American experience: Drama. New York, Macmillan, 1968. 371p (Rev. ed. of Contemporary American Drama)
Albee, E. The sandbox
Anderson, M. Barefoot in Athens
Hellman, L. The little foxes
Wilder, T. The matchmaker
Williams, T. The glass menagerie

BART Barrows, Marjorie Wescott, comp. Currents in drama. Rev. ed. New York, Macmillan [1968] 327p
Benét, S. The devil and Daniel Webster
Čapek, K. R.U.R.
Chekhov, A. The boor
Milne, A. The ugly duckling
Saroyan, W. The man with the heart in the highlands
Shakespeare, W. A midsum-

BART (cont.)
mer night's dream
Tagore, R. The post office

BARU Barrows, Marjorie Wescott, ed. The English tradition: Drama. New York, Macmillan, 1968. 477p
Goldsmith, O. She stoops to conquer
O'Casey, S. The plough and the stars
Osborne, J. A subject of scandal and concern
Shakespeare, W. Macbeth
Shaw, G. Arms and the man

BARV Barrows, Marjorie Wescott and Dolkey, Matthew, eds. Modern English drama. New York, Macmillan [c1964] 358p
Dane, C. Wild Decembers
Priestley, J. They came to the city
Shaw, G. Arms and the man
Sherriff, R. Home at seven

BAS Baskervill, Charles Read; Heltzel, Virgil B., and Nethercot, Arthur H., eds. Elizabethan and Stuart plays ...New York, Holt [c1934] 1660p
Arden of Feversham
Attowell's jig (Francis' new jig)
Beaumont, F., and Fletcher, J. The knight of the burning pestle
Beaumont, F., and Fletcher, J. The maid's tragedy
Beaumont, F., and Fletcher, J. Philaster
Chapman, G. Bussy d'Ambois
Dekker, T. The honest whore, pt. I
Dekker, T. The shoemakers' holiday
Fletcher, J. The faithful shepherdess
Ford, J. The broken heart
Ford, J. Perkin Warbeck
Ford, J., Dekker, T., and Rowley, W. The witch of Edmonton
Gascoigne, G. Supposes
Greene, R. Friar Bacon and Friar Bungay
Greene, R. George a Greene
Heywood, T. A woman killed with kindness
Jonson, B. The alchemist
Jonson, B. Every man in his humor
Jonson, B. The hue and cry after cupid
Jonson, B. The sad shepherd
Jonson, B. Sejanus, his fall
Jonson, B. Volpone
Kyd, T. The Spanish tragedy
Lyly, J. Endymion
Marlowe, C. Doctor Faustus
Marlowe, C. Edward II
Marlowe, C. Tamburlaine, pt. I
Marston, J., and Webster, J. The malcontent
Massinger, P. The maid of honor
Massinger, P. A new way to pay old debts
Middleton, T. A trick to catch the old one
Middleton, T., and Rowley, W. The changeling
Mucedorus
Norton, T., and Sackville, T. Gorboduc
Peele, G. The arraignment of Paris
Peele, G. The old wives' tale
Preston, T. Cambises
Shirley, J. The cardinal
Shirley, J. The lady of pleasure
Stevenson, W. Gammer Gurton's needle
Udall, N. Roister Doister
Webster, J. The Duchess of Malfi

BAT Bates, Alfred...The

drama; Its history, literature and influence on civilization... London, Athenian society, 1903-04. 22v
Aeschylus. Eumenides 1
Alfieri, V. Myrrha 5
Aristophanes. The clouds 2
Aristophanes. Ecclesiazusae 21
Babo, J. Dagobert, king of the Franks 12
Beaumont, F., and Fletcher, J. The knight of the burning pestle 14
Benedix, R. Obstinacy 11
Bjørnson, B. A gauntlet 17
Boucicault, D. London assurance 22
Brougham, J. Pocahontas 20
Bulwer-Lytton, E. Money 16
Burke, C. Rip Van Winkle 19
Calderón de la Barca, P. Belshazzar's feast 4
Chekhov, A. A marriage proposal 18
Colman, G., and Garrick, D. The clandestine marriage 15
Cowley, Mrs. H. The belle's stratagem 15
Dancourt, F. Woman's craze for titles 8
The death stone 3
Euripides. The cyclops 1
Everyman 4
Farquhar, G. The beaux' stratagem 22
The fatal error 21
Fath-Ali, M. The alchemist 3
Gazul, C. [pseud.] Ines Mendo; or, The triumph of prejudice 21
Gilbert, W. Sweethearts 16
Goethe, J. Iphigenia in Tauris 11
Goethe, J. Stella 12
Gogol, N. The inspector (Revisor) 18
Goldoni, C. The post-inn 5
Gorki, M. In the depths 18
Guinon, A., and Marni, J. The yoke 21
Hanshew, T. The forty-niners 20
Hauptmann, G. Hannele 12
Hersha Deva, S. Retnavali 3
Holberg, L. The loquacious barber 17
Home, J. Douglas 14
Ibsen, H. Ghosts 17
Iffland, A. Conscience 11
Ireland, W. Vortigern 22
Jones, J. Solon Shingle 20
Jonson, B. Every man in his humor 14
Kock, P. A happy day 9
Kotzebue, A. Egotist and pseudo-critic (Herr Gottlieb Merks) 11
Kotzebue, A. Lover's vows; or, The natural son 21
Le Sage, A. Crispin, rival of his master 8
Lessing, G. The soldier's fortune (Minna von Barnhelm) 10
Longfellow, H. The Spanish student 19
Maeterlinck, M. The death of Tintagiles 21
The martyrdom of Ali 3
Massinger, P. A new way to pay old debts 13
Maupassant, G. The household peace 9
Metastasio, P. The dream of Scipio 5
"Mr. Punch." A dramatic sequel to The lady of Lyons; or, In the Lyons den 22
"Mr. Punch." A dramatic sequel to Hamlet; or, The new wing at Elsinore 22
"Mr. Punch." Omar and oh my! 21
Molière, J. L'école des maris (School for husbands) 7
Musset, A. The chandelier 9
Ohnet, G. The iron manufacturer 9
Payne, J. Therese, the orphan of Geneva 19

BAT (cont.)
The philosopher duped by love 7
Plautus. Amphitryon; or, Jupiter in disguise 21
The printer's apprentice 4
Racine, J. Les plaideurs (The suitors) 7
Robertson, T. Society 16
Rueda, L. The seventh farce 6
Sachs, H. Raising the devil 10
Scala, F. The faithful friend 5
Schiller, F. The camp of Wallenstein 10
Schnitzler, A. Questioning the irrevocable 12
Shadwell, T. The Lancashire witches, and Tegue O. Divelly 22
Sophocles. Antigone 1
Terence. The eunuch 2
Tobin, J. The honeymoon 16
Torres Naharro, B. Hymen 6
Townley, J. High life below stairs 16
Udall, N. Ralph Roister Doister 13
Vanbrugh, J. The provoked husband 15
Vega Carpio, L. The dog in the manger 6
Voltaire, F. Mahomet 8
Voltaire, F. Socrates 8
The wept of the wish-ton-wish 19
Werner, F. The twenty-fourth of February 10

BAUG Baugh, Albert C., and McClelland, George W., eds. English literature... New York, Appleton-Century-Crofts [c1954] 1480p
Dryden, J. All for love
Marlowe, C. The tragical history of Doctor Faustus
Wilde, O. Lady Windermere's fan

BAUL Bauland, Peter and Ingram, William, comps. The tradition of the theatre. Boston, Allyn and Bacon, 1971. 633p
Brecht, B. The Caucasian chalk circle
Chekhov, A. The cherry orchard
Dürrenmatt, F. The visit
Ibsen, H. Hedda Gabler
Miller, A. The crucible
Molière, J. The would-be gentleman
The second shepherds' play
Shaw, G. The devil's disciple
Sophocles. Antigone
Strindberg, A. A dream play
Webster, J. The duchess of Malfi
Wycherley, W. The country wife

BAYLISS, JOHN <u>See</u> NEWR New road...

BAYM Baylor, Robert and Moore, James, ed. In the presence of this continent; American themes and ideas...New York, Holt, Rinehart and Winston, 1971. 551p
Gurney, A. The golden fleece
Humphrey, H., and Baldwin, J. My childhood
Lamb, M. But what have you done for me lately?
Terry, M. Calm down, Mother
Trombo, D. Opening sequence

BEAC Beacon lights of literature...[Edited by] Marquis E. Shattuck...Rudolph W. Chamberlain...Edwin B. Richards...[Books six-twelve] Syracuse, N.Y., Iroquois, 1940. 7v
Coppée, F. The violin maker

of Cremona 8
Down, O. The maker of dreams 12
Dunsany, E. A night at an inn 11
Glaspell, S. Trifles 11
Goldsmith, O. She stoops to conquer 11
Gregory, I. The rising of the moon 12
Gregory, I. Spreading the news 8
Hall, H., and Middleman, R. The valiant 10
Kaufman, G., and Connelly, M. Merton of the movies 12
MacKaye, P. Sam Average 11
Moeller, P. Helena's husband 12
Moorhouse, A. The grand cham's diamond 10
O'Neill, E. Ile 12
Saunders, L. The knave of hearts 7
Shakespeare, W. Julius Caesar 11
Shakespeare, W. Macbeth 12
Shakespeare, W. The merchant of Venice 10
Shakespeare, W. A midsummer night's dream 9
Walker, S. The medicine show 11

BEAL Beal, Richard S., and Korg, Jacob, eds. The complete reader. Englewood Cliffs, N.J., Prentice-Hall, 1961. 630p
Shakespeare, W. The chronicle history of King Henry the fourth, pt. one
Shaw, G. Arms and the man
Sophocles. Oedipus the King

BEAM Beal, Richard S. and Korg, Jacob, eds. The complete reader. 2d ed. Englewood Cliffs, N.J., Prentice-Hall [1967] 627p
Shakespeare, W. Henry IV, pt. 1
Shaw, G. Arms and the man
Sophocles. Oedipus
Yeats, W. Purgatory

BEAR Beardsley, Monroe C.; Daniel, Robert and Leggett, Glenn, eds. Theme and form... Englewood Cliffs, N.J., Prentice-Hall, 1956. 725p
Shakespeare, W. Othello
Shaw, G. Arms and the man
Sophocles. Antigone
Thomas, D. The doctor and the devils

BECHHOFER, CARL ERIC. <u>See</u> ROE Roberts, Carl Eric Bechhofer, tr. Five Russian plays...

BEN Benedikt, Michael and Wellwarth, George E., eds. and trs. Modern French Theatre: the avant-garde, Dada, and surrealism; an anthology of plays. New York, Dutton, 1964. 406p
Anouilh, J. and Aurenche, J. Humulus the mute
Apollinaire, G. The breasts of Tiresias
Aragon, L. The mirror-wardrobe one fine evening
Artaud, A. Jet of blood
Breton, A. and Soupault, P. If you please
Cocteau, J. The wedding on the Eiffel Tower
Daumal, R. En gggarrrde!
Desnos, R. La Place de l'Etoile
Gilbert-Lecomte, R. The odyssey of Ulysses the Palmiped
Ionesco, E. The painting
Jarry, A. King Ubu
Pinget, R. Architruc
Radiguet, R. The pelicans
Salacrou, A. A circus story
Tardieu, J. One way for another
Tzara, T. The gas heart

BEN (cont.)
Vitrac, R. The mysteries of love

BENA Benedikt, Michael and Wellwarth, George E., eds. Modern Spanish theatre; an anthology of plays. New York, Dutton, 1968. 416p
Alberti, R. Night and war in the Prado Museum
Arrabal, F. First communion
Bellido, J. Football
Casona, A. Suicide prohibited in springtime
García Lorca, F. The shoemaker's prodigious wife
Mihura, M. Three top hats
Olmo, L. The news item
Valle-Inclán, R. Divine words

BENB Benedikt, Michael and Wellwarth, George E., eds. and trs. Postwar German theatre: an anthology of plays. New York, Dutton, 1967. 348p
Borchert, W. The outsider
Dorst, T. Freedom for Clemens
Dürrenmatt, F. Incident at twilight
Frisch, M. The great fury of Philip Hotz
Grass, G. Rocking back and forth
Hildesheimer, W. Nightpiece
Kaiser, G. The raft of the Medusa
Laszlo, C. The Chinese icebox
Laszlo, C. Let's eat hair!
Sylvanus, E. Dr. Korczak and the children
Weiss, P. The tower

BENET, WILLIAM ROSE. See OXF Oxford anthology of American literature... edited by William Rose Benét and Norman Holmes Pearson

BENN Bennett, Henry Garland, ed. ...English literature ...N.Y., American book company [c1935] 603p
Goldsmith, O. She stoops to conquer
Shakespeare, W. Macbeth

BENP Bennett, Henry Garland ...On the high road... N.Y., American book company [c1935] 600p
Dowson, E. The Pierrot of the minute
Everyman
Maeterlinck, M. The intruder
O'Neill, E. Where the cross is made
Riggs, L. Knives from Syria
Shakespeare, W. Julius Caesar
Sheridan, R. The rivals
Wilde, P. Confessional

BENPB Bens, John H., ed. Facing some problems... New York, Holt, Rinehart, and Winston, 1970. 306p
Rattigan, T. Table number seven
Shaw, I. Bury the dead
Steinbeck, J. Of mice and men

BENQ Benson, Carl Frederick and Littleton, Taylor, eds. The idea of tragedy. Glenview, Ill., Scott Foresman [1966] 370p
Aeschylus. Agamemnon
Chekhov, A. Uncle Vanya
Ibsen, H. Rosmersholm
Shakespeare, W. King Lear
Sophocles. King Oedipus
Webster, J. The Duchess of Malfi

BENR Bentley, Eric Russell, ed. The classic theatre [1st ed.]... Garden City, N.Y., Doubleday [1958-

61.] 4v
Beaumarchais, P. Figaro's marriage; or, One mad day 4
Beolco, A. Ruzzante returns from the wars 1
Calderón de la Barca, P. Life is a dream 3
Calderón de la Barca, P. Love after death 3
Calderón de la Barca, P. The wonder-working magician 3
Castro y Bellvis, G. Exploits of the Cid 4
Cervantes Saavedra, M. The siege of Numantia 3
Corneille, P. The cid 4
Goethe, J. Egmont 2
Goldoni, C. Mirandolina 1
Goldoni, C. The servant of two masters 1
Gozzi, C. The king stag 1
Kleist, H. Penthesilea 2
Kleist, H. The Prince of Homburg 2
Lesage, A. Turcaret 4
Machiavelli, N. The mandrake 1
Marivaux, P. The false confessions 4
Molière, J. The misanthrope 4
Racine, J. Phaedra 4
Rojas, F. Celestina; or, The tragi-comedy of Calisto and Melibea 3
Schiller, J. Don Carlos 2
Schiller, J. Mary Stuart 2
Téllez, G. The trickster of Seville and his guest of stone 3
The three cuckolds 1
Vega Carpio, L. Fuente Ovejuna 3

BENS Bentley, Eric Russell, ed. From the modern repertoire. Series one - three. [Denver, Col.] University of Denver press; Bloomington, Ind., Indiana university press. [c1949-1956] 3v

Anouilh, J. Cecile; or, The school for fathers 3
Becque, H. La Parisienne 1
Brecht, B. Galileo 2
Brecht, B. Saint Joan of the stockyards 3
Brecht, B. The threepenny opera 1
Büchner, G. Danton's death 1
Büchner, G. Leonce and Lena 3
Cocteau, J. The infernal machine 1
Cocteau, J. Intimate relations 3
Cummings, E. him 2
Eliot, T. Sweeney Agonistes 1
Fergusson, F. The king and the duke 2
García Lorca, F. The love of Don Perlimplin and Belisa in the garden 1
Giraudoux, J. Electra 2
Jeffers, R. The Cretan woman 3
MacNeice, L. The dark tower 2
Mirbeau, O. The epidemic 2
Musset, A. A door should be either open or shut 3
Musset, A. Fantasio 1
Obey, A. Venus and Adonis 2
Ostrovsky, A. Easy money 2
Pinero, A. The magistrate 3
Romains, J. Dr. Knock 3
Schnitzler, A. Anatol 3
Schnitzler, A. Round dance 1
Sternheim, C. The snob 1
Wedekind, F. The Marquis of Keith 2
Yeats, W. A full moon in March 1
Zola, E. Thérèse Raquin 3

BENSA Bentley, Eric Russell, ed. The genius of the

BENSA (cont.)
Italian theater. New York, New American Library [1964] 584p
Bruno, G. The candle bearer
The deceived
Dovizi da Bibiena, B. The follies of Calandro
Filippo, E. Filumena Marturano
Gozzi, C. Turandot
Pirandello, L. The emperor
Tasso, T. Amyntas

BENSB Bentley, Eric Russell, ed. The great playwrights: 25 plays with commentaries by critics and scholars... Garden City, N.Y., Doubleday, 1972. 2v
Aeschylus. Prometheus bound 1
Brecht, B. The Caucasian chalk circle 2
Brecht, B. Mother Courage 2
Calderón de la Barca, P. Life is a dream 1
Chekhov, A. The three sisters 2
Euripides. The bacchae 1
Ibsen, H. Rosmersholm 2
Ibsen, H. The wild duck 2
Jonson, B. Volpone; or, The fox 1
Kleist, H. Prince Frederick of Hamburg 1
Molière, J. Don Juan; or, The stone guest 1
Molière, J. The misanthrope 1
Pirandello, L. Right you are 2
Pirandello, L. Six characters in search of an author 2
Racine, J. Phaedra 1
Shakespeare, W. King Lear 1
Shakespeare, W. Troilus and Cressida 1
Shaw, G. Major Barbara 2
Shaw, G. Saint Joan 2
Sophocles. Antigone 1
Sophocles. King Oedipus 1
Strindberg, A. Miss Julie 2
Synge, J. The playboy of the western world 2
Vega Carpio, L. Fuente ovejuna 1
Wilde, O. The importance of being earnest 2

BENSC Bentley, Eric Russell, ed. Let's get a divorce! and other plays. New York, Hill and Wang [c1958] 364p
Courteline, G. These cornfields
Feydeau, G. Keep an eye on Amélie!
Labiche, E. and Martin, E. A trip abroad
Prévert, J. A united family
Sardou, V. and Najac, E. Let's get a divorce!

BENT Bentley, Eric Russell, ed. The modern theatre. [Plays] Garden City, N.Y., Doubleday [c1955-1960] 6v
Anouilh, J. Medea 5
Anouilh, J. Thieves' carnival 3
Becque, H. Woman of Paris 1
Beerbohm, M. A social success 6
Brecht, B. The measures taken 6
Brecht, B. Mother courage 2
Brecht, B. The threepenny opera 1
Büchner, G. Woyzeck 1
Büchner, G. Danton's death 5
Conrad, J. One day more 3
Fitch, C. Captain Jinks of the horse marines 4
Ghelderode, M. Escurial 5
Giraudoux, J. Electra 1
Giraudoux, J. Judith 3
Gogol, N. Gamblers 3
Gogol, N. The marriage 5
Labiche, E., and Marc-

Michel. An Italian straw hat 3
Mitchell, L. The New York idea 4
Musset, A. Fantasio 2
Musset, A. Lorenzaccio 6
O'Casey, S. Cock-a-doodle dandy 5
Ostrovsky, A. The diary of a scoundrel 2
Saroyan, W. The man with the heart in the Highlands 4
Schnitzler, A. La ronde 2
Sternheim, C. The underpants 6
Swerling, J., Burrows, A., and Loesser, F. Guys and dolls 4
Verga, G. Cavalleria rusticana 1
Wedekind, F. Spring's awakening 6
Wilder, T. Pullman car Hiawatha 4
Yeats, W. Purgatory 2

BENU Bentley, Eric Russell, ed. The play; a critical anthology... New York, Prentice-Hall, 1951. 774p
Ibsen, H. Ghosts
Miller, A. Death of a salesman
Molière, J. The miser
Rostand, E. Cyrano de Bergerac
Shakespeare, W. Othello
Shakespeare, W. Twelfth night
Sophocles. Antigone
Strindberg, A. The ghost sonata
Wilde, O. The importance of being earnest

BENY Bentley, Gerald Eades, ed. The development of English drama... New York, Appleton-Century-Crofts [c1950] 823p
Abraham and Isaac
Beaumont, F., and Fletcher, J. The knight of the burning pestle
Boucicault, D. London assurance
Congreve, W. Love for love
Congreve, W. The way of the world
Cumberland, R. The West Indian
Dekker, T. The shoemakers' holiday
The deluge; or, Noah's flood
Dryden, J. All for love; or, The world well lost
Dryden, J., and Howard, R. The Indian queen
Everyman
Fletcher, J. The wild-goose chase
Ford, J. 'Tis a pity she's a whore
Goldsmith, O. She stoops to conquer
Greene, R. Friar Bacon and Friar Bungay
Jonson, B. The alchemist
Lillo, G. The London merchant
Marlowe, C. Doctor Faustus
Pinero, A. The second Mrs. Tanqueray
The second shepherds' play
Sheridan, R. The school for scandal
Webster, J. The white devil
Wilde, O. Lady Windermere's fan

BENZ Benton, Charles William, ed. Easy French plays... Chicago, Scott, Foresman, 1901. 236p
Girardin, E. de. La joie fait peur
Labiche, E. La grammaire
Scribe, E. Les doigts de fée

BERGH, ALBERT ELLERY. See DRA Dramatic masterpieces...

BER Bergin, Thomas Goddard

BER (cont.) and Anderson, Theodore, eds. French plays... New York, American book co. [c1941] 452p
Brieux, E. Les trois filles de M. Dupont
Hervieu, P. La course du flambeau
Mirbeau, O. Les affaires sont les affaires

BERKLEY, JAMES. See PATM, PATP Patterns of literature...

BERM Bermel, Albert, ed. The genius of the French theater... New York, New American Library [c1961] 574p
Anouilh, J. The lark
Beaumarchais, P. The barber of Seville
Giraudoux, J. Song of songs
Hugo, V. Hernani
Labiche, E., and Delacour, A. Pots of money
Molière, J. The imaginary invalid
Racine, J. Andromache
Rostand, E. The romantics

BERN Bernbaum, Ernest, ed. Anthology of romanticism ... New York, Ronald [c1948] 1238p
Byron, G. Manfred
Shelley, P. Prometheus unbound

BES Best plays of 1894/1889-1973/74; and The yearbook of the drama in America ... Edited by R. B. Mantle ... G. P. Sherwood... John Chapman... Louis Kronenberger... Henry Hewes... Otis L. Guernsey, Jr.... New York, Dodd, Mead, 1920-74. 57v
Note: Numbers following titles indicate volumes by years, e.g., 27 indicates volume for 1927/28: 28 for 1928/29, etc.
Abbott, G., and Bridgers, A. Coquette 27
Abbott, G., and Gleason, J. The fall guy 24
Ableman, P. Green Julia 72
Ade, G. The county chairman 99
Akins, Z. Declassee 19
Akins, Z. The old maid 34
Albee, E. A delicate balance 66
Albee, E. Tiny Alice 64
Albee, E. Who's afraid of Virginia Woolf? 62
Alfred, W. Hogan's goat 65
Allen, J. Forty carats 68
Anderson, M. Anne of the thousand days 48
Anderson, M. Bad seed 54
Anderson, M. Barefoot in Athens 51
Anderson, M. Both your houses 32
Anderson, M. Candle in the wind 41
Anderson, M. Elizabeth the queen 30
Anderson, M. The eve of St. Mark 42
Anderson, M. Gypsy 28
Anderson, M. High Tor 36
Anderson, M. Joan of Lorraine 46
Anderson, M. Key largo 39
Anderson, M., and Weill, K. Lost in the stars 49
Anderson, M. Mary of Scotland 33
Anderson, M. Saturday's children 26
Anderson, M. The star-wagon 37
Anderson, M. Storm operation 43
Anderson, M. Valley Forge 34
Anderson, M. Winterset 35
Anderson, M., and Stallings, L. What price glory? 24

Anderson, R. I never sang for my father 67
Anderson, R. Tea and sympathy 53
Anderson, R. You know I can't hear you when the water's running 66
Andreyev, L. He who gets slapped 21
Anouilh, J. Becket; or, The honor of God 60
Anouilh, J. The lark 55
Anouilh, J. Poor Bitos 64
Anouilh, J. The rehearsal 63
Anouilh, J. Time remembered 57
Anouilh, J. The waltz of the toreadors 56
Anouilh, J., and Galantière, L. Antigone 45
Ansky, S. The dybbuk 25
Anspacher, L. The unchastened woman 09
Archer, W. The green goddess 20
Archibald, W. The innocents 49
Ardrey, R. Stone and star 61
Arlen, M. The green hat 25
Atlas, L. Wednesday's child 33
Aurthur, R. A very special baby 56
Bagnold, E. The chalk garden 55
Balderston, J. Berkeley Square 29
Barrie, J. The little minister 94
Barrie, J. Mary Rose 20
Barry, P. The animal kingdom 31
Barry, P. Foolish notion 44
Barry, P. Here come the clowns 38
Barry, P. Holiday 28
Barry, P. Paris bound 27
Barry, P. The Philadelphia story 38
Barry, P. Second threshold 50
Barry, P. Tomorrow and tomorrow 30
Barry, P. You and I 22
Barry, P. The youngest 24
Baum, V. Grand hotel 30
Beach, L. The goose hangs high 23
Beckett, S. Waiting for Godot 55
Behan, B. The hostage 60
Behrman, S. Amphitryon 38 37
Behrman, S. Biography 32
Behrman, S. Brief moment 31
Behrman, S. The cold wind and the warm 58
Behrman, S. End of summer 35
Behrman, S. I know my love 49
Behrman, S. Jacobowsky and the Colonel 43
Behrman, S. Jane 51
Behrman, S. No time for comedy 38
Belasco, D. The heart of Maryland 94
Belasco, D., and Long, J. The darling of the gods 99
Benelli, S. The jest 19
Berg, G. Me and Molly 47
Berrigan, D. The trial of the Catonsville nine 70
Besier, R. The Barretts of Wimpole street 30
Bolitho, W. Overture 30
Bolt, R. A man for all seasons 61
Bolt, R. Vivat! Vivat! Regina 71
Bolton, G. Chicken feed 23
Bolton, G., and Middleton, G. Adam and Eva 19
Boothe, C. Kiss the boys good-bye 38
Boothe, C. Margin for error 39
Boothe, C. The women 36
Bowen, J. After the rain 67
Bowles, J. In the summer house 53
Brecht, B. Mother Courage and her children 62
Bricusse, L. and Newley, A.

BES (cont.)
Stop the world--I want to get off 62
Browne, P. The bad man 20
Burrows, A. Cactus flower 65
Burrows, A., Weinstock, J., and Gilbert, W. How to succeed in business without really trying 61
Butler, R. Mamma's affair 19
Camus, A. Caligula 59
Čapek, K. R.U.R. 22
Carroll, P. Shadow and substance 37
Carroll, P. The white steed 38
Casella, A. Death takes a holiday 29
Chase, M. Bernardine 52
Chase, M. Harvey 44
Chase, M. Mrs. McThing 51
Chayefsky, P. Gideon 61
Chayefsky, P. The passion of Josef D. 63
Chayefsky, P. The tenth man 59
Chodorov, E. Decision 43
Christie, A. Witness for the prosecution 54
Coffee, L., and Cowen, W. Family portrait 38
Cohan, G. Pigeons and people 32
Cohan, G. Seven keys to Baldpate 09
Colton, J., and Randolph, C. Rain 22
Comden, B. and Green, A. Applause 69
Conkle, E. Prologue to glory 37
Connelly, M. Green pastures 29
Connelly, M. The wisdom tooth 25
Cormack, B. The racket 27
Coward, N. Blithe spirit 41
Coward, N. Design for living 32
Coward, N. Noel Coward in two keys 73
Coxe, L., and Chapman, R. Billy Budd 50
Craven, F. The first year 20
Crothers, R. As husbands go 30
Crothers, R. Let us be gay 28
Crothers, R. Mary the 3d 22
Crothers, R. Nice people 20
Crothers, R. Susan and God 37
Crothers, R. When ladies meet 32
Crowley, M. The boys in the band 67
Dane, C. A bill of divorcement 21
Davis, O. Icebound 22
Davis, O. Mr. and Mrs. North 40
Davis, O., and Davis, D. Ethan Frome 35
Dayton, K., and Kaufman, G. First lady 35
Delaney, S. A taste of honey 60
Dell, F., and Mitchell, T. Little accident 28
Denker, H. A far country 60
Deval, J. Tovarich 36
Dodd, L. The changelings 23
Drinkwater, J. Abraham Lincoln 19
Driver, D. Your own thing 67
Duerrenmatt, F. The physicists 64
Duerrenmatt, F. The visit 57
Dunning, P., and Abbott, G. Broadway 26
D'Usseau, A., and Gow, J. Deep are the roots 45
Dyer, C. Rattle of a simple man 62
Dyer, C. Staircase 67
Eliot, T. The cocktail

party 49
Eliot, T. The confidential clerk 53
Elser, F. The farmer takes a wife 34
Emery, G. The hero 21
Emery, G. Tarnish 23
England, B. Conduct unbecoming 70
Ervine, St. J. The first Mrs. Fraser 29
Ervine, St. J. Jane Clegg 19
Ervine, St. J. John Ferguson 09
Fauchois, R. The last Christopher Bean 32
Feiffer, J. The White House murder case 69
Field, S. Wedding bells 19
Fields, J. The doughgirls 42
Fields, J., and Chodorov, J. Junior miss 41
Fields, J., and Chodorov, J. My sister Eileen 40
Fields, J., and Chodorov, J. The ponder heart 55
Fields, J., and Chodorov, J. Wonderful town 52
Fitch, W. Barbara Frietchie 99
Fitch, W. The climbers 99
Flavin, M. The criminal code 29
Forbes, J. The famous Mrs. Fair 19
Ford, R., and Faulkner, W. Requiem for a nun 58
Franken, R. Another language 31
Franken, R. Claudia 40
Franken, R. Outrageous fortune 43
Francken, R. Soldier's wife 44
Freeman, D. Creeps 73
Friedman, B. Scuba Duba 67
Friedman, B. Steambath 70
Friel, B. Lovers 68
Friel, B. Philadelphia, here I come! 65
Frings, K. Look homeward angel 57
Frisch, M. Andorra 62
Fry, C. The dark is light enough 54
Fry, C. Venus observed 51
Funt, J. The magic and the loss 53
Fugard, A. Boesman and Lena 70
Furth, G. and Sondheim, S. Company 69
Galsworthy, J. Escape 27
Galsworthy, J. Loyalties 22
Galsworthy, J. The skin game 20
Gardner, D. Eastward in Eden 47
Gardner, H. A thousand clowns 61
Genêt, J. The screens 71
Geraldy, P. The nest 21
Gershe, L. Butterflies are free 69
Gesner, C. You're a good man, Charlie Brown 66
Gibbs, W. Season in the sun 50
Gillette, W. Secret service 94
Gilroy, F. The subject was roses 64
Giraudoux, J. Duel of angels 59
Giraudoux, J. The enchanted 49
Giraudoux, J. The madwoman of Chaillot 48
Giraudoux, J. Tiger at the gates 55
Glaspell, S. Alison's house 30
Goetz, R., and Goetz, A. The heiress 47
Goetz, R., and Goetz, A. The immoralist 53
Goldman, J. The lion in winter 65
Goldman, J. Follies 70
Goldsmith, C. What a life 37
Goodhart, W. Generation 65
Goodrich, F., and Hackett, A. The diary of Anne Frank 55
Gordon, R. Over 21 43

BES (cont.)
Gordon, R. Years ago 46
Gordone, C. No place to be somebody 68
Gow, J., and D'Usseau, A. Tomorrow the world 42
Gray, S. Butley 72
Green, P. The house of Connelly 31
Green, P. In Abraham's bosom 26
Green, P. Johnny Johnson 36
Green, P., and Wright, R. Native son 40
Greene, G. The complaisant lover 61
Greene, G. The living room 54
Greene, G. The potting shed 56
Guare, J. The house of blue leaves 70
Guitry, S. Deburau 20
Hagan, J. One Sunday afternoon 32
Haines, W. Command decision 47
Hamilton, P. Angel street 41
Hammerstein, O., and Rodgers, R. Allegro 47
Hammerstein, O., and Rodgers, R. Oklahoma! 42
Hampton, C. The philanthropist 70
Hanley, W. Slow dance on the killing ground 64
Hansberry, L. A raisin in the sun 58
Harnick, S. and Bock, J. The apple tree 66
Hart, M. Christopher Blake 46
Hart, M. The climate of Eden 52
Hart, M. Lady in the dark 40
Hart, M. Light up the sky 48
Hart, M. Winged victory 43
Hartog, J. The fourposter 51
Hartog, J. Skipper next to God 47
Harwood, H., and Gore-Browne, R. Cynara 31
Hayden, J. Lost horizons 34
Hayes, A. The girl on the Via Flaminia 53
Hayes, J. The desperate hours 54
Hecht, B., and MacArthur, C. The front page 28
Heggen, T., and Logan, J. Mister Roberts 47
Hellman, L. Another part of the forest 46
Hellman, L. The autumn garden 50
Hellman, L. Candide 56
Hellman, L. The children's hour 34
Hellman, L. The little foxes 38
Hellman, L. The searching wind 43
Hellman, L. Toys in the attic 59
Hellman, L. Watch on the Rhine 40
Herbert, F. Kiss and tell 42
Heyward, D., and Heyward, D. Porgy 27
Hochhuth, R. The deputy 63
Hopkins, J. Find your way home 73
Housman, L. Victoria Regina 35
Howard, S. Alien corn 22
Howard, S. Dodsworth 33
Howard, S., and Irwin, W. Lute song 45
Howard, S. The silver cord 26
Howard, S. They knew what they wanted 24
Hughes, H. Hell-bent fer heaven 23
Hurlbut, W. The bride of the lamb 25
Inge, W. Bus stop 54
Inge, W. Come back, little Sheba 49
Inge, W. The dark at the top of the stairs 57
Inge, W. Picnic 52

Ionesco, E. Rhinoceros 60
Itallie, J. America hurrah 66
Itallie, J. The serpent: a ceremony 69
James, D. Winter soldiers 42
Jerome, H. Pride and prejudice 35
Job, T. Uncle Harry 41
Jones, H. The case of rebellious Susan 94
Jones, L. The toilet 64
Jones, T. Celebration 68
Kanin, F. Goodbye, my fancy 48
Kanin, G. Born yesterday 45
Kaufman, G. The butter and egg man 25
Kaufman, G., and Connelly, M. Beggar on horseback 23
Kaufman, G., and Connelly, M. Dulcy 21
Kaufman, G., and Connelly, M. Merton of the movies 22
Kaufman, G., and Ferber, E. Dinner at eight 32
Kaufman, G., and Ferber, E. Minick 24
Kaufman, G., and Ferber, E. The royal family 27
Kaufman, G., and Ferber, E. Stage door 36
Kaufman, G., and Hart, M. The American way 38
Kaufman, G., and Hart, M. George Washington slept here 40
Kaufman, G., and Hart, M. The man who came to dinner 39
Kaufman, G., and Hart, M. Merrily we roll along 34
Kaufman, G., and Hart, M. Once in a lifetime 30
Kaufman, G., and Hart, M. You can't take it with you 36
Kaufman, G., and Ryskind, M. Of thee I sing 31
Kelly, G. Behold the bridegroom 27
Kelly, G. Craig's wife 25
Kelly, G. Daisy Mayme 26
Kelly, G. The fatal weakness 46
Kelly, G. The show-off 23
Kennedy, M., and Hawthorne, R. Mrs. Partridge presents 24
Kerr, J. Finishing touches 72
Kerr, J. Mary, Mary 60
Kesselring, J. Arsenic and old lace 40
Kingsley, S. Darkness at noon 50
Kingsley, S. Dead end 35
Kingsley, S. Detective story 48
Kingsley, S. Men in white 33
Kingsley, S. The patriots 42
Kingsley, S. The world we make 39
Kipphardt, H. In the matter of J. Robert Oppenheimer 68
Knott, F. Dial "M" for murder 52
Koch, H., and Huston, J. In time to come 41
Kopit, A. Indians 69
Kopit, A. Oh dad, poor dad, mamma's hung you in the closet and I'm feelin' so sad 61
Kramm, J. The shrike 51
Krasna, N. Dear Ruth 44
Krasna, N. John loves Mary 46
Kummer, C. Good gracious Annabelle 09
Kummer, C. Her master's voice 33
Lardner, R., and Kaufman, G. June moon 29
Latouche, J. The golden apple 53
Laurents, A. A clearing in the woods 56
Laurents, A. Home of the brave 45
Laurents, A. The time of the cuckoo 52

Lavery, E. The magnificent Yankee 45
Lawler, R. Summer of the 17th doll 57
Lawrence, J., and Lee, R. Inherit the wind 54
Lerner, A., and Loewe, F. Brigadoon 46
Lerner, A. My fair lady 55
Levin, I. No time for sergeants 55
Levitt, S. The Andersonville trial 59
Levy, B. Clutterbuck 49
Levy, B. The devil passes 31
Lindsay, H., and Crouse, R. Life with father 39
Lindsay, H., and Crouse, R. Life with mother 48
Lindsay, H., and Crouse, R. Remains to be seen 51
Lindsay, H., and Crouse, R. State of the union 45
Logan, J. The wisteria trees 49
Lonsdale, F. The last of Mrs. Cheyney 25
Loos, A. Gigi 51
Luke, P. Hadrian VII 68
McCarthy, J. If I were king 99
McCullers, C. The member of the wedding 49
McEnroe, R. The silver whistle 48
McGuire, W. Six cylinder love 21
MacLeish, A. J.B. 58
McLellan, C. Leah Kleschna 99
McNally, T. Bad habits 73
McNally, T. Next 68
McNally, T. Where has Tommy Flowers gone? 71
Marasco, R. Child's play 69
Marceau, F. The egg 61
Marcus, F. The killing of Sister George 66
Marquand, J., and Kaufman, G. The late George Apley 44
Marquis, D. The old soak 22
Martínez Sierra, G. The kingdom of God 28
Martínez Sierra, G., and Martínez Sierra, M. The cradle song 26
Masteroff, J. Cabaret 66
Masteroff, J. She loves me 62
Maugham, W. The circle 21
Maugham, W. The constant wife 26
May, E. Adaptation 68
Mayer, E. The firebrand 24
Medoff, M. When you comin' back, Red Ryder? 73
Michaels, S. Dylan 63
Michaels, S. Tchin-Tchin 62
Miller, A. After the fall 63
Miller, A. All my sons 46
Miller, A. The creation of the world and other business 72
Miller, A. The crucible 52
Miller, A. Death of a salesman 48
Miller, A. Incident at Vichy 64
Miller, A. The price 67
Miller, A. A view from the bridge 55
Miller, J. That champion season 71
Milne, A. The Dover road 21
Milne, A. Michael and Mary 29
Molnár, F. Liliom 20
Molnár, F. The play's the thing 26
Molnár, F. The swan 23
Moody, W. The great divide 99
Moore, E. The sea horse 73
Morley, R., and Langley, N. Edward, my son 48
Mosel, T. All the way home 60
Newman, D., and Benton, R. "It's a bird, it's a plane,

it's superman" 65
Nichols, P. A day in the death of Joe Egg 67
Nichols, R., and Browne, M. Wings over Europe 28
O'Casey, S. The plough and the stars 27
O'Conor, J. The iron harp 56
Odets, C. Awake and sing 34
Odets, C. The country girl 50
Odets, C. The flowering peach 54
Odets, C. Golden boy 37
Odets, C. Rocket to the moon 38
O'Neill, E. Ah, wilderness! 33
O'Neill, E. Anna Christie 21
O'Neill, E. Beyond the horizon 19
O'Neill, E. Desire under the elms 24
O'Neill, E. The Emperor Jones 20
O'Neill, E. The great god Brown 25
O'Neill, E. The iceman cometh 46
O'Neill, E. Long day's journey into night 56
O'Neill, E. A moon for the misbegotten 56
O'Neill, E. Mourning becomes Electra 31
O'Neill, E. Strange interlude 27
O'Neill, E. A touch of the poet 58
Orton, J. What the butler saw 69
Osborn, P. A bell for Adano 44
Osborn, P. The innocent voyage 43
Osborn, P. Morning's at seven 39
Osborn, P. On borrowed time 37
Osborn, P. Point of no return 51
Osborne, J. The entertainer 57
Osborne, J. Inadmissable evidence 65
Osborne, J. Look back in anger 57
Osborne, J. Luther 63
Osborne, J., and Creighton, A. Epitaph for George Dillon 58
Parker, L. Disraeli 09
Patrick, J. The hasty heart 44
Patrick, J. The story of Mary Surratt 46
Patrick, J. The teahouse of the August moon 53
Peterson, L. Take a giant step 53
Pinero, A. Trelawny of the Wells 94
Piñero, M. Short eyes 73
Pinter, H. The caretaker 61
Pinter, H. The collection 62
Pinter, H. The homecoming 66
Pollock, C. The enemy 25
Pollock, C. The fool 22
Priestley, J. An inspector calls 47
Rabe, R. Sticks and bones 71
Randall, B. 6 rms riv vu 72
Raphaelson, S. Accent on youth 34
Raphaelson, S. Jason 41
Raphaelson, S. Skylark 39
Rattigan, T. O mistress mine 45
Rattigan, T. Separate tables 56
Rattigan, T. The Winslow boy 47
Rayfiel, D. P.S. 193 62
Reed, M. Yes, my darling daughter 36
Reizenstein, E. On trial 09
Rice, E. Dream girl 45
Rice, E. Flight to the west 40
Rice, E. The left bank 31
Rice, E. Street scene 28

BES (cont.)
Rice, E. We, the people 32
Richman, A. Ambush 21
Riggs, L. Green grow the lilacs 30
Rotter, F., and Vincent, A. Letters to Lucerne 41
Royle, E. The squaw man 99
Ryerson, F., and Clements, C. Harriet 42
Sackler, H. The great white hope 68
Saroyan, W. The time of your life 39
Saunders, J. Next time I'll sing to you 63
Schary, D. The devil's advocate 60
Schary, D. Sunrise at Campobello 57
Schisgal, M. Luv 64
Schulberg, B., and Breit, H. The disenchanted 58
Selwyn, E., and Goulding, E. Dancing mothers 24
Shaffer, A. Sleuth 70
Shaffer, P. Black comedy 66
Shaffer, P. Five finger exercise 59
Shaffer, P. The Royal hunt of the sun 65
Shairp, M. The green bay tree 33
Shaw, R. The man in the glass booth 68
Sheldon, E. Romance 09
Shelley, E. Pick-up girl 43
Sherriff, R. Journey's end 28
Sherriff, R., and Casalis, J. St. Helena 36
Sherriff, R. Abe Lincoln in Illinois 38
Sherwood, R. Idiot's delight 35
Sherwood, R. The petrified forest 34
Sherwood, R. Reunion in Vienna 31
Sherwood, R. The road to Rome 26
Sherwood, R. The rugged path 45
Sherwood, R. There shall be no night 39
Simon, N. Barefoot in the park 63
Simon, N. The gingerbread lady 70
Simon, N. The good doctor 73
Simon, N. Last of the red hot lovers 69
Simon, N. The odd couple 64
Simon, N. Plaza suite 67
Simon, N. The prisoner of Second Avenue 71
Simon, N. The sunshine boys 72
Smith, D. Call it a day 35
Smith, H. Mrs. Bumpstead-Leigh 09
Spewack, B., and Spewack, S. Boy meets girl 35
Spewack, B., and Spewack, S. My 3 angels 52
Spewack, S. Two blind mice 48
Stein, J. Fiddler on the roof 64
Steinbeck, J. The moon is down 41
Steinbeck, J. Of mice and men 37
Stewart, D. Rebound 29
Stewart, M. Hello, Dolly 63
Stone, P., and Edwards, S. 1776 68
Stoppard, T. Jumpers 73
Stoppard, T. Rosencrantz and Guildenstern are dead 67
Storey, D. The changing room 72
Storey, D. The contractor 70
Storey, D. Home 70
Sturges, P. Strictly dishonorable 29
Swerling, J., and Burrows, A. Guys and dolls 50
Tabori, G. The emperor's clothes 52
Tarkington, B. Clarence 19
Tarkington, B., and Wilson,

H. The man from home 99
Taylor, S. The happy time 49
Taylor, S., and Skinner, C. The pleasure of his company 58
Thomas, A. No more ladies 33
Thomas, A. The witching hour 99
Thomas, D. Under milk wood 57
Thurber, J. A Thurber carnival 59
Thurber, J., and Nugent, E. The male animal 39
Totheroh, D. Wild birds 24
Treadwell, S. Hope for a harvest 41
Treadwell, S. Machinal 28
Turney, R. Daughters of Atreus 36
Ustinov, P. The love of four colonels 52
Van Druten, J. Bell, book and candle 50
Van Druten, J., and Morris, L. The damask cheek 42
Van Druten, J. The distaff side 34
Van Druten, J. I am a camera 51
Van Druten, J. I remember mama 44
Van Druten, J. The voice of the turtle 43
Van Druten, J. Young Woodley 25
Vane, S. Outward bound 23
Varesi, G., and Byrne, D. Enter madame 20
Verneuil, L. Affairs of state 50
Vidal, G. The best man 59
Vidal, G. Visit to a small planet 56
Vollmer, L. Sun-up 23
Walker, J. The River Niger 72
Walter, E. The easiest way 09
Wasserman, D. Man of La Mancha 65
Watkins, M. Chicago 26
Watters, G., and Hopkins, A. Burlesque 27
Weidman, J., and Abbott, G. Fiorello! 59
Weiss, P. The persecution and assassination of Marat as performed by the inmates of the Asylum of Charenton under the direction of the Marquis de Sade 65
Weitzenkorn, L. Five star final 30
Weller, M. Moonchildren 71
Wesker, A. Chips with everything 63
Wexley, J. The last mile 29
Wexley, J. They shall not die 33
Wheeler, H. Big fish, little fish 60
Wheeler, H. A little night music 72
Wilder, T. The matchmaker 55
Wilder, T. Our town 37
Wilder, T. The skin of our teeth 42
Williams, E. The corn is green 40
Williams, J. Why marry? 09
Williams, J. Why not? 22
Williams, T. Cat on a hot tin roof 54
Williams, T. The glass menagerie 44
Williams, T. The milk train doesn't stop here anymore 62
Williams, T. The night of the iguana 61
Williams, T. Orpheus descending 56
Williams, T. Period of adjustment 60
Williams, T. The rose tattoo 50
Williams, T. Small craft warnings 71
Williams, T. A streetcar

BES (cont.)
named desire 47
Williams, T. Sweet bird of youth 58
Wilson, J. Hamp 66
Wilson, L. The hot l Baltimore 72
Wilson, S. The boy friend 54
Wincelberg, S. Kataki 58
Winter, K. The shining hour 33
Wishengrad, M. The rope dancers 57
Wolfson, V. Excursion 36
Wouk, H. The Caine mutiny court-martial 53
Yaffe, J. The deadly game 59
Yordan, P. Anna Lucasta 44
Zindel, P. The effect of gamma rays on man-in-the-moon marigolds 69

BEST PLAYS SERIES; See GARSA, GART, GARU, GARW, GARX, GARZ, GARZA, GAS, GASB. Gassner, John, ed. ...

BEV Bevington, David Martin, ed. The Macro; the castle of perseverance, wisdom, mankind... New York, Johnson Reprint, 1972. 305p
The castle of perseverance
Mankind
Wisdom; or, Mind, will, and understanding

BEVI Bevis, Richard W., ed. Eighteenth century drama: afterpieces. London, Oxford University Press, 1970. 286p
Colman, G. Polly Honeycombe
Fielding, H. The historical register for year 1736
Foote, S. The commissary
Garrick, D. Miss in her teens
The kept mistress
Macklin, C. A will and no will
Murphy, A. The upholsterer
Murphy, A. The way to keep him

BIER Bierman, Judah; Hart, James and Johnson, Stanley, eds. The dramatic experience.. Englewood Cliffs, N.J., Prentice Hall, 1958. 549p
Everyman
García Lorca, F. Blood wedding
Ibsen, H. The wild duck
Hayes, J. The desperate hours
Miller, A. Death of a salesman
Saroyan, W. The time of your life
Shakespeare, W. Othello
Shakespeare, W. Twelfth night; or, What you will
Shaw, G. Caesar and Cleopatra
Sherwood, R. Abe Lincoln in Illinois
Sophocles. Oedipus rex

BIES Bierstadt, Edward Hale, ed. Three plays of the Argentine... New York, Duffield, 1920. 147p
Bayón Herrera, L. Santos Vega
Manco, S. Juan Moreira
Sánchez Gardel, P. The witches' mountain

BIN Bingham, Joel Foote, comp. Gemme della letteratura italiane... London, Frowde, 1904. 1016p
Alfieri, V. Saul
Goldoni, C. Un curioso accidente
Metastasio, P. Attilio rigolo

BIR Birch, Cyril, ed. Anthology of Chinese literature. New York, Grove, 1972. 2v (v1, From early times to the 14th century; v2, From the 14th century to the present day)
K'ang Chin-chih. Li K'uei carries thorns 2

Ma Chih-yüan. Autumn in the palace of Han 1
T'ang Hsien-tsu. Peony pavilion 1
Yao Hsin-nung. The malice of empire 2

BLA A Black quartet: 4 new Black plays by Ben Caldwell, and others...New York, New American Libraries, 1970. 158p
Bullins, E. The gentleman caller
Caldwell, B. Prayer meeting; or, The first militant minister
Jones, L. Great goodness of life
Milner, R. The warning, a theme for Linda

BLAG Blair, Walter, and Gerber, John C., eds. ... Literature (Better Reading vol. 2). Chicago, Scott, Foresman [c1949] 778p
Note: Also published in one volume under the title, The College Anthology
Chekhov, A. The swan song
Dunsany, E. A night at an inn
Ibsen, H. Hedda Gabler
Molière, J. Tartuffe
O'Neill, E. Anna Christie
Sophocles. Oedipus the king

BLAH Blair, Walter and Gerber, John, eds. Repertory ...Chicago, Scott, Foresman [1960] 1173p
Chekhov, A. The cherry orchard
Chekhov, A. The swan song
Chayefsky, P. Marty
Dunsany, E. A night at an inn
Fry, C. A phoenix too frequent
O'Neill, E. Bound east for Cardiff
Shakespeare, W. Romeo and Juliet
Sophocles. Oedipus the king

BLAI Blair, Walter; Hornberger, Theodore, and Stewart, Randall, eds. The literature of the United States...Chicago, Scott, Foresman [c1946-47] 2v
Aiken, G. Uncle Tom's cabin; or, Life among the lowly 2
Mitchell, L. The New York idea 2
O'Neill, E. The hairy ape 2
Tyler, R. The contrast 1

BLAJ Blair, Walter; Hornberger, Theodore and Stewart, Randall. The literature of the United States...Single volume edition. Chicago, Scott, Foresman [c1949] 1313p
O'Neill, E. The hairy ape

BLOC Block, Haskell M., and Shedd, Robert G., eds. Masters of modern drama ...New York, Random House [c1962] 1198p
Anouilh, J. Antigone
Anouilh, J. Thieves' carnival
Beckett, S. Endgame
Brecht, B. The good woman of Setzuan
Brecht, B. Mother courage and her children
Camus, A. Caligula
Chayefsky, P. Marty
Chekhov, A. The cherry orchard
Chekhov, A. The sea gull
Cocteau, J. Orphée
Duerrenmatt, F. The visit
Frisch, M. Biedermann and the firebugs
García Lorca, F. Blood wedding
Giraudoux, J. Electra
Giraudoux, J. The madwoman

BLOC (cont.)
of Chaillot
Gorki, M. The lower depths
Hauptmann, G. The weavers
Hofmannsthal, H. Death and the fool
Ibsen, H. Ghosts
Ibsen, H. Peer Gynt
Ionesco, E. The bald soprano
Kaiser, G. From morn to midnight
Maeterlinck, M. The intruder
Miller, A. Death of a salesman
O'Casey, S. Cock-a-doodle dandy
O'Casey, S. Juno and the paycock
Odets, C. Awake and sing!
O'Neill, E. The Emperor Jones
O'Neill, E. The iceman cometh
Osborne, J. Look back in anger
Pirandello, L. Henry IV
Saroyan, W. The time of your life
Sartre, J. No exit
Schnitzler, A. La ronde
Shaw, G. Major Barbara
Shaw, G. Man and superman
Strindberg, A. The ghost sonata
Strindberg, A. Miss Julie
Synge, J. The playboy of the western world
Synge, J. Riders to the sea
Wedekind, F. The Marquis of Keith
Wilder, T. The matchmaker
Williams, T. The glass menagerie
Yeats, W. At the hawk's well
Zuckmayer, C. The devil's general

BLOD Blodgett, Harold William and Johnson, Burges, eds. Readings for our times... Boston, Ginn [c1942] 2v
Rostand, E. Cyrano de Bergerac 1
Wilder, T. Our town 1

BLON Bloomfield, Morton Wilfred and Elliott, Robert C., eds. Great plays, Sophocles to Brecht. New York, Holt, Rinehart and Winston [1965] 614p
Brecht, B. The Caucasian chalk circle
Chekhov, A. Three sisters
Congreve, W. The way of the world
Ibsen, H. Hedda Gabler
Molière, J. The misanthrope
O'Neill, E. The hairy ape
Shakespeare, W. Othello
Shaw, G. Arms and the man
Sophocles. Antigone
Strindberg, A. Miss Julie
Williams, T. The glass menagerie

BLOO Bloomfield, Morton W. and Elliott, Robert C., eds. Ten plays... New York, Rinehart [c1951] 719p
Chekhov, A. Three sisters
Dekker, T. The shoemakers' holiday
Farquhar, G. The beaux' stratagem
Hellman, L. The little foxes
Ibsen, H. Hedda Gabler
O'Neill, E. The hairy ape
Rostand, E. Cyrano de Bergerac
Shakespeare, W. Othello
Sophocles. Antigone
Thurber, J., and Nugent, E. The male animal

BOA Boas, Frederick Samuel, ed. Five pre-Shakespearean comedies (early Tudor period)... London, Oxford university press [1934] 343p (The world's classics)
Gascoigne, G. Supposes
Heywood, J. The four pp
Medwall, H. Fulgens and

Lucrece
"Mr. S. Mr. of Art." Gammer Gurton's needle
Udall, N. Ralph Roister Doister

BOGO Bogorad, Samuel N. and Trevithick, Jack, eds. The college miscellany... New York, Rinehart [c1952] 621p
Barrie, J. The twelve-pound look
Rattigan, T. The Winslow boy
Shakespeare, W. King Henry the fourth, pt. I

BOH Bohemian club, San Francisco. The Grove plays of the Bohemian club; edited by Porter Garnett... San Francisco, The club, 1918. 3v
Crocker, C. The land of happiness 3
Field, C. The cave man 2
Field, C. The man in the forest 1
Field, C. The owl and cave 1
Garnett, P. The green knight 2
Irwin, W. The Hamadryads 1
Myrtle, F. Gold 3
Pixley, F. Apollo 3
Redding, J. The atonement of Pan 2
Robertson, L. Montezuma 1
Scheffauer, H. The sons of Baldur 1
Shiels, J. Nec-natama 3
Steele, R. The fall of Ug 3
Stephens, H. St. Patrick at Tara 2
Stirling, G. The triumph of Bohemia 1
Tharp, N. The quest of the Gorgon 1

BONA Bonazza, Blaze O., and Roy, Emil, eds. Studies in drama... New York, Harper & Row [c1963] 344p
Ibsen, H. An enemy of the people
Shakespeare, W. A midsummer night's dream
Shaw, G. Candida
Sophocles. Antigone
Williams, T. The glass menagerie

BONB Bonazza, Blaze Odell, and Roy, Emil, eds. Studies in drama. New York, Harper & Row [c1963-64] 378p
Chekhov, A. The cherry orchard
Ibsen, H. An enemy of the people
Ibsen, H. The master builder
O'Neill, E. Desire under the elms
Shakespeare, W. King Lear
Shakespeare, W. A midsummer night's dream
Shaw, G. Candida
Shaw, G. Heartbreak house
Sophocles. Antigone
Wilder, T. Our town
Williams, T. The glass menagerie

BONC Bonazza, Blaze Odell, and Roy, Emil, eds. Studies in drama. 2d ed. New York, Harper and Row [1968] 583p
Brecht, B. Mother Courage and her children
Chekhov, A. Cherry orchard
Ibsen, H. An enemy of the people
O'Neill, E. Desire under the elms
Shakespeare, W. King Lear
Shaw, G. Heartbreak house
Sheridan, R. The school for scandal
Sophocles. Antigone

BONC (cont.)
Strindberg, A. Miss Julie
Synge, J. Riders to the sea
Wilder, T. Our town
Williams, T. The glass menagerie

BOND Bond, Richard Warwick, ed. Early plays from the Italian. Oxford, Clarendon press, 1911. 332p
The buggbears
Gascoigne, G. Supposes
Misogonus

BOO Booth, Michael R., ed. Eighteenth century tragedy ... London, New York, Oxford University Press, 1965. 394p
Colman, G., the Younger. The iron chest
Home, J. Douglas
Johnson, S. Irene
Lillo, G. The London merchant
Moore, E. The gamester

BOOA Booth, Michael, ed. English plays of the nineteenth century. New York, Oxford University Press, 1969-1973. 4v
Boucicault, D. The Corsican brothers 2
Boucicault, D. The Shaughraun 2
Brough, W., and Halliday, A. The area belle 4
Bulwer-Lytton, E. Richelieu; or, The conspiracy 1
Bulwer-Lytton, E. Money 3
Chambers, C. The tyranny of tears 3
Coleman, G. John Bull 3
Coyne, J. How to settle accounts with your laundress 4
Gilbert, W. Engaged 3
Gilbert, W. Tom Cobb 4
Jerrold, D. Black-eyed Susan; or, All in the downs 1
Jerrold, D. Mr. Paul Pry 4
Jones, H. Mrs. Dane's defence 2
Kenney, K. Raising the wind 4
Knowles, J. Virginius 1
Mathews, C. Patter versus clatter 4
Morton, J. Box and Cox 4
Murray, W. Diamond cut diamond 4
Pinero, A. The magistrate 4
Pinero, A. The second Mrs. Tanqueray 2
Pocock, I. The miller and his men 1
Taylor, T. New men and old acres 3
Taylor, T. The ticket-of-leave man 2
Walker, J. The factory lad 1

BOOB Booth, Michael R., comp. Hiss the villain, six English and American melodramas. New York, Benjamin Blom, 1964. 390p
Daly, A. Under the gaslight
Haines, J. My Poll and my partner Joe
Lewis, L. The bells
Phillips, W. Lost in London
Pocock, I. The miller and his men
Pratt, W. Ten nights in a bar-room

BOR Borgerhoff, Joseph Leopold, ed. ... Nineteenth century French plays... New York, Century [c1931] 790p
Augier, E. Le mariage d'Olympe
Augier, E. et Sandeau, J. Le gendre de M. Poirier
Balzac, H. Mercadet
Becque, H. Les corbeaux
Brieux, E. Les trois filles de M. Dupont

Curel, F. L'envers d'une sainte
Delavigne, C. Marino Faliero
Dumas, A. père. Antony
Dumas, A. père. Henri III et sa cour
Dumas, A. fils. La dame aux camélias
Dumas, A. fils. Les idées de Madame Aubray
Hugo, V. Hernani
Musset, A. Les caprices de Marianne
Pailleron, E. Le monde où l'on s'ennuie
Picard, L. Les ricochets
Pixérécourt, R. Coelina; ou, L'enfant du mystère
Rostand, E. Cyrano de Bergerac
Scribe, E. Le verre d'eau
Vigny, A. Chatterton

THE BORZOI READER. See VAN Van Doren, Carl Clinton, ed.

BOV Bovée, Arthur Gibbon; Cattanès, Hélène and Robert, Osmond Thomas, eds. Promenades littéraires et historiques... New York, Harcourt, Brace, 1940. 750p
Beaumarchais, P. Le barbier de Séville
Pailleron, E. Le monde où l'on s'ennuie

BOVE Bovée, Arthur Gibbon; Cattanès, Hélène and Robert, Osmond Thomas, eds. Promenades littéraires et historiques... Nouvelle édition. New York, Harcourt Brace, 1948. 658p
Beaumarchais, P. Le barbier de Séville
Legouvé, E., and Labiche, E. La cigale chez les fourmis

BOW Bowen, James K., and Van Der Beets, Richard, comps. Drama... New York, Harper and Row, 1971. 761p
Aristophanes. Lysistrata
Chekhov, A. The cherry orchard
Dürrenmatt, F. The visit
Everyman
Ibsen, H. Ghosts
Molière, J. The misanthrope
O'Neill, E. Desire under the elms
Racine, J. Phaedra
Shakespeare, W. Othello
Shaw, G. Major Barbara
Sophocles. Oedipus Rex
Strindberg, A. Miss Julie

BOWY Bowyer, John Wilson, and Brooks, John Lee, eds. The Victorian Age... Second edition. New York, Appleton-Century-Crofts [c1954] 1188p
Gilbert, W. Iolanthe; or, The peer and the peri
Jones, H. Michael and his lost angel
Pinero, A. The second Mrs. Tanqueray
Robertson, T. Caste
Shaw, G. Arms and the man
Wilde, O. The importance of being earnest
Yeats, W. The Countess Cathleen

BOY Boynton, Robert Whitney and Mack, Maynard, eds. Introduction to the play. New York, Hayden Book, 1969. 386p
Cocteau, J. The infernal machine
Ibsen, H. Ghosts
Shakespeare, W. Henry the fourth, Pt. I
Shaw, G. The devil's disciple
Sophocles. Oedipus the King

BRA Brandon, James R., comp. Traditional Asian plays.

BRA (cont.)
New York, Hill and Wang, 1972. 308p
Manohra
Namiki Gohei III. The subscription list
The price of wine
Shiko, O. The Zen substitute
Shudraka, K. The toy cart
Zembō, M. Ikkaku sennin

BRAS Brasmer, William, and Consolo, Dominick Peter, eds. Black drama; an anthology... Columbus, Ohio, Charles E. Merrill Publishing Company, 1970. 393p
Davis, O. Purlie victorious
Green, P. Native son
Hughes, L. Mulatto
Kennedy, A. Funny house of a Negro
Shine, T. Contribution
Ward, D. Day of absence
Ward, D. Happy ending

BRE Brenner, Clarence Dietz, and Goodyear, Nolan, A., eds. Eighteenth century French plays... New York, Century [c1927] 561p
Beaumarchais, P. Le mariage de Figaro
Crébillon, P. Rhadamiste et Zénobie
Dancourt, F. Le chevalier à la mode
Destouches, P. Le glorieux
Diderot, D. Le père de famille
Gresset, J. Le méchant
La Chaussée, P. Le préjugé à la mode
Laya, J. L'ami des lois
Lesage, A. Turcaret
Marivaux, P. Le jeu de l'amour et du hazard
Palissot de Montenoy, C. Les philosophes
Regnard, J. Le légataire universel
Sedaine, M. Le philosophe sans le savoir
Voltaire, F. Nanine
Voltaire, F. Zaire

BRET Brett, Lewis Edward ed. ... Nineteenth century Spanish plays... New York, Appleton-Century [c1935] 889p
Benavente y Martínez, J. El nido ajeno
Bréton de los Herreros, M. Muérete ¡y verás!
Echegaray y Eizaguirre, J. El gran Galeoto
García Gutiérrez, A. Juan Lorenzo
Gil y Zárate, A. Guzmán el Bueno
Hartzenbusch, J. Los amantes de Teruel
López de Ayala, A. Consuelo
Moratín, L. El sí de las niñas
Núñez de Arce, G. El haz de leña
Pérez Galdós, B. La de San Quintín
Rivas, A. Don Alvaro
Tamayo y Baus, M. Un drama nuevo
Vega, R. Pepa la frescachona
Vega, V. El hombre de mundo
Zorrilla y Moral, J. Don Juan Tenorio

BRIG Briggs, Thomas Henry; Herzberg, Max J., and Bolenius, Emma Miller, eds. ... English literature ... Boston, Houghton Mifflin [c1934] 770p (Literature in the senior high school. v4)
Shakespeare, W. The tragedy of Macbeth
Sheridan, R. The school for scandal
Synge, J. Riders to the sea

BRIK Briggs, Thomas Henry; Herzberg, Max J., and

Bolenius, Emma Miller, eds. ...Romance...Boston, Houghton Mifflin [c1932] 770p (Literature in the senior high school. v2)
Peabody, J. The piper
Shakespeare, W. As you like it

BRIT Britsch, Ralph A., and others. Literature as art. Provo, Utah, Brigham Young University Press, 1972. 743p
Chekhov, A. The master builder
Goethe, J. Faust, Part I
Sophocles. Antigone

BRIU Brittin, Norman A., comp. A reading apprenticeship literature. New York, Holt, Rinehart, and Winston, 1971. 469p
Miller, A. A view from the bridge
O'Casey, S. Bedtime story
Synge, J. Riders to the sea

BRIX Brockett, Oscar Gross and Brockett, Lenyth, eds. Plays for the theatre; an anthology of world drama... New York, Holt, Rinehart and Winston [1967] 503p
Brecht, B. The good woman of Setzuan
Ibsen, H. The wild duck
Kaiser, G. From morn to midnight
Miller, A. Death of a salesman
Molière, J. Tartuffe; or, The imposter
Plautus, T. The Menaechmi
The second shepherds' play
Shakespeare, W. King Lear
Sheridan, R. The school for scandal

BRN Brodin, Sylvie Bostsarron and Vigneras, Marcel, eds. En scène: trois comédies avec musique...New York, Dryden press [c1942] 295p
Beaumarchais, P. Le barbier de Séville
Labiche, E., and Martin, E. Les trente--sept sous de M. Montaudoin
Le savetier Calbain

BRNB Brodkin, Sylvia Z., and Pearson, Elizabeth J., eds. Close-up: a collection of short plays. New York, Globe, 1970. 282p
Arno, O. The other player
Carroll, R. Heat lightning
Daviot, G. The pen of my aunt
Hailey, A. Flight into danger
McDaniel, C. The ends of justice
Niggli, J. The ring of General Macías
Rose, R. Thunder on Sycamore Street
Watson, M. The dogs of war

BRO Brooke, Charles Frederick Tucker, ed. The Shakespeare apocrypha... Oxford, Clarendon press, 1918. 455p
Arden of Feversham
The birth of Merlin
Edward III
Fair Em
Locrine
The London prodigal
The merry devil of Edmonton
Mucedorus
The puritan
Sir John Oldcastle
Sir Thomas More
Thomas, lord Cromwell
The two noble kinsmen
A Yorkshire tragedy

BROC Brooke, Charles Frederick Tucker and Paradise,

BROC (cont.)
Nathaniel Burton, eds. English drama, 1580-1642 ... Boston, Heath [c1933] 1044p
Beaumont, F., and Fletcher, J. The knight of the burning pestle
Beaumont, F., and Fletcher, J. The maid's tragedy
Beaumont, F., and Fletcher, J. Philaster
Chapman, G. Bussy d'Ambois
Chapman, G., Johnson, B., and Marston, J. Eastward ho!
Dekker, T. The shoemakers' holiday
Fletcher, J. The island princess
Fletcher, J., and Massinger, P. Beggars' bush
Ford, J. The broken heart
Greene, R. Friar Bacon and Friar Bungay
Heywood, T. A woman killed with kindness
Jonson, B. The alchemist
Jonson, B. Epicoene; or, The silent woman
Jonson, B. Every man in his humor
Jonson, B. The gipsies metamorphosed
Jonson, B. Volpone; or, The fox
Kyd, T. The Spanish tragedy
Lyly, J. Endymion
Marlowe, C. Doctor Faustus
Marlowe, C. Edward II
Marlowe, C. The Jew of Malta
Marlowe, C. Tamburlaine, pt. I
Marston, J. The malcontent
Massinger, P. A new way to pay old debts
Middleton, T. A game at chess
Middleton, T., and Rowley, W. The changeling
Peele, G. The arraignment of Paris
Peele, G. The old wives' tale
Shirley, J. The cardinal
Webster, J. The Duchess of Malfi

BROF Brooks, Cleanth; Purser, John Thibaut and Warren, Robert Penn. An approach to literature. Baton Rouge, Louisiana university press, 1936. 578p
Čapek, K. R.U.R. (Rossum's universal robots)
Ibsen, H. Hedda Gabler

BROG Brooks, Cleanth; Purser, John Thibaut and Warren, Robert Penn. An approach to literature. Rev. ed. New York, Crofts, 1939. 634p
Čapek, K. R.U.R. (Rossum's universal robots)
Ibsen, H. Hedda Gabler
Shakespeare, W. Antony and Cleopatra
Wilde, O. The importance of being earnest

BROH Brooks, Cleanth; Purser, John Thibaut and Warren, Robert Penn. An approach to literature. Third edition. New York, Appleton-Century-Crofts [c1952] 820p
Eliot, T. Murder in the cathedral
Ibsen, H. Hedda Gabler
Maugham, W. The circle
Miller, A. All my sons
Shakespeare, W. Antony and Cleopatra

BROJ Brooks, Cleanth, and Heilman, Robert B., eds. Understanding drama... New York, Holt [c1945] 515p
Congreve, W. The way of the world

Everyman
Lillo, G. The London merchant
Ibsen, H. Rosmersholm
Plautus. The twin Menaechmi
Shakespeare, W. Henry IV, pt. I
Sheridan, R. The school for scandal
Wilde, O. Lady Windermere's fan

BROK Brooks, Cleanth and Heilman, Robert B. Understanding drama; twelve plays...New York, Holt [c1948] 674, +64p
Chekhov, A. The sea gull
Congreve, W. The way of the world
Everyman
Ibsen, H. Rosmersholm
Lillo, G. The London merchant; or, The history of George Barnwell
Marlowe, C. Dr. Faustus
Plautus. The twin Menaechmi
Shakespeare, W. Henry IV, pt. I
Shakespeare, W. King Lear
Sheridan, R. The school for scandal
Sophocles. Oedipus the king
Wilde, O. Lady Windermere's fan

BROOKS, VAN WYCK. See AME American caravan...

BROWNE, ELLIOTT MARTIN. See also NEWE New English dramatists...

BROS Browne, Elliott Martin, ed. Four modern verse plays...[Harmondsworth, Middlesex] Penguin Books [1957] 269p
Eliot, T. The family reunion
Fry, C. A phoenix too frequent
MacDonagh, D. Happy as Larry
Williams, C. Thomas Cranmer of Canterbury

BROSA Browne, Elliott Martin, ed. Three European plays ...[Harmondsworth, Middlesex] Penguin Books [1958] 190p
Anouilh, J. Ring round the moon
Betti, U. The queen and the rebels
Sartre, J. In camera

BROT Browne, Elliott Martin, ed. Three Irish plays... Baltimore, Penguin Books [1960, c1959] 236p
Johnston, D. The moon in the Yellow river
MacDonagh, D. Step-in-the-hollow
O'Conor, J. The iron harp

BROTA Brown, Ashley and Kimmey, J. L., eds. Tragedy. Columbus, Ohio, Merrill, 1968. 268p
Lowell, R. Benito Cereno
Shakespeare, W. King Lear
Sophocles. King Oedipus

BROWN, IVOR. See FOUP Four plays of 1936...

BROU Brown, Leonard Stanley; Waite, Harlow O., and Atkinson, Benjamin P., eds. Literature for our time...New York, Holt [c1947] 951p
Anderson, M. Winterset
Barry, P. The Philadelphia story
Behrman, S. Biography
Čapek, K. R.U.R.
Corwin, N. We hold these truths
MacLeish, A. The fall of the city
O'Neill, E. The hairy ape

BROW Brown, Leonard Stanley, and Perrin, Porter Gale, eds. A quarto of modern literature... New York, Scribner [c1935] 436p
Barrie, J. Dear Brutus
Galsworthy, J. Justice
Howard, S. The silver cord
O'Neill, E. In the zone

BROX Brown, Leonard Stanley, and Perrin, Porter Gale, eds. A quarto of modern literature... Third edition. New York, Scribner [c1950] 631p
Galsworthy, J. Loyalties
Giraudoux, J. The madwoman of Chaillot
Howard, S. The silver cord
Miller, A. Death of a salesman
O'Neill, E. The Emperor Jones
Sherwood, R. Abe Lincoln in Illinois

BROY Brown, Leonard Stanley and Perrin, P. G., eds. A quarto of modern literature. 5th ed. New York, Scribner, 1964. 606p
Giraudoux, J. The madwoman of Chaillot
Miller, A. Death of a salesman
Shaw, G. Pygmalion
Williams, T. The glass menagerie

BRR Brown, Sharon Osborne, ed. Present tense... New York, Harcourt, Brace, 1941. 3v
Čapek, K. R.U.R. (Rossum's universal robots) 3
MacLeish, A. The fall of the city 3
Wilder, T. Our town 1

BRS Brown, Sharon Osborne, ed. Present tense. Rev. ed. New York, Harcourt, Brace, 1945. 762p
Corwin, N. Good heavens
Wilder, T. Our town

BRYSON, LYMAN. See THP Three great Greek plays...

BUCK Buck, Philo M., jr., ed. An anthology of world literature... New York, Macmillan, 1934. 1016p
Aeschylus. Agamemnon
Aeschylus. Prometheus bound
Aristophanes. The frogs
Euripides. Iphigenia at Aulis
Goethe, J. Faust, pts. I and II
Hauptmann, G. The sunken bell
Hebbel, F. Maria Magdalena
Ibsen, H. An enemy of the people
Kälidäsa. Sakoontalá
Molière, J. The misanthrope
Molière, J. Tartuffe
Pérez Galdós, B. Electra
Racine, J. Athaliah
Sophocles. Antigone
Sophocles. Oedipus the king

BUCL Buck, Philo M., jr., and Alberson, Hazel, eds. An anthology of world literature. Revised edition... New York, Macmillan, 1940. 1148p
Aeschylus. Agamemnon
Aeschylus. Prometheus bound
Aristophanes. The frogs
Book of Job
Euripides. Iphigenia at Aulis
Euripides. Medea
Goethe, J. Faust, pts. I and II
Hauptmann, G. The sunken bell
Hebbel, F. Maria Magdalena
Ibsen, H. An enemy of the people
Kälidäsa. Sakoontalá

Molière, J. The misanthrope
Molière, J. Tartuffe
Racine, J. Athaliah
Sophocles. Antigone
Sophocles. Oedipus the king

BUCM Buck, Philo M., jr., and Alberson, Hazel Stewart, eds. An anthology of world literature. Third edition... New York, Macmillan [c1951] 1150p
Aeschylus. Agamemnon
Aeschylus. Prometheus bound
Aristophanes. The frogs
Book of Job
Euripides. Iphigenia at Aulis
Euripides. Medea
Goethe, J. Faust
Hauptmann, G. The sunken bell
Hebbel, F. Maria Magdalena
Ibsen, H. An enemy of the people
Kālidāsa. Shakuntalā
Molière, J. The misanthrope
Molière, J. Tartuffe
Plautus. Aulularia
Racine, J. Athaliah
Sophocles. Antigone
Sophocles. Oedipus the king

BUFF Buffington, Albert F., ed. The Reichard collection of early Pennsylvania German plays... Lancaster, Pa., 1962. 439p (v61, Pennsylvania German Society)
Barba, P. An der lumpa parti
Barba, P. Die verrechelte rechler
Birmelin, J. Der gnopp
Birmelin, J. Em Docktor Fogel sei offis schtunn
Brendle, T. Di hoffning
Brendle, T. Die mutter
Fink, E. Noshions duhn
Grumbine, E. Die insurance business
Iobst, C. Die Calline browierts
Iobst, C. Es Heller's Chrischtdag
Miller, D. Per Peter soll en handwerk lernen
Miller, D. En gespräch zwischen zweb demokrate über politiks
Miller, D. Noch eppes vom Peter seim handwerk
Moss, A., and Newhard, E. H. M. S. Pinafore; oder, Das maedle und ihr sailor kerl
Rauch, E. Rip Van Winkle; oder, Die shpooks fum Blowa Barrick
Wieand, P. Der parra kumpt
Wieand, P. Die huchzich um kreitz waig
Wieand, P. Tzu forwitsich
Wollenweber, L. Das lied von der union
Wollenweber, L. Die Margareth und die Lea
Wollenweber, L. Die Sära und die Betz
Wollenweber, L. Eb Refschneider un Susi Leimbach
Wollenweber, L. Ein gespräch

BUL Bullen, Arthur Henry, ed. A collection of old English plays. New York, B. Blom, 1964. 7v. in 4v
Davenport, R. The city nightcap 4
Davenport, R. A crowne for a conquerour 4
Davenport, R. King John and Matilda 4
Davenport, R. A new trick to cheat the divell 4
Davenport, R. A survey of the sciences 4
Davenport, R. Too late to call backe yesterday 4
The distracted emperor 2
The martyr'd souldier 1
The mayde's metamorphosis 1
Nabbes, T. Covent Garden 3
Nabbes, T. Hannibal and

BUL (cont.)
Scipio 3
Nabbes, T. Tottenham Court 3
The noble souldier 1
Sir Gyles Goosecappe 2
Tragedy of Nero 1
The tryall of chevalry 2
The wisdom of Dr. Dodypoll 2

BUR Burgess, Charles Owen. Drama; literature on stage. Philadelphia, Lippincott, 1969. 598p
Beach, L. The clod
Brecht, B. The good woman of Setzuan
Chekhov, A. The sea-gull
Ibsen, H. An enemy of the people
Lowell, R. Benito Cereno
Molière, J. The misanthrope
O'Neill, E. In the zone
Shakespeare, W. Antony and Cleopatra
Shaw, G. Major Barbara
Sophocles. Oedipus rex
Strindberg, A. The stronger
Williams, T. The last of my gold watches

THE BURNS MANTLE YEAR-BOOK... See BES Best plays of 1894/99... etc.

BURR Burrows, David James, and others, eds. Myth and motifs in literature. New York, Free Press, 1973. 470p
Aeschylus. Prometheus bound
Büchner, G. Woyzeck
Yeats, W. The land of the heart's desire

C

CADY Cady, Edwin H., ed. Literature of the early republic... New York, Rinehart [c1950] 495p
Tyler, R. The contrast

CALD Calderwood, James Lee and Tollver, H. E., eds. Forms of drama. Englewood Cliffs, N.J., Prentice-Hall, 1969. 601p
Beckett, S. All that fall
Chekhov, A. The cherry orchard
Dürrenmatt, F. The visit
Everyman
Ibsen, H. The master builder
Molière, J. Tartuffe
Orton, J. Entertaining Mr. Sloane
Racine, J. Phaedra
The second shepherds' pageant
Shakespeare, W. Henry the fourth, pt. I
Shakespeare, W. The tempest
Shakespeare, W. The tragedy of Macbeth
Shaw, G. B. Arms and the man
Sophocles. Oedipus rex
Yeats, W. Purgatory

CALG Campbell, Gladys and Thomas, Russell Brown, eds. Reading American literature... Boston, Little, Brown, 1944. 912p
Sherwood, R. Abe Lincoln in Illinois

CALM Campbell, Oscar James; Van Gundy, Justine and Shrodes, Caroline, eds. Patterns for living. New York, Macmillan, 1940. 1306p
Anderson, M. Winterset
Carroll, P. Shadow and substance
Milne, A. Mr. Pim passes by
Toller, E. No more peace!

CALN Campbell, Oscar James; Van Gundy, Justine and Shrodes, Caroline, eds. Patterns for living... Alter-

nate edition... New York, Macmillan [c1943, c1947] 2v
Anderson, M. Winterset 2
Čapek, K. R.U.R. 1
Franken, R. Claudia 1
Hellman, L. Watch on the Rhine 2

CALP Campbell, Oscar James; Van Gundy, Justine and Shrodes, Caroline, eds. Patterns for living... Third edition. New York, Macmillan, 1949. 951p
Hellman, L. Watch on the Rhine
Sherwood, R. Abe Lincoln in Illinois

CALQ Campbell, Oscar James; Van Gundy, Justine and Shrodes, Caroline, eds. Patterns for living... Fourth edition. New York, Macmillan [c1955] 975p
Hellman, L. Watch on the Rhine
Miller, A. Death of a salesman

CAM Campbell, Thomas Moody, ed. German plays of the nineteenth century... New York, Crofts, 1930. 437p
Anzengruber, L. Das vierte gebot
Grillparzer, F. König Ottokars glück und ende
Hauptmann, G. Einsame menschen
Hebbel, C. Agnes Bernauer
Hebbel, C. Herodes und Mariamne
Hebbel, C. Maria Magdalene
Kleist, B. Der zerbrochene krug
Kleist, B. Prinz Friedrich von Homburg
Ludwig, O. Der erbförster
Tieck, J. Der gestiefelte kater
Werner, Z. Der vierundzwanzigste Februar

CANADIAN PLAYS FROM HART HOUSE THEATRE. See MAS Massey, Vincent, ed.

CAN Canfield, Curtis, ed. Plays of changing Ireland. New York, Macmillan, 1936. 481p
Johnston, D. The old lady says 'No!'
Longford, C. Mr. Jiggins of Jigginstown
Longford, E. Yahoo
Manning, M. Youth's the season...?
Mayne, R. Bridge head
Robinson, L. Church street
Shiels, G. The new gossoon
Yeats, W. The words upon the windowpane

CAP Canfield, Curtis, ed. Plays of the Irish renaissance, 1880-1930... New York, Ives Washburn, 1929. 436p
Colum, P. The land
Fitzmaurice, G. The dandy dolls
Gregory, I. Hyacinth Halvey
Hyde, D. The twisting of the rope
Martyn, E. Maeve
Murray, T. Birthright
O'Casey, S. Juno and the paycock
Pearse, P. The singer
Robinson, L. The big house
Russell, G. Deirdre
Synge, J. Riders to the sea
Yeats, W. On Baile's strand
Yeats, W. The only jealousy of Emer

CAPU Caputi, Anthony Francis, ed. Modern drama; authoritative texts... backgrounds, and criticism. New York, Norton [1966] 494p
Chekhov, A. The three sisters

CAPU (cont.)
Ibsen, H. The wild duck
O'Neill, E. Desire under the elms
Pirandello, L. Henry IV
Shaw, G. The devil's disciple
Strindberg, A. A dream play

CARGILL, OSCAR. See American literature: a period anthology; Oscar Cargill, general editor

CAR Carpenter, Bruce, comp. A book of dramas, an anthology of nineteen plays... New York, Prentice-Hall, 1929. 1111p
Aeschylus. Agamemnon
Archer, W. The green goddess
Behrman, S. The second man
Chekhov, A. The cherry orchard
Congreve, W. Love for love
Dickens, C. The cricket on the hearth
Euripides. The Trojan women
The farce of the worthy master Pierre Patelin
Hugo, V. Hernani
Ibsen, H. Hedda Gabler
Kaufman, G., and Connelly, M. Beggar on horseback
Maeterlinck, M. The intruder
Molière, J. The misanthrope
Parker, L. A minuet
Racine, J. Phaedra
Sophocles. Oedipus, King of Thebes
Strindberg, A. Miss Julia
Synge, J. Riders to the sea
Wilde, O. The importance of being earnest

CARA Carpenter, Bruce, ed. A book of dramas...[Rev. ed.] New York, Prentice-Hall, 1949. 992p
Aeschylus. Agamemnon
Behrman, S. The second man
Chekhov, A. The cherry orchard
Congreve, W. Love for love
Euripides. The Trojan women
Ibsen, H. Hedda Gabler
Kaufman, G., and Connelly, M. Beggar on horseback
Maeterlinck, M. The intruder
Molière, J. The misanthrope
O'Neill, E. The long voyage home
Racine, J. Phaedra
Rostand, E. Cyrano de Bergerac
Sophocles. Oedipus, King of Thebes
Synge, J. Riders to the sea
Wilde, O. The importance of being earnest

CARL Carlsen, George Robert. American literature; themes and writers. St. Louis, Mo., Webster, 1967. 788p
Lardner, R. Thompson's vacation
O'Neill, E. In the zone
Rose, R. Twelve angry men
Wilder, T. Our town

CARM Carlsen, George Robert. Encounters; themes in literature. St. Louis, Mo. Webster, 1967. 758p
Glaspel, S. Trifles
Goodrich, F., and Hackett, A. The diary of Anne Frank
Shakespeare, W. Julius Caesar

CARN Carlsen, George Robert. Western literature; themes and writers. St. Louis, Mo., Webster, 1967. 786p
Shakespeare, W. Macbeth
Shaw, G. Androcles and the lion

Sophocles. Antigone

CARTMELL, VAN H. See also CET... Cerf, Bennett Alfred and Cartmell, Van H., comps.

CART Cartmell, Van H., and Cerf, Bennett Alfred, comps. Famous plays of crime and detection... Philadelphia, Blakiston, 1946. 910p
Cohan, G. Seven keys to Baldpate
Chodorov, E. Kind lady
Dell, J. Payment deferred
Dunning, P., and Abbott, G. Broadway
Gillette, W. Sherlock Holmes
Hamilton, P. Angel street
Megrue, R. Under cover
Rice, E. On trial
Rinehart, M., and Hopwood, A. The bat
Veiller, B. The thirteenth chair
Veiller, B. Within the law
Willard, J. The cat and the canary
Williams, E. Night must fall

CASE Cassell, Richard A. and Knepler, Henry, eds. What is the play? Glenview, Ill., Scott, Foresman [1967] 751p
Anouilh, J. Antigone
Dürrenmatt, F. The visit
Ghelderode, M. Christopher Columbus
Ibsen, H. An enemy of the people
Jonson, B. The alchemist
Lowell, R. My kinsman, Major Molineux
Molière, J. Scapin
O'Neill, I. Hughie
Shakespeare, W. King Henry IV, pt. I
Shaw, G. Arms and the man
Sophocles. Antigone
Wilder, T. The matchmaker

CASS Cassidy, Frederic G., ed. Modern American plays... New York, Longmans, Green, 1949. 501p
Anderson, M. Winterset
Hellman, L. Watch on the Rhine
Lindsay, H., and Crouse, R. Life with father
Odets, C. Waiting for Lefty
O'Neill, E. Anna Christie
Sherwood, R. Abe Lincoln in Illinois

CASU Casson, Lionel, ed. and tr. Masters of ancient comedy... New York, Macmillan, 1960. 424p
Aristophanes. The Acharnians
Menander. The arbitration
Menander. The grouch
Menander. She who was shorn
Menander. The woman of Samos
Plautus, T. The haunted house
Plautus, T. The rope
Terentius Afer, P. The brothers
Terentius Afer, P. Phormio

CATH Catholic University of America. Committee for the revision of English curricula... American profile. (The Catholic high school literature series. Book III) New York, W. H. Sadlier [c1944] 752p
Barry, P. The joyous season
Wilder, T. Our town

CAWL Cawley, Arthur C., ed. Everyman and medieval miracle plays... New York, Dutton [c1959] 266p
Abraham and Isaac
The annunciation
Cain and Abel
The creation, and the fall of Lucifer

CAWL (cont.)
The creation of Adam and Eve
The crucifixion
The death of Pilate
Everyman
The fall of man
The harrowing of hell
Herod the great
The judgment
Noah's flood
The resurrection
The second shepherds' pageant
The woman taken in adultery

CAWM Cawley, Arthur C., ed. The Wakefield pageants in the Towneley cycle...[Manchester] Manchester University Press [c1958] 187p (Old and Middle English texts)
Coliphizacio
Mactacio Abel
Magnus Herodes
Prima pastorum
Processus Noe cum filiis
Secundus pastorum

CERF, BENNETT ALFRED.
See also CART Cartmell, Van H., and Cerf, Bennett Alfred, comps. Famous plays of crime and detection...

CEQ Cerf, Bennett Alfred, comp. Four contemporary American plays...New York, Vintage Books [c1961] 386p
Chayefsky, P. The tenth man
Hansberry, L. A raisin in the sun
Hellman, L. Toys in the attic
Levitt, S. The Andersonville trial

CEQA Cerf, Bennett Alfred, comp. Plays of our time ...New York, Random House [1967] 782p
Bolt, R. A man for all seasons
Hansberry, L. A raisin in the sun
Heggen, T. and Logan, J. Mister Roberts
Inge, W. Come back, little Sheba
Miller, A. Death of a salesman
O'Neill, E. The iceman cometh
Osborne, J. Look back in anger
Schisgal, M. Luv
Williams, T. A streetcar named desire

CER Cerf, Bennett Alfred, ed. The pocket book of modern American plays...New York, Pocket books [1942] 430p
Behrman, S. No time for comedy
Boothe, C. Margin for error
Odets, C. Awake and sing
Rice, E. Street scene

CES Cerf, Bennett Alfred, ed. Six American plays for today...New York, Modern Library [c1961] 599p
Chayefsky, P. The tenth man
Hansberry, L. A raisin in the sun
Hellman, L. Toys in the attic
Inge, W. The dark at the top of the stairs
Schary, D. Sunrise at Campobello
Williams, T. Camino Real

CET Cerf, Bennett Alfred and Cartmell, Van H., eds. Sixteen famous American plays...Garden City, N.Y., Garden City publishing co. [c1941] 1049p
Behrman, S. Biography
Boothe, C. The women
Connelly, M. The green pastures
Hart, M., and Kaufman, G.

The man who came to dinner
Hecht, B., and MacArthur, C. The front page
Hellman, L. The little foxes
Howard, S. They knew what they wanted
Kingsley, S. Dead end
Kober, A. "Having wonderful time"
Lindsay, H., and Crouse, R. Life with father
Odets, C. Waiting for Lefty
O'Neill, E. Ah, wilderness!
Saroyan, W. The time of your life
Sherwood, R. The petrified forest
Spewack, B., and Spewack, S. Boy meets girl
Wilder, T. Our town

CEU Cerf, Bennett Alfred and Cartmell, Van H., comps. Sixteen famous British plays... Garden City, N.Y., Garden City publishing co. [1942] 1000p
Archer, W. The green goddess
Barrie, J. What every woman knows
Bennett, A., and Knoblock, E. Milestones
Besier, R. The Barretts of Wimpole street
Coward, N. Cavalcade
Galsworthy, J. Loyalties
Housman, L. Victoria Regina
Maugham, W. The circle
Milne, A. Mr. Pim passes by
Pinero, A. The second Mrs. Tanqueray
Priestley, J. Dangerous corner
Shairp, M. The green bay tree
Sherriff, R. Journey's end
Vane, S. Outward bound
Wilde, O. The importance of being earnest
Williams, E. The corn is green

CEW Cerf, Bennett Alfred, and Cartmell, Van H., comps. Sixteen famous European plays... Garden City, N.Y., Garden City publishing co. [1943] 1052p
Ansky, S. The dybbuk
Baum, V. Grand hotel
Čapek, K. R.U.R.
Carroll, P. Shadow and substance
Chekhov, A. The sea gull
Deval, J. Tovarich
Giraudoux, J. Amphitryon 38
Gorky, M. The lower depths
Hauptmann, G. The weavers
Ibsen, H. The wild duck
Martínez Sierra, G. The cradle song
Molnár, F. Liliom
Pirandello, L. Six characters in search of an author
Rostand, E. Cyrano de Bergerac
Schnitzler, A. Anatol
Synge, J. The playboy of the western world

CEY Cerf, Bennett Alfred, and Cartmell, Van H., comps. S.R.O.; the most successful plays in the history of the American stage... Garden City, N.Y., Doubleday, Doran, 1944. 920p
Aiken, G. Uncle Tom's cabin
Boucicault, D. Rip Van Winkle
D'Ennery, A., and Cormon, E. The two orphans
Hammerstein, O., and Rodgers, R. Oklahoma!
Kesselring, J. Arsenic and old lace
Kirkland, J. Tobacco road
Lindsay, H., and Crouse, R. Life with father
Manners, J. Peg o' my heart
Nichols, A. Abie's Irish Rose

CEY (cont.)
Rinehart, M., and Hopwood, A. The bat
Smith, W., and Bacon, F. Lightnin'
Tarkington, B., and Wilson, H. The man from home
Thompson, D. The old homestead
Wood, Mrs. H. East Lynne

CHA Chandler, Frank Wadleigh and Cordell, Richard Albert, eds. Twentieth century plays...New York, Nelson, 1934. v.p.
Alvarez Quintero, S., and Alvarez Quintero, J. Doña Clarines
Anderson, M., and Stallings, L. What price glory
Čapek, K., and Čapek, J. And so ad infinitum
Chlumberg, H. The miracle at Verdun
Connelly, M. The green pastures
Coward, N. Private lives
Crothers, R. As husbands go
Ervine, St. J. John Ferguson
Hankin, St. J. The last of the De Mullins
Jones, H. Dolly reforming herself
Lenormand, H. The coward
Maugham, W. The breadwinner
Molnár, F. The swan
O'Neill, E. Marco Millions
Pinero, A. The thunderbolt
Pirandello, L. Each in his own way
Rice, E. Street scene
Robinson, L. The far-off hills
Sherriff, R. Journey's end
Tolstoy, L. The live corpse

CHAN Chandler, Frank Wadleigh and Cordell, Richard Albert, eds. Twentieth century plays...Rev. New York, Nelson, 1939. v.p.
Alvarez Quintero, S., and Alvarez Quintero, J. Doña Clarines
Anderson, M. Winterset
Behrman, S. Rain from heaven
Čapek, K., and Čapek, J. And so ad infinitum
Chlumberg, H. The miracle at Verdun
Connelly, M. The green pastures
Coward, N. Private lives
Ervine, St. J. John Ferguson
Hankin, St. J. The last of the De Mullins
Howard, S. The silver cord
Jones, H. Dolly reforming herself
Kaufman, G., and Connelly, M. Beggar on horseback
Lenormand, H. The coward
Maugham, W. The breadwinner
Molnár, F. The swan
O'Neill, E. Anna Christie
Pinero, A. The thunderbolt
Pirandello, L. Each in his own way
Rice, E. Street scene
Robinson, L. The far-off hills
Sherriff, R. Journey's end
Tolstoy, L. The live corpse

CHAP Chandler, Frank Wadleigh and Cordell, Richard Albert, eds. Twentieth century plays, American ...Rev. New York, Nelson, 1939. 295p
Anderson, M. Winterset
Behrman, S. Rain from heaven
Connelly, M. The green pastures
Howard, S. The silver cord
Kaufman, G., and Connelly, M. Beggar on horseback
O'Neill, E. Anna Christie
Rice, E. Street scene

CHAR Chandler, Frank Wadleigh, and Cordell, Richard Albert, eds. Twentieth century plays, British... Rev. and enl. New York, Nelson, 1941. 399p
Barrie, J. The admirable Crichton
Coward, N. Private lives
Ervine, St. J. John Ferguson
Galsworthy, J. The silver box
Hankin, St. J. The last of the De Mullins
Jones, H. Dolly reforming herself
Maugham, S. The breadwinner
Pinero, A. The thunderbolt
Robinson, L. The far-off hills
Sherriff, R. Journey's end

CHAPMAN, JOHN ARTHUR See BES Best plays of 1894/99...etc.; THEA Theater, 1953/56...

CHARLTON, J. M. See PLAJ Plays of the sixties...; PLAL Plays of the thirties...

CHES The Chester mystery plays... Adapted into modern English by Maurice P. Hussey. London, William Heinemann [c1957] 160p
Abraham and Isaac
The adoration of the magi
The adoration of the shepherds
Antichrist
The betrayal of Christ
Christ's ascension
Christ's passion
Christ's resurrection
The creation of man: Adam and Eve
The fall of Lucifer
The last judgment
The magi's oblation
The nativity
Noah's deluge
Simon the leper
The slaying of the innocents

CHI Child, Clarence Griffin, ed. and tr. The second shepherds' play, Everyman, and other early plays... Boston, Houghton Mifflin [c1910] 138p
The Brome Abraham and Isaac
Everyman
The Oxfordshire St. George play
The Quem quaeritis
Robin Hood and the friar
Robin Hood and the knight
Robin Hood and the potter
The second shepherds' play

CHR Christy, Arthur, and Wells, Henry Willis, eds. World literature... Freeport, N.Y., Books for Libraries, 1971. 1115p (Reprint)
Aeschylus. Agamemnon
Andreyev, L. An incident
Molnár, F. Still life
Pirandello, L. The jar

CHU Church, Mrs. Virginia Woodson (Frame), ed. Curtain! A book of modern plays... New York, Harper, 1932. 504p
Bennett, A. The great adventure
Church, V. What men live by
Dunsany, E. The lost silk hat
Green, P. The man who died at twelve o'clock
MacKaye, P. Napoleon crossing the Rockies
Millay, E. Aria da capo
Milne, A. The great Broxopp
Morley, C. Good theatre
Nichols, R., and Brown, M. Wings over Europe
O'Neill, E. The Emperor Jones

CHU (cont.)
Wilder, T. The angel on the ship

CLARK, BARRETT HARPER. See also AMP America's lost plays.

CLA Clark, Barrett Harper, ed. Favorite American plays of the nineteenth century... Princeton, N. J., Princeton university press, 1943. 553p
Alfriend, E., and Wheeler, A. The great diamond robbery
Belasco, D. The heart of Maryland
Boucicault, D. Flying scud; or, A four-legged fortune
Campbell, B. My partner
Fechter, C. Monte Cristo
Howard, B. The banker's daughter
Hoyt, C. A trip to Chinatown; or, An idyll of San Francisco
Murdoch, F. Davy Crockett; or, Be sure you're right, then go ahead
Stone, J. Metamora; or, The last of the Wampanoags
Woolf, B. The mighty dollar

CLD Clark, Barrett Harper, tr. Four plays of the Free theater... Cincinnati, Stewart & Kidd, 1915. 257p
Ancey, G. The dupe
Curel, F. The fossils
Julien, J. The serenade
Porto-Riche, G. Françoise' luck

CLDM Clark, Barrett Harper, ed. Masterpieces of modern Spanish drama... New York, Cuffield, 1917. 290p
Echegaray [y Eizaguirre], J. The great Galeoto
Guimerá, A. Daniela
Pérez Galdós, B. The Duchess of San Quentin

CLDP Clark, Barrett Harper, and Davenport, William H., eds. Nine modern plays ... New York, Appleton-Century-Crofts [c1951] 432p
Anderson, M. High Tor
Ferber, E., and Kaufman, G. Stage door
Haines, W. Command decision
Hart, M., and Kaufman, G. You can't take it with you
O'Neill, E. The hairy ape
Rice, E. Street scene
Riggs, L. Green grow the lilacs
Sherwood, R. Abe Lincoln in Illinois
Williams, T. The glass menagerie

CLF Clark, Barrett Harper, ed. World drama... New York, Appleton, 1933. 2v
Abstraction 1
Adam 1
Aeschylus. Prometheus bound 1
Alfieri, V. Saul 2
Aristophanes. The clouds 1
Augier, E., and Sandeau, J. M. Poirier's son-in-law 2
Beaumarchais, P. The barber of Seville 2
Beaumont, F., and Fletcher, J. The maid's tragedy 1
Beolco, A. Bilora 2
Calderón de la Barca, P. The constant prince 2
Cervantes Saavedra, M. The cave of Salamanca 2
The chalk circle 1
Chikamatsu Monzaemon. Fair ladies at a game of poemcards 1
Corneille, P. The cid 2
Dumas, A. fils. The demi-monde 2
Euripides. Alcestis 1
Everyman 1
The farce of the worthy

Master Pierre Patelin 1
Farquhar, G. The beaux' stratagem 1
Goethe, J. Egmont 2
Goldoni, C. The fan 2
Goldsmith, O. She stoops to conquer 1
Heywood, T. A woman killed with kindness 1
Holberg, L. Jeppe of the hill 2
Hugo, V. Hernani 2
Ibsen, H. A doll's house 2
Jonson, B. Every man in his humour 1
Kālidāsa. Sakoontalá 1
Lessing, G. Miss Sara Sampson 2
Marlowe, C. The tragical history of Dr. Faustus 1
Molière, J. The cit turned gentleman 2
Ostrovsky, A. The thunderstorm 2
Plautus, T. The captives 1
The play of St. George 1
Racine, J. Berenice 2
Sachs, H. The wandering scholar from Paradise 1
Scala, F. The portrait 2
Schiller, J. William Tell 2
Seami, M. Nakamitsu 1
The second shepherds' play 1
Seneca. Medea 1
Sheridan, R. The school for scandal 1
Sophocles. Antigone 1
Terence. Phormio 1
Vega Carpio, L. The king, the greatest Alcalde 2
The wise virgins and the foolish virgins 1

CLK Clark, David Lee; Gates, William Bryan and Leisy, Ernest Erwin, eds. The voices of England and America... New York, Nelson, 1939. 2v

Dryden, J. All for love 1
Everyman 1
Farquhar, G. The beaux' stratagem 1
Jonson, B. Every man in his humor 1
Marlowe, C. The tragical history of Doctor Faustus 1
Milton, J. Comus 1
O'Neill, E. The Emperor Jones 2
Pinero, A. The second Mrs. Tanqueray 2
The second shepherds' play 1
Sheridan, R. The rivals 1

CLKJ Clark, Justus Kent and Piper, Henry D., eds. Dimensions in drama; six plays of crime and punishment. New York, Scribner [1964] 573p

Gay, J. The beggar's opera
Ibsen, H. Rosmersholm
Miller, A. All my sons
Sartre, J. No exit
Shakespeare, W. Macbeth
Sophocles. Oedipus rex

CLKW Clark, William Smith II, ed. Chief patterns of world drama... [Boston] Houghton Mifflin [c1946] 1152p

Aeschylus. Prometheus bound
Anderson, M. Mary of Scotland
Aristophanes. The birds
Barrie, J. The admirable Crichton
Beaumont, F., and Fletcher, J. The maid's tragedy
Čapek, J., and Čapek, K. The life of the insects
Chekhov, A. The sea-gull
Dekker, T. The shoemakers' holiday
Euripides. Alcestis
Etherege, G. The man of mode; or, Sir Fopling Flutter
Galsworthy, J. The silver box
Gogol, N. The inspector-

CLKW (cont.)
general
Green, P. Roll sweet chariot
Hebbel, J. Maria Magdalena
Ibsen, H. Hedda Gabler
Jonson, B. Epicoene; or, The silent woman
Marlowe, C. The troublesome reign and lamentable death of Edward the Second
Molière, J. The miser
Nice wanton
O'Neill, E. The hairy ape
Pirandello, L. Naked
Plautus. The pot of gold
Racine, J. Andromache
The second shepherds' play
Sheridan, R. The school for scandal
Sophocles. Electra
Synge, J. The playboy of the western world
Terence. Phormio
Vega, Lope de. The star of Seville

CLM Clayes, Stanley A., and Spencer, David G., eds. Contemporary drama... New York, Scribner [c1962] 512p
Chekhov, A. Uncle Vanya
García Lorca, F. The house of Bernarda Alba
Giraudoux, J. Ondine
Hellman, L. The autumn garden
Ibsen, H. The wild duck
Maugham, W. The circle
Miller, A. A view from the bridge
O'Casey, S. Juno and the paycock
Odets, C. The country girl
Shaw, G. The devil's disciple
Sophocles. Antigone (Cocteau, J. adapter)
Sophocles. Antigone
Strindberg, A. Miss Julie
Williams, T. The rose tattoo

CLN Clayes, Stanley and Spencer, David. Contemporary drama: 13 plays. 2d ed. New York, Scribner, 1970. 512p
Brecht, B. The Caucasian chalk circle
Bullins, E. A son come home
Chekhov, A. Uncle Vanya
García Lorca, F. The house of Bernarda Alba
Giraudoux, J. Ondine
Ibsen, H. The wild duck
Itallie, J. America hurrah
Miller, A. A view from the bridge
O'Casey, S. Juno and the paycock
Odets, C. The country girl
Shaw, G. The devil's disciple
Strindberg, A. Miss Julie
Williams, T. The rose tattoo

CLO Clayes, Stanley A., ed. Drama and discussion... New York, Appleton-Century-Crofts [1967] 651p
Aeschylus. Libation bearers
Anouilh, J. The lark
Beckett, S. All that fall
Brecht, B. Mother Courage and her children
Chekhov, A. The cherry orchard
Euripides. The Trojan women
García Lorca, F. Blood wedding
Giraudoux, J. Tiger at the gates
Ibsen, H. Ghosts
Shakespeare, W. Hamlet
Shaw, G. Saint Joan
Sophocles. Electra
Synge, J. Riders to the sea
Williams, T. A streetcar named desire

CLOU Clouard, Henri, and Leggewie, Robert, eds. Anthologie de la litterature française. Tome II... New

York, Oxford University Press, 1960. 468p
Giraudoux, J. La guerre de Troie n'aura pas lieu
Musset, A. Fantasio
Sartre, J. Huis clos

CLUR Clurman, Harold, ed. Famous American plays of the 1930s...[New York, Dell publishing co. c1959] 480p (Laurel drama series)
Behrman, S. End of summer
Odets, C. Awake and sing!
Saroyan, W. The time of your life
Sherwood, R. Idiot's delight
Steinbeck, J. Of mice and men

CLURMAN, HAROLD. See also SEVD Seven plays of the modern theatre

COD Coffman, George Raleigh, ed. ...A book of modern plays...Chicago, Scott, Foresman [c1925] 490p
Bennett, A., and Knoblock, E. Milestones
Gregory, I. The workhouse ward
Ibsen, H. An enemy of the people
O'Neill, E. Where the cross is made
Robertson, T. Caste
Rostand, E. The romancers
Synge, J. Riders to the sea

COF Coffman, George Raleigh, ed. Five significant English plays...New York, Nelson, 1930. 433p
Dekker, T. The shoemakers' holiday
Marlowe, C. Dr. Faustus
Pinero, A. The second Mrs. Tanqueray
Sheridan, R. The school for scandal
Steele, R. The conscious lovers

COH Cohen, Helen Louise, ed. Longer plays by modern authors (American)...New York, Harcourt, Brace [c1922] 353p
Fitch, C. Beau Brummell
Kaufman, G., and Connelly, M. Dulcy
Tarkington, B. The intimate strangers
Thomas, A. The copperhead

COJ Cohen, Helen Louise, ed. Milestones of the drama. New York, Harcourt, Brace [c1940] 580p
Everyman
Ibsen, H. A doll's house
Marlowe, C. Doctor Faustus
O'Neill, E. The Emperor Jones
Rostand, E. Cyrano de Bergerac
Sheridan, R. The school for scandal
Sophocles. Oedipus, king of Thebes

COK Cohn, Ruby; Dukore, Bernard F. and Block, Haskett M., eds. Twentieth century drama: England, Ireland [and] The United States...New York, Random House [1966] 692p
Albee, E. The zoo story
Beckett, S. Embers
Eliot, T. Murder in the cathedral
Odets, C. Awake and sing
O'Neill, E. The iceman cometh
Osborne, J. Look back in anger
Pinter, H. The dumb waiter
Shaw, G. Major Barbara
Synge, J. The playboy of the western world
Wilder, T. Our town
Williams, T. The glass menagerie
Yeats, W. The only jealousy of Emer

THE COLLEGE OMNIBUS. See MCCA, MCCB, MCCD, MCCF, MCCG McCallum, James Dow, ed. See also FUL Fullington, James Fitz-James. The new college omnibus

COL College survey of English literature...[Edited by B. J. Whiting; Fred B. Millett; Alexander M. Whiterspoon and others] New York, Harcourt, Brace, 1942. 2v
- Congreve, W. The way of the world 1
- Goldsmith, O. She stoops to conquer 1
- Marlowe, C. The tragical history of Doctor Faustus 1
- The second play of the shepherds (Wakefield) 2
- Shakespeare, W. King Henry IV, pt. I 1
- Synge, J. The playboy of the western world 2

COLLETTE, ELIZABETH. See WORL The world in literature

COLI Collins, Margaret, and Collins, Fletcher, eds. Theater wagon plays of place and any place. Charlottesville, Va., University Press of Virginia, 1973. 299p
- Collins, M. Love is a daisy
- Collins, M. 3 filosofers in a firetower
- Evreinov, N. A merry death
- Evreinov, N. Styopic and Manya
- Hite, B. Birdwatchers
- Hite, B. Sandcastle
- Lee, J. On the corner of Cherry and elsewhere

COMFORT, ALEX See NEWR New road...

COM Comfort, William Wistar, ed. French romantic plays ...New York, Scribner [c1933] 628p
- Dumas, A. père. Antony
- Hugo, V. Hernani
- Hugo, V. Ruy Blas
- Musset, A. On ne badine pas avec l'amour
- Vigny, A. Chatterton

CONB Conflict in social drama: plays for education. London, Methuen, 1972. 2v (v1, The personal conflict; v2, The social conflict)
- Arden, J. Soldier, soldier 2
- Cregan, D. Transcending 1
- Livings, H. There's no room for you here for a start 2
- Mortimer, J. David and broccoli 1
- Pinter, H. A night out 1
- Wesker, A. The kitchen 2

CONG Congdon, S. Perry, ed. The drama reader...New York, Odyssey Press [c1962] 418p
- Čapek, K. R.U.R.
- Cohan, G. Seven keys to Baldpate
- Kaufman, G., and Connelly, M. Dulcy
- Shakespeare, W. Richard III
- Sophocles. Antigone

CONN Connolly, Francis Xavier, ed. Literature, the channel of culture...New York, Harcourt, Brace, 1948. 714p
- Connelly, M. The green pastures
- Shakespeare, W. The tempest
- Synge, J. Riders to the sea

CONO Connolly, Francis Xavier, ed. Man and his measure. New York, Harcourt, Brace & World [1964] 139p
- Betti, U. Corruption in the

palace of justice
Marlowe, C. The tragical history of Doctor Faustus
Molière, J. The misanthrope
Sophocles. Oedipus rex

CONP Connolly, Francis X., ed. The types of literature... New York, Harcourt, Brace [c1955] 810p
Barrie, J. The twelve-pound look
Eliot, T. Murder in the cathedral
O'Neill, E. Bound east for Cardiff
Sheridan, R. The school for scandal
Sophocles. Antigone

CONT Contemporary Danish plays... London, Thames and Hudson, 1955. 557p
Abell, K. The Queen on tour
Branner, H. The judge
Clausen, S. The bird of contention
Fischer, L. The mystery tour
Locher, J. Tea for three
Munk, K. Herod the king
Schlüter, K. Off the rails
Sønderby, K. A woman too many
Soya, C. Two threads

CONTINENTAL DRAMA. See HARC Harvard classics, v26

COOA Cook, Albert Spaulding, and Dolin, Edwin, eds. An anthology of Greek tragedy. Indianapolis, Ind., Bobbs-Merrill, 1972. 400p
Aeschylus. Agamemnon
Aeschylus. Prometheus bound
Euripides. Andromache
Euripides. The bacchae
Euripides. The Trojan women
Sophocles. Oedipus at Colonus
Sophocles. Oedipus Rex
Sophocles. Philoctetes

COOJ Cook, Luella Bussey; Loban, Walter; McDowell, Tremaine and Stauffer, Ruth M., eds. America through literature... Harcourt, Brace, 1948. 750p (Living literature)
Sherwood, R. Abe Lincoln in Illinois
Wilder, T. Our town

COOK Cook, Luella Bussey; Norvell, George W., and McCall, William A., eds. Hidden treasures in literature. New York, Harcourt, Brace, 1934. 3v
Coppée, F. The violin-maker of Cremona 1
Dunsany, E. A night at an inn 3
Field, R. The patchwork quilt 2
Fitch, C. Nathan Hale 2
Monkhouse, A. The grand cham's necklace 2
Pillot, E. Two crooks and a lady 3
Rostand, E. The romancers 2
Saunders, L. The knave of hearts 1
Shakespeare, W. Julius Caesar 3

COOP Cooper, Charles W. Preface to drama... New York, Ronald press [c1955] 773p
Coward, N. Fumed oak
Gilbert, W. H. M. S. Pinafore
Housman, L. "A good lesson!"
Ibsen, H. Hedda Gabler
Lindsay, H., and Crouse, R. Life with father
Miller, A. The crucible
Molière, J. The ridiculous précieuses
O'Neill, E. The long voyage home
Shakespeare, W. Othello
Shaw, G. Candida

COOP (cont.)
Sophocles. Antigone
Wilder, T. The happy journey to Trenton and Camden
Williams, T. The glass menagerie

COOPA Cooper, Joshua, ed., and tr. Four Russian plays. Harmondsworth, Middlesex, Penguin, 1972. 394p
Fonvizin, D. The infant
Gogol, N. The inspector
Griboiedov, A. Chatsky
Ostrovskiĭ, A. Thunder

COOPER, LANE. See TEN Ten Greek plays...

COP Copeland, Charles Townsend, ed. The Copeland reader. New York, Scribner, 1926. 1687p
Sheridan, R. The critic; or, A tragedy rehearsed

COPB Copeland, Charles Townsend, ed. The Copeland translations...New York, Scribner, 1934. 1080p
Molière, J. The physician in spite of himself

COPC Copeland, Charles Townsend, ed. Copeland's treasury for booklovers... New York, Scribner, 1927. 5v
Sheridan, R. The critic; or, A tragedy rehearsed 1

CORB Corbin, Richard K. and Balf, Miriam, eds. Twelve American plays, 1920-1960. New York, Scribner, 1969. 480p
Albee, E. The sandbox
Chase, M. Harvey
Hellman, L. The little foxes
Kesselring, J. Arsenic and old lace
Nash, R. The rainmaker
O'Neill, E. Beyond the horizon
Patrick, J. The teahouse of the August moon
Rodgers, R. and Hammerstein, O. The king and I
Serling, R. Requiem for a heavyweight
Sherwood, R. There shall be no night
Wilder, T. Our town
Williams, T. The glass menagerie

CORD Cordell, Kathryn (Coe) and Cordell, William Howard, eds. The Pulitzer prize plays, 1918-1934... New York, Random House [1935] 856p
Anderson, M. Both your houses
Connelly, M. The green pastures
Davis, O. Icebound
Gale, Z. Miss Lulu Bett
Glaspell, S. Alison's house
Green, P. In Abraham's bosom
Howard, S. They knew what they wanted
Hughes, H. Hell-bent fer heaven
Kaufman, G., and Ryskind, M. Of thee I sing
Kelly, G. Craig's wife
Kingsley, S. Men in white
O'Neill, E. Anna Christie
O'Neill, E. Beyond the horizon
O'Neill, E. Strange interlude
Rice, E. Street scene
Williams, J. Why marry?

CORE Cordell, Kathryn (Coe) and Cordell, William Howard, eds. The Pulitzer prize plays...New ed. New York, Random house [1938?] 983p
Anderson, M. Both your houses
Connelly, M. The green

pastures
Davis, O. Icebound
Gale, Z. Miss Lulu Bett
Glaspell, S. Alison's house
Green, P. In Abraham's bosom
Hart, M., and Kaufman, G. You can't take it with you
Howard, S. They knew what they wanted
Hughes, H. Hell-bent fer heaven
Kaufman, G., and Ryskind, M. Of thee I sing
Kelly, G. Craig's wife
Kingsley, S. Men in white
O'Neill, E. Anna Christie
O'Neill, E. Beyond the horizon
O'Neill, E. Strange interlude
Rice, E. Street scene
Sherwood, R. Idiot's delight
Williams, J. Why marry?

CORF Cordell, Kathryn (Coe) and Cordell, William Howard, eds. A new edition of the Pulitzer prize plays ... New York, Random house [1940] 1091p
Anderson, M. Both your houses
Connelly, M. The green pastures
Davis, O. Icebound
Gale, Z. Miss Lulu Bett
Glaspell, S. Alison's house
Green, P. In Abraham's bosom
Hart, M., and Kaufman, G. You can't take it with you
Howard, S. They knew what they wanted
Hughes, H. Hell-bent fer heaven
Kaufman, G., and Ryskind, M. Of thee I sing
Kelly, G. Craig's wife
Kingsley, S. Men in white
O'Neill, E. Anna Christie
O'Neill, E. Beyond the horizon
O'Neill, E. Strange interlude
Rice, E. Street scene
Sherwood, R. Abe Lincoln in Illinois
Sherwood, R. Idiot's delight
Wilder, T. Our town
Williams, J. Why marry?

CORDELL, RICHARD ALBERT. See also CHA, CHAN, CHAP, CHAR Chandler, Frank Wadleigh and Cordell, Richard Albert, eds. Twentieth century plays...

COT Cordell, Richard Albert, ed. Represntative modern plays... New York, Nelson, 1929. 654p
Ade, G. The college widow
Bennett, A. The great adventure
Crothers, R. Expressing Willie
Dane, C. A bill of divorcement
Fitch, C. The climbers
Gilbert, W. Sweethearts
Hughes, H. Hell-bent fer heaven
Jones, H. Mrs. Dane's defence
Kaufman, G., and Connelly, M. Beggar on horseback
Maugham, W. The circle
Milne, A. Success
O'Casey, S. Juno and the paycock
O'Neill, E. Diff'rent
Pinero, A. Iris
Robertson, T. Caste
Wilde, O. A woman of no importance

COTE Cordell, Richard Albert, ed. Twentieth century plays, American... Third edition. New York, Ronald press [c1947] 329p
Anderson, M. Winterset
Connelly, M. The green pastures
Hellman, L. The little foxes
Howard, S. The silver cord

COTE (cont.)
Marquand, J., and Kaufman, G. The late George Apley
O'Neill, E. Anna Christie
Rice, E. Street scene
Sherwood, R. Abe Lincoln in Illinois

COTH Cordell, Richard Albert, ed. Twentieth century plays, British, American, Continental...Third edition. New York, Ronald press [c1947] 447p
Anderson, M. Winterset
Barrie, J. The admirable Crichton
Čapek, K. R.U.R.
Galsworthy, J. The silver box
Hellman, L. The little foxes
Maugham, W. The circle
Marquand, J., and Kaufman, G. The late George Apley
O'Neill, E. Anna Christie
Rice, E. Street scene
Rostand, E. Cyrano de Bergerac
Sherwood, R. Abe Lincoln in Illinois

COTK Cordell, Richard Albert, and Matson, Lowell, eds. The off-Broadway theatre... New York, Random house [c1959] 481p
Anouilh, J. Ardèle
Barkentin, M. Ulysses in Nighttown
Forsyth, J. Héloise
Hayes, A. The girl on the Via Flaminia
Lee, J. Career
O'Casey, S. Purple dust
Priestley, J., and Hawkes, J. Dragon's mouth

CORRIGAN, ROBERT WILLOUGHBY. See also NEWA New American plays...

COTKC Corrigan, Robert Willoughby and Rosenberg, James L., eds. The art of the theatre, a critical anthology of drama...San Francisco, Chandler [1964] 609p
Aristophanes. Lysistrata
Chekhov, A. Uncle Vanya
Ionesco, E. The new tenant
Molière, J. Tartuffe
Shakespeare, W. Macbeth
Sophocles. Antigone
Strindberg, A. Miss Julie
Synge, J. Riders to the sea
Wilde, O. The importance of being earnest
Williams, T. The rose tattoo

COTKF Corrigan, Robert Willoughby, comp. Laurel British drama: the nineteenth century. [New York, Dell, 1967] 464p
Boucicault, D. London assurance
Gilbert, W. Patience
Lewis, L. The bells
Pinero, A. The second Mrs. Tanqueray
Shaw, G. Arms and the man
Wilde, O. The importance of being earnest

COTKH Corrigan, Robert Willoughby, ed. Laurel British drama: the twentieth century. [New York, Dell, 1965] 511p
Bagnold, E. The chalk garden
Bolt, R. A man for all seasons
Coward, N. Private lives
Galsworthy, L. Loyalties
Jellicoe, A. The knack
Shaw, G. Heartbreak house

COTKI Corrigan, Robert Willoughby, ed. Comedy; a critical anthology. Boston, Houghton Mifflin, 1971. 769p
Aristophanes. Lysistrata
Bellow, S. The last analysis

Brecht, B. Puntila and his hired man
Chekhov, A. The cherry orchard
Giraudoux, J. The madwoman of Chaillot
Jonson, B. Volpone
Molière, J. Tartuffe
Shakespeare, W. Twelfth night
Shaw, G. Misalliance
Sheridan, R. The school for scandal
Synge, J. The playboy of the western world
Wilde, O. The importance of being earnest

COTKIR Corrigan, Robert Willoughby, comp. The forms of drama. Boston, Houghton Mifflin, 1972. 746p
Büchner, G. Woyzeck
Congreve, W. The way of the world
Ibsen, H. Ghosts
Jellicoe, A. The knack
Labiche, E., and Michel, M. An Italian straw hat
Miller, A. A view from the bridge
Molière, J. The miser
Plautus, T. The Menaechmi
Shakespeare, W. Othello
Shaw, G. Arms and the man
Sophocles. Antigone
Webster, J. The duchess of Malfi

COTKJ Corrigan, Robert Willoughby, ed. Masterpieces of the modern central European theatre; five plays. New York, Collier Books, 1967. 382p
Čapek, K. R.U.R.
Hofmannstal, H. Electra
Molnár, F. The play's the thing
Schnitzler, A. The game of love
Schnitzler, A. La ronde

COTKR Corrigan, Robert Willoughby, ed. Masterpieces of the modern English theatre. New York, Collier Books, 1967. 476p
Barrie, J. Dear Brutus
Galsworthy, J. Loyalties
Kops, B. Enter Solly Gold
Shaw, G. Major Barbara
Wilde, O. The importance of being earnest

COTKW Corrigan, Robert Willoughby, ed. Masterpieces of the modern French theatre; 6 plays. New York, Collier Books, 1967. 442p
Anouilh, J. Euridice
Becque, H. The Parisian woman
Ghelderode, M. Christopher Columbus
Giraudoux, J. Electra
Ionesco, E. Improvisation; or, The shepherd's chameleon
Montherlant, H. Queen after death

COTL Corrigan, Robert Willoughby, ed. Masterpieces of the modern German theatre; five plays. New York, Collier Books, 1967. 416p
Brecht, B. The Caucasian chalk circle
Büchner, G. Woyzeck
Hauptmann, G. The weavers
Hebbel, F. Maria Magdalena
Wedekind, F. The Marquis of Keith

COTM Corrigan, Robert Willoughby, ed. Masterpieces of the modern Irish theatre; five plays. New York, Collier Books, 1967. 317p
O'Casey, S. Cock-a-doodle dandy
O'Casey, S. The silver tassie

COTM (cont.)
Synge, J. The playboy of the western world
Synge, J. Riders to the sea
Yeats, W. The Countess Cathleen

COTN Corrigan, Robert Willoughby, ed. Masterpieces of the modern Italian theatre; six plays. New York, Collier Books [1967] 352p
Betti, U. Crime on Goat Island
Filippo, E. Filumena Marturano
Fratti, M. The academy
Fratti, M. The return
Pirandello, L. The pleasure of honesty
Pirandello, L. Six characters in search of an author

COTO Corrigan, Robert Willoughby, ed. Masterpieces of the modern Russian theatre; five plays. New York, Collier Books [c1967] 414p
Chekhov, A. The cherry orchard
Chekhov, A. Uncle Vanya
Gorki, M. The lower depths
Mayakovsky, V. The bed bug
Turgenev, I. A month in the country

COTP Corrigan, Robert Willoughby, ed. Masterpieces of the modern Spanish theatre. New York, Collier Books, 1967. 384p
Benavente y Martínez, J. The witches' sabbath
Buero Vallejo, A. The dream weaver
García Lorca, F. The love of Don Perlimplín and Belisa in the garden
Martínez Sierra, G. The cradle song
Sastre, A. Death thrust

COTQ Corrigan, Robert Willoughby, ed. The modern theatre. New York, Macmillan, 1964. 1267p
Anouilh, J. Eurydice
Beckett, S. Endgame
Betti, U. The queen and the rebels
Brecht, B. The Caucasian chalk circle
Büchner, G. Woyzeck
Chekhov, A. The cherry orchard
Chekhov, A. Uncle Vanya
Duerrenmatt, F. The visit
Eliot, T. Murder in the cathedral
Frisch, M. The Chinese wall
Fry, C. A sleep of prisoners
García Lorca, F. Yerma
Genêt, J. Deathwatch
Giraudoux, J. Electra
Gorki, M. The lower depths
Hauptmann, G. The weavers
Hebbel, F. Maria Magdalena
Hellman, L. The little foxes
Hofmannsthal, H. Electra
Ibsen, H. Hedda Gabler
Ibsen, H. The wild duck
Ionesco, E. The chairs
Miller, A. A view from the bridge
O'Casey, S. The plough and the stars
O'Neill, E. Desire under the elms
Pirandello, L. The emperor
Pirandello, L. Six characters in search of an author
Saroyan, W. The time of your life
Sartre, J. The victors
Sastre, A. Anna Kleiber
Schnitzler, A. La ronde
Shaw, G. Major Barbara
Strindberg, A. The ghost sonata
Strindberg, A. Miss Julie
Synge, J. Playboy of the western world
Synge, J. Riders to the sea
Wedekind, F. The marquis

of Keith
Wilder, T. The skin of our teeth
Williams, T. The glass menagerie
Yeats, W. On Baile's strand

COTR Corrigan, Robert W., ed. The new theatre of Europe ...[New York, Dell Publishing Co., c1962] 399p
Betti, U. Corruption in the palace of justice
Bolt, R. A man for all seasons
Ghelderode, M. Pantagleize
Peryalis, N. Masks of angels
Sastre, A. Anna Kleiber

COTS Corrigan, Robert Willoughby, ed. The new theatre of Europe, 2; 5 contemporary plays from the European stage...New York, Dell, 1964. 320p
Brecht, B. Mother Courage
Fratti, M. The cage
Fratti, M. The suicide
Grass, G. The wicked cooks
Schehadé, G. Vasco

COTT Corrigan, Robert Willoughby, ed. The new theatre of Europe, 3; 4 contemporary plays from the European stage...New York, Dell, 1968. 309p
Dorst, T. The curve
Forssell, L. The Sunday promenade
Guerdon, D. The laundry
Osborne, J. Inadmissable evidence

COTU Corrigan, Robert Willoughby, ed. Roman drama, in modern translations. [New York, Dell, 1966] 380p
Horatius Flaccus, Q. Ars poetica
Plautus, T. The Menaechmi
Plautus, T. The merchant
Seneca, L. Medea
Terentius Afer, P. Adelphi
Terentius Afer, P. Phormio

COTX Corrigan, Robert Willoughby, comp. Tragedy: a critical anthology. Boston, Houghton Mifflin, 1971. 787p
Coxe, L., and Chapman, R. Billy Budd
Dryden, J. All for love
Euripides. The bacchae
Ibsen, H. The master builders
MacLeish, A. J.B.
Marlowe, C. Doctor Faust
Miller, A. Death of a salesman
Racine, J. Phaedra
Shakespeare, W. The tragedy of King Lear
Shaw, G. Saint Joan
Sophocles. Oedipus the King
Strindberg, A. Miss Julie

COUR Cournos, John, ed. A treasury of classic Russian literature...New York, Capricorn Books [c1961] 580p and index
Gogol, N. The inspector-general
Ostrovskiĭ, A. A domestic picture
Tolstoi, L. Condemnation
Tolstoi, L. Taxes

COUS Cournos, John, ed. A treasury of Russian life and humor...New York, Coward-McCann [c1943] 676p
Gogol, N. The inspector

COX Cox, Martha Heasley, ed. Image and value; an invitation to literature. New York, Harcourt, Brace & World [1966] 630p
Arrabal, F. Picnic on the battlefield
Giraudoux, J. The Apollo of

COX (cont.)
Bellac
O'Neill, E. A touch of the poet
Shaw, G. Pygmalion
Sophocles. Antigone

COY Coyle, William and Damaser, H. G., eds. Six early American plays, 1798-1890. Columbus, Ohio, Merrill, 1968. 313p
Boucicault, D. The octoroon
Dunlap, W. André
Herne, J. Margaret Fleming
Howard, B. Shenandoah
Mowatt, A. Fashion
Stone, J. Metamora

CRAF Craft, Harry M., comp. Logic, style and arrangement... Beverly Hills, Calif., Glencoe Press, 1971. 501p
Shakespeare, W. King Lear
Sophocles. Antigone
Wilde, O. The importance of being earnest

CRAN Crane, William Garrett [and others] eds. Twelve hundred years; the literature of England... Harrisburg, Pa. Stackpole and Heck [c1949] 2v
Wilde, O. The importance of being earnest 2

CRE Creeth, Edmund, comp. Tudor plays; an anthology of early English drama. Garden City, New York, Anchor Books (Doubleday) [1966] 569p
Bale, J. Kyng Johan
Heywood, J. Johan Johan the husbande
Medwall, H. Fulgens and Lucres
Preston, T. Cambises
Sackville, T., and Norton, T. Ferrex and Porrex; or, Gorboduc
Stevenson, W. Gammer Gurton's nedle
Udall, N. Royster Doyster

CRIT The Critics' prize plays. Introduction by George Jean Nathan. Cleveland, Ohio, World publishing co. [c1945] 377p
Anderson, M. High Tor
Anderson, M. Winterset
Hellman, L. Watch on the Rhine
Kingsley, S. The patriots
Saroyan, W. The time of your life
Steinbeck, J. Of mice and men

CROS Cross, Ethan Allen, ed. World literature. New York, American book co. [c1935] 1396p
Aeschylus. Prometheus bound
Bulwer-Lytton, E. Richelieu; or, The conspiracy
Euripides. Iphigenia in Aulis
Galsworthy, J. The silver box
Ibsen, H. The master builder
Molière, J. The miser
Plautus. Menaechmi; or, The twin brothers
Seneca. Medea
Shakespeare, W. Antony and Cleopatra
Sophocles. Antigone
Terence. Andria

CROV Cross, Tom Peete and Slover, Clark H., eds. Heath readings in the literature of Europe... Boston, Heath [c1933] 1194p
Adam, The play of
Aeschylus. Prometheus bound
Aristophanes. The birds
Corneille, P. Le cid
Goethe, J. Faust, pt. I
Goldoni, C. A curious mishap

Ibsen, H. Ghosts
Lessing, G. Minna von Barnhelm
Molière, J. The misanthrope
Plautus. The captives
Seneca. Medea
Vega Carpio, L. The star of Seville

CROX Cross, Tom Peete; Smith, Reed; Stauffer, Elmer C., and Collette, Elizabeth. American writers. Revised edition.. Boston, Ginn [c1955] 708p
Wilder, T. Our town

CROZ Cross-section... Edited by Edwin Seaver. New York, L. B. Fischer [c1944-48] 4v
Miller, A. The man who had all the luck 1
Peters, P. Nat Turner 1
Whittington, R. The death of García Lorca 1

CUBE Cubeta, Paul M., ed. ... Modern drama for analysis. New York, William Sloane Associates [c1950] 584p
Chekhov, A. The cherry orchard
Hellman, L. Watch on the Rhine
Ibsen, H. The wild duck
O'Casey, S. Juno and the paycock
O'Neill, E. The Emperor Jones
Synge, J. The playboy of the western world
Wilder, T. The skin of our teeth
Williams, T. The glass menagerie

CUBG Cubeta, Paul M. Modern drama for analysis. Revised edition. [New York, Dryden, c1955] 785p
Chekhov, A. The cherry orchard
Ibsen, H. The wild duck
Inge, W. Come back, little Sheba
O'Casey, S. Juno and the paycock
O'Neill, E. Anna Christie
Shaw, G. Arms and the man
Synge, J. The playboy of the western world
Wilder, T. The skin of our teeth
Williams, T. The glass menagerie

CUBH Cubeta, Paul M. Modern drama for analysis... 3rd ed. New York, Holt, Rinehart and Winston [c1962] 613p
Albee, E. The sandbox
Anouilh, J. Becket; or, The honor or God
Chekhov, A. The cherry orchard
Eliot, T. Murder in the cathedral
Ibsen, H. Rosmersholm
Miller, A. A view from the bridge
O'Neill, E. Desire under the elms
Shaw, G. The devil's disciple
Wilder, T. The skin of our teeth
Williams, T. The glass menagerie

CUN Cunliffe, John William, ed. Early English classical tragedies... Oxford, Clarendon press, 1912. 352p
Gascoigne, G., and Kinwelmersh, F. Jocasta
Hughes, T. The misfortunes of Arthur
Norton, T., and Sackville, T. Gorboduc; or, Ferrex and Porrex
[Wilmot, R., and others] Gismond of Salerne

D

DAI Daiches, David; Jewett, Arno; Havighurst, Walter and Searles, John, comps. English literature. Boston, Houghton Mifflin, 1968. 848p
- Goldsmith, O. She stoops to conquer
- Shakespeare, W. Macbeth
- Shaw, G. Pygmalion
- Synge, J. Riders to the sea

DANA, H. W. L. See SEVP Seven Soviet plays...

DANI Daniel, Robert Woodham, and Leggett, G. H., eds. The written word... Englewood Cliffs, N. J., Prentice Hall, 1960. 726p
- Shaw, G. The man of destiny

DAV Davenport, William H.; Wimberley, Lowry C., and Shaw, Harry, eds. Dominant types in British and American literature... New York, Harper [c1949] 2v
- Anderson, M. Winterset 1
- Barrie, J. The 12-pound look 1
- O'Neill, E. The hairy ape 1
- Rice, E. The adding machine 1
- The second shepherds' play 1
- Shakespeare, W. King Henry the fourth 1
- Sheridan, R. The school for scandal 1
- Synge, J. Riders to the sea 1
- Wilde, O. Lady Windermere's fan 1

DAVI David, Sister Mary Agnes. Modern American Drama... New York, Macmillan [c1961] 235p (The pageant of literature)
- Barry, P. The joyous season
- Coxe, L., and Chapman, R. Billy Budd
- Van Druten, J. I remember mama

DAVJ Davies, Reginald Trevor, ed. The Corpus Christi play of the English middle ages. Totowa, N. J., Rowman and Littlefield, 1972. 458p
- Abraham (Wakefield)
- Abraham (York)
- Abraham and Isaac (Brome)
- Abraham and Isaac (Dublin)
- Abraham and Isaac (Ludus Coventriae)
- Abraham, Melchisedec and Isaac (Chester)
- The apostles at the tomb
- Appearance to Cleopas and Luke
- Appearance to Mary Magdalen
- Appearance to Thomas
- Ascension
- Assumption
- Birth of the Son
- Cain and Abel
- Creation and fall of Lucifer
- Creation and fall of man
- Doomsday
- Harrowing of Hell II
- Herod and the three kings
- Jesse
- Jesus and the doctors
- Matthias
- Moses
- Mother of Mercy: Conception
- Mother of Mercy: Joseph
- Mother of Mercy: Parliament of Heaven and Annunciation
- Mother of Mercy: Salutation
- Noah
- Passion I: Agony at Olivet
- --I: Betrayal
- --I: Council of Jews I
- --I: Council of Jews II
- --I: Entry into Jerusalem
- --I: Maundy I
- --I: Maundy II
- --I: Maundy III
- --I: Prologues
- --I: Taking of Jesus
- Passion II: Before Annas and Caiphas
- --II: Before Herod II
- --II: Before Pilate

Passion II: Before Pilate II
--II: Centurion
--II: Crucifixion
--II: Dream of Pilate's wife
--II: Harrowing of Hell I
--II: Jesus before Herod
--II: Longeus and burial
--II: Peter's denial
--II: Prologue
--II: Setting of watch
--II: Way of the cross
Pentecost
Presentation and purification
Raising of Lazarus
Resurrection and appearance to mother
The shepherds' play
Slaughter of the innocents
Story of the watch
Three Marys at the tomb
Trial of Joseph and Mary
Woman taken in adultery

DAVK Davis, Earle R., and Hummel, William C., eds. Readings for enjoyment. Englewood Cliffs, N.J., Prentice-Hall, 1959. 611p
The book of Job
Kaufman, G., and Hart, M. The man who came to dinner
O'Neill, E. Ah, wilderness
Shakespeare, W. Hamlet, Prince of Denmark
Sophocles. Oedipus rex

DAVM Davis, Muriel, comp. Inscape; stories, plays, poems... Philadelphia, Lippincott, 1971. 632p
Aristophanes. Lysistrata
Chayefsky, P. Marty
Saroyan, W. The time of your life
Williams, T. The glass menagerie

DAVR Davison, Dennis, ed. Restoration comedies. London, Oxford, 1970. 399p
Dryden, J. Marriage a la mode
Etherege, G. She would if she could
Sedley, C. The mulberry garden
Vanbrugh, J. The relapse
Wycherley, W. The country wife

DEAN Dean, Leonard, ed. ... Elizabethan drama... New York, Prentice-Hall, 1950. 334p (English masterpieces. v2)
Marlowe, C. Doctor Faustus
Shakespeare, W. Henry the fourth, pt. I
Shakespeare, W. King Lear
Webster, J. The Duchess of Malfi

DEAO Dean, Leonard Fellows, ed. Elizabethan drama... Second edition. Englewood Cliffs, N.J., Prentice-Hall, 1961. 364p (English masterpieces. v2)
Jonson, B. Volpone; or, The fox
Marlowe, C. The tragical history of Doctor Faustus
Shakespeare, W. King Lear
Webster, J. The Duchess of Malfi

DEAP Dean, Leonard Fellows, ed. Nine great plays from Aeschylus to Eliot. New York, Harcourt, Brace [c1950] 595p
Aeschylus. Agamemnon
Chekhov, A. The cherry orchard
Congreve, W. The way of the world
Eliot, T. Murder in the cathedral
Ibsen, H. The wild duck
Jonson, B. Volpone; or, The fox
Molière, J. The misanthrope
O'Neill, E. The Emperor Jones
Sophocles. King Oedipus

DEAR Dean, Leonard, F., ed. Nine great plays, from Aeschylus to Eliot. Revised edition...New York, Harcourt Brace [c1956] 695p
- Aeschylus. Agamemnon
- Chekhov, A. The cherry orchard
- Congreve, W. The way of the world
- Eliot, T. Murder in the cathedral
- Ibsen, H. An enemy of the people
- Jonson, B. Volpone
- Molière, J. The would-be invalid
- Shaw, G. Pygmalion
- Sophocles. Oedipus Rex

DEAS Dean, Leonard F., ed. Twelve great plays. New York, Harcourt, Brace, Jovanovich, 1970. 789p
- Abse, D. House of cowards
- Aeschylus. Agamemnon
- Brecht, B. The Caucasian chalk circle
- Chekhov, A. The cherry orchard
- Ibsen, H. Ghosts
- Jonson, B. The alchemist
- Marlowe, C. The Jew of Malta
- Molière, J. Tartuffe
- Pirandello, L. Six characters in search of an author
- Shakespeare, W. Henry IV, Part 1
- Sophocles. Oedipus Rex
- Williams, T. The glass menagerie

DEBENHAM, A. H. See SEVE Seven sacred plays

DEM De Mille, Alban Bertram, ed. Three English comedies...Boston, Allyn and Bacon [c1924] 479p
- Goldsmith, O. She stoops to conquer
- Sheridan, R. The rivals
- Sheridan, R. The school for scandal

DENSMORE, H. B. See TEN Ten Greek plays...

DIC Dickinson, Thomas Herbert, ed. Chief contemporary dramatists...[first series] Boston, Houghton, Mifflin [c1915] 676p
- Barker, G. The Madras house
- Bjørnson, B. Beyond human power
- Brieux, E. The red robe
- Chekhov, A. The cherry orchard
- Fitch, C. The truth
- Galsworthy, J. Strife
- Gregory, A. The rising of the moon
- Hauptmann, G. The weavers
- Hervieu, P. Know thyself
- Jones, H. Michael and his lost angel
- MacKaye, P. The scarecrow
- Maeterlinck, M. Pélléas and Mélisande
- Moody, W. The great divide
- Pinero, A. The second Mrs. Tanqueray
- Strindberg, A. The father
- Sudermann, H. The vale of content
- Synge, J. Riders to the sea
- Thomas, A. The witching hour
- Wilde, O. Lady Windermere's fan
- Yeats, W. The hour-glass

DID Dickinson, Thomas Herbert, ed. Chief contemporary dramatists, second series...Boston, Houghton Mifflin [c1921] 734p
- Annunzio, G. d'. Gioconda
- Bahr, H. The concert
- Benavente (y Martínez), J. The bonds of interest
- Bennett, A., and Knoblock, E. Milestones

Drinkwater, J. Abraham Lincoln
Dunsany, E. King Argimenes and the unknown warrior
Ervine, St. J. Mixed marriage
Gorki, M. The lower depths
Guitry, S. Pasteur
Hazelton, G., and Benrimo, J. The yellow jacket
Heiberg, G. The tragedy of love
Maugham, W. Our betters
Peabody, J. The piper
Porto-Riche, G. de. A loving wife
Rostand, E. Cyrano de Bergerac
Schnitzler, A. Living hours
Thoma, L. Moral
Walter, E. The easiest way

DIE Dickinson, Thomas Herbert, ed. Chief contemporary dramatists, third series... Boston, Houghton, Mifflin [c1930] 698p
Alvarez Quintero, S., and Alvarez Quintero, J. Malvaloca
Andreyev, L. He who gets slapped
Ansky, S. The dybbuk
Benelli, S. The love of the three kings
Čapek, K. R.U.R.
Green, P. In Abraham's bosom
Hofmannsthal, H. von. Electra
Howard, S. The silver cord
Kaiser, G. From morn to midnight
Lenormand, H. Time is a dream
Martínez Sierra, G., and Martínez Sierra, M. A lily among thorns
Milne, A. The Dover road
Molnár, F. Liliom
O'Casey, S. Juno and the paycock
O'Neill, E. The Emperor Jones
Pirandello, L. Naked
Sigurjónsson, J. Eyvind of the hills
Vildrac, C. The steamship Tenacity
Wedekind, F. Such is life
Yevreinov, N. The theatre of soul

DIG Dickinson, Thomas Herbert, and Crawford, Jack Randall, eds. Contemporary plays... Boston, Houghton Mifflin [c1925] 650p
Anspacher, L. The unchastened woman
Baker, E. Chains
Crothers, R. Mary the third
Davies, H. The mollusc
Davis, O. Icebound
Drinkwater, J. Oliver Cromwell
Granville-Barker, H. The Voysey inheritance
Hankin, St. J. The Cassilis engagement
Houghton, S. Hindle wakes
Kenyon, C. Kindling
Maugham, W. The circle
O'Neill, E. The hairy ape
Phillips, S. Paolo and Francesca
Rice, E. The adding machine
Sowerby, G. Rutherford and son
Sutro, A. John Gladye's honour

DIK Dickinson, Thomas Herbert, ed. ... Continental plays... Boston, Houghton Mifflin [c1935] 2v (Types contemporary drama)
Alvarez Quintero, S., and Alvarez Quintero, J. A bright morning 1
Andreyev, L. The life of man 2
Annunzio, G. d'. Francesca da Rimini 1
Bernard, J. L'invitation au

DIK (cont.)
voyage 2
Brieux, E. The red robe 2
Čapek, K. R. U. R. 1
Chekhov, A. The cherry orchard 1
Claudel, P. The tidings brought to Mary 1
Echegaray [y Eizaguirre], J. The great Galeoto 2
Gorky, M. The lower depths 2
Hauptmann, G. The weavers 1
Kaiser, G. The coral 2
Maeterlinck, M. Pelléas and Mélisande 1
Molnár, F. Liliom 1
Pirandello, L. Six characters in search of an author 2
Rostand, E. Cyrano de Bergerac 2
Schnitzler, A. Light-o'-love 1
Strindberg, A. A dream play 2
Tolstoy, L. The power of darkness 1
Wedekind, F. Erdgeist 2

DIT Dietrich, Richard Farr, and others, comps. The art of drama. New York, Holt, 1969. 669p
Brecht, B. The Caucasian chalk circle
Chekhov, A. The cherry orchard
Hansberry, L. Raisin in the sun
Ibsen, H. The wild duck
Miller, A. A view from the bridge
Molière, J. The misanthrope
Osborne, J. Luther
Pirandello, L. Six characters in search of an author
Shakespeare, W. Antony and Cleopatra
Shaw, G. Caesar and Cleopatra
Sophocles. Antigone
Sophocles. Oedipus
Williams, T. The glass menagerie

DIV Dietrich, Richard Farr, comp. The realities of literature. Waltham, Mass., Xerox College Publications, 1971. 656p
Hansberry, L. A raisin in the sun
Ionesco, E. The picture
Pirandello, L. Six characters in search of an author
Shaw, G. Caesar and Cleopatra
Sophocles. Oedipus Rex

DIZ Disch, Robert, and Schwartz, Barry N., eds. Killing time; a guide to life in the happy valley. Englewood Cliffs, N.J., Prentice-Hall, 1972. 500p
Aeschylus. Agamemnon
Chekhov, A. The cherry orchard
Davis, O. Purlie victorious
Fratti, M. The bridge
Terry, M. The magic realists

DOA Dobrée, Bonamy, ed. Five heroic plays... London, Oxford University Press, 1960. 417p
Crowne, J. The destruction of Jerusalem
Dryden, J. Aureng-zebe
Lee, N. Sophonisba
Orrery, R. The tragedy of Mustapha, the son of Solyman the magnificent
Settle, E. The Empress of Morocco

DOB Dobrée, Bonamy, ed. Five restoration tragedies ...[London] Oxford university press [1928] 450p (The world's classics)
Addison, J. Cato

Dryden, J. All for love
Otway, T. Venice preserv'd
Rowe, N. The fair penitent
Southerne, T. Oroonoko

DOD Dodge, Richard H., and Lindblom, Peter D., comps. Of time and experience: literary themes. Cambridge, Mass., Winthrop Publishers, 1972. 725p
Chayefsky, P. Marty
Dolan, H. Losers weepers
Lowell, R. My kinsman, Major Molineaux
Richardson, J. Gallows humor
Shaw, G. Arms and the man

DOT Dodson, Daniel Boone, comp. Twelve modern plays. Belmont, Calif., Wadsworth Publishers, 1970. 471p
Anouilh, J. Antigone
Brecht, B. The good woman of Setzuan
Chekhov, A. The three sisters
García Lorca, F. The house of Bernarda Alba
Giraudoux, J. Tiger at the gates
Hellman, L. The little foxes
Ibsen, H. The wild duck
Miller, A. The crucible
Pirandello, L. Henry IV
Shaw, G. Heartbreak house
Strindberg, A. Miss Julie
Synge, J. The playboy of the western world

DOV Dolan, Paul J., and Dolan, Grace M., eds. Introduction to drama. New York, Wiley, 1974. 642p
Chekhov, A. The cherry orchard
Ibsen, H. An enemy of the people
Jones, L. Dutchman
Lowell, R. Benito Cereno
Molière, J. The misanthrope
Pirandello, L. Henry IV
Racine, J. Phaedre
The second shepherds' play
Shakespeare, W. Othello
Shaw, G. Saint Joan
Sophocles. Antigone
Sophocles. Oedipus
Strindberg, A. Miss Julie
Yeats, W. Purgatory

DOWM Downer, Alan S., ed. American drama... New York, Thomas Y. Crowell [c1960] 261p (American literary forms)
Herne, J. Shore acres
Moody, W. The great divide
O'Neill, E. The hairy ape
Sherwood, R. The petrified forest
Tyler, R. The contrast
Wilder, T. The long Christmas dinner
Williams, T. The glass menagerie

DOWN Downer, Alan S. The art of the play... New York, Henry Holt [c1955] 451p
Aeschylus. Prometheus bound
Chekhov, A. The sea-gull
Ibsen, H. Ghosts
Marlowe, C. Doctor Faustus
Molière, J. Tartuffe
O'Neill, E. The Emperor Jones
Shakespeare, W. Antony and Cleopatra
Sophocles. Oedipus rex
Vega Carpio, L. Fuente ovejuna

DOWS Downer, Seymoud, ed. Great world theatre; an introduction to drama. New York, Harper & Row [1964] 867p
Chekhov, A. The three sisters

DOWS (cont.)
Euripides. The Bacchae
Everyman
Ibsen, H. Solness, the master builder
Giraudoux, J. Tiger at the gates
Goldsmith, O. She stoops to conquer
Miller, A. A view from the bridge
Molière, J. The misanthrope
Pirandello, A. Six characters in search of an author
Plautus, T. The little ghost
Shudraka. The toy cart
Sophocles. Antigone
Webster, J. The Duchess of Malfi
Wilder, T. The skin of our teeth

DRA Dramatic masterpieces by Greek, Spanish, French, German and English dramatists; with a special introduction by Albert Ellery Bergh. Rev. ed. New York, Collier [c1900] 2v (The world's greatest literature)
Aeschylus. Prometheus bound 1
Aristophanes. The knights 1
Calderón de la Barca, P. Life is a dream 1
Euripides. Medea 1
Goethe, J. Faust 2
Goldsmith, O. She stoops to conquer 1
Ibsen, H. A doll's house 2
Molière, J. The misanthrope 1
Racine, J. Phaedra 1
Sardou, V. Les pattes de mouche 2
Schiller, F. Mary Stuart 2
Sophocles. Oedipus rex 1
Sheridan, R. The rivals 2

DRU Drummond, Alexander Magnus, and Gard, Robert E., eds. The lake guns of Seneca and Cayuga and eight other plays of upstate New York. Port Washington, N.Y., Kennikat Press, 1972. 273p (Reprint)
Baker, E. and Drummond, A. A day in the vineyard
Drummond, A. The lake guns of Seneca and Cayuga
Gard, R. Let's get on with the marrin'
Gard, R. Raisin' the devil
Gard, R. Mixing up the rent
Kamarck, E. Chenango crone
O'Connell, L. Donalds O'Rourk
Thurston, E. Family cooperative
Williams, L. Over fourteen: and single

DUC Duckworth, George Eckel, ed. The complete Roman drama... New York, Random house [c1942] 2v
Plautus. Amphytryon 1
Plautus. The braggart warrior 1
Plautus. The captives 1
Plautus. The Carthaginian 1
Plautus. Casina 1
Plautus. The casket 1
Plautus. The comedy of asses 1
Plautus. Curculio 1
Plautus. Epidicus 1
Plautus. The girl from Persia 1
Plautus. The haunted house 1
Plautus. The merchant 1
Plautus. The pot of gold 1
Plautus. Pseudolus 1
Plautus. The rope 1
Plautus. Stichus 2
Plautus. The three penny day 2
Plautus. Truculentus 2
Plautus. The twin Menaechmi 1
Plautus. The two bacchides 1

Querolus 2
Seneca. Agamemnon 2
Seneca. Hercules on Oeta 2
Seneca. Mad Hercules 2
Seneca. Medea 2
Seneca. Octavia 2
Seneca. Oedipus 2
Seneca. Phaedra 2
Seneca. The Phoenician women 2
Seneca. Thyestes 2
Seneca. The Trojan women 2
Terence. The brothers 2
Terence. The eunuch 2
Terence. The mother-in-law 2
Terence. Phormio 2
Terence. The self-tormentor 2
Terence. The woman of Andros 2

DUH Duhamel, Pierre Albert and Hughes, Richard E., eds. Literature: form and function... Englewood Cliffs, N.J., Prentice-Hall, 1965. 634p
Chekhov, A. The cherry orchard
Goldsmith, O. She stoops to conquer
Shakespeare, W. Richard II
Sophocles. Oedipus rex

DUN Dunn, Esther Cloudman, ed. Eight famous Elizabethan plays... New York, Modern library [1932] 721p
Beaumont, F., and Fletcher, J. The maid's tragedy
Dekker, T. The shoemakers' holiday
Ford, J. 'Tis a pity she's a whore
Heywood, T. A woman killed with kindness
Jonson, B. Volpone; or, The fox
Marlowe, C. The tragical history of Doctor Faustus
Massinger, P. A new way to pay old debts
Webster, J. The Duchess of Malfi

DUP Duran, Lee, tr. Plays of old Japan. Folcroft, Pa., Folcroft Library Editions, 1973. 127p (Reprint)
The Daimyo
Forsaken love
The hands in the box
The honor of Danzo
The horns

DUR Durham, Willard Higley and Dodds, John W., eds. British and American plays. 1830-1945... New York, Oxford university press, 1947. 796p
Anderson, M. Winterset
Barrie, J. The admirable Crichton
Bulwer-Lytton, E. Richelieu
Carroll, P. Shadow and substance
Connelly, M. The green pastures
Ervine, St. J. John Ferguson
Galsworthy, J. Strife
Ibsen, H. An enemy of the people
Jones, H. The liars
Kaufman, G., and Ryskind, M. Of thee I sing
Maugham, W. The circle
O'Casey, S. Juno and the paycock
Odets, C. Waiting for Lefty
O'Neill, E. The great god Brown
Pinero, A. The second Mrs. Tanqueray
Rice, E. The adding machine
Robertson, T. Caste
Sherwood, R. There shall be no night
Synge, J. The playboy of the western world
Yeats, W. Cathleen ni Houlihan

DUSE, ELEONORA. See SAY Sayler, Oliver Martin, ed. The Eleonora Duse series of plays...

E

EAVE Eaves, Thomas Cary Duncan and Kimpe, Ben D., eds. The informal reader ...New York, Appleton-Century-Crofts [c1955] 743p
Shaw, G. Pygmalion

EDAD Edades, Jean and Fosdick, Carolyn E., eds. Drama of the east and west. Manila, Bookman, 1956. 656p
Alvarez Quintero, S., and J. A sunny morning
Chekhov, A. The cherry orchard
Euripides. Medea
Guerrero, W. Forever
Ibsen, H. A doll's house
Joaquín, N. A portrait of the artist as Filipino
Kālidāsa. Shakuntalā
Molière, J. The misanthrope
Montano, S. Sabina
Palarca, J. Other tomorrows
Plautus. The Menaechmi
Shakespeare, W. Romeo and Juliet
Shaw, I. Bury the dead
Sicam, G., and Casiño, J. Mir-i-nisa
The sorrows of Han
Villa, L. Educating Josefina
Wilde, O. The importance of being earnest
Wilder, T. Our town
Williams, E. The corn is green

EIGH Eighteenth-century plays with an introduction by Ricardo Quintana...New York, Modern library [c1952] 484p
Addison, J. Cato
Fielding, H. The tragedy of tragedies
Gay, J. The beggar's opera
Goldsmith, O. She stoops to conquer
Lillo, G. The London merchant
Rowe, N. The tragedy of Jane Shore
Sheridan, R. The rivals
Steele, R. The conscious lovers

THE ELEONORA DUSE SERIES OF PLAYS. See SAY Sayler, Oliver Martin, ed.

ELEVEN PLAYS OF THE GREEK DRAMATISTS. See PLAG Plays of the Greek dramatists...

ELIOT, CHARLES W. See HARC Harvard classics...

ELK Elkins, William R. and others, comps. Literary reflections. New York, McGraw, 1967. 757p
Shakespeare, W. Antony and Cleopatra
Sophocles. Oedipus rex
Williams, T. The glass menagerie

ELLI Ellis, Harold Milton; Pound, Louise, and Spohn, George Weida, eds. A college book of American literature...New York, American book co. [c1939] 2v
Boker, G. Francesca da Rimini 1
O'Neill, E. The rope 2
Tyler, R. The contrast 1

ELLK Ellis, Harold Milton; Pound, Louise; Spohn, George Weida and Hoffman, Frederick J., eds. A college book of American lit-

erature.. Second edition. New York, American book co. [c1949] 1107p
O'Neill, E. The Emperor Jones

ELLIS, HAVELOCK. See NER Nero (Tragedy); Nero and other plays...

ELIZABETHAN DRAMA. See HARC Harvard classics, v46-7

EMB Embassy successes... London, Sampson, Low, Marston [1946-48] 3v
Bagnold, E. National velvet 2
Delderfield, R. Peace comes to Peckham 3
Delderfield, R. Worm's eye view 1
Doherty, B. Father Malachy's miracle 1
Gielgud, V. Away from it all 3
Hartog, J. Skipper next to God 2
Hay, I. "Let my people go!" 3
Pollock, R. Zoo in Silesia 1
Temple, J. No room at the inn 2

ENG England, Alan William, ed. Two ages of man. Edinburgh, Oliver and Boyd, 1971. 206p
Cooper, G. Unman, Wittering and Zigo
Kaiser, G. The raft of Medusa
Leonard, H. Stephen D
Shaffer, P. The private ear

ENGLISH MASTERPIECES. v2. See DEAN Dear, Leonard, ed. Elizabethan drama; v5. See MACK Mack, Maynard, ed. The Augustans...

ESS Esslin, Martin, ed. The genius of the German theater... New York, New American Library, 1968. 638p
Brecht, B. The Caucasian chalk circle
Büchner, G. Leonce and Lena
Goethe, J. Faust, a tragedy, pt. I
Kleist, H. Prince Frederick of Homburg
Lessing, G. Emilia Galotti
Schiller, J. The death of Wallenstein
Wedekind, F. King Nicolo; or, Such is life

EVA Everett, Edwin Mallard; Brown, Calvin S., and Wade, John D., eds. Masterworks of world literature... New York, Dryden press [c1947] 2v
Euripides. Medea 1
Goethe, J. Faust, pt. I 2
Ibsen, H. An enemy of the people 2
Molière, J. Tartuffe 2
Racine, J. Phaedra 2
Shakespeare, W. Romeo and Juliet 2
Sophocles. Antigone 1
Sophocles. Oedipus the king 1

EVB Everett, Edwin Mallard; Brown, Calvin S., and Wade, John D., eds. Masterworks of world literature... Revised edition ... New York, Dryden [c1955] 2v
Aeschylus. Agamemnon 1
Euripides. Medea 1
Goethe, J. Faust, pt. I 2
Ibsen, H. The enemy of the people 2
Molière, J. Tartuffe 2
Racine, J. Phaedra 2
Shakespeare, W. Romeo and Juliet 2
Sophocles. Antigone 1

EVB (cont.)
Sophocles. Oedipus the king 1

EVC Everett, Edwin Mallard, and others, ed. Masterworks of world literature. 3d ed. New York, Holt, Rinehart, and Winston, 1970. 2v
Aeschylus. Agamemnon 1
Aristophanes. Lysistrata 1
Euripides. Medea 1
Goethe, J. Faust 2
Molière, J. Tartuffe 2
Racine, J. Phaedra 2
Shakespeare, W. Antony and Cleopatra 2
Sophocles. Oedipus the King 1

EVE Everyman and other plays. [London] Chapman and Hall, 1925. 201p
Everyman
The nativity
The shepherds' play

EVER "Everyman," with other interludes, including eight miracle plays. London, Dent [1928] 198p (Everyman's library)
Abraham, Melchisedec, and Isaac
Bale, J. God's promises
The crucifixion
The deluge
Everyman
The harrowing of hell
Mary Magdalene
Pageant of shearmen and taylors
St. George and the dragon
Second shepherds' play
The three Maries

F

FAL Falle, George G., ed. Three restoration comedies... London, Macmillan, 1964. 342p
Buckingham, G. The rehearsal
Congreve, W. The way of the world
Wycherley, W. The country wife

FAM Famous American plays of the 1950's. Selected and introduced by Lee Strasberg. [New York, Dell, c 1962] 415p
Albee, E. The zoo story
Anderson, R. Tea and sympathy
Gazzo, M. A hatful of rain
Hellman, L. The autumn garden
Williams, T. Camino real

FAMA Famous plays of 1931... London, Gollancz [1931] 672p
Anthony, C. Autumn crocus
Besier, R. The Barretts of Wimpole street
Delafield, E. To see ourselves
Fagan, J. The improper duchess
Van Druten, J. After all
Van Druten, J. London wall

FAMB Famous plays of 1932... London, Gollancz, 1932. 654p
Bax, C. The rose without a thorn
Hart, M., and Kaufman, G. Once in a life time
Mackenzie, R. Musical chairs
Rice, E. See Naples and die
Van Druten, J. Somebody knows
Van Druten, J. There's always Juliet

FAMC Famous plays of 1932-33... London, Gollancz, 1933. 727p
Ackland, R. Strange orchestra

Anthony, C. Service
Chlumberg, H. Miracle at Verdun
Rice, E. Counsellor-at-law
Van Druten, J. Behold we live
Winsloe, C. Children in uniform

FAMD Famous plays of 1933... London, Gollancz, 1933. 702p
Armstrong, A. Ten-minute alibi
Chetham-Strode, W. Sometimes even now
Daviot, G. Richard of Bordeaux
Fauchois, R. The late Christopher Bean
Howard, S. Alien corn
Kaufman, G., and Ryskind, M. Of thee I sing

FAME Famous plays of 1933-34... London, Gollancz, 1934. 712p
Daviot, G. The laughing woman
Hodge, M. The wind and the rain
Lipscomb, W., and Minney, R. Clive of India
Sherwood, R. Reunion in Vienna
Stuart, A., and Stuart, P. Sixteen
Van Druten, J. The distaff side

FAMF Famous plays of 1934... London, Gollancz, 1934. 688p
Anthony, C. Touch wood
Daviot, G. Queen of Scots
Harwood, H. Old folks at home
Jennings, G. Family affairs
Kingsley, S. Men in white
Mackenzie, R. The Maitlands

FAMG Famous plays of 1934-35... London, Gollancz, 1935. 695p
Ackland, R. The old ladies
Egan, M. The dominant sex
Ginsbury, M. Viceroy Sarah
Johnson, P. Lovers' leap
Pryce, R. Frolic wind
Van Druten, J. Flowers of the forest

FAMH Famous plays of 1935... London, Gollancz, 1935. 622p
Hodge, M. Grief goes over
Raphaelson, S. Accent on youth
Somin, W. Close quarters (Attentat)
Sternheim, C. The mask of virtue
Vulpius, P. Youth at the helm
Williams, E. Night must fall

FAMI Famous plays of 1935-36... London, Gollancz, 1936. 701p
Ackland, R. After October
Anthony, C. Call it a day
Deevy, T. Katie Roche
Hodson, J. Red night
Odets, C. Awake and sing
Sherriff, R., and De Casalis, J. St. Helena

FAMJ Famous plays of 1936 ... London, Gollancz, 1936. 568p
Farjeon, E., and Farjeon, H. The two bouquets
Odets, C. Till the day I die
Schauffler, E. Parnell
Schnitzler, A. Professor Bernhardi
Shaw, I. Bury the dead
Spewack, B., and Spewack, S. Boy meets girl

FAMK Famous plays of 1937... London, Gollancz, 1937. 775p
Boothe, C. The women
Lenormand, H. In Theatre street

FAMK (cont.)
Reid, A. People in love
Rice, E. Judgment day
Sayers, D., and Bryne, M. Busman's honeymoon
Turgenev, I. A month in the country

FAML Famous plays of 1938-39 ... London, Gollancz, 1939. 661p
Egan, M. To love and to cherish
Hodson, J. Harvest in the north
MacOwan, N. Glorious morning
Malleson, M., and Brooks, H. Six men of Dorset
Odets, C. Golden boy
Sayers, D. The zeal of thy house

FAMO Famous plays of 1954... London, Gollancz, 1954. 592p
Christie, A. Witness for the prosecution
Christie, D., and C. Carrington, V. C.
Hunter, N. A day by the sea
Odets, C. The big knife
Van Druten, J. I am a camera

FAO Famous plays of to-day... London, Gollancz, 1929. 671p
Berkeley, R. The lady with a lamp
Dukes, A. Such men are dangerous
Hoffe, M. Many waters
Levy, B. Mrs. Moonlight
Sherriff, R. Journey's end
Van Druten, J. Young Woodley

FAOS Famous plays of today... London, Gollancz, 1953. 373p
Hunter, N. Waters of the moon
Knott, F. Dial "M" for murder
Priestley, J., and Hawkes, J. Dragon's mouth
Rattigan, T. The deep blue sea

FAR Farmer, John Stephen, ed. ...Anonymous plays. 3rd series... London, Early English drama society, 1906. 302p (Early English dramatists)
Gammer Gurton's needle
Jack Juggler
King Darius
New custom
Trial of treasure

FARM Farmer, John Stephen, ed. ... Five anonymous plays. 4th series... London, Early English drama society, 1908. 328p (Early English dramatists)
Appius and Virginia
Common conditions
Grim the collier of Croydon
The marriage of wit and science
The marriage of wit and wisdom

FARN Farmer, John Stephen, ed. ...Recently recovered "lost" Tudor plays with some others. London, Early English drama society, 1907. 427p (Early English dramatists)
An interlude of impatient poverty
The interlude of John the evangelist
An interlude of wealth and health
Mankind
Medwall, H. Nature
Redford, J. The play of wit and science
Respublica

FARO Farmer, John Stephen,

ed. ... Six anonymous plays. 1st series (c1510-1537)... London, Early English drama society, 1905. 286p (Early English dramatists)

The beauty and good properties of women (commonly called Calisto and Melibaea)
Hickscorner
The nature of the four elements
The summoning of Every man
Thersites
The world and the child

FARP Farmer, John Stephen, ed. ... Six anonymous plays. 2d series... London, Early English drama society, 1906. 478p (Early English dramatists)

A comedy called Misogonus
The history of Jacob and Esau
An interlude of godly Queen Hester
The interlude of youth
A moral play of Albion, knight
Tom Tyler and his wife

FAY, W. G. See FIT Five three-act plays...

FED Federal council of the churches of Christ in America. Committee on religious drama. Religious dramas, 1924-25... New York, Century [c1923-26] 2v

Bates, E. The two thieves 2
Cropper, M. Two sides of the door 2
Currie, C. Whither goest thou? 2
Goodman, K. Dust of the road 1
Goold, M. The quest divine 2
Goold, M. St. Claudia 2
Goold, M. The shepherds 2
Hamlin, M. The rock 1
Harnwell, A., and Meaker, I. The alabaster box 2
Kimball, R. The resurrection 1
Leamon, D. Barabas 2
McCauley, C. The seeker 1
MacKaye, P. The pilgrim and the book 1
Mason, H. At the gate beautiful 2
Mygatt, T. The sword of the Samurai 2
Osgood, P. A sinner beloved 1
Willcox, H. Larola 1
Woodbridge, E. The crusade of the children 1

FEDERAL THEATRE PLAYS. See FEE, FEF Federal theatre project

FEE Federal theatre project. Federal theatre plays... ["Edited for the Federal Theatre by Pierre de Rohan"] New York, Random house [c1938] v.p.

Arent, A., ed. One-third of a nation
Conkle, E. Prologue to glory
Dubois, W. Haiti

FEF Federal theatre project. Federal theatre plays... ["Edited for the Federal theatre by Pierre de Rohan."] New York, Random house [c1938] v.p.

Arent, A. Power, a living newspaper
Sundgaard, A. Spirochete
Triple-A plowed under, by the staff of the Living newspaper

FEFH Feise, Ernst and Steinhauer, Harry, eds. German literature since Goethe ... Boston, Houghton Mifflin [c1958] 2v

Brecht, B. Das verhör des Lukullus 2

FEFH (cont.)
Grillparzer, F. Der traum ein leben 1
Hauptmann, G. Michael Kramer 2
Hebbel, F. Maria Magdalene 1
Hofmannsthal, H. Das Salzburger grosse welttheater 2
Kaiser, G. Gas II 2
Schnitzler, A. Der grüne kakadu 2

FEFL Felheim, Marvin, ed. Comedy; plays, theory, and criticism... New York, Harcourt, Brace [c1962] 288p
Aristophanes. The birds
Chekhov, A. A wedding; or, A joke in one act
Fry, C. A phoenix too frequent
Molière, J. The misanthrope
Shakespeare, W. Twelfth night; or, What you will
Shaw, G. The man of destiny
Sheridan, R. The critic; or, A tragedy rehearsed
Wilde, O. The importance of being earnest

FEFM Felperin, Howard Michael, ed. Dramatic romance... New York, Harcourt, Brace, Jovanovich, 1973. 258p
Brecht, B. The Caucasian chalk circle
Eliot, T. The cocktail party
Euripides. Alcestis
Gay, J. The beggar's opera
Ibsen, H. When we dead awaken
Shakespeare, W. The tempest

FEFT Fifteen Greek plays translated into English... New York, Oxford university press, 1943. 794p
Aeschylus. Agamemnon
Aeschylus. Choephoroe
Aeschylus. The Eumenides
Aeschylus. Prometheus bound
Aristophanes. The birds
Aristophanes. The clouds
Aristophanes. The frogs
Euripides. Electra
Euripides. Hippolytus
Euripides. Iphigenia in Tauris
Euripides. Medea
Sophocles. Antigone
Sophocles. Electra
Sophocles. Oedipus at Colonus
Sophocles. Oedipus, king of Thebes

FIF Fifteenth century prose and verse, with an introduction by Alfred W. Pollard. New York, Dutton [1903] 324p (An English garner. [v1])
Everyman
The pageant of the shearmen and tailors

FIFR Fitts, Dudley, ed. Four Greek plays... New York, Harcourt, Brace [c1960] 310p
Aeschylus. Agamemnon
Aristophanes. The birds
Euripides. Alcestis
Sophocles. Oedipus rex

FIFT Fitts, Dudley, ed. Greek plays in modern translation ... New York, Dial press, 1947. 596p (The permanent library series)
Aeschylus. Agamemnon
Aeschylus. Eumenides
Aeschylus. Prometheus bound
Euripides. Alcestis
Euripides. Hippolytus
Euripides. Medea
Euripides. The Trojan women
Sophocles. Antigone
Sophocles. Electra
Sophocles. King Oedipus
Sophocles. Oedipus at Colonus

FIFV Fitts, Dudley, ed. Six Greek plays in modern translation...New York, Dryden [c1955] 294p
Aeschylus. Agamemnon
Aeschylus. Choephoroe
Aeschylus. Eumenides
Aristophanes. The birds
Euripides. Andromache
Sophocles. Philoctetes

FIG Five great modern Irish plays...with a foreword by George Jean Nathan. New York, Modern Library [1941] 332p
Carroll, P. Shadow and substance
Gregory, I. Spreading the news
O'Casey, S. Juno and the paycock
Synge, J. The playboy of the western world
Synge, J. Riders to the sea

FIL Five modern Scandinavian plays. New York, Twayne Publishers. 1971. 424p
Chorell, W. The sisters
Grieg, N. Our power and our glory
Lagerkvist, P. The man who lived his life over
Soya, C. Lion with corset
Stefánsson, D. The golden gate

FIN Five new full-length plays for all-women casts... London, Dickson & Thompson [1935] 375p
Box, M. Angels of war
Box, S. The woman and the walnut tree
Popplewell, O. This bondage
Rye, E. The three-fold path
Smee, L. No thoroughfare

FIP Five plays of 1937... [London] Hamilton [1937] v.p.
Hellman, L. The children's hour
Jerome, H. Charlotte Corday
Lyndon, B. They came by night
Rattigan, T. French without tears
Savory, G. George and Margaret

FIR Five plays of 1940...London, Hamilton [1940] v.p.
Ardrey, R. Thunder rock
Boothe, C. Margin for error
Ginsbury, N. The first gentleman
Morgan, D. A house in the square
Stuart, A. Jeannie

FIT Five three-act plays; foreword by W. G. Fay. [London] Rich and Cowan [1933] 448p
Bennett, A. Flora
Gielgud, V. Chinese white
Holme, C. "I want!"
Pertwee, R. Heat wave
Wilson, T. Champion north

FLAN Flanagan, John Theodore and Hudson, Arthur Palmer, eds. Folklore in American literature...Evanston, Ill., Rowe, Peterson [c1958] 511p
Green, P. Unto such glory
MacKaye, P. The scarecrow; or, The glass of truth

FLOR Flores, Angel, ed. Masterpieces of the Spanish golden age...New York, Rinehart [c1957] 395p
Calderón de la Barca. The great theater of the world
Téllez, G. The trickster of Seville and the guest of stone
Vega Carpio, L. Fuenteovejuna

FLOS Flores, Angel, ed. Spanish drama...New York,

FLOS (cont.)
Bantam Books [c1962] 473p (Library of world drama)
Benavente y Martínez, J. The bonds of interest
Calderón de la Barca, P. Life is a dream
Cervantes Saavedra, M. The vigilant sentinel
Echegaray y Eizaguirre, J. The great Galeoto
García Lorca, F. Blood wedding
Moratín, L. When a girl says yes
Rueda, L. The olives
Ruiz de Alarcón y Mendoza, J. The truth suspected
Téllez, G. The rogue of Seville
Vega Carpio, L. Fuenteovejuna

FOR Force, William M., comp. Orestes and Electra; myth and dramatic form... Boston, Houghton Mifflin [1968] 329p
Aeschylus. The libation-bearers
Euripides. Electra
Giraudoux, J. Electra
Richardson, J. The prodigal
Sophocles. Electra

FORD Ford, Nick Aaron, ed. Black insights: significant literature by Black Americans - 1760 to the present. Boston, Ginn, 1971. 373p
Hansberry, L. A raisin in the sun (Act I only)
Peterson, L. Take a giant step
Watson, H. Those golden gates fall down

FOU Foulke, Robert, and Smith, Paul, comps. An anatomy of literature. New York, Harcourt, Brace, Jovanovich, 1972. 1125p
Jonson, B. Volpone; or, The fox
Shakespeare, W. King Lear
Synge, J. The playboy of the western world

FOUA Four contemporary French plays... New York, Modern library, 1967. 265p
Anouilh, J. Antigone
Camus, A. Caligula
Giraudoux, J. The madwoman of Chaillot
Sartre, J. No exit

FOUB Four great comedies of the restoration and 18th century... With an introduction by Brooks Atkinson. New York, Bantam Books [c1958] 321p
Congreve, W. The way of the world
Goldsmith, O. She stoops to conquer; or, The mistakes of a night
Sheridan, R. The school for scandal
Wycherley, W. The country wife

FOUD Four great Elizabethan plays. With an introduction by John Gassner. New York, Bantam Books [c1960] 316p
Dekker, T. The shoemakers' holiday; or, A pleasant comedy of the gentle craft
Jonson, B. Volpone; or, The fox
Marlowe, C. The tragical history of Doctor Faustus
Webster, J. The Duchess of Malfi

FOUF Four modern French comedies... With an introduction by Wallace Fowlie. New York, Capricorn Books [c1960] 256p
Adamov, A. Professor Toranne

Aymé, M. Clérambard
Courteline, G. The commissioner
Jarry, A. Ubu Roi

FOUK Four modern plays; first series...rev. ed. New York, Holt, Rinehart and Winston, 1963. 292p
Chekhov, A. The cherry orchard
Ibsen, H. Hedda Gabler
O'Neill, H. Emperor Jones
Shaw, B. Pygmalion

FOUM Four modern verse plays. First [and] second series...ed. by Henry Popkin. New York, Holt, Rinehart and Winston [c1957, 1961] 2v
Gorky, M. The lower depths
Ibsen, H. Hedda Gabler
Ibsen, H. Rosmersholm
Miller, A. Death of a salesman
O'Neill, E. The Emperor Jones
Rostand, E. Cyrano de Bergerac
Shaw, G. Pygmalion
Wilde, O. The importance of being earnest

FOUR Four Renaissance tragedies; with an introduction and glossary by Donald Stone, Jr. Cambridge, Mass., Harvard University Press, 1966. 224p
Bèze, T. Abraham sacrifiant
Buchanan, G. Jephté; ou, Le voeu
Jodelle, E. Didon se sacrifiant
Taille, J. Saul le furieux

FOUP Four plays of 1936... with an introduction by Ivor Brown. [London] Hamilton [1936] 624p
Jerome, H. Jane Eyre
Jerome, H. Pride and prejudice
Lyndon, B. The amazing Dr. Clitterhouse
Turney, C. Bitter harvest

FOUS Four...Soviet...plays ...New York, International publishers, 1937. 427p
Gorky, M. Yegor Bulichov and others
Kocherga, I. Masters of time
Pogodin, N. Aristocrats
Vishnevskiĭ, V. An optimistic tragedy

FOUT Four Soviet war plays ...London, Hutchinson [1944] 208p
Korneichuk, A. The front
Korneichuk, A. Guerillas of the Ukrainian Steppes
Leonov, L. Invasion
Simonov, K. The Russians

FOWLIE, WALLACE. <u>See also</u> FOUF Four modern French comedies...

FOWL Fowlie, Wallace, ed., and tr. Classical French drama...New York, Bantam Books [c1962] 277p
Beaumarchais, P. The barber of Seville
Corneille, P. The cid
Marivaux, P. The game of love and chance
Molière, J. The intellectual ladies
Racine, J. Phaedra

FRA Francke, Kuno, ed. The German classics of the nineteenth and twentieth centuries...New York, German publication society [c1913-14] 20v
Anzengruber, L. The farmer foresworn 16
Freytag, G. The journalists 12
Fulda, L. Tête-à-tête 17

FRA (cont.)
Goethe, J. Faust, pt. I 1
Goethe, J. Faust, pt. II 1
Goethe, J. Iphigenia in Tauris 1
Grillparzer, F. The Jewess of Toledo 6
Grillparzer, F. Medea 6
Gutzkow, K. Sword and queue 7
Halbe, M. Mother earth 20
Hardt, E. Tristram the jester 20
Hauptmann, G. Michael Kramer 18
Hauptmann, G. The sunken bell 18
Hauptmann, G. The weavers 18
Hebbel, F. Maria Magdalena 9
Hebbel, F. Siegfried's death 9
Hofmannsthal, H. Death and the fool 17
Hofmannsthal, H. The death of Titian 17
Hofmannsthal, H. The marriage of Sobeide 20
Kleist, H. The prince of Homburg 4
Ludwig, O. The hereditary forester 9
Schiller, F. The death of Wallenstein 3
Schiller, F. The homage of the arts 3
Schiller, F. William Tell 3
Schnitzler, A. The green cockatoo 20
Schnitzler, A. Literature 20
Schönherr, K. Faith and fireside 16
Sudermann, H. John the Baptist 17
Tieck, J. L. Puss in boots 4
Wedekind, F. The court singer 20
Wilbrandt, A. The master of Palmyra 16
Wildenbruch, E. King Henry 17

FRAN Franklin, Alexander, ed. Seven miracle plays. New York, Oxford University Press, 1963. 158p
Abraham and Isaac
Adam and Eve
Cain and Abel
King Herod
Noah's flood
The shepherds
The three kings

FREE Freedley, George, ed. Three plays about crime and criminals... New York, Washington Square Press [c1962] 278p
Chodorov, E. Kind lady
Kesselring, J. Arsenic and old lace
Kingsley, S. Detective story

FREF Freedman, Morris and Davis, P. B., eds. Controversy in literature; fiction, drama and poetry with related criticism. New York, Scribner, 1968. 750p
Abraham and Isaac (Brome)
Ferlinghetti, L. Our little trip
Ibsen, H. An enemy of the people
Kopit, A. Oh dad, poor dad, mamma's hung you in the closet and I'm feelin' so sad
Shaw, G. The devil's disciple
Sophocles. Antigone

FREG Freedman, Morris, ed. Tragedy; texts and commentary... New York, Scribner, 1969. 641p
Aeschylus. Agamemnon
Betti, U. Corruption in the palace of justice
Chekhov, A. The three sisters
Dryden, J. All for love
Euripides. Medea

Everyman
García Lorca, F. Yerma
Ibsen, H. Ghosts
Marlowe, C. The tragic history of Doctor Faustus
Milton, J. Samson Agonistes
O'Neill, E. Desire under the elms
Pirandello, L. Henry IV
Racine, J. Phaedra
Shakespeare, W. Othello, The Moor of Venice
Sophocles. Oedipus rex
Strindberg, A. The father

FREI Freier, Robert; Lazarus, Arnold Leslie and Potell, Herbert, eds. Adventures in modern literature. Fourth edition. New York, Harcourt Brace [c1956] 690p (Adventures in literature series)
Glaspell, S. Trifles
O'Casey, S. The end of the beginning
Shaw, G. Caesar and Cleopatra
Sherriff, R. Journey's end

FRO From classroom to stage. Three new plays. London, Longmans, 1966. 214p
Grant, D. The king cat
Holt, B. Noah's ark
Mitson, R. Beyond the bourn; or, The night time stood still

FULLINGTON, JAMES FITZ-JAMES. See also MCCA, MCCB, MCCD, MCCF, MCCG McCallum, James Dow, ed. The college omnibus...

FUL Fullington, James Fitz-James; Reed, Harry B., and McCorkle, Julia Norton, eds. The new college omnibus...New York, Harcourt, Brace, 1938. 1241p
Connelly, M. The green pastures
Howard, S. The silver cord
O'Neill, E. The hairy ape
Sherriff, R. Journey's end

FULT Fulton, Albert Rondthaler, ed. Drama and theatre, illustrated by seven modern plays...New York, Holt [c1946] 556p
Barrie, J. A well-remembered voice
Coward, N. Blithe spirit
Lawson, J. Roger Bloomer
O'Neill, E. Beyond the horizon
Pinero, A. The second Mrs. Tanqueray
Rice, E. Street scene
Wilder, T. Our town

G

GALB Galbraith, Esther, E., ed. Plays without footlights...New York, Harcourt, Brace [c1945] 358p
Anderson, M. Journey to Jerusalem
Greene, P. Papa is all
Niggli, J. This bull ate nutmeg
Reely, M. Flittermouse
Rickert, V. The bishop's candlesticks
Roberts, C. Tails up
Saroyan, W. The people with light coming out of them
Smith, B. Fun after supper
Upson, W. The master salesman
Wilder, T. The happy journey to Trenton and Camden

GARNETT, PORTER. See BOH Bohemian club, San Francisco. The Grove plays of the Bohemian club...

GARSA Gassner, John, ed. Best American plays; 5th ser., 1957-1963...New York, Crown, 1963. 678p
- Albee, E. Who's afraid of Virginia Woolf?
- Anderson, R. Silent night, lonely night
- Chayefsky, P. Gideon
- Frings, K. Look homeward, angel
- Gardner, H. A thousand clowns
- Gibson, W. Two for the see-saw
- Inge, W. The dark at the top of the stairs
- Kerr, J. Mary, Mary
- Kopit, A. Oh dad, poor dad, mamma's hung you in the closet and I'm feelin' so sad
- MacLeish, A. J. B.
- Mosel, T. All the way home
- O'Neill, E. A touch of the poet
- Saroyan, W. The cave dwellers
- Vidal, G. The best man
- Williams, T. The night of the iguana
- Williams, T. Orpheus descending
- Wishengrad, M. The rope dancers

GART Gassner, John, ed. Best American plays. Fourth series...1951-57...New York, Crown [c1958] 648p
- Anderson, R. Tea and sympathy
- Axelrod, G. The seven year itch
- Gazzo, M. A hatful of rain
- Hartog, J. The fourposter
- Inge, W. Bus stop
- Inge, W. Picnic
- Kaufman, G., and Teichman, H. The solid gold Cadillac
- Lawrence, J., and Lee, R. Inherit the wind
- Levin, I. No time for sergeants
- Miller, A. The crucible
- Miller, A. A view from the bridge
- O'Neill, E. A moon for the misbegotten
- Van Druten, J. I am a camera
- Wilder, T. The matchmaker
- Williams, T. Cat on a hot tin roof
- Williams, T. The rose tattoo
- Wouk, H. The Caine mutiny

GARU Gassner, John, ed. Best American plays; supplementary vol., 1918-58...New York, Crown [c1961] 687p
- Barry, P. Here come the clowns
- Behrman, S. Biography
- Chase, M. Harvey
- Colton, J. Rain
- Davis, O., and Davis, D. Ethan Frome
- Goodrich, F., and Hackett, A. The diary of Anne Frank
- Green, P. The house of Connelly
- Howard, S., and DeKruif, P. Yellow jack
- Kingsley, S. Men in white
- Mayer, E. Children of darkness
- Odets, C. Awake and sing
- Osborn, P. Morning's at seven
- Osborn, P. On borrowed time
- Patrick, J. The teahouse of the August moon
- Rice, E. The adding machine
- Riggs, L. Green grow the lilacs
- Tarkington, B. Clarence

GARV Gassner, John, and Barnes, Olive, eds. Best American plays. 6th series,

1963-1967. New York, Crown, 1971. 594p
Albee, E. Tiny Alice
Alfred, W. Hogan's goat
Anderson, R. You know I can't hear you when the water's running
Baldwin, J. Blues for Mister Charlie
Bellow, S. The last analysis
Duberman, M. In white America
Gilroy, F. The subject was roses
Goldman, J. The lion in winter
Hanley, W. Slow dance on the killing ground
Hansberry, L. A raisin in the sun
Jones, L. The toilet
Jones, T. The fantasticks
Lowell, R. Benito Cereno
Manhoff, B. The owl and the pussycat
O'Neill, E. Hughie
Simon, N. The odd couple
Stein, J. Fiddler on the roof

GARW Gassner, John, ed. Best American plays. Third series - 1945-51...New York, Crown [c1952] 707p
Anderson, M. Anne of the thousand days
Coxe, L., and Chapman, R. Billy Budd
Euripides. Medea
Heggen, T., and Logan, J. Mister Roberts
Hellman, L. The autumn garden
Herbert, F. The moon is blue
Inge, W. Come back, little Sheba
Kingsley, S. Darkness at noon
Kingsley, S. Detective story
Lindsay, H., and Crouse, R. State of the union
McCullers, C. The member of the wedding
Miller, A. All my sons
Miller, A. Death of a salesman
O'Neill, E. The iceman cometh
Van Druten, J. Bell, book and candle
Williams, T. A streetcar named desire
Williams, T. Summer and smoke

GARX Gassner, John, comp. Best plays of the early American theatre; from the beginning to 1916... New York, Crown [1967] 716p
Aiken, G. Uncle Tom's cabin
Barker, J. Superstition
Boucicault, D. The octoroon
Fechter, C. The Count of Monte Cristo
Fitch, C. The truth
Gillette, W. Secret service
Howells, W. The mousetrap
MacKaye, P. The scarecrow
Mitchell, L. The New York idea
Moody, W. The great divide
Mowatt, A. Fashion
Payne, J. and Irving, W. Charles the second
Sheldon, E. Salvation Nell
Thomas, A. The witching hour
Tyler, R. The contrast
Walter, E. The easiest way

GARZ Gassner, John, ed. Best plays of the modern American theatre: Second series...New York, Crown [c1947] 776p
Barry, P. The Philadelphia story
Gow, J., and D'Usseau, A. Tomorrow the world
Hellman, L. Watch on the Rhine
Kanin, G. Born yesterday

GARZ (cont.)
Kaufman, G., and Hart, M. The man who came to dinner
Kesselring, J. Arsenic and old lace
Kingsley, S. The patriots
Laurents, A. Home of the brave
Lindsay, H., and Crouse, R. Life with father
Patrick, J. The hasty heart
Rice, E. Dream girl
Saroyan, W. The time of your life
Sherwood, R. Abe Lincoln in Illinois
Thurber, J., and Nugent, E. The male animal
Van Druten, J. I remember mama
Van Druten, J. The voice of the turtle
Williams, T. The glass menagerie

GARZA Gassner, John and Barnes, Olive, comps. 50 Best plays of the American theater. New York, Crown, 1969. 4v
Aiken, G. Uncle Tom's cabin 1
Albee, E. Who's afraid of Virginia Woolf? 4
Anderson, M. High Tor 2
Anderson, R. Tea and sympathy 4
Axelrod, G. The seven year itch 4
Barry, P. The Philadelphia story 2
Chase, M. Harvey 3
Colton, J. and Randolph, C. Rain 1
Connelly, M. Green pastures 1
Davis, O. and Davis, D. Ethan Frome 2
Frings, K. Look homeward, angel 4
Gibson, W. Two for the seesaw 4
Goodrich, F. and Hackett, A. The diary of Anne Frank 4
Hartog, J. The fourposter 4
Hecht, B. and MacArthur, C. The front page 1
Heggen, T. and Logan, J. Mister Roberts 3
Hellman, L. The children's hour 2
Heyward, D. and Heyward, D. Porgy 1
Inge, W. Come back, little Sheba 4
Jeffers, R. Medea 3
Kanin, G. Born yesterday 3
Kaufman, G. and Hart, M. The man who came to dinner 2
Kaufman, G. and Hart, M. You can't take it with you 2
Kesselring, J. Arsenic and old lace 3
Kingsley, S. Men in white 1
Kirkland, J. Tobacco road 1
Kopit, A. Oh dad, poor dad, mamma's hung you in the closet and I'm feelin' so sad 4
Lindsay, H. and Crouse, R. Life with father 2
Lindsay, H. and Crouse, R. The state of the union 3
McCullers, C. The member of the wedding 3
Miller, A. The crucible 4
Miller, A. Death of a salesman 3
Odets, C. Awake and sing 2
Odets, C. Golden boy 2
O'Neill, E. Desire under the elms 1
O'Neill, E. The hairy ape 1
Osborn, P. On borrowed time 2
Patrick, J. The teahouse of the August moon 4
Rice, E. Dream girl 3
Rice, E. Street scene 1

Saroyan, W. The time of your life 3
Shaw, I. Bury the dead 2
Sheldon, E. Salvation Nell 1
Sherwood, R. Abe Lincoln in Illinois 2
Simon, N. The odd couple 4
Stein, J. Fiddler on the roof 4
Tyler, R. The contrast 1
Wilder, T. The matchmaker 2
Williams, T. The glass menagerie 3
Williams, T. A streetcar named desire 3

GARZAE Gassner, John, and Green, William, comps. Elizabethan drama. New York, Bantam Books, 1967. 639p
Arden of Feversham
Dekker, T. The shoemaker's holiday
Greene, R. Friar Bacon and Friar Bungay
Heywood, T. A woman killed with kindness
Jonson, B. Everyman in his humor
Kyd, T. The Spanish tragedy
Marlowe, C. Doctor Faustus
Marlowe, C. Edward II

GARZAL Gassner, John, ed. Four new Yale playwrights. New York, Crown [1965] 235p
Eisenstein, M. The fighter
Ingham, R. A simple life
Kleb, W. Honeymoon in Haiti
Murray, R. The good lieutenant

GARZAP Gassner, John and Sweetkind, Morris, eds. Introducing the drama, an anthology...New York, Holt, Rinehart and Winston [1963] 583p
Besier, R. The Barretts of Wimpole Street
Chekhov, A. Then and now
Dunsany, E. A night at an inn
Everyman
Giraudoux, J. The Apollo of Bellac
Howard, S. The late Christopher Bean
Ibsen, H. An enemy of the people
Mackaye, P. The scarecrow
Molière, J. The pretentious ladies
Shakespeare, W. Romeo and Juliet
Shaw, G. Arms and the man
Sheridan, R. The school for scandal
Sophocles. Antigone
Williams, T. The glass menagerie

GARZB Gassner, John, ed. Medieval and Tudor drama ...New York, Bantam Books [c1963] 457p (Library of world drama)
Abraham and Isaac
The betrayal of Christ
A Christmas mumming; the play of Saint (Prince) George
The creation and the fall of Lucifer
The crucifixion
The death of Herod
The death of Pilate
The deluge
An Easter resurrection play
Everyman
Man's disobedience and the fall of man
The murder of Abel
The Orléans sepulcher
The pageant of the shearmen and tailors
A pantomime for Easter day
The quem quaeritis
The resurrection, harrowing of hell, and the last judgment
The second shepherds' play
Heywood, J. The play called

GARZB (cont.)
the four pp
Hrotsvit. Dulcitius
Hrotsvit. Paphnutius
Sackville, T., and Norton, T. Gorboduc
Stevenson, W. Gammer-Gurton's needle
Udall, N. Ralph Roister Doister

GARZE Gassner, John, ed. 19th century Russian drama... with introduction and prefaces by Marc Slonin. New York, Bantam Books [c1963] 342p (Library of world drama)
Gogol, N. The inspector general
Ostrovsky, A. The thunderstorm
Pushkin, A. The stone guest
Tolstoy, L. The power of darkness
Turgenev, I. A month in the country

GARZF Gassner, John and Sweetkind, Morris, comps. Tragedy, history and romance. New York, Holt, Rinehart and Winston, 1968. 419p
Miller, A. The crucible
Rostand, E. Cyrano de Bergerac
Shakespeare, W. Henry IV, pt. I
Sophocles. Oedipus the king

GARZH Gassner, John, ed. Twenty best European plays on the American stage... New York, Crown [c1957] 733p
Anouilh, J. The lark
Behrman, S. Jacobowsky and the Colonel
Benavente y Martínez, J. The passion flower
Čapek, J., and Čapek, K. The world we live in
Chekhov, A. The sea gull
Giraudoux, J. The madwoman of Chaillot
Giraudoux, J. Ondine
Giraudoux, J. Tiger at the gates
Heijermans, H. The good hope
Howard, S. The late Christopher Bean
Kaiser, G. From morn to midnight
Molnár, F. The play's the thing
Obey, A. Noah
Pirandello, L. As you desire me
Rappaport, S. The dybbuk
Sartre, J. No exit
Spewack, S. My three angels
Tolstoy, L. Redemption
Turgenev, I. A month in the country
Zweig, S. Volpone

GARZJ Gassner, John, ed. 20th century Russian drama. Translated with an introduction and prefaces by Andrew R. MacAndrew. New York, Bantam Books [c1963] 376p (Library of world drama)
Andreyev, L. He who gets slapped
Chekhov, A. The three sisters
Gorky, M. The lower depths
Mayakóvsky, V. The bathhouse
Olesha, Y. A list of assets

GAS Gassner, John, ed. Twenty best plays of the modern American theatre... New York, Crown [c1939] 874p
Abbott, G., and Holm, J. Three men on a horse
Anderson, M. High Tor
Anderson, M. Winterset
Barry, P. The animal kingdom

Behrman, S. End of summer
Boothe, C. The women
Connelly, M. Green pastures
Ferber, E., and Kaufman, G. Stage door
Green, P. Johnny Johnson
Hart, M., and Kaufman, G. You can't take it with you
Hellman, L. The children's hour
Kingsley, S. Dead end
Kirkland, J., and Caldwell, E. Tobacco road
MacLeish, A. The fall of the city
Odets, C. Golden boy
Reed, M. Yes, my darling daughter
Shaw, I. Bury the dead
Sherwood, R. Idiot's delight
Spewack, B., and Spewack, S. Boy meets girl
Steinbeck, J. Of mice and men

GASB Gassner, John, ed. Twenty-five best plays of the modern American theatre: Early series...New York, Crown [c1949] 756p
Anderson, M., and Hickerson, H. Gods of the lightning
Anderson, M. Saturday's children
Balderston, J. Berkeley Square
Barry, P. Paris bound
Beach, L. The clod
Behrman, S. The second man
Conkle, E. Minnie Field
Dunning, P., and Abbott, G. Broadway
Glaspell, S. Trifles
Green, P. White dresses
Hecht, B., and MacArthur, C. The front page
Heyward, D., and Heyward, D. Porgy
Howard, S. They knew what they wanted
Kaufman, G., and Connelly, M. Beggar on horseback
Kelly, G. Craig's wife
Kelly, G. Poor Aubrey
Millay, E. Aria da Capo
O'Neill, E. Desire under the elms
O'Neill, E. The hairy ape
O'Neill, E. Ile
Rice, E. Street scene
Sherwood, R. The road to Rome
Stallings, L., and Anderson, M. What price glory?
Sturges, P. Strictly dishonorable
Treadwell, S. Machinal

GASS Gassner, John, and Sweetkind, Morris, eds. Introducing the drama...New York, Holt, Rinehart and Winston [1963] 583p
Everyman
Besier, R. The Barretts of Wimpole Street
Dunsany, E. A night at an inn
Gassner, J. Then and now
Giraudoux, J. The Apollo of Bellac
Howard, S. The late Christopher Bean
Ibsen, H. An enemy of the people
MacKaye, P. The scarecrow
Molière, J. The pretentious ladies
Shakespeare, W. The tragedy of Romeo and Juliet
Shaw, G. Arms and the man
Sheridan, R. The school for scandal
Sophocles. Antigone
Williams, T. The glass menagerie

GASY Gassner, John, ed. The Yale School of Drama presents...[1st ed.] New York, Dutton, 1964. 315p
Hailey, O. Hey you, light man!
Hill, E. Man better man
Oliansky, J. Here comes Santa Claus

GASSNER, JOHN. See also FOUD Gour great Elizabethan plays; TRE, TREA, TREB, TREBA, TREC, TREE, TREI, A treasury of the theatre...

GAUB Gaubert, Helen A. Four classic French plays... New York, Washington Square Press [c1961] 260p
- Corneille, P. The cid
- Molière, J. The would-be gentleman
- Racine, J. Athaliah
- Racine, J. Phaedra

GAVE Gaver, Jack, ed. Critics' choice. New York Drama Critics' Circle prize plays 1935-55... New York, Hawthorn books [c1955] 661p
- Anderson, M. High tor
- Anderson, M. Winterset
- Hellman, L. Watch on the Rhine
- Inge, W. Picnic
- Kingsley, S. Darkness at noon
- Kingsley, S. The patriots
- McCullers, C. The member of the wedding
- Miller, A. All my sons
- Miller, A. Death of a salesman
- Patrick, J. The teahouse of the August moon
- Saroyan, W. The time of your life
- Steinbeck, J. Of mice and men
- Van Druten, J. I am a camera
- Williams, T. Cat on a hot tin roof
- Williams, T. The glass menagerie
- Williams, T. A streetcar named desire

GAY Gayley, Charles Mills, ed. Representative English comedies... New York, Macmillan, 1903-36. 4v
- Brome, R. The antipodes 3
- Chapman, G.; Jonson, B., and Marston, J. Eastward hoe 2
- Congreve, W. The way of the world 4
- Cowley, A. Cutter of Coleman-street 4
- Dekker, T. The shoemaker's holiday 3
- Dryden, J. The Spanish fryar 4
- Farquhar, G. The recruiting officer 4
- Fletcher, J. Rule a wife and have a wife 3
- Greene, R. The honorable historie of Frier Bacon and Frier Bungay 1
- Heywood, J. A mery play betweene Johan Johan, Tyb, his wyfe, and Syr Jhan the preest 1
- Heywood, J. The play of the wether 1
- Jonson, B. The alchemist 2
- Jonson, B. Epicoene; or, The silent woman 2
- Jonson, B. Every man in his humour 2
- Lyly, J. Alexander and Campaspe 1
- Massinger, P. A new way to pay old debts 3
- The merry devill of Edmonton 2
- Middleton, T., and Rowley, W. The Spanish gipsie 3
- Peele, G. The old wives' tale 1
- Porter, H. The two angry women of Abington 1
- Shirley, J. The royall master 3
- Stevenson, W. Gammer Gurton's nedle 1
- Udall, N. Roister Doister 1
- Vanbrugh, J. The provok'd wife 4
- Wycherley, W. The plain-dealer 4

GEST, MORRIS. See MOSA
Moscow art theatre series
of Russian plays...

GIA Gianos, Mary P., ed. and
tr. Introduction to modern
Greek literature; an anthology of fiction, drama, and
poetry. New York, Twayne,
1969. 548p
Akritas, L. Hostages
Prevelakis, P. The last
tournament
Theotokas, G. The game of
folly vs. wisdom
Xenopoulos, G. Divine dream

GLE Glenny, Michael, ed. Three
Soviet plays. [Middlesex,
Eng.] Penguin Books [1966]
217p
Babel, I. Marya
Mayakóvsky, V. The bedbug
Schwartz, Y. The dragon

GLI Gliner, Robert and Raines,
Robert Arnold, eds.
Munching on existence; contemporary American society
through literature. New
York, Free Press, 1971.
465p
Koch, K. The academic
murders
McNally, T. Tour
Pinter, H. Trouble in the
works
Van Itallie, J. Interview

GLO Glorfeld, Louis E., and
others, eds. Plays by
four tragedians. Columbus,
Ohio, Merrill, 1968. 529p
Ibsen, H. Ghosts
Ibsen, H. Hedda Gabler
Shakespeare, W. Othello
Shakespeare, W. Romeo and
Juliet
Sophocles. Antigone
Sophocles. Oedipus the king
Strindberg, A. The father
Strindberg, A. Miss Julie

GOL Goldberg, Isaac, tr.
Plays of the Italian theatre...Boston, Luce, 1921.
202p
Lopez, S. The sparrow
Morselli, E. Gastone the
animal tamer
Morselli, E. Water upon
fire
Pirandello, L. Sicilian limes
Verga, G. The wolf-hunt

GOLD Goldman, Mark and
Traschen, Isadore, eds.
The drama; traditional and
modern...Rockleigh, N.J.,
Allyn and Bacon [1968]
690p
Beckett, S. Happy days
Brecht, B. Mother Courage
Chekhov, A. The cherry orchard
Ibsen, H. The wild duck
Molière, J. The misanthrope
Pirandello, L. Six characters
in search of an author
Shakespeare, W. King Lear
Shakespeare, W. Twelfth
night
Shaw, G. Arms and the man
Sophocles. Oedipus rex

GOLH Goldstone, Richard Henry, comp. Contexts of
the drama...New York,
MaGraw-Hill [1968] 775p
Albee, E. The zoo story
Anouilh, J. Becket
Chekhov, A. Three sisters
Euripides. Hippolytus
Ibsen, H. Hedda Gabler
Molière, J. The miser
O'Neill, E. Hughie
Shakespeare, W. Antony
and Cleopatra
Shaw, G. Caesar and Cleopatra
Sophocles. Antigone
Wilder, T. The matchmaker
Williams, T. Summer and
smoke

GOLK Goldstone, Richard Hen-

GOLK (cont.)
ry, comp. Mentor masterworks of modern drama: five plays. New York, New American Library, 1969. 478p
Ibsen, H. An enemy of the people
Miller, A. The crucible
Rostand, E. Cyrano de Bergerac
Shaw, G. Pygmalion
Wilder, T. Our town

GOM Gomme, Andor Harvey, ed. Jacobean tragedies... New York, Oxford University Press, 1969. 398p
Marston, J. The malcontent
Middleton, T. Women beware women
Middleton, T., and Rowley, W. The changeling
Tourneur, C. The atheist's tragedy
Tourneur, C. The revenger's tragedy

GOOD Goodman, Randolph, ed. Drama on stage... New York, Holt, Rinehart and Winston [c1961] 475p
Everyman
Duerrenmatt, F. The visit
Euripides. Medea
Molière, J. The misanthrope
Shakespeare, W. The tragedy of Macbeth
Williams, T. A streetcar named desire

GOOR Goodman, G., ed. From script to stage: eight modern plays. San Francisco, Rinehart Press, 1971. 623p
Aspenström, W. The apes shall inherit the earth
Brecht, B. The seven deadly sins of the lower middle classes
Chekhov, A. The seagull
Ibsen, H. Hedda Gabler
O'Neill, E. Desire under the elms
Pinget, R. The old tune
Shaw, G. Pygmalion
Strindberg, A. A dream play

GORDON, DUDLEY CHADWICK. See TOD Today's literature

GORDP Gordon, Edward J., comp. Introduction to tragedy. Rochelle Park, N.J., Hayden Books, 1973. 349p
Anouilh, J. Antigone
Ibsen, H. Hedda Gabler
O'Neill, E. Beyond the horizon
Sophocles. Oedipus the king

GORE Gordon, Walker K., ed. Literature in critical perspectives: an anthology. New York, Appleton-Century-Crofts. 1968. 795p
Shakespeare, W. The tragedy of Hamlet, Prince of Denmark
Shaw, G. Major Barbara
Sophocles. Oedipus rex
Williams, T. Orpheus descending

GOS Gosse, Edmund William. Restoration plays from Dryden to Farquhar. London, Dent [1929] 431p (Everyman's library)
Congreve, W. The way of the world
Dryden, J. All for love
Farquhar, G. The beaux-stratagem
Otway, T. Venice preserved
Vanbrugh, J. The provok'd wife
Wycherley, W. The country wife

GOSA Gosse, Edmund William. Restoration plays from

Dryden to Farquhar. London, Dent [1932] 509p (Everyman's library)
Congreve, W. The way of the world
Dryden, J. All for love
Etherege, G. The man of mode
Farquhar, G. The beaux-stratagem
Otway, T. Venice preserved
Vanbrugh, J. The provok'd wife
Wycherley, W. The country wife

GOU Gould, James Adams, and Kiefer, Harry Christian, eds. The western humanities. New York, Holt, Rinehart, and Winston, 1971. 2v
Aristophanes. Lysistrata 1
Brecht, B. The Caucasian chalk circle 2
Goethe, J. Faust, Part I 2
Goldsmith, O. She stoops to conquer; or, The mistakes of a night 2
Ibsen, H. Hedda Gabler 2
Racine, J. Phaedra 2
Sophocles. Oedipus the king 1

GOW Gow, J. Rodger and Hanlon, Helen J., eds. Five Broadway plays... New York, Harper [c1948] 432p
Anderson, M. High Tor
Besier, R. The Barretts of Wimpole Street
Chodorov, J., and Fields, J. Junior miss
Osborn, P. On borrowed time
Sherwood, R. Abe Lincoln in Illinois

GOWA Gow, J. Rodger and Hanlon, Helen J., eds. Five Broadway plays. 2d ed. New York, Globe Book Co., 1968. 432p
Anderson, M. High Tor
Besier, R. The Barretts of Wimpole Street
Chodorov, J., and Fields, J. Junior miss
Osborn, P. On borrowed time
Sherwood, R. Abe Lincoln in Illinois

GPA Graham, Cary B. Freshman English program... Chicago, Scott, Foresman [c1960] 946p
Ibsen, H. Hedda Gabler
O'Neill, E. Bound east for Cardiff
Shakespeare, W. Romeo and Juliet
Sophocles. Oedipus the king

GRA Grant, Elliott Mansfield, ed. Chief French plays of the nineteenth century... New York, Harper, 1934. 934p
Augier, E. Le gendre de M. Poirier
Becque, H. Les corbeaux
Brieux, E. La robe rouge
Dumas, A. fils. La dame aux camélias
Dumas, A. père. Henri III et sa cour
Hugo, V. Hernani
Hugo, V. Ruy Blas
Musset, A. On ne badine pas avec l'amour
Rostand, E. Cyrano de Bergerac
Vigny, A. Chatterton

GRAF Grant, Elliott Mansfield, ed. Four French plays of the twentieth century... New York, Harper [c1949] 338p
Anouilh, J. Antigone
Bernard, J. Le secret d'Arvers
Giraudoux, J. Siegfried
Pagnol, M., and Nivoix, P. Les marchands de gloire

GRD Great American parade. Garden City, N.Y., Doubleday, Doran, 1935. 611p
Connelly, M. The green pastures

GRDB Great books of the western world...[Robert Maynard Hutchins, editor in chief]...[Chicago] W. Benton [1952] 54v
Aeschylus. Agamemnon 5
Aeschylus. Choephoroe 5
Aeschylus. Eumenides 5
Aeschylus. The Persians 5
Aeschylus. Prometheus bound 5
Aeschylus. The seven against Thebes 5
Aeschylus. The suppliant maidens 5
Aristophanes. Acharnians 5
Aristophanes. Birds 5
Aristophanes. Clouds 5
Aristophanes. Ecclesiazusae 5
Aristophanes. Frogs 5
Aristophanes. Knights 5
Aristophanes. Lysistrata 5
Aristophanes. Peace 5
Aristophanes. Plutus 5
Aristophanes. Thesmaphoriazusae 5
Aristophanes. Wasps 5
Euripides. Alcestis 5
Euripides. Andromache 5
Euripides. The bacchantes 5
Euripides. The cyclops 5
Euripides. Electra 5
Euripides. Hecuba 5
Euripides. Helen 5
Euripides. Heracleidae 5
Euripides. Heracles mad 5
Euripides. Hippolytus 5
Euripides. Ion 5
Euripides. Iphigenia among the Tauri 5
Euripides. Iphigenia at Aulis 5
Euripides. Medea 5
Euripides. The Phoenician maidens 5
Euripides. Rhesus 5
Euripides. The suppliants 5
Euripides. The Trojan women 5
Goethe, J. Faust 47
Shakespeare, W. All's well that ends well 27
Shakespeare, W. Antony and Cleopatra 27
Shakespeare, W. As you like it 26
Shakespeare, W. The comedy of errors 26
Shakespeare, W. Coriolanus 27
Shakespeare, W. Cymbeline 27
Shakespeare, W. Hamlet, Prince of Denmark 27
Shakespeare, W. Julius Caesar 26
Shakespeare, W. King Henry the eighth 27
Shakespeare, W. King Henry the fifth 26
Shakespeare, W. King Henry, IV, Part 1 26
Shakespeare, W. King Henry, IV, Part 2 26
Shakespeare, W. King Henry, VI, Part 1 26
Shakespeare, W. King Henry, VI, Part 2 26
Shakespeare, W. King Henry, VI, Part 3 26
Shakespeare, W. King John 26
Shakespeare, W. King Richard II 26
Shakespeare, W. King Richard III 26
Shakespeare, W. King Lear 27
Shakespeare, W. Love's labour's lost 26
Shakespeare, W. Macbeth 27
Shakespeare, W. Measure for measure 27
Shakespeare, W. The merchant of Venice 26
Shakespeare, W. The merry wives of Windsor 27
Shakespeare, W. A midsummer night's dream 26

Shakespeare, W. Much ado about nothing 26
Shakespeare, W. Othello, the Moor of Venice 27
Shakespeare, W. Pericles, Prince of Tyre 27
Shakespeare, W. Romeo and Juliet 26
Shakespeare, W. The taming of the shrew 26
Shakespeare, W. The tempest 27
Shakespeare, W. Timon of Athens 27
Shakespeare, W. Titus Andronicus 26
Shakespeare, W. Troilus and Cressida 27
Shakespeare, W. Twelfth night 27
Shakespeare, W. The two gentlemen of Verona 26
Shakespeare, W. The winter's tale 27
Sophocles. Ajax 5
Sophocles. Antigone 5
Sophocles. Electra 5
Sophocles. Oedipus at Colonus 5
Sophocles. Oedipus the king 5
Sophocles. Philoctetes 5
Sophocles. Trachiniae 5

GRE Great plays (English)... with biographical notes and a critical introduction by Joseph O'Connor...[Aldine ed.] New York, Appleton, 1900. 421p (The world's great books)
Browning, R. A blot in the 'scutcheon
Fletcher, J. The faithful shepherdess
Jonson, B. The alchemist
Marlowe, C. Edward the second
Payne, J. Brutus; or, The fall of Tarquin
Sheridan, R. The school for scandal

GREA Great plays (French and German)... with biographical notes, and a critical introduction by Brander Matthews...[Aldine ed.] New York, Appleton, 1901. 504p (The world's great books)
Corneille, P. The cid
Hugo, V. Ruy Blas
Lessing, G. Minna von Barnhelm
Molière, J. Tartuffe
Racine, J. Athaliah
Schiller, J. Wilhelm Tell

GREB Grebanier, Bernard D. N., and Thompson, Stith, eds. English literature and its backgrounds...New York, Cordon co. [c1939-40] 2v
Aeschylus. Prometheus bound 2
Byron, G. Manfred 2
Congreve, W. The way of the world 1
Everyman 1
Marlowe, C. The tragical history of Doctor Faustus 1
Milton, J. Samson Agonistes 1
Molière, J. The misanthrope 1
Shelley, P. Prometheus unbound 2
Sheridan, R. The school for scandal 1
Wilde, O. The importance of being earnest 2

GREC Grebanier, Bernard D. N.; Middlebrook, Samuel; Thompson, Stith, and Watt, William, eds. English literature and its backgrounds. Revised edition...New York, Dryden press [c1949] 2v
Abraham and Isaac 1
Browning, R. In a balcony 2
Congreve, W. The way of the world 1
Dekker, T. The shoemaker's

GREC (cont.)
holiday 1
Everyman 1
Marlowe, C. Doctor Faustus 1
Milton, J. Samson Agonistes 1
Molière, J. The misanthrope 1
Shakespeare, W. Othello 1
Sheridan, R. The school for scandal 1
Sophocles. Oedipus the king 1
Synge, J. The playboy of the western world 2
Wilde, O. The importance of being earnest 2
Williams, E. The corn is green 2

GRED Grebanier, Bernard D.N., and Reiter, Seymour, eds. Introduction to imaginative literature. New York, Thomas Y. Crowell Company...[c1960] 969p
Coward, N. Brief encounter
Milton, J. Samson Agonistes
O'Neill, E. In the zone
Sapensley, A. Even the weariest river
Shakespeare, W. King Lear
Shaw, G. Caesar and Cleopatra
Synge, J. The playboy of the western world
Turque, M. Shoptalk
Williams, T. The rose tattoo

GREE Greek dramas...with biographical notes and a critical introduction by Bernadotte Perrin...[Aldine ed.] New York, Appleton, 1900. 390p (The world's great books)
Aeschylus. Agamemnon
Aeschylus. Prometheus bound
Aristophanes. The clouds
Aristophanes. Plutus
Euripides. Alcestis
Euripides. Medea
Sophocles. Antigone
Sophocles. Oedipus tyrannus

GREG Greenfield, Ralph, and Side, Ronald K., eds. Temper of the times;... New York, McGraw-Hill, 1969. 557p
Hailey, A. Shadow of suspicion
Odets, C. Waiting for Lefty
Synge, J. Riders to the sea
Williams, N. The mountain

GREJ Greenspan, Charlotte L., and Hirsch, Lester M., eds. All those voices: The minority experience. New York, Macmillan, 1971. 484p
Nkosi, L. The rhythm of violence
Shakespeare, W. The merchant of Venice
Shaw, G. John Bull's other island. (Act I only)

GREN Grene, David, tr. Three Greek tragedies in translation...Chicago, University of Chicago press [c1942] 228p
Aeschylus. Prometheus bound
Euripides. Hippolytus
Sophocles. Oedipus the king

GREP Grene, David, and Lattimore, Richmond, eds. The complete Greek tragedies...[Chicago] University of Chicago Press [1959] 4v
Aeschylus. Agamemnon 1
Aeschylus. The eumenides 1
Aeschylus. The libation bearers 1
Aeschylus. The Persians 1
Aeschylus. Prometheus bound 1
Aeschylus. Seven against Thebes 1
Aeschylus. The suppliant

maidens 1
Euripides. Alcestis 3
Euripides. Andromache 3
Euripides. The bacchae 4
Euripides. The cyclops 3
Euripides. Electra 4
Euripides. Hecuba 3
Euripides. Helen 3
Euripides. The Heracleidae 3
Euripides. Heracles 3
Euripides. Hippolytus 3
Euripides. Ion 4
Euripides. Iphigenia in Aulis 4
Euripides. Iphigenia in Tauris 3
Euripides. The Medea 3
Euripides. Orestes 4
Euripides. The Phoenician women 4
Euripides. Rhesus 4
Euripides. The suppliant women 4
Euripides. The Trojan women 3
Sophocles. Ajax 2
Sophocles. Antigone 2
Sophocles. Electra 2
Sophocles. Oedipus at Colonus 2
Sophocles. Oedipus the king 2
Sophocles. Philoctetes 2
Sophocles. The women of Trachis 2

GRER Grene, David, and Lattimore, Richmond, eds. Greek tragedies... [Chicago] University of Chicago Press [1960] 3v
Aeschylus. Agamemnon 1
Aeschylus. The eumenides 3
Aeschylus. The libation bearers 2
Aeschylus. Prometheus bound 1
Euripides. Alcestis 3
Euripides. The bacchae 3
Euripides. Electra 2
Euripides. Hippolytus 1
Euripides. Iphigenia in Tauris 2
Euripides. The Trojan women 2
Sophocles. Antigone 1
Sophocles. Electra 2
Sophocles. Oedipus at Colonus 3
Sophocles. Oedipus the king 1
Sophocles. Philoctetes 3

GRIF Griffin, Alice Sylvia (Venezky), ed. Living theatre ...New York, Twayne [c1953] 510p
Aeschylus. Oresteia
Anderson, M. Winterset
Chekhov, A. The sea gull
Everyman
Giraudoux, J. The madwoman of Chaillot
Hebbel, F. Maria Magdalena
Ibsen, H. Hedda Gabler
Marlowe, C. Faustus
Molière, J. The misanthrope
Odets, C. Awake and sing
Plautus, T. Mostellaria
Rice, E. Street scene
Shakespeare, W. Romeo and Juliet

THE GROVE PLAYS OF THE BOHEMIAN CLUB. <u>See</u> BOH Bohemian club, San Francisco

GUE Guerney, Bernard Guilbert, ed. A treasury of Russian literature... New York, Vanguard press [c1943] 1048p
Chekhov, A. The three sisters
Gogol, N. The inspector general
Gorki, M. The lowest depths

GUI Guinagh, Kevin and Dorjahn, Alfred Paul, eds. Latin literature in translation... New York, Longmans, Green, 1942. 822p
Plautus, T. The menaechmi
Plautus, T. The rudens; or, The rope
Terence. The Adelphi; or,

GUI (cont.)
The brothers
Terence. The Phormio

GUIN Guinagh, Kevin and Dorjahn, Alfred P., eds. Latin literature in translation ... Second edition. New York, Longmans, Green [c1952] 822p
Plautus. The menaechmi
Plautus. The rudens
Seneca. Medea
Terence. The Adelphi
Terence. The Phormio

GUSTAFSON, ALRIK. See SCAN Scandinavian plays of the twentieth century...

GUTH Guth, Hans Paul. Idea and image... Belmont, Calif., Wadsworth Pub. Co. [c1962] 838p
Ibsen, H. The master builder
Miller, A. The crucible
Molière, J. The misanthrope
Shakespeare, W. Antony and Cleopatra
Sophocles. Antigone

GUTL Guth, Hans Paul, comp. Literature. 2d ed... Belmont, Calif., Wadsworth Pub. Co. [1968] 923p
Ibsen, H. The master builder
Miller, A. The crucible
Shakespeare, W. Antony and Cleopatra
Sophocles. Antigone

H

HAH Halliday, Frank Ernest, ed. The legend of the rood ... London, Gerald Duckworth [c1955] 142p
The death of Pilate
The legend of the rood
The three Maries

HALLINE, ALLAN GATES. See also SIXC Six modern American plays...

HAL Halline, Allan Gates, ed. American plays. New York, American book co. [c1935] 787p
Barker, J. Superstition
Barry, P. You and I
Bird, R. The gladiator
Boker, G. Francesca da Rimini
Daly, A. Horizon
Davis, O. Icebound
Dunlap, W. André
Green, P. The field god
Howard, B. The Henrietta
Miller, J. The Danites in the Sierras
Mitchell, L. The New York idea
Moeller, P. Madame Sand
Mowatt, A. Fashion
O'Neill, E. The great god Brown
Paulding, J. The bucktails; or, Americans in England
Tyler, R. The contrast
Willis, N. Bianca Visconti

HALU Hamalian, Leo, and Volpe, Edmond L., eds. Pulitzer prize reader... New York, Popular Library [c1961] 607p
Williams, T. 27 wagons full of cotton

HAM Hamilton, Edith, tr. Three Greek plays... New York, Norton [c1937] 239p
Aeschylus. Agamemnon
Aeschylus. Prometheus bound
Euripides. The Trojan women

HAMI Hamilton (Hamish) ltd., London Majority: 1931-52... London, Hamish Hamilton [1952] 1035p
Rattigan, T. The Browning

version
Sartre, J. In camera

HAN Hampden, John, comp. Eighteenth century plays. ...London, Dent [1928] 408p (Everyman's library)
Addison, J. Cato
Colman, G., and Garrick, D. The clandestine marriage
Cumberland, R. The West Indian
Fielding, H. The tragedy of tragedies; or, Tom Thumb the great
Gay, J. The beggar's opera
Lillo, G. The London merchant; or, George Barnwell
Rowe, N. Jane Shore

HANG Hanger, Eunice, comp. Three Australian plays. Minneapolis, Minn., Univ. of Minnesota Press, 1968. 274p
Elliott, S. Rusty bugles
McKinney, J. The well
Mathew, R. We find the bunyip

HAO Happé, Peter, ed. Tudor interludes. New York, Penguin, 1972. 434p
Apius and Virginia
Fulwell, U. Like will to like
Heywood, J. The play of the wether
Medwall, H. Fulgens and Lucres. (Extracts)
Redford, J. Wit and science
Respublica. (Extracts)
Youth

HAP Harbrace omnibus...edited by H. B. Reed, J. N. McCorkle, W. H. Hildreth, and J. D. McCallum. New York, Harcourt, Brace, 1942. v.p.
Anderson, M. High Tor
O'Neill, E. In the zone

HAPD Harding, Helen Elizabeth, ed. ...Tragedies old and new...New York, Noble & Noble [c1939] 486p
Note: Also published under the title, Hamlet and other tragedies...
O'Neill, E. Beyond the horizon
Shakespeare, W. Hamlet
Sophocles. Electra

HAPO Hardison, Osborne Bennett, and Mills, Jerry Leath, eds. The forms of imagination...Englewood Cliffs, N.J., Prentice-Hall, 1972. 615p
Chekhov, A. Uncle Vanya
Hansberry, L. A raisin in the sun
Sophocles. Oedipus Rex
Williams, T. The glass menagerie

HAPRA Harrier, Richard C., ed. The Anchor anthology of Jacobean drama...Garden City, N.Y., Doubleday (Anchor Books). 1963. 2v
Chapman, G. Bussy D'Ambois 1
Ford, J. The broken heart 2
Jonson, B. Everyman in his humour 1
Marston, J. and Webster, J. The malcontent 1
Middleton, T. and Rowley, W. The changeling 2
Shirley, J. The lady of pleasure 2
Tourneur, C. The revenger's tragedy 2
Webster, J. The white devil 1

HAPRB Harrier, Richard C., ed. Jacobean drama; an anthology...New York, Norton, 1968. 2v
Chapman, G. Bussy D'Ambois 1
Ford, J. The broken heart 2

HAPRB (cont.)
Jonson, B. Everyman in his humour 1
Marston, J. and Webster, J. The malcontent 1
Middleton, T. and Rowley, W. The changeling 2
Shirley, J. The lady of pleasure 2
Tourneur, C. The revenger's tragedy 2
Webster, J. The white devil 1

HAPS Harrison, G. B., ed. Major British Writers... New York, Harcourt [c1954] 2v
Shakespeare, W. Hamlet, Prince of Denmark
Shakespeare, W. King Henry the fourth, pt. I
Shakespeare, W. The tempest
Shaw, G. Man and superman

HAPT Harrison, George Bagshawe [and others], eds. Major British writers... Enl. ed., New York, Harcourt, Brace [c1959] 2v
Byron, G. Manfred 2
Dryden, J. The secular masque 1
Milton, J. Samson Agonistes 1
Shakespeare, W. Hamlet 1
Shakespeare, W. Henry IV, part I 1
Shakespeare, W. The tempest 1
Shaw, G. Man and superman 2
Shelley, P. Prometheus unbound 2

HAPV Harsh, Philip Whaley, ed. An anthology of Roman drama... New York, Holt, Rinehart and Winston [c1960] 317p
Plautus, T. The rope
Plautus, T. The twin Menaechmi
Seneca, L. The Medea
Seneca, L. The Phaedra
Seneca, L. The Thyestes
Terentius Afer, P. The brothers
Terentius Afer, P. The Phormio

HARA Hart, James David, and Gohdes, Clarence, eds. America's literature. New York. Dryden [c1955] 958p
O'Neill, E. The hairy ape

HARB Hartley, Lodwick Charles and Ladu, Arthur Irish, eds. Patterns in modern drama... New York, Prentice-Hall, 1948. 496p
Chekhov, A. Uncle Vanya
Galsworthy, J. The pigeon
Hellman, L. The little foxes
Ibsen, H. An enemy of the people
Kelly, G. Craig's wife
O'Neill, E. The Emperor Jones
Thurber, J., and Nugent, E. The male animal

HARC Harvard classics, edited by Charles W. Eliot. New York, Collier [c1909-10] 50v
Aeschylus. Agamemnon 8
Aeschylus. The furies 8
Aeschylus. The libation-bearers 8
Aeschylus. Prometheus bound 8
Aristophanes. The frogs 8
Beaumont, F., and Fletcher, J. Philaster 47
Browning, R. A blot in the 'scutcheon 18
Byron, R. Manfred 18
Calderón de la Barca, P. Life is a dream 26
Corneille, P. Polyeucte 26
Dekker, T. The shoemaker's holiday 47
Dryden, J. All for love; or,

The world well lost 18
Euripides. The bacchae 8
Euripides. Hippolytus 8
Goethe, J. Egmont 19
Goethe, J. Faust, pt. I 19
Goldsmith, O. She stoops to conquer 18
Jonson, B. The alchemist 47
Lessing, G. Minna von Barnhelm; or, The soldier's fortune 26
Marlowe, C. Doctor Faustus 19
Marlowe, C. Edward the second 46
Massinger, P. A new way to pay old debts 47
Milton, J. Comus 4
Milton, J. Samson Agonistes 4
Molière, J. Tartuffe; or, The hypocrite 26
Racine, J. Phaedra 26
Schiller, J. Wilhelm Tell 26
Shakespeare, W. The tempest 46
Shakespeare, W. The tragedy of Hamlet Prince of Denmark 46
Shakespeare, W. The tragedy of King Lear 46
Shakespeare, W. The tragedy of Macbeth 46
Shelley, P. The Cenci 18
Sheridan, R. The school for scandal 18
Sophocles. Antigone 8
Sophocles. Oedipus the king 8
Webster, J. The Duchess of Malfi 47

HARPL Harris, Stephen LeRoy, comp. The humanist tradition in world literature: an anthology of masterpieces from Gilgamesh to the divine comedy. Columbus, Ohio, Merrill, 1970. 1008p
Aeschylus. Agamemnon
Aeschylus. Prometheus bound
Aristophanes. Lysistrata
Euripides. The bacchae
Euripides. Medea
Sophocles. Oedipus the King
Sophocles. Philoctetes

HARRIS, BRICE. See REST Restoration plays...

THE HARVARD DRAMATIC CLUB MIRACLE PLAYS. See ROHD Robinson, Donald Fay, ed.

HART Harvitt, Hélène Josephine and Schwartz, H. Stanley, eds. Promenade littéraire au vintième siècle...New York, Dryden press [c1949] 407p
Vildrac, C. Le paquebot Tenacity

HARV Harvitt, Hélène Josephine, ed. Representative plays from the French theatre of today. ...Boston, Heath [c1940] 442p
Bernstein, H. Le secret
Claudel, P. L'annonce faite à Marie
Lenormand, H. Le simoun
Sarment, J. Le pêcheur d'ombres
Vildrac, C. Le paquebot Tenacity

HARW Harwood, A. C., tr. Christmas plays from Oberufer...London, Anthroposophical publishing co. [1944] 64p
The Paradise play
The Shepherds' play
The Three kings' play

HARY Hatch, James Vernon, ed. Black theater, U.S.A.; 45 plays by Black Americans, 1847-1974. New York, Free Press, 1974. 886p
Aldridge, I. The Black doctor
Anderson, G. Appearances
Baldwin, J. The amen corner
Bonner, M. The purple flower

HARY (cont.)
Branch, W. In splendid error
Brown, W. The escape; or, A leap to freedom
Browne, T. Natural man
Bullins, E. Goin' a Buffalo
Burrill, M. They that sit in darkness
Charles, M. Job security
Childress, A. Wine in the wilderness
Cotter, J. Caleb the degenerate
Dodson, O. Divine comedy
Dunbar-Nelson, A. Mine eyes have seen
Edmonds, R. Bad man
Edward, H. Job hunters
Ferdinand, V. Blk love song #1
Gaines-Shelton, R. The church fight
Grimke, A. Rachel
Hansberry, L. The drinking gourd
Hill, A. Walk hard
Hughes, L. Don't you want to be free
Hughes, L. Limitations of life
Hughes, L. Little ham
Jackson, C. Fly blackbird
Johnson, G. A Sunday morning in the south
Jones, L. The slave
Kennedy, A. The owl answers
Livingston, M. For unborn children
Matheus, J. 'Cruiter
Miller, M. Graven images
Mitchell, L. Star of the morning
Pawley, T. The tumult and the shouting
Peterson, L. Take a giant step
Richards, S. District of Columbia
Richardson, W. The flight of the natives
Richardson, W. The idle head
Sebree, C. The dry August
Sejour, V. The brown overcoat
Shine, T. Herbert III
Spence, E. Undertow
Toomer, J. Balo
Ward, D. Day of absence
Ward, T. Big white fog
Wright, R. Native son

HAT Hatcher, Harlan Henthorne, ed. Modern American dramas... New York, Harcourt, Brace, 1941. 394p
Anderson, M. Winterset
Howard, S. Dodsworth
Odets, C. Awake and sing
O'Neill, E. Beyond the horizon
Rice, E. The adding machine
St. Joseph, E. A passenger to Bali
Sherwood, R. Abe Lincoln in Illinois
Wilder, T. Our town

HATA Hatcher, Harlan Henthorne, ed. Modern American dramas. New edition ... New York, Harcourt, Brace [c1949] 378p
Anderson, M. Winterset
Heggen, T. Mister Roberts
Miller, A. All my sons
O'Neill, E. The Emperor Jones
Rice, E. The adding machine
Saroyan, W. The time of your life
Sherwood, R. Abe Lincoln in Illinois
Williams, T. The glass menagerie

HAU Hatcher, Harlan Henthorne, ed. Modern British dramas... New York, Harcourt, Brace, 1941. 374p
Dunsany, E. If
Galsworthy, J. Justice
Maugham, W. The constant

wife
Monkhouse, A. The conquering hero
O'Flaherty, L. The informer
Pinero, A. Mid-channel
Synge, J. The playboy of the western world

HAV Hatcher, Harlan Henthorne, ed. Modern continental dramas... New York, Harcourt, Brace, 1941. 747p
Čapek, K. R.U.R.
Chekhov, A. The cherry orchard
Claudel, P. The tidings brought to Mary
Gorky, M. The lower depths
Hauptmann, G. Hannele
Ibsen, H. Hedda Gabler
Katayev, V. Squaring the circle
Lenormand, H. Time is a dream
Maeterlinck, M. Pelléas and Mélisande
Martínez Sierra, G. The cradle song
Molnár, F. Liliom
Pirandello, L. As you desire me
Rostand, E. Cyrano de Bergerac
Strindberg, A. The ghost sonata
Strindberg, A. Miss Julia
Toller, E. Transfiguration

HAVD Hatcher, Harlan Henthorne, ed. Modern dramas. Shorter edition... New York, Harcourt, Brace [c1944] 495p
Anderson, M. Winterset
Čapek, K. R.U.R.
Chekhov, A. Cherry orchard
Galsworthy, J. Justice
Hellman, L. Watch on the Rhine
Ibsen, H. Hedda Gabler
O'Flaherty, L. The informer
O'Neill, E. Beyond the horizon
Sherwood, R. Abe Lincoln in Illinois

HAVE Hatcher, Harlan Henthorne, ed. Modern dramas. New shorter edition. New York, Harcourt, Brace [c1948] 479p
Anderson, M. Winterset
Čapek, K. R.U.R.
Galsworthy, J. Justice
Hellman, L. The little foxes
Ibsen, H. Hedda Gabler
Katayev, V. Squaring the circle
Maugham, W. The circle
O'Neill, E. Beyond the horizon
Sherwood, R. Abe Lincoln in Illinois

HAVG Hatcher, Harlan Henthorne... A Modern repertory. New York, Harcourt, Brace [c1953] 714p
Coxe, L., and Chapman, R. Billy Budd
Eliot, T. Murder in the cathedral
Fry, C. Venus observed
Giraudoux, J. The madwoman of Chaillot
Kingsley, S. Detective story
O'Casey, S. Juno and the paycock
O'Neill, E. Ah, wilderness!
Shaw, G. Candida
Williams, T. Summer and smoke

HAVH Hatlen, Theodore W., comp. Drama; principles and plays... New York, Appleton-Century-Crofts [1967] 522p
Beckett, S. Act without words, I
Brecht, B. The Caucasian chalk circle
Ibsen, H. An enemy of the people
Ionesco, E. The leader
Molière, J. The miser

HAVH (cont.)
O'Neill, E. Desire under the elms
Shakespeare, W. Hamlet
Shaw, G. Major Barbara
Sheridan, R. The school for scandal
Sophocles. Antigone
Strindberg, A. Miss Julie
Williams, T. The glass menagerie

HAVHA Haugen, Einar Ingvald, ed. Fire and ice; 3 Icelandic plays... Madison, University of Wisconsin Press, 1967. 266p
Sigurjónsson, J. The wish
Stefánsson, D. The golden gate
Thórdarson, A. Atoms and madams

HAVI Havighurst, Walter; Almy, Robert F., Wilson, Gordon D., and Middlebrook, L. Ruth, eds. ...Selection: a reader for college writing. New York, Dryden [c1955] 740p
Shaw, G. Arms and the man
Sophocles. Antigone
Synge, J. Riders to the sea
Williams, T. The glass menagerie

HAVL Hay, David L. and Howell, James F., comps. Contact with drama. Chicago, Science Research Associates, 1974. 550p
Cornish, R. Open twenty-four hours
Enrico, R. On Owl Creek
Ibsen, H. Hedda Gabler
Miller, A. Death of a salesman
O'Neill, E. The Emperor Jones
Pirandello, L. Six characters in search of an author
Shaffer, P. Black comedy
Shakespeare, W. Othello
Synge, J. Riders to the sea
Van Itallie, J. Motel
Wycherley, W. The country wife
Zindel, P. The effect of gamma rays on man-in-the moon marigolds

HAY Haydn, Hiram Collins, ed. The portable Elizabethan reader... New York, Viking, 1946. 688p
Dekker, T. The shoemaker's holiday; or, A pleasant comedy of the gentle craft
Marlowe, C. Doctor Faustus

HAYD Haydn, Hiram Collins and Nelson, John Charles, eds. ...A renaissance treasury... New York, Doubleday, 1953. 432p
Machiavelli, N. Mandragola
Tasso, T. Aminta

HAYES, HELEN. See GRIF Griffin, Alice Sylvia (Venezky), ed. Living theatre...

HAYE Hayes, Richard, ed. Port-Royal and other plays ...New York, Hill and Wang [c1962] 267p (Mermaid dramabook)
Claudel, P. Tobias and Sara
Copeau, J. The little poor man
Mauriac, F. Asmodée
Montherlant, H. Port-Royal

HEI Heisch, Elizabeth, ed. Discovery and recollection; an anthology of literary types. New York, Holt, Rinehart and Winston, 1970. 566p
Benét, S. The devil and Daniel Webster
Chayevsky, P. Marty
Fletcher, L. Sorry, wrong number
Hansberry, L. A raisin in the sun

Shaw, G. Pygmalion

HEIL Heilman, Robert B., ed. An anthology of English drama before Shakespeare ...New York, Rinehart [c1952] 405p
The betrayal
The crucifixion
Everyman
Greene, R. The honorable history of Friar Bacon and Friar Bungay
Kyd, T. The Spanish tragedy
Marlowe, C. The tragical history of Dr. Faustus
Noah
The second shepherds' play
Stevenson, W. Gammer Gurton's needle

HEWES, HENRY. See also BES Best plays of 1894/99-1961/62...

HEWE Hewes, Henry, ed. Famous American plays of the 1940's...[New York, Dell, c1960] 447p (Laurel drama series)
Anderson, M., and Weil, K. Lost in the stars
Laurents, A. Home of the brave
McCullers, C. The member of the wedding
Miller, A. All my sons
Wilder, T. The skin of our teeth

HIB Hibbard, Clarence Addison, ed. Writers of the western world. Boston, Houghton, Mifflin [c1942] 1261p
Aeschylus. Agamemnon
Aristophanes. The frogs
Euripides. Medea
Evreinov, N. The theatre of the soul
Goethe, J. Faust, pt. I
Ibsen, H. The master builder
Molière, J. The misanthrope
O'Neill, E. The hairy ape
Racine, J. Phaedra
Shakespeare, W. King Lear
Sophocles. Antigone

HIBA Hibbard, Clarence Addison, ed. ... Writers of the western world...[Rev. ed.] Boston, Houghton, Mifflin [c1946] 1033p (United States Naval Academy edition edited by Cyril B. Judge)
Aeschylus. Agamemnon
Aristophanes. The frogs
Evreinov, N. The theatre of the soul
Goethe, J. Faust, pt. I
Ibsen, H. The master builder
Molière, J. The misanthrope
O'Neill, E. The hairy ape
Shakespeare, W. King Lear

HIBB Hibbard, Clarence Addison, and Frenz, Horst, eds. Writers of the western world...Second edition ...Boston, Houghton Mifflin [c1954] 1239p
Aeschylus. Agamemnon
Aristophanes. The frogs
Chekhov, A. The cherry orchard
Claudel, P. The satin slipper; or, The worst is not the surest
Euripides. Medea
Goethe, J. Faust, pt. I
Ibsen, H. The master builder
Molière, J. The misanthrope
O'Neill, E. The hairy ape
Pirandello, L. The jar
Racine, J. Phaedra
Shakespeare, W. King Lear
Sophocles. Antigone

HIG Higgins, V. Louise and Kerr, Walter, eds. Five world plays. New York, Harcourt, Brace and World, 1964. 550p
Chekhov, A. The cherry orchard

HIG (cont.)
Shakespeare, W. Hamlet
Shaw, G. Saint Joan
Sheridan, R. The rivals
Sophocles. Antigone

HILDRETH, WILLIAM HENRY. See also HAP Harbrace omnibus...

HIL Hildreth, William Henry and Dumble, Wilson Randle, eds. Five contemporary American plays...New York, Harper [c1939] 410p
Anderson, M. Winterset
Kaufman, G., and Ryskind, M. Of thee I sing
Odets, C. Waiting for Lefty
O'Neill, E. Ah, wilderness
Sherwood, R. Idiot's delight

HILL Hill, John McMurray and Harlan, Mabel Margaret, eds. Cuatro comedias... New York, Norton [c1941] 699p
Calderón de la Barca, P. No siempre lo peor es cierto
Ruiz de Alarcón y Mendoza, J. No hay mal que por bien no venga (Don Domingo de Don Blas)
Téllez, G. (Tirso de Molina [pseud.]). El burlador de Sevilla
Vega [Carpio], L. de. Peribáñez y el comendador de Ocaña

HILP Hill, Philip George, comp. The living art; an introduction to theatre and drama. New York, Holt, Rinehart and Winston, 1971. 578p
Brecht, B. Galileo
Hellman, L. The little foxes
MacLeish, A. J.B.
Miller, A. A view from the bridge
Molière, J. Tartuffe
Oldenburg, C. Fotodeath
Rostand, E. Cyrano de Bergerac
Shakespeare, W. Twelfth night
Sophocles. Oedipus Rex
Wilde, O. The importance of being earnest

HOFFMAN, WILLIAM M. See NEWA New American plays...

HOGA Hogan, Robert Goode and Molin, Sven Eric, eds. Drama; the major genres. ...New York, Dodd, Mead, 1962. 652p
Chekhov, A. The three sisters
García Lorca, F. The house of Bernarda Alba
Gorky, M. Yegor Bulychov and the others
Inge, W. Bus stop
James, H. The American
Jonson, B. The silent woman
Molière, J. Tartuffe
O'Casey, S. The plough and the stars
Shakespeare, W. The tragedy of King Lear
Shaw, G. The six of Calais
Sophocles. Antigone

HOGE Hogan, Robert Goode, comp. Seven Irish plays, 1946-1964...Minneapolis, University of Minnesota Press [1967] 472p
Byrne, S. Design for a headstone
Douglas, J. The ice goddess
Keane, J. Many young men of twenty
Keane, J. Sharon's grave
MacMahon, B. Song of the anvil
Molloy, M. The visiting house
O'Donovan, J. Copperfaced Jack

HOGI Hogins, James B., comp. Literature; a collection of mythology and folklore, short stories, poetry, drama... Chicago, Science Research Associates, 1973. 962p
Arrabal, F. Picnic on the battlefield
Bullins, E. The electronic nigger
Miller, A. A view from the bridge
Molière, J. Sganarelle
Shakespeare, W. Macbeth
Shaw, G. How he lied to her husband
Sophocles. Oedipus Rex
Synge, J. Riders to the sea

HOLM Holmes, John Albert and Towle, Carroll S., eds. A complete college reader ... Boston, Houghton, Mifflin [c1950] 1063p
Anderson, M. Winterset
Ibsen, H. An enemy of the people
O'Neill, E. Ah, wilderness!

HOLP Holmes, Paul C., and Lehman, A. J., eds. Keys to understanding; receiving and sending; drama. New York, Harper and Row, 1970. 459p
Aristophanes. Lysistrata
Cowen, R. Summertime
Gardner, H. A thousand clowns
Ionesco, E. The gap
Jones, L. Dutchman
Saroyan, W. Hello out there
Shakespeare, W. Romeo and Juliet
Sophocles. Antigone
Ward, D. Happy ending

HOLT Holt, Marion P., ed. The modern Spanish stage: four plays. New York, Hill and Wang, 1970. 388p
Buero Vallejo, A. The concert at Saint Ovide
Casona, A. The boat without fisherman
López Rubio, J. The blindfold
Sastre, A. Condemned squad

HOPP Hopper, Vincent Foster, and Lahey, Gerald B., eds. Medieval mystery plays... morality plays... and interludes. Great Neck, N.Y., Barron's Educational Series [c1962] 299p
Abraham and Isaac
The castle of perseverance
Everyman
Noah's flood
The second shepherds' play
Heywood, J. Johan Johan
Heywood, J. The play called the four pp

HORN Horn, Gunnar. A cavalcade of world writing... Boston, Allyn and Bacon, 1961. 718p
Čapek, K. R.U.R. (Rossum's universal robots)

HORNE, HERBERT P. See NER Nero (Tragedy). Nero & other plays...

HOUE Houghton, Norris, ed. The golden age... [New York, Dell, 1963] 349p (Laurel masterpieces of continental drama, v1)
Calderón de la Barca, P. Life is a dream
Corneille, P. The cid
Molière, J. The misanthrope
Racine, J. Phaedra
Vega Carpio, L. The sheep well

HOUG Houghton, Norris, ed. Great Russian plays... [New York, Dell, c1960] 511p (Laurel drama series)
Andreyev, L. He who gets slapped

HOUG (cont.)
Chekhov, A. The cherry orchard
Gogol, N. The inspector general
Gorky, M. The lower depths
Tolstoy, L. The power of darkness
Turgenev, I. A month in the country

HOUK Houghton, Norris, ed. The romantic influence. [New York, Dell, 1963] 542p (Laurel masterpieces of continental drama, v2)
Goethe, J. Faust, pt. 1
Hugo, V. Hernani
Rostand, E. Cyrano de Bergerac
Schiller, F. Mary Stuart

HOUP Houghton, Norris, ed. Seeds of modern drama. [New York, Dell, 1963] 413p (Laurel masterpieces of continental drama, v3)
Chekhov, A. The sea gull
Hauptmann, G. The weavers
Ibsen, H. An enemy of the people
Strindberg, A. Miss Julie
Zola, E. Thérèse Raquin

HOUS Houston, Percy Hazen and Smith, Robert Metcalf, eds. Types of world literature... Garden City, N.Y., Doubleday, Doran [c1930] 1200p
Aeschylus. Agamemnon
Aristophanes. The birds
Euripides. Hippolytus
Everyman
Ibsen, H. A doll's house
Molière, J. The misanthrope
Plautus, T. The captives
Racine, J. Athaliah
Shakespeare, W. As you like it
Shakespeare, W. King Lear
Sheridan, R. The rivals
Sophocles. Antigone
Wilde, O. The importance of being earnest

HOW Howard, Edwin Johnson, ed. Ten Elizabethan plays ... New York, Nelson, 1931. 451p
Beaumont, F., and Fletcher, J. The knight of the burning pestle
Beaumont, F., and Fletcher, J. Philaster
Dekker, T. The shoemaker's holiday
Greene, R. The honorable history of Friar Bacon and Friar Bungay
Jonson, B. The alchemist
Kyd, T. The Spanish tragedy
Marlowe, C. Tamburlaine the great
Marlowe, C. The tragical history of Dr. Faustus
Massinger, P. A new way to pay old debts
Webster, J. The Duchess of Malfi

HOWE Howe, George and Harrer, Gustave Adolphus, eds. ... Greek literature in translation... New York, Harper [c1924] 642p
Aeschylus. Agamemnon
Aristophanes. The clouds
Euripides. Alcestis
Euripides. Medea
Menander. The arbitration
Sophocles. Oedipus the king

HOWF Howe, George, and Harrer, Gustave Adolphus, eds. Greek literature in translation... Revised edition by Preston Herschel Epps. New York, Harper [c1948] 903p
Aeschylus. Agamemnon
Aristophanes. The clouds
Aristophanes. The frogs
Euripides. Alcestis
Euripides. Medea
Menander. The arbitration

Sophocles. Oedipus the king

HOWJ Howe, George, and Harrer, Gustave, eds. ... Roman literature in translation...New York, Harper, 1924. 630p
Plautus. Menaechmi
Seneca. Octavia
Terence. Phormio

HOWK Howe, George, and Harrer, Gustave, eds. Roman literature in translation... Revised by Albert Suskin ...New York, Harper [c1959] 649p
Horatius Flaccus, Q. The bore; a dramatic version of Horace (Satires I, 9)
Plautus, T. The braggart soldier
Seneca, L. Octavia
Terentius Afer, P. The brothers

HOWP Howe, Irving, [and others], comps. The literature of America. New York, McGraw-Hill, 1971. 2v
Albee, E. The zoo story 2
Jones, L. Dutchman 2
O'Neill, E. Desire under the elms 2
Tyler, R. The contrast 1
Wilder, T. The skin of our teeth 2

HUB Hubbell, Jay Broadus, ed. American life in literature ...New York, Harper [c1936] 849p
O'Neill, E. Marco millions

HUBA Hubbell, Jay Broadus, ed. American life in literature...New York, Harper [c1949] 2v
O'Neill, E. The Emperor Jones 2

HUD Hubbell, Jay Broadus and Beatty, John Owen, eds. An introduction to drama ...New York, Macmillan, 1927. 838p
Abraham and Isaac
Beaumont, F., and Fletcher, J. Philaster
Chekhov, A. The boor
Dunsany, E. A night at an inn
Everyman
Farquhar, G. The beaux' stratagem
Gerstenberg, A. Overtones
Gilbert, W., and Sullivan, A. Iolanthe
Glaspell, S. Trifles
Goldsmith, O. She stoops to conquer
Hauptmann, G. The assumption of Hannele
Ibsen, H. A doll's house
Jones, H. The goal
Jonson, B. Volpone
Maeterlinck, M. The intruder
Marlowe, C. Doctor Faustus
Molière, J. Tartuffe
O'Neill, E. The Emperor Jones
Pinero, A. The second Mrs. Tanqueray
Plautus, T. Menaechmi
Quem quaeritis
Rostand, E. Cyrano de Bergerac
The second shepherds' play
Sheridan, R. The school for scandal
Sophocles. Antigone
Synge, J. Riders to the sea
Wilde, O. Lady Windermere's fan
Williamson, H. Peggy
Yeats, W. The land of heart's desire

HUDE Huberman, Edward, and Raymo, Robert R., eds. Angles of vision...Boston, Houghton Mifflin [c1962] 679p
Harburg, E., and Saidy, F. Finian's rainbow

HUDE (cont.)
Inge, W. The dark at the top of the stairs
Priestley, J. An inspector calls
Shakespeare, W. A midsummer night's dream
Wedekind, F. The tenor

HUDS Hudson, Arthur Palmer; Hurley, Leonard Buswell and Clark, Joseph Deadrick, eds. Nelson's college caravan...New York, Nelson, 1936. 4v
Green, P. Unto such glory 2
O'Neill, E. Marco millions 2
Rostand, E. Cyrano de Bergerac 2
Sherriff, R. Journey's end 2
Sophocles. Antigone 2

HUDT Hudson, Arthur Palmer; Hurley, Leonard Buswell and Clark, Joseph Deadrick, eds. Nelson's college caravan...3rd ed. New York, Nelson, 1942. 1418p (4v in 1)
Čapek, K. R.U.R.
O'Neill, E. Marco millions
Sophocles. Antigone

HUGH Hughes, Leo, and Scouten, A. H., eds. Ten English farces...Austin, Texas, University of Texas press, 1948. 286p
Behn, A. The emperor of the moon
The bilker bilk'd
Dogget, T. Hob; or, The country wake
Hoare, P. No song no supper
Inchbald, E. Appearance is against them
Jevon, T.; Coffey, C.; Mottley, J., and Cibber, T. The devil to pay; or, The wives metamorphos'd
Johnson, C. The cobbler of Preston
Ravenscroft, E., and Motteux, P. The anatomist; or, The sham doctor
Sheridan, T. The brave Irishman
Tate, N. A duke and no duke

HUNT Hunt, Kellogg, W., and Stoakes, Paul, eds. Our living language...Boston, Houghton Mifflin [c1961] 631p
Miller, A. Death of a salesman
Serling, R. Patterns

HUSSEY, MAURICE P. See CHES Chester mystery plays

HUST Huston, John Dennis and Kernan, A. B., comps. Classics of the renaissance theater: English plays. New York, Harcourt, 1969. 735p
Ford, J. 'Tis a pity she's a whore
Jonson, B. Volpone
Kyd, T. The Spanish tragedy
Marlowe, C. Tamburlaine the Great
Middleton, T. and Rowley, W. The changeling
Tourneur, C. The revenger's tragedy
Webster, J. The Duchess of Malfi

HUTC Hutchens, John K., ed. The American twenties... Philadelphia, Lippincott [c1952] 480p
O'Neill, E. The Emperor Jones

HUTCHINS, ROBERT MAYNARD. See GRDB Great books of the western world...

I

ING Inglis, Rewey Belle; Gehlmann, John; Bowman, Mary Rives and Foerster, Norman, eds. Adventures in American literature. 3rd ed. ...New York, Harcourt, Brace, 1941. v.p.
Anderson, S. Textiles
O'Neill, E. Where the cross is made
Wilder, T. Our town

INGA Inglis, Rewey Belle; Bowman, Mary Rives; Gehlmann, John and Schramm, Wilbur. Adventures in American literature... Fourth...edition. New York, Harcourt, Brace [c1947] 811p
Buck, P. Will this earth hold?
Gallico, P. The snow goose
O'Neill, E. Where the cross is made
Wilder, T. Our town

INGB Inglis, Rewey Belle; Gehlmann, John; Bowman, Mary Rives and Schramm, Wilbur, eds. Adventures in American literature. Mercury edition. [5th edition] New York, Harcourt, Brace, 1952. 783p
Clarke, W. The ghost patrol
Gallico, P. The snow goose
Wilder, T. Our town

INGE Inglis, Rewey Belle; Cooper, Alice Cecilia; Sturdevant, Marion A., and Benét, William Rose, eds. Adventures in English literature. Rev. ed. ...New York, Harcourt, Brace, 1938. 1178p
Galsworthy, J. Strife
Shakespeare, W. Macbeth
Synge, J. Riders to the sea

INGG Inglis, Rewey Belle; Cooper, Alice Cecilia; Oppenheimer, Celia, and Benét, William Rose, eds. Adventures in English literature... Fourth edition. New York, Harcourt, Brace [c1946] 775p
Barrie, J. The old lady shows her medals
Galsworthy, J. Strife
Shakespeare, W. Macbeth
Synge, J. Riders to the sea

INGH Inglis, Rewey Belle; Stauffer, Donald A., and Larsen, Cecil Evva, eds. Adventures in English literature. Mercury edition. New York, Harcourt, Brace. 1952. 782p
Barrie, J. The old lady shows her medals
Besier, R. The Barretts of Wimpole Street
Synge, J. Riders to the sea

INGW Inglis, Rewey Belle, and Stewart, William Kilbourne, eds. Adventures in world literature...New York, Harcourt, Brace, 1936. 1268p
Benavente y Martínez, J. No smoking
The bird-catcher in hell
Ibsen, H. An enemy of the people
Molière, J. The physician in spite of himself
Sachs, H. The horse thief
Sophocles. Antigone

INTE International modern plays...London, Dent [1950] 304p (Everyman's library)
Čapek, K., and Čapek, J. The life of the insects
Chiarelli, L. The mask and the face
Cocteau, J. The infernal machine

INTE (cont.)
Hauptmann, G. Hannele
Strindberg, A. Lady Julie

IRW Irwin, Vera Rusforth, comp. and tr. Four classical Asian plays in modern translation. Baltimore, Penguin, 1972. 333p
Bhasa. The vision of Vasavadatta
Danjuro, I. Narukami
Wang Shih-fu. The west chamber
Zembō, M. Ikkaku sennin

J

JACKSON, SIR BARRY. See MAL Malvern festival plays...

JAFF Jaffe, Adrian H., and Weisinger, Herbert, eds. The laureate fraternity... Evanston, Ill., Row, Peterson [c1960] 720p
Goldsmith, O. She stoops to conquer; or, The mistakes of a night
Kingsley, S. Detective story
O'Neill, E. Ah, wilderness!
Shakespeare, W. Othello, the Moor of Venice
Sophocles. Oedipus rex
Wilde, O. An ideal husband

THE JOHNS HOPKINS STUDIES IN ROMANCE LITERATURE AND LANGUAGES v29. See LAN Lancaster, Henry Carrington, ed. Five French farces, 1655-1694?...

JOH [Johnson, Rossiter] ed. An anthology of Italian authors from Cavalcanti to Fogazzaro (1270-1907)...[New York] National alumni [c1907] 388p (The literature of Italy, 1265-1907)
Metastasio, P. Achilles in Scyros

JOHN Johnson, Stanley Lewis; Bierman, Judah and Hart, James, eds. The play and the reader. Englewood Cliffs, N.J., Prentice-Hall, 1966. 442p
Aristophanes. Lysistrata
Brecht, B. Mother Courage
Giraudoux, J. The madwoman of Chaillot
Ibsen, H. Rosmersholm
Ionesco, E. The chairs
Pirandello, L. Henry IV
Shakespeare, W. King Lear
Shaw, G. Caesar and Cleopatra
Sophocles. Oedipus rex

JOHO Johnson, Stanley Lewis, [and others], eds. The play and the reader. Englewood Cliffs, N.J., Prentice-Hall, 1971. 583p
Anouilh, J. Antigone
Brecht, B. The Caucasian chalk circle
Frisch, M. Firebugs
Ibsen, H. An enemy of the people
Molière, J. Tartuffe
Pirandello, L. Right you are if you think you are
Shakespeare, W. Hamlet
Shakespeare, W. Twelfth night
Sophocles. Antigone
Wilder, T. The skin of our teeth

JON Jones, Le Roi, and Neal, Larry, eds. Black fire: an anthology of Afro-American writing. New York, Apollo Eds., 1969. 670p
Bullins, E. How do you do
Caldwell, B. Prayer meeting; or, The first militant minister
Drayton, R. Notes from a strange God
Freeman, C. The suicide
Garrett, J. We own the night

Jackson, M. Flowers for the trash-man
Jones, L. Madheart
Patterson, C. Black ice
White, J. The leader

JONA Jones, Willis Knapp, tr. and comp. Men and angels: three South American comedies. Carbondale, Ill., Southern Illinois University Press, 1970. 191p
Darthes, J., and Damel, C. The quack doctor
Frank, M. The man of the century
Matto, J. The fate of Chipí González

JORG Jorgenson, Paul A., and Shroyer, Frederick B., eds. A college treasury ... New York, Charles Scribner's sons [c1956] 598p
Howard, S. The silver cord
Rice, E. The adding machine
Shakespeare, W. Romeo and Juliet
Shaw, G. Arms and the man
Sherriff, R. The colonel's lady

JORH Jorgensen, Paul A. and Shroyer, Frederick B., eds. A college treasury: prose, fiction, drama, poetry... 2d ed. New York, Scribner [1967] 604p
Shakespeare, W. The tragedy of Hamlet, Prince of Denmark
Shaw, G. Arms and the man
Sophocles. Oedipus rex
Wilder, T. The skin of our teeth

K

KAT Katzin, Mrs. Winifred, comp. Eight European plays... New York, Brentano, 1927. 426p
Bernard, J. Glamour
Bernard, J. Martine
Harlan, W. The Nüremberg egg
Kaiser, G. The fire in the opera house
Mann, H. Madame Legros
Rosso di san Secondo, P. The stairs
Sternheim, C. A place in the world
Vollmöller, K. Uncle's been dreaming

KAU Kauver, Gerald B., and Sorensen, Gerald Charles, comps. Nineteenth century English verse drama. Cranbury, N.J., Fairleigh Dickinson University Press, 1973. 355p
Arnold, M. Empedocles on Etna
Browning, R. King Victor and King Charles
Coleridge, S. Remorse
Gordon, G. Manfred
Keats, J. Otho the Great
Shelley, P. The Cenci
Swinburne, A. Atlanta in Calydon
Tennyson, A. Becket
Wordsworth, W. The borderers

KEE Keene, Donald, ed. and comp. Twenty plays of the Nō theatre. New York, Columbia University Press, 1970. 336p
The iron crown
Kanze Kiyotsugu Kan'ami. Komachi and the hundred nights
Kanze Kiyotsugu Kan'ami. Matsukaze
Kanze Kiyotsugu Kan'ami. The sought-for grave
Kanze Kojiro Nobumitsu. Dōjōji
Kanze Kojiro Nobumitsu. The priest and the willow

KEE (cont.)
Komparu-Zenchiku. The queen mother of the West
Komparu-Zenchiku. Yōkihi
Kongō Yagorō. The bird-scaring boat
Seami, M. The brocade tree
Seami, M. The deserted crone
Seami, M. The imperial visit to Ohara
Seami, M. Kanehira
Seami, M. Komachi at Sekidera
Seami, M. Lady Han
Seami, M. The reed cutter
Seami, M. Semimaru
Shōkun
The shrine in the fields
The valley rite

KER Kermode, John Frank, ed. The anthology of English literature. New York, Oxford University Press, 1973. 2v
Congreve, W. The way of the world 1
Everyman 1
Gay, J. The beggar's opera 1
Marlowe, C. Doctor Faustus 1
The second shepherds' play 1
Shakespeare, W. The tempest 1
Shaw, G. Saint Joan 2
Wilde, O. The importance of being earnest 2

KERN Kernan, Alvin B., ed. Character and conflict: An introduction to drama... New York, Harcourt, Brace [c1963] 757p
Brecht, B. Mother Courage and her children
Chekhov, A. The cherry orchard
Everyman
Ibsen, H. Hedda Gabler
MacLeish, A. The fall of the city
Molière, J. The misanthrope
Saroyan, W. The time of your life
Shakespeare, W. King Henry the fourth, part 1
Shakespeare, W. The tragedy of Hamlet, Prince of Denmark
Sophocles. Antigone
Strindberg, A. The stronger

KERO Kernan, Alvin Bernard, ed. Character and conflict; an introduction to drama. 2d ed. New York, Harcourt, Brace and World, 1969. 721p
Arrabal, F. Picnic on the battlefield
Brecht, B. Mother Courage and her children
Chekhov, A. The cherry orchard
Everyman
Giraudoux, J. Tiger at the gates
Ibsen, H. Hedda Gabler
Molière, J. The misanthrope
Shakespeare, W. Hamlet
Sophocles. Antigone
Strindberg, A. The stronger
Synge, J. Riders to the sea
Wilder, T. The skin of our teeth

KERP Kernan, Alvin Bernard, ed. Classics of the modern theater, realism and after. New York, Harcourt, Brace and World [1965] 538p
Albee, E. The zoo story
Betti, U. Corruption in the palace of justice
Brecht, B. Mother Courage and her children
Chekhov, A. The cherry orchard
García Lorca, F. Blood wedding
Ibsen, H. Ghosts
Ionesco, E. The chairs
Pirandello, L. Six characters in search of an author

Shaw, G. Arms and the man
Strindberg, A. The father
Strindberg, A. The ghost sonata

KET Ketchum, Roland and Billis, Adolph, eds. Three masters of English drama ...New York, Dodd, Mead, 1934. 469p
Dryden, J. All for love
Shakespeare, W. Julius Caesar
Shaw, G. Caesar and Cleopatra

KEY Keyes, Rowena Keith and Roth, Helen M., eds. ... Comparative comedies present and past...New York, Noble & Noble [c1935] 628p
Barry, P. Holiday
Beach, L. The goose hangs high
Goldsmith, O. She stoops to conquer
Sheridan, R. The rivals

KIN Kincheloe, Isabel Mary, and Cook, Lester H., comps. Adventures in values. New York, Harcourt, Brace, Jovanovich, 1969. 784p
Anderson, M. Feast of Ortolans
Hansberry, L. A raisin in the sun
Jeffers, R. Medea
Shakespeare, W. Macbeth
Shaw, G. Devil's disciple
Vidal, G. Visit to a small planet

KING, VERNON RUPERT. See TOD Today's literature...

KINH King, Woodie, and Milner, Ron, comps. Black drama anthology. New York, Columbia University Press, 1971. 671p
Branch, W. A medal for Willie
Bullins, E. The corner
Caldwell, B. All white caste
Charles, M. Black cycle
Dean, P. The owl killer
DeAnda, P. Ladies in waiting
Elder, L. Charades on East Fourth Street
Gordon, C. The breakout
Greaves, D. The marriage
Hill, E. Strictly matrimony
Hughes, L. Mother and child
Jackson, E. Toe jam
Jones, L. Bloodrites
Jones, L. Junkies are full of (SHHH...)
Mackey, W. Requiem for Brother X
Mason, C. Gabriel
Milner, R. Who's got his own
Mitchell, L. Star of the morning
Pitcher, O. The one
Shepp, A. Junebug graduates tonight
Walker, J. Ododo
Ward, D. Brotherhood
Zuber, R. Three X love

KINN Kinney, Arthur Frederick, and others, eds. Symposium on love. Boston, Houghton, Mifflin, 1970. 268p
Abraham and Isaac
Molière, J. Tartuffe
Pirandello, L. Six characacters in search of an author
Shakespeare, W. The tragedy of King Lear
Sophocles. Oedipus the king
Zembō, M. Early snow

KNIC Knickerbocker, Kenneth L. and Reninger, H. Willard, eds. ...Interpreting literature. New York, Henry Holt [c1955] 850p

KNIC (cont.)
Chekhov, A. The boor
Connelly, M. The green pastures
Ibsen, H. A doll's house
O'Neill, E. Ile
Rostand, E. Cyrano de Bergerac
Shaw, G. Candida
Williams, T. The glass menagerie

KNID Knickerbocker, Kenneth L., and Reninger, H. Willard, eds. Interpreting literature, Revised edition... New York, Holt, Rinehart and Winston [c1960] 832p
Chekhov, A. The boor
Connelly, M. The green pastures
Ibsen, H. A doll's house
O'Neill, E. Ile
Frost, R. A masque of reason
Shakespeare, W. The tragedy of Macbeth
Shaw, G. Candida
Sophocles. Antigone
Williams, T. The glass menagerie

KNIE Knickerbocker, Kenneth L., and Reninger, H. Willard. Interpreting literature... 3d ed., New York, Holt, Rinehart and Winston [1969] 908p
Besier, R. The Barretts of Wimpole Street
Chekhov, A. The boor
Connelly, M. The green pastures
Ibsen, H. An enemy of the people
Molière, J. The physician in spite of himself
O'Neill, E. "Ile"
Shakespeare, W. The tragedy of Macbeth
Shaw, G. Arms and the man
Sophocles. Antigone

KNO Knott, John Ray, and Reaske, Christopher Russell, eds. Mirrors; an introduction to literature. San Francisco, Canfield Press, 1972. 508p
Bergman, I. The seventh seal
Frisch, M. Biedermann and the firebugs
Ibsen, H. Hedda Gabler
Jones, L. Dutchman
Sophocles. Oedipus rex

KNOW Knowland, A. S., ed. Six Caroline plays... London, Oxford University Press, 1962. 553p
Brome, R. The antipodes
Brome, R. The mad couple well matched
D'Avenant, W. The wits
Killigrew, T. The parson's wedding
Shirley, J. The lady of pleasure
Shirley, J. The wedding

KOH Kohut, George Alexander, ed. A Hebrew anthology. ... Cincinnati, Bacharach, 1913. 2v
Byron, G. Cain 2
Byron, G. Heaven and earth 2
Cayzer, C. David and Bathshua 2
Davidson, R. Elijah 2
Ewing, T. Jonathan 2
Francis, A. The song of songs which is Solomon's 2
Leavitt, J. The Jewish captives 2
Lessing, G. Nathan the wise 2
Milman, H. Belshazzar 2
Milman, H. The fall of Jerusalem 2
Milton, J. Samson Agonistes 2
More, H. Belshazzar 2
More, H. Daniel 2

More, H. David and Goliath 2
More, H. Moses in the bulrushes 2
Racine, J. Athaliah 2
Rives, A. Herod and Mariamne 2

KON Konick, Marcus, ed. Six complete world plays and a history of the drama. New York, Globe [c1963] 701p
Chekhov, A. The cherry orchard
Everyman
Ibsen, H. An enemy of the people
Rostand, E. Cyrano de Bergerac
Shaw, G. Caesar and Cleopatra
Sophocles. Antigone

KOZ Kozlenko, William, ed. The best short plays of the social theatre... New York, Random house [c1939] 456p
Auden, W., and Isherwood, C. The dog beneath the skin
Bengal, B. Plant in the sun
Blitzstein, M. The cradle will rock
Green, P. Hymn to the rising sun
Kozlenko, W. This earth is ours
Maltz, A. Private Hicks
Odets, C. Waiting for Lefty
Shaw, I. Bury the dead
Sifton, C., and Sifton, P. Give all thy terrors to the wind
Wexley, J. Running dogs

KREYMBORG, ALFRED. See also AME American caravan...

KRE Kreymborg, Alfred, ed. Poetic drama... New York, Modern age [c1941] 855p
Abraham, Melchisedec, and Isaac
Adam
Aeschylus. Agamemnon
Aristophanes. The Acharnians
Auden, W., and Isherwood, C. The dog beneath the skin
Bottomley, G. Gruach
The chalk circle
Corneille, P. Cinna
Euripides. Ion
Everyman
Goethe, J. Torquato Tasso
Hauptmann, G. The white saviour
Jonson, B. Volpone
Kreymborg, A. Hole in the wall
MacLeish, A. The fall of the city
Marlowe, C. Tamburlaine the great, pt. I
Massinger, P. A new way to pay old debts
Millay, E. Aria da capo
Molière, J. The misanthrope
Moody, W. The death of Eve
Racine, J. Athaliah
Rostand, E. The last night of Don Juan
Sachs, H. The wandering scholar from Paradise
Schiller, F. The death of Wallenstein
Schwartz, D. Shenandoah
Seami. Nakamitsu
The second shepherds' play
Shakespeare, W. Measure for measure
Shelley, P. The Cenci
Sophocles. Oedipus coloneus
Vega Carpio, L. de. The sheep well
Webster, J. The white devil
Yeats, W. The king's threshold

KRM Kronenberger, Louis, ed. Cavalcade of comedy... New York, Simon and Schuster [c1953] 715p
Congreve, W. Love for love

KRM (cont.)
Congreve, W. The way of the world
Coward, N. Blithe spirit
Etherege, G. The man of mode
Goldsmith, O. She stoops to conquer
Jonson, B. The alchemist
Jonson, B. Volpone
Kelly, G. The show-off
Maugham, W. The circle
Mayer, E. Children of darkness
O'Casey, S. Juno and the paycock
Osborn, P. Morning's at seven
Shaw, G. Androcles and the lion
Shaw, G. Pygmalion
Sheridan, R. The school for scandal
Synge, J. The playboy of the western world
Thurber, J., and Nugent, E. The male animal
Vanbrugh, J. The confederacy
Van Druten, J. The voice of the turtle
Wilde, O. The importance of being earnest
Wycherley, W. The country wife

KRO Kronenberger, Louis, ed. An eighteenth century miscellany... New York, Putnam, 1936. 578p
Gay, J. The beggar's opera
Sheridan, R. The school for scandal

KRON Kronenberger, Louis, ed. The pleasure of their company... New York, Knopf, 1946. 653p
Congreve, W. The way of the world

KRONENBERGER, LOUIS <u>See also</u> BES Best plays of 1894/99-1961/62

<u>L</u>

LAB Labiche, Eugène and Gondinet, Edmond, eds. Three French farces. [Le plus heureux des trois] The happiest of the three ... Harmondsworth, Middlesex, Penguin, 288p
Labiche, E., and Gondinet, E. The happiest of the three
Feydeau, G. Get out of my hair
Sardou, V., and Najac, E. Let's get a divorce!

LAH Lahr, John, ed. Showcase 1; plays from Eugene O'Neill foundation. New York, Grove, 1970. 220p
Gagliano, F. Father Uxbridge wants to marry
Guare, J. Muzeeka
Hailey, O. Who's happy now?
Horovitz, I. The Indian wants the Bronx

LAL Lal, Paul, ed. and tr. Great Sanscrit plays... [New York, New Directions, 1964] 396p
Bhāsa. The dream of Vāsavadatta
Bhavabhūti. The later story of Rama
Harsha. Ratnavali
Kālidāsa. Shakuntalā
Shudraka, K. The toy cart
Vishakadatta. The signet ring of Rakshasa

LAM Lambert, Robert and Lynn, Kenneth S., eds. The range of literature; drama. Boston, Houghton, Mifflin, 1969. 502p
Duberman, M. In white America
Hart, M., and Kaufman, G. You can't take it with you
Ibsen, H. An enemy of the people

Rostand, E. Cyrano de Bergerac
Wilder, T. Our town

LAMP Lamport, Francis John, ed. and tr. Five German tragedies. Harmondsworth, Middlesex, Penguin, 1969. 503p
Goethe, J. Egmont
Grillparzer, F. Medea
Kleist, H. Penthesilea
Lessing, G. Emelia Galotti
Schiller, J. Mary Stuart

LAN Lancaster, Henry Carrington, ed. ...Five French farces, 1655-1694?...Baltimore, Johns Hopkins press, 1937. 141p (The Johns Hopkins studies in Romance literatures and languages, v29)
Boisrobert, F. L'amant ridicule
Le docteur amoureux
Donneau de Visé, J. Le gentilhomme guespin
Raisin, J. Merlin gascon
Villiers, C. L'apoticaire devalisé

LAO Landis, Joseph C., ed. and tr. The dybbuk, and other great Yiddish plays. New York, Bantam Books [1966] 356p
Anski, S. The dybbuk
Asch, S. God of vengeance
Hirshbein, P. Green fields
Leivick, H. The golem
Pinski, D. King David and his wives

LAOG Landis, Joseph C., ed. and tr. The great Jewish plays. New York, Horizon, 1972. 356p
Asch, S. God of vengeance
Halper, L. The golem
Hirshbein, P. Green fields
Pinski, D. King David and his wives
Rappoport, S. The dybbuk

LAP Landis, Paul Nissley, ed. Four famous Greek plays ...New York, Modern library [1929] 285p
Aeschylus. Agamemnon
Aristophanes. The frogs
Euripides. Medea
Sophocles. Oedipus the king

LAUGHLIN, JAMES. See NEW New directions in prose and poetry...

LAUREL DRAMA SERIES. See HEWE Hewes, Henry, ed. Famous American plays of The 1940's...HOUG Houghton, Norris, ed. Great Russian plays...MACG Macgowan, Kenneth, ed. Famous American plays of the 1920's...

LAUREL MASTERPIECES OF CONTINENTAL DRAMA, v1-3. See HOUE, HOUK, HOUP Houghton, Norris, ed.

LAV Laverty, Carroll D., and others, comps. The unity of English...New York, Harper, 1971. 556p
Hansberry, L. A raisin in the sun
Saroyan, W. The time of your life
Williams, T. The glass menagerie

LAW Law, Frederick Houk, ed. Modern plays, short and long...New York, Century, 1924. 429p
Archer, W. The green goddess
Church, V. What men live by
Corneau, P. Masks
Dean, A. Just neighborly
Gilbert, W. Iolanthe

Idzumo, T. Bushido
Mackay, C. Benjamin Franklin journeyman
MacMillan, D. Off Nags head
Macmillan, M. The pioneers
Mick, H. The maid who wouldn't be proper
Rip van Winkle

LAWR Lawrence, Robert G., ed. Early seventeenth century drama... New York, Dutton [c1963] 390p
Dekker, T. The shoemaker's holiday; or, The gentle craft
Heywood, T. A woman killed with kindness
Marston, J., and Webster, J. The malcontent
Massinger, P. A new way to pay old debts
Middleton, T., and Rowley, W. The changeling

LAWS Lawrence, Robert Gilford, ed. Jacobean and Caroline comedies. London, Dent, 1973. 241p
Brome, R. A jovial crew
Ford, J. and Rowley, W. The witch of Edmonton
Middleton, T. A trick to catch the old one

LEG Le Gallienne, Eva, ed. Eva Le Gallienne's Civic repertory plays... New York, Norton [c1928] 327p
Chekhov, A. Three sisters
Goldoni, C. La locandiera
Ibsen, H. Hedda Gabler
Wied, G. 2 x 2 = 5

LEIS Leishman, J. B., ed. The three Parnassus plays (1598-1601)... London, Ivor Nicholson & Watson, 1949. 398p
The first part of the return from Parnassus
The pilgrimage to Parnassus
The second part of the return from Parnassus

LEV Leverton, Garrett Hasty, ed. Plays for the college theater... New York, French, 1932. 629p
Ames, W. A kiss in Xanadu
Atlas, L. "L"
Barry, P. Hotel Universe
Boucicault, D. Belle Lamar
Britton, K., and Hargrave, R. Houseparty
Buckingham, G. The rehearsal
Elser, F. Low bridge
Everyman
France, A. The man who married a dumb wife
Gammer Gurton's needle
Green, P. The Lord's will
Ibsen, H. The wild duck
Kaufman, G. The butter and egg man
Kreymborg, A. Lima beans
Levy, B. Springtime for Henry
Martinez Sierra, G. The two shepherds
Molière, J. The doctor in spite of himself
Molnár, F. Liliom
O'Neill, E. The moon of the Caribbees
Riggs, L. Green grow the lilacs
Rostand, E. Cyrano de Bergerac
Sardou, V. Patrie!
Scala, F. The portrait
Schnitzler, A. The green cockatoo
Shay, F. A Christmas carol
Strong, A. The drums of Oude
Vildrac, C. Michel Auclair
The York nativity

LEVE Leverton, Garrett Hasty, ed. Plays for the college theater... New York, French, 1934. 601p
Ames, W. A kiss in Xanadu

Atlas, L. "L"
Barry, P. Hotel Universe
Boucicault, D. Belle Lamar
Britton, K., and Hargrave, R. Houseparty
Buckingham, G. The rehearsal
Everyman
France, A. The man who married a dumb wife
Gammer Gurton's needle
Green, P. The Lord's will
Ibsen, H. The wild duck
Kaufman, G. The butter and egg man
Kreymborg, A. Lima beans
Levy, B. Springtime for Henry
Martínez Sierra, G. The two shepherds
Molière, J. The doctor in spite of himself
Molnár, F. Liliom
O'Neill, E. The moon of the Caribbees
Riggs, L. Green grow the lilacs
Rostand, E. Cyrano de Bergerac
Sardou, V. Patrie!
Scala, F. The portrait
Schnitzler, A. The green cockatoo
Shay, F. A Christmas carol
Strong, A. The drums of Oude
Vildrac, C. Michel Auclair
The York nativity

LEVI Levin, Richard Louis, ed. Tragedy; Plays, theory, criticism... New York, Harcourt, Brace & World [c1960] 217p
Ibsen, H. Ghosts
O'Neill, E. The hairy ape
Seneca, L. Oedipus
Shakespeare, W. Othello
Sophocles. Oedipus rex

LEVJ Levin, Richard Louis, ed. Tragedy: plays, theory and criticism... Alternate ed. ... New York, Harcourt Brace and World [1965] 233p
Eliot, T. Murder in the cathedral
Ibsen, H. The wild duck
Shakespeare, W. Coriolanus
Sophocles. Antigone

LEWI Lewisohn, Ludwig, ed. Among the nations... New York, Farrar. Strauss [c1948] 270p
Galsworthy, J. Loyalties

LIBRARY OF BEST AMERICAN PLAYS. See GARW, GARZ, GAS, GASB Gassner, John, ed. ...

LIBRARY OF WORLD DRAMA. See FLOS Flores, Angel, ed. Spanish drama... GARZB Gassner, John, ed. Medieval and Tudor drama... GARZE Gassner, John, ed. 19th cent. Russian drama... GARZJ Gassner, John, ed. 20th cent. Russian drama... MACD MacAndrew, Andrew Robert, tr. 19th century Russian drama... MACE MacAndrew, Andrew Robert, tr. 20th century Russian drama

LIBR Library of universal literature... New York, Alden bros. [c1906] [701]p
Addison, J. Cato

LIC Lieberman, Samuel and Miller, Frank Justus, eds. and trs. Roman drama... New York, Bantam Books [1964] 376p
Plautus, T. Menaechmi twins
Plautus, T. Prisoners of war
Plautus, T. The rope

LIC (cont.)
Seneca, L. Medea
Seneca, L. Oedipus
Seneca, L. Phaedra
Terence, P. Adelphi
Terence, P. Phormio
Terence, P. The woman of Andros

LID Lid, Richard Wald and Bernd, Daniel, comps. Plays, classic and contemporary. Philadelphia, Lippincott, [1967] 623p
Chekhov, A. The cherry orchard
Etherege, G. The man of mode; or, Sir Fopling Flutter
Ibsen, H. Little Eyolf
Ionesco, E. Maid to marry
Molière, J. Don Juan
Shakespeare, W. The tragedy of Antony and Cleopatra
Shaw, G. The doctor's dilemma
Sophocles. Oedipus rex

LIE Lieder, Paul Robert; Lovett, Robert Morss and Root, Robert Kilburn, eds. British drama... Boston, Houghton Mifflin [c1929] 374p
Beaumont, F., and Fletcher, J. Philaster; or, Love lies a-bleeding
The Brome Abraham and Isaac
Congreve, W. The way of the world
Dryden, J. All for love; or, The world well lost
Everyman
Jonson, B. The alchemist
Marlowe, C. The tragical history of Dr. Faustus
The second shepherds' play
Sheridan, R. The school for scandal
Wilde, O. Lady Windermere's fan

LIED Lieder, Paul Robert; Lovett, Robert Morss and Root, Robert Kilburn, eds. British prose and poetry. Revised ed. Boston, Houghton Mifflin [c1938] 2v
Dryden, J. All for love 1
Jonson, B. Volpone 1
Marlowe, C. Dr. Faustus 1
Second shepherds' play 1
Sheridan, R. The school for scandal 1
Synge, J. The playboy of the western world 2
Wilde, O. Lady Windermere's fan 2

LIEE Lieder, Paul Robert; Lovett, Robert Morss and Root, Robert Kilburn, eds. British poetry and prose. Third edition... Boston, Houghton Mifflin [c1950] 2v
Dryden, J. All for love 1
Jonson, B. Alchemist 1
Marlowe, C. Dr. Faustus 1
The second shepherds' play 1
Sheridan, R. The school for scandal 1
Synge, J. Playboy of the western world 2
Wilde, O. Lady Windermere's fan 2

LIEF Lief, Leonard, and Light, James Forest, [eds]. The modern age; literature. 2d ed. New York, Holt, 1972. 744p
Feiffer, J. Little murders
Miller, A. A memory of two Mondays
O'Neill, E. Desire under the elms
Shaw, G. Major Barbara
Wilder, T. The skin of our teeth
Williams, T. Suddenly last summer

LIND Lind, Levi Robert, ed. Ten Greek plays in con-

temporary translations... Boston, Houghton Mifflin [c1957] 419p
Aeschylus. Agamemnon
Aeschylus. Prometheus bound
Aristophanes. Lysistrata
Euripides. Alcestis
Euripides. Andromache
Euripides. Bacchae
Euripides. Suppliants
Sophocles. Antigone
Sophocles. Oedipus rex
Sophocles. Philoctetes

THE LITERATURE OF ITALY, 1265-1907. See JOH Johnson, Rossiter, ed. An anthology of Italian authors from Cavalcanti to Fogazzaro...

LITT Litto, Fredric M., ed. Plays from Black Africa... New York, Hill and Wang, 1968. 316p
Clark, J. Song of a goat
Henshaw, J. The jewels of the shrine
Hutchinson, A. The rain-killers
Nkosi, L. The rhythm of violence
Ofori, H. The literary society
Sutherland, E. Edufa

LIU Liu, Jung-en, comp. and tr. Six Yuan plays. Harmondsworth, Middlesex, Penguin, 1972. 285p
Chêng, T. The soul of Ch'ien-nu leaves her body
Chi, C. The orphan of Chao
Kaan, H. The injustice done to Tou Ngo
Li, H. Chang boils the sea
Ma, C. Autumn in Han Palace
A stratagem of interlocking rings

LOC Locke, Alain Le Roy, and Montgomery, Gregory, eds. Plays of Negro life...New York, Harper, 1927. 430p
Bruce, R. Sahdji, an African ballet
Culbertson, E. Rackey
Duncan, T. The death dance
Green, P. In Abraham's bosom
Green, P. The no'count boy
Green, P. White dresses
Johnson, G. Plumes
Matheus, J. 'Cruiter
O'Neill, E. The dreamy kid
O'Neill, E. The Emperor Jones
Richardson, W. The broken banjo
Richardson, W. The flight of the natives
Rogers, J. Judge Lynch
Spence, E. The starter
Toomer, J. Balo
Torrence, R. The danse Calinda
Torrence, R. Granny Maumee
Torrence, R. The rider of dreams
White, L. The bird child
Wilson, F. Sugar cane

LOCK Locke, Louis Glenn; Gibson, William M., and Arms, George, eds. Introduction to literature... New York, Rinehart [c1948] 592p (Readings for liberal education, v2)
Euripides. Alcestis
Marlowe, C. Doctor Faustus
O'Neill, E. The Emperor Jones
Thurber, J., and Nugent, E. The male animal

LOCL Locke, Louis Glenn; Gibson, William M., and Arms, George, eds. Introduction to literature... Revised edition. New York, Rinehart [c1952] 749p (Readings for liberal education, v2)
Cocteau, J. The infernal machine

LOCL (cont.)
Ibsen, H. Hedda Gabler
Marlowe, C. The tragical history of Doctor Faustus
O'Neill, E. The long voyage home
Sophocles. Oedipus the king

LOCLA Locke, Louis Glenn; Gibson, William M., and Arms, George, eds. Introduction to literature. Third edition...New York, Rinehart [c1957] 864p (Readings for liberal education, v2)
Cocteau, J. The infernal machine
Ibsen, H. Hedda Gabler
Molière, J. The bourgeois gentleman
O'Neill, E. The long voyage home
Shaw, G. The devil's disciple
Sophocles. Oedipus the king
Synge, J. In the shadow of the glen

LOCLB Locke, Louis Glenn; Gibson, William and Arms, George, eds. Introduction to literature. Fourth edition...New York, Holt, Rinehart and Winston [c1962] (Readings for liberal education, v2)
Cocteau, J. The infernal machine
García Lorca, F. Blood wedding
Ibsen, H. Hedda Gabler
O'Neill, E. The long voyage home
Shaw, G. Candida
Sophocles. Oedipus the king

LOCM Locke, Louis Glenn; Kirby, John P., and Porter, M. E., eds. Literature of western civilization...New York, Ronald [c1952] 2v
Aeschylus. Agamemnon 1
Aristophanes. Lysistrata 1
Euripides. Medea 1
Goethe, J. Faust, pt. I 2
Ibsen, H. Rosmersholm 2
Molière, J. The misanthrope 2
Plautus, T. Amphitryon 1
Racine, J. Phaedra 2
Shakespeare, W. Hamlet 1
Vega Carpio, L. The king the greatest Alcalde 1
Sophocles. Oedipus the king 1

LOCR Lockert, Lacy, ed., and tr. The chief rivals of Corneille and Racine... Nashville, Vanderbilt University Press, c1956. 605p
Campistron, J. Andronicus
Corneille, T. The earl of Essex
Corneille, T. Laodice
Crebillon, P. Rhadamistus and Zenobia
Du Ryer, P. Saul
Du Ryer, P. Scaevola
Hermite, T. Mariamne
La Fosse, A. Manlius Capitolinus
Mairet, J. Sophonisba
Rotrou, J. Chosroes
Rotrou, J. Wenceshaus
Voltaire, F. Zaire

LOCU Lockert, Lacy, ed. and tr. More plays by rivals of Corneille and Racine... Nashville, Vanderbilt University Press, 1968. 694p
Boyer, C. Oropaste
Campistron, J. Tiridate
Corneille, T. Ariane
Corneille, T. Maximian
Corneille, T. Timocrate
Du Ryer, P. Esther
Hardy, A. Mariamne
Hermite, T. La mort de Seneque
Hermite, T. Osman
La Grange-Chancel. Ino et Mélicerte

Péchantré. Geta
Quinault, P. Astrate
Rotrou, J. Saint Genest

LOGG Loggins, Vernon, ed. Three great French plays ... Greenwich, Connecticut, Fawcett [c1961] 256p
Corneille, P. Polyeucte
Molière, J. The hypochrondriac
Racine, J. Phèdre

LON London omnibus, with an introduction by Carl Van Doren, Garden City, N.Y., Doubleday, Doran, 1932. v.p.
Coward, N. Private lives

LOND London, Ephraim, ed. The world of law; a treasury of great writing about and in the law, short stories, plays...New York, Simon and Schuster [1960] 2v
The farce of the worthy master 1
Mortimer, J. The dock brief 1
Rattigan, T. The Winslow boy 1

LOO Loomis, Roger Sherman and Clark, Donald Leman, eds. Modern English readings...New York, Farrar and Rinehart, 1934. 892p
Lawson, J. Success story
O'Neill, E. The moon of the Caribbees
Wilde, O. The importance of being earnest

LOOA Loomis, Roger Sherman, and Clark, Donald Leman, eds. Modern English readings. Rev. ed. ...New York, Farrar and Rinehart, 1936. 1074p
Anderson, M. Both your houses
Connelly, M. The green pastures
O'Neill, E. Beyond the horizon
Synge, J. Riders to the sea
Wilde, O. The importance of being earnest

LOOB Loomis, Roger Sherman, and Clark, Donald Leman, eds. Modern English readings. 3rd ed. ...New York, Farrar and Rinehart, 1939. 1147p
Anderson, M. Both your houses
Connelly, M. The green pastures
MacLeish, A. The fall of the city
O'Neill, E. Beyond the horizon
Synge, J. Riders to the sea

LOOC Loomis, Roger Sherman, and Clark, Donald Leman, eds. Modern English readings. 4th ed. ...New York, Farrar and Rinehart, 1942. 968p
Connelly, M. The green pastures
Hart, M., and Kaufman, G. You can't take it with you
MacLeish, A. The fall of the city
O'Neill, E. Beyond the horizon
Synge, J. Riders to the sea

LOOD Loomis, Roger Sherman, and Clark, Donald Leman, eds. Modern English readings. Fifth edition...New York, Rinehart [c1946] 1062p
Connelly, M. The green pastures
Corwin, N. Good heavens
Hart, M., and Kaufman, G. You can't take it with you
MacLeish, A. The Fall of the city

LOOD (cont.)
O'Neill, E. Beyond the horizon
Synge, J. Riders to the sea

LOOE Loomis, Roger Sherman, and Clark, Donald Leman, eds. Modern English readings. Sixth edition...New York, Rinehart [c1950] 1061p
Connelly, M. The green pastures
Hart, M., and Kaufman, G. You can't take it with you
MacLeish, A. The fall of the city
O'Neill, E. Beyond the horizon
Synge, J. Riders to the sea

LOOF Loomis, Roger Sherman; Clark, Donald Leman, and Middendorf, John Harlan, eds. Modern English readings. Seventh edition... New York, Rinehart [c1956] 1097p
Hart, M., and Kaufman, G. You can't take it with you
O'Neill, E. Beyond the horizon
Shaw, G. Arms and the man
Synge, J. Riders to the sea

LOOM Loomis, Roger Sherman and Wells, Henry Willis, eds. Representative medieval and Tudor plays, translated and modernized...New York, Sheed & Ward, 1942. 301p
The annunciation
Heywood, J. John, Tyb, and Sir John
Heywood, J. The pardoner and the friar
Hilarius. The miracle of Saint Nicholas and the image
La Vigne, A. The miracle of the blind man and the cripple
The miracle of Saint Nicholas and the school boys
The miracle of Saint Nicholas and the virgins
The mystery of the redemption
The second shepherds' play
The summoning of Everyman

LOR Lovell, Ernest James, and Pratt, Willis W., eds. Modern drama: An anthology of nine plays...Boston, Ginn [c1963] 425p
Anderson, M. The wingless victory
Duncan, R. The death of Satan
Euripides. Medea
Giraudoux, J. Electra
Ibsen, H. Hedda Gabler
Maugham, W. The constant wife
Miller, A. The crucible
O'Neill, E. A moon for the misbegotten
Shaw, G. Caesar and Cleopatra

LOV Lovett, Robert Morss, and Jones, Howard Mumford, eds. The college reader...Boston, Houghton Mifflin [c1936] 1099p
Archer, W. The green goddess
Sherriff, R. Journey's end

LOVR Lovrien, Marian; Potell, Herbert and Bostwich, Prudence, eds. Adventures in living...New York, Harcourt, Brace, 1955. 626p (Adventures in literature series)
Corwin, N. Ann Rutledge
Duffield, B. The lottery
Law, W. Indomitable blacksmith
Lindsay, H., and Crouse, R. Life with father
Martens, A. Blue beads
Richmond, S. Career for Ralph

LOW Lowe, Orton, ed. Our land and its literature... New York, Harper, 1936. 666p
Vollmer, L. Sun-up

LUCA Lucas, Frank Laurence, ed. and tr. Greek drama for everyman... London, J. M. Dent [1954] 454p
Aeschylus. Agamemnon
Aeschylus. Prometheus bound
Aristophanes. The clouds
Euripides. The bacchae
Euripides. Hippolytus
Sophocles. Antigone
Sophocles. Oedipus the king

LUCAB Lucas, Frank Laurence, ed. and tr. Greek drama for the common reader; reissued with corrections. London, Chatto, 1967. 459p
Aeschylus. Agamemnon
Aeschylus. Prometheus bound
Aristophanes. The clouds
Euripides. The bacchae
Euripides. Hippolytus
Sophocles. Antigone
Sophocles. Oedipus the king

LUCAF Lucas, Frank Laurence, ed. and tr. Greek tragedy and comedy. New York, Viking, 1968. 454p
Aeschylus. Agamemnon
Aeschylus. Prometheus bound
Aristophanes. The clouds
Euripides. The bacchae
Euripides. Hippolytus
Sophocles. Antigone
Sophocles. Oedipus the king

LUCAS, HARRIET MARCELLA. See PROD Prose and poetry for appreciation...

LUST Lustig, Theodore H., tr. Classical German drama... With an introduction by Victor Lange... New York, Bantam Books [c1963] 466p
Büchner, G. Danton's death
Goethe, J. Egmont
Kleist, H. The prince of Homburg
Lessing, G. Nathan the wise
Schiller, J. Mary Stuart

LYMAN, WILLIAM WHITTINGHAM. See TOD Today's literature...

LYK Lyons, Eugene, ed. ... Six Soviet plays... Boston, Houghton Mifflin, 1934. [469]p
Afinogenyev, A. Fear
Bulgakov, M. Days of the Turbins
Glebov, A. Inga
Katayev, V. Squaring the circle
Krishon, V. Bread
Pogodin, N. Tempo

LYO Lyons, John Coriden and Searles, Colbert, eds. Eight French classic plays ...New York, Holt [c1932] 609p
Corneille, P. Le cid
Corneille, P. Le menteur
Corneille, P. Polyeucte
Molière, J. Le misanthrope
Molière, J. Les précieuses ridicules
Molière, J. Le Tartuffe; ou L'imposteur
Racine, J. Andromaque
Racine, J. Phèdre

M

MACD MacAndrew, Andrew Robert, tr. 19th century Russian drama... New York, Bantam Books [1963] 342p (The library of world drama)
Gogol, N. The inspector general
Ostrovsky, A. The thunder-

MACD (cont.)
storm
Pushkin, A. The stone guest
Tolstoy, L. The power of darkness
Turgenev, I. A month in the country

MACE MacAndrew, Andrew Robert, tr. 20th century Russian drama. New York, Bantam Books [1963] 376p (The library of world drama)
Andreyev, L. He who gets slapped
Chekhov, A. The three sisters
Gorky, M. The lower depths
Mayakóvsky, V. The bathhouse
Olesha, Y. A list of assets

MACF MacDonald, J. W. and Saxton, J. C. W., comps. Four stages...New York, St. Martin's Press [1967, c1966] 398p
Ibsen, H. Pillars of society
Marlowe, C. Doctor Faustus
Miller, A. All my sons
Sophocles. Oedipus rex

MACG Macgowan, Kenneth, ed. Famous American plays of the 1920's...[New York, Dell, c1959] 511p (Laurel drama series)
Anderson, M., and Stallings, L. What price glory?
Barry, P. Holiday
Heyward, D., and Heyward, D. Porgy
Howard, S. They knew what they wanted
O'Neill, E. The moon of the Caribbees
Rice, E. Street scene

MACH Machiz, Herbert, ed. Artists' theatre: four plays ...New York, Grove [c1960] 224p
Abel, L. Absalom
Ashbery, J. The heroes
Merrill, J. The bait
O'Hara, F. Try! Try!

MACJ Mack, Maynard [and others], eds. The continental edition of world masterpieces...New York, W. W. Norton [c1962] 1971p
Aeschylus. Agamemnon
Euripides. Medea
Goethe, J. Faust, pts. 1 & 2
Ibsen, H. The wild duck
Molière, J. The bourgeois gentleman
Racine, J. Phaedra
Sophocles. King Oedipus

MACK Mack, Maynard, ed. ... The Augustans...New York, Prentice-Hall, 1950. 343p (English masterpieces, v5)
Gay, J. The beggar's opera

MACL Mack, Maynard [and others] eds. World masterpieces...New York, W. W. Norton [c1956] 2v
Aeschylus. Agamemnon 1
Euripides. Medea 1
Goethe, J. Faust, pts. 1 & 2 2
Ibsen, H. The wild duck 2
Molière, J. The bourgeois gentleman 2
Racine, J. Phaedra 2
Shakespeare, W. Hamlet, Prince of Denmark 1
Sophocles. King Oedipus 1
Synge, J. The playboy of the western world 2

MACM Mack, Maynard [and others] eds. World masterpieces...Rev. ed. New York, Norton [1965] 2v
Aeschylus. Agamemnon 1
Aeschylus. Prometheus bound 1
Aristophanes. Lysistrata 1

Brecht, B. The Caucasian chalk circle 2
Calderón de la Barca, P. Life is a dream 1
Eliot, T. Murder in the cathedral 2
Euripides. Medea 1
Euripides. Trojan women 1
Everyman 1
Goethe, J. Faust (abridged ed.) 2
Ibsen, H. The wild duck 2
Marlowe, C. The tragical history of the life and death of Doctor Faustus 1
Molière, J. Tartuffe; or, The imposter 2
Molina, T. The trickster of Seville and his guest of stone 1
Racine, J. Phaedra 2
Sartre, J. No exit 2
Shakespeare, W. Hamlet 1
Sophocles. Antigone 1
Sophocles. Oedipus at Colonus 1
Sophocles. Oedipus the king 1

MACN Mack, Maynard, and others, eds. World masterpieces. 3d ed. New York, Norton, 1973. 2v
Aeschylus. Agamemnon 1
Aristophanes. Lysistrata 1
Calderón de la Barca, P. Life is a dream 1
Chekhov, A. The cherry orchard 2
Euripides. Medea 1
Goethe, J. Faust, Part 1 2
Ibsen, H. The wild duck 2
Marlowe, C. The tragical history of the life and death of Doctor Faustus 1
Molière, J. Tartuffe 2
Pirandello, L. Henry IV 2
Racine, J. Phaedra 2
Sartre, J. No exit 2
Shakespeare, W. Hamlet, Prince of Denmark 1
Shaw, G. Saint Joan 2
Sophocles. Antigone 1
Sophocles. Oedipus tyrannus 1

MAGA Magarshack, David, tr. The storm, and other Russian plays... New York, Hill and Wang [c1960] 362p (Mermaid dramabook)
Chekhov, A. Uncle Vanya
Gogol, N. The government inspector
Gorky, M. The lower depths
Ostrovsky, A. The storm
Tolstoy, L. The power of darkness

MAK Malcolmson, Anne (Burnett), adapter. Miracle plays; seven medieval plays for modern players ... Boston, Houghton Mifflin [c1956, 1959] 142p
Abraham and Isaac
Herod and the magi
The nativity
Noah's flood
Saint Nicholas and the three scholars
The shepherds' play
Hilarius. The statue of Saint Nicholas

MALINE, JULIAN L. See PATM, PATP Patterns of literature... PROI Prose and poetry of America...

MALLON, WILFRED M. See PROI Prose and poetry of America...

MAL Malvern festival plays MCMXXXIII, arranged for production by H. K. Ayliff. With an introduction by Hugh Walpole and a preface by Sir Barry Jackson. London, Heath Cranton, 1933. 343p
The conversion of St. Paul
Dryden, J. All for love
Heywood, T. The fair maid of the west

MAL (cont.)
Jones, H. The dancing girl
Knowles, J. The love-chase
"Mr. S., master of arts."
Gammer Gurton's needle

MAN Mandel, Oscar, comp. and tr. Five comedies of medieval France. New York, Dutton, 1970. 158p
The chicken pie and the chocolate cake
Bodel, J. The play of Saint Nicholas
Adam de la Halle. The play of Robin and Marion
Peter Quill's shenanigans

MANO Mandel, Oscar, ed. The theatre of Don Juan; a collection of plays and views, 1630-1963... Lincoln, University of Nebraska Press, c1963. 731p
Don Juan and Don Pietro; or, The dead stone's banquet
Grabbe, C. Don Juan and Faust
Molière, J. Don Juan; or, The libertine
Molina, T. The playboy of Seville; or, Supper with a statue
Moncrieff, W. Giovanni in London; or, The libertine reclaimed
Ponte, L. The punished libertine; or, Don Giovanni
Rostand, E. The last night of Don Juan
Shadwell, T. The libertine
Zorrilla y Moral, J. Don Juan Tenorio

MANTLE, R. BURNS. See BES Best plays of 1894/1899... etc. See also TRE, TREA A treasury of the theatre...

MARNAU, FRED. See NEWR New road...

MAO Marowitz, Charles, ed. New American drama. Harmondsworth, Middlesex, Penguin, [1966] 203p
Albee, E. The American dream
Miller, A. Incident at Vichy
Richardson, J. Gallows humour
Schisgal, M. The typists

MAOC Marowitz, Charles, comp. Open space plays. Harmondsworth, Middlesex, Penguin, 1974. 310p
Burgess, J., and Marowitz, C. The Chicago conspiracy
Burns, A., and Marowitz, C. Palach
Herbert, J. Fortune and men's eyes
McGough, R. The puny little life show
Marowitz, C. An Othello

MAP Marriott, James William, ed. Great modern British plays... London, Harrap [1932] 1083p
Bennett, A., and Knoblock, E. Milestones
Berkeley, R. The white château
Besier, R. The virgin goddess
Brighouse, H. Hobson's choice
Chapin, H. The new morality
Coward, H. The young idea
Dane, C. A bill of divorcement
Dukes, A. The man with a load of mischief
Galsworthy, J. Strife
Gilbert, W. Pygmalion and Galatea
Hankin, St. J. The return of the prodigal
Jones, H. The liars
McEvoy, C. The likes of her
Maugham, W. The circle
Munro, C. At Mrs. Beam's

Pinero, A. Trelawny of the "Wells"
Robertson, T. Caste
Sutro, A. The walls of Jericho
Vane, S. Outward bound

MAS Massey, Vincent, ed. Canadian plays from Hart house theatre... Toronto, Macmillan, 1926-27. 2v
Aikins, C. The god of gods 2
Borsook, H. Three weddings of a hunchback 1
Cooke, B. The translation of John Snaith 1
Denison, M. Balm 1
Denison, M. Brothers in arms 1
Denison, M. The weather breeder 1
Mackay, I. The second lie 1
Mackay, L. The freedom of Jean Guichet 2
Osborne, M. The point of view 1
Reid, L. Trespassers 2
Scott, D. Pierre 1

MAST Masterpieces of Greek literature... Supervising editor John Henry Wright. Boston, Houghton Mifflin [c1902] 456p
Aeschylus. Prometheus bound
Euripides. Alcestis
Sophocles. Antigone

MASW Matlow, Myron, comp. The black crook, and other nineteenth century American plays. New York, Dutton, 1967. 511p
Barras, C. The black crook
Boker, G. Francesca da Rimini
Boucicault, D. The octoroon; or, Life in Louisiana
Herne, J. Margaret Fleming
Howard, B. Shenandoah
Mowatt, A. Fashion; or, Life in New York
Rip Van Winkle

MAT Matthews, Brander and Lieder, Paul Robert, eds. The chief British dramatists excluding Shakespeare ... Boston, Houghton Mifflin [c1924] 1084p
Beaumont, F., and Fletcher, J. Philaster; or, Love lies a-bleeding
Boucicault, D. London assurance
The Brome Abraham and Isaac
Bulwer-Lytton, E. Richelieu; or, The conspiracy
Congreve, W. The way of the world
Dryden, J. All for love; or, The world well lost
Farquhar, G. The beaux' stratagem
Gilbert, W. Pygmalion and Galatea
Goldsmith, O. She stoops to conquer; or, The mistakes of a night
Heywood, T. A woman killed with kindness
Jones, H. The liars
Jonson, B. Every man in his humour
Kyd, T. The Spanish tragedy; or, Hieronimo is mad again
Marlowe, C. The troublesome reign and lamentable death of Edward the second
Massinger, P. A new way to pay old debts
Otway, T. Venice preserved; or, A plot discovered
Pinero, A. The second Mrs. Tanqueray
Robertson, T. Caste
The second shepherds' play
Sheridan, R. The school for scandal
Udall, N. Ralph Roister Doister
Vanbrugh, J. The provoked wife
Webster, J. The Duchess of Malfi

MAT (cont.)
Wilde, O. Lady Windermere's fan
Wycherley, W. The plain dealer

MAU Matthews, Brander, ed. The chief European dramatists... Boston, Houghton Mifflin [c1916] 786p
Aeschylus. Agamemnon
Aristophanes. The frogs
Augier, E., and Sandeau, J. The son-in-law of M. Poirier
Beaumarchais, P. The barber of Seville
Calderón de la Barca, P. Life is a dream
Corneille, P. The cid
Dumas, A. fils. The outer edge of society
Euripides. Medea
Goethe, J. Goetz von Berlichingen
Goldoni, C. The mistress of the inn
Holberg, L. Rasmus Montanus
Hugo, V. Hernani
Ibsen, H. A doll's house
Lessing, G. Minna von Barnhelm
Molière, J. Tartuffe
Plautus, T. The captives
Racine, J. Phaedra
Schiller, J. William Tell
Sophocles. Oedipus the king
Terence, P. Phormio
Vega Carpio, L. de. The star of Seville

MATTHEWS, BRANDER. See also GREA Great plays (French and German)...

MCA McAvoy, William C., ed. Dramatic tragedy. New York, Webster Division, McGraw-Hill, 1971. 390p
Everyman
Ibsen, H. Ghosts
Marlowe, C. The tragical history of Doctor Faustus
Miller, A. All my sons
Shakespeare, W. The tragedy of Hamlet, Prince of Denmark
Sophocles. Oedipus rex
Williams, T. The glass menagerie

McCALLUM, JAMES DOW. See also HAP Harbrace omnibus...

MCCA McCallum, James Dow, ed. The college omnibus ...New York, Harcourt, Brace, 1933. 832p
O'Neill, E. The Emperor Jones
Synge, J. Riders to the sea

MCCB McCallum, James Dow, ed. The college omnibus ...New York, Harcourt, Brace [c1934] 982p
Galsworthy, J. Strife
O'Neill, E. The Emperor Jones
Synge, J. Riders to the sea

MCCD McCallum, James Dow, ed. The 1936 college omnibus...in collaboration with Marston Balch, Percy Marks...[and others]. New York, Harcourt, Brace [c1936] 1193p
Galsworthy, J. Strife
O'Neill, E. The Emperor Jones
Rostand, E. Cyrano de Bergerac

MCCF McCallum, James Dow, ed. The revised college omnibus...in collaboration with Marston Balch, Ralph P. Boas, Percy Marks [and others]. New York, Harcourt, Brace, 1939. 1258p
Galsworthy, J. Strife
MacLeish, A. Air raid

O'Neill, E. The Emperor Jones
Rostand, E. Cyrano de Bergerac

MCCG McCallum, James Dow, ed. The college omnibus. 6th edition... in collaboration with Marston Balch, Ralph P. Boas, Percy Marks, Benfield Pressey, Louis Untermeyer. New York, Harcourt, Brace [c1947] 1288p
Galsworthy, J. Strife
Nichols, R., and Browne, M. Wings over Europe
O'Neill, E. The Emperor Jones
Rostand, E. Cyrano de Bergerac

MCCL MacClelland, George Williams, and Baugh, Albert Croll, eds. Century types of English literature chronologically arranged... New York, Century, 1925. 1144p
Dekker, T. The shoemaker's holiday
Dryden, J. All for love
Sheridan, R. The school for scandal
Wilde, O. Lady Windermere's fan

MCCP McClintock, Marshall, ed. The Nobel prize treasury... Garden City, N.Y., Doubleday, 1948. 612p
Benavente, J. His widow's husband
Bjørnson, B. Between the battles
Echegaray, J. The street singer
Hauptmann, G. The sunken bell
Maeterlinck, M. Interior
O'Neill, E. Desire under the elms
Pirandello, L. Our lord of the ships
Yeats, W. The land of heart's desire

McCORKLE, J. N. See HAP Harbrace omnibus...

MCD McDermott, John Francis, ed. Modern plays... New York, Harcourt, Brace [c1932] 427p
Čapek, K. R.U.R.
Howard, S. They knew what they wanted
Hughes, H. Hell bent fer heaven
Ibsen, H. A doll's house
Maugham, W. The circle
Milne, A. Mr. Pim passes by
O'Neill, E. The Emperor Jones

MCDL McDowell, Tremaine, ed. America in literature ... New York, Crofts, 1944. 540p
Connelly, M. The green pastures
Wilder, T. Our town

MCDO McDowell, Tremaine, ed. The romantic triumph; American literature from 1830 to 1860... New York, Macmillan, 1933. 744p (American literature: a period anthology; Oscar Cargill, general editor. v2)
Boker, G. Francesca da Rimini

McGRAW, H. WARD. See PROB Prose and poetry for appreciation... PROF, PROG, PROH Prose and poetry of America... PROM, PRON Prose and poetry of England...

MCI McIlwraith, Archibald Kennedy, ed. Five Elizabe-

MCI (cont.)
than comedies... London, Oxford university press [1934] 308p (The world's classics)
Dekker, T. The shoemaker's holiday
Greene, R. Friar Bacon and Friar Bungay
Lyly, J. Campaspe
The merry devil of Edmonton
Peele, G. The old wives' tale

MCJ McIlwraith, Archibald Kennedy, ed. Five Elizabethan tragedies... London, Oxford university press [1938] 399p (The world's classics)
Arden of Feversham
Heywood, T. A woman killed with kindness
Kyd, T. The Spanish tragedy
Norton, T., and Sackville, T. Gorboduc
Seneca, L. Thyestes

MCK McIlwraith, Archibald Kennedy, ed. Five Stuart tragedies... London, Oxford university press [1953] 497p (The world's classics)
Beaumont, F., and Fletcher, J. The maid's tragedy
Chapman, G. Bussy D'Ambois
Ford, J. 'Tis a pity she's a whore
Massinger, P. The Roman actor
Webster, J. The Duchess of Malfi

MCKK MacKendrick, Paul, and Howe, Herbert M., eds. Classics in translation. Madison, Wisconsin. The university of Wisconsin press, 1952. 2v
Aeschylus. Agamemnon 1
Aristophanes. Frogs 1
Euripides. Medea 1
Plautus. The haunted house 2
Seneca. Medea 2
Sophocles. Antigone 1
Terence. Woman from Andros 2

MCKL McLean, Hugh and Vickery, Walter N., eds. and trs. The year of protest, 1956: An anthology of Soviet literary materials... New York, Random House [c1961] 269p
Alyoshin, S. Alone

MCKM McLeish, Kenneth, comp. and tr. The frogs and other Greek plays. Harlow, Longmans, 1970. 202p
Aeschylus. Prometheus bound
Aristophanes. The birds
Aristophanes. The frogs
Euripides. Medea

MCL McMahon, Agnes; Krauss, Franklin Brunell, and Carter, James Franklin, eds. Explorations in French literature... New York, Nelson, 1939. 538p
Labiche, E. Le voyage de Monsieur Perrichon

MCM MacMillan, Dougald, and Jones, Howard Mumford, eds. Plays of the restoration and eighteenth century ...New York, Holt, 1931. 896p
Addison, J. Cato
Cibber, G. Love's last shift
Colman, G., and Garrick, D. the clandestine marriage
Congreve, W. The way of the world
Cumberland, R. The West Indian
D'Avenant, W. The siege of Rhodes, pt. I
Dryden, J. All for love
Dryden, J., and Howard, R. The Indian queen
Etherege, G. The man of mode

Farquhar, G. The beaux' stratagem
Gay, J. The beggar's opera
Goldsmith, O. She stoops to conquer
Home, J. Douglas
Kelly, H. False delicacy
Kotzebue, A. The stranger
Lee, N. The rival queens
Lillo, G. The London merchant
Otway, T. Venice preserved
Rowe, N. The fair penitent
Shadwell, T. The squire of Alsatia
Sheridan, R. The school for scandal
Steele, R. The conscious lovers
Vanbrugh, J. The relapse
Villiers, G., and others. The rehearsal

MCMI MacMillan, Dougald and Jones, Howard Mumford, eds. Plays of the restoration and eighteenth century ... New York, Holt [1938] 961p
Addison, J. Cato
Cibber, C. Love's last shift
Colman, G., and Garrick, D. The clandestine marriage
Congreve, W. The way of the world
Cumberland, R. The West Indian
D'Avenant, W. The siege of Rhodes, pt. I
Dryden, J. All for love
Dryden, J., and Howard, R. The Indian queen
Etherege, G. The man of mode
Farquhar, G. The beaux' stratagem
Gay, J. The beggar's opera
Goldsmith, O. She stoops to conquer
Home, J. Douglas
Kelly, H. False delicacy
Kotzebue, A. The stranger
Lee, N. The rival queens
Lillo, G. The London merchant
Otway, T. Venice preserved
Rowe, N. The fair penitent
Shadwell, T. The squire of Alsatia
Sheridan, R. The school for scandal
Steele, R. The conscious lovers
Vanbrugh, J. The relapse
Villiers, G., and others. The rehearsal
Wycherley, W. The plain-dealer

MCMS McMillin, Scott, ed. Restoration and eighteenth-century comedy. New York, Norton, 1973. 565p
Congreve, W. The way of the world
Etherege, G. The man of mode
Sheridan, R. The school for scandal
Steele, R. The conscious lovers
Wycherley, W. The country wife

MCNA McNamee, Maurice B.; Cronin, James E., and Rogers, Joseph A., eds. Literary types and themes. New York, Rinehart [c1960] 705p
Anouilh, J. Antigone
Barrie, J. The twelve-pound look
Chayefsky, P. Marty
Miller, A. Death of a salesman
Williams, T. The glass menagerie

MCNB McNamee, Maurice Basil [and others], eds. Literary types and themes. 2d ed. New York, Rinehart and Winston, 1971. 773p
Albee, E. The American dream

MCNB (cont.)
Miller, A. Death of a salesman
Pirandello, L. Six characters in search of an author
Wilder, T. Pullman car Hiawatha
Williams, T. Glass menagerie

MCNI McNiff, William T., ed. The beginnings of English literature... New York, Macmillan [c1961] 198p
Everyman
Marlowe, C. The tragedy of Doctor Faustus

MEN Mendenhall, John Cooper, ed. English literature, 1650-1800... Chicago, Lippincott [c1940] 1166p
Congreve, W. The way of the world
Dryden, J. Aureng-zebe
Otway, T. Venice preserv'd

MERC Mercier, Vivian, and Greene, David H., eds. 1000 years of Irish prose. Part I. The literary revival... New York, Devin-Adair, 1952. 607p
O'Casey, S. The shadow of a gunman
Synge, J. In the shadow of the glen
Yeats, W. Cathleen ni Houlihan
Yeats, W. The resurrection

MERS Mersand, Joseph E., ed. Three comedies of American family life... New York, Washington Square Press [c1961] 314p
Kaufman, G., and Hart, M. You can't take it with you
Lindsay, H., and Crouse, R. Life with father
Van Druten, J. I remember mama

MERT Mersand, Joseph, ed. Three dramas of American individualism... New York, Washington Square Press [c1961] 266p
Anderson, M. High Tor
Lavery, E. The magnificent Yankee
Odets, C. Golden boy

MERU Mersand, Joseph E., ed. Three dramas of American realism... New York, Washington Square Press [c1961] 312p
Rice, E. Street scene
Saroyan, W. The time of your life
Sherwood, R. Idiot's delight

MERV Mersand, Joseph E., ed. Three plays about doctors ... New York, Washington Square Press [c1961] 294p
Howard, S., and DeKruif, P. Yellow jack
Ibsen, H. An enemy of the people
Kingsley, S. Men in white

MERW Mersand, Joseph E., ed. Three plays about marriage... New York, Washington Square Press [c1962] 298p
Barry, P. Holiday
Howard, S. They knew what they wanted
Kelly, G. Craig's wife

MESE Meserve, Walter J., Jr., and Meserve, Ruth I., eds. Modern drama from Communist China. New York, New York University Press, 1970. 368p
Han-ching, K. Snow in midsummer
Hsun, L. The passer-by
Ou-hung, W. and Chia, A. The red lantern
Pao-Hua, C. and Yi-ping, C. Yesterday

Seh, S., To, F., Yung, M. and Chi-huang, L. Letters from the south
Sheh, L. Dragon beard ditch
Teh-yao, J. Magic aster
Yi, T. and Ching-chih, H. The white haired girl
Yu, S. The women's representative

MESERVE, WALTER J. See AMPA America's lost plays, v21, edited by Walter J. Meserve and William R. Reardon

MESS Messner, Nancy Shingler [and others], comps. Collection: literature for the seventies. Lexington, Mass., Heath, 1972. 915p
Aristophanes. Lysistrata
Bermange, B. Scenes from family life
Chekhov, A. Uncle Vanya
Ibsen, H. An enemy of the people
Roemer, M. and Young, R. Nothing but a man
Shakespeare, W. Othello
Williams, T. Suddenly last summer

MIJ Miller, Edwin Lillie, ed. Explorations in literature ... Chicago, Lippincott [c1933-34] 2v
Gilbert, W. The mikado 2
Shakespeare, W. Macbeth 2

MIJA Miller, Edwin Lillie, ed. Explorations in literature ... Rev. ed. ... Chicago, Lippincott [c1937-38] 2v
O'Neill, E. The Emperor Jones 1
Shakespeare, W. Macbeth 2
Tompkins, F. Sham 1

MIJB Miller, James Edwin and Slate, Bernice, comps. The dimensions of literature... New York, Random House [1967] 808p
Brecht, B. The Caucasian chalk circle
O'Neill, E. In the zone
Shaw, G. Arms and the man
Sophocles. Oedipus rex

MIJE Miller, James Edwin [and others], comps. Translations from the French... Glenview, Ill., Scott, Foresman, 1971. 402p
Anouilh, J. Antigone
Cocteau, J. The Eiffel Tower wedding party
Duras, M. The rivers and forests
Giraudoux, J. The Apollo of Bellac
Molière, J. The forced marriage

MIJY Miller, Jordan Yale, ed. American dramatic literature... New York, McGraw-Hill, 1961. 641p
Behrman, S. Biography
Chase, M. Harvey
Haines, W. Command decision
Hellman, L. The little foxes
Heyward, D., and Heyward, D. Porgy
McCullers, C. The member of the wedding
Miller, A. The crucible
O'Neill, E. Desire under the elms
Thurber, J., and Nugent, E. The male animal
Williams, T. Camino real

MIK Miller, Marion Mills, ed. The classics, Greek & Latin... New York, V. Parke [c1909-10] 15v
Aeschylus. Prometheus bound 7
Aristophanes. The clouds 7
Euripides. Medea 7
Plautus, T. Captivi 8
Plautus, T. Menaechmi 8

MIK (cont.)
Plautus, T. Miles gloriosus 8
Seneca, L. The phaedra; or, Hippolytus 8
Sophocles. Antigone 7
Terence. Adelphi 8
Terence. Heautonimorumenos 8

MIKE Miller, Perry [and others], eds. Major writers of America...New York, Harcourt, Brace & World [c1962] 2v
O'Neill, E. The iceman cometh 2

MIL Millett, Fred Benjamin, and Bentley, Gerald Eades, eds. The play's the thing ...New York, Appleton-Century [c1936] 571p
Belasco, D. The return of Peter Grimm
Chekhov, A. Uncle Vanya
Chester play of the deluge
Congreve, W. Love for love
Cumberland, W. The West Indian
Dryden, J. All for love
Euripides. Hippolytus
Gregory, I. Hyacinth Halvey
Howard, S. Ned McCobb's daughter
Ibsen, H. Ghosts
Maeterlinck, M. Interior
Marlowe, C. Doctor Faustus
Molière, J. The misanthrope
O'Neill, E. The hairy ape
Plautus, T. The haunted house
Racine, J. Phaedra
Rostand, E. Cyrano de Bergerac
Shakespeare, W. Antony and Cleopatra
Shakespeare, W. Twelfth night
Sophocles. Oedipus, king of Thebes
Strong, A. The drums of Oude

MILL Millett, Fred Benjamin. Reading drama; a method of analysis with selections for study...New York, Harper [c1950] 252p
Barrie, J. The will
O'Neill, E. Beyond the horizon
Schnitzler, A. A farewell supper
Synge, J. Riders to the sea
Wilder, T. The long Christmas dinner
Yeats, W. Cathleen ni Houlihan

MIN Minor Elizabethan drama ...London, Dent [1913] 2v (Everyman's library)
Arden of Feversham 1
Greene, R. Friar Bacon and Friar Bungay 2
Greene, R. James the fourth 2
Kyd, T. The Spanish tragedy 1
Lyly, J. Endimion 2
Norton, T., and Sackville, T. (Lord Buckhurst) Gorboduc 1
Peele, G. David and Bethsabe 1
Peele, G. The old wives' tale 2
Udall, N. Ralph Roister Doister 2

MIO Minor Elizabethan drama ...London, Dent [1939] 2v (Everyman's library)
Arden of Feversham 1
Greene, R. Friar Bacon and Friar Bungay 2
Greene, R. James the fourth 2
Kyd, T. The Spanish tragedy 1
Lyly, J. Endimion 2
Norton, T., and Sackville, T. (Lord Buckhurst) Gorboduc 1
Peele, G. David and Bethsabe 1

Peele, G. The old wives' tale 2
Preston, T. Cambyses 1
Udall, N. Ralph Roister Doister 2

MOD Modern plays...London, Dent [1937] 354p (Everyman's library)
Bennett, A., and Knoblock, E. Milestones
Coward, N. Hay fever
Maugham, W. For services rendered
Milne, A. The Dover road
Sherriff, R. Journey's end

MODERN ENGLISH DRAMA. See HARC Harvard classics, v18

MODS Modern Scandinavian plays...New York, Liveright [c1954] 366p
Kielland, T. Queen Margaret of Norway
Munk, K. Egelykke
Strindberg, A. The great highway
Sveinbjörnsson, T. Bishop Jón Arason

MOL Mondala; literature for critical analysis [by] Wilfred L. Guerin [and others], eds. New York, Harper and Row, 1970. 766p
Miller, A. A view from the bridge
Shakespeare, W. Othello
Sophocles. Oedipus the King

MON Montague, Gene and Henshaw, Marjorie, comps. The experience of literature ...Englewood Cliffs, N.J., Prentice-Hall [1966] 404p
Shakespeare, W. Othello, the Moor of Venice
Sheridan, R. The school for scandal
Sophocles. Antigone
Wilde, O. The importance of being earnest
Williams, T. The glass menagerie

MONA Montague, Gene; Henshaw, Marjorie and Salerno, Nicholas A., comps. The experience of literature...2d ed. Englewood Cliffs, N.J., Prentice-Hall [1970] 803p
Hansberry, L. A raisin in the sun
Shakespeare, W. Hamlet
Sophocles. Antigone
Williams, T. The glass menagerie

MONR Moody, Richard, ed. Dramas from the American theatre, 1762-1909. Cleveland, World, [c1966] 873p (New World literature series, v1)
Aiken, G. Uncle Tom's cabin
Bird, R. The gladiator
Boker, G. Francesca da Rimini
Brougham, J. Po-ca-hon-tas
Burk, J. Bunker-Hill
Dunlap, W. The glory of Columbia
Dunlap, W. A trip to Niagara
Fitch, C. The city
Harrigan, E. The Mulligan guard ball
Herne, J. Shore acres
Hopkinson, F. A dialogue and ode
Howard, B. Shenandoah
Howells, W. A letter of introduction
Hoyt, C. A temperance town
McCloskey, J. Across the continent
Minstrel show
Mitchell, L. The New York idea
Moody, W. The great divide
Mowatt, A. Fashion
Munford, R. The candidates
Noah, M. She would be a soldier
Smith, J. A dialogue between an Englishman and an Indian

Smith, J. A little teatable chitchat
Smith. W. The drunkard
Stone, J. Metamora
Tyler, R. The contrast
Woodworth, S. The forest rose

MONV Moore, Harry Thornton, ed. Elizabethan age...[N.Y., Dell, 1965] 544p
Arden of Feversham
Dekker, T. The shoemaker's holiday
Marlowe, C. The tragical history of Doctor Faustus

MOO Moore, John Robert, ed. Representative English dramas... Boston, Ginn [c1929] 461p
Dryden, J. All for love
Everyman
Goldsmith, O. She stoops to conquer
Marlowe, C. The tragical history of Doctor Faustus
Sheridan, R. The school for scandal
Wilde, O. Lady Windermere's fan

MOR Morgan, Arthur Eustace, comp. English plays, 1660-1820... New York, Harper, 1935. 1157p
Addison, J. Cato
Buckstone, J. Luke, the labourer
Colman, G., and Garrick, D. The clandestine marriage
Congreve, W. The way of the world
Cumberland, R. The West Indian
Dryden, J. All for love; or, The world well lost
Dryden, J. Almanzor and Almahide; or, The conquest of Granada by the Spaniards
Etherege, G. The man of mode; or, Sir Fopling Flutter
Farquhar, G. The beaux' stratagem
Foote, S. The mayor of Garret
Gay, J. The beggar's opera
Goldsmith, O. She stoops to conquer; or, The mistakes of a night
Hoadly, B. The suspicious husband
Home, J. Douglas
Lillo, G. The London merchant
Morton, T. Speed the plough
Murphy, A. All in the wrong
Otway, T. Venice preserv'd; or, A plot discover'd
Reynolds, F. The dramatist; or, Stop him who can!
Shadwell, T. Bury-fair
Sheridan, R. The rivals
Steele, R. The conscious lovers
Townley, J. High life below the stairs
Vanbrugh, J. The relapse; or, Virtue in danger
Wycherley, W. The plain-dealer

MORR Morrell, Janet M., ed. Four English comedies of the 17th and 18th centuries ... Baltimore, Penguin [Harmondsworth, Middlesex, 1950,...1962] 414p
Congreve, W. The way of the world
Goldsmith, O. She stoops to conquer; or, The mistakes of a night
Jonson, B. Volpone; or, The fox
Sheridan, R. The school for scandal

MORRIS, ALTON CHESTER. See also WISD, WISE, WISF Wise, Jacob Hooper [and others] eds. College English...

MORT Morris, Alton Chester; Walker, Biron; Bradshaw, Philip; Hodges, John C. and Whitten, Mary E., eds. College English: the first year

... 4th ed. New York, Harcourt, Brace and World [1964] 944p
Hughes, R. The sister's tragedy
O'Casey, S. Red roses for me
Shaw, G. Caesar and Cleopatra
Sophocles. Antigone
Strindberg, A. The stronger

MORV Morris, Alton Chester; Walker, Biron; Bradshaw, Philip; Hodges, John C. and Whitten, Mary E., eds. College English: the first year ... 5th ed. New York, Harcourt, Brace and World [1968] 957p
Anouilh, J. Becket; or, The honor of God
Miller, A. The crucible
Sophocles. Antigone
Strindberg, A. The stronger
Synge, J. The playboy of the western world

MORW Morris, Alton Chester; Walker, Biron; Bradshaw, Philip; Hodges, John C. and Whitten, Mary E., eds. College English: the first year... 6th ed. New York, Harcourt Brace Jovanovich, 1973. 878p
Camus, A. Caligula
Miller, A. The crucible
Sophocles. Antigone
Strindberg, A. The stronger
Synge, J. The playboy of the western world

MORX Morris, Alton Chester; Walker, Biron and Bradshaw, Philip, comps. Imaginative literature; fiction, drama, poetry... N.Y., Harcourt, Brace and World [1968] 353p
Anouilh, J. Becket; or, The honor of God
Miller, A. The crucible
Sophocles. Antigone
Synge, J. The playboy of the western world

MOS Moscow art theatre series of Russian plays, ed. by Oliver M. Sayler... New York, Brentano [c1923] v.p.
Chekhov, A. The cherry orchard
Chekhov, A. The three sisters
Chekhov, A. Uncle Vanya
Gorky, M. The lower depths
Tolstoi, A. Tsar Fyodor Ivanovitch

MOSA Moscow art theatre series of Russian plays, direction of Morris Gest, ed. by Oliver M. Sayler. [2nd series] New York, Brentano [c1923] v.p.
Chekhov, A. Ivanoff
Dostoievsky, F. The brothers Karamazoff
Goldoni, C. The mistress of the inn
Ibsen, H. An enemy of the people
Ostrovsky, A. Enough stupidity in every wise man

MOSE Moses, Montrose Jonas, ed. British plays from the restoration to 1820... Boston, Little, Brown, 1929. 2v
Cibber, C. The careless husband 1
Colman, G., and Garrick, D. The clandestine marriage 2
Congreve, W. The way of the world 1
Cumberland, R. The fashionable lover 2
Dryden, J. The Spanish Fryar; or, The double discovery 1
Etherege, G. The man of mode; or, Sir Fopling Flutter 1
Farquhar, G. The beaux' stratagem 2
Gay, J. The beggar's opera 2
Goldsmith, O. She stoops to conquer; or, The mistakes of a night 2
Home, J. Douglas 2

Otway, T. Venice preserv'd; or, A plot discover'd 1
Rowe, N. Jane Shore 2
Shelley, P. The Cenci 2
Sheridan, R. The school for scandal 2
Steele, R. The conscious lovers 1
Vanbrugh, J. The provok'd wife 1
Villiers, G. The rehearsal 1
Wycherley, W. The plain-dealer 1

MOSG Moses, Montrose Jonas, ed. Dramas of modernism and their forerunners... Boston, Little Brown, 1931. 741p
Andreyev, L. He who gets slapped
Čapek, K., and Čapek, J. Adam the creator
Chekhov, A. The cherry orchard
Gorky, M. Night's lodging (The lower depths)
Howard, S. The silver cord
Kaiser, G. From morn to midnight
Kelly, G. Craig's wife
Lenormand, H. The dream doctor
Maugham, W. The circle
Milne, A. The truth about Blayds
Molnár, F. Liliom
Nichols, R., and Browne, M. Wings over Europe
O'Neill, E. Desire under the elms
Pirandello, L. Right you are! (If you think so)
Strindberg, J. There are crimes and crimes
Toller, E. The machine-wreckers

MOSH Moses, Montrose Jonas and Campbell, Oscar James, eds. Dramas of modernism and their forerunners...Rev. ed. ...Boston, Little, Brown, 1941. 946p
Anderson, M. Winterset
Andreyev, L. He who gets slapped
Čapek, K., and Čapek, J. Adam the creator
Carroll, P. Shadow and substance
Chekhov, A. The cherry orchard
Gorky, M. Night's lodging (The lower depths)
Howard, S. The silver cord
Kaiser, G. From morn to midnight
Kelly, G. Craig's wife
Lenormand, H. The dream doctor
Maugham, W. The circle
Milne, A. The truth about Blayds
Molnár, F. Liliom
Nichols, R., and Browne, M. Wings over Europe
Odets, C. Golden boy
O'Neill, E. Desire under the elms
Pirandello, L. Right you are! (If you think so)
Sherwood, R. Idiot's delight
Strindberg, J. There are crimes and crimes
Toller, E. The machine-wreckers

MOSJ Moses, Montrose Jonas, ed. Representative American dramas, national and local...Boston, Little, Brown, 1926. 681p
Belasco, D. The girl of the golden west
Crothers, R. Nice people
Davis, O. The detour
Fitch, C. The city
Forbes, J. The famous Mrs. Fair
Hoyt, C. A Texas steer
Kaufman, G., and Connelly, M. Dulcy
Kelly, G. The show-off
MacKaye, P. The scarecrow
Megrue, R., and Hackett, W. It pays to advertise
O'Neill, E. The Emperor Jones

Peabody, J. The piper
Rice, E. The adding machine
Smith, H. Mrs. Bumpstead-Leigh
Thomas, A. The witching hour

MOSK Moses, Montrose Jonas, ed. Representative American dramas, national and local...Rev. ed. Boston, Little, Brown, 1933. 890p
Barry, P. Holiday
Behrman, S. The second man
Belasco, D. The girl of the golden west
Connelly, M. The green pastures
Crothers, R. Nice people
Davis, O. The detour
Fitch, C. The city
Forbes, J. The famous Mrs. Fair
Howard, S. Lucky Sam McCarver
Hoyt, C. A Texas steer
Kaufman, G., and Connelly, M. Dulcy
Kelly, G. The show-off
MacKaye, P. The scarecrow
Megrue, R., and Hackett, W. It pays to advertise
O'Neill, E. The Emperor Jones
Peabody, J. The piper
Rice, E. The adding machine
Smith, H. Mrs. Bumpstead-Leigh
Thomas, A. The witching hour

MOSL Moses, Montrose Jonas and Krutch, Joseph Wood, eds. Representative American dramas, national and local...Rev. and brought up-to-date...Boston, Little, Brown, 1941. 1041p
Anderson, M. The masque of kings
Barry, P. Holiday
Behrman, S. The second man
Belasco, D. The girl of the golden west
Connelly, M. The green pastures
Crothers, R. Nice people
Davis, O. The detour
Fitch, C. The city
Forbes, J. The famous Mrs. Fair
Howard, S. Lucky Sam McCarver
Hoyt, C. A Texas steer
Kaufman, G., and Connelly, M. Dulcy
Kelly, G. The show-off
MacKaye, P. The scarecrow
Megrue, R., and Hackett, W. It pays to advertise
Odets, C. Awake and sing
O'Neill, E. The Emperor Jones
Peabody, J. The piper
Rice, E. The adding machine
Sherwood, R. The petrified forest
Smith, H. Mrs. Bumpstead-Leigh
Thomas, A. The witching hour

MOSN Moses, Montrose Jonas, ed. Representative British dramas, Victorian and modern... Boston, Little, Brown, 1918. 861p
Barker, G. The Madras house
Boucicault, D. London assurance
Browning, R. A blot in the 'scutcheon
Bulwer-Lytton, E. Richelieu; or, The conspiracy
Colum, P. Thomas Muskerry
Dunsany, E. The gods of the mountain
Galsworthy, J. The silver box
Gilbert, W. H.M.S. Pinafore; or, The lass that loved a sailor
Gregory, I. The workhouse ward
Hankin, St. J. The Cassilis engagement
Jerrold, D. Black-ey'd Susan; or, All in the downs
Jones, H. The masqueraders
Knowles, J. Virginius
Masefield, J. The tragedy of Pompey the Great
Pinero, A. The gay Lord Quex
Robertson, T. Caste

Synge, J. Riders to the sea
Taylor, T. The ticket-of-leave man
Tennyson, A. Becket
Wilde, O. The importance of being earnest
Yeats, W. Cathleen ni Houlihan

MOSO Moses, Montrose Jonas, ed. Representative British dramas, Victorian and modern. New rev. ed. ...Boston, Little, Brown, 1931. 996p
Boucicault, D. London assurance
Browning, R. A blot in the 'scutcheon
Bulwer-Lytton, E. Richelieu; or, The conspiracy
Coward, N. Easy virtue
Dane, C. A bill of divorcement
Dunsany, E. The gods of the mountain
Galsworthy, J. The silver box
Gilbert, W. H.M.S. Pinafore; or, The lass that loved a sailor
Granville-Barker, H. The Madras house
Gregory, I. The workhouse ward
Hankin, St. J. The Cassilis engagement
Jerrold, D. Black-ey'd Susan; or, All in the downs
Jones, H. The masqueraders
Knowles, J. Virginius
Maugham, W. Our betters
Monkhouse, A. First blood
Munro, C. At Mrs. Beam's
Pinero, A. The gay Lord Quex
Robertson, T. Caste
Synge, J. Riders to the sea
Taylor, T. The ticket-of-leave man
Wilde, O. The importance of being earnest
Yeats, W. Cathleen ni Houlihan

MOSQ Moses, Montrose Jonas, ed. Representative continental dramas, revolutionary and transitional...Boston, Little, Brown, 1924. 688p
Andreyeff, L. The life of man
Annunzio, G. d'. The daughter of Jorio
Becque, H. The vultures
Benavente y Martínez, J. The bonds of interest
Chekhov, A. The sea-gull
Donnay, M. Lovers
Giacosa, G. Like falling leaves
Hauptmann, G. The sunken bell
Ibsen, H. The wild duck
Maeterlinck, M. Monna Vanna
Nirdlinger, C. The world and his wife
Rostand, E. Cyrano de Bergerac
Schnitzler, A. The lonely way
Sudermann, H. The fires of St. John
Verhaeren, E. The dawn

MOSS Moses, Montrose Jonas, ed. Representative plays by American dramatists... New York, Dutton, 1918-25. 3v
Aiken, G. Uncle Tom's cabin 2
Barker, J. The Indian princess; or, La belle sauvage 1
Bateman, Mrs. S. Self 2
Belasco, D. The return of Peter Grimm 3
Boker, G. Francesca da Rimini 3
Brackenridge, H. The battle of Bunkershill 1
Brown, D. Sertorius; or, The Roman patriot 2
Bunce, O. Love in '76 3
Burke, C. Rip Van Winkle 3
Conrad, R. Jack Cade 2

Dunlap, W. André 1
Fitch, C. The moth and the flame 3
Godfrey, T. The prince of Parthia 1
Howard, B. Shenandoah 3
Hutton, J. Fashionable follies 2
Jones, J. The people's lawyer 2
Leacock, J. The fall of British tyranny; or, American liberty 1
Low, S. The politician outwitted 1
MacKaye, S. Paul Kauvar; or, Anarchy 3
Mitchell, L. The New York idea 3
Mowatt, Mrs. A. Fashion 2
Noah, M. She would be a soldier; or, The plains of Chippewa 1
Payne, J. Brutus; or, The fall of Tarquin 2
Rogers, R. Ponteach; or, The savages of America 1
Tayleure, C. Horse-shoe Robinson 2
Thomas, A. In Mizzoura 3
Tyler, R. The contrast 1
Walter, E. The easiest way 3
Warren, Mrs. M. The group 1
Willis, N. Tortesa, the usurer 2

MUMFORD, LEWIS. See AME American caravan...

MURP Murphy, Charles T.; Guinagh, Kevin and Oates, Whitney J., eds. Greek and Roman classics in translation... New York, Longmans, Green [c1947] 1052p
Aeschylus. Prometheus bound
Aristophanes. The clouds
Euripides. Hippolytus
Sophocles. Oedipus the king

MURRAY, GILBERT. See TEN Ten Greek plays...

MYB My best play... London, Faber & Faber [1934] 590p
Bax, C. The Venetian
Coward, N. Hay fever
Dane, C. Granite
Maugham, W. The circle
Milne, A. Success
Munro, C. The rumour
Robinson, L. The whiteheaded boy
Van Druten, J. After all

N

NAGE Nagelberg, Munjou Moses. Drama in our time... New York, Harcourt, Brace [c1948] 478p
Arent, A. One-third of a nation
Čapek, K. R.U.R.
Corwin, N. El Capitan and the corporal
Hellman, L. Watch on the Rhine
Howard, S. Yellow Jack
Saroyan, W. The human comedy
Sherwood, R. Abe Lincoln in Illinois
Wilder, T. Our town

NATHAN, GEORGE JEAN. See CRIT The Critics' prize plays... FIG Five great modern Irish plays... WORP World's great plays...

NEI Neilson, William Allan, ed. The chief Elizabethan dramatists, excluding Shakespeare... Boston, Houghton Mifflin [1911] 878p
Beaumont, F., and Fletcher, J. The knight of the burn-

NEI (cont.)
ing pestle
Beaumont, F., and Fletcher, J. The maid's tragedy
Beaumont, F., and Fletcher, J. Philaster
Chapman, G. Bussy D'Ambois
Dekker, T. The honest whore, pt. I
Dekker, T. The honest whore, pt. II
Dekker, T. The shoekamer's holiday
Fletcher, J. The faithful shepherdess
Fletcher, J. The wild-goose chase
Ford, J. The broken heart
Greene, R. The honourable history of Friar Bacon and Friar Bungay
Heywood, T. A woman killed with kindness
Jonson, B. The alchemist
Jonson, B. Every man in his humour
Jonson, B. Sejanus, his fall
Jonson, B. Volpone; or, The fox
Kyd, T. The Spanish tragedy; or, Hieronimo is mad again
Lyly, J. Endymion, the man in the moon
Marlowe, C. The Jew of Malta
Marlowe, C. Tamburlaine, pt. I
Marlowe, C. The tragical history of Doctor Faustus
Marlowe, C. The troublesome reign and lamentable death of Edward the second
Marston, J. The malcontent
Massinger, P. A new way to pay old debts
Middleton, T. A trick to catch the old one
Middleton, T., and Rowley, W. The changeling
Peele, G. The old wives' tale
Shirley, J. The cardinal
Shirley, J. The lady of pleasure
Webster, J. The Duchess of Malfi

NELS Nelson, John Herbert and Cargill, Oscar, eds. Contemporary trends; American literature since 1900. Revised edition. New York, Macmillan [c1949] 1263p (American literature; a period anthology. [v4] Oscar Cargill, gen. ed.)
Anderson, M. Winterset
MacLeish, A. The fall of the city
O'Neill, E. Bound east for Cardiff
O'Neill, E. Lazarus laughed

NER Nero (Tragedy)...Nero & other plays; edited...by Herbert P. Horne; Havelock Ellis; Arthur Symons and A. Wilson Verity... New York, Scribner [1904-48] 488p
Day, J. Humour out of breath
Day, J. The parliament of bees
Field, N. Amends for ladies
Field, N. Woman is a weathercock
Nero
Porter, H. The two angry women of Abington

NES Nethercot, Arthur Hobart [and others], eds. Elizabethan plays. New York, Holt, 1971. 845p
Chapman, G. Bussy d'Ambois
Dekker, T. The honest whore, pt. I
Dekker, T. The shoemaker's holiday
Gascoigne, G. Supposes
Greene, R. George A.

Greene, the pinner of Wakefield
Greene, R. The honorable history of Friar Bacon and Friar Bungay
Heywood, T. A woman killed with kindness
Kyd, T. The Spanish tragedy
Lyly, J. Endymion
Marlowe, C. Attowell's jig (Francis' new jig)
Marlowe, C. Edward the second
Marlowe, C. Doctor Faustus
Marlowe, C. Mucedorus
Marlowe, C. Tamburlaine, pt. I
Marston, J. The malcontent
Norton, T. and Sackville, T. Gorboduc
Peele, G. The arraignment of Paris
Peele, G. The old wives' tale
Preston, T. Cambises, King of Persia
Stevenson, W. Gammer Gurton's needle
Udall, N. Ralph Roister Doister

NET Nettleton, George Henry and Case, Arthur Ellicott, eds. British dramatists from Dryden to Sheridan... Boston, Houghton Mifflin [c1939] 957p
Addison, J. Cato
Buckingham, G. The rehearsal
Cibber, C. The careless husband
Colman, G. The jealous wife
Congreve, W. The way of the world
Cumberland, R. The West Indian
Dryden, J. All for love; or, The world well lost
Dryden, J. The conquest of Granada by the Spaniards, pt. I
Etherege, G. The man of mode; or, Sir Fopling Flutter
Farquhar, G. The beaux' stratagem
Fielding, H. Tom Thumb
Garrick, D. The lying valet
Gay, J. The beggar's opera
Goldsmith, O. She stoops to conquer; or, The mistakes of a night
Home, J. Douglas
Lillo, G. The London merchant; or, The history of George Barnwell
Otway, T. Venice preserved; or, A plot discovered
Rowe, N. The tragedy of Jane Shore
Sheridan, R. The critic; or, A tragedy rehearsed
Sheridan, R. The rivals
Sheridan, R. The school for scandal
Steele, R. The conscious lovers
Vanbrugh, J. The relapse; or, Virtue in danger
Wycherley, W. The plain dealer

NEVI Neville, Mary Anthony and Herzberg, Max J., eds. This England... Chicago, Rand McNally [c1956] 786p
Shakespeare, W. Macbeth
Wilde, O. The importance of being earnest

NEW AMERICAN CARAVAN. 1929. See AME American caravan, v3

NEW AMERICAN PLAYS. See NEWA New American plays. Edited by Robert Willoughby Corrigan (v1) and William M. Hoffman (v2, v3, v4)

NEW CARAVAN. 1936. See AME American caravan. v5

NEW DIRECTIONS. See NEW New directions in prose and poetry... James Laughlin, ed. See also PLAA Playbook...; SPC Spearhead...

NEW New directions in prose and poetry... James Laughlin, ed. Norfolk, Ct., New Directions, 1936-1955. 15v

Brecht, B. The exception and the rule 55
Brecht, B. Mother courage 41
Büchner, G. Woyzeck 50
Cocteau, J. Les maries de la Tour Eiffel 37
García Lorca, F. In the frame of Don Cristóbal 44
Goodman, P. The tower of Babel 40
Hutchins, M. The case of Astrolable 44
Hutchins, M. A play about Joseph Smith, jr. 44
Hutchins, M. The wandering Jew 51
Moss, H. No strings attached 44
Ortiz de Montellano, B. Salome's head 44
Reid, B. The fourth room 44
Rexroth, K. Iphigenia at Aulis 44
Rexroth, K. Phaedra 44
Schwartz, D. Paris and Helen 41
Second, L. Apollinaris 42
Stein, G. Daniel Webster, eighteen in America 37
Williams, T. Dos ranchos; or, The purification 44
Williams, W. Trial horse no. 1: Many loves 42

NEWA New American plays. Edited by Robert Willoughby Corrigan (v1) and William H. Hoffman (v2, v3, v4). New York, Hill and Wang, 1965-71. 4v

Barlow, A. Mr. Biggs 1
Bullins, E. The electronic nigger 3
Bush, J. French gray 2
Cameron, K. The hundred and first 1
Dey, J. Passacaglia 2
Estrin, M. An American playground sampler 3
Eyen, T. The white whore and the bit player 2
Fredericks, C. A summer ghost 1
Harris, T. Always with love 3
Heide, R. At war with the mongols 4
Herndon, V. Until the monkey comes 2
Hoffman, B. The king of Spain 3
Hoffman, W. Thank you, Miss Victoria 3
Jasudowicz, D. Blood money 1
Kennedy, A. The owl answers 2
Levinson, A. Socrates wounded 1
Magnuson, J. African Medea 4
Maljean, J. A message from cougar 2
Mee, C. Constantinople Smith 1
Molinaro, U. The abstract wife 2
Owens, R. Futz 2
Patrick, R. The golden circle 3
Peluso, E. Moby Tick 4
Rosenberg, J. The death and life of Sneaky Fitch 1
Rubenstein, K. Icarus 4
Smith, M. Captain Jack's revenge 4
Starkweather, D. The poet's papers 3
Washburn, D. Ginger Anne 1
Yankowitz, S. Slaughterhouse 4
Yerby, L. The golden bull of boredom 1

NEWE New English dramatists ...Edited by E. Martin Browne...Tom Maschler... [Harmondsworth, Middlesex] Penguin Books [1958-1971] 14v

Arden, J., and D'Arcy, M. The happy haven 4
Arden, J. Live like pigs 3
Bermange, B. No quarter 12
Bolt, R. A man for all seasons 6
Churchill, C. The ants 12
Conn, S. The king 14
Cooper, G. Everything in the garden 7
Cooper, G. Happy family 11
Cooper, G. The object 12
Finley, I. The estate hunters 14
Finley, I. Walking through seaweed 14
Fugard, A. The blood knot 13
Hall, W. The long and the short and the tall 3
Hastings, M. Yes, and after 4
Howarth, D. A lily in little India 9
Johnson, B. You're human like the rest of them 14
Kops, B. The hamlet of Stepney Green 1
Lessing, D. Each his own wilderness 1
Livings, H. Nil carborundum 6
Livings, H. Stop it, whoever you are 5
Lynne, J. The trigon 8
MacBeth, G., and Bingham, J. The doomsday show 14
Orton, J. Entertaining Mr. Sloane 8
Orton, J. Loot 13
Osborne, J., and Creighton, A. Epitaph for George Dillon 2
Owen, A. Progress to the park 5
Pinner, D. Dickon 10
Pinner, D. The drums of snow 13
Pinter, H. The dumb waiter 3
Reckord, B. Skyvers 9
Rudkin, D. Afore night come 7
Sanford, J. The whelks and the cromium 12
Shaffer, P. Five finger exercise 4
Sharp, A. The long-distance piano player 12
Simpson, N. A resounding tinkle 2
Storey, D. The restoration of Arnold Middleton 14
Taylor, C. Bread and butter 10
Taylor, C. Happy days are here again 12
Terson, P. The mighty reservoy 14
Terson, P. A night to make angels weep 11
Wesker, A. Chicken soup with barley 1
Wesker, A. Chips with everything 7
Wesker, A. The four seasons 9
Wesker, A. The kitchen 2
Wesker, A. Their very own and golden city 10
Whiting, J. The devils 6
Whiting, J. Marching song 3
Wood, C. Cockade 8
Wood, C. Fill the stage with happy hours 11

NEWL New Lafayette theatre presents: plays with aesthetic comments by 6 Black playwrights;...Garden City, N.Y., (Anchor Press Books) Doubleday, 1974. 301p

Bullins, E. The fabulous Miss Marie
Gaines, J. What if it had turned up heads?
Goss, C. On being hit
Oyamo. His first step

NEWL (cont.)
Sánchez, S. Uh, uh, but how do it free us?
Wesley, R. Black terror

NEWR New road...edited by Fred Marnau...Alex Comfort...John Bayliss...1943-1947. London, The grey walls press [1943-1947] 5v
Carroll, P. The strings, my Lord, are false 1
Gardiner, W. The last refuge 1

NEWV New voices in the American theatre. Foreword by Brooks Atkinson. New York, Modern library [c1955] 559p
Anderson, R. Tea and sympathy
Axelrod, G. The seven year itch
Inge, W. Come back little Sheba
Miller, A. Death of a salesman
Williams, T. A streetcar named desire
Wouk, H. The Caine mutiny court-martial

NEW WORLD LITERATURE SERIES, v1. <u>See</u> MONR Moody, Richard, ed. Dramas from the American theatre, 1762-1909

NEWW New world writing... New York, New American library, 1952-1956. 10v
Bellow, S. The wrecker 6
Bercovici, E. The heart of age 4
Brunson, B. A bastard of the blood 10
Denney, R. September lemonade 7
Eberhart, R. The visionary farms 3
García Lorca, F. Don Cristobita and Doña Rosita 8
Ionesco, E. The bald soprano 9
MacDonagh, D. Happy as Larry 6
Meldon, M. Purple path to the poppy field 5
Picasso, P. Desire trapped by the tail 2
Williams, T. I rise in flame, cried the Phoenix 1

NIC Nicoll, Allardyce, ed. Lesser English comedies of the eighteenth century... London, Oxford university press [1927] [537]p (The world's classics)
Colman, G. The jealous wife
Inchbald, E. Every one has his fault
Morton, T. Speed the plough
Murphy, A. The way to keep him
Reynolds, F. The dramatist

NINE GREEK DRAMAS. <u>See</u> HARC Harvard classics, v8

NOY Noyes, George Rapall, ed. and tr. Masterpieces of the Russian drama...New York, Appleton-Century, 1933. 902p
Andreyev, L. Professor Storitsyn
Chekhov, A. The cherry orchard
Fonvízin, D. The young hopeful
Gogol, N. The inspector
Gorky, M. Down and out
Griboyedov, A. Wit works woe
Mayakóvsky, V. Mystery-Bouffe
Ostrovsky, A. The poor bride
Pisemsky, A. A bitter fate
Tolstoy, A. The death of Ivan the terrible
Tolstoy, L. The power of

darkness
Turgenev, I. A month in the country

O

OAT Oates, Whitney Jennings and O'Neill, Eugene Gladstone, eds. The complete Greek drama... New York, Random house [c1938] 2v
Aeschylus. Agamemnon 1
Aeschylus. The choephori 1
Aeschylus. The eumenides 1
Aeschylus. The Persians 1
Aeschylus. Prometheus bound 1
Aeschylus. The seven against Thebes 1
Aeschylus. The suppliants 1
Aristophanes. The Acharnians 2
Aristophanes. The birds 2
Aristophanes. The clouds 2
Aristophanes. The ecclesiazusae 2
Aristophanes. The frogs 2
Aristophanes. The knights 2
Aristophanes. Lysistrata 2
Aristophanes. Peace 2
Aristophanes. Plutus 2
Aristophanes. Thesmophoriazusae 2
Aristophanes. The wasps 2
Euripides. Alcestis 1
Euripides. Andromache 1
Euripides. The bacchae 2
Euripides. The cyclops 2
Euripides. Electra 2
Euripides. Hecuba 1
Euripides. Helen 2
Euripides. The Heracleidae 1
Euripides. Heracles 1
Euripides. Hippolytus 1
Euripides. Ion 1
Euripides. Iphigenia in Aulis 2
Euripides. Iphigenia in Tauris 1
Euripides. Medea 1
Euripides. Orestes 2
Euripides. The Phoenissae 2
Euripides. Rhesus 2
Euripides. The suppliants 1
Euripides. The Trojan women 1
Menander. The arbitration 2
Menander. The girl from Samos 2
Menander. The shearing of Glycera 2
Sophocles. Ajax 1
Sophocles. Antigone 1
Sophocles. Electra 1
Sophocles. Oedipus at Colonus 1
Sophocles. Oedipus the king 1
Sophocles. Philoctetes 1
Sophocles. The trachiniae 1

OATE Oates, Whitney Jennings and Murphy, Charles Theophilus, eds. Greek literature in translation... New York, Longmans, Green, 1944. 1072p
Aeschylus. Agamemnon
Aeschylus. The Eumenides
Aeschylus. Prometheus bound
Aristophanes. Lysistrata
Euripides. The bacchae
Euripides. Hippolytus
Menander. The arbitration
Sophocles. Antigone
Sophocles. Oedipus the king

OATH Oates, Whitney Jennings and O'Neill, Eugene, jr., eds. ...Seven famous Greek plays... New York, Modern library [c1950] 446p (Modern library college editions)
Aeschylus. Agamemnon
Aeschylus. Prometheus bound
Aristophanes. The frogs
Euripides. Alcestis
Euripides. Medea
Sophocles. Antigone
Sophocles. Oedipus the king

OBERUFER, CHRISTMAS PLAYS

FROM. See HARW Harwood, A. C., tr.

OBSE The observer plays, with a preface by Kenneth Tynan. London, Faber and Faber [c1958] 475p
- Beynon, R. The shifting heart
- Campbell, M., and Athas, D. Sit on the earth
- Cavan, R. All my own work
- Davis, A. Four men, a tragicomedy
- Jellicoe, A. The sport of my mad mother
- John, E. Moon on a rainbow shawl
- Simpson, N. A resounding tinkle

O'CONNOR, JOSEPH. See GRE Great plays (English)...

OFF Off Broadway plays. Harmondsworth, Middlesex, Penguin. 1971-72. 2v
- Dizenzo, C. The drapes come 1
- Dizenzo, C. An evening for Merlin Finch 1
- Guare, J. Cop-out 1
- Guare, J. Muzeeka 1
- Horovitz, I. It's called the sugar plum 1
- Horivitz, I. The Indian wants the Bronx 1
- Kopit, A. Oh dad, poor dad, momma's hung you in the closet and I'm feeling so sad 1
- McNally, T. Botticelli 2
- McNally, T. Sweet eros 2
- Peluso, E. Good day 2
- Peluso, E. Little fears 2
- Shepard, S. Red cross 2
- Weller, M. The bodybuilders 2
- Weller, M. Now there's just the three of us 2

OHL Ohlsen, Woodrow, and Hammond, Frank L., eds. Frames of reference: an introduction to literature. Belmont, Calif., Wadsworth Pub., 1974. 399p
- Anderson, M. Anne of the thousand days
- Arrabal, F. Picnic on the battlefield
- Ibsen, H. An enemy of the people
- Vidal, G. Visit to a small planet

OLH Oliphant, Ernest Henry Clark, ed. Elizabethan dramatists other than Shakespeare... New York, Prentice-Hall, 1931. 1511p
- Arden of Feversham
- Beaumont, F., and Fletcher, J. The knight of the burning pestle
- Beaumont, F., and Fletcher, J. The maid's tragedy
- Beaumont, F., and Fletcher, J. Philaster
- Brome, R. A jovial crew
- Dekker, T. The honest whore, pt. II
- Drayton, M. The merry devil of Edmonton
- Ford, J. The broken heart
- Greene, R. Friar Bacon and Friar Bungay
- Heywood, T. A woman killed with kindness
- Jonson, B. The alchemist
- Jonson, B. Bartholomew fair
- Jonson, B. Volpone
- Jonson, B., Chapman, G., and Marston, J. Eastward hoe!
- Kyd, T. The Spanish tragedy
- Lyly, J. Campaspe
- Marlowe, C. Edward II
- Marlowe, C. Faustus
- Massinger, P. A new way to pay old debts
- Middleton, T. Women, beware women
- Middleton, T., and Rowley, W. The changeling
- Milton, J. Comus
- Peele, G. The old wives'

tale
Porter, H. The two angry women of Abington
Rowley, W., and Middleton, T. A fair quarrel
Shirley, J. The traitor
Tourneur, C. The revenger's tragedy
Webster, J. The Duchess of Malfi
Webster, J. The white devil
A Yorkshire tragedy

OLI Oliphant, Ernest Henry Clark, ed. Shakespeare and his fellow dramatists ...New York, Prentice-Hall, 1929. 2v

Arden of Feversham 1
Beaumont, F., and Fletcher, J. The knight of the burning pestle 2
Beaumont, F., and Fletcher, J. The maid's tragedy 2
Beaumont, F., and Fletcher, J. Philaster 2
Brome, R. A jovial crew 2
Dekker, T. The honest whore, pt. II 1
Drayton, M. The merry devil of Edmonton 1
Ford, J. The broken heart 2
Greene, R. Friar Bacon and Friar Bungay 1
Heywood, T. A woman killed with kindness 1
Jonson, B. The alchemist 2
Jonson, B. Bartholomew fair 2
Jonson, B. Volpone 1
Jonson, B., Chapman, G., and Marston, J. Eastward hoe! 1
Kyd, T. The Spanish tragedy 1
Lyly, J. Campaspe 1
Marlowe, C. Edward II 1
Marlowe, C. Faustus 1
Massinger, P. A new way to pay old debts 2
Middleton, T. Women, beware women 2
Middleton, T., and Rowley, W. The changeling 2
Milton, J. Comus 2
Peele, G. The old wives' tale 1
Porter, H. The two angry women of Abington 1
Rowley, W., and Middleton, T. A fair quarrel 2
Shakespeare, W. Antony and Cleopatra 2
Shakespeare, W. As you like it 1
Shakespeare, W. Coriolanus 2
Shakespeare, W. Cymbeline 2
Shakespeare, W. Hamlet 1
Shakespeare, W. Henry IV, pt. I 1
Shakespeare, W. Julius Caesar 1
Shakespeare, W. King Lear 1
Shakespeare, W. Macbeth 2
Shakespeare, W. The merchant of Venice 1
Shakespeare, W. Midsummer night's dream 1
Shakespeare, W. Othello 1
Shakespeare, W. Romeo and Juliet 1
Shakespeare, W. Twelfth night 1
Shakespeare, W. The winter's tale 2
Shirley, J. The traitor 2
Tourneur, C. The revenger's tragedy 2
Webster, J. The Duchess of Malfi 2
Webster, J. The white devil 2
A Yorkshire tragedy 2

OLIV Oliver, Clinton S. and Sills, Stephanie, eds. Contemporary black drama... New York, Scribner, 1970. 360p

Baldwin, J. Blues for Mr. Charlie
Bullins, E. Gentleman caller

OLIV (cont.)
Davis, O. Purlie victorious
Gordone, C. No place to be somebody
Hansberry, L. A raisin in the sun
Jones, L. Dutchman
Kennedy, A. Funnyhouse of a Negro
Ward, D. Day of absence
Ward, D. Happy ending

OLIW Oliver, William Irvin, ed. and tr. Voices of change in the Spanish American theater. Austin, Texas, University of Texas Press, 1971. 294p
Buenaventura, E. In the right hand of God the Father
Carbillido, E. The day they let the lions loose
Gambargo, G. The camp
Hernández, L. The mullatto's orgy
Maggi, C. The library
Vodāhovic, S. Three beach plays

ORI Oriental literature... Rev. ed. New York, Colonial press [c1960] 4v (The world's great classics)

Abstraction	2
Kālidāsa. Sakoontalā	3
Nakamitsu	2
The sorrows of Han	4

ORNC Ornstein, Robert and Spencer, Hazelton, eds. Elizabethan and Jacobean comedy... Boston, Heath [1964] 315p (A companion volume to the editors' Elizabethan and Jacobean tragedy...)
Beaumont, F. The knight of the burning pestle
Dekker, T. The shoemaker's holiday
Gascoine, G. Supposes
Greene, R. Friar Bacon and Friar Bungay
Jonson, B. The alchemist
Jonson, B. Every man in his humour
Lyly, J. Endymion, the man in the moon
Massinger, P. A new way to pay old debts

ORNT Ornstein, Robert and Spencer, Hazelton, eds. Elizabethan and Jacobean tragedy... Boston, Heath [1964] 308p (A companion volume to the editors' Elizabethan and Jacobean comedy...)
Chapman, G. Bussy D'Ambois
Ford, J. The broken heart
Kyd, T. The Spanish tragedy
Marlowe, C. The tragical history of Doctor Faustus
Middleton, T. and Rowley, W. The changeling
Webster, J. The white devil

ORZ Orzel, Nick, and Smith, Michael, eds. Eight plays from off-Broadway. Indianapolis, Bobbs, Merrill, 1966. 281p
Fornés, M. The successful life of 3: a skit for vaudeville
Foster, P. Balls
O'Hara, F. The general returns from one place to another
Oppenheimer, J. The great American desert
Shepard, S. Chicago
Terry, M. Calm down, Mother
Van Itallie, J. America hurrah
Wilson, L. The madness of Lady Bright

OULD Ould, Herman, ed. The book of the P.E.N. ... London, Arthur Barker [1950] 254p
Farjeon, E. The plane-tree

Jameson, S. William the defeated
Johnson, P. The Duchess at sunset

OWE Owens, Rochelle, ed. Spontaneous combustion; 8 new American plays. New York, Winter House, 1972. 224p (Winter Repertory, 6)
Bovasso, J. Schubert's last serenade
Bullins, E. Dialect determinism
Hoffman, W. A quick nut bread to make your mouth water
Jones, L. Ba-Ra-Ka
Kennedy, A. Sun
Melfi, L. Cinque
Owens, R. He wants shih
Terry, M. Sanibel and Captiva

OXF Oxford anthology of American literature, chosen and edited by William Rose Benét and Norman Holmes Pearson. New York, Oxford university press, 1938. 1705p
O'Neill, E. Lazarus laughed

P

PAJ Parker, John W., ed. Adventures in playmaking; 4 plays by Carolina playmakers. Chapel Hill, Univ. of North Carolina Press, c1968. 333p
Brower, B. A little to the left
Graves, R. The battle of the carnival and Lent
McDonald, C. and Mason, W. Spring for sure
Niggli, J. Singing valley

PAR Parks, Edd Winfield, and Beatty, Richard Croom, eds. The English drama, an anthology, 900-1642... New York, Norton [c1935] 1495p
Abraham and Isaac
Beaumont, F., and Fletcher, J. Philaster; or, Love lies a-bleeding
Daniel, S. The vision of the twelve goddesses
Dekker, T. The shoemaker's holiday
Everyman
Fletcher, J., and Shakespeare, W. Two noble kinsmen
Ford, J. 'Tis a pity she's a whore
Greene, R. The honorable history of Friar Bacon and Friar Bungay
Heywood, J. A merry play between John John the husband
Heywood, T. A woman killed with kindness
Jonson, B. Every man in his humour
Jonson, B. Oberon, the fairy prince
Jonson, B. Sejanus, his fall
Jonson, B. Volpone; or, The fox
Kyd, T. The Spanish tragedy
Lyly, J. Endymion
Marlowe, C. Edward II
Marlowe, C. The Jew of Malta
Marlowe, C. The tragical history of Dr. Faustus
Massinger, P. A new way to pay old debts
Milton, J. Comus
Oxfordshire St. George play
Peele, G. The old wives' tale
Plautus, T. The miles gloriosus
The quem quaeritis
Robin Hood and the friar
The second shepherds' play
Seneca, L. Thyestes
Shetland sword dance
Shirley, J. The cardinal
Sidney, P. The Lady of May

PAR (cont.)
Udall, N. Ralph Roister Doister
Webster, J. The white devil

PARNASSUS PLAYS (1598-1601) ...See LEIS Leishman, J. B., ed.

PARR Parry, W. Dyfed. Old plays for modern players ...London, Arnold [1930] 156p
Abraham and Isaac
Heywood, J. The four p's
Jonson, B. Volpone; or, The fox
Noah's flood
Peele, G. The old wives' tale
The shepherds' play

PARV Patt, Beatrice P., and Nozick, Martin, eds. The generation of 1898 and after ...New York, Dodd, Mead, 1961. 427p
García Lorca, F. La casa de Bernarda Alba

PATM Patterns of literature. Edited by Julian L. Maline and James Berkley. New York, Singer-Random House, 1967. 4v (v3, Dramatic literature)
Chekhov, A. The boor 3
Ibsen, H. An enemy of the people 3
McCullers, C. The member of the wedding 3
Maeterlinck, M. The intruder 3
Mukerji, D. The judgment of Indra 3
Rostand, E. The romancers 3
Seami, M. The dwarf trees 3
Shakespeare, W. Macbeth 3
Sophocles. Antigone 3
Synge, J. Riders to the sea 3

PATP Patterns of literature. Edited by Julian L. Maline and James Berkley. New York, Singer-Random House [1969] 734p
Anouilh, J. Antigone
McCullers, C. The member of the wedding
Mukerji, D. The judgment of Indra
Seami, M. The dwarf trees
Shakespeare, W. Macbeth
Sophocles. Antigone
Synge, J. Riders to the sea

PATR Patterson, Lindsay, [comp.] Black theatre; a 20th century collection of the best playwrights. New York, Dodd, Mead, 1971. 493p
Baldwin, J. The amen corner
Bontemps, A., and Cullen, C. The St. Louis woman
Branch, W. In splendid error
Bullins, E. In the wine time
Childress, A. Trouble in mind
Davis, O. Purlie victorious
Elder, L. Ceremonies in dark old men
Gordone, C. No place to be somebody
Hansberry, L. A raisin in the sun
Hughes, L. Simply heaven
Jones, L. Dutchman
Peterson, L. Take a giant step

PATT Pattison, Walter Thomas. Representative Spanish authors...New York, Oxford university press, 1942. 2v in 1
Rivas, A. Don Alvaro; o, La fuerza del sino
Rueda, L. Paso séptimo: de las aceitunas
Ruiz de Alarcón y Mendoza, J. Las paredes oyen

PEARSON, NORMAN HOLMES. See OXF Oxford anthology of American literature... edited by William Rose Benét and Norman Holmes Pearson

PEN Pence, Raymond Woodbury, ed. Dramas by present-day writers...New York, Scribner [c1927] 690p
- Bennett, A., and Knoblock, E. Milestones
- Davies, M. The slave with two faces
- Drinkwater, J. Cophetua
- Dunsany, E. A night at an inn
- Galsworthy, J. Loyalties
- Glaspell, S. Trifles
- Gregory, I. Spreading the news
- Jacobs, W. A love passage
- Jones, H. The goal
- Kaufman, G., and Connelly, M. Merton of the movies
- Mackay, C. Counsel retained
- Morley, C. Thursday evening
- O'Neill, E. "Ile"
- Sutro, A. A marriage has been arranged
- Tarkington, B. Monsieur Beaucaire
- Wilde, P. Confessional

PENNSYLVANIA GERMAN SOCIETY. See BUFF Buffington, Albert F., ed. The Richard collection of early Pennsylvania German plays...

PERRIN, BERNADOTTE. See GREE Greek dramas...

PERS Perrine, Laurence, comp., Dimensions of drama. New York, Harcourt, Brace, Jovanovich, 1973. 567p
- Chekhov, A. The brute
- Everyman
- García Lorca, F. Blood wedding
- Ibsen, H. An enemy of the people
- Miller, A. Death of a salesman
- Molière, J. The misanthrope
- Shakespeare, W. Othello
- Sophocles. Oedipus rex
- Strindberg, A. The stronger
- Williams, T. The glass menagerie

PERT Perrine, Laurence, comp. Literature; structure, sound and sense. New York, Harcourt, Brace, Jovanovich, 1970. 1426p
- Albee, E. The sandbox
- Chekhov, A. The brute
- García Lorca, F. Blood wedding
- Ibsen, H. An enemy of the people
- Miller, A. Death of a salesman
- Molière, J. The misanthrope
- Shakespeare, W. Othello
- Shaw, G. Candida
- Sophocles. Oedipus rex
- Strindberg, A. The stronger
- Williams, T. The glass menagerie

PERU Perrine, Laurence, ed. Literature, structure, sound and sense. 2d ed. New York, Harcourt, Brace, Jovanovich, 1974. 1508p
- Albee, E. The sandbox
- Chekhov, C. The brute: A joke in one act
- Everyman
- García Lorca, F. Blood wedding
- Hansberry, L. A raisin in the sun
- Ibsen, H. An enemy of the people
- Miller, A. Death of a salesman
- Molière, J. The misanthrope
- Shakespeare, W. Othello
- Shaw, G. Candida

PERU (cont.)
Sophocles. Antigone
Strindberg, A. The stronger

PHI Philbrick, Norman, ed. Trumpets sounding: propaganda plays of the American revolution. New York, 1972. 367p
The battle of Brooklyn, a farce of two acts
The blockheads; or, The affrighted officers
Brackenridge, H. The death of General Montgomery, in storming the City of Quebec
A dialogue, between a Southern delegate, and his spouse, on his return from the grand Continental Congress
The fall of British tyranny; or, American liberty triumphant
The motley assembly
Munford, R. The patriots

PIE Pierce, Frederick Erastus and Schreiber, Carl Frederick, eds. Fiction and fantasy of German romance. New York, Oxford university press, 1927. 392p
Kleist, H. Kaethchen of Heilbronn

PIET Pieterse, Cosmo, ed. Five African plays. London, Heinemann, 1972. 217p
Bart-Williams, G. The drug
Kay, K. Laughter and hubbub in the house
Kimmel, H. The cell
Oyono, F. Houseboy

PLAYBOOK: FIVE PLAYS FOR A NEW THEATRE (PLAA). See also PLAC Plays for a new theater; Playbook 2...

PLAA Playbook: Five plays for a new theatre. [1] [New York] New Directions [c1956] 298p
Abel, L. The death of Odysseus
Hivnor, R. The ticklish acrobat
Kinoshita, J. Twilight crane
Merrill, J. The immortal husband
Richards, I. A leak in the universe

PLAB Plays by Greek, Spanish, French, German and English dramatists...Rev. ed. New York, Colonial press [c1900] 2v (The world's great classics)
Aeschylus. Prometheus bound 1
Aristophanes. The knights 1
Calderón de la Barca, P. Life a dream 1
Euripides. Medea 1
Goethe, J. Faust, pt. I 2
Goldsmith, O. She stoops to conquer 1
Ibsen, H. A doll's house 2
Molière, J. The misanthrope 1
Racine, J. Phaedra 1
Sardou, V. Les pattes de mouche 2
Schiller, F. Mary Stuart 2
Sheridan, R. The rivals 2
Sophocles. Oedipus rex 1

PLAC Plays for a new theater; playbook 2...[New York] New Directions [1966] 282p
Alvaro, C. The long night of Medea
Goll, Y. Methusalem; or, The eternal bourgeois
Hawkes, J. The wax museum
Hivnor, R. The assault upon Charles Sumner
Vian, B. Knackery for all

PLAD Plays of a half-decade ...[London] Gollancz [1933] 1008p

Anthony, C. Autumn crocus
Bax, C. The rose without a thorn
Berkeley, R. The lady with a lamp
Besier, R. The Barretts of Wimpole street
Dealfield, E. To see ourselves
Fagan, J. The improper duchess
Hoffe, M. Many waters
Mackenzie, R. Musical chairs
Sherriff, R. Journey's end
Van Druten, J. After all
Van Druten, J. Young Woodley

PLAG ...Plays of the Greek dramatists...New York, Caxton house [c1946] 360p
Note: Variant title: Eleven plays of the Greek dramatists...
Aeschylus. Agamemnon
Aeschylus. Choephoroe
Aeschylus. The Eumenides
Aristophanes. The clouds
Aristophanes. The frogs
Aristophanes. Lysistrata
Euripides. The cyclops
Euripides. Iphigenia in Tauris
Sophocles. Antigone
Sophocles. Electra
Sophocles. Oedipus, the king

PLAH Plays of the Moscow art theatre musical studio... English translation from the Russian by George S., and Gilbert Seldes, with introductions by Oliver M. Sayler. New York, Brentano [c1925] v.p.
Aristophanes. Lysistrata
Lecocq, C. The daughter of Madame Angot
Lipskeroff, C. Carmencita and the soldier
Offenbach, J. La périchole
Pushkin, A Love and death, featuring "Aleko," by Rachmaninoff

PLAJ Plays of the sixties. Selected by J. M. Charlton. London, Pan Books, 1966-1967. 2v
Campton, D. Soldier from the wars returning 2
Chapman, J. Simple spymen 2
Lessing, D. Play with a tiger 1
Millar, R. The affair 2
Murdock, I. and Priestley, J. A severed head 2
Rattigan, T. Ross 1
Shaffer, P. The royal hunt of the sun 1
Waterhouse, K. and Hall, W. Billy Liar 1

PLAL Plays of the thirties. Selected by J. M. Charlton. London, Pan Books, 1966-1967. 2v
Besier, R. The Barretts of Wimpole Street 2
Bridie, J. Tobias and the angel 1
Coward, N. Private lives 2
Daviot, G. Richard of Bordeaux 1
Gow, R. and Greenwood, W. Love on the dole 1
Rattigan, T. French without tears 2
Smith, D. Autumn crocus 2
Smith, D. Dear Octopus 1

PLAN Plays of the year, chosen by J. C. Trewin...London, Paul Elek; New York, Frederick Ungar [c1949-1972] 42v
Abse, D. House of cowards 23
Achard, M. Rollo 20
Ackland, R. Before the party 2
Ackland, R. A dead secret 16
Albery, P. Anne Boleyn 14
Anouilh, J. The ermine 13
Anouilh, J. Medea 15
Anouilh, J. The waltz of

PLAN (cont.)
the toreadors 8
Arden, J. The party 18
Arout, G. Beware of the dog 33
Babel, I. Marya 35
Bagnold, E. Call me Jacky 34
Boland, B. Cockpit 1
Boland, B. Gordon 25
Boland, B. The prisoner 10
Boland, B. The return 9
Braddon, R. Naked island 22
Browne, W. The holly and the ivy 3
Chekhov, A. Uncle Vanya 39
Chetham-Strode, W. Background 4
Christie, D. and Christie, C. His excellency 4
Coffee, L. and Cowen, W. Family portrait 1
Cooper, G. Out of the crocodile 27
Corlett, W. Tinker's curse 34
Cross, B. The mines of sulphur 30
Dewhurst, K. Rafferty's chant 33
Dighton, J. The happiest days of your life 1
Dighton, J. Who goes there! 6
Dinner, W., and Morum, W. The late Edwina Black 2
Dobie, L., and Sloman, R. The tinker 24
Dowling, J., and Letton, F. The young Elizabeth 7
Dyer, C. Rattle of a simple man 26
Exton, C. Have you any dirty washing, mother dear? 37
Fairchild, W. The sound of murder 20
Feely, T. Don't let summer come 29
Fletcher, J. The chances 25
Francis, W. Portrait of a queen 30
Frisby, T. There's a girl in my soup 32
Frost, R. Small hotel 13
Gear, B. The sky is green 27
Gilbert, M. The bargain 23
Gilbert, M. A clean kill 21
Goldoni, C. The servant of two masters 36
Gow, R. Ann Veronica 2
Gow, R. The Edwardians 20
Green, J. Murder mistaken 8
Green, J. South 12
Guitry, S. Don't listen ladies! 1
Guthrie, T. Top of the ladder 3
Hale, J. The black swan winter 37
Hale, J. Spithead 38
Hanley, J. Say nothing 27
Harrison, J. Knight in four acts 38
Harrison, J. Unaccompanied cello 40
Hastings, C. Bonaventure 3
Hastings, C. Uncertain joy 12
Hastings, C. Seagulls over Sorrento 4
Hellman, L. The children's hour 5
Hochwälder, F. The public prosecutor 16
Hochwälder, F. The strong are lonely 14
Home, W. The jockey club stakes 40
Home, W. Lloyd George knew my father 42
Home, W. The queen's highland servant 35
Home, W. The secretary bird 36
Horne, K. Trial and error 9
Horne, W. The thistle and the rose 4
Howarth, D. Three months gone 39
Ibsen, H. John Gabriel Borkman 23
Jeans, R. Count your blessings 5

Jeans, R. Young wives' tale 3
Jones, P. Birthday honours 9
Jones, P., and Jowett, J. The party spirit 11
Kennaway, J. Country dance 33
Kimmins, A. The amorous prawn 21
King, N. The shadow of doubt 12
King, P. Serious charge 11
King, P. and Cary, F. Sailor, beware! 12
King, P. and Cary, F. Watch it, sailor! 22
Kleist, H. The Prince of Homburg 36
Launder, F. and Guilliat, S. Meet a body 10
Leonard, H. The Patrick Pearse motel 41
Leonard, H. The poker session 28
Lethbridge, N. The Portsmouth defence 32
Levy, B. The member for Gaza 32
Lewis, S. Siwan 21
Lonsdale, F. Let them eat cake 19
Luke, P. Hadrian VII 33
Macauley, P. The creeper 29
MacDougall, R. The gentle gunman 5
MacDougall, R. To Dorothy, a son 4
MacIlwraith, B. The anniversary 31
Mackie, P. The big killing 25
Mackie, P. The whole truth 13
Macrae, A. Both ends meet 10
Marcus, F. Formation dancers 28
Marcus, F. The killing of Sister George 31
Marcus, F. Mrs. Mouse are you within? 35
Marcus, F. Notes on a love affair 42
Massinger, P. The city madam 28
Maugham, R. Enemy 39
Maurette, M. Anastasia 9
May, V. and Rowell, G. Sixty thousand nights 31
Melville, A. Castle in the air 3
Melville, A. Dear Charles 8
Melville, A. Simon and Laura 11
Millar, R. Abelard and Heloise 39
Millar, R. Waiting for Gillian 10
Miller, H. The house by the lake 14
Miller, S. One bright day 14
Mills, H. The little glass clock 11
Milner, R. How's the world treating you? 30
Mitchell, J. A heritage and its history 30
Mitchell, Y. The same sky 6
Molière, J. Doctor's delight 5
Molière, J. The imaginary invalid 19
Molière, J. The misanthrope 11
Molière, J. The miser 1
Molière, J. The prodigious snob 6
Molière, J. The school for wives 10
Molière, J. Sganarelle 11
Molière, J. Tartuffe 3
Molloy, M. The King of Friday's men 2
Montherlant, H. The cardinal of Spain 37
Mortimer, J. The dock brief 17
Mortimer, J. What shall we tell Caroline? 17
O'Brien, E. A cheap bunch of nice flowers 26
Oulton, B. Mr. Sydney Smith

PLAN (cont.)
coming upstairs 42
Passeur, S. A measure of cruelty 29
Peacock, J. Children of the wolf 40
Pertwee, R. and Pertwee, M. The paragon 1
Pinero, A. The magistrate 38
Popple, W. The double deceit; or, A cure for jealousy 26
Popplewell, J. Dead on nine 13
Popplewell, J. Dear delinquent 16
Pulman, J. The happy apple 34
Regnier, M. Paddle your own canoe 17
Richardson, H. and Berney, W. Dark of the moon 2
Ronder, J. This year, next year 22
Rosenthal, A. Third person 7
Ross, G. and Singer, C. Any other business 18
Ross, G. and Singer, C. Difference of opinion 27
Ross, G. and Singer, C. Guilty party 24
Ross, G. The sacking of Norman Banks 37
Sardou, V. and Najac, E. Let's get a divorce! 31
Sharp, A. Nightmare abbey 7
Shaw, R. The man in the glass booth 34
Sherriff, R. The long sunset 12
Sherriff, R. A shred of evidence 22
Sherriff, R. The telescope 15
Sieveking, L. The strange case of Dr. Jekyll and Mr. Hyde 15
Sisson, R. The Queen and the Welshman 18
Sisson, R. The splendid outcasts 19
Spewack, S. Under the sycamore tree 7
Storey, D. The contractor 40
Storey, D. Home 41
Storey, D. In celebration 38
Storey, D. The restoration of Arnold Middleton 35
Storey, R. Touch it light 18
Storm, L. Black chiffon 2
Strindberg, A. Creditors 21
Strindberg, A. The dance of death 32
Stuart, A. Lace on her petticoat 5
Sudraka, K. The little clay cart 29
Sylvaine, V. As long as they're happy 9
Taylor, C. The wings of the dove 28
Thomas, G. Jackie the jumper 26
Thomas, G. The keep 24
Ustinov, P. The unknown soldier and his wife 36
Verneuil, L. Affairs of state 8
Vian, B. The empire builders 25
Watkyn, A. For better, for worse 8
Watkyn, A. Not in the book 17
Webber, C. Be good, sweet maid 15
Whiting, J. Saint's day 21
Williams, H. and Williams, M. By accident 21
Williams, H. and Williams, M. Double yolk 21
Williams, H. and Williams, M. The grass is greener 19
Williams, H. and Williams, M. The happy man 17
Williams, H. and Williams, M. The irregular verb to love 23
Williams, H. and Williams, M. Plaintiff in a pretty hat 15
Williams, H. and Williams,

M. With intent 21
Williamson, H. Diamond cut diamond 7
Williamson, H. Gunpowder, treason and plot 6
Williamson, H. Heart of Bruce 20
Williamson, H. Teresa of Avila 24
Woods, A., Slade, J. and Rowell, G. Trelawny 41

PLAP Plays of to-day... London, Sidgwick and Jackson [1925-1930] 3v
Alvarez Quintero, S. and Alvarez Quintero, J. A hundred years old 3
Baker, E. Chains 1
Drinkwater, J. Abraham Lincoln 1
Dukes, A. The man with a load of mischief 3
Ervine, St. J. Jane Clegg 1
Granville-Barker, H. The Voysey inheritance 1
Hastings, B. The new sin 2
Houghton, S. Hindle wakes 1
Housman, L. and Granville-Barker, H. Prunella 2
Masefield, J. Pompey the Great 2
Mayor, B. The pleasure garden 3
Monkhouse, A. Mary Broome 2
Munro, C. At Mrs. Beam's 3
Robinson, L. The white-headed boy 3
Sowerby, G. Rutherford and son 2

PLAYS OF THE SOUTHERN AMERICAS. See SSTE Stanford university. Dramatists' Alliance

POCH Pochman, Henry August and Allen, Gay Wilson, eds. Masters of American literature... New York, Macmillan, 1949. 2v

O'Neill, E. The great god Brown 2

POLLARD, ALFRED WILLIAM. See also FIF Fifteenth century prose and verse

POLL Pollard, Alfred William, ed. English miracle plays, moralities and interludes... 8th edition revised. Oxford, Clarendon Press, 1927. 250p
Abraham and Isaac
The castell of perseverance
The creation and the fall of Lucifer
Everyman
The four elements
The harrowing of hell
Ludus super iconia Sancti Nicolai
Mary Magdalen
Mysterium resurrectionis D.N. Jhesu Christi
Noah's flood
The sacrifice of Isaac
The salutation and conception
Secunda pastorum
Thersytes
Bale, J. King John
Heywood, J. The pardoner and the frere
Skelton, J. Magnyfycence

POOL Pooley, Robert C.; Farmer, Paul; Thornton, Helen and Anderson, George K., eds. England in literature... Chicago, Scott, Foresman [c1953] 752p
Fry, C. The boy with a cart
Goldsmith, O. She stoops to conquer
Shakespeare, W. Macbeth

POP Popkin, Henry, ed. The new British drama... New York, Grove Press [1964] 606p
Arden, J. Serjeant Musgrave's

POP (cont.)
dance
Behan, B. The hostage
Delaney, S. A taste of honey
Pinter, H. The caretaker
Simpson, N. One way pendulum
Wesker, A. Roots

PRAT Pratt, Robert A. [and others] eds. Masters of British literature... Second edition. Boston, Houghton Mifflin [c1958, 1962] 2v
Arnold, M. Empedocles on Etna 2
Arnold, M. The strayed reveler 2
Shakespeare, W. The first part of Henry the fourth 1
Shakespeare, W. The tragedy of King Lear 1
Shakespeare, W. The winter's tale 1
Shelley, P. Prometheus unbound 2

PRO Pronko, Leonard Cabell, ed. Three modern French plays of the imagination... [New York, Dell, 1966] 252p (The Laurel language library, French series)
Ghelderode, M. Christophe Colomb
Ionesco, E. Les chaises
Neveux, G. Juliette ou la clé des songes

PROB Prose and poetry for appreciation... edited by H. Ward McGraw... Syracuse, N. Y., Singer [c1934] 1971p (The prose and poetry series)
Dunsany, E. A night at an inn
Gregory, A. The rising of the moon
Monkhouse, A. The grand cham's diamond
Tarkington, B. Monsieur Beaucaire

PROC Prose and poetry for appreciation, edited by Elizabeth Frances Ansorge [and others] Syracuse, N. Y., Singer [c1942] 787p (The prose and poetry series)
Corwin, N. They fly through the air
Gregory, A. Spreading the news
Kaufman, G., and Hart, M. The American way
Knight, E. Never come Monday
Knight, V. Cartwheel

PROD Prose and poetry for appreciation, edited by Harriet Marcelia Lucas [and others] Fourth edition. Syracuse, N. Y. Singer [c1950] 822p (The prose and poetry series)
Corwin, N. The odyssey of Runyon Jones
Gilbert, W. and Sullivan, A. The Mikado
Glaspell, S. Trifles
Sherwood, R. Abe Lincoln in Illinois

PROF Prose and poetry of America; edited by H. Ward McGraw... Syracuse, N. Y., Singer [c1934] 1034p (The prose and poetry series)
Fitch, C. Nathan Hale
Glaspell, S. Trifles
Hopkins, A. Moonshine

PROG Prose and poetry of America... edited by H. Ward McGraw... Syracuse, N. Y., Singer [c1934] 1198p (The new prose and poetry series. Southwestern edition)
Bowen, M. Crude and unrefined
Fitch, C. Nathan Hale
Fortune, J. The cavalier

from France
Glaspell, S. Trifles
Hopkins, A. Moonshine
Rogers, J. Judge Lynch

PROH Prose and poetry of America; edited by H. Ward McGraw [and others] Catholic edition... Syracuse, N. Y., Singer [c1940] 1133p (The new prose and poetry series)
Fitch, C. Nathan Hale
Hopkins, A. Moonshine
Kelly, G. Poor Aubrey

PROI Prose and poetry of America... edited by Julian L. Maline... Wilfred M. Mallon [and others] Syracuse, N. Y., Singer [c1949] 822p (At head of title: The St. Thomas More series)
Connelly, M. The green pastures
Hopkins, A. Moonshine
Mulvey, T. Letter to Tuffy

PROM Prose and poetry of England... edited by H. Ward McGraw. Syracuse, N. Y., Singer [c1934] 1196p (The new prose and poetry series)
Dunsany, E. The lost silk hat
Goldsmith, O. She stoops to conquer
Shakespeare, W. Macbeth

PRON Prose and poetry of England; edited by H. Ward McGraw. Catholic edition ... Syracuse, N. Y., Singer [c1940] 1150p (The new prose and poetry series)
Benson, R. The upper room
Dunsany, E. The lost silk hat
Shakespeare, W. Macbeth

PROW Prose and poetry of the world; edited by John R. Barnes [and others] Syracuse, N. Y., Singer [c1941] 1010p (The prose and poetry series)
Euripides. Medea
Ibsen, H. A doll's house
O'Neill, E. Where the cross is made
Sachs, H. The wandering scholar from Paradise
Synge, J. Riders to the sea

PROX Prose and poetry of the world; edited by James K. Agnew and Agnes L. McCarthy... Syracuse, N. Y., Singer [c1954] 788p
Čapek, K. R. U. R.
Miller, A. Pussycat and the expert plumber who was a man
Williams, E. Corn is green

PUCC Pucciani, Oreste F., ed. The French theater since 1930... Boston, Ginn and Company [c1954] 400p
Camus, A. Le malentendu
Cocteau, J. La machine infernale
Giraudoux, J. La guerre de Troie n'aura pas lieu
Montherlant, H. La reine morte
Sartre, J. Les mains sales

THE PULITZER PRIZE PLAYS. See CORD, CORE, CORF Cordell, Kathryn (Coe) and Cordell, William Howard, eds.

Q

QUI Quinn, Arthur Hobson, ed. Contemporary American plays... New York, Scribner [c1923] 382p
Crothers, R. Nice people
Emery, G. The hero
Kaufman, G., and Connelly, M. To the ladies!

QUI (cont.)
O'Neill, E. The Emperor Jones
Williams, J. Why marry?

QUIG Quinn, Arthur Hobson, ed. Representative American plays from 1880 to the present day... Modern drama ed. New York, Century [c1928] 495-1052p
Belasco, D., and Long, J. Madame Butterfly
Crothers, R. He and she
Fitch, C. Her great match
Gillette, W. Secret service
Howard, B. Shenandoah
MacKaye, P. The scarecrow
MacKaye, S. Hazel Kirke
Mitchell, L. The New York idea
Moody, W. The faith healer
O'Neill, E. Beyond the horizon
Sheldon, E. The boss
Thomas, A. The witching hour
Vollmer, L. Sun-up

QUIJ Quinn, Arthur Hobson, ed. Representative American plays... New York, Century, 1917. 968p
Barker, J. Superstition
Belasco, D. and Long, J. Madame Butterfly
Bird, R. The broker of Bogota
Boker, G. Francesca da Rimini
Boucicault, D. The octoroon; or, Life in Louisiana
Crothers, R. He and she
Custis, G. Pocahontas; or, The settlers of Virginia
Dunlap, W. André
Fitch, C. Her great match
Gillette, W. Secret service
Godfrey, T. The prince of Parthia
Howard, B. Shenandoah
Howe, J. Leonora; or, The world's own
MacKaye, P. The scarecrow
MacKaye, S. Hazel Kirke
Mitchell, L. The New York idea
Moody, W. The faith healer
Payne, J. and Irving, W. Charles the second
Rip Van Winkle
Ritchie, A. Fashion
Sheldon, E. The boss
Smith, R. The triumph at Plattsburg
Thomas, A. The witching hour
Tyler, R. The contrast
Willis, N. Tortesa the usurer

QUIK Quinn, Arthur Hobson, ed. Representative American plays, 1767-1923... 3rd ed. rev. and enl. New York, Century, 1925. 1052p
Barker, J. Superstition
Belasco, D. and Long, J. Madame Butterfly
Bird, R. The broker of Bogota
Boker, G. Francesca da Rimini
Boucicault, D. The octoroon; or, Life in Louisiana
Crothers, R. He and she
Custis, G. Pocahontas; or, The settlers of Virginia
Dunlap, W. André
Fitch, C. Her great match
Gillette, W. Secret service
Godfrey, T. The prince of Parthia
Howard, B. Shenandoah
Howe, J. Leonora; or, The world's own
MacKaye, P. The scarecrow
MacKaye, S. Hazel Kirke
Mitchell, L. The New York idea
Moody, W. The faith healer
O'Neill, E. Beyond the horizon
Payne, J. and Irving, W. Charles the second

Rip Van Winkle
Ritchie, A. Fashion
Sheldon, E. The boss
Smith, R. The triumph at Plattsburg
Thomas, A. The witching hour
Tyler, R. The contrast
Vollmer, L. Sun-up
Willis, N. Tortesa the usurer

QUIL Quinn, Arthur Hobson, ed. Representative American plays from 1767 to the present day... 5th ed. rev. and enl. New York, Century [c1930] 1107p
Barker, J. Superstition
Barry, B. Paris bound
Belasco, D. and Long, J. Madame Butterfly
Bird, R. The broker of Bogota
Boker, G. Francesca da Rimini
Boucicault, D. The octoroon; or, Life in Louisiana
Crothers, R. He and she
Custis, G. Pocahontas; or, the settlers of Virginia
Dunlap, W. André
Fitch, C. The girl with the green eyes
Gillette, W. Secret service
Godfrey, T. The prince of Parthia
Herne, J. Margaret Fleming
Howard, B. Shenandoah
Howard, S. The silver cord
MacKaye, P. The scarecrow
MacKaye, S. Hazel Kirke
Mitchell, L. The New York idea
Moody, W. The faith healer
O'Neill, E. Beyond the horizon
Payne, J. and Irving, W. Charles the second
Rip Van Winkle
Ritchie, A. Fashion
Sheldon, E. The boss
Thomas, A. The witching hour
Tyler, R. The contrast
Vollmer, L. Sun-up
Willis, N. Tortesa the usurer

QUIM Quinn, Arthur Hobson, ed. Representative plays from 1767 to the present day... 6th ed. rev. and enl. New York, Appleton-Century [c1938] 1157p
Anderson, M. Winterset
Barker, J. Superstition
Barry, P. Paris bound
Belasco, D. and Long, J. Madame Butterfly
Bird, R. The broker of Bogota
Boker, G. Francesca da Rimini
Boucicault, D. The octoroon; or, Life in Louisiana
Crothers, R. He and she
Custis, G. Pocahontas; or, The settlers of Virginia
Dunlap, W. André
Fitch, C. The girl with the green eyes
Gillette, W. Secret service
Godfrey, T. The prince of Parthia
Herne, J. Margaret Fleming
Howard, B. Shenandoah
Howard, S. The silver cord
MacKaye, P. The scarecrow
MacKaye, S. Hazel Kirke
Mitchell, L. The New York idea
Moody, W. The faith healer
O'Neill, E. Beyond the horizon
Payne, J. and Irving, W. Charles the second
Rip Van Winkle
Fitchie, A. Fashion
Sheldon, E. The boss
Thomas, A. The witching hour
Tyler, R. The contrast
Vollmer, L. Sun-up
Willis, N. Tortesa the usurer

QUIN Quinn, Arthur Hobson, ed. Representative American plays from 1767 to the present day... 7th ed., rev. and enl. New York, Appleton-Century-Crofts [c1953] 1248p
- Anderson, M. Winterset
- Barker, J. Superstition
- Barry, P. Paris bound
- Belasco, D. and Long, J. Madame Butterfly
- Bird, R. The broker of Bogota
- Boker, G. Francesca da Rimini
- Boucicault, D. The octoroon; or, Life in Louisiana
- Crothers, R. He and she
- Custis, G. Pocahontas; or, The settlers of Virginia
- Dunlap, W. André
- Fitch, C. The girl with the green eyes
- Gillette, W. Secret service
- Godfrey, T. The prince of Parthia
- Haines, W. Command decision
- Hammerstein II, O.; Rodgers, R.; Logan, J. and Michener, J. South Pacific
- Herne, J. Margaret Fleming
- Howard, B. Shenandoah
- Howard, S. The silver cord
- Jefferson, J. Rip Van Winkle
- MacKaye, P. The scarecrow
- MacKaye, S. Hazel Kirke
- Mitchell, L. The New York idea
- Moody, W. The faith healer
- O'Neill, E. Beyond the horizon
- Payne, J. Charles the second
- Ritchie, A. Fashion; or, Life in New York
- Sheldon, E. The boss
- Thomas, A. The witching hour
- Tyler, R. The contrast
- Vollmer, L. Sun-up
- Willis, N. Tortesa the usurer

QUINTANA, RICARDO. See EIGH Eighteenth century plays...

QUIO Quinn, Arthur Hobson; Baugh, Albert Croll and Howe, Will David, eds. The literature of America ...New York, Scribner [c1929] 2v
- Belasco, D. and Long, J. Madame Butterfly 2
- Boker, G. Francesca da Rimini 1
- Howells, W. The unexpected guests 2
- O'Neill, E. Lazarus laughed 2
- Tyler, R. The contrast 1

R

RAI Raines, Robert Arnold, ed. Modern drama and social change. Englewood Cliffs, N.J., Prentice-Hall, 1972. 339p
- Brecht, B. Galileo
- Camus, A. Caligula
- Ionesco, E. The leader
- O'Neill, E. The hairy ape
- Shaw, G. Major Barbara
- Ward, D. Day of absence

RAV Ravicz, Marilyn Ekdahl, ed. Early colonial religious drama in Mexico: from Tzompantli to Golgotha. Washington, D.C., Catholic University of America Press, 1970. 263p
- The adoration of the kings
- The destruction of Jerusalem
- The final judgment
- How the Blessed Saint Helen found the holy cross
- The merchant
- The sacrifice of Isaac
- Souls and testamentary executors

RAVA Ravitz, Abe C., ed. The disinherited: plays;

Myrna J. Harrison and Robert J. Griffin, consulting editors. Encino, Calif., Dickenson Pub., 1974. 273p
Anderson, M. Winterset
Brown, W. The escape; or, A leap for freedom
Caldwell, B. The king of soul; or, The Devil and Otis Redding
The double Dutch act
The double Wop act
Figueroa, J. Everybody's a Jew
Green, P., and Green, E. Fixin's: the tragedy of a tenant farm woman
Hughes, L. Soul gone home
Jones, L. Great goodness of life (A coon show)
Lamb, M. But what have you done for me lately?
Levine, M., McNamee, G., and Greenberg, D. The tales of Hoffman--a series of excerpts from the "Chicago Conspiracy" trial
Miller, J. The Danites in the Sierras
Moore, E. Angela is happening
O'Neill, E. All God's chillun got wings
Rice, E. The adding machine
The school act
The straight and the Jew
Terkel, L. Monologues from "Division Street, USA"
Van Itallie, C. Motel: a masque for three dolls
Williams, T. Hello from Bertha
Williams, T. Talk to me like the rain and let me listen

RAY Ray, Gordon Norton; Edel, Leon; Johnson, Thomas H.; Paul, Sherman and Simpson, Claude, eds. Masters of American literature... Boston, Houghton [c1959] 2v
O'Neill, E. Desire under the elms 2
O'Neill, E. The long voyage home 2

READINGS FOR LIBERAL EDUCATION, v. 2. See LOCLA, LOCLB Locke, Louis Glenn [and others] eds. Introduction to literature...

REARDON, WILLIAM R. See AMPA America's lost plays, v21, edited by Walter J. Meserve and William R. Reardon

RED Redman, Crosby E., comp. Designs in drama. Rev. ed. New York, Macmillan, 1968. 365p
Barrie, J. The admirable Crichton
Rattigan, T. The Winslow boy
Shakespeare, W. Julius Caesar
Wouk, H. The Caine mutiny court martial

REDM Redman, Crosby E., comp. Drama II... New York, Macmillan [c1962] 357p
Barrie, J. The admirable Crichton
Rattigan, T. The Winslow boy
Shakespeare, W. Julius Caesar
Van Druten, J. I remember mama

REED, HARRY B. See HAP Harbrace omnibus...

REEV Reeve, Franklin D., ed. and tr. An anthology of Russian plays... New York, Vintage Books [c1961, 1963] 2v
Andreyev, L. He who gets slapped 2

REEV (cont.)
Blok, A. The puppet show 2
Bulgakov, M. The days of the Turbins 2
Chekhov, A. The sea gull 2
Fonvizin, D. The minor 1
Gogol, N. The inspector general 1
Gorky, M. The lower depths 2
Griboyedov, A. The trouble with reason 1
Mayakovsky, V. The bedbug 2
Ostrovsky, A. The storm 1
Pushkin, A. Boris Godunov 1
Shvarts, E. The shadow 2
Tolstoy, L. The power of darkness 1

REIL Reinert, Otto, ed. Classic through modern drama... Boston, Little, Brown, 1970. 949p
Albee, E. Who's afraid of Virginia Woolf?
Brecht, B. The Caucasian chalk circle
Chekhov, A. The three sisters
Etherege, G. The man of mode; or, Sir Fopling Flutter
Everyman
Ibsen, H. The wild duck
Jones, L. Dutchman
Molière, J. Tartuffe
O'Neill, E. The Emperor Jones
Shakespeare, W. Hamlet
Shaw, G. Caesar and Cleopatra
Sophocles. Oedipus rex
Strindberg, A. The ghost sonata
Synge, J. Riders to the sea
Weiss, P. The persecution and assassination of Jean-Paul Marat as performed by the inmates of the Asylum of Charenton under the direction of the Marquis de Sade

REIN Reinert, Otto, ed. Drama, an introductory anthology... Boston, Little, Brown [c1961] 672p
Brecht, B. The good woman of Setzuan
Chekhov, A. Three sisters
Everyman
Ibsen, H. The wild duck
Ionesco, E. The lesson
Miller, A. A view from the bridge
Molière, J. Tartuffe
Shakespeare, W. Macbeth
Shaw, G. Arms and the man
Sophocles. Oedipus rex
Strindberg, A. The ghost sonata
Yeats, W. Purgatory

REIO Reinert, Otto, ed. Drama, an introductory anthology. Alternate ed. Boston, Little Brown [1964] 889p
Albee, E. The American dream
Brecht, B. The Caucasian chalk circle
Chekhov, A. The cherry orchard
Ibsen, H. Hedda Gabler
Jonson, B. The alchemist
Molière, J. The misanthrope
Pirandello, L. Six characters in search of an author
Shakespeare, W. Othello
Shaw, G. Caesar and Cleopatra
Sheridan, R. The rivals
Sophocles. Antigone
Strindberg, A. Miss Julie
Synge, J. The playboy of the western world

REIP Reinert, Otto, ed. Modern drama, nine plays... Boston, Little, Brown [c1961, 1962] 491p
Brecht, B. The good woman of Setzuan
Chekhov, A. Three sisters
Ibsen, H. The wild duck

Ionesco, E. The lesson
Pirandello, L. Six characters in search of an author
Shaw, G. Arms and the man
Strindberg, A. The ghost sonata
Williams, T. The glass menagerie
Yeats, W. Purgatory

REIT Reinert, Otto, ed. Modern drama. Alternate ed. Boston, Little, Brown [1966] 630p
Albee, E. The zoo story
Brecht, B. The Caucasian chalk circle
Chekhov, A. The cherry orchard
Ghelderode, M. Chronicles of hell
Ibsen, H. The wild duck
Pirandello, L. Six characters in search of an author
Shaw, G. Caesar and Cleopatra
Strindberg, A. The father
Synge, J. The playboy of the western world
Williams, T. The glass menagerie
Yeats, W. The hour-glass

REIV Reinert, Otto, ed. Six plays, an introductory anthology. Boston, Little, Brown, 1973. 401p
Chekhov, A. The cherry orchard
Ibsen, H. Hedda Gabler
Molière, J. The misanthrope
Shakespeare, W. Othello
Sophocles. Antigone
Williams, T. The glass menagerie

RELIGIOUS DRAMAS, 1924-25. See FED Federal council of the churches of Christ in America

REST Restoration plays; with an introduction by Brice Harris... New York, Modern library [c1955] 674p
Congreve, W. The way of the world
Dryden, J. All for love
Etherege, G. The man of mode
Farquhar, G. The beaux' stratagem
Otway, T. Venice preserved
Vanbrugh, J. The relapse
Villiers, G. The rehearsal
Wycherley, W. The country wife

RHE Rhode, Eric, ed. Novelists' theatre. Harmondsworth, Middlesex, Penguin, 1966. 279p
Dennis, N. August for the people
Spark, M. Doctors of philosophy
Wilson, A. The mulberry bush

RHO Rhodes, Solomon Alhadef, ed. The contemporary French theatre... New York, Crofts, 1942. 431p
Bernard, J. Martine
Claudel, P. L'annonce faite á Marie
Curel, F. Le repas du lion
Lenormand, H. L'homme et ses fantômes
Maeterlinck, M. Pelléas et Mélisande
Porto-Riche, G. Amoureuse
Raynal, P. Le tombeau sous l'Arc de triomphe
Romains, J. Cromedeyre-le-Vieil
Sarment, J. Les plus beaux yeux du monde

RICH Rich, Mabel Irene... A study of the types of literature... New York, Century [c1921] 542p
Gibson, W. The family's pride
Milton, J. Comus

RICH (cont.)
Shakespeare, W. The tragedy of Hamlet, Prince of Denmark
Wilde, P. The traitor

RICI Richards, Stanley, ed. Best mystery and suspense plays of the modern theatre. New York, Dodd, Mead, 1971. 800p
Anderson, M. The bad seed
Christie, A. Witness for the prosecution
Deane, H. and Warburton, H. Dracula
Hamilton, P. Angel Street
Kesselring, J. Arsenic and old lace
Knott, F. Dial "M" for murder
Marasco, R. Child's play
Maugham, W. The letter
Priestley, J. Dangerous corner
Shaffer, A. Sleuth

RICIS Richards, Stanley, ed. Best plays of the sixties... Garden City, N.Y., Doubleday, 1970. 1036p
Anouilh, J. Becket
Crowley, M. The boys in the band
Friel, B. Philadelphia, here I come
Luke, P. Hadrian VII
Marcus, F. The killing of Sister George
Sackler, H. The great white hope
Shaffer, P. The royal hunt of the sun
Simon, N. The odd couple
Stein, J. Fiddler on the roof
Williams, T. Night of the iguana

RICJ Richards, Stanley, ed. Best short plays of the world theatre, 1958-1967. New York, Crown, 1968. 334p
Anouilh, J. Madame de...
Anouilh, J. The orchestra
Behan, B. The new house
Brophy, B. The waste disposal unit
Coward, N. Come into the garden, Maud
Feiffer, J. Crawling Arnold
Fratti, M. The academy
Frisch, M. The firebugs
Inge, W. The disposal
Jones, L. The great goodness of life
Lowell, R. Benito Cereno
Macauley, P. Monica
Marcus, F. The window
Melfi, L. Birdbath
Mercer, D. The governor's lady
O'Casey, S. Nannie's night out
Osborne, J. A subject of scandal and concern
Pirandello, L. Bellavita
Shaffer, P. White lies
Weiss, P. The tower

RICK Richards, Stanley, ed. Best short plays of the world theatre, 1968-1973. New York, Crown, 1973. 303p
Anouilh, J. Episode in the life of an author
Bellow, S. Orange souffle
Bentley, E. Larry Parks' day in court
Bowen, J. The waiting room
Childress, A. Mojo
Duncan, R. The gift
Ginsbury, N. The safety match
Horovitz, I. Line
Inge, W. Margaret's bed
Kennedy, A., Lennon, J., and Spinetti, V. The Lennon play: in his own write
Miller, J. Lou Gehrig did not die of cancer
Mortimer, J. Bermondsday
Owen, A. Male of the species
Salacrou, A. Marguerite
Schisgal, M. The Chinese

Shepard, S. The holy ghostly
Simon, N. Visitor from Forest Hills
Ward, D. Day of absence
Williams, T. Confessional

RICL Richardson, Lyon Norman; Orians, George H., and Brown, Herbert R., eds. The heritage of American literature... Boston, Ginn [c1951] 2v
O'Neill, E. Anna Christie 2

RITS Ritchie, James M. and Garten, H. F., eds. and trs. Seven expressionist plays; Kokoschka to Barlach. London, Calder and Boyars [1968] 201p
Barlach, E. Squire Blue Boll
Brust, A. The wolves
Goll, I. Methusalem
Kafka, F. The guardian of the tomb
Kaiser, T. The protagonist
Kokoschka, O. Murderer hope of womankind
Stramm, A. Awakening

RITV Ritchie, James M. and Stowell, J. D., eds. and trs. Vision and aftermath: four expressionist war plays... London, Calder and Boyars, 1969. 208p
Goering, R. Naval encounter
Haesenclever, W. Antigone
Hauptmann, C. War, a Te Deum
Toller, E. Hinkelmann

ROB Robbins, Harry Wolcott and Coleman, William Harold, eds. Western world literature... New York, Macmillan, 1938. 1422p
Aeschylus. Agamemnon
Aristophanes. The frogs
Calderón de la Barca, P. Keep your own secret
Euripides. Iphigenia at Aulis
Everyman
Goethe, J. Faust, pt. I
Ibsen, H. Ghosts
Molière, J. Misanthrope
O'Neill, E. Beyond the horizon
Plautus, T. The captives
Racine, J. Phaedra
Shakespeare, W. King Lear
Sheridan, R. The rivals

ROBE Robertson, Durant Waite, ed. The literature of medieval England. New York, McGraw-Hill, 1970. 612p
Everyman
Mactacio Abel
Secunda pastorum

ROBI Robinson, Charles Alexander, jr., ed. An anthology of Greek drama, first series... New York, Rinehart [c1949] 269p (Rinehart editions)
Aeschylus. Agamemnon
Aristophanes. Lysistrata
Euripides. Hippolytus
Euripides. Medea
Sophocles. Antigone
Sophocles. Oedipus the king

ROBJ Robinson, Charles Alexander, Jr., ed. An anthology of Greek drama, second series... New York, Rinehart [c1954] 398p (Rinehart editions)
Aeschylus. Choëphoroe
Aeschylus. Eumenides
Aeschylus. Prometheus bound
Aristophanes. The clouds
Aristophanes. The frogs
Euripides. The bacchae
Euripides. The Trojan women
Sophocles. Oedipus at Colonus
Sophocles. Philoctetes

ROBJA Robinson, Charles Alexander, Jr., ed. The spring of civilization, Periclean Athens. New York, Dutton, 1954. 464p

ROBJA (cont.)
Aeschylus. Agamemnon
Euripides. Medea
Euripides. The Trojan women
Sophocles. Antigone
Sophocles. Oedipus at Colonus
Sophocles. Oedipus the king

ROBK Robinson, Cyril Edward, tr. The genius of the Greek drama... Oxford, Clarendon press, 1921. 96p
Aeschylus. Agamemnon
Euripides. Medea
Sophocles. Antigone

ROBM Robinson, Donald Fay, ed. The Harvard Dramatic Club miracle plays; ten plays translated and adapted by various hands... New York, French, 1928. 241p
The Benediktbeuren play
Bourlet, K. The nativity
The Hessian Christmas play
The Maastricht play
The pageant of the shearmen and the tailors
The provençal play
The star
The Towneley play
The Umbrian play
The wisemen

ROE Roberts, Carl Eric Bechhofer, tr. Five Russian plays, with one from the Ukrainian... New York, Dutton, 1916. 173p
Chekhov, A. The jubilee
Chekhov, A. The wedding
Evreinov, N. The beautiful despot
Evreinov, N. A merry death
Fonvizin, D. The choice of a tutor
Ukrainka, L. [pseud.] The Babylonian captivity

ROET Roby, Robert C., and Ulanov, Barry, eds. Introduction to drama... New York, McGraw-Hill, 1962. 704p
Chekhov, A. The cherry orchard
Congreve, W. The way of the world
Euripides. Medea
Giraudoux, J. Tiger at the gates
Ibsen, H. Rosmersholm
Jonson, B. The alchemist
Kaiser, G. From morn to midnight
Lindsay, D. The satire of the three estates
Molière, J. The misanthrope
Plautus, T. Miles gloriosus
Racine, J. Phaedra
Shaw, G. Man and superman
Sophocles. Oedipus rex
Strindberg, A. The dance of death
Webster, J. The Duchess of Malfi

ROGE Rogers, Winfield Heyser; Redinger, Ruby V., and Haydn II, Hiram C., eds. Explorations in living... New York, Reynal & Hitchcock [c1941] 783p
Ibsen, H. An enemy of the people
Shakespeare, W. Hamlet
Wilder, T. Our town

ROHAN, PIERRE DE. See FEE, FEF Federal theatre project. Federal theatre plays... ["Edited for the Federal theatre by Pierre de Rohan"]

ROHR Rohrberger, Mary; Woods, Samuel H., Jr. and Dukore, Bernard F., comps. An introduction to literature... New York, Random House [1968] 983p
Everyman
Shakespeare, W. The tragedy of Macbeth

Shaw, G. Pygmalion
Sophocles. Antigone
Strindberg, A. A dream play
Williams, T. The glass menagerie

ROLF Rolfe, Franklin Prescott; Davenport, William H. and Bowerman, Paul, eds. The modern omnibus... New York, Harcourt, Brace [c1946] 1071p
Anderson, M. Key Largo
Kaufman, G. and Ryskind, M. Of thee I sing
Sherwood, R. Abe Lincoln in Illinois
Thurber, J. and Nugent, E. The male animal

ROM Roman drama... Indianapolis Bobbs-Merrill [c1965] 463p
Plautus, T. The Menaechmi
Plautus, T. The haunted house
Plautus, T. The rope
Seneca, L. Medea
Seneca, L. Oedipus
Seneca, T. Thyestes
Terence, P. The brothers
Terence, P. Phormio
Terence, P. The woman of Andros

ROSE, MARTIAL. <u>See</u> TOWN Towneley plays. The Wakefield mystery plays...

ROSENFIELD, JOHN. <u>See</u> THX Three Southwest plays...

ROSENFIELD, PAUL. <u>See</u> AME American caravan...

ROSS Ross, Ralph Gilbert; Berryman, John and Tate, Allen, eds. The arts of reading. New York, Thomas Y. Crowell [c1960] 488p
Chekhov, A. A marriage proposal
Shakespeare, W. The tragedy of Macbeth

ROWC Rowell, George, ed. Late Victorian plays, 1890-1914. New York, Oxford, 1968. 507p
Davies, H. The mollusc
Galsworthy, J. Justice
Granville-Barker, H. The Voysey inheritance
Hankin, St. J. The Cassilis engagement
Houghton, S. Hindle wakes
Jones, H. The liars
Pinero, A. The second Mrs. Tanqueray

ROWE Rowell, George, ed. Nineteenth century plays... London, Oxford university press [c1953] 567p
Albery, J. Two roses
Boucicault, D. The colleen bawn
Bulwer-Lytton, E. Money
Grundy, S. A pair of spectacles
Hazelwood, C. Lady Audley's secret
Jerrold, D. Black-ey'd Susan
Lewis, L. The bells
Robertson, T. Caste
Taylor, T. The ticket-of-leave man
Taylor, T. and Reade, C. Masks and faces

RUA Rubinstein, Harold Frederick, ed. Four Jewish plays... London, Gollancz, 1948. 303p
Bernhard, E. The Marranos
Block, T. You must stay to tea
Hemro. Poor ostrich
Scott, P. Pillars of salt

RUB Rubinstein, Harold Frederick, ed. Great English plays... New York, Harper, 1928. 1136p
Beaumont, F. and Fletcher, J. The maid's tragedy
Congreve, W. The way of the world

RUB (cont.)
Dekker, T. The shoemaker's holiday
Everyman
Farquhar, G. The recruiting officer
Fletcher, J. The chances
Ford, J. 'Tis a pity she's a whore
Goldsmith, O. She stoops to conquer
Heywood, J. John, Tyb, and the curate
Jones, H. Judah
Jonson, B. The silent woman
Jonson, B., Chapman, G. and Marston, J. Eastward ho!
Kyd, T. The Spanish tragedy
Marlowe, C. Doctor Faustus
Marlowe, C. Edward the second
Massinger, P. The bondman
Massinger, P. A new way to pay old debts
Otway, T. Venice preserved
Peele, G. The old wives' tale
Robertson, T. Society
Sheridan, R. The school for scandal
Vanbrugh, J. The provoked wife
A Wakefield nativity
Webster, J. The white devil
Wilde, O. Lady Windermere's fan
A Yorkshire tragedy

RUSS Russell, Harry Kitsun; Wells, William and Stauffer, Donald A., eds. Literature in English... New York, Holt [c1948] 1174p
Shakespeare, W. King Lear
Sheridan, R. The school for scandal

RUSV Russell, John David, and Brown, Ashley, eds. Satire ... Cleveland, World Books, [c1967] 420p
Euripides. The cyclops
Mayakóvsky, V. The bedbug
Molière, J. Love is the best doctor

RYL Rylands, George Humphrey Wolfestan, ed. Elizabethan tragedy... London, Bell, 1933. 623p
Chapman, G. Bussy d'Ambois
Ford, J. 'Tis a pity she's a whore
Heywood, T. A woman killed with kindness
Marlowe, C. Tamburlaine the great, pt. I
Tourneur, C. The revenger's tragedy
Webster, J. The white devil

S

SAFF Saffron, Robert, ed. Great farces... New York, Collier Books, 1966. 316p
Aristophanes. Lysistrata
Gogol, N. The inspector general
Molière, J. Le bourgeois gentilhomme
Spewack, B. and Spewack, S. Boy meets girl
Wilde, O. The importance of being earnest

SAFM Saffron, Robert, ed. Great melodramas... New York, Collier Books, 1966. 341p
Dumas, A. Monte Cristo
Gillette, W. Secret service
Hamilton, P. Angel street
Maugham, W. The letter

SALE Salerno, Henry Frank, ed. English drama in transition 1880-1920... New York, Pegasus [1968] 544p
Barrie, J. The admirable Crichton
Galsworthy, J. The silver box

Jones, H. The liars
Maugham, W. Our betters
Pinero, A. The second Mrs. Tanqueray
Shaw, G. Major Barbara
Synge, J. The playboy of the western world
Wilde, O. The importance of being earnest
Yeats, M. Deirdre

SALG Salgãdo, Ramsay Gãmini Norton, ed. Three Jacobean tragedies... Baltimore, Penguin Books [1965] 363p
Middleton, T. The changeling
Tourneur, C. The revenger's tragedy
Webster, J. The white devil

SALR Salgãdo, Ramsay Gãmini Norton, ed. Three restoration comedies... Baltimore, Penguin Books [1968] 365p
Congreve, W. Love for love
Etherege, G. The man of mode
Wycherley, W. The country wife

SAND Sanderlin, George. College reading... Boston, Heath [c1953] 849p
Ibsen, H. An enemy of the people
O'Neill, E. Bound east for Cardiff
Shaw, G. Androcles and the lion

SANE Sanders, Charles [and others] eds. Synthesis: responses to literature. New York, Knopf, 1971. 750p
Chekhov, A. The three sisters
Euripides. The bacchae
Ibsen, H. The master builder
Itallie, J. America hurrah
Molière, J. Tartuffe
Pirandello, L. Henry IV

SANK Sanders, Thomas S. The discovery of drama. Glenview, Ill., Scott, Foresman, 1968. 637p
Bellow, S. Orange souffle
Chayefsky, P. The latent heterosexual
Giraudoux, J. Sodom and Gomorrah
Shakespeare, W. Macbeth
Sophocles. Oedipus rex
Synge, J. Riders to the sea
Williams, T. Camino real

SANM Sanderson, James L. and Zimmerman, Everett, eds. Medea: myth and dramatic form... Boston, Houghton Mifflin [1967] 337p
Anderson, M. The wingless victory
Anouilh, J. Medea
Euripides. Medea
Jeffers, R. Medea
Seneca. Medea

SANO Sanderson, James L. and Zimmerman, Everett, eds. Oedipus: myth and dramatic form... Boston, Houghton Mifflin [1968] 341p
Cocteau, J. The infernal machine
Gide, A. Oedipus
Seneca. Oedipus
Sophocles. King Oedipus
Voltaire. Oedipus

SANP Sanderson, James L. and Gopnik, Irwin, eds. Phaedra and Hippolytus: myth and dramatic form. Boston, Houghton Mifflin, 1966. 338p
Euripides. Hippolytus
Jeffers, F. The Cretan woman
O'Neill, E. Desire under the elms
Racine, J. Phaedra
Seneca. Phaedra

SATA Satan, Socialites, and Solly Gold: Three new plays from England. New York, Coward-McCann [c1961] 280p
Duncan, R. The death of Satan
Jupp, K. The socialites
Kops, B. Enter Solly Gold

SATI Satin, Joseph Henry, comp. Reading literature ... Boston, Houghton Mifflin [1964] 1338p (Pt. III, Reading drama)
Albee, E. The sand box
Betti, U. Corruption in the palace of justice
Chekhov, A. Uncle Vanya
Hill, F. The six degrees of crime
Molière, J. The physician in spite of himself
Steinbeck, J. Of mice and men
Strindberg, A. Miss Julie
Wilde, O. The importance of being earnest

SATJ Satin, Joseph Henry, ed. Reading literature; stories, plays and poems... Boston, Houghton Mifflin [1968] 683p
Albee, E. The sand box
Chekhov, A. Uncle Vanya
Giraudoux, J. The tiger at the gates
Shaw, G. Arms and the man
Sophocles. Oedipus the king

SAYLER, OLIVER MARTIN, <u>See also</u> MOS, MOSA Moscow art theatre series of Russian plays... and PLAM Plays of the Moscow art theatre musical studio...

SAY Sayler, Oliver Martin, ed. The Eleonora Duse series of plays... New York, Brentano [c1923] v.p.
Annunzio, G. d'. The dead city
Gallarati-Scotti, T. Thy will be done
Ibsen, H. Ghosts
Ibsen, H. The lady from the sea
Praga, M. The closed door

SCAN ... Scandinavian plays of the twentieth century... Princeton, N. J., Princeton university press, 1944-1951. 3v
Abell, K. Anna Sophie Hedvig 2
Bergman, H. Mr. Sleeman is coming 1
Bergman, H. The Swedenhielms 3
Dagerman, S. The condemned 3
Grieg, N. The defeat; a play about the Paris Commune 2
Josephson, R. Perhaps a poet 1
Krog, H. The sounding shell 2
Lagerkvist, P. Let man live 3
Lagerkvist, P. The man without a soul 1
Munk, K. Niels Ebbesen 2
Schildt, R. The Gallows man: a midwinter story 1

SCAR Scanlan, David, comp. 5 comedies. Boston, Houghton, Mifflin, 1971. 343p
Giraudoux, J. The madwoman of Chaillot
Pritchard, B. Captain Fantastio meets the ectomorph
Saroyan, W. The time of your life
Shaw, G. Arms and the man
Sheridan, R. The rivals

SCAT Schell, Edgar Thomas, ed. English morality plays and moral interludes... New York, Holt, Rinehart and

Winston, 1969. 554p
The castle of perseverance
Everyman
The interlude of youth
Lupton, T. All for money
Redford, J. Wit and science
Respublica
Wager, W. Enough is as good as a feast
Wapull, G. The tide tarrieth no man
Woodes, N. The conflict of conscience
World and the child

SCH Schelling, Felix Emmanuel, ed. Typical Elizabethan plays...New York, Harper, 1926. 797p
Beaumont, F. and Fletcher, J. The maid's tragedy
Beaumont, F. and Fletcher, J. Philaster; or, Love lies a-bleeding
Chapman, G., Jonson, B. and Marston, J. Eastward ho!
Dekker, T. The pleasant comedy of Old Fortunatus
Fletcher, J. Rule a wife and have a wife
Ford, J. The chronical history of Perkin Warbeck, a strange truth
Greene, R. A pleasant conceited comedy of [George a Greene], the pinner of Wakefield
Heywood, T. A woman killed with kindness
Jonson, B. The hue and cry after cupid
Jonson, B. The sad shepherd
Jonson, B. Volpone; or, The fox
The lamentable and true tragedy of Master Arden of Feversham in Kent
Lyly, J. Endymion, the man in the moon
Marlowe, C. The tragical history of Doctor Faustus
Marlowe, C. The troublesome reign and lamentable death of Edward II
Massinger, P. A new way to pay old debts
Middleton, T. and Rowley, W. The changeling
Munday, A. Sir Thomas More (An ill May-day)
The return from Parnassus; or, The scourge of simony, pt. II
Shirley, J. The lady of pleasure
Webster, J. The tragedy of The Duchess of Malfi

SCI Schelling, Felix Emmanuel and Black, Matthew, W., eds. Typical Elizabethan plays...Rev. and enl. ed. New York, Harper [c1931] 1033p
Beaumont, F. and Fletcher, J. The knight of the burning pestle
Beaumont, F. and Fletcher, J. The maid's tragedy
Beaumont, F. and Fletcher, J. Philaster; or, Love lies a-bleeding
Chapman, G., Jonson, B. and Marston, J. Eastward ho!
Dekker, T. The pleasant comedy of Old Fortunatus
Dekker, T. The shoemaker's holiday; or, The gentle craft
Fletcher, J. The faithful shepherdess
Fletcher, J. Rule a wife and have a wife
Ford, J. The broken heart
Greene, R. The honorable history of Friar Bacon and Friar Bungay
Heywood, T. A woman killed with kindness
Jonson, B. Every man in his humour
Jonson, B. The hue and cry after cupid
Jonson, B. Volpone; or, The fox
Kyd, T. The Spanish tragedy

SCI (cont.)
Lyly, J. Endymion, the man in the moon
Marlowe, C. Tamburlaine the great, pt. I
Marlowe, C. The tragical history of Doctor Faustus
Marlowe, C. The troublesome reign and lamentable death of Edward II
Massinger, P. A new way to pay old debts
Middleton, T. Michaelmas term
Middleton, T. and Rowley, W. The changeling
Munday, A. Sir Thomas More (An ill May-day)
Peele, G. The old wives' tale
The return from Parnassus; or, The scourge of simony, pt. II
Shirley, J. The lady of pleasure
Webster, J. The tragedy of The Duchess of Malfi

SCJ Schelling, Felix Emmanuel and Black, Matthew W., eds. Typical Elizabethan plays...Third edition, revised and enlarged...New York, Harper [c1949] 1065p
Beaumont, F. and Fletcher, J. The knight of the burning pestle
Beaumont, F. and Fletcher, J. The maid's tragedy
Beaumont, F. and Fletcher, J. Philaster; or, Love lies a-bleeding
Chapman, G., Jonson, B. and Marston, J. Eastward ho!
Dekker, T. The shoemaker's holiday; or, The gentle craft
Fletcher, J. The faithful shepherdess
Ford, J. The broken heart
Greene, R. The honorable history of Friar Bacon and Friar Bungay
Heywood, T. A woman killed with kindness
Jonson, B. Every man in his humour
Jonson, B. The hue and cry after cupid
Jonson, B. Volpone; or, The fox
Kyd, T. The Spanish tragedy
Lyly, J. Endymion, the man in the moon
Marlowe, C. Tamburlaine the great, pt. I
Marlowe, C. The tragical history of Doctor Faustus
Marlowe, C. The troublesome reign and lamentable death of Edward II
Massinger, P. A new way to pay old debts
Middleton, T. Michaelmas term
Middleton, T. and Rowley, W. The changeling
Munday, A. Sir Thomas More (An ill May-day)
Peele, G. The old wives' tale
The return from Parnassus; or, The scourge of simony, pt. II
Shirley, J. The lady of pleasure
Webster, J. The tragedy of the Duchess of Malfi

SCN Schinz, Albert; Robert, Osmond Thomas and Giroud, Pierre François, eds. Nouvelle anthologie française. New York, Harcourt, Brace, 1936. 680p
Corneille, P. Le cid
La farce de maître Pierre Pathelin
Hugo, V. Ruy Blas
Labiche, E. et Martin, E. La poudre aux yeux
Molière, J. Le bourgeois gentilhomme
Racine, J. Andromaque

SCNN Schneider, Elizabeth W.;

Walker, Albert L. and Childs, Herbert E., eds. The range of literature... New York, American Book Company [c1960] 732p
Chekhov, A. The cherry orchard
Rice, E. The adding machine
Shakespeare, W. Othello, the Moor of Venice
Shaw, G. Arms and the man
Sophocles. Oedipus rex

SCNO Schneider, Elizabeth Wintersteen; Walker, Albert L. and Childs, Herbert E., eds. The range of literature... 2d ed. New York, American Book Co. [1967] 702p
Beckett, S. All that fall
Chekhov, A. The cherry orchard
Ionesco, E. Improvisation; or, The shepherd's chameleon
Shakespeare, W. Othello
Shaw, G. Arms and the man
Sophocles. Oedipus rex
Wilder, T. The skin of our teeth

SCNP Schneider, Elizabeth Wintersteen [and others] eds. The range of literature. 3d ed. New York, Van Nostrand-Reinhold, 1973. 1116p
Chekhov, A. The cherry orchard
Hansberry, L. A raisin in the sun
Ibsen, H. A doll's house
MacLeish, A. J. B.
Mrożek, S. The police
Shakespeare, W. Othello
Shaw, G. Arms and the man
Sophocles. Antigone

SCNR Schorer, Mark, comp. Galaxy: literary modes and genres. New York, Harcourt, Brace and World [1967] 620p
Chekhov, A. The three sisters
Euripides. The Trojan women
Giraudoux, J. Tiger at the gates
Lowell, R. My kinsman, Major Molineux

SCNT Schorer, Mark, comp. The literature of America: twentieth century... New York, McGraw-Hill, 1970. 1159p
Albee, E. The zoo story
Jones, L. Dutchman
O'Neill, E. Desire under the elms
Wilder, T. The skin of our teeth

SCV Schotter, Richard, ed. The American place theatre. New York, Dell Publishing Company, 1973. 270p
Cameron, K. Papp
Ribman, R. Fingernails blue as flowers
Russell, C. Five on the black hand side
Tabori, G. The cannibals
Tesich, S. The carpenters

SCW Schweikert, Harry Christian, ed. Early English plays... New York, Harcourt, Brace [c1928] 845p
Abraham and Isaac
Banns
Dekker, T. The shoemaker's holiday
Everyman
The fall of Lucifer
Greene, R. The honorable history of Friar Bacon and Friar Bungay
Jonson, B. Every man in his humour
The judgment day
Kyd, T. The Spanish tragedy
Lyly, J. Endymion

SCW (cont.)
Marlowe, C. Tamburlaine the great, pts. I and II
Marlowe, C. The tragical history of Doctor Faustus
Noah
Peele, G. The old wives' tale
Quem quaeritis
Robin Hood and the friar
Sackville, T. and Norton, T. Gorboduc
Saint George and the dragon
The second shepherds' play
Udall, N. Ralph Roister Doister

SCWE Schweikert, Harry Christian; Inglis, Rewey Belle and Gehlmann, John, eds. Adventures in American literature... New York, Harcourt, Brace [c1930] 1064p
Fitch, C. Nathan Hale
O'Neill, E. Where the cross is made
Tarkington, B. The trysting place

SCWG Schweikert, Harry Christian; Inglis, Rewey Belle; Gehlmann, John and Foerster, Norman, eds. Adventures in American literature. Rev. ed. New York, Harcourt Brace, 1936. 1217p
Kelly, G. Poor Aubrey
O'Neill, E. The Emperor Jones
Tarkington, B. The trysting place

SCWI Schweikert, Harry Christian; Miller, Harry Augustus and Cook, Luella Bussey, eds. Adventures in appreciation... New York, Harcourt, Brace, 1935. 1965p
Dunsany, E. The lost silk hat
Howard, S. and DeKruif, P. Yellow jack
Shakespeare, W. As you like it

SCX Scott, Adolphe Clarence, ed. and tr. Traditional Chinese plays. Madison, University of Wisconsin Press, 1967-69. 2v
The butterfly dream (Hu tieh meng) 1
Ssu Lang visits his mother (Ssu Lang t'an mu) 1
Fifteen strings of cash (Shih wu kuan) 2
Longing for worldly pleasures (Ssu fan) 2

SEA Searles, Colbert, ed. Seven French plays (1730-1897)... New York, Holt [c1935] 749p
Augier, E. Le gendre de M. Poirier
Beaumarchais, P. Le mariage de Figaro
Becque, H. Les corbeaux
Hugo, V. Hernani
Marivaux, P. Le jeu de l'amour et du hasard
Rostand, E. Cyrano de Bergerac
Voltaire, F. Zaire

SEAVER, EDWIN. See CROZ Cross-section...

SEBO Seboyar, Gerald Edwin and Brosius, Rudolph Frederic, eds. Readings in European literature. New York, Crofts, 1928. 876p
Aeschylus. Prometheus bound
Aristophanes. The frogs
Euripides. Medea
Ibsen, H. Ghosts
Molière, J. The high-brow ladies
Plautus. The crock of gold
Racine, J. Phaedra
Sophocles. Antigone

Terence. Andria; the fair Andrian

SEBP Seboyar, Gerald Edwin and Brosius, Rudolph Frederic, eds. Readings in European literature [Second edition] New York, Crofts, 1946. 900p
Aeschylus. Prometheus bound
Aristophanes. The frogs
Euripides. Medea
Ibsen, H. Ghosts
Molière, J. The high-brow ladies
Plautus. The Menaechmi
Racine, J. Phaedra
Sophocles. Antigone
Terence. Andria; the fair Andrian

SECK Secker, Martin. The eighteen-nineties... London, Richards [1948] 616p
Dowson, E. The pierrot of the minute
Yeats, W. The Countess Cathleen

SECOND AMERICAN CARAVAN. 1928. See AME American caravan, v2

SELDES, GEORGE S. See PLAM Plays of the Moscow art theatre musical studio...

SELDES, GILBERT. See PLAM Plays of the Moscow art theatre musical studio...

SEN Seng, Peter J., ed. Plays; Wadsworth handbook and anthology. Belmont, Calif., Wadsworth Publishing Company, 1970. 487p
Chekhov, A. The cherry orchard
Everyman
García Lorca, F. The house of Bernarda Alba
Ibsen, H. The wild duck
Jonson, B. Volpone, or; The fox
O'Neill, E. Desire under the elms
Pirandello, L. Six characters in search of an author
The second shepherds' play
Shakespeare, W. Macbeth
Shakespeare, W. A midsummer night's dream
Shaw, G. Heartbreak house
Sophocles. Oedipus rex
Strindberg, A. The ghost sonata
Synge, J. Riders to the sea
Webster, J. The Duchess of Malfi
Wycherly, W. The country wife

SER Seronde, Joseph and Peyre, Henri, eds. ...Nine classic French plays... Boston, Heath [c1936] 748p
Corneille, P. Le cid
Corneille, P. Horace
Corneille, P. Polyeucte
Molière, J. Le précieuses ridicules
Molière, J. Le misanthrope
Molière, J. Le Tartuffe
Racine, J. Andromaque
Racine, J. Esther
Racine, J. Phèdre

SERD Seronde, Joseph and Peyre, Henri, eds. ... Three classic French plays ... Boston, Heath [c1935] 253p
Corneille, P. Le cid
Molière, J. Les précieuses ridicules
Racine, J. Andromaque

SET Setchanove, L. J. Five French comedies... Boston, Allyn and Bacon [c1925] 276p
Bernard, T. L'anglais tel qu'on le parle
La farce de maitre Pathelin
Forest, L. Par un jour de

SET (cont.)
pluie
France, A. La comèdie de celui qui épousa une femme muette
Maurey, M. Rosalie

SEV Seven plays... London, Heinemann [1935] 775p
Coward, N. Conversation piece
Dane, C. Moonlight is silver
Kennedy, M. Escape me never!
Lonsdale, F. Aren't we all?
Priestley, J. Laburnum grove
Winter, J. The shining hour
Wooll, E. Libel

SEVD Seven plays of the modern theatre. With an introduction by Harold Clurman. New York, Grove Press [c1962] 548p
Beckett, S. Waiting for Godot
Behan, B. The quare fellow
Delaney, S. A taste of honey
Gelber, J. The connection
Genêt, J. The balcony
Ionesco, E. Rhinoceros
Pinter, H. The birthday party

SEVE Seven sacred plays with an introduction by Sir Francis Younghusband and notes by A. H. Debenham. London, Methuen [1934] v.p.
Bulkley, A. The crown of light
Debenham, A. Good will toward men
Debenham, A. The Prince of Peace
Gonne, F. In the city of David
Hines, L. Simon
Mell, M. The apostle play
The passion play of Alsfeld

SEVP Seven Soviet plays... with introductions by H. W. L. Dana. New York, Macmillan, 1946. 520p
Afinogenov, A. On the eve
Korneichuk, A. The front
Leonov, L. The orchards of Polovchansk
Rokk, V. Engineer Sergeyev
Simonov, K. The Russian people
Solovyov, V. Field Marshall Kutuzov
Tur, L., Tur, P. and Sheinin, L. Smoke of the fatherland

SHA Shafer, Robert, ed. American literature... New York, Doubleday, Doran [c1926] 2v
Fitch, C. The girl with the green eyes 2
O'Neill, E. "The hairy ape" 2

SHAH Shafer, Robert, ed. From Beowulf to Thomas Hardy... New York, Doubleday, Page [c1924] 2v
Dryden, J. All for love 1
Everyman 1
Goldsmith, O. She stoops to conquer 1
Marlowe, C. The tragical history of Doctor Faustus 1

SHAI Shafer, Robert, ed. From Beowulf to Thomas Hardy... Rev. ed. New York, Doubleday, Doran [c1931] 2v
Congreve, W. The way of the world 1
Everyman 1
Marlowe, C. The tragical history of Doctor Faustus 1
Sheridan, R. The rivals 2

SHAJ Shafer, Robert, ed. From Beowulf to Thomas Hardy. New ed. ... New York, Doubleday, Doran

[c1939] 2v
Dekker, T. The shoemaker's holiday 1
Dryden, J. All for love; or, The world well lost 1
Everyman 1
Marlowe, C. The tragical history of Doctor Faustus 1
The second shepherds' play 1
Sheridan, R. The rivals 2
Wilde, O. The importance of being earnest 2

SHAR Sharp, Russell, A.; Brewton, John E.; Lemon, Babette, and Abney, Louise, eds. English and continental literature... Chicago, Laidlaw [c1950] 800p (Cultural Growth series)
Gregory, I. The rising of the moon
Molière, J. The physician in spite of himself
Shakespeare, W. Macbeth

SHAV Shaw, Harry, ed. A collection of readings for writers; book three of A complete course in freshman English. 6th ed. New York, Harper and Row [1967] 722p
Shakespeare, W. The tragedy of Macbeth
Shaw, G. Pygmalion
Sophocles. Antigone

SHAW Shaw, Harry, ed. A complete course in freshman English... Fifth edition. New York, Harper & Brothers [c1959] 1306p
Shakespeare, W. The tragedy of Romeo and Juliet
Shaw, G. Pygmalion
Wilder, T. The long Christmas dinner

SHAX Shaw, Harry Lee, ed. A complete course in freshman English. 7th ed. New York, Harper, 1973. 836p
Shaw, G. Arms and the man
Sophocles. Antigone
Wilder, T. The long Christmas dinner

SHAY Shay, Frank, ed. A treasury of plays for women... Boston, Little, Brown, 1922. 443p
Clements, C. Columbine
Clements, C. The siege
Dransfield, J. The lost Pleiad
Emig, E. The china pig
Gerstenberg, A. Ever young
Gerstenberg, A. A patroness
Knox, F. For distinguished service
Kreymborg, A. Manikin and Minikin
Kreymborg, A. Rocking chairs
McCauley, C. The conflict
Maeterlinck, M. The death of Tintagiles
Millay, E. The lamp and the bell
Morley, C. Rehearsal
O'Neill, E. Before breakfast
Pillot, E. My lady dreams
Smith, H. Blackberryin'
Strindberg, A. Motherly love
Strindberg, A. The stronger woman

SHER Sheratsky, Rodney E. and Reilly, John L., eds. The lively arts; 4 representative types. New York, Globe Book Co. [1964] 544p
Agee, J. Abraham Lincoln, the early years
Chayefsky, P. Marty
Lawrence, J. and Lee, R. Inherit the wind

SHERWOOD, GARRISON P. See BEST plays of 1894/1899... etc.

SHR Shrodes, Caroline; Van Gundy, Justine and Dorius

SHR (cont.)
Joel, comps. Reading for understanding: fiction, drama, poetry...New York, Macmillan [1968] 716p
Albee, E. The zoo story
Chekhov, A. The sea-gull
Ibsen, H. Ghosts
Shakespeare, W. Antony and Cleopatra
Sophocles. King Oedipus
Yeats, W. The words upon the window pane

SHRO Shroyer, Frederick Benjamin, and Gardemal, Louis G., comps. Types of drama. Glenview, Ill., Scott, Foresman, 1970. 678p
Aristophanes. The frogs
Brecht, B. The good woman of Setzuan
Everyman
Molière, J. Tartuffe
Powell, A. The death of everymom
Rostand, E. Cyrano de Bergerac
Shakespeare, W. Hamlet
Sheridan, R. The school for scandal
Sophocles. Oedipus the king
Wilder, T. The matchmaker
Williams, T. The glass menagerie

SILM Simonson, Harold Peter, ed. Trio; a book of stories, plays, and poems...New York, Harper & Brothers [c1962] 489p
Chekhov, A. The cherry orchard
Ibsen, H. Ghosts

SILN Simonson, Harold Peter, ed. Trio: a book of stories, plays and poems. 3d ed. New York, Harper, 1970. 747p
Chekhov, A. Uncle Vanya
Ibsen, H. Ghosts
Strindberg, A. Miss Julie
Synge, J. Riders to the sea
Williams, T. The glass menagerie

SILQ Simonson, Harold Peter, ed. Quartet: a book of stories, plays, poems and critical essays. New York, Harper and Row, 1970. 1019p
Chekhov, A. Uncle Vanya
Ibsen, H. Ghosts
Strindberg, A. Miss Julie
Synge, J. Riders to the sea
Williams, T. The glass menagerie

SIM Simpson, Claude Mitchell and Nevins, Allan, eds. The American reader... Boston, Heath [c1941] 866p
Connelly, M. The green pastures
Riggs, L. Green grow the lilacs
Wilder, T. Our town

SIN Singleton, Ralph H. and Millet, Stanton, eds. An introduction to literature ...Cleveland, World [1966] 1237p
Ibsen, H. Hedda Gabler
Shakespeare, W. Measure for measure
Shakespeare, W. Othello
Shaw, G. Pygmalion
Sophocles. Antigone
Sophocles. Oedipus rex

SIXB Six great modern plays... [New York, Dell, c1956] 512p
Chekhov, A. Three sisters
Ibsen, H. The master builder
Miller, A. All my sons
O'Casey, S. Red roses for me
Shaw, G. Mrs. Warren's profession
Williams, T. The glass menagerie

SIXC Six modern American plays. Introduction by Allan G. Halline... New York, Modern library [c1951] 419p
Anderson, M. Winterset
Heggen, T. and Logan, J. Mister Roberts
Hellman, L. The little foxes
Kaufman, G. and Hart, M. The man who came to dinner
O'Neill, E. The Emperor Jones
Williams, T. The glass menagerie

SIXD Six plays... London, Gollancz, 1930. 672p
Bax, C. Socrates
Connelly, M. The green pastures
George, E. Down our street
Glaspell, S. Alison's house
Rice, E. Street scene
Sherriff, R. Badger's green

SIXH Six plays... London, Heinemann [1934] 746p
Coward, N. Design for living
Dane, C. Wild Decembers
Kaufman, G. and Ferber, E. Dinner at eight
Maugham, W. Sheppey
Priestley, J. Dangerous corner
Winter, K. The rats of Norway

SIXL Six plays of 1939... [London] Hamilton [1939] v.p.
Behrman, S. No time for comedy
Hellman, L. The little foxes
Jones, J. Rhondda roundabout
Lyndon, B. The man in Half moon street
McCracken, E. Quiet wedding
Rattigan, T. After the dance

SIXP Six plays of today... London, Heinemann [1939] 716p
Coppel, A. I killed the count
Coward, N. Point Valaine
Hodge, M. The island
Priestley, J. Cornelius
Sherwood, R. Idiot's delight
Wolfe, H. The silent knight

SLM Smith, Michael Townsend, ed. The best off off-Broadway. New York, Dutton, 1969. 256p
Agenoux, S. Charles Dickens' Christmas carol
Fornés, M. Dr. Kheal
Heide, R. Moon
Kvares, D. Mushrooms
Shepard, S. Forensic and the navigators
Smith, M. The next thing
Tavel, R. Gorilla queen

SMA Small, Norman M., and Sutton, Maurice Lewis, eds. The making of drama. Boston, Holbrook Press, 1972. 691p
Brecht, B. The Caucasian chalk circle
Chekhov, A. The cherry orchard
Goldoni, C. The servant of two masters
Gorki, M. The lower depths
Kopit, A. Oh dad, poor dad, mama's hung you in the closet and I'm feelin' so sad
Molière, J. Tartuffe
Rice, E. The adding machine
Shakespeare, W. Hamlet
Sophocles. Oedipus the king

SME Smith, Michael Townsend, ed. More plays from off-off Broadway. Indianapolis, Bobbs Merrill, 1972. 409p
Birmisa, G. Georgie porgie
Eyen, T. Grand tenement and November 22
Hadler, W. Flite cage
Hoffman, W. X
X
X X
X

SME (cont.)
Kennedy, A. A rat's mass
Koutoukas, H. Tidy passions, or kill, kaleidoscope, kill
Ludlam, C. Bluebeard
Mednick, M. Willie the germ
Williams, A. The poor little watch girl

SMI Smith, Robert Metcalf, ed. ...Types of domestic tragedy...New York, Prentice-Hall, 1928. 576p (World drama series)
Annunzio, G. d'. Gioconda
Hebbel, F. Maria Magdalena
Heywood, T. A woman killed with kindness
Ibsen, H. Hedda Gabler
Lillo, G. George Barnwell; or, The London merchant
Pinero, A. Mid-channel
Strindberg, A. The father

SMK Smith, Robert Metcalf, ed. ...Types of historical drama...New York, Prentice-Hall, 1928. 635p (World drama series)
Hebbel, C. Agnes Bernauer
Ibsen, H. The pretenders
Kleist, H. The prince of Homburg
Schiller, F. William Tell
Shakespeare, W. King Henry the fourth, pt. I
Tennyson, A. Becket

SML Smith, Robert Metcalf, ed. ...Types of philosophic drama...New York, Prentice-Hall, 1928. 524p (World drama series)
Aeschylus. Prometheus bound
Andreev, L. The life of man
The book of Job
Byron, G. Manfred
Everyman
Marlowe, C. Dr. Faustus
Milton, J. Samson Agonistes
Shelley, P. Prometheus unbound

SMN Smith, Robert Metcalf, ed. ...Types of romantic drama...New York, Prentice-Hall, 1928. 621p (World drama series)
Corneille, P. The Cid
Dryden, J. All for love
Grillparzer, F. Sappho
Maeterlinck, M. Pelléas and Mélisande
Phillips, S. Paolo and Francesca
Rostand, E. Cyrano de Bergerac
Shakespeare, W. Romeo and Juliet

SMO Smith, Robert Metcalf, ed. ...Types of social comedy ...New York, Prentice-Hall, 1928. 759p (World drama series)
Congreve, W. The way of the world
Goldsmith, O. She stoops to conquer
Massinger, P. A new way to pay old debts
Maugham, W. Our betters
Molière, J. Tartuffe
Pinero, A. The gay Lord Quex
Sheridan, R. The school for scandal
Wilde, O. Lady Windermere's fan

SMP Smith, Robert Metcalf, ed. ...Types of world tragedy ...New York, Prentice-Hall, 1928. 667p (World drama series)
Euripides. Medea
Gorki, M. The lower depths
Hauptmann, G. The weavers
Ibsen, H. Ghosts
Racine, J. Phaedra
Shakespeare, W. Othello, the Moor of Venice
Shelley, P. The Cenci
Sophocles. Oedipus the king

SMR Smith, Robert Metcalf and

Rhoads, Howard Garrett, eds. ...Types of farce comedy...New York, Prentice-Hall, 1928. 598p (World drama series)
Aristophanes. The frogs
France, A. The man who married a dumb wife
Gay, J. The beggar's opera
Gilbert, W. and Sullivan, A. Patience
Molière, J. The doctor in spite of himself
Pinero, A. The magistrate
Plautus, T. The Menaechmi
Shakespeare, W. The taming of the shrew
Wilde, O. The importance of being earnest

SNO Snow, Lois Wheeler, ed. and tr. China on stage; an American actress in the People's Republic. New York, Random House, 1972. 328p
Ou-hung, W., and Chia, A. Red lantern
Red detachment of women
Shachiapang
Taking Tiger Mountain by strategy

SNYD Snyder, Franklyn Bliss and Martin, Robert Grant, eds. A book of English literature...4th edition. New York, Macmillan [c1942-43] 2v
Abraham and Isaac 1
Dryden, J. All for love 1
Everyman 1
Galsworthy, J. Loyalties 2
Marlowe, C. Doctor Faustus 1
Noah's flood 1
O'Casey, S. Juno and the paycock 2
Sheridan, R. The rivals 1

SOK Sokel, Walter Herbert, ed. Anthology of German expressionist drama; a prelude to the absurd. Garden City, N.Y., Doubleday, 1963. 365p
Brecht, B. Baal
Goll, Y. The immortal one
Hasenclever, W. Humanity
Kaiser, G. Alkibiades saved
Kokoschka, O. Job
Kokoschka, O. Murderer the women's hope
Lauckner, R. Cry in the street
Sorge, R. The beggar
Sternheim, C. The strongbox

SOM Somer, John L., comp. Dramatic experience: the public voice. Glenview, Ill., Scott, Foresman, 1970. 282p
Ibsen, H. Hedda Gabler
Shakespeare, W. Romeo and Juliet
Sophocles. Antigone
Synge, J. The playboy of the western world
Williams, T. The glass menagerie

SOMA Somer, John L., and Cozzo, Joseph, comps. Literary experience: public and private voices. Glenview, Ill., Scott, Foresman, 1971. 681p
Ibsen, H. Hedda Gabler
Shakespeare, W. Romeo and Juliet
Sophocles. Antigone
Synge, J. The playboy of the western world
Williams, T. The glass menagerie

SOU Soule, George, comp. The theatre of the mind. Englewood Cliffs, N.J., Prentice-Hall, 1974. 665p
Aeschylus. Agamemnon
Aristophanes. Lysistrata
Chekhov, A. The cherry orchard
Ibsen, H. Hedda Gabler

SOU (cont.)
Molière, J. The miser
Pinter, H. The dumb waiter
Shakespeare, W. As you like it
Shakespeare, W. King Lear
Shaw, G. Pygmalion
Williams, T. The glass menagerie

SPC Spearhead. 10 years' experimental writing in America [New York, New directions, c1947] 604p
Hutchins, M. Aunt Julia's Caesar
Stein, G. Daniel Webster eighteen in America
Williams, T. 27 wagons full of cotton

SPE Spencer, Hazelton, ed. Elizabethan plays... Boston, Little, Brown, 1933. 1173p
Beaumont, F. [and Fletcher, J.] The knight of the burning pestle
Beaumont, F. and Fletcher, J. The maid's tragedy
Beaumont, F. and Fletcher, J. Philaster; or, Love lies a-bleeding
Chapman, G. Bussy d'Ambois
Chapman, G.; Jonson, B. and Marston, J. Eastward ho!
Dekker, T. The honest whore, pt. I
Dekker, T. The honest whore, pt. II
Dekker, T. The shoemaker's holiday
Fletcher, J. The wild-goose chase
Ford, J. The broken heart
Greene, R. The honourable history of Friar Bacon and Friar Bungay
Heywood, T. A woman killed with kindness
Jonson, B. The alchemist
Jonson, B. Bartholomew fair
Jonson, B. Every man in his humour
Jonson, B. Volpone; or, The fox
Kyd, T. The Spanish tragedy; or, Hieronimo is mad again
Lyly, J. Endymion, the man in the moon
Marlowe, C. The Jew of Malta
Marlowe, C. Tamburlaine, pt. I
Marlowe, C. The tragical history of Doctor Faustus
Marlowe, C. The troublesome reign and lamentable death of Edward the second
Marston, J. The malcontent
Massinger, P. A new way to pay old debts
Middleton, T. A trick to catch the old one
Middleton, T. and Rowley, W. The changeling
Shirley, J. The lady of pleasure
Webster, J. The white devil; or; Vittoria Corombona

SPER Sper, Felix, ed. Favorite modern plays... New York, Globe Book Company [c1953] 530p
Barrie, J. The admirable Crichton
Besier, R. The Barretts of Wimpole Street
Galsworthy, J. Loyalties
Lindsay, H. and Crouse, R. Life with father
Rattigan, T. The Winslow boy

SPES Sper, Felix, ed. Living American plays... New York, Globe Book [c1954] 454p
Hart, M. and Kaufman, G. You can't take it with you
Howard, S. The late Christopher Bean
Lavery, E. The magnificent Yankee
Van Druten, J. I remember Mama

Williams, T. The glass menagerie

SPF Spencer, Hazleton; Houghton, Walter E. and Barrows, Herbert. British literature... Boston, Heath [c1951, 1952] 2v
Congreve, W. The way of the world 1
Dekker, J. The shoemaker's holiday 1
Marlowe, C. Doctor Faustus 1
The second shepherds' play 1
Sheridan, R. The school for scandal 1
Webster, J. The Duchess of Malfi 1

SPI Spiller, Robert Ernest, ed. The roots of national culture; American literature to 1830... New York, Macmillan, 1933. 758p (American literature: a period anthology; Oscar Cargill, general editor, v1)
Tyler, R. The contrast

SPR Sprinchorn, Evert, ed. The genius of the Scandinavian theater. New York, New American Library [1964] 637p
Avell, K. Days on a cloud
Holberg, L. Jeppe of the hill
Ibsen, H. The master builder
Ibsen, H. The wild duck
Lagerkvist, P. The difficult hour
Strindberg, A. Crimes and crimes
Strindberg, A. To Damascus, Part I

SRY Srygley, Ola Pauline and Betts, Otsie Verona, eds. Highlights in English literature and other selections... Dallas, Texas, Banks, Upshaw [1940] 868p
Goldsmith, O. She stoops to conquer
Milne, A. The boy comes home
Shakespeare, W. Macbeth

SRYG Srygley, Ola Pauline and Betts, Otsie Verona, eds. Highlights in English literature... Dallas, Texas, Banks Upshaw [c1940] 868p
Goldsmith, O. She stoops to conquer
Milne, A. The boy comes home
Shakespeare, W. Macbeth
Tolstoy, L. What men live by

SSSF Stafford, William T., ed. Twentieth century American writing... New York Odyssey Press [1965] 712p (The Odyssey surveys of American writing)
O'Neill, E. Desire under the elms
Rice, E. The adding machine
Williams, T. The glass menagerie

SSST Stallman, R. W. and Watters, R. E. The creative reader... New York, Ronald [c1954] 923p
Chekhov, A. The cherry orchard
Coxe, L. and Chapman, R. Billy Budd
Ibsen, H. The wild duck
Shakespeare, W. The tempest
Sophocles. Antigone

SSSU Stallman, R. W. and Watters, R. E. The creative reader... Second edition. New York, Ronald [c1962] 992p
Anouilh, J. Antigone
Coxe, L. and Chapman, R. Billy Budd
Ibsen, H. The wild duck
Shakespeare, W. The tempest

SSSU (cont.)
Sophocles. Antigone

SSTA Stamm, Rudolf, ed. ... Three Anglo-Irish plays... Bern, Switzerland, A. Francke, 1943. 114p (Bibliotheca Anglicana...v5)
Gregory, I. The rising of the moon
Synge, J. Riders to the sea
Yeats, W. Deirdre

SSTE Stanford University. Dramatists' Alliance. Plays of the southern Americas ...Stanford Univ., Dramatists' Alliance, 1942. v.p.
Acevedo Hernández, A. Cabrerita
Sánchez, F. La Gringa
Vargas Tejada, L. Las convulsiones

SSTF Stanley, Linda, and Gillespie, Sheena, comps. The treehouse: an introduction to literature. Cambridge, Mass., Winthrop Pubs., 1974. 368p
Čapek, K., and Čapek, J. The insect play
Euripides. Medea
Miller, A. A memory of two Mondays

SSTG Stanton, Stephen S., ed. Camille and other plays... New York, Hill and Wang [1957] 306p (Mermaid dramabook)
Augier, E. Olympe's marriage
Dumas, A. Camille
Sardou, V. A scrap of paper
Scribe, E. The glass of water
Scribe, E. and Bayard, J. A peculiar position

SSTW Starkie, Walter Fitzwilliam, ed. and tr. Eight Spanish plays of the golden age...New York, Modern Library [1964] 328p
Calderón de la Barca, P. The mayor of Zalamea
Cervantes Saavedra, M. The jealous old man
Cervantes Saavedra, M. Pedro, the artful dodger
The mystery play of Elche
Rueda, L. The mask
Ruiz, J. The gallant, the bawd, and the fair lady
Téllez, G. The playboy of Seville
Vega Carpio, L. Peribáñez and the commander of Ocaña

SSTY Stasio, Marilyn, ed. Broadway's beautiful losers. New York, Delacorte Press, 1972. 425p
Bellow, S. The last analysis
Mercier, M. Johnny no-trump
Perelman, S. The beauty part
Richardson, J. Xmas in Las Vegas
Wheeler, H. Look: we've come through

STA Stauffer, Ruth Matilda, comp. The progress of drama through the centuries ...New York, Macmillan, 1927. 696p
Bulwer-Lytton, E. The lady of Lyons; or, Love and pride
Calderón de la Barca, P. The constant prince
Corneille, P. Polyeucte
Euripides. The Trojan women
Everyman
Fitch, C. The truth
Goldsmith, O. She stoops to conquer; or, The mistakes of a night
Ibsen, H. An enemy of the people
Jonson, B. Epicoene; or, The silent woman

Marlowe, C. Faustus
Molière, J. L'avare
Plautus, T. Aulularia; or, The pot of gold
Racine, J. Berenice
Schiller, J. William Tell
The second shepherds' play
Shakespeare, W. Hamlet
Sheridan, R. The school for scandal
Sophocles. Antigone

STAT Stauffer, Ruth Matilda and Cunningham, William H., eds. Adventures in modern literature. New York, Harcourt, Brace [c1939] 1170p
Anderson, M. The feast of Ortolans
Galsworthy, J. The silver box
Gibney, S. and Collings, P. The story of Louis Pasteur
Glaspell, S. Trifles
Goodman, K. and Hecht, B. The hand of Siva
Sherriff, R. Journey's end

STAU Stauffer, Ruth Matilda and Cunningham, William H., eds. Adventures in modern literature... Second edition. New York, Harcourt, Brace, 1944. 1042p
Čapek, K. R.U.R.
Gibney, S. and Collings, P. The story of Louis Pasteur
Glaspell, S. Trifles
Goodman, K. and Hecht, B. The hand of Siva
Sherriff, R. Journey's end
Wilde, P. Blood of the martyrs

STAUFFER, R. M. See also FREI Freier, Robert... Adventures in modern literature

STAV Stauffer, Ruth Matilda; Cunningham, William H. and Sullivan, Catherine J., eds. Adventures in modern literature. Third edition... New York, Harcourt, Brace, 1951. 747p
Corwin, N. My client Curley
Glaspell, S. Trifles
O'Casey, S. The end of the beginning
Sherriff, R. Journey's end
Van Druten, J. I remember mama

STE Steeves, Harrison Ross, ed. Plays from the modern theatre... Boston, Heath [c1931] 526p
Chekhov, A. The cherry orchard
Donnay, M. Lovers
Hauptmann, G. The beaver coat
Ibsen, H. Ghosts
Molnár, F. Liliom
O'Neill, E. The great god Brown
Pinero, A. The second Mrs. Tanqueray
Schnitzler, A. Intermezzo
Wilde, O. The importance of being earnest

STEI Steinberg, M. W., ed. Aspects of modern drama ...[New York] Henry Holt [c1960] 633p
Anderson, M. Elizabeth the queen
Galsworthy, J. Strife
Miller, A. Death of a salesman
O'Neill, E. The great god Brown
Saroyan, W. The time of your life
Shaw, G. Candida
Shaw, G. Man of destiny
Synge, J. The playboy of the western world
Synge, J. Riders to the sea
Wilde, O. The importance of being earnest
Williams, T. The glass menagerie
Yeats, W. The dreaming of the bones

STI Steinhauer, Harry, ed. Das Deutsche drama, 1880-1933 ...New York, Norton [c1938] 2v
- Hauptmann, G. Das friedensfest 1
- Hofmannsthal, H. Der tor und der tod 1
- Kaiser, G. Gas I 2
- Schnitzler, A. Lebendige stunden 1
- Toller, E. Masse mensch 2
- Unruh, F. Heinruch aus Andernach 2
- Wedekind, F. Der kammersänger 1
- Wiechert, E. Das spiel vom deutschen bettelmann 2

STJ Steinhauer, Harry and Walter, Felix, eds. Omnibus of French literature... New York, Macmillan, 1941. 2v
- Beaumarchais, P. Le barbier de Seville 1
- Becque, H. Les corbeaux 2
- Corneille, P. Le cid 1
- Hugo, V. Ruy Blas 2
- Marivaux, P. Le jeu de l'amour et du hasard 1
- Molière, J. Le misanthrope 1
- Racine, J. Andromaque 1

STJM Steinmann, Martin, Jr. and Willen, Gerald, eds. Literature for writing... Belmont, Cal., Wadsworth Publishing Co. [c1962] 692p
- Gay, J. The beggar's opera
- Miller, A. Death of a salesman
- Shakespeare, W. Henry IV

STJN Steinmann, Martin and Willen, Gerald, ed. Literature for writing; an anthology of major British and American authors...2d ed. Belmont, Calif., Wadsworth [1967] 719p
- Miller, A. Death of a salesman
- Shakespeare, W. Henry IV
- Synge, J. Riders to the sea (one act only)
- Wilde, O. The importance of being earnest

STL Stern, Milton R. and Cross Seymour L., eds. American literature survey... New York, Viking [c1962] 4v
- O'Neill, E. The hairy ape 4
- Tyler, R. The contrast 1

STM Stevens, David Harrison, ed. Types of English drama, 1660-1780... Boston, Ginn [c1923] 920p
- Addison, J. Cato
- Buckingham, G., and others. The rehearsal
- Congreve, W. Love for love
- Congreve, W. The way of the world
- Dryden, J. All for love; or, The world well lost
- Dryden, J. Aureng-Zebe
- Etherege, G. The man of mode; or, Sir Fopling Flutter
- Farquhar, G. The beaux' stratagem
- Fielding, H. The tragedy of tragedies; or, The life and death of Tom Thumb the great
- Gay, J. The beggar's opera
- Goldsmith, O. The good-natured man
- Goldsmith, O. She stoops to conquer; or, The mistakes of a night
- Home, J. Douglas
- Lillo, G. The London merchant; or, The history of George Barnwell
- Otway, T. Venice preserved; or, A plot discovered
- Rowe, N. Jane Shore
- Shadwell, T. Bury fair
- Sheridan, R. The critic

Sheridan, R. The duenna
Sheridan, R. The rivals
Sheridan, R. The school for scandal
Steele, R. The conscious lovers

STOC Stock, Dora and Stock, Marie, eds. ...Recueil de lectures... Boston, Heath [c1950] 240p
Labiche, E. La grammaire

STONE, DONALD, JR. See FOUR Four Renaissance tragedies...

STRASBERG, LEE. See FAM Famous American plays of the 1950's...

STRB Stroud, Theodore Albert, and Gordon, E. J., eds. The literature of comedy; an anthology. Boston, Ginn, 1968. 763p
Day, C. Life with father
Rostand, E. Cyrano de Bergerac
Shaw, G. Androcles and the lion
Wilde, O. The importance of being earnest

STY Styan, J. L., comp. The challenge of the theatre. Encino, Calif., Dickenson Publishing Co., 1972. 421p
Aeschylus. Agamemnon
Chekhov, A. The cherry orchard
Everyman
Frisch, M. The firebugs
Ibsen, H. The wild duck
Pirandello, L. Six characters in search of an author
Shakespeare, W. King Lear
Shakespeare, W. Twelfth night
Sophocles. Oedipus the king
Strindberg, A. Miss Julie
Synge, J. The shadow of the glen
Wilde, O. The importance of being earnest
Williams, T. The glass menagerie

SUB Sullivan, Victoria, and Hatch, James V., eds. Plays by and about women. New York, Random House, 1973. 425p
Boothe, C. The women
Childress, A. Wine in the wilderness
Duffy, M. Rites
Gerstenberg, A. Overtones
Ginsberg, N. Advertisement
Hellman, L. The children's hour
Lessing, D. Play with a tiger
Terry, M. Calm down, Mother

SUL Summers, Hollis Spurgeon and Whan, Edgar, eds. Literature: An introduction. New York, McGraw-Hill, 1960. 706p
Jonson, B. Volpone; or, The fox
MacLeish, A. The music crept by me upon the waters
Miller, A. The crucible
Shaw, G. The devil's disciple
Sophocles. Antigone
Wilder, T. The matchmaker
Williams, T. Something unspoken

SUM Summers, Montague, ed. Restoration comedies... London, Cape, 1921. 400p
Crowne, J. Sir Courtly Nice; or, It cannot be
Killigrew, T. The parson's wedding
Ravenscroft, E. The London cuckolds

SUMB Summers, Montague, ed. Shakespeare adaptations...

SUMB (cont.)
London, Cape, 1922. 282p
D'Avenant, W. and Dryden, J. The tempest; or, The enchanted island
Duffett, T. The mock-tempest; or, The enchanted castle
Tate, N. The history of King Lear

SUT Sutton, John F. and others, comps. Ideas and patterns in literature... New York, Harcourt, Brace, Jovanovich, 1970. 4v
Agee, J. The bride comes to Yellow sky 3
Anouilh, J. Antigone 2
Chekhov, A. The marriage proposal 1
Gibson, W. The miracle worker 1
O'Casey, S. The end of the beginning 4
O'Neill, E. Ile 3
Serling, R. Requiem for a heavyweight 3
Serling, R. The shelter 2
Shakespeare, W. Julius Caesar 2
Shakespeare, W. Macbeth 4
Shaw, G. Arms and the man 4
Waugh, E. The man who liked Dickens 1
Wilder, T. Our town 3

SUTL Sutton, Larry M. and others, comps. Journeys: an introduction to literature. Boston, Holbrook Press, 1971. 510p
Hughes, R. The sister's tragedy
Odets, C. Waiting for Lefty
Shakespeare, W. Othello
Sophocles. Antigone

SWA Swander, Homer D., ed. Man and the gods; three tragedies. Harcourt, Brace and World [c1964] 215p
Aeschylus. Agamemnon
Marlowe, C. The tragical history of Doctor Faustus
Shaw, G. Saint Joan

SWI Swire, Willard, ed. Three distinctive plays about Abraham Lincoln... New York, Washington Square Press [c1961] 208p
Conkle, E. Prologue to glory
Drinkwater, J. Abraham Lincoln
Van Doren, M. The last days of Lincoln

SWIT Switz, Theodore MacLean and Johnston, Robert A., eds. Great Christian plays... Greenwich, Conn., Seabury, 1956. 306p
Abraham and Isaac
Conversion of St. Paul
Everyman
Resurrection
Totentanz

SYMONS, ARTHUR. See NER Nero (Tragedy). Nero & other plays

T

TAFT Taft, Kendall B. Minor knickerbockers... New York, American book company [c1947] 410p
Payne, J. Charles the second

TAT Tatlock, John Strong Perry and Martin, Robert Grant, eds. Representative English plays... New York, Century, 1916. 838p
Abraham and Isaac
Addison, J. Cato
Beaumont, F. and Fletcher, J. Philaster; or, Love lies a-bleeding
Browning, R. A blot in the 'scutcheon

Bulwer-Lytton, E. The lady of Lyons; or, Love and pride
Congreve, W. The way of the world
Dekker, T. The shoemaker's holiday; or, The gentle craft
Dryden, J. Almanzor and Almahide; or, The conquest of Granada
Everyman
Fielding, H. The tragedy of tragedies; or, The life and death of Tom Thumb the great
Fletcher, J. The wild-goose chase
Goldsmith, O. She stoops to conquer; or, The mistakes of a night
Heywood, T. A woman killed with kindness
Jonson, B. The alchemist
Lyly, J. Mother Bombie
Marlowe, C. The troublesome reign and lamentable death of Edward the second
Middleton, R. and Rowley, W. The changeling
Noah's flood
Otway, T. Venice preserved; or, A plot discovered
The second shepherds' play
Shelly, P. The Cenci
Sheridan, R. The school for scandal
Steele, R. The conscious lovers
Webster, J. The Duchess of Malfi
Wilde, O. Lady Windermere's fan

TAU Tatlock, John Strong Perry and Martin, Robert Grant, eds. Representative English plays...2d ed. rev. and and enl. New York, Appleton-Century [c1938] 914p
Abraham and Isaac
Addison, J. Cato
Beaumont, F. and Fletcher, J. Philaster; or, Love lies a-bleeding
Bulwer-Lytton, E. The lady of Lyons; or, Love and pride
Congreve, W. The way of the world
Dekker, T. The shoemaker's holiday; or, The gentle craft
Dryden, J. Almanzor and Almahide; or, The conquest of Granada
Everyman
Fielding, H. The tragedy of tragedies; or, The life and death of Tom Thumb the great
Fletcher, J. The wild-goose chase
Goldsmith, O. She stoops to conquer; or, The mistakes of a night
Heywood, T. A woman killed with kindness
Jonson, B. The alchemist
Lillo, G. The London merchant; or, The history of George Barnwell
Lyly, J. Mother Bombie
Marlowe, C. The troublesome reign and lamentable death of Edward the second
Middleton, T. and Rowley, W. The changeling
Noah's flood
Otway, T. Venice preserved; or, A plot discovered
Pinero, A. The second Mrs. Tanqueray
Robertson, T. Caste
The second shepherds' play
Shelley, P. The Cenci
Sheridan, R. The school for scandal
Steele, R. The conscious lovers
Webster, J. The Duchess of Malfi
Wilde, O. Lady Windermere's fan

TAUJ Taylor, John Chesley,

TAUJ (cont.)
and Thompson, Gary Richard, comps. Ritual, realism, and revolt; major traditions in the drama. New York, Scribner, 1972. 816p
Adamov, A. Professor Toranne
Camus, A. Caligula
Eliot, T. Murder in the cathedral
Euripides. Medea
Euripides. Orestes
Ibsen, H. Hedda Gabler
Jones, L. The slave
Middleton, T. and Rowley, W. The changeling
Miller, A. The crucible
O'Neill, E. The great god Brown
Osborne, J. The entertainer
Shakespeare, W. Othello
Sophocles. Antigone
Synge, J. Riders to the sea
Williams, T. Summer and smoke
Wycherley, W. The country wife
Yeats, W. Purgatory

TAV Taylor, Joseph Richard, ed. European and Asiatic plays... Boston, Expression co., 1936. 730p
Aristophanes. The frogs
Calderón de la Barca, P. Life is a dream
Corneille, P. The cid
Dekker, T. The shoemaker's holiday
Enamai No Sayemon. The cormorant fisher
Esashi Jūō. The bird catcher in hell
Euripides. Medea
Everyman
Heywood, J. The four p's
Hroswitha. Dulcitius
Kālidāsa. Shakuntalā
Massinger, P. A new way to pay old debts
Plautus, T. The Menaechmi
Sackville, T. and Norton, T. Gorboduc
Seami, M. Atsumori
The second shepherds' play
Seneca, L. Medea
Shakespeare, W. The comedy of errors
Shirley, J. The traitor
The sorrows of Han
Udall, N. Ralph Roister Doister

TAY Taylor, William Duncan, ed. Eighteenth century comedy... London, Oxford university press [1929] 413p (The world's classics)
Farquhar, G. The beaux' stratagem
Fielding, H. The tragedy of tragedies; or, The life and death of Tom Thumb the great
Gay, J. The beggar's opera
Goldsmith, O. She stoops to conquer
Steele, R. The conscious lovers

TEN Ten Greek plays, translated into English by Gilbert Murray and others; with an introduction by Lane Cooper, and a preface by H. B. Densmore. New York, Oxford university press, 1930. 475p
Aeschylus. Agamemnon
Aeschylus. The choephoroe
Aeschylus. The eumenides
Aristophanes. The frogs
Aristophanes. Plutus, the god of riches
Euripides. Electra
Euripides. Iphigenia in Tauris
Euripides. Medea
Sophocles. Antigone
Sophocles. Oedipus, king of Thebes

THA Thayer, William Roscoe, ed. The best Elizabethan plays... Boston, Ginn

[c1890] 611p
Beaumont, F. and Fletcher, J. Philaster; or, Love lies a-bleeding
Fletcher, J. And Shakespeare, W. The two noble kinsmen
Jonson, B. The alchemist
Marlowe, C. The Jew of Malta
Webster, J. The Duchess of Malfi

THEA Theatre. 1953-56. Edited by John Chapman...New York, Random House [c1953-56] 4v
Abbott, G. and Bissell, R. The pajama game 54
Anderson, M. The bad seed 55
Anderson, R. Tea and sympathy 54
Axelrod, G. The seven year itch 53
Bagnold, E. The chalk garden 56
Behrman, S. and Logan, J. Fanny 55
Chase, M. Bernardine 53
Chodorov, E. Oh, men! Oh, women! 54
Christie, A. Witness for the prosecution 55
Denker, H. and Berkey, R. Time limit! 56
Eliot, T. The confidential clerk 54
Fields, J. and Chodorov, J. The ponder heart 56
Fields, J. and Chodorov, J. Wonderful town 53
Gazzo, M. A hatful of rain 56
Giraudoux, J. Ondine 54
Giraudoux, J. Tiger at the gates 56
Hackett, A. and Goodrich, F. The diary of Anne Frank 56
Hart, M. The climate of Eden 53
Hayes, J. The desperate hours 55
Howard, S. Madam, will you walk 54
Inge, W. Bus stop 55
Inge, W. Picnic 53
Kingsley, S. Lunatics and lovers 55
Knott, F. Dial "M" for murder 53
Kober, A. and Logan, J. Wish you were here 53
Kurnitz, H. Reclining figure 55
Latouche, J. The golden apple 54
Laurents, A. The time of the cuckoo 53
Lawrence, J. and Lee, R. Inherit the wind 55
Levin, I. No time for sergeants 56
Loesser, F. The most happy fella 56
Maurette, M. Anastasia 55
Menotti, G. The saint of Bleecker Street 55
Miller, A. The crucible 53
Miller, A. A view from the bridge 56
O'Brien, L. The remarkable Mr. Pennypacker 54
Patrick, J. The teahouse of the August moon 54
Rosten, N. Mister Johnson 56
Shulman, M. and Smith, R. The tender trap 55
Spewack, S. and Spewack, B. My three angels 53
Taylor, S. Sabrina fair 54
Teichman, H. and Kaufman, G. The solid gold Cadillac 54
Ustinov, P. The love of four colonels 53
Wilder, T. The matchmaker 56
Williams, T. Cat on a hot tin roof 55
Wouk, H. The Caine mutiny court-martial 54
Young, S. Mr. Pickwick 53

THEC Theatre for tomorrow... London, Longmans, Green,

THEC (cont.)
1940. 397p
Breen, R. and Schnibble, H. "Who ride on white horses," the story of Edmund Campion
Lavery, E. and Murphy, G. Kamiano, the story of Damien
Nagle, U. Savonarola, the flame of Florence

THF Theatre guild. The Theatre guild anthology... New York, Random house [c1936] 961p
Anderson, M. Mary of Scotland
Andreyev, L. He who gets slapped
Barry, B. Hotel Universe
Behrman, S. Rain from heaven
Ervine, St. J. John Ferguson
Heyward, D. and Heyward, D. Porgy
Howard, S. The silver cord
Milne, A. Mr. Pim passes by
Molnár, F. Liliom
O'Neill, E. Strange interlude
Rice, E. The adding machine
Shaw, G. Saint Joan
Sherwood, R. Reunion in Vienna
Werfel, F. Goat song

THH Theatre omnibus...[London] Hamilton [1938] v.p.
Behrman, S. Amphitryon 38
Jerome, H. Jane Eyre
Jerome, H. Pride and prejudice
Lyndon, B. The amazing Dr. Clitterhouse
Rattigan, T. French without tears
Savoy(!), G. George and Margaret

THO Thomas, Russell Brown, ed. Plays and the theatre ...Boston, Little, Brown, 1937. 729p
Anderson, M. Elizabeth the queen
Besier, R. The Barretts of Wimpole street
Ibsen, H. An enemy of the people
Kelly, G. Poor Aubrey
Master Pierre Patelin
Molière, J. The miser
Morton, J. Box and Cox
O'Neill, E. In the zone
Shakespeare, W. Romeo and Juliet
Sheridan, R. The school for scandal
Sophocles. Antigone
Steele, W. The giant's stair

THOD Thompson, David, ed. Theatre today. London, Longmans, 1965. 206p
Albee, E. The sand box
Campton, D. Then...
Donleavy, J. The interview
Ionesco, E. The new tenant
Mankowitz, W. It should happen to a dog
O'Casey, S. Hall of healing
Pinter, H. The black and white
Pinter, H. Last to go
Saroyan, W. The oyster and the pearl
Shaw, G. Passion, poison and petrifaction

THOM Thompson, Stith, ed. Our heritage of world literature... New York, Dryden press [c1938] 1246p
Aeschylus. Agamemnon
Aristophanes. The frogs
Chekhov, A. The cherry orchard
Euripides. Alcestis
Goethe, J. Faust, pt. I
Ibsen, H. A doll's house
Molière, J. The miser
Plautus, T. The captives
Racine, J. Phaedra
Shakespeare, W. Hamlet
Sophocles. Antigone

Wilde, O. The importance of being earnest

THON Thompson, Stith and Gassner, John, eds. Our heritage of world literature... Rev. ed. New York, Dryden press [c1942] 1416p
Aeschylus. Agamemnon
Aristophanes. The frogs
Chekhov, A. The cherry orchard
Euripides. Alcestis
Goethe, J. Faust, pt. I
Hauptmann, G. The weavers
Ibsen, H. A doll's house
Molière, J. The miser
Plautus, T. The captives
Racine, J. Phaedra
Shakespeare, W. Hamlet
Sophocles. Antigone
Wilde, O. The importance of being earnest

THOP Three Australian plays... Harmondsworth, Middlesex, Penguin [1963] 311p
Porter, H. The tower
Seymour, A. The one day of the year
Stewart, D. Ned Kelly

THOR Three East European plays. Hammondsworth, Middlesex, Penguin, 1970. 271p
Hay, J. The horse
Havel, V. The memorandum
Slawomir, M. Tango

THP Three great Greek plays ... Selected [with an introduction] by Lyman Bryson. Greenwich, Conn., Fawcett [c1960]
Aeschylus. Agamemnon
Euripides. Hippolytus
Sophocles. Oedipus the king

THR Three modern plays from the French... New York, Holt, 1914. 272p
Donnay, M. The other danger
Lavedan, H. The prince d'Aurec
Lemaître, J. The pardon

THT Three Negro plays... Harmondsworth, Middlesex, Penguin, 1969. 207p
Hansberry, L. The sign in Sidney Brustein's window
Hughes, L. Mulatto
Jones, L. The slave

THTN Three Nigerian plays. London, Longmans, 1967. 89p
Ijimere, O. Born with the fire on his head
Ladipo, D. Moremi
Ogunyemi, W. The scheme

THU Three plays. London, Gardner, Darton [1926] v.p.
Ouless, E. Our pageant
Pakington, M. The queen of hearts
Paul, Mrs. C. The fugitive king

THX Three Southwest plays... With an introduction by John Rosenfield. Dallas, Southwest review, 1942. 326p
Acheson, S. We are besieged
Rogers, J. Where the dear antelope play
Witherspoon, K. Jute

THY Three Soviet plays... Moscow, Foreign Language Publishing House [1961] 247p
Arbuzov, A. It happened in Irkutsk
Korneichuk, A. Platon Krechet
Pogodin, N. Kremlin chimes

TICK Tickner, Frederick James, ed. Restoration dramatists... London, Nel-

TICK (cont.)
son [1930] 229p
Dryden, J. Aureng-zebe
Farquhar, G. The beaux' stratagem
Otway, T. Venice preserved; or, A plot discovered
Vanbrugh, J. A journey to London

TICO Tickner, Frederick James, ed. Shakespeare's predecessors... London, Nelson [1929] 278p
Greene, R. Friar Bacon and Friar Bungay
Heywood, J. The four p's
Kyd, T. The Spanish tragedy
Marlowe, C. Tamburlaine the great [pt. I]

TOBI Tobin, James Edward; Hamm, Victor M. and Hines, William H., eds. College book of English literature... New York, American book co. [c1949] 1156p
Marlowe, C. The tragical history of Doctor Faustus
The second shepherds' play
Synge, J. Riders to the sea

TOD Today's literature... edited by Dudley Chadwick Gordon, Vernon Rupert King and William Whittingham Lyman... New York, American book co. [c1935] 998p
Bernard, L. Lars killed his son
Flavin, M. Amaco
Ford, H. Youth must be served
Galsworthy, J. The silver box
Green, P. In Abraham's bosom
Gregory, I. The workhouse ward
Hopkins, A. Moonshine
Jennings, T. No more frontier
O'Neill, E. Where the cross is made
Riggs, L. Knives from Syria

TOWN Towneley plays. The Wakefield mystery plays. Ed. by Martial Rose... London, Evans, c1961. 464p
Abraham
The annunciation
The ascension of the Lord
The buffeting
Caesar Augustus
The conspiracy
The creation
The crucifixion
The deliverance of souls
The first shepherds' play
The flight into Egypt
The hanging of Judas
Herod the Great
Isaac
Jacob
John the Baptist
The judgment
The killing of Abel
Lazarus
Noah
The offering of the magi
Pharaoh
The pilgrims
The play of the doctors
The procession of the prophets
The purification of Mary
The resurrection
The salutation of Elizabeth
The scourging
The second shepherds' play
The talents
Thomas of India

TRE A treasury of the theatre ...from Aeschylus to Eugene O'Neill; edited by Burns Mantle and John Gassner. New York, Simon and Schuster, 1935. 1643p
Aeschylus. Agamemnon
Anderson, M. Elizabeth the queen
Anderson, M. and Stallings,

L. What price glory?
Aristophanes. Lysistrata
Chekhov, A. The cherry orchard
Congreve, W. The way of the world
Connelly, M. The green pastures
Euripides. Electra
Everyman
Galsworthy, J. Escape
Goethe, J. Faust, pt. I
Gorki, M. The lower depths
Hauptmann, G. The weavers
Ibsen, H. Hedda Gabler
Job
Jonson, B. Volpone
Kālidāsa. Shakuntalā
Kaufman, G. and Ryskind, M. Of thee I sing
Kiyotsugu, K. Sotoba Komachi
Molière, J. The misanthrope
Molnár, F. Liliom
O'Neill, E. Anna Christie
Pirandello, L. Six characters in search of an author
Racine, J. Phaedra
Rostand, E. Cyrano de Bergerac
Shakespeare, W. Hamlet
Shaw, G. Candida
Shelley, P. The Cenci
Sherriff, R. Journey's end
Sophocles. Antigone
Strindberg, A. The father
Synge, J. Riders to the sea
Webster, J. The Duchess of Malfi
Wilde, O. The importance of being earnest

TREA A treasury of the theatre ...[edited by Burns Mantle and John Gassner] rev. and adapted for colleges by Philo M. Buck, jr., John Gassner [and] H. S. Alberson. New York, Simon and Schuster [c1940] 2v (v1, From Ibsen to Odets; v2, Aeschylus to Hebbel)
Abraham and Isaac 2
Aeschylus. Agamemnon 2
Anderson, M. Elizabeth the queen 1
Anderson, M. and Stallings, L. What price glory? 1
Aristophanes. Lysistrata 2
Chekhov, A. The cherry orchard 1
Congreve, W. The way of the world 2
Connelly, M. The green pastures 1
Euripides. Electra 2
Everyman 2
Galsworthy, J. Escape 1
Goethe, J. Faust, pt. I 2
Gorki, M. The lower depths 1
Hauptmann, G. The weavers 1
Hebbel, F. Maria Magdalena 2
Ibsen, H. Hedda Gabler 1
Job 2
Jonson, B. Volpone 2
Kālidāsa. Shakuntalā 2
Molière, J. The misanthrope 2
Molnár, F. Liliom 1
Odets, C. Awake and sing 1
O'Neill, E. Anna Christie 1
Pirandello, L. Six characters in search of an author 1
Plautus, T. The Menaechmi 2
Racine, J. Phaedra 2
Rostand, E. Cyrano de Bergerac 1
Shakespeare, W. Hamlet 2
Shaw, G. Candida 1
Sherriff, R. Journey's end 1
Sophocles. Antigone 2
Strindberg, A. The father 1
Synge, J. Riders to the sea 1
Webster, J. The Duchess of Malfi 2
Wilde, O. The importance of being earnest 1

TREB A treasury of the theatre...from Aeschylus to

TREB (cont.)
Ostrovsky. 3d ed. Edited by John Gassner. New York, Simon and Schuster, 1967. 1033p
Abraham and Isaac
Aeschylus. Agamemnon
Aristophanes. The frogs
Büchner, G. Danton's death
Calderón de la Barca, P. Life is a dream
Cervantes Saavedra, M. The cave of Salamanca
Congreve, W. The way of the world
Corneille, P. The cid
The death of Pilate
Euripides. The bacchae
Euripides. The Trojan women
Everyman
Gay, J. The beggar's opera
Goethe, J. Faust, pt. I
Gogol, N. The inspector
Hebbel, F. Maria Magdalena
Hrotsvitha. Paphnutius
Hugo, V. Hernani
Jonson, B. The vision of delight
Jonson, B. Volpone
Kālidāsa. Shakuntalā
Kiyotsugu, K. Sotoba Komachi
Lillo, G. The London merchant
Marlowe, C. The tragical history of Doctor Faustus
Molière, J. The misanthrope
Musset, A. No trifling with love
Ostrovsky, A. The thunderstorm
Plautus. The Menaechmi
Racine, J. Phaedra
Scala, F. The portrait
Schiller, J. Mary Stuart
The second shepherds' play
Seneca. Thyestes
Shakespeare, W. Hamlet
Sheridan, R. The school for scandal
Sophocles. Oedipus the king
Sophocles. The searching satyrs
Terence. The brothers
Turgenev, I. A month in the country
Vega Carpio, L. Fuente ovejuna
Webster, J. The Duchess of Malfi

TREBA A treasury of the theatre; from Henrik Ibsen to Eugene Ionesco. 3d college edition. Edited by John Gassner. New York, Simon and Schuster [1960] 1275p
Anderson, M. Elizabeth the queen
Anouilh, J. The lark
Barrie, J. The admirable Crichton
Becque, H. The vultures
Brecht, B. The private life of the master race
Čapek, K. R.U.R.
Chekhov, A. The cherry orchard
Claudel, P. The tidings brought to Mary
Connelly, M. The green pastures
Coward, N. Blithe spirit
Galsworthy, J. Escape
García Lorca, F. Blood wedding
Genêt, J. The maids
Giraudoux, J. The madwoman of Chaillot
Gorki, M. The lower depths
Gregory, I. The workhouse ward
Hauptmann, G. The weavers
Hellman, L. The little foxes
Ibsen, H. Ghosts
Ibsen, H. Hedda Gabler
Ionesco, E. The chairs
Maeterlinck, M. The intruder
Maugham, W. The circle
Miller, A. Death of a salesman
Molnár, F. Liliom
O'Casey, S. The plough and the stars
Odets, C. Golden boy

O'Neill, E. Anna Christie
O'Neill, E. The hairy ape
Pirandello, L. Six characters in search of an author
Rostand, E. Cyrano de Bergerac
Saroyan, W. My heart's in the highlands
Sartre, J. The flies
Shaw, G. Candida
Sherriff, R. Journey's end
Stallings, L. and Anderson, M. What price glory?
Strindberg, A. A dream play
Strindberg, A. The father
Strindberg, A. There are crimes and crimes
Synge, J. Riders to the sea
Tolstoy, L. The power of darkness
Wedekind, F. The tenor
Wilde, O. The importance of being earnest
Wilder, T. Our town
Williams, T. The glass menagerie

TREBJ A treasury of the theatre. 4th ed. Edited by John Gassner and Bernard F. Dukore. New York, Simon and Schuster, 1970. 1298p
Albee, E. Who's afraid of Virginia Woolf?
Anderson, M. Elizabeth the queen
Anouilh, J. The lark
Artaud, A. The spurt of blood
Becque, H. The vultures
Brecht, B. Galileo
Brecht, B. The good woman of Setzuan
Chekhov, A. The cherry orchard
Claudel, P. The tidings brought to Mary
García Lorca, F. Blood wedding
Giraudoux, J. The madwoman of Chaillot
Gorki, M. The lower depths
Hauptmann, G. The weavers
Hellman, L. The little foxes
Ibsen, H. Ghosts
Ibsen, H. Hedda Gabler
Jarry, A. Ubu the king
Jones, L. Dutchman
Lowell, R. Benito Cereno
Maeterlinck, M. The intruder
Maugham, W. The circle
Miller, A. Death of a salesman
O'Casey, S. The plough and the stars
Odets, C. Golden boy
O'Neill, E. The hairy ape
O'Neill, E. A moon for the misbegotten
Osborne, J. and Creighton, A. Epitaph for George Dillon
Pinter, H. A slight ache
Pirandello, L. Six characters in search of an author
Rostand, E. Cyrano de Bergerac
Saroyan, W. My heart's in the highlands
Sartre, J. The flies
Shaw, G. Candida
Shaw, G. Heartbreak house
Strindberg, A. A dream play
Strindberg, A. The father
Synge, J. Playboy of the western world
Synge, J. Riders to the sea
Tolstoy, L. The power of darkness
Wedekind, F. The tenor
Wilde, O. The importance of being earnest
Wilder, T. Our town
Williams, T. The glass menagerie
Witkiewicz, S. The cuttlefish
Yeats, W. Purgatory

TREC A treasury of the theatre... Revised edition for colleges. Edited by John

TREC (cont.)
Gassner... New York, Simon and Schuster [c1950-51] 2v (v1, From Aeschylus to Turgenev; v2, From Henrik Ibsen to Arthur Miller)

Abraham and Isaac 1
Aeschylus. Agamemnon 1
Anderson, M. Elizabeth the queen 2
Aristophanes. The frogs 1
Barrie, J. The admirable Crichton 2
Becque, H. The vultures 2
Brecht, B. The private life of the master race 2
Büchner, G. Danton's death 1
Čapek, K. R.U.R. 2
Chekhov, A. The cherry orchard 2
Congreve, W. The way of the world 1
Connelly, M. The green pastures 2
Coward, N. Blithe spirit 2
Euripides. The Trojan women 1
Everyman 1
Galsworthy, J. Escape 2
García Lorca, F. Blood wedding 2
Goethe, J. Faust 1
Gogol, N. The inspector 1
Gorki, M. The lower depths 2
Gregory, I. The workhouse ward 2
Hauptmann, G. The weavers 2
Hebbel, F. Maria Magdalena 1
Hellman, L. The little foxes 2
Ibsen, H. Ghosts 2
Ibsen, H. Hedda Gabler 2
Jonson, B. Volpone 1
Kālidāsa. Shakuntalā 1
Kiyotsugu, K. Sotoba Komachi 1
Maeterlinck, M. The intruder 2
Marlowe, C. The tragical history of Doctor Faustus 1
Maugham, W. The circle 2
Miller, A. Death of a salesman 2
Molière, J. The misanthrope 1
Molnár, F. Liliom 2
Musset, A. No trifling with love 1
O'Casey, S. The plough and the stars 2
Odets, C. Golden boy 2
O'Neill, E. Anna Christie 2
O'Neill, E. The hairy ape 2
Pirandello, L. Six characters in search of an author 2
Plautus. The Menaechmi 1
Racine, J. Phaedra 1
Rostand, E. Cyrano de Bergerac 2
Saroyan, W. My heart's in the highlands 2
Sartre, J. The flies 2
The second shepherds' play 1
Shakespeare, W. Hamlet 1
Shaw, G. Candida 2
Sheridan, R. The school for scandal 1
Sherriff, R. Journey's end 2
Sophocles. Oedipus the king 1
Stallings, L. and Anderson, M. What price glory? 2
Strindberg, A. The father 2
Strindberg, A. There are crimes and crimes 2
Synge, J. Riders to the sea 2
Terence. The brothers 1
Tolstoy, L. The power of darkness 2
Turgenev, I. A month in the country 1
Vega Carpio, L. Fuente ovejuna 1
Webster, J. The Duchess of Malfi 1
Wedekind, F. The tenor 2
Wilde, O. The importance of

being earnest 2
Wilder, T. Our town 2
Williams, T. The glass menagerie 2

TREE A treasury of the theatre...Revised edition, edited by John Gassner. New York, Simon and Schuster [c1951] 3v (v1, World drama: From Aeschylus to Turgenev; v2, Modern European drama: From Henrik Ibsen to Jean-Paul Sartre; v3, Modern British and American drama: From Oscar Wilde to Arthur Miller)
Abraham and Isaac 1
Aeschylus. Agamemnon 1
Anderson, M. Elizabeth the queen 3
Aristophanes. The frogs 1
Barrie, J. The admirable Crichton 3
Becque, H. The vultures 2
Brecht, B. The private life of the master race 2
Büchner, G. Danton's death 1
Čapek, K. R.U.R. 2
Chekhov, A. The cherry orchard 2
Congreve, W. The way of the world 1
Connelly, M. The green pastures 3
Coward, N. Blithe spirit 3
Euripides. The Trojan women 1
Everyman 1
Galsworthy, J. Escape 3
García Lorca, F. Blood wedding 2
Goethe, J. Faust 1
Gogol, N. The inspector 1
Gorki, M. The lower depths 2
Gregory, I. The workhouse ward 3
Hauptmann, G. The weavers 2
Hebbel, F. Maria Magdalena 1
Hellman, L. The little foxes 3
Ibsen, H. Ghosts 2
Ibsen, H. Hedda Gabler 2
Jonson, B. Volpone 1
Kālidāsa. Shakuntalā 1
Kiyotsugu, K. Sotoba Komachi 1
Maeterlinck, M. The intruder 2
Marlowe, C. The tragical history of Doctor Faustus 1
Maugham, W. The circle 3
Miller, A. Death of a salesman 3
Molière, J. The misanthrope 1
Molnár, F. Liliom 2
Musset, A. No trifling with love 1
O'Casey, S. The plough and the stars 3
Odets, C. Golden boy 3
O'Neill, E. Anna Christie 3
O'Neill, E. The hairy ape 3
Pirandello, L. Six characters in search of an author 2
Plautus. The Menaechmi 1
Racine, J. Phaedra 1
Rostand, E. Cyrano de Bergerac 2
Saroyan, W. My heart's in the highlands 3
Sartre, J. The flies 2
The second shepherds' play 1
Shakespeare, W. Hamlet 1
Shaw, G. Candida 3
Sheridan, R. The school for scandal 1
Sherriff, R. Journey's end 3
Sophocles. Oedipus the king 1
Stallings, L. and Anderson, M. What price glory? 3
Strindberg, A. The father 2
Strindberg, A. There are crimes and crimes 2
Synge, J. Riders to the sea 3
Terence. The brothers 1

TREE (cont.)

Tolstoy, L. The power of darkness 2
Turgenev, I. A month in the country 1
Vega Carpio, L. Fuente ovejuna 1
Webster, J. The Duchess of Malfi 1
Wedekind, F. The tenor 2
Wilde, O. The importance of being earnest 3
Wilder, T. Our town 3
Williams, T. The glass menagerie 3

TREI A treasury of the theatre--Revised edition, edited by John Gassner. New York, Simon, 1963. 3v (v1, World drama: From Aeschylus to Turgenev; v2, Modern European drama: From Henrik Ibsen to Jean-Paul Sartre; v3, Modern drama: From Oscar Wilde to Eugène Ionesco)...

Abraham and Isaac 1
Aeschylus. Agamemnon 1
Anderson, M. Elizabeth the queen 3
Anouilh, J. The lark 3
Aristophanes. The frogs 1
Barrie, J. The admirable Crichton 3
Becque, H. The vultures 2
Brecht, B. The private life of the master race [excerpts] 2
Büchner, G. Danton's death 1
Čapek, K. R.U.R. 2
Chekhov, A. The cherry orchard 2
Claudel, P. The tidings brought to Mary 3
Congreve, W. The way of the world 1
Connelly, M. The green pastures 3
Coward, N. Blithe spirit 3
Euripides. The Trojan women 1
Everyman 1
Galsworthy, J. Escape 3
García Lorca, F. Blood wedding 2
Genêt, J. The maids 3
Giraudoux, J. The madwomen of Chaillot 3
Goethe, J. Faust, pt. I 1
Gogol, N. The inspector 1
Gorki, M. The lower depths 2
Gregory, I. The workhouse ward 3
Hauptmann, G. The weavers 2
Hebbel, F. Maria Magdalena 1
Hellman, L. The little foxes 3
Ibsen, H. Ghosts 2
Ibsen, H. Hedda Gabler 2
Ionesco, E. The chairs 3
Jonson, B. Volpone 1
Kālidāsa. Shakuntalā 1
Kiyotsugu, K. Sotoba Komachi 1
Maeterlinck, M. The intruder 2
Marlowe, C. The tragical history of Doctor Faustus 1
Maugham, W. The circle 3
Miller, A. Death of a salesman 3
Molière, J. The misanthrope 1
Molnár, F. Liliom 2
Musset, A. No trifling with love 1
O'Casey, S. The plough and the stars 3
Odets, C. Golden boy 3
O'Neill, E. Anna Christie 3
O'Neill, E. The hairy ape 3
Pirandello, L. Six characters in search of an author 2
Plautus. The Menaechmi 1
Racine, J. Phaedra 1
Rostand, E. Cyrano de Bergerac 2
Saroyan, W. My heart's in the highlands 3

Sartre, J. The flies 2
The second shepherds' play 1
Shakespeare, W. Hamlet 1
Shaw, G. Candida 3
Sheridan, R. The school for scandal 1
Sherriff, R. Journey's end 3
Sophocles. Oedipus the king 1
Stallings, L. and Anderson, M. What price glory? 3
Strindberg, A. A dream play 3
Strindberg, A. The father 2
Strindberg, A. There are crimes and crimes 2
Synge, J. Riders to the sea 3
Terence. The brothers 1
Tolstoy, L. The power of darkness 2
Turgenev, I. A month in the country 1
Vega Carpio, L. Fuente ovejuna 1
Webster, J. The Duchess of Malfi 1
Wedekind, F. The tenor 2
Wilde, O. The importance of being earnest 3
Wilder, T. Our town 3
Williams, T. The glass menagerie 3

TRES Tres dramas románticos ... Garden City, New York, Doubleday, 1962. 319p
García Gutiérrez, A. El trovador
Rivas, A. Don Alvaro; ó, La fuerza del Sino
Zorrilla y Moral, J. Don Juan Tenorio

TREWIN, J. C. See PLAN Plays of the year...

TRI Trilling, Lionel, comp. The experience of literature ... Garden City, N.Y., Doubleday, 1967. 1320p
Brecht, B. Galileo
Chekhov, A. The three sisters
Ibsen, H. The wild duck
Pirandello, L. Six characters in search of an author
Shakespeare, W. The tragedy of King Lear
Shaw, G. The doctor's dilemma
Sophocles. Oedipus rex
Yeats, W. Purgatory

TRIA Trilling, Lionel, comp. The experience of literature... New York, Holt, Rinehart and Winston [1967] 1320p
Brecht, B. Galileo
Chekhov, A. The three sisters
Ibsen, H. The wild duck
Pirandello, L. Six characters in search of an author
Shakespeare, W. The tragedy of King Lear
Shaw, G. The doctor's dilemma
Sophocles. Oedipus rex
Yeats, W. Purgatory

TUCD Tucker, Samuel Marion, ed. Modern American and British plays... New York, Harper [c1931] 946p
Anderson, M. Saturday's children
Barry, P. In a garden
Brighouse, H. Hobson's choice
Colton, J. and Randolph, C. Rain
Coward, N. The vortex
Crothers, R. Mary the third
Dane, C. Granite
Emery, G. The hero
Ervine, St. J. John Ferguson
Glover, H. The king's jewry
Granville-Barker, H. Waste
Green, P. The field god
Houghton, S. Hindle wakes
Howard, S. The silver cord

TUCD (cont.)
Kaufman, G. and Connelly, M. To the ladies!
Maugham, W. The circle
Millay, E. The king's henchman
Milne, A. The truth about Blayds
Moeller, P. Madame Sand
O'Neill, E. The great god Brown
Pinero, A. The thunderbolt
Vollmer, L. Sun-up
Wilde, O. The importance of being earnest

TUCG Tucker, Samuel Marion, ed. Modern continental plays...New York, Harper, 1929. 836p
Andreyev, L. He who gets slapped
Annunzio, G. d'. Francesca da Rimini
Benavente y Martínez, J. La malquerida
Bjørnson, B. Beyond our power
Bracco, R. Phantasms
Brieux, E. False gods
Čapek, K. R.U.R.
Chekhov, A. The cherry orchard
Claudel, P. The tidings brought to Mary
Gorki, M. The lower depths
Hauptmann, G. The rats
Kaiser, G. The coral
Kaiser, G. Gas, pt. I
Kaiser, G. Gas, pt. II
Maeterlinck, M. Pelléas and Mélisande
Molnár, F. Liliom
Pérez Galdós, B. Electra
Rostand, E. Cyrano de Bergerac
Schnitzler, A. Light-o'-love
Strindberg, A. Comrades
Vildrac, C. S.S. Tenacity
Wedekind, F. Such is life

TUCJ Tucker, Samuel Marion, ed. Modern plays...New York, Macmillan [c1932] 400p
Bennett, A. and Knoblock, E. Milestones
Crothers, R. Mary the third
Hughes, H. Hell bent fer heaven
Milne, A. The ivory door
O'Neill, E. The Emperor Jones

TUCM Tucker, Samuel Marion, ed. Twenty-five modern plays...New York, Harper [c1931] 1045p
Andreyev, L. He who gets slapped
Annunzio, G. d'. Francesca da Rimini
Barry, P. In a garden
Benavente y Martínez, J. La malquerida
Čapek, K. R.U.R.
Chekhov, A. The cherry orchard
Coward, N. The vortex
Crothers, R. Mary the third
Ervine, St. J. John Ferguson
Green, P. The field god
Hauptmann, G. The rats
Howard, S. The silver cord
Kaiser, G. The coral
Kaiser, G. Gas, pt. I
Kaiser, G. Gas, pt. II
Maeterlinck, M. Pelléas and Mélisande
Maugham, W. The circle
Milne, A. The truth about Blayds
Molnár, F. Liliom
O'Neill, E. The great god Brown
Pinero, A. The thunderbolt
Rostand, E. Cyrano de Bergerac
Schnitzler, A. Light-o'-love
Strindberg, A. Comrades
Vildrac, C. S.S. Tenacity
Vollmer, L. Sun-up
Wilde, O. The importance of being earnest

TUCN Tucker, Samuel Marion

and Downer, Alan S., eds. Twenty-five modern plays ...Revised edition by Alan S. Downer, New York, Harper [c1948] 1009p
Andreyev, L. He who gets slapped
Auden, W. and Isherwood, C. The ascent of F6
Benavente, [y Martínez, J.] La malquerida
Čapek, K. R.U.R.
Chekhov, A. The cherry orchard
Cocteau, J. The infernal machine
Ervine, St. J. John Ferguson
Gorki, M. The lower depths
Green, P. The field god
Haines, W. Command decision
Hauptmann, G. The rats
Howard, S. The silver cord
Ibsen, H. Rosmersholm
Kaiser, G. The coral
Kaiser, G. Gas I
Kaiser, G. Gas II
Maeterlinck, M. Pelléas and Mélisande
Molnár, F. Liliom
O'Casey, S. The plough and the stars
O'Neill, E. The great god Brown
Pinero, A. The thunderbolt
Riggs, L. Roadside
Rostand, E. Cyrano de Bergerac
Schnitzler, A. Light-o'-love
Strindberg, A. Comrades
Synge, J. Riders to the sea
Wilde, O. The importance of being earnest

TUCO Tucker, S. Marion and Downer, Alan S., eds. Twenty-five modern plays ...Third edition...New York, Harper [c1953] 1008p
Andreyev, L. He who gets slapped
Benavente, J. La malquerida
Čapek, K. R.U.R.
Chekhov, A. The cherry orchard
Cocteau, J. The infernal machine
Eliot, T. Murder in the cathedral
Ervine, St. J. John Ferguson
Gorki, M. The lower depths
Hauptmann, G. The rats
Howard, S. The silver cord
Ibsen, H. Rosmersholm
Kaiser, G. The coral
Kaiser, G. Gas, Parts 1 and 2
Maeterlinck, M. Pelléas and Mélisande
Miller, A. Death of a salesman
Molnár, F. Liliom
O'Casey, S. The plough and the stars
O'Neill, E. The great god Brown
Pinero, A. The thunderbolt
Riggs, L. Roadside
Rostand, E. Cyrano de Bergerac
Schnitzler, A. Light-o'-love
Strindberg, A. Comrades
Synge, J. Riders to the sea
Wilde, O. The importance of being earnest
Williams, T. A streetcar named desire

TUP Tupper, Frederick and Tupper, James Waddell, eds. Representative English dramas from Dryden to Sheridan...New York, Oxford university press, 1914. 460p
Addison, J. Cato
Congreve, W. The way of the world
Dryden, J. All for love
Dryden, J. The conquest of Granada
Farquhar, G. The beaux' stratagem
Fielding, H. Tom Thumb the great

TUP (cont.)
Gay, J. The beggar's opera
Goldsmith, O. She stoops to conquer
Otway, T. Venice preserved
Sheridan, R. The rivals
Sheridan, R. The school for scandal
Steele, R. The conscious lovers

TUQ Tupper, Frederick and Tupper, James Waddell, eds. Representative English dramas from Dryden to Sheridan...New and enl. ed. New York, Oxford university press [c1934] 722p
Addison, J. Cato
Cibber, C. Love's last shift
Congreve, W. The way of the world
Dryden, J. All for love
Dryden, J. The conquest of Granada
Etherege, G. The man of mode
Farquhar, G. The beaux' stratagem
Fielding, H. Tom Thumb the great
Gay, J. The beggar's opera
Goldsmith, O. She stoops to conquer
Lillo, G. The London merchant
Otway, T. Venice preserved
Rowe, N. The tragedy of Jane Shore
Sheridan, R. The rivals
Sheridan, R. The school for scandal
Steele, R. The conscious lovers
Vanbrugh, J. The relapse
Wycherley, W. The country wife

TUQH Turkish literature...tr. into English for the first time, with a special introduction by Epiphanius Wilson...Rev. ed. New York, Colonial press [1901] 462p (The world's great classics)
Mirza Feth-Ali, A. The magistrates

TUQT Turner, Darwin T., comp. Black drama in America: an anthology. Greenwich, Conn., Fawcett, 1971. 630p
Bass, K. We righteous bombers
Davis, O. Purlie victorious
Dodson, O. Bayou legend
Edmands, R. Earth and stars
Hughes, L. Emperor of Haiti
Jones, L. The toilet
Peterson, L. Take a giant step
Richardson, W. The chip woman's fortune
Ward, T. Our lan'

TUR Turrell, Charles Alfred, ed. and tr. Contemporary Spanish dramatists...Boston, Badger [c1919] 397p
Alvarez Quintero, S. and Alvarez Quintero, J. The women's town
Dicenta y Benedicto, J. Juan José
Linares Rivas, M. The claws
Marquina, E. When the roses bloom again
Pérez Galdós, B. Electra
Zamacois, E. The passing of the magi

TWE Twelve famous plays of the restoration and eighteenth century...New York, Modern library [c1933] 952p
Congreve, W. Love for love
Congreve, W. The way of the world
Dryden, J. All for love; or, the world well lost

Farquhar, G. The beaux' stratagem
Garrick, D. The clandestine marriage
Gay, J. The beggar's opera
Goldsmith, O. She stoops to conquer; or, The mistakes of a night
Otway, T. Venice preserv'd; or, A plot discover'd
Sheridan, R. The rivals
Sheridan, R. The school for scandal
Vanbrugh, J. The provok'd wife
Wycherley, W. The country wife

U

UHL Uhler, John Earle, ed. The best eighteenth century comedies...New York, Knopf, 1929. 480p
Farquhar, G. The beaux' stratagem
Gay, J. The beggar's opera
Goldsmith, O. She stoops to conquer
Sheridan, R. The rivals
Sheridan, R. The school for scandal

ULAN Ulanov, Barry, ed. Makers of the modern theater...New York, McGraw-Hill [c1961] 743p
Anouilh, J. Antigone
Betti, U. The queen and the rebels
Chekhov, A. Ivanov
García Lorca, F. Yerma
Giraudoux, J. Sodom and Gomorrah
Giraudoux, J. Song of songs
Hauptmann, G. Hannele
Ibsen, H. John Gabriel Borkman
Ionesco, E. The bald soprano
Marcel, G. Ariadne
Miller, A. A view from the bridge
Montherlant, H. The master of Santiago
O'Casey, S. Purple dust
O'Neill, E. The long voyage home
Pirandello, L. Henry IV
Shaw, G. Getting married
Strindberg, A. To Damascus, part 1
Synge, J. The well of the saints
Toller, E. Hoppla! Such is life!
Williams, T. Camino real
Yeats, W. On Baile's strand
Yeats, W. Purgatory

UNTE Untermeyer, Louis, ed. The Britannica library of great American writing... Chicago, J. B. Lippincott [c1960] 2v
O'Neill, E. The Emperor Jones 2

V

VAN DOREN, CARL CLINTON. See also AMI American omnibus...LON London omnibus...

VAN Van Doren, Carl Clinton, ed. The Borzoi reader... New York, Knopf, 1936. 1033p
Kaufman, G., Ryskind, M. and Gershwin, I. Of thee I sing

VANM Van Doren, Carl, ed. Modern American prose... New York, Harcourt, Brace [c1934] 939p
Anderson, M. and Stallings, L. What price glory?

VANV Van Ghent, Dorothy (Bendon) and Brown, Joseph S., eds. Continental literature; an anthology...Philadelphia, Lippin-

VANV (cont.)
cott [1968] 2v
Aeschylus. Agamemnon 1
Aristophanes. Lysistrata 1
Brecht, B. The good woman of Setzuan 2
Euripides. Hippolytus 1
García Lorca, F. The king of Harlem 2
García Lorca, F. Lament for Ignacio Sánchez Mejías 2
Goethe, J. Faust, pt. I 2
Ibsen, H. Hedda Gabler 2
Molière, J. Tartuffe 2
Pirandello, L. Such is life 2
Racine, J. Phaedra 2
Sophocles. Oedipus rex 1

VENEZKY, ALICE. See GRIF Griffin, Alice Sylvia (Venezky), ed. ...

VOAD Voaden, Herman Arthur, ed. Four good plays to read and act... Toronto, Longmans Green [c1944] 297p
Coward, N. Cavalcade
Jerome, H. Price and prejudice
MacLeish, A. The fall of the city
Saroyan, W. My heart's in the highlands

VOLI Volpe, Edward Loris, and Magalaner, Marvin, comps. An introduction to literature: drama. New York, Random House, 1967. 467p
Chekhov, A. The cherry orchard
Ibsen, H. The wild duck
Molière, J. Tartuffe
O'Neill, E. Desire under the elms
Shakespeare, W. Othello
Sophocles. Oedipus rex

VOLP Volpe, Edward Loris [and others] eds. Poetry, drama, fiction... New York, Random House [c1967] 808p
O'Neill, E. Desire under the elms
Shakespeare, W. Othello
Sophocles. Oedipus rex

VON Von Staden, H., comp. Western literature... New York, Harcourt, Brace, Jovanovich, 1971. 3v
Aeschylus. Agamemnon 1
Aristophanes. Lysistrata 1
Euripides. Bacchae 1
Goethe, J. Faust, Part 1 3
Ibsen, H. The master builder 3
Lowell, R. Old glory: Benito Cereno 3
Molière, J. The misanthrope 2
Pirandello, L. Six characters in search of an author 3
Shakespeare, W. Othello 2
Sophocles. Oedipus the king 1

W

WAGC Wagenheim, Harold H.; Brattig, Elizabeth Voris and Dolkey, Matthew, eds. Our reading heritage... New York, Henry Holt [c1956] 4v
Bennett, A. and Knoblock, E. Milestones 4
Cohan, G. Pigeons and people 3
Gilsdorf, F. and Gibson, P. The ghost of Benjamin Sweet 1
Gordon, R. Years ago 1
Hoote, H. The dancers 2
Kelly, G. Finders'-keepers 3
O'Neill, E. In the zone 2
Osborn, P. Point of no return 3
Rattigan, T. The Winslow

boy 2
Shakespeare, W. Macbeth 4
Shaw, G. Saint Joan 4

WAGE Wagenheim, Harold H.; Brattig, Elizabeth Voris and Flesch, Rudolf, eds. Read up on life...New York, Henry Holt, 1952. 507p (Holt literature series)
Gordon, R. Years ago

WAIT Waite, Harlow O. and Atkinson, Benjamin P., eds. Literature for our time... New York, Henry Holt [c1953] 998p
Anderson, M. Winterset
Barry, P. The Philadelphia story
Behrman, S. Biography
MacLeish, A. The fall of the city
O'Neill, E. The hairy ape
Williams, T. The glass menagerie

WAIU Waite, Harlow O. and Atkinson, Benjamin P., eds. Literature for our time...New York, Henry Holt [c1958] 1009p
Barry, P. The Philadelphia story
Giraudoux, J. Tiger at the gates
O'Neill, E. The hairy ape
Shaw, G. Major Barbara
Williams, T. The glass menagerie

WAIW Waith, Eugene M., ed. The dramatic moment... Englewood Cliffs, N.J., Prentice-Hall [1967] 505p
Albee, E. The zoo story
Brecht, B. Mother Courage and her children
Chekhov, A. The seagull
Ibsen, H. Hedda Gabler
Jonson, B. Volpone; or, The fox
Molière, J. The misanthrope
Pirandello, L. Six characters in search of an author
Shakespeare, W. King Lear
Shaw, G. Major Barbara
Sophocles. Oedipus rex
Strindberg, A. The ghost sonata
Summoning of everyman

WALB Wall, Vincent and McCormick, James Patton, eds. Seven plays of the modern theater...New York, American book co. [c1950] 521p
Anderson, M. Winterset
Chekhov, A. Uncle Vanya
Coward, N. Blithe spirit
Ibsen, H. Hedda Gabler
Maugham, W. The circle
O'Neill, E. The hairy ape
Williams, T. The glass menagerie

WALJ Walley, Harold Reinoehl. The book of the play... New York, Scribner [c1950] 699p
Chekhov, A. The sea gull
Congreve, W. The way of the world
Ibsen, H. An enemy of the people
Molière, J. The misanthrope
O'Neill, E. Desire under the elms
Racine, J. Phaedra
Rostand, E. Cyrano de Bergerac
Shakespeare, W. The tragedy of Hamlet, Prince of Denmark
Shakespeare, W. Twelfth night; or, What you will
Sophocles. Oedipus the king
Strindberg, A. The dream play
Synge, J. The playboy of the western world

WALL Walley, Harold Reinoehl and Wilson, John Harold,

WALL (cont.)
eds. Early seventeenth century plays, 1600-1642... New York, Harcourt, Brace [c1930] 1120p
Beaumont, F. and Fletcher, J. A king or no king
Brome, R. A mad couple well matched
Chapman, G. The revenge of Bussy D'Ambois
Chapman, G., Jonson, B. and Marston, J. Eastward ho!
D'Avenant, W. Love and honor
Dekker, T. and Middleton, T. The honest whore, pt. I
Fletcher, J. The wild-goose chase
Ford, J. 'Tis a pity she's a whore
Heywood, T. A woman killed with kindness
Jonson, B. Volpone; or, The fox
Marston, J. The Dutch courtesan
Massinger, P. A new way to pay old debts
Middleton, T. A chaste maid in Cheapside
Shirley, J. The cardinal
Webster, J. The white devil

WALPOLE, HUGH. See MAL Malvern festival plays...

WAR Warfel, Harry Redcay; Gabriel, Ralph Henry and Williams, Stanley Thomas, eds. The American mind ...New York, American book co. [c1937] 1520p
O'Neill, E. The Emperor Jones

WARH Warnock, Robert. Representative modern plays... American. Chicago, Scott, Foresman [c1952] 758p
Anderson, M. Valley Forge
Behrman, S. Biography
Howard, S. The late Christopher Bean
Kaufman, G. and Connelly, M. Beggar on horseback
Miller, A. Death of a salesman
Odets, C. Waiting for Lefty
O'Neill, E. Mourning becomes Electra
Williams, T. The glass menagerie

WARI Warnock, Robert, ed. Representative modern plays, British. Chicago, Scott, Foresman [1953] 710p
Barrie, J. The admirable Crichton
Coward, N. The blithe spirit
Eliot, T. Murder in the cathedral
Fry, C. A phoenix too frequent
Galsworthy, J. Loyalties
Maugham, W. The constant wife
O'Casey, S. Juno and the paycock
Shaw, G. The doctor's dilemma
Synge, J. Riders to the sea

WARL Warnock, Robert, comp. Representative modern plays: Ibsen to Tennessee Williams. Chicago, Scott, Foresman [1964] 696p
Behrman, S. Biography
Chekhov, A. The sea-gull
Fry, C. A phoenix too frequent
Ibsen, H. The master builder
Maugham, W. The constant wife
O'Casey, S. Juno and the paycock
O'Neill, E. Desire under the elms
Shaw, G. The doctor's dilemma
Strindberg, A. Miss Julie

Synge, J. Riders to the sea
Williams, T. The glass menagerie

WARN Warnock, Robert and Anderson, George K., eds. The world in literature... Chicago, Scott, Foresman [c1950] 2v in 1
Aeschylus. Agamemnon 1
Aristophanes. The clouds 1
Euripides. Hippolytus 1
Kālidāsa. Shakuntalā 1
Shakespeare, W. Hamlet, Prince of Denmark 2
Sophocles. Oedipus the king 1
Vega Carpio, L. The sheep well 2

WAT Watrous, George Ansel, ed. Elizabethan dramatists ...New York, Crowell [1903] 293p
Beaumont, F. and Fletcher, J. Philaster
Jonson, B. Every man in his humour
Marlowe, C. Dr. Faustus

WATA Watson, Ernest Bradlee and Pressey, Benfield, eds. Contemporary drama: American, English and Irish, European...New York, Scribner [c1959] 577p
Chekhov, A. Uncle Vanya
Eliot, T. Murder in the cathedral
Frings, K. Look homeward, angel
García Lorca, F. Blood wedding
Ibsen, H. Hedda Gabler
Inge, W. Comeback, little Sheba
Miller, A. The crucible
O'Casey, S. Purple dust
O'Neill, E. Ah, wilderness!
Pirandello, L. Henry IV
Shaw, G. Man and superman
Strindberg, A. The dream play

Synge, J. Riders to the sea
Wilde, O. The importance of being earnest
Wilder, T. The skin of our teeth

WATC Watson, Ernest Bradlee and Pressey, Benfield, comps. Contemporary drama; American plays... New York, Scribner [c1931-38] 2v
Anderson, M. Elizabeth the queen 2
Barry, P. Hotel Universe 2
Howard, S. The silver cord 1
Kaufman, G. and Connelly, M. Beggar on horseback 1
Lawson, J. Processional 1
Mitchell, L. The New York idea 1
O'Neill, E. The Emperor Jones 1
O'Neill, E. The hairy ape 2
Rice, E. Street scene 2
Sherwood, R. The petrified forest 2

WATE Watson, Ernest Bradlee and Pressey, Benfield, eds. Contemporary drama, eleven plays: American, English, European...New York, Scribner's [c1956] 341p
Anouilh, J. Antigone
Connelly, M. The green pastures
Coward, N. Ways and means
Fry, C. Venus observed
Giraudoux, J. The madwoman of Chaillot
Hellman, L. Another part of the forest
Miller, A. Death of a salesman
Saroyan, W. Hello out there
Shaw, G. Pygmalion
Wilder, T. The happy journey to Trenton and Camden

WATE (cont.)
Williams, T. The glass menagerie

WATF Watson, Ernest Bradlee and Pressey, Benfield, comps. Contemporary drama: English and Irish plays...New York, Scribner [c1931] 2v
Barrie, J. Dear Brutus 2
Barrie, J. What every woman knows 1
Dunsany, E. The glittering gate 1
Galsworthy, J. Justice 1
Galsworthy, J. Loyalties 2
Gregory, I. Hyacinth Halvey 1
Maugham, W. The circle 2
Milne, A. Mr. Pim passes by 2
O'Casey, S. Juno and the paycock 2
Pinero, A. Mid-channel 1
Synge, J. Riders to the sea 1

WATI Watson, Ernest Bradlee and Pressey, Benfield, comps. Contemporary drama: European, English and Irish, American plays... New York, Scribner [c1941] 1177p
Anderson, M. Elizabeth the queen
Andreyev, L. He who gets slapped
Barrie, J. Dear Brutus
Barrie, J. What every woman knows
Barry, P. Hotel Universe
Benavente y Martínez, J. The passion flower
Čapek, K. R.U.R. (Rossum's universal robots)
Chekhov, A. The cherry orchard
Chekhov, A. Uncle Vanya
Curel, F. de. The fossils
Dunsany, E. The glittering gate
Galsworthy, J. Justice
Galsworthy, J. Loyalties
Gorki, M. Night's lodging; or, The lower depths
Gregory, I. Hyacinth Halvey
Hauptmann, G. The beaver coat
Howard, S. The silver cord
Ibsen, H. A doll's house
Ibsen, H. Hedda Gabler
Kaufman, G. and Connelly, M. Beggar on horseback
Lawson, J. Processional
Maeterlinck, M. Pelléas and Mélisande
Maugham, W. The circle
Milne, A. Mr. Pim passes by
O'Casey, S. Juno and the paycock
O'Neill, E. The Emperor Jones
O'Neill, E. "The hairy ape"
Pinero, A. Mid-channel
Pirandello, L. "Henry IV"
Rice, E. Street scene
Rostand, E. Cyrano de Bergerac
Schnitzler, A. Light-o'-love
Sherwood, R. Abe Lincoln in Illinois
Strindberg, A. The dream play
Sudermann, H. Magda
Synge, J. Riders to the sea
Toller, E. Man and the masses

WATL Watson, Ernest Bradlee and Pressey, Benfield, comps. Contemporary drama: European plays... New York, Scribner [c1931-34] 4v
Andreyev, L. He who gets slapped 4
Annunzio, G. d'. Francesca da Rimini 3
Becque, H. The vultures 1
Benavente y Martínez, J. The passion flower 3
Čapek, K. R.U.R. 4
Chekhov, A. The cherry orchard 1

Chekhov, A. The sea gull 3
Chekhov, A. Uncle Vanya 2
Curel, F. de. The fossils 1
Gorki, M. Night's lodging 3
Hauptmann, G. The beaver coat 1
Ibsen, H. A doll's house 1
Ibsen, H. Hedda Gabler 2
Maeterlinck, M. Pelléas and Mélisande 2
Pirandello, L. Henry IV 4
Rostand, E. Cyrano de Bergerac 2
Schnitzler, A. Light-o'-love 1
Strindberg, A. The dream play 3
Sudermann, H. Magda 2
Toller, E. Man and the masses 4

WATO Watson, Ernest Bradlee and Pressey, Benfield, comps. Contemporary drama, nine plays: American, English, European... New York, Scribner [c1941] 362p
Barrie, J. What every woman knows
Čapek, K. R.U.R. (Rossum's universal robots)
Galsworthy, J. Justice
Howard, S. The silver cord
Maugham, W. The circle
O'Neill, E. "The hairy ape"
Rice, E. Street scene
Rostand, E. Cyrano de Bergerac
Sherwood, R. Abe Lincoln in Illinois

WATR Watson, Ernest Bradlee and Pressey, Benfield, comps. Five modern plays ...New York, Scribner [c1933] v.p.
Chekhov, A. The cherry orchard
Galsworthy, J. Justice
Ibsen, H. Hedda Gabler
Maeterlinck, M. Pelléas and Mélisande
Rostand, E. Cyrano de Bergerac

WATS Watt, Homer Andrew and Cargill, Oscar, eds. College reader. New York, Prentice-Hall, 1948. 949p
Behrman, S. End of summer
Corwin, N. Radio primer
Galsworthy, J. Strife
Gregory, A. Spreading the news

WATT Watt, Homer Andrew and Munn, James Buell, eds. Ideas and forms in English and American literature... Chicago, Scott, Foresman [c1932] 2v
Gregory, I. Hyacinth Halvey 2
Milne, A. The Dover road 2
Mr. S. Mr. of Art. Gammer Gurton's needle 2
Pinero, A. The second Mrs. Tanqueray 2
Sheridan, R. The school for scandal 2
Synge, J. Riders to the sea 2
Webster, J. The Duchess of Malfi 2
Yeats, W. The land of heart's desire 2

WEAL Weales, Gerald Clifford, ed. Edwardian plays... New York, Hill and Wang [1962] 429p (Mermaid dramabook)
Granville-Barker, H. The Madras house
Hankin, J. The return of the prodigal
Maugham, W. Loaves and fishes
Pinero, A. Mid-channel
Shaw, G. Getting married

WEAN Weales, Gerald Clifford, ed. Eleven plays...New York, Norton [1964] 617p
Anouilh, J. The lark
Barker, G. Rococo
Euripides. Alcestis

WEAN (cont.)
Ibsen, H. The wild duck
Miller, A. All my sons
Musset, A. Camille and Perdican
Pirandello, L. Tonight we improvise
Shakespeare, W. Troilus and Cressida
Shaw, G. Arms and the man
Wilder, T. The matchmaker
Wycherley, W. The country wife

WEAT Weatherley, Edward Howell; Moffet, Harold Y.; Prouty, Charles T. and Noyes, Henry H. The English heritage... Boston, Ginn [c1945] 2v
Barrie, J. The twelve-pound look 2
Everyman 1
Farquhar, G. The beaux' stratagem 1
Marlowe, C. The tragical history of Doctor Faustus 1
Noah's flood 1
Sheridan, R. The rivals 1
Synge, J. Riders to the sea 2

WEAV Weatherly, Edward Howell; Wagener, A. Pelzer; Zeydel, Edwin H. and Yarmolinsky, Avrahm, eds. The heritage of European literature. Boston, Ginn [c1948-49] 2v
Aeschylus. Agamemnon 1
Chekhov, A. The cherry orchard 2
Euripides. Electra 1
Goethe, J. Faust, pt. I 2
Ibsen, H. The wild duck 2
Molière, J. Tartuffe; or, The imposter 2
Molière, J. The physician in spite of himself 2
Racine, J. Phaedra 2
Schiller, J. William Tell 2
Sophocles. Oedipus the king 1
Terence. Phormio 1
Vega Carpio, L. The king the greatest Alcalde 1

WEB Webber, James Plaisted and Webster, Hanson Hart, eds. Typical plays for secondary schools... Boston, Houghton Mifflin [c1929] 343p
Note: Re-issued in 1930 as Typical plays for young people, 291p. Same contents
Baring, M. The rehearsal
Chapin, H. Augustus in search of a father
Frank, M. A mistake at the manor
Gilbert, W. Sweethearts
Gregory, I. The dragon
Healey, F. The copper pot
Hsiung, C. The thrice promised bride
Kotzebue, A. Pharaoh's daughter
Mackay, C. The prince of court painters
Tarkington, B. and Wilson, H. The Gibson upright
Webber, J. Frances and Francis

WED Wedeck, Harry Ezekiel, ed. Classics of Greek literature... New York, Philosophical Library, 1963. 385p
Aeschylus. The Persians
Aristophanes. The birds
Euripides. Iphigenia in Tauris
Sophocles. Electra

WEE Week-end library. 3rd issue [1930] Garden City, N.Y., Doubleday Page, 1930. v.p.
Maugham, W. The circle
Morley, C. Really, my dear...
Morley, C. Wagon-lits

WEIM Weiss, Samuel Abba, ed. Drama in the modern

world... Boston, Heath [1964] 555p
Arbuzov, A. It happened in Irkutsk
Beckett, S. All that fall
Brecht, B. The good woman of Setzuan
Chekhov, A. The cherry orchard
García Lorca, F. The house of Bernarda Alba
Giraudoux, J. Ondine
Ibsen, H. The wild duck
Ionesco, E. The bald soprano
O'Neill, E. Desire under the elms
Pirandello, L. Six characters in search of an author
Shaw, G. Major Barbara
Strindberg, A. Miss Julie
Synge, J. The playboy of the western world
Williams, T. The glass menagerie

WEIS Weiss, Samuel A., comp. Drama in the western world; 15 plays with essays. Boston, Heath. 1968. 794p
Aristophanes. Lysistrata
Beckett, S. All that fall
Brecht, B. The Caucasian chalk circle
Chekhov, A. Uncle Vanya
Euripides. The bacchae
Ibsen, H. Ghosts
Kleist, H. The Prince of Homburg
Molière, J. The misanthrope
O'Neill, E. Desire under the elms
Pirandello, L. Six characters in search of an author
Racine, J. Phaedra
Shaw, G. Caesar and Cleopatra
Sophocles. Oedipus the king
Strindberg, A. A dream play
Williams, T. The glass menagerie

WEIW Weiss, Samuel A., comp. Drama in the western world; 9 plays with essays. Boston, Heath, 1968. 506p
Aristophanes. Lysistrata
Brecht, B. The Caucasian chalk circle
Chekhov, A. Uncle Vanya
Ibsen, H. Ghosts
Molière, J. The misanthrope
Pirandello, L. Six characters in search of an author
Shaw, G. Caesar and Cleopatra
Sophocles. Oedipus the king
Williams, T. The glass menagerie

WEL Wells, Henry Willis, ed. Six Sanskrit plays, in English translation. New York, Asia Publishing House [1964] 487p
Bhāsa. The vision of Vāsavadatta
Bhavabhūti. Rama's later history
Harsha. Nagananda
Kālidāsa. Shakuntalā
Kālidāsa. Vikramorvacie; or, The hero and the nymph
Sūdraka. The little clay cart

WELG Wellwarth, George, ed. German drama between the wars. New York, Dutton, 1972. 366p
Broch, H. The atonement
Hasenclaver, W., and Tucholsky, K. Christopher Columbus
Kokoschka, O. Job
Kraus, K. The last days of mankind (excerpt)
Toller, E. No more peace!
Zuckmayer, C. The captain of Köpenick

WELL Wellwarth, George Emanuel, ed. The new wave of Spanish drama. New York, New York Uni-

WELL (cont.)
versity press, 1970. 321p
Ballesteros, A. The best of all possible worlds
Ballesteros, A. The hero
Bellido, J. Bread and rice or geometry in yellow
Bellido, J. Train to H...
Ruibal, J. The man and the fly
Ruibal, J. The jackass
Sastre, A. Sad are the eyes of William Tell

WELT Wellwarth, George Emanuel, ed. Themes of drama: an anthology. New York, Crowell, 1973. 647p
Adamov, A. All against all
Aristophanes. Lysistrata
Ballesteros, A. The best of all possible worlds
Büchner, G. Woyzeck
Cornish, R. Open twenty-four hours
Dennis, N. Cards to identify
Dürrenmatt, F. Incident at twilight
Everyman
Euripides. The bacchae
Fugard, A. The blood knot
Hochenwälder, F. The holy experiment
Jarry, A. King Ubu
Molière, J. The would-be gentleman
Nkosi, L. The rhythm of violence
Pirandello, L. Henry IV
Richardson, J. Gallows humor
Ruibal, J. The man and the fly
Schnitzler, A. Round dance
Shakespeare, W. Antony and Cleopatra
Shaw, G. Mrs. Warren's profession

WHE Wheeler, Charles Bickersteth, ed. Six plays by contemporaries of Shakespeare... London, Oxford university press [1928] 595p (The world's classics)
Beaumont, F. and Fletcher, J. The knight of the burning pestle
Beaumont, F. and Fletcher, J. Philaster
Dekker, T. The shoemaker's holiday
Massinger, P. A new way to pay old debts
Webster, J. The Duchess of Malfi
Webster, J. The white devil

WHF White, Elizabeth A. and others, eds. Understanding literature. Boston, Ginn, 1967. 751p
Alvarez Quintero, S. and Alvarez Quintero, J. A sunny morning
Fletcher, L. Sorry, wrong number
MacLeish, A. The trojan horse
Shakespeare, W. The life of King Henry the fifth

WHFA White, Elizabeth A. and others, eds. Understanding literature. Boston, Ginn, 1970. 756p
Gibson, W. The miracle worker
Goodrich, F. and Hackett, A. The diary of Anne Frank
Shakespeare, W. The life of King Henry the fifth

WHFM White, Melvin R., and Whiting, Frank M. Playreader's repertory: an anthology for introduction to theatre. Glenview, Ill., Scott, Foresman, 1970. 804p
Aristophanes. The birds
Chekhov, A. The cherry orchard

Everyman
Hansberry, L. A raisin in the sun
Ibsen, H. Ghosts
Kopit, A. Oh dad, poor dad, mamma's hung you in the closet and I'm feelin' so sad
Molière, J. Tartuffe
O'Neill, E. Desire under the elms
Pirandello, L. Six characters in search of an author
Shakespeare, W. Hamlet, Prince of Denmark
Shaw, G. Arms and the man
Sophocles. King Oedipus
Wilde, O. The importance of being earnest

WHITING, B. J. See COL College survey of English literature. [Edited by B. J. Whiting...and others]

WHI Whitman, Charles Huntington, ed. Representative modern dramas...New York, Macmillan, 1936. 1121p
Anderson, M. Elizabeth the queen
Barry, P. Hotel Universe
Behrman, S. Biography
Benavente y Martínez, J. The bonds of interest
Brieux, E. The red robe
Chekhov, A. The cherry orchard
Galsworthy, J. Strife
Gorki, M. The lower depths
Green, P. In Abraham's bosom
Hauptmann, G. The weavers
Howard, S. The silver cord
Ibsen, H. The wild duck
Maeterlinck, M. Pelléas and Mélisande
Maugham, W. Our betters
Molnár, F. Liliom
O'Casey, S. Juno and the paycock
O'Neill, E. The hairy ape
Pinero, A. Mid-channel
Pirandello, L. Six characters in search of an author
Rostand, E. Cyrano de Bergerac
Schnitzler, A. The lonely way
Strindberg, A. The father
Synge, J. Riders to the sea
Wilde, O. The importance of being earnest

WHK Whitman, Charles Huntington, ed. Seven contemporary plays...Boston, Houghton Mifflin [c1931] 565p
Chekhov, A. The cherry orchard
Galsworthy, J. Strife
Hauptmann, G. The sunken bell
Ibsen, H. An enemy of the people
O'Neill, E. Beyond the horizon
Rostand, E. Cyrano de Bergerac
Synge, J. Riders to the sea

WHT Whittaker, Charlotte C., ed. Youth and the world ...Chicago, Ill., Lippincott [c1955] 512p (Reading for life series)
Ibsen, H. A doll's house

WILE Wilson, John Harold, ed. Six eighteenth century plays. Boston, Houghton Mifflin [c1963] 374p
Gay, J. The beggar's opera
Goldsmith, O. She stoops to conquer
Lillo, G. The London merchant
Rowe, N. The fair penitent
Sheridan, R. The school for scandal
Steele, R. The conscious lovers

WILS Wilson, John Harold, ed. Six Restoration plays... Boston, Houghton Mifflin [c1959] 463p

WILS (cont.)
Congreve, W. The way of the world
Dryden, J. All for love; or, The world well lost
Etherege, G. The man of mode; or, Sir Fopling Flutter
Farquhar, G. The beaux' stratagem
Otway, T. Venice preserved; or, A plot discovered
Wycherley, W. The country wife

WILSON, EPIPHANIUS. See TUQH Turkish literature...

WINE Wine, Martin L., ed. Drama of the English renaissance. New York, Modern Library, 1969. 786p
Beaumont, F. and Fletcher, J. The knight of the burning pestle
Beaumont, F. and Fletcher, J. Philaster; or, Love lies a-bleeding
Dekker, T. The shoemaker's holiday: a pleasant comedy of a gentle craft
Ford, J. The broken heart
Jonson, B. The masque of blackness
Jonson, B. Volpone; or, The fox
Marlowe, C. The tragical history of the life and death of Doctor Faustus
Middleton, T. and Rowley, W. The changeling
Webster, J. The Duchess of Malfi

WINN Winny, James, ed. Three Elizabethan plays... London, Chatto and Windus [c1959] 223p
Lyly, J. Midas
Mucedorus
The reign of King Edward III

WISD Wise, Jacob Hooper; Congleton, J. E.; Morris, Alton C. and Hodges, John C. ... College English: the first year... New York, Harcourt, Brace [c1952] 959p
Kingsley, S. Darkness at noon
Rostand, E. Cyrano de Bergerac
Thurber, J. and Nugent, E. The male animal

WISE Wise, Jacob Hooper; Congleton, J. E.; Morris, Alton C. and Hodges, John C. ... College English: the first year... Revised edition. New York, Harcourt, Brace [c1956] 982p
Miller, A. Death of a salesman
Rostand, E. Cyrano de Bergerac
Shaw, G. Pygmalion

WISF Wise, Jacob Hooper; Morris, Alton C. and Hodges, John C., eds. College English: the first year. Third edition... New York, Harcourt, Brace [c1960] 982p
Anouilh, J. Antigone
Capote, T. The grass harp
Miller, A. Death of a salesman
Shaw, G. Androcles and the lion

WOO Woods, George Benjamin; Watt, Homer Andrew and Anderson, George Kumler, eds. The literature of England... Chicago, Scott, Foresman [c1936] 2v
Dekker, T. The shoemaker's holiday 1
Galsworthy, J. Strife 2
Marlowe, C. The tragical history of Doctor Faustus 1

The second shepherds' play 1
Sheridan, R. The rivals 1
Wilde, O. The importance of being earnest 2

WOOD Woods, George Benjamin; Watt, Homer Andrew and Anderson, George Kumler, eds. The literature of England...[Rev. ed.] Chicago, Scott, Foresman [c1941] 2v
Everyman 1
Jonson, B. Epicoene; or, The silent woman 1
Marlowe, C. Doctor Faustus 1
Sheridan, R. The school for scandal 1
The second shepherds' play 1
Synge, J. Riders to the sea 1
Wilde, O. The importance of being earnest 2

WOOE Woods, George Benjamin; Watt, Homer A. and Anderson, George K., eds. ... The literature of England... [Third edition] Chicago, Ill., Scott, Foresman [1947] 2v
Congreve, W. The way of the world 1
Dryden, J. All for love 1
Everyman 1
Marlowe, C. The tragical history of Doctor Faustus 1
The second shepherds' play 1
Shakespeare, W. The tragedy of Antony and Cleopatra 1
Sheridan, R. The school for scandal 1
Synge, J. Riders to the sea 2
Wilde, O. The importance of being earnest 2

WOOG Woodyard, George, ed. The modern stage in Latin America: six plays. New York, Dutton, 1971. 331p
Carballido, E. I too speak of roses
Diaz, J. The place where the mammals die
Dragún, O. And they told us we were immortal
Gomes, A. Payment as pledged
Marqués, R. The fanlights
Triana, J. The criminals

WORL The world in literature [edited by] Elizabeth Collette; Tom Peete Cross and Elmer C. Stauffer. Boston, Ginn [c1949] 4v
Barrie, J. Shall we join the ladies? 4
Shakespeare, W. Julius Caesar 2
Shakespeare, W. Macbeth 4
Wilder, T. Our town 3

WORLD DRAMA SERIES. See SMI, SMK, SML, SMN, SMO, SMP, SMR Smith, Robert Metcalf, ed.

THE WORLD'S GREAT BOOKS. See GRE Great plays (English)...GREA Great plays (French and German) ...GREE Greek dramas...

THE WORLD'S GREAT CLASSICS. See ORI Oriental literature...PLAB Plays by Greek, Spanish, French, German and English dramatists...TUQH Turkish literature...

WORP World's great plays; with an introduction by George Jean Nathan. Cleveland, Ohio, World publishing co. [1944] 491p
Aristophanes. Lysistrata
Chekhov, A. The cherry orchard
Goethe, J. Faust
Ibsen, H. The master builder
O'Casey, S. The plough and the stars

WORP (cont.)
O'Neill, E. The Emperor Jones
Rostand, E. Cyrano de Bergerac

THE WORLD'S GREATEST LITERATURE. See DRA Dramatic masterpieces...

WRIGHT, JOHN HENRY. See MAST Masterpieces of Greek literature...

WRIH Wright, Louis Booker and LaMar, Virginia A., eds. Four famous Tudor and Stuart plays. New York, Washington Square Press [1963] 422p
Dekker, T. The shoemaker's holiday
Jonson, B. Volpone
Marlowe, C. Doctor Faustus
Webster, J. The Duchess of Malfi

WRIR Wright, Louis Booker and LaMar, Virginia A., eds. Four great Restoration plays... New York, Washington Square Press [1964] 477p
Congreve, W. The way of the world
Dryden, J. All for love
Farquhar, G. The beaux' stratagem
Wycherley, W. The country wife

X, Y, Z

YOHA Yohannan, John D., ed. A treasury of Asian literature... New York, John Day [c1956] 487p
Kālidāsa. Shakuntalā
Motokiyo, S. Atsumori

ZDA Zdanowicz, Casimir Douglas, ed. Four French comedies of the eighteenth century... New York, Scribner [c1933] 488p (The modern student's library)
Beaumarchais, P. Le barbier de Séville
Lesage, A. Turcaret
Marivaux, P. Le jeu de l'amour et du hasard
Sedaine, M. Le philosophe sans le savoir

ZIM Zimmermann, Armand, ed. Four European plays ...New York, Macmillan [1965] 547p
Anouilh, J. Thieves' carnival
Chekhov, A. The cherry orchard
Ibsen, H. An enemy of the people
Rostand, E. Cyrano de Bergerac

TITLE INDEX

Abe Lincoln in Illinois. Sherwood, R.
Abelard and Heloise. Millar, R.
Abendstunde im Spätherbst. See Duerrenmatt, F. Incident at twilight
Abhijnanashakuntala. See Kālidāsa. Shakuntalā
Abie's Irish rose. Nichols, A.
Abiko. Euba, F.
Abraham (Wakefield). Anonymous plays
Abraham and Isaac (Brome). Anonymous plays
Abraham Lincoln. Drinkwater, J.
Abraham Lincoln, the early years. Agee, J.
Abraham, Melchisedec and Isaac (Chester). Anonymous plays
Abraham, Melchizedek and Lot, with the sacrifice of Isaac. See Anonymous plays. Abraham, Melchisedec and Isaac
Abraham sacrifiant. Bèze, T.
Absalom. Abel, L.
Abstract wife, The. Molinaro, U.
Abstraction. Anonymous plays
Academic murders, The. Koch, K.
Academy, The. Fratti, M.
L'accademia. See Fratti, M. The academy
Accent on youth. Raphaelson, S.
Las aceitunas. See Rueda, L. The olives
Acharians, The. Aristophanes
L'acheteuse. See Passeur, S. A measure of cruelty
Achilles in Scyros. Metastasio, P.
Acqua sul fuoco. See Morselli, E. Water upon fire
Across the continent; or, Scenes from New York life and the Pacific Railroad. McCloskey, J.
Act of love. See Hayes, A. The girl on the Via Flaminia
Act without words. Beckett, S.
Adam. Anonymous plays
Adam and Eva. Bolton, G. and Middleton, G.
Adam and Eve. Anonymous plays.
Adam stvoritel. See Čapek, K. and Čapek, J. Adam the creator
Adam the creator. Čapek, K. and Čapek, J.
Adaptation. May, E.
Adding machine, The. Rice, E.
Adelphi. Terentius Afer, P.
Admirable Crichton, The. Barrie, J.
Adoration of the kings, The. Anonymous plays
Adoration of the magi, The. Anonymous plays
Adoration of the shepherds, The. Anonymous plays
Adventures of a shawl. See Inchbald, E. Appearance is against them
Advertisement, The. Ginsbury, N.
Affair, The. Millar, R.
Affaires sont les affaires, Les. Mirbeau, O.
Affairs of Anatol, The. See Schnitzler, A. Anatol
Affairs of state. Verneuil, L.
Affected young ladies, The. See

Molière, J. Les précieuses ridicules
Afore night come. Rudkin, D.
African Medea. Magnuson, J.
Afsporet. See Schluter, K. Off the rails
After all. Van Druten, J.
After dark. Boucicault, D.
After October. Ackland, R.
After the dance. Rattigan, T.
After the fall. Miller, A.
After the rain. Bowen, J.
Agamemnon. Aeschylus
Agamemnon. Seneca, L.
Agnes Bernauer. Hebbel, C.
Ah, wilderness! O'Neill, E.
Aim of the law, The. See Brieux, E. La robe rouge
Air raid. MacLeish, A.
Ajax. Sophocles
Alabaster box, The. Harnwell, A. and Meaker, I.
Albion, knight. See Anonymous plays. A moral play of Albion, knight
El alcalde de Zalamea. See Calderón de la Barca, P. The mayor of Zalamea
Alcestis. Euripides
Alchemist, The. Fath'Ali, A.
Alchemist, The. Jonson, B.
"Aleko." See Nemirovich-Danchenko, V. Love and death
Alexander and Campaspe. See Lyly, J. Campaspe
Alien corn. Howard, S.
Alkibiades saved. Kaiser, G.
All against all. Adamov, A.
All for love; or, The world well lost. Dryden, J.
All for money. Lupton, T.
All God's chillun got wings. O'Neill, E.
All in the downs. See Jerrold, D. Black-ey'd Susan
All in the wrong. Murphy, A.
All my own work. Cavan, R.
All my sons. Miller, A.
All that fall. Beckett, S.
All the way home. Mosel, T.
All white caste. Caldwell, B.
Allegro. Hammerstein, O.
Allison's house. Glaspell, S.
All's one, or, one of the foure plaies in one, called a York-Shire tragedy. See Anonymous plays. A York-Shire tragedy
All's well that ends well. Shakespeare, W.
Almanzor and Almahide; or, The conquest of Granada. Dryden, J.
Almighty dollar, The. See Woolf, B. The mighty dollar
Alone. Alyoshin, S.
L'alouete. See Anouilh, J. The lark
Alsfeld, passion play. See Anonymous plays. The passion play of Alsfeld
Always with love. Harris, T.
Amaco. Flavin, M.
L'amant ridicule. Bois-Robert, F.
Amantes de Teruel, Los. Hartzenbusch, J.
Amants, Les. See Donnay, M. The lovers
Amar después de la muerte. See Calderón de la Barca, P. Love after death
Amazing Dr. Clitterhouse, The. Lyndon, B.
Ambush. Richman, A.
Amen corner, The. Baldwin, J.
Amends for ladies. Field, N.
America hurrah. Van Itallie, J.
American, The. James, H.
American dream, The. Albee, E.
American liberty triumphant. See Leacock, J. The fall of British tyranny
American orphan in Germany, The. See Dunlap, W. False shame
American playground sampler, An. Estrin, M.
American power: The master. See Schevill, J. The master
American power: the space fan. See Schevill, J. The space fan

American way, The. Kaufman, G. and Hart, M.
Americans in England. See Paulding, J. The bucktails
Americans in Tripoli. See Jones, J. S. The usurper
L'ami des lois. Laya, J.
Aminta. Tasso, T.
El amor de don Perlimplín con Belisa en su jardín. See García Lorca, F. The love of Don Perlimplin and Belisa in the garden
L'amore dei tre re. See Benelli, S. The love of the three kings
Amorous prawn, The. Kimmins, A.
L'amour médecin. See Molière, J. Love is the best doctor
L'amour puni. See Anouilh, J. The rehearsal
Amoureuse. Porto-Riche, G.
Amphitryon. Plautus, T.
Amphitryon 38. Behrman, S.
Amphitryon 38. Giraudoux, J. See Behrman, S. Amphitryon 38
Amyntas. See Tasso, T. Aminta
Ana Kleiber. See Sastre, A. Anna Kleiber
Anarchy. See MacKaye, S. Paul Kauvar
Anastasia. Maurette, M.
Anatol. Schnitzler, A.
Anatomist, The; or, The sham doctor... with the loves of Mars and Venus. Ravenscroft, E. and Motteux, P.
An der lumpa parti. Barba, P.
And so ad infinitum. Čapek, K. and Čapek, J.
And so they were married. See Williams, J. Why marry?
And that's the truth. See Pirandello, L. Right you are! If you think so
... and the boy who came to leave. Kalcheim, L.
And they told us that we were immortal. Dragun, O.
And things that go bump in the night. McNally, T.
Andersonville trial, The. Levitt, S.
Andorra. Frisch, M.
André. Dunlap, W.
Andria, The. See Terentius Afer, P. The woman of Andros
Andria, the fair Andrian. See Terentius Afer, P. The woman of Andros
Androboros. Hunter, G.
Androcles and the lion. Shaw, G.
Andromache. Euripides
Andromaque. Racine, J.
Andronic. See Campistron, J. Andronicus
Andronicus. Campistron, J.
Angel on the ship, The. Wilder, T.
Angel street. Hamilton, P.
Angela is happening. Moore, E.
Angels of war. Box, M.
L'anglais tel qu'on le parle. Bernard, T.
Animal kingdom, The. Barry, P.
Ann Rutledge. Corwin, N.
Ann Veronica. Gow, R.
Anna Christie. O'Neill, E.
Anna Kleiber. Sastre, A.
Anna Lucasta. Yordan, P.
Anna Sophie Hedvig. Abell, K.
Anne Boleyn. Albery, P.
Anne Frank, the diary of a young girl. See Hackett, A. and Goodrich, F.
Anne of the thousand days. Anderson, M.
Anniversary on weedy hill. Allen, J.
Anniversary, The. See Chekhov, A. The jubilee
Anniversary, The. MacIlwraith, B.
L'annonce faite à Marie. Claudel, P.
Annunciation, The. Anonymous plays
Another language. Franken, R.
Another part of the forest.

Hellman, L.
Antichrist. Anonymous plays
Antigone. Anouilh, J.
Antigone. Hasenclever, W.
Antigone. Sophocles.
Antigone and the tyrant. See Anouilh, J. Antigone
Antigone et le tyrant. See Anouilh, J. Antigone
Antipodes, The. Brome, R.
Antony. Dumas, A., père
Antony and Cleopatra. Shakespeare, W.
Ants, The. Churchill, C.
Any other business. Ross, G.
Aoi no Uye. Zenchiku, U.
Apes shall inherit the earth, The. Aspenström, W.
Apius and Virginia. Anonymous plays
Apollinaris. Second, L.
Apollo. Pixley, F.
Apollo of Bellac, The. Giraudoux, J.
L'Apollon de Bellac. See Giraudoux, J. The Apollo of Bellac
L'Apollon de Marsac. See Giraudoux, J. The Apollo of Bellac
Apostle play, The. Mell, M.
L'apoticaire devalisé. Villiers, C.
Appearance is against them. Inchbald, E.
Appearances. Anderson, G.
Appius and Virginia. See Anonymous plays. Apius and Virginia
Applause. Comden, B. and Green, A.
Apple tree, The. Harnick, S. and Bock, J.
Arbitration, The. Menander
Architruc. Pinget, R.
Archives of Palermo, The. See Stone, J. Tancred, King of Sicily
Ardèle. Anouilh, J.
Ardèle; ou, La Marguerite. See Anouilh, J. Ardèle
Arden of Feversham. Anonymous plays
Are you now or have you ever been: The investigation of show business by the Un-American Activities Committee, 1947-48. Bentley, E.
Area belle, The. Brough, W. and Halliday, A.
Aren't we all? Lonsdale, F.
Aria da capo. Millay, E.
Ariadne. Corneille, T.
Ariadne. Marcel, G.
Ariane. See Corneille, T. Ariadne
Aristocrats. Pogodin, N.
Aristokraty. See Pogodin, N. Aristocrats
Arm of the law, The. Brieux, E.
L'armoire à glace un beau soir. See Aragon, L. The mirror-wardrobe one fine evening
Arms and the man. Shaw, G.
Arraignment of Paris, The. Peele, G.
Arrant knave, An. MacKaye, S.
Ars poetica. Horatius Flaccus, Q.
Arsenic and old lace. Kesselring, J.
Art of being bored, The. See Pailleron, E. Le monde ou l'on s'ennuie
Arvers' secret. See Bernard, J. Le secret d'Arvers
As a man thinks. Thomas, A.
As husbands go. Crothers, R.
As it was in the beginning. See Hodge, M. The wind and the rain
As long as they're happy. Sylvaine, V.
As the leaves fall. See Giacosa, G. Like falling leaves
As you desire me. Pirandello, L.
As you like it. Shakespeare, W.
Ascension of the Lord, The. (Wakefield). Anonymous plays

Ascent of F6, The. Auden, W. and Isherwood, C.
Ashikara. See Seami, M. The reed cutter
Asinaria. See Plautus, T. The comedy of asses
Asmodée. Mauriac, F.
El asno. See Ruibal, J. The jackass
Assassin. Ball, D.
Assault upon Charles Sumner, The. Hivnor, R.
Assumption of Hannele, The. See Hauptmann, G. Hannele
Astrate. See Quinault, P. Astrates
Astrates. Quinault, P.
At Mrs. Beam's. Munro, C.
At the bottom. See Gorki, M. [pseud.] The lower depths
At the gate beautiful. Mason, H.
At the hawk's well. Yeats, W.
At war with the Mongols. Heide, R.
Athaliah. Racine, J.
Atheist's revenge, The. Tourneur, C.
Atlanta in Calydon. Swinburne, A.
Atoms and madams. Thórdarson, A.
Atonement, The. Broch, H.
Atonement of Pan, The. Redding, J.
Atsumori. Seami, M.
Atsumori at Ikuta. Zembō, M.
En attendant Godot. See Beckett, S. Waiting for Godot
Attentant. See Somin, W. Close quarters
Attilio Rigolo. Metastasio, P.
Attowell's jig. Anonymous plays
Les aubes. See Verhaeren, E. The dawn
August for the people. Dennis, N.
Augustus in search of a father. Chapin, H.
Aulularia. Plautus, T.
Aunt Julia's Caesar. Hutchins, M.
Auprès de ma blonde. Achard, M. See Behrman, S. I know my love
Aureng-zebe. Dryden, J.
Die ausnahme und die regel. See Brecht, B. The exception and the rule
L'autre danger. See Donnay, M. The other danger
Autumn crocus. Smith, D. G.
Autumn garden, The. Hellman, L.
Autumn in Han Palace. See Ma C. Autumn in the Palace of Han
Autumn in the Palace of Han. Ma C.
Autumn morning, An. See Alvarez Quintero, S. and Alvarez Quintero, J. A bright morning
L'avare. See Molière, J. The miser
Avenger, The. See Bird, R. Caridorf
Aves. See Aristophanes. The birds
Awake and sing. Odets, C.
Awakening. Stramm, A.
Away from it all. Gielgud, V.

B

Baal. Brecht, B.
Babylonian captivity, The. Kosach, L.
Bacchae, The. Euripides
Bacchantes, The. See Euripides. The bacchae
Back stage of the soul, The. See Evreinov, N. The theatre of the soul
Background. Chetham-Strode, W.
Bad habits. McNally, T.
Bad man. Edmonds, R.
Bad man, The. Brown, P.
Bad play for an old lady, A. Johnson, E.
Bad seed, The. Anderson, M.
Badger's green. Sherriff, R.
Bait, The. Merrill, J.
Le bal des voleurs. See

Anouilh, J. Thieves' carnival
Le balcon. See Genêt, J. The balcony
Balcony, The. Genêt, J.
Bald prima donna, The. See Ionesco, E. The bald soprano
Bald soprano, The. Ionesco, E.
Balls. Foster, P.
Balm. Denison, M.
Balo. Toomer, J.
Banker's daughter, The. Howard, B.
Bankrupt, The. Boker, G.
Banns (Coventry). Anonymous plays
Barabas. Leamon, D.
Ba-ra-ka. Jones, L.
Barbara Allen. See Richardson, H. and Berney, W. Dark of the moon
Barbara Frietchie. Fitch, C.
Barber of Seville, The. See Beaumarchais, P. Le barbier de Seville
Le barbier de Seville; ou, La précaution inutile. Beaumarchais, P.
La barca sin pescador. See Rodríguez, A. The boat without a fisherman
Barefoot in Athens. Anderson, M.
Barefoot in the park. Simon, N.
Bargain, The. Gilbert, M.
Baron Rudolph. Howard, B.
Barretts of Wimpole street, The. Besier, R.
Bartholomew Fair. Jonson, B.
Bastard of the blood, A. Brunson, B.
Bat, The. Rinehart, M. and Hopwood, A.
Bathhouse, The. Mayakóvsky, V.
Les bâttisseurs d'empire. See Vian, B. The empire builders
Battle of Brooklyn, The. Anonymous plays
Battle of Bunkers-hill, The. Brackenridge, H.
Battle of Stillwater, The; or, The maniac. Conway, H.
Battle of the carnival and Lent, The. Graves, R.
Bayou legend. Dodson, O.
Be good, sweet maid. Webber, C.
Be sure you're right, then go ahead. See Murdoch, F. Davy Crockett
Bear, The. See Chekhov, A. The boor
Beau Brummell. Fitch, C.
Beautiful despot, The. Evreinov, N.
Beauty and good properties of women, The. Anonymous plays
Beauty part, The. Perelman, S.
Les beaux jours. See Beckett, S. Happy days
Beaux' stratagem, The. Farquhar, G.
Beaver coat, The. Hauptmann, G.
Becket. Tennyson, A.
Becket; or, The honor of God. Anouilh, J.
Becket; ou, L'honneur de Dieu. See Anouilh, J. Becket
Becky Sharp. Mitchell, L.
Bedbug, The. Mayakóvsky, V.
Bedtime story. O'Casey, S.
Before and behind the curtain. See Taylor, T. and Reade, C. Masks and faces
Before breakfast. O'Neill, E.
Before the party. Ackland, R.
Before the throne. See Dowling, J. and Letton, F. The young Elizabeth
Beggar, The. Sorge, R.
Beggar on horseback. Kaufman, G. and Connelly, M.
Beggars' bush. Fletcher, J., Massinger, P. [and Beaumont, F.]
Beggar's opera, The. Gay, J.
Behind the curtain of the soul. See Evreinov, N. The theatre of the soul

Behold the bridegroom. Kelly, G.
Behold we live. Van Druten, J.
Bell, book and candle. Van Druten, J.
Bell for Adano, A. Osborn, P.
Bellavita. Pirandello, L.
Belle Lamar. Boucicault, D.
La belle Russe. Belasco, D.
La belle sauvage. See Baker, J. The Indian princess
Belle's stratagem, The. Cowley, Mrs. H.
Bells, The. Lewis, L.
Belshazzar. Milman, H.
Belshazzar. More, H.
Belshazzar's feast. Calderón de la Barca, P.
Beneath four eyes. See Fulda, L. Tête-à-tête
Benediktbeuren play, The. Anonymous plays
Benito Cereno. Lowell, R.
Benjamin Franklin, journeyman. Mackay, C.
Benkei on the bridge. Hiyoshi, S.
Bérénice. Racine, J.
Beritten hin und zurück. See Grass, G. Rocking back and forth
Berkeley square. Balderston, J.
Bermondsey. Mortimer, J.
Bernardine. Chase, M.
Bertram; or, The castle of St. Aldobrand. Maturin, C.
Best man, The. Vidal, G.
Best of all possible worlds, The. Ballesteros, A.
Besuch der alten dame, Der. See Duerrenmatt, F. The visit
Betrayal, The. (Wakefield). Anonymous plays
Betrayal of Christ, The. (Chester). Anonymous plays
Betraying of Christ, The. (Coventry). Anonymous plays
Die Bettler. See Sorge, R. The beggar
Between the battles. Bjørnson, B.
Between two worlds. See Rappaport, S. The dybbuk
Beware of the dog. Arout, G.
Beyond human power. See Bjørnson, B. Beyond our power
Beyond our power. Bjørnson, B.
Beyond the bourn; or, The night time stood still. Mitson, R.
Beyond the horizon. O'Neill, E.
Bianca Viconti; or, The heart overtasked. Willis, N.
Bias of the world, The. See Benavente y Martínez, J. The bonds of interest
Der biberpeiz, eine diebskomödie. See Hauptmann, G. The beaver coat
Biedermann and the firebugs. Frisch, M.
Biedermann und die brandstifter. See Frisch, M. Biedermann and the firebugs
Bierce takes on the railroad. Bosakowski, P.
Big bonanza, The. Daly, A.
Big fish, little fish. Wheeler, A.
Big house, The. Robinson, L.
Big killing, The. Mackie, P.
Big knife, The. Odets, C.
Big white fog. Ward, D.
Bilker bilk'd, The. Anonymous plays
Bill of divorcement, A. Ashton, W.
Billy Budd. Coxe, L. and Chapman, R.
Billy liar. Waterhouse, K. and Hall, W.
Billy the kid. Woods, W.
Bilora. Beolco, A.
Bilsen play. See Anonymous plays. The star
Biography. Behrman, S.
Bird catcher in hell, The. Esashi Juō
Bird child, The. White, L.
Bird of contention, The. Clausen, S.

Birdbath. Melfi, L.
Birds, The. Aristophanes
Bird-scaring boat, The. Kongō Yagorō
Birdwatchers. Hite, B.
Birth of Jesus, The (York). Anonymous plays
Birth of Merlin, The; or, The child hath found his father. Anonymous plays
Birthday honours. Jones, P.
Birthday party, The. Pinter, H.
Birthright. Murray, T.
Bishop Jon Arason. Sveinbjörnsson, T.
Bishop's candlesticks, The. Rickert, V.
Bitter fate, A. Pisemkii, A.
Bitter harvest. Turney, C.
Bitter oleander. See García Lorca, F. Blood wedding
Bjaerg-Ejvind og hans hustru. See Sigurjónsson, J. Eyvind of the hills
Black and white, The. Pinter, H.
Black chiffon. Storm, L.
Black comedy. Shaffer, P.
Black crook, The. Barras, C.
Black cycle. Charles, M.
Black doctor, The. Aldridge, I.
Black ice. Patterson, C.
Black man, The; or, The spleen. Payne, J.
Black Rip Van Winkle, The. See Gold, M. Hoboken blues
Black swan winter, The. Hale, J.
Black terror. Wesley, R.
Blackberryin'. Smith, H. F.
Black-ey'd Susan; or, All in the downs. Jerrold, D.
Blind man and the cripple, The. See La Vigne, A. The miracle of the blind man and the cripple
Blindfold, The. López Rubio, J.
Blithe spirit. Coward, N.
Blk love song #1. Ferdinand, V̌.
Blockheads, The; or, The affrighted officers. Anonymous plays
Blood knot, The. Fugard, A.
Blood money. Jasudowicz, D.
Blood of the martyrs. Wilde, P.
Bloodrites. Jones, L.
Blood wedding. García Lorca, F.
Blot in the 'scutcheon, A. Browning, R.
Blue beads. Martens, A.
Bluebeard. Ludlam, C.
Blues for Mr. Charlie. Baldwin, J.
Bluffers. See Labiche, E. and Martin, E. La poudre aux yeux
Boat without the fisherman, The. Rodriguez, A.
Boarding schools, The; or, Life among the little folks. Payne, J.
Bockgesang. See Werfel, F. Goat song
Bodas de sangre. See García Lorca, F. Blood wedding
Bodies in our cellar. See Kesselring, J. Arsenic and old lace
Body was well nourished, The. See Launder, F. and Gilliat, S. Meet a body
Bodybuilder, The. Weller, M.
Boesman and Lena. Fugard, A.
Bombardment of Algiers, The. Smith, R.
Bonaventure. Hastings, C.
Bondman, The. Massinger, P.
Bonds of interest, The. Benavente y Martínez, J.
Les bonnes. See Genêt, J. The maids
Book of Job, The. See Anonymous plays. Job
Boor, The. Chekhov, A.
Borderers, The. Wordsworth, W.
Boris Godunov. Pushkin, A.
Born with the fire on his head. Ijimere, O.
Born yesterday. Kanin, G.
Die bösen Köche. See Grass, G. The wicked cooks
Boss, The. Sheldon, E.

Botticelli. McNally, T.
Both ends meet. Macrae, A.
Both your houses. Anderson, M.
Les Boulingrin. See Courteline, G. These cornfields
Bound east for Cardiff. O'Neill, E.
Le bourgeois gentilhomme. Molière, J.
Bourgeois gentleman, The. See Molière, J. Le bourgeois gentilhomme
Les bourgeois de qualité. See Dancourt, F. Woman's craze for titles
Boursiquot. See Boucicault, D. The colleen bawn
Box and Cox. Morton, J.
Boxes. Yankowitz, S.
Boy comes home, The. Milne, A.
Boy friend, The. Wilson, S.
Boy meets girl. Spewack, B. and Spewack, S.
Boy with a cart, The. Fry, C.
Boys in the band, The. Crowley, M.
Braggart captain, The. See Plautus, T. Miles gloriosus
Braggart soldier, The. See Plautus, T. Miles gloriosus
Braggart warrior, The. See Plautus, T. Miles gloriosus
Der brand in opernhaus. See Kaiser, G. The fire in the opera house
Brass butterfly, The. Golding, W.
Brave Irishman, The; or, Captain O'Blunder. Sheridan, T.
Bread. Kirshon, V.
Bread and butter. Taylor, C.
Bread and rice or geometry in yellow. Bellido, J.
Breadwinner, The. Maugham, W.
Breakfast in bed. See Feydeau, G. Keep an eye on Amélie
Breaking point. See Denker, H. and Berkey, R. Time limit!
Breakout, The. Gordone, C.
Breasts of Tiresias, The. Kostrowisky, G.
Bride comes to yellow sky, The. Agee, J.
Bride of the lamb, The. Hurlbut, W.
Brides of Garryowen, The. See Boucicault, D. The colleen bawn
Bridge, The. Fratti, M.
Bridge head. Waddell, S.
Brief encounter. Coward, N.
Brief moment. Behrman, S.
Brigadoon. Lerner, A. and Loewe, F.
Bright morning, A. Alvarez Quintero, S. and Alvarez Quintero, J.
Broadway. Dunning, P. and Abbott, G.
Brocade tree, The. Seami, M.
Broken banjo, The. Richardson, W.
Broken heart, The. Ford, J.
Broken jug, The. See Kleist, H. Der zerbrochene krug
Broker of Bogota, The. Bird, R.
Brome Abraham and Isaac, The. See Anonymous plays. Abraham and Isaac
Brome plays. See Anonymous plays. Abraham and Isaac
Brotherhood. Ward, D.
Brothers, The. See Terentius Afer, P. Adelphi
Brothers in arms. Denison, M.
Brothers Karamazoff, The. Nemirovich-Danchenko, V.
Brott och brott. See Strindberg, A. There are crimes and crimes
Brown overcoat, The. Sejour, V.
Las brujas del domingo. See Benavente y Martínez, J. The witches' sabbath
Brute: A joke in one act, The. Chekhov, A.
Brutus; or, The fall of Tarquin. Payne, J.
Bucktails, The; or, Americans in England. Paulding, J.
Buffeting, The (Wakefield).

Anonymous plays
Buggbears, The. Jeffere, J.
Bunch of keys, A; or, The hotel. Hoyt, C.
Bunker-Hill; or, The death of General Warren. Burk, J.
Bunthorne's bride. See Gilbert, W. and Sullivan, A. Patience
El burlador de Sevilla. Téllez, G.
Burlesque. Watters, G. and Hopkins, A.
Bury fair. Shadwell, T.
Bury the dead. Shaw, I.
Bus stop. Inge, W.
Bushido. Idzumo, T.
Business is business. See Mirbeau, O. Les affaires sont les affaires
Busman's honeymoon. Sayers, D. and Byrne, M.
Bussy D'Ambois. Chapman, G.
Bussy D'Ambois. The revenge of. Chapman, G.
But what have you done for me lately? See Lamb, M. Scyklon Z
Butter and egg man, The. Kaufman, G.
Butterflies are free. Gershe, L.
Butley. Gray, S.
Butterfly dream, The. Anonymous plays
By accident. Williams, H. and Williams, M.
By ourselves. See Fulda, L. Tête-à-tête
Bygmester Solness. See Ibsen, H. The master builder

C

Cabaret. Masteroff, J.
Cabrerita. Acevedo Hernández, A.
La caccia al lupo. See Verga, G. The wolfhunt
Cactus flower. Burrows, A.
Caesar and Cleopatra. Shaw, G.
Caesar Augustus (Wakefield). Anonymous plays
Cage, The. Fratti, M.
La Cagnolte. See Labiche, E. and Delacour, A. Pots of money
Cain. Byron, G.
Cain and Abel. Anonymous plays
Caine mutiny court-martial, The. Wouk, H.
La Calandria. See Dovizi da Bibiena, B. The follies of Calandro
Caleb the degenerate. Cotter, J.
Caligula. Camus, A.
Calisto and Melibaea. See Anonymous plays. The beauty and good properties of women
Call it a day. Smith, D.
Call me Jacky. Bagnold, E.
Calline browierts, Die. Iobst, C.
Calm down, Mother. Terry, M.
Cambises, King of Persia. Preston, T.
Cambyses. See Preston, T. Cambises, King of Persia
Camilla; or, The fate of a coquette. See Dumas, A., fils. La dame aux camélias
Camille. See Dumas, A., fils. La dame aux camélias
Camille and Perdican. Musset, A.
Camino real. Williams, T.
Camp, The. Gambargo, G.
Camp of Wallenstein, The. Schiller, J.
Campaspe. Lyly, J.
Campion, Edmund. See Breen, R. and Schnibbe, H. "Who ride on white horses"
Campo dei fiori. See Ilyenkov, V. The square of flowers
Canavans, The. Gregory, I.
Canción de cuna. See Martínez Sierra, G. and Martínez Sierra, M. The cradle song
Il candelaio. See Bruno, G.

The candle bearer
Candida. Shaw, G.
Candidates; or, The humours of a Virginia election, The. Munford, R.
Candide. Hellman, L.
Candle bearer, The. Bruno, G.
Candle in the wind. Anderson, M.
Cannibals. Tabori, G.
La cantatrice chauve. See Ionesco, E. The bald soprano
Cantique des cantiques. See Giraudoux, J. Song of songs
Canvas. Roszkowski, D.
Capitan and the corporal, El. Corwin, N.
Les caprices de Marianne. Musset, A.
Captain Fantastic meets the ectomorph. Pritchard, B.
Captain from Koepenick, The. See Zuckmayer, C. The captain of Köpenick
Captain Jack's revenge. Smith, M.
Captain Jinks of the horse marines. Fitch, C.
Captain O'Blunder. See Sheridan, T. The brave Irishman
Captain of Köpenick, The. Zuckmayer, C.
Captives, The. Plautus, T.
Captivi. See Plautus, T. The captives
La carátula. See Rueda, L. The mask
Cardinal d'Espagne, Le. See Montherlant, H. Cardinal of Spain, The
Cardinal, The. Shirley, J.
Cardinal of Spain, The. Montherlant, H.
Cards to identify. Dennis, N.
Care for jealousy, A. See Peeple, W. The double deceit
Career. Lee, J.
Career for Ralph. Richmond, S.
Careless husband, The. Cibber, C.
Caretaker, The. Pinter, H.
Caridorf; or, The avenger. Bird, R.
Carmencita and the soldier. Lipskeroff, K.
Carpenters, The. Tesich, S.
Carthaginian, The. Plautus, T.
Cartwheel. Knight, V.
La casa de Bernarda Alba. See García Lorca, F. The house of Bernarda Alba
Casa paterna. See Sudermann, H. Magda
Case of Astrolable, The. Phelps, M.
Case of rebellious Susan, The. Jones, H.
Casina. Plautus, T.
Casket, The. Plautus, T.
Cassilis engagement, The. Hankin, St. J.
Caste. Robertson, T.
Castle in the air. Melville, A.
Castle of St. Aldobrand, The. See Maturin, C. Bertram
Castle of perserverance, The. Anonymous plays
Cat and the canary, The. Willard, J.
Cat on a hot tin roof. Williams, T.
Cathleen ni Houlihan. Yeats, W.
Cato. Addison, J.
Caucasian chalk circle, The. Brecht, B.
Cavalcade. Coward, N.
Cavalier from France, The. Fortune, J.
Cavalleria rusticana. Verga, G.
Cave dwellers, The. Saroyan, W.
Cave man, The. Field, C.
Cave of Salamanca, The. Cervantes Saavedra, M.
Cecile; or, The school for fathers. Anouilh, J.
Cécile; ou, L'école des pères. See Anouilh, J. Cecile
Celebration. Jones, T.
Celestina; or, The tragi-comedy of Calisto and Melibea.

Rojas, F.
La Celestina. See Rojas, F. Celestina
Célimare. Labiche, E. and Delacour, A.
Célimare le bien-aimé. See Labiche, E. and Delacour, A. Célimare
Cell, The. Kimmel, H.
La cena de Baltasar. See Calderón de la Barca, P. Belshazzar's feast
La cena delle beffe. See Benelli, S. The jest
Cenci, The. Shelley, P.
Centenarian, The. See Alvarez Quintero, S. and Alvarez Quintero, J. A hundred years old
Centenario. See Alvarez Quintero, S. and Alvarez Quintero, J. A hundred years old
Ceremonies in dark old men. Elder, L.
Chains. Baker, E.
Chairs, The. See Ionesco, E. Les chaises
Les chaises. Ionesco, E.
Chalk circle, The. Anonymous plays
Chalk garden, The. Bagnold, E.
Chamber pieces. O'Keefe, J.
Champion north. Wilson, T.
Champions of morality. See Thomas, L. Moral
La chance de Françoise. See Porto-Riche, G. Françoise' luck
Chances, The. Fletcher, J.
Chandelier, The. Musset, A.
Chang boils the sea. Li H.
Changeling, The. Middleton, T. and Rowley, W.
Changelings, The. Dodd, L.
Changing room, The. Storey, D.
Chantilly play, The. See Courlet, Katherine. The nativity
Charades on East Fourth Street. Elder, L.
Charity ball, The. Belasco, D. and De Mille, H.
Charles Dickens' Christmas carol. Agenoux, S.
Charles the second; or, The merry monarch. Payne, J. and Irving, W.
Charlotte Corday. Jerome, H.
Chaste maid in Cheapside, A. Middleton, T.
Chatsky; or, The misery of having a mind. Griboiedov, A.
Chatterton. Vigny, A.
Cheap bunch of nice flowers, A. O'Brien, E.
Le chemin de Crête. See Marcel, G. Ariadne
Chenango crone. Kamarck, E.
Cherry orchard, The. Chekhov, A.
Chester play of the deluge. See Anonymous plays. The deluge
Chester plays. See Anonymous plays: Abraham, Melchisedec and Isaac; The adoration of the magi; The adoration of the shepherds; Antichrist; The betrayal of Christ; Christ's ascension; Christ's ministry; Christ's passion; Christ's resurrection; The creation of man: Adam and Eve; The death of Herod; The deluge; The fall of Lucifer; The last judgment; The magi's oblation; The nativity; The prophets; The resurrection, harrowing of hell, and the last judgment; The sacrifice of Isaac; Simon the leper; The slaying of the innocents
Le cheval Tartare. See Payne, J. Mazeppa
Le chevalier à la mode. Dancourt, F.
Chicago. Shepard, S.
Chicago. Watkins, M.
Chicago conspiracy, The. Burgess, J. and Marowitz, C.
Chicago "conspiracy" trials. See Levine, M.; McNamee,

G.; and Greenberg, D. The tales of Hoffman - a series of excerpts from the "Chicago conspiracy" trial
Chicken feed. Bolton, G.
Children of the kingdom. Opper, D.
Chicken soup with barley. Wesker, A.
Child hath found his father, The. See Anonymous plays. The birth of Merlin
Child of Grace. See Funt, J. The magic and the loss
Child wife, The. See Ibsen, H. A doll's house
Children in uniform. Winsloe, C.
Children of darkness. Mayer, E.
Children of Heracles, The. See Euripides. The Heracleidae
Chicken pie and the chocolate cake, The. Anonymous plays
Children of the wolf. Peacock, J.
Children's hour, The. Hellman, L.
Child's play. Marasco, R.
Chimes of the Kremlin, The. Pogodin, N.
China pig, The. Emig, E.
Chinese, The. Schisgal, M.
Chinese icebox, The. Laszlo, C.
Chinese wall, The Frisch, M.
Chinese white. Gielgud, V.
Der Chinesische Kühlschrank. See Laszlo, C. The Chinese icebox
Die Chinesische Mauer. See Frisch, M. The Chinese wall
Ch'ing kung yüan. See Yao Hsin-nung. The malice of empire
Chip woman's fortune, The. Richardson, W.
Chips with everything. Wesker, A.
Choephori, The. See Aeschylus. Choephoroe
Choephoroe. Aeschylus
Choice of a tutor, The. Fonvizin, D.
Choosing company. Schwartz, D.
Chosroes. Rotrou, J.
Christmas carol, A. Shay, F.
Christmas mumming, A. Anonymous plays
Christmas play of St. George. See Anonymous plays. A Christmas mumming
Christophe Colomb. Ghelderode, M.
Christopher Blake. Hart, M.
Christopher Columbus. Hasenclever, W. and Tucholsky, K.
Christopher Columbus. See Ghelderode, M. Christophe Colomb
Christ's ascension (Chester). Anonymous plays
Christ's ministry (Chester). Anonymous plays
Christ's passion (Chester). Anonymous plays
Christ's resurrection (Chester). Anonymous plays
Chronicle history of Perkin Warbeck, The. Ford, J.
Chronicles of hell. Ghelderode, M.
Church fight, The. Gaines-Shelton, R.
Church street. Robinson, L.
Churl, The. See Plautus, T. Truculentus
Ciascuno a suo modo. See Pirandello, L. Each in his own way
Le cid. Corneille, P.
Cid, The. See Corneille, P. Le cid
Cigale chez les fourmis, La. Legouvé, E. and Labiche, E.
Cinna; or, The mercy of Augustus. Corneille, P.
Cinque. Melfi, L.
Circle, The. Maugham, W.
Circular staircase, The. See Rinehart, M. and Hopwood, A. The bat
Circus story, A. Tardieu, J.

Cistellaria. See Plautus, T. The casket
Cit turned gentleman, The. See Molière, J. Le bourgeois gentilhomme
La città morta. See Annunzio, G. d'. The dead city
City, The. Anonymous plays.
City, The. Fitch, C.
City night-cap, The. Davenport, R.
City madam, The. Massinger, P.
Clandestine marriage, The. Colman, G. and Garrick, D.
Clarence. Tarkington, B.
Claudia. Franken, R.
Claws, The. Linares Rivas, M.
Clean kill, A. Gilbert, M.
Clearing in the woods, A. Laurents, A.
Clérambard. Aymé, M.
Climate of Eden, The. Hart, M.
Climbers, The. Fitch, C.
Clive of India. Lipscomb, W. and Minney, R.
Clod, The. Beach, L.
Close quarters. Somin, W.
Closed door, The. Praga, M.
Clouds, The. Aristophanes
Clutterbuck. Levy, B.
Cobler of Preston, The. Johnson, C.
Cock of the village, The. See Smith, R. The last man
Cockade. Wood, C.
Cock-a-doodle dandy. O'Casey, S.
Cockpit. Boland, B.
Cocktail party, The. Eliot, T.
Coelina; ou, L'enfant du mystère. Pixérécourt, R.
La coeur a gaz. See Tzara, T. The gas heart
Cold wind and the warm, The. Behrman, S.
Coliphizacio (Wakefield). Anonymous plays
Collection, The. Pinter, H.
Colleen bawn, The; or, The brides of Garryowen. Boucicault, D.
College widow, The. Ade, G.
Colonel's lady, The. Sherriff, R.
Columbine. Clements, C.
Come back, little Sheba. Inge, W.
Come into the garden Maud. Coward, N.
Come le foglie. See Giacosa, G. Like falling leaves
Come tu mi vuoi. See Pirandello, L. As you desire me
Comedia de Calisto y Melibea. See Rojas, F. Celestina
Comedia Himenea. See Torres Naharro, B. Hymen
La comédie de celui qui épousa une femme muette. France, A.
Comedy called Misogonus, A. See Anonymous plays. Misogonus
Comedy of asses, The. Plautus, T.
Comedy of errors, The. Shakespeare, W.
Coming of peace, The. See Hauptmann, G. Das friedensfest
Command decision. Haines, W.
Commercial drummer, The. See Jessop, G. Sam'l of Posen
Commissary, The. Foote, S.
Commissioner, The. Courteline, G.
Common conditions. Anonymous plays
Company. Furth, G. and Sondheim, S.
Complaisant lover, The. Greene, G.
Comrades. Strindberg, A.
Le comte D'Essex. See Corneille, T. The earl of Essex
Comus. Milton, J.
Conceited count, The. See Destouches, P. Le glorieux
Concert, The. Bahr, H.
Concert at Saint Ovide, The.

Buero Vallejo, A.
El concierto de San Ovideo. See Buero Vallejo, A. The concert at Saint Ovide
Condemnation. Tolstoi, L.
Condemned, The. Dagerman, S.
Condemned squad. Sastre, A.
Conduct unbecoming. England, B.
Confederacy, The. Vanbrugh, J.
Confessional. Wilde, P.
Confessional, The. Williams, T.
Confidential clerk, The. Eliot, T.
Conflagration of the opera house, The. See Kaiser, G. The fire in the opera house
Conflict, The. McCauley, C.
Conflict of conscience. Woodes, N.
Connection, The. Gelber, J.
Connais-toi. See Hervieu, P. Know thyself
Conquering hero, The. Monkhouse, A.
Conquest of Granada, The. See Dryden, J. Almanzor and Almahide
Conscience. Iffland, A.
Conscious lovers, The. Steele, R.
Conspiracy, The. See Bulwer-Lytton, E. Richelieu
Conspiracy, The (Wakefield). Anonymous plays
Constant prince, The. Calderón de la Barca, P.
Constant wife, The. Maugham, W.
Constantinople Smith. Mee, C.
Consuelo. López de Ayala, A.
Contract of marriage between wit and wisdom, The. Anonymous plays
Contractor, The. Storey, D.
Contrast, The. Tyler, R.
Contribution. Shine, T.
Conversation piece. Coward, N.
Conversion of St. Paul, The. Anonymous plays
Convulsiones, Las. Vargas Tejada, L.
Cophetua. Drinkwater, J.
Cop-out. Guare, J.
Copper pot, The. Healey, F.
Copperfaced Jack. O'Donovan, J.
Copperhead, The. Thomas, A.
Le coq de village. Décour, C. and Théodore, A. See Smith, R. The last man
Coquette. Abbott, G. and Bridgers, A.
Coral, The. Kaiser, G.
Les corbeaux. Becque, H.
Coriolanus. Shakespeare, W.
Cormorant fisher, The. Enamai No Sayemon
Corn is green, The. Williams, E.
Cornelius. Priestley, J.
Corner, The. Bullins, E.
Cornish play of the three Maries, The. See Anonymous plays. The three Maries
Cornish plays. See Anonymous plays. The death of Pilate; The legend of the rood; The three Maries
Corruption in the palace of justice. Betti, U.
Corruzione al Palazzo di Giustizia. See Betti, U. Corruption in the palace of justice
Corsican brothers, The. Boucicault, D.
Cosî è se vi pare! See Pirandello, L. Right you are! If you think so
Cosi sia. See Gallarati-Scotti, T. Thy will be done
Cosroès. See Rotrou, J. Chosroes
Cottage on the cliff, The. See Wood, H. East Lynne
Council of women, The. See Aristophanes. The ecclesiazusae
Council retained. Mackay, C.
Counsellor-at-law. Rice, E.
Count of Clerambard, The. See Aymé, M. Clérambard

Count of Monte Cristo, The. See Fletcher, C. Monte Cristo
Count your blessings. Jeans, R.
Countess Cathleen, The. Yeats, W.
Countess Julie. See Strindberg, A. Miss Julia
Country dance. Kennaway, J.
Country girl, The. Odets, C.
Country wake, The. See Dogget, T. Hob
Country wife, The. Wycherley, W.
County chairman, The. Ade, G.
Courier for hell, The. Chikamatsu
La course du flambeau. Hervieu, P.
Court singer, The. See Wedekind, F. Der kammersänger
Courtois d'Arras. Anonymous plays
Cousin Billy. See Labiche, E. and Martin, E. Le voyage de Monsieur Perrichon
Covent Garden. Nabbes, T.
Coventry plays. See Ludus Coventriae plays
Coward, The. Lenormand, H.
Cowled lover, The. Bird, R.
Cradle song, The. Martínez Sierra, G. and Martínez Sierra, M.
Cradle will rock. The. Blitzstein, M.
Crawling Arnold. Feiffer, J.
Craig's wife. Kelly, G.
Creation, The (Wakefield). Anonymous plays
Creation and the fall of Lucifer, The (York). Anonymous plays
Creation of Adam and Eve, The (York). Anonymous plays
Creation of Eve, The, with the expelling of Adam and Eve out of Paradise. Anonymous plays
Creation of man: Adam and Eve, The (Chester). Anonymous plays
Creation of the world and other business, The. Miller, A.
Creditors. Strindberg, A.
Creeper, The. Macauley, P.
Creeps. Freeman, D.
Crépuscule du théatre. See Lenormand, H. In Theatre street
Cretan woman, The. Jeffers, R.
Cricket and the hearth, The. Smith, A.
Crime on Goat Island. Betti, U.
Crime passionel. See Sartre, J. Les mains sales
Crimes and crimes. See Strindberg, A. There are crimes and crimes
Criminal code, The. Flavin, M.
Criminals, The. Triana, A.
Crispin médecin. Hauteroche, N. See Ravenscroft, E. and Motteux, P. The anatomist
Crispin, rival de son maître. See Le Sage, A. Crispin rival of his master
Crispin, rival of his master. Le Sage, A.
Critic, The; or, A tragedy rehearsed. Sheridan, R.
Crock of gold, The. See Plautus. Aulularia
Crock of gold, The; or, The toiler's trials. Steele, S.
Cromedeyre-le-vieil. Romains, J.
Crown matrimonial. Ryton, R.
Crown of light, The. Bulkley, A.
Crowne for a conquerour, A. Davenport, R.
Crows, The. See Becque, H. Les corbeaux
Crucible, The. Miller, A.
Crucifixion, The (Wakefield). Anonymous plays
Crucifixion, The (York). Anonymous plays
Crude and unrefined. Bowen, M.
Cruel fate. See Pisemskiĭ, A.

A bitter fate
'Cruiter. Mathews, J.
Crusade of children, The. Morris, E.
Cry in the street. Lauckner, R.
Csendélet. Molnár, F.
Cuando florezcan las rosales. See Marquina, E. When the roses bloom again
La cueva de Salamanca. See Cervantes Saavedra, M. The cave of Salamanca
Cult of boredom, The. See Pailleron, E. Le monde où l'on s'ennuie
Cupid's rival. See Porto-Riche, G. Amoureuse
Curculio. Plautus, T.
Cure for jealousy, A. See Popple, W. The double deceit
Un curioso accidente. Goldoni, C.
Curious mishap, A. See Goldini, C. Un curioso accidente
Curious misunderstanding, A. See Goldoni, C. Un curioso accidente
Curve, The. Dorst, T.
Cutter of Colman-street. Cowley, A.
Cuttlefish, The. Witkiewicz, S.
Le cuvier. See Anonymous plays. The washtub
Cyclops, The. Euripides
Cymbeline. Shakespeare, W.
Cynara. Harwood, H. and Gore-Browne, R.
Cyrano de Bergerac. Rostand, E.

D

Dagobert, der Franken könig. See Babo, J. Dagobert, king of the Franks
Dagobert, king of the Franks. Babo, J.
Daisy, The. See Molnár, F. Liliom
Daisy Mayme. Kelly, G.
Damask cheek, The. Van Druten, J. and Morris, L.
La dame aux camélias. Dumas, A., fils
Damien. See Lavery, E. and Murphy, G. Kamiano, the story of Damien
Damon and Pithias. Edwards, R.
Dance of death, The. See Anonymous plays. Totentanz
Dance of death, The. Strindberg, A.
Dancers, The. Hoote, H.
Dancing girl, The. Jones, H.
Dancing mothers. Selwyn, E. and Goulding, E.
Dandy dolls, The. Fitzmaurice, G.
Dangerous corner. Priestley, J.
Daniel. More, H.
Daniel Webster eighteen in America. Stein, G.
Daniela. Guimerá, A.
Danites of the Sierras, The. Miller, J. [pseud.]
Dans les fonds. See Gorki, M. [pseud.] The lower depths
Danse Calinda, The. Torrence, F.
Danton's death. Büchner, G.
Dantons tod. See Büchner, G. Danton's death
Darby's return. Dunlap, W.
Dark at the top of the stairs, The. Inge, W.
Dark is light enough, The. Fry, C.
Dark of the moon. Richardson, H. and Berney, W.
Dark tower, The. Macneice, L.
Darkness at noon. Kingsley, S.
Darling of the gods, The. Belasco, D. and Long, J.
Daughter of Jorio, The. Annunzio, G. d'
Daughter of Madame Angot, The. Lecocq, A.
Daughters of Atreus. Turney, R.
David and Bathshua. Cayzer, C.

David and Bethsabe. Peele, G.
David and broccoli. Mortimer, J.
David and Goliath. More, H.
Davy Crockett; or, Be sure you're right, then go ahead. Murdoch, F.
Dawn, The. Verhaeren, E.
Day after the fair, The. Harvey, F.
Day by the sea, A. Hunter, N.
Day in the death of Joe Egg, A. Nichols, P.
Day in the vineyard, A. Baker, A.
Day of absence. Ward, D.
The day the lions got loose. See Carballido, E. The day they let the lions loose
Day they let the lions loose, The. Carballido, E.
Days of the Turbins. Bulgakov, M.
Days on a cloud. Avell, K.
La de San Quintín. Pérez Galdós, B.
Dead are free, The. Kreymborg, A.
Dead city, The. Annunzio, G. d'
Dead end. Kingsley, S.
Dead on nine. Popplewell, J.
Dead secret, A. Ackland, R.
Dead stone's banquet, The. See Anonymous plays. Don Juan and Don Pietro
Deadly game, The. Yaffe, J.
Dear Brutus. Barrie, J.
Dear Charles. Melville, A.
Dear delinquent. Popplewell, J.
Dear octopus. Smith, D.
Dear Ruth. Krasna, N.
Death and life of sneaky Fitch, The. Rosenberg, J.
Death and the fool. See Hofmannsthal, H. von. Der tor und der tod
Death dance, The. Duncan, T.
Death of a salesman. Miller, A.
Death of Alexander the great, The. See Lee, N. The rival queens
Death of Eve, The. Moody, W.
Death of everymom, The. Powell, A.
Death of García Lorca, The. Whittington, R.
Death of General Montgomery, in storming the city of Quebec. Brackenridge, H.
Death of General Warren, The. See Burk, J. Bunker-Hill
Death of Herod, The (Chester). Anonymous plays
Death of Ivan the terrible, The. Tolstoĭ, A.
Death of Odysseus, The. Abel, L.
Death of Pilate, The (Cornish). Anonymous plays
Death of Satan, The. Duncan, R.
Death of Seneca, The. Hermite, l' T.
Death of Tintagiles, The. Maeterlinck, M.
Death of Titian, The. Hofmannsthal, H. von
Death of Wallenstein, The. Schiller, J.
Death squad. Sastre, A.
Death stone, The. Anonymous plays
Death takes a holiday. Casella, A.
Death thrust. Sastre, A.
Deathwatch. Genêt, J.
Deburau. Guitry, S.
Deceived, The. Anonymous plays
Decision. Chodorov, E.
Declassee. Akins, Z.
Deep are the roots. Gow, J. and D'Usseau, A.
Deep blue sea, The. Rattigan, T.
Defeat, The; a play about the Paris Commune. Grieg, N.
Deidre of the sorrows. Synge, J.
Deirdre. Russell, G.
Deirdre. Yeats, W.
Del rey abajo, ninguno. Rojas

Zorrilla, F.
Delicate balance, A. Albee, E.
Delitto all' Isola della Capre. See Betti, U. Crime on Goat Island
Deliverance of souls, The (Wakefield). Anonymous plays
Deluge, The (Chester). Anonymous plays
Deluge, The (Wakefield). Anonymous plays
Le demi-monde. See Dumas, A., fils. The outer edge of society
Department of forestry. See Duras, M. The rivers and forests
Depositio cornuti typographici. See Anonymous plays. The printer's apprentice
Deputy, The. Hochhuth, R.
Los derechos de la salud. Sánchez, F.
La dernière nuit de Don Juan. See Rostand, E. The last night of Don Juan
El desdén con el desdén. Moreto y Cavana, A.
Deserted crone, The. Seami, M.
Design for a headstone. Byrne, S.
Design for living. Coward, N.
Le désir attrapé par la queue. See Picasso, P. Desire trapped by the tail
Desire trapped by the tail. Picasso, P.
Desire under the elms. O'Neill, E.
Desperate hours, The. Hayes, J.
Destinies of Haman and Mordecai, The. See Tyler, R. The origin of the feast of Purim; or, The destinies of Haman and Mordecai
Destruction of Jerusalem, The. Anonymous plays
Destruction of Jerusalem, The. Crowne, J.
Detective story. Kingsley, S.
Detour, The. David, O.
Les deux gendres. Etienne, C. See Payne, J. The two sons-in-law
Deux orphelines, Les. See D'Ennery, A. and Cormon, E. The two orphans
Devil and Daniel Webster, The. Benét, S.
Devil and his dame, The. See Anonymous plays. Grim the collier of Croydon
Devil and Otis Redding, The. See Caldwell, B. The king of soul
Devil of a wife. Jevon, T. See Jevon, T.; Coffey, C.; Mottley, J.; Cibber, T. The devil to pay
Devil passes, The. Levy, B.
Devil to pay, The; or, The wives metamorphos'd. Jevon, T.; Coffey, C.; Mottley, J. and Cibber, T.
Devils, The. Whiting, J.
Devil's disciple, The. Shaw, G.
Devil's general, The. Zuckmayer, C.
Devourer of dreams, The. See Lenormand, H. The dream doctor
El día que se soltaron los leones. See Carballido, E. The day they let the lions loose
Dial "M" for murder. Knott, F.
Dialect determinism. Bullins, E.
Dialogue and ode, A. Hopkinson, F.
Dialogue between a southern delegate, and his spouse, on his return from the grand Continental Congress, A. Anonymous plays
Dialogue between an Englishman and an Indian, A. Smith, J.
Dialogue between Don Melón Ortiz and Doña Endrina. See Ruiz, J. The gallant, the bawd and the fair lady

Diamond cut diamond. Murray, W.
Diamond cut diamond. Williamson, H.
Diary of a scoundrel, The. Ostrovskii, A.
Diary of a young girl. See Hackett, A. and Goodrich, F. The diary of Anne Frank
Diary of Anne Frank, The. Hackett, A. and Goodrich, F.
Dickon. Pinner, D.
Didon se sacrifiant. Jodelle, E.
Difference of opinion. Ross, G. and Singer, C.
Difficult hour, I-III, The. Lagerkvist, P.
Diff'rent. O'Neill, E.
Digby plays. See Anonymous plays. The conversion of St. Paul
Le diner des têtes. See Anouilh, J. Poor Bitos
Dinner at eight. Kaufman, G. and Ferber, E.
Dirty hands. See Sartre, J. Les mains sales
Disenchanted, The. Schulbert, B.
Disposal, The. Inge, W.
Disraeli. Parker, L.
Distaff side, The. Van Druten, J.
Distant point. See Afinogenyev, A. Far taiga
Distracted emperor, The. Anonymous plays
District of Columbia. Richards, S.
Divinas palabras. See Valle-Inclán, R. Divine words
Divine comedy. Dodson, O.
Divine dream. Xenopoulos, G.
Divine words. Valle-Inclán, R.
Division Street, USA. See Terkel, L. Monologues from "Division Street, USA"
Divorce. Daly, A.
Divorcio nupcial. Eichelbaum, S.
Divorçons. See Sardou, V. and Najac, E. Let's get a divorce
Dock brief, The. Mortimer, J.
Em docktor Fogel sic offis schtunn. Birmelin, J.
Le docteur amoureux. Anonymous plays
Doctor and the devils, The. Thomas, D.
Doctor Faustus. See Marlowe, C. The tragical history of Doctor Faustus
Doctor in spite of himself, The. Molière, J.
Dr. Kheal. Fornés, M.
Dr. Knock. Romains, J.
Dr. Korczak and the children. Sylvanus, E.
Dr. Kranich's sprechstunde. See Anonymous plays. Em Doctor Fogel sei offis schtunn (based on book by John Birmelin)
Doctor's daughter, The. See Goetz, R. and Goetz, A. The heiress
Doctor's delight. Molière, J.
Doctor's dilemma, The. Shaw, G.
Doctors of philosophy. Spark, M.
Dodsworth. Howard, S.
Den dödsdörnde. See Dagerman, S. The condemned
Dog beneath the skin, The. Auden, W. and Isherwood, C.
Dog in the manger, The. Vega Carpio, L.
Dogs of war, The. Watson, M.
Les doigts de fée. Scribe, A.
Dōjōji. Kanze Kojiro Nobumitsu
Doll's house, A. Ibsen, H.
Dolly reforming herself. Jones, H.
Dom Juan, ou le festin de Pierre. See Molière, J. Don Juan
Il domatore Gastone. See Morselli, E. Gastone the animal tamer
Domestic picture, A. Ostrovskii, A.
Dominant sex, The. Egan, M.

Dominion of darkness, The. See Tolstoi, L. The power of darkness
Don Alvaro; ó la fuerza del sino. Rivas, A.
Don Carlos. Schiller, J.
Don Cristobita and Doña Rosita, The. García Lorca, F.
Don Giovanni. See Ponte, L. Da. The punished libertine
Don John; or, The libertine. See Molière, J. Don Juan
Don Juan. Molière, J.
Don Juan; or, The stone guest. See Molière, J. Don Juan
Don Juan. See also Rostand, E. The last night of Don Juan
Don Juan and Don Pietro; or, The dead stone's banquet. Anonymous plays
Don Juan and Faust. Grabbe, C.
Don Juan in hell. Shaw, G.
Don Juan Tenorio. Zorrilla y Moral, J.
Don Juan and Faust. See Grabbe, C. Don Juan and Faust
Don Juan's last night. See Rostand, E. The last night of Don Juan
Doña Clarines. Alvarez Quintero, S. and Alvarez Quintero, J.
Donalds O'Rourk. O'Connell, L.
Donna Diana. See Moreto y Cavaña, A. El desdén con el desdén
Don't let summer come. Feely, T.
Don't listen, ladies! Guitry, S.
Don't you want to be free. Hughes, L.
Doomsday circus. See Basshe, E. The dream of the dollar
Doomsday show, The. MacBeth, G. and Bingham, J.
Door should be either open or shut, A. Musset, A. de
Dot. Boucicault, D.
Double deceit, The; or, A cure for jealousy. Popple, W.
Double discovery, The. See Dryden, J. The Spanish fryar
Double Dutch act, The. Anonymous plays
Double Wop, The. See Anonymous plays
Double yolk. Williams, H. and Williams, M.
Doughgirls, The. Fields, J.
Douglas. Home, J.
Dover road, The. Milne, A.
Down and out. See Gorki, M. [pseud.] The lower depths
Down our street. Wise, E.
Dracula. Deane, H. and Warburton, H.
Dragon, The. Gregory, I.
Dragon, The. Schwartz, Y.
Dragon beard ditch. Sheh, L.
Dragon's mouth. Priestley, J. and Hawkes, J.
Un drama nuevo. Tamayo y Baus, M.
Dramatic sequel to Hamlet, A; or, The new wing at Elsinor. "Mr. Punch" [pseud.]
Dramatic sequel to The lady of Lyons, A; or, In the Lyons den. "Mr. Punch" [pseud.]
Dramatist, The; or, Stop him who can! Reynolds, F.
Drapes come, The. Dizenzo, C.
Draussen vor der Tür. See Borchert, W. The outsider
Dream doctor, The. Lenormand, H.
Dream girl. Rice, E.
Dream of Scipio, The. Metastasio, P.
Dream of the dollar, The. Basshe, E.
Dream of Vāsavadatta, The. Bhāsa
Dream play, A. Strindberg, A.
Dream weaver, The. Buero Vallejo, A.
Dreaming of the bones, The. Yeats, W.
Dreamy kid, The. O'Neill, E.
Dreigroschenoper. See Brecht, B. The threepenny opera
Drifting apart. Herne, J.
Drinking gourd, The. Hansberry, L.

Drive-in. Kranes, D.
Ett drömspel. See Strindberg, A. The dream play
Dronning gaar igen. See Abell, K. The queen on tour
Dronningen og hennes menn. See Kielland, T. Queen Margaret of Norway
Drug, The. Bart-Williams, G.
Drums of Oude, The. Strong, A.
Drums of snow, The. Pinner, D.
Drunkard, The. Smith, W.
Dry August, The. Sebree, C.
Duchess at sunset, The. Johnson, P.
Duchess of Malfi, The. Webster, J.
Duchess of San Quentin, The. See Pérez Galdós, B. La de San Quintín
Duel of angels. Giraudoux, J.
Duenna, The. Sheridan, R.
Duk Moraud. Anonymous plays
Duke and no duke, A; or, Trapolin's vagaries. Tate, N.
Duke and the actress, The. See Schnitzler, A. The green cockatoo
Duke's motto, The; or, I am here! Brougham, J.
Et dukkehjem. See Ibsen, H. A doll's house
Dulcitius. Hrotsvit
Dulcy. Kaufman, G. and Connelly, M.
Dumb waiter, The. Pinter, H.
Dupe, The. Ancey, G. [pseud.]
Dust in the eyes. See Labiche, E. and Martin, E. La poudre aux yeux
Dust of the road. Goodman, K.
Dutch courtesan, The. Marston, J.
Dutchman. Jones, L.
Dwarf trees, The. Seami, M.
Dybbuk, The. Rappoport, S.
Dylan. Michaels, S.
Dyskolos. See Menander. The grouch

E

Each his own wilderness. Lessing, D.
Each in his own way. Pirandello, L.
Earl of Essex, The. Corneille, T.
Early snow. Zembō, M.
Earth and stars. Edmonds, R.
Earth-spirit, The. See Wedekind, F. Erdgeist
Easiest way, The. Walter, E.
East Lynne. Palmer, T.
East Lynne. Wood, H.
Easter resurrection play, An. Anonymous plays
Eastward ho! Chapman, G., Jonson, B. and Marston, J.
Eastward hoe. See Chapman, G., Jonson, B. and Marston, J. Eastward ho!
Eastward in Eden. Gardner, D.
Easy virtue. Coward, N.
Les eaux et forêts. See Duras, M. The rivers and forests
Eb refschneider un Susi Leimbach. Wollenweber, L.
Eboshi-ori. See Miyamasu. The hatmaker
Ecclesiazusae. Aristophanes
L'école de maris. See Molière, J. School for husbands
L'école des pères. See Anouilh, J. Cecile
Edmund Campion. See Breen, R. and Schnibbe, H. "Who ride on white horses"
Educating Josefina. Villa, L.
Edufa. Sutherland, E.
Edward, my son. Morley, R.
Edward II. See Marlowe, C. The troublesome reign and lamentable death of Edward the second
Edward III. See Anonymous plays. The reign of King Edward the third

Edwardians, The. Gow, R.
Effect of gamma rays on man-in-the-moon marigolds, The. Zindel, P.
Egelykke. Munk, K.
Egg, The. Marceau, F.
Egmont. Goethe, J.
Der egoist und kritikus. See Kotzebue, A. Egotist and pseudo-critic Herr Gottlieb Merks
Egotist and pseudo-critic Herr Gottlieb Merks. Kotzebue, A.
Eiffel Tower wedding party. See Cocteau, J. Les mariés de la Tour Eiffel
Eigensinn. See Benedix, R. Obstinacy
Ein gesprach. Wollenweber, L.
Einsame menschen. Hauptmann, G.
Der einsame weg. See Schnitzler, A. The lonely way
El capitan and the corporal. Corwin, N.
Elche mystery play, The. See Anonymous plays. The mystery play of Elche
Elckerlijk. See Anonymous plays. Everyman
Electra. Euripides
Electra. Giraudoux, J.
Electra. Hofmannsthal, H. von
Electra. Pérez Galdós, B.
Electra. Sophocles
Electre. See Giraudoux, J. Electra
Electronic nigger, The. Bullins, E.
Elijah. Davidson, R.
Elizabeth the queen. Anderson, M.
Elvira. See Calderón de la Barca, P. No siempre lo peor es cierto
Embers. Beckett, S.
Emilia Galotti. Lessing, G.
Empedocles on Etna. Arnold, M.
Emperor, The. See Pirandello, L. Henry IV
Emperor Jones, The. O'Neill, E.
Emperor of Haiti. Hughes, L.
Emperor of the moon, The. Behn, A.
Emperor's clothes, The. Tabori, G.
Empire builders, The. Vian, B.
Empress of Morocco, The. Settle, E.
En gespräch zwischen zweb demokrate über politiks. Miller, D.
En gggarrrde! Daumal, R.
En idealist. See Munk, K. Herod the king
En kvinde er overflodig. See Sonderby, K. A woman too many
Enchanted, The. Giraudoux, J.
Enchanted castle, The. See Duffett, T. The mock-tempest
Enchanted island, The. See Dryden, J. and D'Avenant, W. The tempest
Encore. Korr, D.
End of summer. Behrman, S.
End of the beginning, The. O'Casey, S.
End of the world, The; or, Fragments from a work in progress. Neilson, K.
Endgame. Beckett, S.
Endimion. See Lyly, J. Endymion
Ends of justice, The. McDaniel, C.
Endymion, the man in the moon. Lyly, J.
Enemy. Maugham, R.
Enemy, The. Pollock, C.
Enemy, The. See Wincelberg, S. Kataki
Enemy of society, An. See Ibsen, H. An enemy of the people
Enemy of the people, An. Ibsen, H.
L'enfant du mystère. See Pixérécourt, R. Coelina
Engaged. Gilbert, W. and Sullivan, A.
Engineer Sergeyev. Rokk, V.
English as it is spoken. See

Bernard, T. L'anglais tel qu'on le parle
Enough is as good as a feast. Wager, W.
Enough stupidity in every wise man. See Ostrovskii, A. The diary of a scoundrel
Enrico IV. See Pirandello, L. Henry IV
Enter madame. Varesi, G. and Byrne, D.
Enter Solly Gold. Kops, B.
Entertainer, The. Osborne, J.
Entertaining Mr. Sloane. Orton, J.
L'envers d'une sainte. Curel, F. de
Epicoene; or, The silent woman. Jonson, B.
Epicurean, The. See Wedekind, F. The Marquis of Keith
L'epidémic. See Mirbeau, O. The epidemic
Epidemic, The. Mirbeau, O.
Epidicus. Plautus, T.
Episode de la vie d'un auteur. See Anouilh, J. Episode in the life of an author
Episode in the life of an author. Anouilh, J.
Epitaph for George Dillon. Osborne, J. and Creighton, A.
Epitrepontes. See Menander. The arbitration
Equal match, An. See Fletcher, J. Rule a wife and have a wife
L'équarrissage pour tous. See Vian, B. Knackery for all
Equites. See Aristophanes. The knights
Erasmus Montanus. See Holberg, L. Rasmus Montanus
Der erbförster. Ludwig, O.
Erdgeist. Wedekind, F.
Ermine, The. Anouilh, J.
Es Heller's Chrischtdag. Iobst, C.
Escape. Galsworthy, J.
Escape by balloon. La Farge, W.
Escape me never! Kennedy, M.
Escape, The; or, A leap to freedom. Brown, W.
El esclavo del demonio. Mira de Amescua, A.
Escuadra hacia la muerte. See Sastre, A. Death squad
Escurial. Ghelderode, M.
Esposa del vengador, La. See Echegaray y Eizaguirre, J. The street singer
Essen wir Haare. See Laszlo, C. Let's eat hair!
Esther. Du Ryer, P.
Esther. Racine, J.
La estrella de Sevilla. Vega Carpio, L.
Eternal bourgeois, The. See Goll, I. Methusalem
Ethan Frome. Davis, O. and Davis, D.
Eumenides. Aeschylus
Eunuch, The. Terentius Afer, P.
Eunuchus. See Terentius Afer, P. The eunuch
Euridice. See Anouilh, J. Eurydice
Eurydice. Anouilh, J.
Eurydice (legend of lovers). See Anouilh, J. Eurydice
Eve of St. Mark, The. Anderson, M.
Even a wise man stumbles. See Ostrovskii, A. The diary of a scoundrel
Evening for Merlin Finch, An. Dizenzo, C.
Ever young. Gerstenberg, A.
Everybody's a Jew. Figueroa, J.
Every man in his humour. Jonson, B.
Every one has his fault. Inchbald, E.
Everyman. Anonymous plays
Everything in the garden. Cooper, G.
Det eviga. See Aspenström, W. The apes shall inherit the earth
Der ewige Bürger. See Goll, I. Methusalem
Ex-Miss Copper Queen on a set of pills. Terry, M.

Exception and the rule, The. Brecht, B.
Excursion. Wolfson, V.
Exercise containing a dialogue and ode on the accession of His present gracious Majesty George III, An. See Hopkinson, F. A dialogue and ode
Exploits of the Cid. See Castro y Bellvis, G. Las mocedades del Cid
Expressing Willie. Crothers, R.
Extraction of souls from hell, The (Wakefield). See Anonymous plays. The harrowing of hell
Eyvind of the hills. Sigurjónsson, J.

F

Fabulous Miss Marie, The. Bullins, E.
Face of wood, The. See Núñez de Arce, G. El haz de leña
Factory lad, The. Walker, J.
Fadren. See Strindberg, A. The father
Der fahrende schüler im Paradies. See Sachs, H. The wandering scholar from Paradise
Der fahrende schüler mit dem teufelbanner. See Sachs, H. Raising the devil
Fair beckoning one. Koebnick, S.
Fair Em. The miller's daughter of Manchester with the love of William the conqueror. Anonymous plays
Fair ladies at a game of poem cards. Chikamatsu
Fair maid of the west, The. Heywood, T.
Fair penitent, The. Rowe, N.
Fair quarrel, A. Middleton, T. and Rowley, W.
Fairfax. Campbell, B.
Faith and fireside. Schönherr, K.
Faith healer, The. Moody, W.
Faithful friend, The. Scala, F.
Faithful shepherdess, The. Fletcher, J.
Fall guy, The. Abbott, G. and Gleason, J.
Fall of British tyranny, The; or, American liberty triumphant. Leacock, J.
Fall of Jerusalem, The. Milman, H.
Fall of Lucifer, The (Coventry). Anonymous plays
Fall of man, The (York). Anonymous plays
Fall of Tarquin, The. See Payne, J. Brutus
Fall of the city, The. MacLeish, A.
Fall of Ug, The. Steele, R.
Falsche scham. Kotzebue, A. See Dunlap, W. False shame
False confessions, The. Marivaux, P.
False delicacy. Kelly, H.
False gods. Brieux, E.
False shame; or, The American orphan in Germany. Dunlap, W.
Une famille bien unie. See Prévert, J. A united family
La famille tuyare de poële; ou, Une famille bien unie. See Prévert, J. A united family
Family affairs. Jennings, G.
Family cooperative. Thurston, E.
Family portrait. Coffee, L. and Cowen, W.
Family reunion, The. Eliot, T.
Family's pride, The. Gibson, W.
Famous Mrs. Fair, The. Forbes, J.
Famous victories of Henry the fifth, The. Anonymous plays
Fan, The. Goldoni, G.
Fanlights, The. Marqués, R.
Fanny. Behrman, S. and Logan, J.

Fanny Hawthorne. See Houghton, S. Hindle wakes
Fantasio. Musset, A.
Fantasmi, I. See Bracco, R. Phantasms
Fantasticks, The. Jones, T.
Fantasticks, The. See Rostand, E. The romancers
Far country, A. Denker, H.
Far taiga. Afinogenyev, A.
La farce de Maître Pathelin. See Anonymous plays. La farce de Maître Pierre Pathelin
La farce de Maître Pierre Pathelin. Anonymous plays
Farce of the worthy Master Pierre Patelin, The. See Anonymous plays. La farce de Maître Pierre Pathelin
Farce of the worthy master, Pierre Patelin, the lawyer, The. See Anonymous plays. La farce de Maître Pierre Pathelin
Farmer forsworn, The. Anzengruber, L.
Farmer takes a wife, The. See Elser, F. and Connelly, M. Low bridge
Far-off hills, The. Robinson, L.
Farther off from Heaven. See Inge, W. The dark at the top of the stairs
Fashion; or, Life in New York. Ritchie, A.
Fashionable follies. Hutton, J.
Fashionable lover, The. Cumberland, R.
Fashionable prejudice. See La Chaussée, P. Le préjugé à la mode
Fatal error, The. Anonymous plays
Fatal ring, The. See Kālidāsa. Shakuntalā
Fatal weakness, The. Kelly, G.
Fate of a coquette, The. See Dumas, A., fils. La dame aux camélias
Fate of Chipí González, The. Matto, J.
Father, The. Strindberg, A.
Father, The. See Diderot, D. Le père de famille
Father Malachy's miracle. Doherty, B.
Father unknown. Shkvarkin, V.
Father Uxbridge wants to marry. Gagliano, F.
Fatherland. See Sardou, V. Patrie!
Les fausses confidences. See Marivaux, P. The false confessions
Faust. Goethe, J.
Faust, pt. I. Goethe, J.
Faustus. See Marlowe, C. The tragical history of Doctor Faustus
Le faux Tonoxare. See Boyer, C. Oropastes
Fear. Afinogenyev, A.
Fear and misery of the Third Reich. See Brecht, B. The private life of the master race
Feast of Ortolans, The. Anderson, M.
Le feint véritable. See Rotrou, J. Saint Genesius
Les femmes savantes. See Molière, J. The intellectual ladies
Ferrex and Porrex. See Sackville, T. and Norton, T. Gorboduc
Festa de Elche. See Anonymous plays. The mystery play of Elche
Festival of peace, The. See Hauptmann, G. Das friedensfest
Die feuerprobe. See Kleist, H. Kaethchen of Heilbronn
Fiddler on the roof. Stein, J.
Il fido amico. See Scala, F. The faithful friend
Field god, The. Green, P.
Field Marshal Kutuzov. Solovev, V.
Fifteen strings of cash. Anonymous plays
Fighter, The. Eisenstein, M.

La figlia di Jorio. See Annunzio, G. d'. The daughter of Jorio
Fill the stage with happy hours. Wood, C.
La fille de Madame Angot. See Lecocq, A. The daughter of Madame Angot
Filumena Marturano. Filippo, E.
El fin de Chipí González. See Matto, J. The fate of Chipí González
Fin de partie. See Beckett, S. Endgame
Final judgment, The. Anonymous plays
Financier, The. See Le Sage, A. Turcaret
Find your way home. Hopkins, J.
Finders-keepers. Kelly, G.
Fingernails blue as flowers. Ribman, R.
Finian's rainbow. Harburg, E.
Finishing touches. Kerr, J.
Fiorello! Weidman, J. and Abbott, G.
Fire in the opera house, The. Kaiser, G.
Fire raisers, The. See Frisch, M. Biedermann and the firebugs
Firebrand, The. Mayer, E.
Firebugs, The. See Frisch, M. Biedermann and the firebugs
Fires of St. John, The. Sudermann, H.
First and last love. See Payne, J. The Spanish husband
First blood. Monkhouse, A.
First communion. Arrabal, F.
First gentleman, The. Ginsbury, N.
First lady. Dayton, K. and Kaufman, G.
First militant minister, The. See Caldwell, B. Prayer meeting
First Mrs. Fraser, The. Ervine, St. J.
First part of the reign of King Richard the second; or, Thomas of Woodstock, The. See Anonymous plays. Woodstock
First part of the return from Parnassus, The. See Anonymous plays. The return from Parnassus
First president, The. Williams, W.
First shepherds' play, The (Wakefield). Anonymous plays
First year, The. Craven, F.
Fishermen's child, The. See Herne, A. Drifting apart
Five easy payments. Lewis, J.
Five finger exercise. Shaffer, P.
Five fingers on the black hand side. Russell, C.
Five star final. Weitzenkorn, L.
Fixin's: The tragedy of a tenant farm woman. Green, P., and Green, E.
Flies, The. Sartre, J.
Flight into danger. Hailey, A.
Flight into Egypt, The (Wakefield). Anonymous plays
Flight of the natives, The. Richardson, W.
Flight to the west. Rice, E.
Flirtation. See Schnitzler, A. Light-o'-love
Flite cage. Hadler, W.
Flittermouse. Reely, M.
Flora. Bennett, A.
Flora; or, Hob in the well. See Dogget, T. Hob
Florentine wager, A. See Benelli, S. The jest
Das Floss der Medusa. See Kaiser, G. The raft of the Medusa
Flowering peach, The. Odets, C.
Flowers for the trashman. Jackman, M.
Flowers of the forest. Van Druten, J.

Fly blackbird. Jackson, C.
Flying scud; or, A four-legged fortune. Boucicault, D.
La foi. Brieux, E.
En folkefiende. See Ibsen, H. An enemy of the people
Folle de Chaillot, La. See Giraudoux, J. The madwoman of Chaillot
Follies. Goldman, J.
Follies of Calandro, The. Dovizi da Bibiena, B.
Follies of Marianne, The. See Musset, A. de. Les caprices de Marianne
Fool, The. Pollock, C.
Fool in fashion, The. See Cibber, C. Love's last shift
Fool there was, A. See Benelli, S. The jest
Foolish notion. Barry, P.
Football. Bellido, J.
For better, for worse. Watkyn, A.
For distinguished service. Knox, F.
For services rendered. Maugham, W.
For unborn children. Livingston, M.
Forbidden fruit. Boucicault, D.
Force of destiny, The. See Rivas, A. Don Alvaro ó la fuerza del sino
Forced marriage, The. Molière, J.
Fordringsägre. See Strindberg, A. Creditors
Foreign girl, The. See Sánchez, F. La gringa
Forensic and the navigators. Shepard, S.
Forest rose, The. Woodworth, S.
Forever. Guerrero, W.
Forge master, The. See Ohnet, G. The iron manufacturer
Forgiveness. See Lemaître, J. The pardon
Formation dancers. Marcus, F.
Fortune and men's eyes. Herbert, J.
Fortunes and death of King Ottokar, The. See Grillparzer, F. König Ottokars glück und ende
Forty carats. Allen, J.
Forty-niners, The. Hanshew, T.
La forza del destino. See Rivas, A. Don Alvaro
Fossils, The. Curel, F. de
Fotodeath. Oldenburg, C.
Four elements, The. See Anonymous plays. The nature of the four elements
Four-legged fortune, A. See Boucicault, D. Flying scud
Four men. David, A.
Four pp, The. Heywood, J.
Four p's, The. See Heywood, J. The four pp
Four seasons, The. Wesker, A.
Les fourberies de Scapin. See Molière, J. Scapin
Fourposter, The. Hartog, J. de
Fourth commandment, The. See Anzengruber, L. Das vierte gebot
Fourth room, The. Reid, B.
Fox, The. See Jonson, B. Volpone
Fox, hound and huntress. Lee, L.
Die frage an das schicksal. See Schnitzler, A. Questioning the irrevocable
Fragments from a work in progress. See Neilson, K. The end of the world
Frances and Francis. Webber, J.
Francesca da Rimini. Annunzio, G. d'
Francesca da Rimini. Boker, G.
Francis' new jig. See Anonymous plays. Attowell's jig
Françoise' luck. Porto-Riche, G.
Freddie the pigeon. Leichman, S.
Freedom for Clemens. Dorst, T.

Freedom for Clement. See Dorst, T. Freedom for Clemens
Freedom of Jean Guichet, The. Mackay, L.
Freiheit für Clemens. See Dorst, T. Freedom for Clemens
French gray. Bush, J.
French without a master. See Bernard, T. L'anglais tel qu'on le parle
French without tears. Rattigan, T.
Friar Bacon and Friar Bungay. See Greene, R. The honorable history of Friar Bacon and Friar Bungay
Das friedensfest. Hauptmann, G.
Frock and thrills. See Scribe, A. Les doigts de fée
Frogs, The. Aristophanes
Fröken Julie. See Strindberg, A. Miss Julia
Frolic wind. Pryce, R.
From morn to midnight. Kaiser, G.
From rags to riches. Taylor, G.
From the depths. See Gorki, M. [pseud.] The lower depths
Front, The. Korneichuk, A.
Front page, The. Hecht, B. and MacArthur, C.
La frontière de Savoie. See Scribe, E. A peculiar position
Fruen fra havet. See Ibsen, H. The lady from the sea
Fuente ovejuna. Vega Carpio, L.
La fuerza del sino. See Rivas, A. Don Alvaro
Fugitive king, The. Paul, C.
Fulgens and Lucrece. See Medwall, H. Fulgens and Lucres
Fulgens and Lucres. Medwall, H.
Full moon in March, A. Yeats, W.
Fumed oak. Coward, N.
Fun after supper. Smith, B.
Funnyhouse of a Negro. Kennedy, A.
Furcht und Elend des Dritten Reiches. See Brecht, B. The private life of the master race
Furies, The. See Aeschylus. Eumenides
Futz. Owens, R.

G

La gabbia. See Fratti, M. The cage
Gabriel. Mason, C.
Galatea. See Gilbert, W. and Sullivan, A. Pygmalion and Galatea
Galgamannen; en midvintersaga. See Schildt, R. The gallows man
Galileo. Brecht, B.
Gallant, the bawd, and the fair lady, The. Ruiz, J.
Galley slave, The. Campbell, B.
Gallows humour. Richardson, J.
Gallows man, The: a midwinter story. Schildt, R.
Galtra-Loftur. See Sigurjónsson, J. The wish
Gamblers. Gogol, N.
Gambler's fate, The. See Dunlap, W. Thirty years
Game at chess, A. Middleton, T.
Game of folly vs. wisdom, The. Theotokas, G.
Game of love, The. See Schnitzler, A. Light-o'-love
Game of love and chance, The. See Marivaux, P. Le jeu de l'amour et du hazard
Gamester, The. Moore, E.
Gammer Gurton's nedle. See Stevenson, W. Gammer Gurton's needle
Gammer Gurton's needle.

Stevenson, W.
Gap, The. Ionesco, E.
Le garçon et l'aveugle. Anonymous plays
Gardener's dog, The. See Vega Carpio, L. The dog in the manger
La garra. See Linares Rivas, M. The claws
Gas heart, The. Tsara, T.
Gas I. Kaiser, G.
Gas II. Kaiser, G.
Gaslight. See Hamilton, P. Angel street
Gastone the animal tamer. Morselli, E.
Gauntlet, A. Bjørnson, B.
Gay invalid, The. See Molière, J. Doctor's delight
Gay Lord Quex, The. Pinero, A.
Le gendre de M. Poirier. Augier, E. and Sandeau, J.
General returns from one place to another, The. O'Hara, F.
Generation. Goodhart, W.
Generous Portugal, The. See Fletcher, J. The island princess
Gengangere. See Ibsen, H. Ghosts
Le gentilhomme Guespin. Donneau de Visé, J.
Gentle craft, The. See Dekker, T. The shoemaker's holiday
Gentle gunman, The. MacDougall, R.
Gentle savage, The. See Brougham, J. Pocahontas
Gentleman caller. Bullins, E.
George a Greene, the pinner of Wakefield. Greene, R.
George and Margaret. Savory, G.
George Barnwell. See Lillo, G. The London merchant
George Washington slept here. Kaufman, G. and Hart, M.
Georgie porgie. Birmisa, G.
Der gerettete Alkibiades. See Kaiser, G. Alkibiades saved
Gestern und heute. See Winsloe, C. Children in uniform
Der gestiefelte kater. Tieck, J.
Get out of my hair. Feydeau, G.
Getting married. Shaw, G.
Das gewissen. See Iffland, A. Conscience
Ghost of Benjamin Sweet, The. Gilsdorf, F. and Gibson, P.
Ghost patrol, The. Clarke, W.
Ghost sonata, The. Strindberg, A.
Ghosts. Ibsen, H.
Giant's stair, The. Steele, W.
La giara. See Pirandello, L. The jar
Gibson upright, The. Tarkington, B. and Wilson, H.
Gideon. Chayefsky, P.
Gift, The. Duncan, R.
Gigi. Loos, A.
Ginger Anne. Washburn, D.
Gingerbread lady, The. Simon, N.
Gioconda. Annunzio, D. d'
Giovanni in London; or, The libertine reclaimed. Moncrieff, W.
Gipsies metamorphosed, The. Jonson, B.
Girl from Lorraine, A. See Anderson, M. Joan of Lorraine
Girl from Persia, The. Plautus, T.
Girl from Samos, The. Menander
Girl I left behind me, The. Belasco, D. and Fyles, F.
Girl of the golden west, The. Belasco, D.
Girl on the Via Flaminia, The. Hayes, A.
Girl with the green eyes, The. Fitch, C.
Girls' acquiescence, The. See Moratín, L. El sí de las niñas
Girls in uniform. See Winsloe, C. Children in uniform
Gismond of Salerne. See Wil-

mot, R. Tancred and Gismond
Give all the terrors to the wind. Sifton, C. and Sifton, P.
Gladiator, The. Bird, R.
Glamour. Bernard, J.
Glass menagerie, The. Williams, T.
Glass of water, A. See Scribe, A. Le verre d'eau
Glaube und heimat. See Schönherr, K. Faith and fireside
Glaucus. Boker, G.
Glittering gate, The. Dunsany, E.
Gloaming, oh my darling, The. Terry, M.
Le glorieux. Destouches, P.
Glorious morning. MacOwan, N.
Glory of Columbia: Her yeomancy!, The. Dunlap, W.
Glove, A. See Bjørnson, B. A gauntlet
Das glück im winkel. See Suderman, H. The vale of content
Der gnopp. Birmelin, J.
Goal, The. Jones, H.
Goat song. Werfel, F.
God bless our home. See Barry, P. The youngest
God of Gods, The. Aikins, C.
God of vengeance. Asch, S.
Godley Queen Hester. Anonymous plays
God of the lightning. Anderson, M. and Hickerson, H.
Gods of the mountain, The. Dunsany, E.
God's promises. Bale, J.
Goetz von Berlichingen. Goethe, J.
Goin' a Buffalo. Bullins, E.
Gold. Myrtle, F.
Golden apple, The. Latouche, J.
Golden boy. Odets, C.
Golden bull of boredom, The. Yerby, L.
Golden circle, The. Patrick, R.
Golden fleece, The. Gurney, A.
Golden gate, The. Stefánsson, D.
Golem, The. Halper, L.
Good day. Peluso, E.
Good doctor, The. Simon, N.
Good gracious Annabelle. Kummer, C.
Good heavens. Corwin, N.
Good hope, The. Heijermans, H.
Good lieutenant, The. Murray, R.
Good-natured man, The. Goldsmith, O.
Good theatre. Morley, C.
Good will toward men. Debenham, A.
Good woman of Setzuan, The. Brecht, B.
Goodbye, my fancy. Kanin, F.
Goose hangs high, The. Beach, L.
Gorboduc; or, Ferrex and Porrex. Sackville, T. and Norton, T.
Gordon. Boland, B.
Gorilla queen. Tavel, R.
Gottlieb Merks. See Kotzebue, A. Egotist and pseudo-critic Herr Gottlieb Merks
Government inspector, The. See Gogol, N. The inspector
Governor's lady, The. Mercer, D.
Grace and George and God. Hierholzer, A.
Gracious ones, The. See Aeschylus. Eumenides
La grammaire. Labiche, E. and Leveaux, A.
El gran Galeoto. Echegaray y Eizaguirre, J.
Gran teatro del mundo. See Calderón de la Barca, P. The great theater of the world
Grand cham's diamond, The. Monkhouse, A.
Grand cham's necklace. See Monkhouse, A. The grand

cham's diamond
Grand hotel. Baum, V.
Grand tenement and November 22. Eyen, T.
Granite. Ashton, W.
Granny Maumee. Torrence, F.
Grass harp, The. Capote, T.
Grass is greener, The. Williams, H. and Williams, M.
Grasshopper at the home of the ants. See Legouvé, E. and Labiche, E. La cigale chez les fourmis
Graven images. Miller, M.
Great adventure, The. Bennett, A.
Great American desert, The. Oppenheimer, J.
Great Broxopp, The. Milne, A.
Great diamond robbery, The. Alfriend, E. and Wheeler, A.
Great divide, The. Moody, W.
Great fury of Philip Hotz, The. Frisch, M.
Great Galeoto, The. See Echegaray y Eizaguirre, J. El gran Galeoto
Great git-away, The. Muller, R.
Great god Brown, The. O'Neill, E.
Great goodness of life. Jones, L.
Great highway, The. Strindberg, A.
Great rage of Philip Hotz, The. See Frisch, M. The great fury of Philip Hotz
Great theater of the world, The. Calderón de la Barca, P.
Great white hope, The. Sackler, H.
Green bay tree, The. Shairp, M.
Green cockatoo, The. Schnitzler, A.
Green fields. Hirshbein, P.
Green goddess, The. Archer, W.
Green grow the lilacs. Riggs, L.
Green hat, The. Arlen, M.
Green Julia. Ableman, P.
Green knight, The. Garnett, P.
Green pastures, The. Connelly, M.
Grief goes over. Hodge, M.
Grim the collier of Croydon; or, The devil and his dame. Anonymous plays
Die grosse wut des Philipp Hotz. See Frisch, M. The great fury of Philip Hotz
Grouch, The. Menander.
Group, The. Warren, M.
Gruach. Bottomley, G.
Der gruene kakadu. See Schnitzler, J. The green cockatoo
La guarda cuidadosa. See Cervantes Saavedra, M. The vigilant sentinel
Guárdate del agua mansa. See Calderón de la Barca, P. Keep your own secret
Guardian of the tomb, The. Kafka, F.
Guerillas of the Ukrainian Steppes. Korneichuk, A.
La guerre de Troie n'aura pas lieu. See Giraudoux, J. Tiger at the gates
Guillermo Tell tiene los ojos tristes. See Sastre, A. Sad are the eyes of William Tell
Guilty party. Ross, G.
Gullna hlidid. See Stefánsson, D. The golden gate
Gun play, A. Udoff, Y.
Gunpowder, treason and plot. Williamson, H.
Der gute mensch von Sezuan. See Brecht, B. The good woman of Setzuan
Guys and dolls. Swerling, J.; Burrows, A. and Loesser, F.
Guzmán el Bueno. Gil y Zárate, A.
Gypsy. Anderson, M.

H

H. M. S. Pinafore; or, The lass that loved a sailor. Gilbert, W. and Sullivan, A.
Hachi no ki. See Seami, M. The dwarf trees
Hadrian VII. Luke, P.
Hairy ape, The. O'Neill, E.
Haiti. Dubois, W.
Haku Rakuten. Seami, M.
Half a loaf. See Lonsdale, F. Let them eat cake
Hall of healing. O'Casey, S.
Hamadryads, The. Irwin, W.
Hamlet. Shakespeare, W.
Hamlet of Stepney Green, The. Kops, B.
Hamlet; or, The new wing at Elsinore. See "Mr. Punch" [pseud.] A dramatic sequel to Hamlet
Hamp. Wilson, J.
Han Kung Ch'in. See Ma, C. Autumn in the Palace of Han
Hand of Siva, The. Goodman, K. and Hecht, B.
Hands around. See Schnitzler, A. Round dance
Hanging of Judas, The (Wakefield). Anonymous plays
Hanjo. See Seami, M. Lady Han
Hannele. Hauptmann, G.
Hannele's assumption. See Hauptmann, G. Hannele
Hanneles himmelfahrt. See Hauptmann, G. Hannele
Hannibal and Scipio. Nabbes, T.
En hanske. See Bjørnson, B. A gauntlet
Happiest days of your life. Dighton, J.
Happiest of the three, The. Labiche, E. and Gondinet, E.
Happiness in a nook. See Sudermann, H. The vale of content
Happy apple, The. Pulman, J.
Happy as Larry. MacDonagh, D.
Happy day, A. Kock, C.
Happy days. Beckett, S.
Happy days are here again. Taylor, C.
Happy ending. Ward, D.
Happy family. Cooper, G.
Happy haven, The. Arden, J. and D'Arcy, M.
Happy journey to Trenton and Camden, The. Wilder, T.
Happy man, The. Williams, H. and Williams, M.
Happy time, The. Taylor, S.
Hard fate, A. See Pisemskiĭ, A. A bitter fate
Harriet. Ryerson, F. and Clements, C.
Harrowing of hell, The (Chester). Anonymous plays
Harrowing of hell, The; or, The extraction of souls from hell (Wakefield). Anonymous plays
Harvest in the north. Hodson, J.
Harvey. Chase, M.
Hashi-Benki. See Hiyoshi, S. Benkei on the bridge
Haste to the wedding. See Labiche, E. and Marc-Michel, L. An Italian straw hat
Hasty heart, The. Patrick, J.
Hatful of rain, A. Gazzo, M.
Hatmaker, The. Miyamasu
Hatsuyuki. See Zembō, M. Early snow
Haunted house, The. Plautus, T.
Der Hauptmann von Koepenick. See Zuckmayer, C. The captain from Köpenick
Haute surveillance. See Genêt, J. Deathwatch
Have you any dirty washing, mother dear? Exton, C.
"Having wonderful time." Kober, A.
Hay fever. Coward, N.
El haz de leña. Núñez de Arce, G.
Hazel Kirke. MacKaye, S.
He and she. Crothers, R.

He wants shih. Owens, R.
He who gets slapped. Andreev, L.
Headshrinkers, The. See Regnier, M. Paddle your own canoe
Heart of age, The. Bercoveci, E.
Heart of Bruce. Williamson, H.
Heart of Maryland, The. Belasco, D.
Heart overtasked, The. See Willis, N. Bianca Visconti
Heartbreak house. Shaw, G.
Heat lightning. Alpert, H.
Heat wave. Pertwee, R.
Heautontimorumenos. Terentius Afer, P.
Heaven and earth. Byron, G.
Hecuba. Euripides
Hecyra. See Terentius Afer, P. The mother-in-law
Hedda Gabler. Ibsen, H.
Hegge plays. See Ludus Coventriae plays
Das heilige experiment. See Hochwalder, F. The strong are lonely
Heimat. See Sudermann, H. Magda
Heinrich aus Andernach. Unruh, F.
Heinrich und Heinrichs geschlecht. See Wildenbruch, E. von. King Henry
Heiress, The. Goetz, R. and Goetz, A.
Helen. Euripides.
Helena's husband. Moeller, P.
Hell-bent fer heaven. Hughes, H.
Hello, Dolly! Stewart, M.
Hello from Bertha. Williams, T.
Hello out there. Saroyan, W.
Héloise. Forsyth, J.
Henri III et sa cour. Dumas, A., père
Henrietta, The. Howard, B.
Henry IV. Pirandello, L.
Henry IV. See Shakespeare, W. King Henry the fourth
Henry IV of Germany, pt. I. See Wildenbruch, E. von. King Henry
Henry the fifth. See Anonymous plays. The famous victories of Henry the fifth
Hepta epi Thebas. See Aeschylus. The seven against Thebes
Her great match. Fitch, C.
Her master's voice. Kummer, C.
Heracleidae, The. Euripides
Heracles. Euripides
Heracles mad. See Euripides. Heracleidae
Herbert III. Shine, T.
Hercules furens. See Seneca, L. Mad Hercules
Hercules Oetaeus. See Seneca, L. Hercules on Oeta
Hercules on Oeta. Seneca, L.
Here choose I. See Mitchell, Y. The same sky
Here come the clowns. Barry, P.
Here comes Santa Claus. Oliansky, J.
Hereditary forester, The. See Ludwig, O. Der erbförster
Herfords, The. See Crothers, R. He and she
Heritage and its history, A. Mitchell, J.
La hermana Josefina. See Darthes, J. and Damel, C. The quack doctor
L'hermine. See Anouilh, J. The ermine
Hernani. Hugh, V.
Hero, The. Ballesteros, A.
Hero, The. Pottle, E.
Hero and the nymph, The. See Kālidāsa. Vikramorvacie
Herod (Coventry). See Anonymous plays. The magi, Herod and the slaughter of the innocents
Herod and Mariamne. Troubetzkoy, A.
Herod and the magi. See Anonymous plays. The magi
Herod the great (Wakefield).

Anonymous plays
Herod the king. Munk, K.
Herodes und Mariamne. Hebbel, C.
Heroes, The. Ashbery, J.
Herr Gottlieb Merks. See Kotzebue, A. Egotist and pseudo-critic...
Herr Puntila und sein knecht matti. See Brecht, B. Puntila and his hired man
Herr Sleeman kommer. See Bergman, J. Mr. Sleeman is coming
Hessian Christmas play, The. Anonymous plays
Hey you, light man! Hailey, O.
Hickscorner. Anonymous plays
Hieronimo is mad again. See Kyd, T. The Spanish tragedy
High life below stairs. Townley, J.
High Tor. Anderson, M.
High-brow, The. See Molière, J. Les prêcieuses ridicules
Hiketides. See Aeschylus. The suppliants; Euripides. The suppliants
him. cummings, e. e.
Hindle wakes. Houghton, D.
Hinkelmann. Toller, E.
Hiob. See Kokoschka, O. Job
Hippolytus. Euripides
Hippolytus. Howe, J.
His first step. Oyamo
His widow's husband. Benavente y Martínez, J.
L'histoire de Tobie et de Sara. See Claudel, P. Tobias and Sara
Histoire de Vasco. See Schehadé, G. Vasco
L'histoire du cirque. See Salacrou, A. A circus story
Historical register for year 1736, The. Fielding, H.
Histories of Lot and Abraham, The. See Anonymous plays. Abraham, Melchisedec and Isaac
History of George Barnwell, The. See Lillo, G. The London merchant
History of Jacob and Esau, The. See Anonymous plays. Jacob and Esau
History of King Lear, The. Tate, N.
History of Vasco, The. See Schéhadé, G. Vasco
Hob; or, The country wake. Dogget, T.
Hob in the well. See Dogget, T. Hob
Hoboken blues; or, The black Rip Van Winkle. Gold, M.
Hobson's choice. Brighouse, H.
Die hochzeit der Sobeide. See Hofmannsthal, H. von. The marriage of Sobeide
Di hoffning. Brendle, T.
Hogan's goat. Alfred, W.
Hole in the wall. Kreymborg, A.
Holiday. Barry, P.
Holly and the ivy, The. Browne, W.
Holy experiment, The. See Hochwalder, F. The strong are lonely
Holy ghostly, The. Shepard, S.
Homage of the arts, The. Schiller, J.
El hombre de mundo. Vega, V.
El hombre del siglo. See Frank, M. The man of the century
El hombre y la mosca. See Ruibal, J. The man and the fly
Home. See Maeterlinck, M. Interior; Sudermann, H. Magda
Home. Storey, D.
Home at seven. Sherriff, R.
Home of the brave. Laurents, A.
Homecoming, The. Pinter, H.
L'homme et ses fantômes. Lenormand, H.
Honest whore, The. Dekker, T. and Middleton, T.

Honeymoon, The. Tobin, J.
Honeymoon in Haiti. Kleb, W.
L'honneur de Dieu. See Anouilh, J. Becket
Honor of God, The. See Anouilh, J. Becket
Honorable history of Friar Bacon and Friar Bungay, The. Greene, R.
Hope for a harvest. Treadwell, S.
Hoppla! See Toller, E. Hoppla! Such is life!
Hoppla! Such is life! Toller, E.
Hoppla, wir leben. See Toller, E. Hoppla! Such is life!
Horace. Corneille, P.
Horizon. Daly, A.
Horse, The. Hay, J.
Horse-shoe Robinson. Tayleure, C.
Horse thief, The. Sachs, H.
Hostage, The. Behan, B.
Hostages. Akritas, L.
Hot l Baltimore, The. Wilson, L.
Hotel, The. See Hoyt, C. A bunch of keys
Hotel Universe. Harry, P.
Hour-glass, The. Yeats, W.
House by the lake, The. Mills, H.
House in the square, A. Morgan, D.
House of Atreus, The (Trilogy). See Aeschylus. Agamemnon; Choephoroe; Eumenides
House of Bernarda Alba, The. García Lorca, F.
House of blue leaves, The. Guare, J.
House of Connelly, The. Green, P.
House of cowards. Abse, D.
Houseboy. Oyono, F.
Household peace, The. Maupassant, G. de
Houseparty. Britton, K. and Hargraves, R.
How do you do. Bullins, E.
How he lied to her husband. Shaw, G.
How the Blessed Saint Helen found the holy cross. Anonymous plays
How to settle accounts with your laundress. Coyne, J.
How to succeed in business without really trying. Burrows, A., Weinstock, J. and Gilbert, W.
How's the world treating you? Milner, R.
Hu tieh meng. See Anonymous plays. The butterfly dream
Huan hun chi. See T'ang Hsien-tsu. Peony pavilion
Die huchzich um kreitz waig? Wieand, P.
Hue and cry after cupid, The. Jonson, B.
Hughie. O'Neill, E.
Huis clos. Sartre, J.
Die huldigung des künste. See Schiller, J. The homage of the arts
Human comedy, The. Estabrook, H.
Humanity. Hasenclever, W.
Humour out of breath. Day, J.
Humours of a Virginia election, The. See Munford, R. The candidates
Humulus le muet. See Anouilh, J. and Aurenche, J. Humulus the mute
Humulus the mute. Anouilh, J. and Aurenche, J.
Hundred and first, The. Cameron, K.
Hundred years old, A. Alvarez Quintero, S. and Alvarez Quintero, J.
Hurricanes. Howard, B.
Hyacinth Halvey. Gregory, I.
Hymen. Torres Naharro, B.
Hymn to the rising sun. Green, P.
Hypochrondriac, The. See Molière, J. Le malade imaginaire
Hypocrite, The. See Molière, J. Le Tartuffe

I

I also speak of the rose. See Carballido, E. I too speak of roses
I am a camera. Van Druten, J.
I am here! See Broucham, J. The duke's motto
I, Elizabeth Otis, being of sound mind. Barber, P.
I fantasmi. See Bracco, R. Phantasms
I killed the count. Coppel, A.
I know my love. Behrman, S.
I never sang for my father. Anderson, R.
I remember mama. Van Druten, J.
I rise in flame, cried the Phoenix. Williams, T.
I suppositi. Ariosto, L. See Gascoigne, G. Supposes
I too speak of roses. Carballido, E.
"I want!" Holme, C.
Icarus. Rubenstein, K.
Ice goddess, The. Douglas, J.
Icebound. David, O.
Iceman cometh, The. O'Neill, E.
Ideal husband, An. Wilde, O.
Ideas of Madame Aubray, The. See Dumas, A., fils. Les idées de Madame Aubray.
Les idées de Madame Aubray. Dumas, A., fils
Idiot's delight. Sherwood, R.
Idle head, The. Richardson, W.
Idyl of San Francisco. See Hoyt, C. A trip to Chinatown
If. Dunsany, E.
If a claw is caught the bird is lost. See Tolstoĭ, L. The power of darkness
If I were king. McCarthy, J.
If you please. Breton, A. and Soupault, P.
Ikkaku sennin. Zembō, M.
Ikuta. See Zembō, M. Atsumori at Ikuta
Ikuta Atsumori. See Zembō, M. Atsumori at Ikuta
Il faut qu'une porte soit ouverte ou fermée. See Musset, A. A door should be either open or shut
Il reduce. See Beolco, A. Ruzzante returns from the wars
"Ile." O'Neill, E.
Ill May-day, An. See Anonymous plays. Sir Thomas More
Imaginary invalid, The. See Molière, J. Le malade imaginaire
Immoralist, The. Goetz, R. and Goetz, A.
Immortal husband, The. Merrill, J.
Immortal one, The. Goll, I.
Impassioned wife, The. See Porto-Riche, G. Amoureuse
Impatient poverty. Anonymous plays
Imperial visit to Ohara, The. Seami, M.
Importance of being earnest, The. Wilde, O.
Imposter, The. See Molière, J. Le Tartuffe
L'imposteur. See Molière, J. Le Tartuffe
L'impromptu de l'alma. See Ionesco, E. Improvisation
Improper duchess, The. Fagan, J.
Improvisation; or, The shepherd's chameleon. Ionesco, E.
In a balcony. Browning, R.
In a garden. Barry, P.
In Abraham's bosom. Green, P.
In camera. See Sartre, J. Huis clos
In celebration. Storey, D.
In der Sache J. Robert Oppenheimer. See Kipphardt, H. In the matter of J. Robert Oppenheimer
In Mizzoura. Thomas, A.
In spite of all. MacKaye, S.

In splendid error. Branch, W.
In the city of David. Gonne, F.
In the depths. See Gorki, M. [pseud.] The lower depths
In the frame of don Cristóbal. García Lorca, F.
In the Lyons den. See "Mr. Punch" [pseud.] A dramatic sequel to The Lady of Lyons
In the matter of J. Robert Oppenheimer. Kipphardt, H.
In the right hand of God the Father. Buenaventura, E.
In the shadow of the glen. Synge, J.
In the summer house. Bowles, J.
In the train. O'Donovan, M.
In the wine time. Bullins, E.
In the zone. O'Neill, E.
In Theatre Street. Lenormand, H.
In time to come. Kock, H. and Huston, J.
In white America. Duberman, M.
Inadmissable evidence. Osborne, J.
Incident, An. Andreyev, L.
Incident at twilight. Duerrenmatt, F.
Incident at Vichy. Miller, A.
Indian princess, The; or, La belle sauvage. Barker, J.
Indian queen, The. Dryden, J. and Howard, R.
Indian wants the Bronx, The. Horovitz, I.
Indians. Kopit, A.
Indomitable blacksmith. Law, W.
Ines Mendo; or, The triumph of prejudice. Mérimée, P.
Infant, The. Fonvizin, D.
Infernal machine, The. Cocteau, J.
Informer, The. O'Flaherty, L.
Inga. Glebov, A.
Gl'ingannati. See Anonymous plays. The deceived
Inherit the wind. Lawrence, J. and Lee, R.
Injustice done to Tou Ngo, The. Kuan, H.
Innocent voyage, The. Osborn, P.
Innocents, The. Archibald, W.
Ino and Melicertes. La Grange-Chancel
Ino et Mélicerte. See La Grange-Chancel. Ino and Melicertes
Die inschurens bissness. See Grumbine, E. Die insurance business
Insect comedy, The. See Čapek, K. and Čapek, J. And so ad infinitum
Insect play, The. See Čapek, K. and Čapek, J. And so ad infinitum
Inspector, The. Gogol, N.
Inspector calls, An. Priestley, J.
Inspector-general, The. See Gogol, N. The inspector
Insurance business, Die. Grumbine, E.
Intellectual ladies, The. See Molière, J. Les femmes savantes
Intelligence comes to grief. See Griboîedov, A. Wit works woe
Los intereses creados. See Benavente y Martínez, J. The bonds of interest
Interests created. See Benavente y Martínez, J. The bonds of interest
L'intérieur. See Maeterlinck, M. Interior
Interior. Maeterlinck, M.
Interlude of Godley Queen Hester, An. See Anonymous plays. Godley Queen Hester
Interlude of impatient poverty, An. See Anonymous plays. Impatient poverty
Interlude of John the evangelist, The. See Anonymous plays. John the evangelist
Interlude of wealth and health, An. See Anonymous plays.

Wealth and health
Interlude of youth, The. See Anonymous plays. Youth
Intermezzo. See Giraudoux, J. The enchanted
Intermezzo. Schnitzler, A.
Interview. Van Itallie, J.
Interview, The. Donleavy, J.
Intimate relations. Cocteau, J.
Intimate strangers, The. Tarkington, B.
Intruder, The. Maeterlinck, M.
L'intruse. See Maeterlinck, M. The intruder
Invasion. Leonov, L.
L'invitation au chateau. See Anouilh, J. Ring round the moon
L'invitation au voyage. See Bernard, J. Glamour
Iolanthe; or, The peer and the peri. Gilbert, W. and Sullivan, A.
Ion. Euripides
Iphigenia among the Tauri. See Euripides. Iphigenia in Tauris
Iphigenia at Aulis. Euripides
Iphigenia at Aulis. Rexroth, K.
Iphigenia in Aulis. See Euripides. Iphigenia at Aulis
Iphigenia in Tauris. Euripides
Iphigenia in Tauris. Goethe, J.
Iphigenia of Tauris. See Goethe, J. Iphigenia in Tauris
Iphigenie auf Tauris. See Goethe, J. Iphigenia in Tauris
Irene. Johnson, S.
Irene. See Verneuil, L. Affairs of state
Iris. Pinero, A.
Iron chest, The. Colman, G., the younger
Iron crown, The. Anonymous plays
Iron harp, The. O'Conor, J.
Iron manufacturer, The. Ohnet, G.
Iron master, The. See Ohnet, G. The iron manufacturer
Irregular verb to love, The. Williams, H. and Williams, M.
Isaac. Anonymous plays.
Island, The. Hodge, M.
Island of Barrataria, The. Tyler, R.
Island of Goats. See Betti, U. Crime on Goat Island
Island princess, The; or, The generous Portugal. Fletcher, J.
It cannot be. See Crowne, J. Sir Courtly Nice
It happened in Irkutsk. Arbuzov, A.
It is so (if you think so). See Pirandello, L. Right you are! If you think so
It pays to advertise. Megrue, R. and Hackett, W.
It should happen to a dog. Mankowitz, W.
Italian bride, The. Payne, J.
Italian straw hat, An. Labiche, E. and Michel, M.
"It's a bird, it's a plane, it's superman." Newman, D. and Benton, R.
It's called the sugar plum. Horovitz, I.
Ivanoff. Chekhov, A.
Ivory door, The. Milne, A.

J

J. B. MacLeish, A.
Jack Cade. Conrad, R.
Jack Juggler. Anonymous plays
Jackass, The. Ruibal, J.
Jackie the jumper. Thomas, G.
Jacob (Wakefield). Anonymous plays
Jacob and Esau. Anonymous plays
Jacobowsky and the Colonel. Behrman, S.
James the fourth. Greene, R.

Jane. Behrman, S.
Jane Clegg. Ervine, St. J.
Jane Eyre. Jerome, H.
Jane Shore. See Rowe, N. The tragedy of Jane Shore
Jar, The. Pirandello, L.
Jason. Raphaelson, S.
Jealous old man, The. Cervantes Saavedra, M.
Jealous wife, The. Colman, G.
Jeannie. Stuart, A.
Jephté; ou, Le voeu. Buchanan, G.
Jeppe of the hill. Holberg, L.
Jeppe paa bjerget. See Holberg, L. Jeppe of the hill
Jest, The. Benelli, S.
Jest, satire, irony, and deeper significance. Grabbe, C.
Jesters' supper, The. See Benelli, S. The jest
Le jet de sang. See Artaud, A. The jet of blood
Jet of blood, The. Artaud, A.
Le jeu d'Adam. See Anonymous plays. Adam
Le jeu de l'amour et du hasard. Marivaux, P.
Le jeu de la feuillée. Adam de la Halle
Le jeu de Robin et Marion. Adam de la Halle
Le jeu de Saint Nicolas. See Bodel, J. The play of Saint Nicholas
La jeune fille a marier. See Ionesco, E. Maid to marry
Jew of Malta, The. Marlowe, C.
Jewels of the shrine, The. Henshaw, J.
Jewess of Toledo, The. Grillparzer, F.
Jewish captives, The. Leavitt, J.
Joan of Lorraine. Anderson, M.
Job. Anonymous plays
Job. Kokoschka, O.
Job and his children. Field, J.
Job hunters. Edward, H.
Job security. Charles, M.
Jocasta. Gascoigne, G. and Kinwelmersh, F.
Jockey club stakes, The. Home, W.
Johan Johan. See Heywood, J. John, Tyb and Sir John
Johan Johan the husbande. See Heywood, J. John, Tyb and Sir John
Johan, Tyb his wife and Sir Jhan the preest. See Heywood, J. John, Tyb and Sir John
Johannes. See Sudermann, H. John the Baptist
Johannisfeuer. See Sudermann, H. The fires of St. John
John Bull. Colman, G.
John Bull's other island. Shaw, G.
John Gabriel Borkman. Ibsen, H.
John Ferguson. Ervine, St. J.
John Glayde's honour. Sutro, A.
John John, Tyb, and Sir John. See Heywood, J. John, Tyb and Sir John
John loves Mary. Krasna, N.
John the Baptist (Wakefield). Anonymous plays.
John the Baptist. Sudermann, H.
John the evangelist. Anonymous plays
John, Tyb and Sir John. Heywood, J.
John, Tyb and the curate. See Heywood, J. John, Tyb and Sir John
Johnny Johnson. Green, P.
Johnny no-trump. Mercier, M.
La joie fait peur. Girardin, D.
Joke in one act, A. See Chekhov, A. A wedding
Jonathan. Ewing, T.
Joseph and his brethren. Tyler, R.
Joseph Smith, jr., A play about. Phelps, M.
Joshua Whitcomb. See Thomp-

son, D. The old homestead
Le joug. See Guinon, A. and Marnière, J. The yoke
Die journalisten. See Freytag, G. The journalists
Journalists, The. Freytag, G.
Une journée de bonheur. See Kock, C. A happy day
Journey to heaven of Hannele, The. See Hauptmann, G. Hannele
Journey to Jerusalem. Anderson, M.
Journey to London, A. Vanbrugh, J.
Journey's end. Sherriff, R.
Jovial crew, A. Brome, R.
Joyous season, The. Barry, P.
Juan José. Dicenta y Benedicto, J.
Juan Lorenzo. García Gutiérrez, A.
Juan Moreira. Manco, S.
Jubilee, The. Chekhov, A.
Judah. Jones, H.
Judge, The. Branner, H.
Judge Lynch. Rogers, J.
Judgment, The (Wakefield). Anonymous plays
Judgment day. Rice, E.
Judgment Day, The (York). Anonymous plays
Judgment of Indra, The. Mukerji, D.
Judgment of Solomon, The. Tyler, R.
Die Jüdin von Toledo. See Grillparzer, F. The Jewess of Toledo
Judith. Giraudoux, J.
Juliette ou la clé des songes. Neveux, G.
Julius Caesar. Shakespeare, W.
Jumpers. Stoppard, T.
June moon. Lardner, R. and Kaufman, G.
Junebug graduates tonight. Shepp, A.
Junior miss. Fields, J. and Chodorov, J.
Junkies are full of (SHHH...) Jones, L.
Juno and the paycock. O'Casey, S.
Jupiter in disguise. See Plautus, T. Amphitryon
Just neighborly. Dean, A.
Justice. Galsworthy, J.
Justice. Saavedra, G.
Jute. Witherspoon, K.

K

Kaethchen of Heilbronn; or, The test of fire. Kleist, H.
Kaga-Sodo. See Anonymous plays. The fatal error
Kamiano, the story of Damien. Lavery, E. and Murphy, G.
Der kammersänger. Wedekind, F.
Kamraterna. See Strindberg, A. Comrades
Kanawa. See Anonymous plays. The iron crown
Kanehira. Seami, M.
Kanjinchō. See Namiki, G. The subscription list
Kanske en diktare. See Josephson, R. Perhaps a poet
Die Kassette. See Sternheim, C. The strongbox
Kataki. Wincelberg, S.
Das Käthchen von Heilbronn; oder, Die feuerprobe. See Kleist, H. Kaetchen of Heilbronn
Katie Roche. Deevy, T.
Der kaukasische Kreidekreis. See Brecht, B. The Caucasian chalk circle
Kayoi Komachi. See Kanze Kiyotsugu Kan'ami. Komachi and the hundred nights
Keep an eye on Amélie. Feydeau, G.
Keep, The. Thomas, G.
Keep your own secret. Calderón de la Barca, P.
Kept mistress, The. Anonymous plays
Key Largo. Anderson, M.

Kill, kaleidoscope, kill. See Koutoukas, H. Tidy passions
Killing of Abel, The (Wakefield). Anonymous plays
Killing of Sister George, The. Marcus, F.
Das kind der liebe. See Kotzebue, A. Lovers' vows
Kind lady. Chodorov, E.
Kindling. Kenyon, C.
King, The. Conn, S.
King and I, The. Hammerstein II, O. and Rodgers, R.
King Argimenes and the unknown warrier. Dunsany, E.
King cat, The. Grant, D.
King Darius. Anonymous plays
King David and his wives. Pinski, D.
King Edward the third. See Anonymous plays. The reign of King Edward the third
King Henry. Wildenbrugh, E.
King Henry the eighth. Shakespeare, W.
King Henry the fifth. Shakespeare, W.
King Henry the fourth. Shakespeare, W.
King Henry the fourth, pt. I. Shakespeare, W.
King Henry VI, pt. I. Shakespeare, W.
King Henry VI, pt. II. Shakespeare, W.
King Herod (Chester). Anonymous plays
King John. Bale, J.
King John. See Shakespeare, W. The life and death of King John
King John and Matilda. Davenport, R.
King Lear. Shakespeare, W.
King Lear. See Tate, N. The history of King Lear
King Nicolo; or, Such is life. See Wedekind, F. Such is life
King Oedipus. See Sophocles. Oedipus the king
King of Friday's men, The. Molly, M.
King of Harlem, The. García Lorca, F.
King of soul, The. Caldwell, B.
King of Spain, The. Hoffman, B.
King or no king, A. Beaumont, R. and Fletcher, J.
King Richard II. Shakespeare, W.
King Richard III. Shakespeare, W.
King Stag, The. Gozzi, C.
King, the greatest Alcalde, The. Vega Carpio, L.
King Victor and King Charles. Browning, R.
King Ubu. Jarry, A.
Kingdom of God, The. Martínez Sierra, G. and Martínez Sierra, M.
King's daughter. See Lewis, S. Siwan
King's henchman, The. Millay, E.
King's jewry, The. Glover, H.
King's threshold, The. Yeats, W.
Kirflugen. See Clausen, S. The bird of contention
Kiss and tell. Herbert, F.
Kiss in Xanadu, A. Ames, W.
Kiss the boys good-bye. Boothe, C.
Kitchen, The. Wesker, A.
Kjaerlighedens tragedie. See Heiberg, G. The tragedy of love
Kjarnorka og kvenkylli. See Thórdarson, A. Atoms and madams
Knack, The. Jellicoe, A.
Knacker's ABC, The. See Vian, B. Knackery for all
Knackery for all. Vian, B.
Knave and queen. Young, C. and Howard, B.
Knight in four acts. Harrison, J.
Knight of the burning pestle, The. Beaumont, F. and

Fletcher, J.
Knights, The. Aristophanes
Knives from Syria. Riggs, L.
Knock about, The. See Andreev, L. He who gets slapped
Know thyself. Hervieu, P.
Komachi and the hundred nights. Kanze Kiyotsugu Kan'ami
Komachi at Sekidera. Seami, M.
Kongsemnerna. See Ibsen, H. The pretenders
König Nikolo. See Wedekind, F. Such is life
König Ottokars glück und ende. Grillparzer, F.
Konkylien. See Krog, H. The sounding shell
Das konzert. See Bahr, H. The concert
Die koralle. See Kaiser, G. The coral
Korczak und die Kinder. See Sylvanus, E. Dr. Korczak and the children
Kreig, ein Te Deum. See Hauptmann, C. War, a Te Deum
Kremlevskie kuranty. See Pogodin, N. The chimes of the Kremlin
Kremlin chimes. See Pogodin, N. The chimes of the Kremlin
Die Kurve. See Dorst, T. The curve
Kynge Johan. See Bale, J. King John

L

"L." Atlas, L.
La la noo. Yeats, J.
La noche de los asesinos. See Triana, J. The criminals
Laburnum grove. Priestley, J.
Lace on her petticoat. Stuart, A.
Le lâche. See Lenormand, H. The coward
Ladies in waiting. De Anda, P.
Lady Aoi. See Zenchiku, U. Aoi no Uye
Lady Audley's secret. Hazlewood, C.
Lady from the sea, The. Ibsen, H.
Lady Han. Seami, A.
Lady in the dark. Hart, M.
Lady Margaret. See Scribe, A. Les doigts de fée
Lady of Lyons, The; or, In the Lyons den. See "Mr. Punch" [pseud.] A dramatic sequel to The Lady of Lyons
Lady of Lyons, The; or, Love and pride. Bulwer-Lytton, E.
Lady of May, The. Sidney, P.
Lady of pleasure, The. Shirley, J.
Lady of the camelias, The. See Dumas, A., fils. La dame aux camélias
Lady Windermere's fan. Wilde, O.
Lady with a lamp, The. Berkeley, R.
Das lager. See Schiller, J. The camp of Wallenstein
Lake guns at Seneca and Cayuga, The. Drummond, A.
Lament for Ignacio Sánchez Mejías. García Lorca, F.
Lament for the death of a bullfighter. See García Lorca, F. Lament for Ignacio Sánchez Mejías
Lamentable and true tragedie of M. Arden of Feversham in Kent, The. See Anonymous plays. Arden of Feversham
Lamentable tragedy of Locrine, The. Anonymous plays
Lamp and the bell, The. Millay, E.
Lancashire witches, The, and Tegue O. Divelly, the Irish priest. Shadwell, T.
Land, The. Colum, P.
Land of happiness, The.

Crocker, C.
Land of heart's desire, The. Yeats, W.
Laodice. Corneille, T.
Lark, The. Anouilh, J.
Larola. Willcox, H.
Larry Parks' day in court. See Bentley, E. Are you now or have you ever been: The investigation of show business by the Un-American Activities Committee, 1947-48
Lars killed his son. Bernard, L.
Lass that loved a sailor, The. See Gilbert, W. and Sullivan, A. H.M.S. Pinafore
Last analysis, The. Bellow, S.
Last days of mankind. Kraus, K.
Last duel in Spain, The. Calderón de la Barca, P. See Payne, J. The last duel in Spain
Last duel in Spain, The. Payne, J.
Last judgment, The (Chester). Anonymous plays
Last man, The; or, The cock of the village. Smith, R.
Last mile, The. Wexley, J.
Last night of Don Juan, The. Rostand, E.
Last of Mrs. Cheyney, The. Lonsdale, F.
Last of my gold watches, The. Williams, T.
Last of the De Mullins, The. Hankin, St. J.
Last of the red hot lovers. Simon, N.
Last of the Turbins. See Bulgakov, M. Days of the Turbins
Last of the Wampanoags, The. See Stone, J. Metamora
Last refuge, The. Gardiner, W.
Last to go. Pinter, H.
Last tournament, The. Prevelakis, P.
Lăt människan leva. See Lagerkvist, P. Let man live
Late Christopher Bean, The. Fauchois, R.
Late Edwina Black, The. Dinner, W. and Morum, W.
Late George Apley, The. Marquand, J. and Kaufman, G.
Latent heterosexual, The. Chayefsky, P.
Later story of Rama, The. Bhavabhūti
Laughing woman, The. MacKintosh, E.
Laughter and hubbub in the house. Kay, K.
Laundry, The. Guerdon, D.
Lazarus. Anonymous plays
Lazarus laughed. O'Neill, E.
Leader, The. Ionesco, E.
Leader, The. White, J.
Leah Kleschna. McLellan, C.
Leak in the universe, A. Richards, I.
Das Leben des Galilei. See Brecht, B. Galileo
Lebendige stunden. Schnitzler, A.
La leçon. See Ionesco, E. The lesson
Left bank, The. Rice, E.
Le légataire universel. Regnard, J.
Legend of lovers. See Anouilh, J. Eurydice
Legend of the rood, The (Cornish). Anonymous plays
Leicestershire St. George play. Anonymous plays
Lennon play: in his own write, The. Kennedy, A. and Lennon, J.
Leonce and Lena. Büchner, G.
Leonora; or, The world's own. Howe, J.
Lesson, The. Ionesco, E.
Lesson, The. See Kelly, G. Finders-keepers
Let man live. Lagerkvist, P.
"Let my people go!" Hay, I.
Let them eat cake. Lonsdale, F.
Let us be gay. Crothers, R.
Let's eat hair! Laszlo, C.
Let's get a divorce! Sardou,

V. and Najac, E.
Let's get on with the marrin'. Gard, R.
Letter, The. Maugham, W.
Letter of introduction, A. Howells, W.
Letter of the law, The. See Brieux, E. La robe rouge
Letter to Tuffy. Mulvay, T.
Letters from the south. Seh, S.
Letters to Lucerne. Rotter, F. and Vincent, A.
Die letzten tage der menschheit. See Kraus, K. The last days of mankind
Li K'uei carries thorns. K'ang Chin-chih
Li K'uei fu ching. See Kang Chin-chih. Li K'uei carries thorns
Liar, The. See Corneille, P. Le menteur
Liars, The. Jones, H.
Libation-bearers, The. See Aeschylus. Choephoroe
Libel! Wooll, E.
Libertine, The. Shadwell, T.
Libertine, The. See also Molière, J. Don Juan
Libertine reclaimed, The. See Moncrieff, W. Giovanni in London
Library, The. Maggi, C.
El libro de buen amor. See Ruiz, J. The gallant, the bawd and the fair lady (adapted from El libro de buen amor)
Liebelei. See Schnitzler, A. Light-o'-love
Das lied von der union. Wollenweber, L.
Life a dream. See Calderón de la Barca, P. La vida es sueño
Life among the little folks. See Payne, J. The boarding schools
Life among the lowly. See Aiken, G. Uncle Tom's cabin
Life and death of King John, The. Shakespeare, W.
Life and death of Lord Cromwell, The. See Anonymous plays. Thomas Lord Cromwell
Life and death of Tom Thumb the great, The. See Fielding, H. The tragedy of tragedies
Life in Louisiana. See Boucicault, D. The octoroon
Life in New York. See Ritchie, A. Fashion
Life is a dream. See Calderón de la Barca, P. La vida es sueño
Life of Cambises, King of Percia, The. See Preston, T. Cambises, King of Persia
Life of King Henry the Fifth, The. See Shakespeare, W. King Henry the fifth
Life of man, The. Andreev, L.
Life of the insects, The. See Čapek, K. and Čapek, J. And so ad infinitum
Life with father. Lindsay, H. and Crouse, R.
Life with Mother. Lindsay, H. and Crouse, R.
Light up the sky. Hart, M.
Lightnin'. Smith, W. and Bacon, F.
Light-o'-love. Schnitzler, A.
Like falling leaves. Giacosa, G.
Like will to like. Fulwell, U.
Likes of her, The. McEvoy, C.
Liliom. Molnár, F.
Lille Eyolf. See Ibsen, H. Little Eyolf
Lily, The. See Molnár, F. Liliom
Lily among the thorns, A. Martínez Sierra, G. and Martínez Sierra, M.
Lily in little India, A. Howarth, D.
Lima beans. Kreymborg, A.
Limitations of life. Hughes, L.
Line. Horovitz, I.
Lion in winter, The. Goldman, J.

Lion with corset. Soya, C.
Lion's share, The. See Curel, F. de. Le repas du lion
Lirio entre espinas. See Martínez Sierra, G. and Martínez Sierra, M. A lily among thorns
List of assets, A. Olesha, Y.
Literary society, The. Ofori, H.
Literatur. See Schnitzler, A. Literature
Literature. Schnitzler, A.
Little accident. Dell, F. and Mitchell, T.
Little clay cart, The. Shudraka.
Little Eyolf. Ibsen, H.
Little fears. Peluso, E.
Little foxes, The. Hellman, L.
Little ghost, The. See Plautus, T. The haunted house
Little glass clock, The. Mills, H.
Little ham. Hughes, L.
Little minister, The. Barrie, J.
Little murders. Feiffer, J.
Little night music, A. Wheeler, H.
Little poor man, The. Copeau, J.
Little teatable chitchat..., A. Smith, J.
Little to the left, A. Brower, B.
Live corpse, The. Tolstoǐ, L.
Live like pigs. Arden, J.
Living corpse, The. See Tolstoǐ, L. The live corpse
Living hours. See Schnitzler, A. Lebendige stunden
Living mask, The. See Pirandello, L. Henry IV
Living newspaper, A. See Arent, A. Power
Living room, The. Greene, G.
Llanto por Ignacio Sánchez Mejías. See García Lorca, F. Lament for Ignacio Sánchez Mejías
Lloyd George knew my father. Home, W.
Loaves and fishes. Maugham, W.
La locandiera. See Goldoni, C. The mistress of the inn
Locrine. See Anonymous plays. The lamentable tragedy of Locrine
Loftur the magician. See Sigurjónsson, J. The wish
London assurance. Boucicault, D.
London cuckolds, The. Ravenscroft, E.
London merchant, The; or, The history of George Barnwell. Lillo, G.
London prodigal, The. Anonymous plays
London wall. Van Druten, J.
Lonely lives. See Hauptmann, G. Einsame menschen
Lonely way, The. Schnitzler, A.
Long and the short and the tall, The. Hall, W.
Long Christmas dinner, The. Wilder, T.
Long day's journey into night. O'Neill, E.
Long-distance piano player, The. Sharp, A.
Long night of Medea, The. Alvaro, C.
Long sunset, The. Sherriff, R.
Long voyage home, The. O'Neill, E.
Long way, The. O'Morrison, K.
Longing for worldly pleasures. Anonymous plays
Look back in anger. Osborne, J.
Look homeward angel. Frings, K.
Look: we've come through. Wheeler, H.
Loot. Orton, J.
Loquacious barber, The. Holberg, L.
Lord Chumley. Belasco, D. and De Mille, H.
Lord's will, The. Green, P.
Lorenzaccio. Musset, A.
Losers weepers. Dolan, H.
Lost horizons. Hayden, J.

Lost in London. Phillips, W.
Lost in the stars. Anderson, M. and Weill, K.
Lost pleiad, The. Dransfield, J.
Lost silk hat, The. Dunsany, E.
Lost son, The. See Buckstone, J. Luke the labourer
Lot and Abraham. See Anonymous plays. Abraham, Melchisedec and Isaac
Lottery, The. Duffield, B.
Lou Gehrig did not die of cancer. Miller, J.
Louis XI. Boucicault, D.
Love after death. Calderón de la Barca, P.
Love and death, featuring "Aleko." Nemīrovīch-Danchenko, V.
Love and honor. Davenant, W.
Love and pride. See Bulwer-Lytton, E. The lady of Lyons
Love as a doctor. See Molière, J. Love is the best doctor
Love-chase, The. Knowles, J.
Love feast, The. See Benelli, S. The jest
Love for love. Congreve, W.
Love in a Dutch garden. See Housman, L. and Granville-Barker, H. Prunella
Love in idleness. See Rattigan, T. O mistress mine
Love in '76. Bunce, O.
Love is a daisy. Collins, M.
Love is the best doctor. Molière, J.
Love lies a-bleeding. See Beaumont, F. and Fletcher, J. Philaster
Love of Don Perlimplín and Belisa in the garden, The. García Lorca, F.
Love of four colonels, The. Ustinov, P.
Love of the three kings, The. Benelli, S.
Love on the dole. Gow, R. and Greenwood, W.
Love passage, A. Jacobs, W.
Love-rogue, The. See Téllez, G. El burlador de Sevilla
Love thief, The. See Benelli, S. The jest
Lovers. Donnay, C.
Lovers. Friel, B.
Lovers' leap. Johnson, P.
Lovers of Teruel, The. See Hartzenbusch, J. Los amantes de Teruel
Lovers' vows; or, The natural son. Kotzebue, A.
Love's labour's lost. Shakespeare, W.
Love's last shift; or, The fool in fashion. Cibber, C.
Loves of Mars and Venus. See Ravenscroft, E. and Motteux, P. The anatomist
Love's victory; or, The school for pride. See Moreto y Cavaña, A. El desdén con el desdén
Loving wife, A. See Porto-Riche, G. Amoureuse
Low bridge. Elser, F.
Lower depths, The. Gorki, M. [pseud.]
Loyalties. Galsworthy, J.
Lucky Sam McCarver. Howard, S.
Ludus Coventriae plays. See Abraham and Isaac; The annunciation; The apostles at the tomb; Appearance to Cleopas and Luke; Appearance to Mary Magdalen; Appearance to Thomas; Ascension; Assumption; Banns; The betraying of Christ; Cain and Abel; Doomsday; The fall of Lucifer; Harrowing of hell II, Jesse; Jesus and the doctors; The magi, Herod, and the slaughter of the innocents; Matthias; Moses; Mother of Mercy; The mystery of the redemption; Noah; The pageant of the shearmen and tailors; Passion I; Passion II; Passion III; Pentecost; Presentation and purification; Raising of

Lazarus; Resurrection and appearance to Mother; The salutation and conception; The shepherds' play; Story of the watch; Three Marys at the tomb; The trial of Christ; Trial of Joseph and Mary; The woman taken in adultery
Ludus super iconia Sancti Nicolai. See Hilarius. The statue of Saint Nicholas
El lugar donde mueren los mamíferos. See Díaz, J. The place where the mammals die
Luke the labourer; or, The lost son. Buckstone, J.
Lumie di Sicilia. See Pirandello, L. Sicilian limes
Lunatics and lovers. Kingsley, S.
Lute song. Howard, S. and Irwin, W.
Luther. Osborne, J.
Le luthier de Crémone. See Coppée, F. The violin maker of Cremona
Luv. Schisgal, M.
Lying-in room, The. Holberg, L.
Lying valet, The. Garrick, D.
Lysistrata. Aristophanes
Lyubov Yarovaya. Trenev, K.

M

Maastricht play, The. Anonymous plays
Macbeth. Shakespeare, W.
Machinal. Treadwell, S.
Machine infernale, La. See Cocteau, J. The infernal machine
Machine-wreckers, The. Toller, E.
Macro Morals. See Anonymous plays. The castle of perseverance; Mankynd; and, Mind, will, and understanding
Mactacio Abel (Wakefield). Anonymous plays
Mad couple well matched, A. Brome, R.
Mad Hercules. Seneca, L.
Madam Popov. Schrock, G.
Madam, will you walk. Howard, S.
Madame Butterfly. Belasco, D. and Long, J.
Madame de... Anouilh, J.
Madame Legros. Mann, H.
Madame Sand. Moeller, P.
Madheart. Jones, L.
Madness of Heracles, The. See Euripides. Heracles
Madness of Lady Bright. Wilson, L.
Madras house, The. Granville-Barker, H.
Madwoman of Chaillot, The. Giraudoux, J.
Maedchen in uniform. See Winsloe, C. Children in uniform
Maeve. Martyn, E.
Magda. Sudermann, H.
Magi, Herod, and the slaughter of the innocents, The (Coventry). Anonymous plays
Magic and the loss, The. Funt, J.
Magic aster. Teh-yao, J.
Magic realist, The. Terry, M.
Mágico prodigioso, El. See Calderón de la Barca, P. The wonder-working magician
Magi's oblation, The (Chester). Anonymous plays
Magistrate, The. Pinero, A.
Magistrates, The. Fath'Ali, A.
Magnificent Yankee, The. Lavery, E.
Magnus Herodes (Wakefield). Anonymous plays
Magnyfycence. Skelton, J.
Magpie and the maid, The. See Payne, J. Trial without jury
Mahomet. Voltaire, F.
Maid of honor, The. Massinger, P.
Maid to Marry. Ionesco, E.
Maid who wouldn't be proper, The. Mick, H.
Maids, The. Genêt, J.

Maid's tragedy, The. Beaumont, F. and Fletcher, J.
Main line, The; or, Rawson's Y. De Mille, H. and Barnard, C.
Les mains sales. Sartre, J.
Maitlands, The. Mackenzie, R.
Le maître. See Ionesco, E. The leader
Le maître des forges. See Ohnet, G. The iron manufacturer
Le maître de Santiago. See Montherlant, H. The master of Santiago
Major Barbara. Shaw, G.
Maker of dreams, The. Down, O.
Le malade imaginaire. See Molière, J. Doctor's delight
Malcontent, The. Marston, J.
Male animal, The. Thurber, J. and Nugent, E.
Male of the species. Owen, A.
Le malentendu. Camus, A.
Malice of empire, The. Yao Hsin-nung
La malquerida. See Benavente y Martínez, J. The passion flower
Malvaloca. Alvarez Quintero, S. and Alvarez Quintero, J.
Les mamelles de Tirésias. See Kostrowisky, G. The breasts of Tiresias
The mammals' graveyard. See Díaz, J. The place where the mammals die
Mamma's affair. Butler, R.
Man and his phantoms. See Lenormand, H. L'homme et ses fantômes
Man and superman. Shaw, G.
Man and the fly, The. Ruibal, J.
Man and the masses. See Toller, E. Masse mensch
Man and wife. Daly, A.
Man better man. Hill, E.
Man for all seasons, A. Bolt, R.
Man from home, The. Tarkington, B. and Wilson, H.
Man in Half Moon street, The. Lyndon, B.
Man in the forest, The. Field, C.
Man in the glass booth, The. Shaw, R.
Man in the moon, The. See Lyly, J. Endymion
Man of destiny, The. Shaw, G.
Man of La Mancha. Wasserman, D.
Man of mode, The; or, Sir Fopling Flutter. Etherege, G.
Man of the century, The. Frank, M.
Man of the world, A. See Vega, V. El hombre de mundo
Man outside, The. See Borchert, W. The outsider
Man who came to dinner, The. Kaufman, G. and Hart, M.
Man who died at twelve o'clock, The. Green, P.
Man who had all the luck, The. Miller, A.
Man who liked Dickens, The. Waugh, E.
Man who lived his life over, The. Lagerkvist, P.
Man who married a dumb wife, The. See France, A. La comédie de celui qui épousa une femme muette
Man who was dead, The. See Tolstoĭ, L. The live corpse
Man with a load of mischief, The. Dukes, A.
Man with the heart in the highlands, The. See Saroyan, W. My heart's in the highlands
Man without a soul, The. Lagerkvist, P.
Mañana de sol. See Alvarez Quintero, S. and Alvarez Quintero, J. A bright morning
Mandragola. Machiavelli, N.
La mandragola. See Machiavelli, N. Mandragola

Mandrake, The. See Machiavelli, N. Mandragola
Manfred. Byron, G.
Le mangeur des rêves. See Lenormand, H. The dream doctor
Maniac, The. See Conway, H. The battle of Stillwater
Manikin and minikin. Kreymborg, A.
La manivelle. See Pinget, R. The old tune
Mankind. See Anonymous plays. Mankynd
Mankynd. Anonymous plays
Manlius Capitolinus. La Fosse, A.
Mannen utan själ. See Lagerkvist, P. The man without a soul
Manohra. Anonymous plays
Man's disobedience and the fall of man (York). Anonymous plays
"Man's extremity is God's opportunity." See Sheldon, E. Salvation Nell
Many waters. Hoffe, M.
Many young men of twenty. Keane, J.
Marat/Sade. See Weiss, P. The persecution and assassination of Jean-Paul Marat as performed by the inmates of the Asylum of Charenton under the direction of the Marquis de Sade
La marca de fuego. Alsina, A.
Marching song. Whiting, J.
Marco millions. O'Neill, E.
Marchands de gloire, Les. Pagnol, M. and Nivoix, P.
Margaret Fleming. Herne, J.
Die Margareth un die Lea. Wollenweber, L.
Margaret's bed. Inge, W.
Margin for error. Boothe, C.
Marguerite. Salacrou, A.
La Marguerite. See Anouilh, J. Ardéle
La Marguerite. See Salacrou, A. Marguerite
Maria Magdalena. Hebbel, C.
Le mariage de Figaro. Beaumarchais, P.
Le mariage d'Olympe. Augier, E.
Le mariage forcé. See Molière, J. The forced marriage
Mariamne. Hardy, A.
Mariamne. Hermite, l'T.
La Mariane. See Hermite, l'T. Mariamne
Marido de su viuda, El. See Benavente y Martínez, J. His widow's husband
Les mariés de la Tour Eiffel. Cocteau, J.
Marino Faliero. Delavigne, J.
Marius, Fanny and César. See Behrman, S. and Logan, J. Fanny
Marodörer. See Strindberg, A. Comrades
Marquis of Keith, The. Wedekind, F.
Die marquis von Arcis. See Sternheim, C. The mask of virtue
Marranos, The. Bernhard, E.
Marranos, The. Cohn, E.
Marriage, The. Gogol, N.
Marriage, The. Greaves, D.
Marriage a la mode. Dryden, J.
Marriage bells, The. See Wood, H. East Lynne
Marriage has been arranged, A. Sutro, A.
Marriage of Figaro, The. See Beaumarchais, P. Le mariage de Figaro
Marriage of Sobeide, The. Hofmannsthal, H. von
Marriage of wit and science, The. Anonymous plays
Marriage of wit and wisdom, The. See Anonymous plays. The contract of marriage between wit and wisdom
Marriage proposal, A. Chekhov, A.
Marriage test, The. Gillman, J.
Mars and Venus. See Ravenscroft, E. and Motteux, P.

The anatomist
Martine. Bernard, J.
Marty. Chayefsky, P.
Martyr'd souldier. Anonymous plays.
Martyrdom of Ali, The. Anonymous plays
Mary Bonaventure. See Hastings, C. Bonaventure
Mary Broome. Monkhouse, A.
Mary loves. See Williams, W. Trial horse no. 1
Mary Magdalene. Anonymous plays
Mary Magdalene and the apostles. See Anonymous plays. The mystery of Mary Magdalene and the apostles
Mary, Mary. Kerr, J.
Mary of Scotland. Anderson, M.
Mary Rose. Barrie, J.
Mary Stuart. Schiller, J.
Mary Surratt, The story of. Patrick, J.
Mary the third. Crothers, R.
Marya. Babel, I.
Maschera ed il volto, La. See Chiarelli, L. The mask and the face
Die maschinen-stuermer. See Toller, E. The machine-wreckers
Mask, The. Rueda, L.
Mask and the face, The. Chiarelli, L.
Mask of virtue, The. Sternheim, C.
Masks. Corneau, P.
Masks and faces; or, Before and behind the curtain. Taylor, T. and Reade, C.
Masks of angels. Peryalis, N.
Masque for three dolls, A. See Van Itallie, J. Motel (part of America hurrah)
Masque of blackness, The. Jonson, B.
Masque of kings, The. Anderson, M.
Masque of reason, A. Frost, R.
Masqueraders, The. Jones, H.
Massacre of the innocents, The. See Anonymous plays. The magi, Herod and the slaughter of the innocents
Masse mensch. Toller, E.
Massnahme, Die. See Brecht, B. The measures taken
Master, The. Schevill, J.
Master builder, The. Ibsen, H.
Master of Palmyra, The. Wilbrandt, A. von
Master of Santiago, The. Montherlant, H.
Master Pierre Patelin. See Anonymous plays. La farce de Maître Pierre Pathelin
Master salesman, The. Upson, W.
Masters of time. Kocherga, I.
Matchmaker, The. Wilder, T.
Matchmaker, The. See also Stewart, M. Hello, Dolly!
Matsukase. Kanze Kiyotsugu Kan'ami
Maximian. Corneille, T.
Mayde's metamorphosis, The. Anonymous plays.
Mayor of Garret, The. Foote, S.
Mayor of Zalamea, The. Calderón de la Barca, P.
Mazeppa; or, The wild horse of Tartary. Payne, J.
Mazeppa; ou, Le cheval Tartare. Chandezon, L. and Cuvelier de Trye, J. See Payne, J. Mazeppa
Me and Molly. Berg, G.
Measure for measure. Shakespeare, W.
Measure of cruelty, A. Passeur, S.
Measures taken, The. Brecht, B.
Meat joy. Schneeman, C.
Le méchant. Gresset, J.
Medal for Willie, A. Branch, W.
Medea. Anouilh, J.
Medea. Euripides
Medea. Grillparzer, F.
Medea. Jeffers, R.

Medea. Seneca, L.
Le médecin malgré lui. See Molière, J. The doctor in spite of himself
Médéé. See Anouilh, J. Medea
Meet a boy. Launder, F. and Gilliat, S.
Meido No Hikyaku. See Chikamatsu, M. The courier for hell
Meineidbauer. See Anzengruber, L. The farmer forsworn
Der meister von Palymra. See Wilbrandt, A. von. The master of Palmyra
El mejor Alcalde el rey. See Vega Carpio, L. The king, the greatest Alcalde
Member for Gaza, The. Levy, B.
Member of the wedding, The. McCullers, C.
Memorandum, The. Havel, V.
Memory of two Mondays, A. Miller, A.
Men and women. Belasco, D. and De Mille, H.
Men in white. Kingsley, S.
Men without shadows. See Sartre, J. The victors
Menaechmi, The. Plautus, T.
Menaechmi twins. See Plautus, T. The Menaechmi
Die Menschen. See Hasenclever, W. Humanity
Menschen im hotel. See Baum, V. Grand Hotel
Menschenhass und reue. See Kotzebue, A. The stranger
Le menteur. Corneille, P.
Mercadet. Balzac, H.
Mercator. See Plautus, T. The merchant
Merchant, The. Anonymous plays
Merchant, The. Plautus, T.
Merchant of Venice, The. Shakespeare, W.
Merchant of Yonkers, The. See Wilder, T. The matchmaker
Mercy Dodd; or, Presumptive evidence. Boucicault, D.
Mercy of Augustus, The. See Corneille, P. Cinna
Merlin gascon. Raisin, J.
Merrily we roll along. Kaufman, G. and Hart, M.
Merry death, A. Evreinov, N.
Merry devil of Edmonton, The. Anonymous plays
Merry go round. See Schnitzler, A. La ronde
Merry monarch, The. See Payne, J. and Irving, W. Charles the second
Merry play, A. See Heywood, J. John, Tyb and Sir John
Merry wives of Windsor, The. Shakespeare, W.
Merton of the movies. Kaufman, G. and Connelly, M.
Mery play betweene Johan Johan, the husbande, Tyb his wife, and Syr Jhan, the preest, A. See Heywood, J. John, Tyb and Sir John
Mery play betweene Johan Johan, Tyb, his wife and Syr Jhan, the preest, A. See Heywood, J. John, Tyb and Sir John
Mery playe betwene the pardoner and the frere, the curate and neybour Pratte. See Heywood, J. The pardoner and the friar
Message from cougar, A. Maljean, J.
Mester Gert Westphaler eller den meget talende barbeer. See Holberg, L. The loquacious barber
Metamora; or, The last of the Wampanoags. Stone, J.
Methusalem; oder, Der ewige Bürger. See Goll, I. Methusalem
Methusalem, or, The eternal bourgeois. Goll, I.
Michael and his lost angel. Jones, H.
Michael and Mary. Milne, A.
Michael Kramer. Hauptmann, G.
Michaelmas term. Middleton, T.

Michel Auclair. Vildrac, C.
Midas. Lyly, J.
Mid-channel. Pinero, A.
Midnight bell, A. Hoyt, C.
Midsummer night's dream. Shakespeare, W.
Midwinter story, A. See Schildt, R. The gallows man
Mighty dollar, The. Woolf, B.
Mighty reservoy, The. Terson, P.
Mikado, The; or, The town of Titipu. Gilbert, W. and Sullivan, A.
Miles gloriosus. Plautus, T.
Milestones. Bennett, A. and Knoblock, E.
Milk white flag, A. Hoyt, C.
Milk train doesn't stop here anymore, The. Williams, T.
Miller and his men, The. Pocock, I.
Miller's daugher of Manchester, The, with the love of William the conqueror. See Anonymous plays. Fair Em
Mind, will, and understanding. Anonymous plays
Mine eyes have seen. Dunbar-Nelson, A.
Mines of sulphur, The. Cross, B.
Minick. Kaufman, G. and Ferber, E.
Minna von Barnhelm; or, The soldier's fortune. Lessing, G.
Minnie Field. Conkle, E.
Minor, The. Fonvizin, D.
Minstrel show. Anonymous plays
Minuet, A. Parker, L.
Minute men of 1774-1775, The. Herne, J.
Miracle at Verdun, The. Chlumberg, H.
Le miracle de Theophile. Rutebeuf
Miracle of Saint Nicholas and the image, The. Hilarius
Miracle of Saint Nicholas and the schoolboys, The. Anonymous plays
Miracle of Saint Nicholas and the virgins, The. Anonymous plays
Miracle of the blind man and the cripple, The. La Vigne, A. de
Miracle worker, The. Gibson, W.
Mirandolina. See Goldoni, C. The mistress of the inn
Mir-i-nisa. Sicam, G. and Casino, J.
Mirror-wardrobe one fine evening, The. Aragon, L.
Misalliance. Shaw, G.
Le misanthrope. Molière, J.
Misanthrope, The. See Molière, J. Le misanthrope
Miser, The. Molière, J.
The misery of having a mind. See Griboîedov, A. Chatsky
Misfortune of being clever, The. See Griboîedov, A. Wit works woe
Misfortunes of Arthur, The. Hughes, T.
Misogonus. Anonymous plays
Miss in her teens. Garrick, D.
Miss Julia. Strindberg, A.
Miss Julie. See Strindberg, A. Miss Julia
Miss Lulu Bett. Gale, Z.
Miss Sara Sampson. Lessing, G.
Miss Thompson. Maugham, W.
Mistake at the manor, A. Frank, M.
Mistake upon mistake; or, Appearance is against them. See Inchbald, E. Appearance is against them
Mistakes of a night, The. See Goldsmith, O. She stoops to conquer
Mr. and Mrs. North. Davis, O.
Mr. Attowell's jig. See Anonymous plays. Attowell's jig
Mr. Biggs. Barlow, A.
Mr. Jiggins of Jigginstown. Longford, C.

Mister Johnson. Rosten, N.
Mr. Paul Pry. Jerrold, D.
Mr. Pickwick. Young, S.
Mr. Pim passes by. Milne, A.
Mister Roberts. Heggen, T. and Logan, J.
Mr. Sidney Smith coming upstairs. Oulton, B.
Mr. Sleeman is coming. Bergman, H.
Mr. Thing. See Chase, M. Mrs. McThing
Mrs. Bumpstead-Leigh. Smith, H. J.
Mrs. Dane's defence. Jones, H.
Mrs. McThing. Chase, M.
Mrs. Moonlight. Levy, B.
Mrs. Mouse are you within? Marcus, F.
Mistress Nell. Hazelton, G.
Mistress of the inn, The. Goldoni, C.
Mrs. Partridge presents. Kennedy, M. and Hawthorne, R.
Mrs. Warren's profession. Shaw, G.
Mixed marriage. Ervine, St. J.
Mixing up the rent. Gard, R.
Moby tick. Peluso, E.
Las mocedades del Cid. Castro y Bellvis, G.
Mock emperor, The. See Pirandello, L. The mock emperor
Mock-tempest, The; or, The enchanted castle. Duffett, T.
Moderskärlek. See Strindberg, A. Motherly love
Mojo. Childress, A.
Mollusc, The. Davies, H.
Le monde où l'on s'ennuie. Pailleron, E.
Money. Bulwer-Lytton, E.
"Money makes the mare go." See Hoyt, C. A Texas steer
Monica. Macauley, P.
Monna Vanna. Maeterlinck, M.
Monologues from "Division Street, USA." Terkel, L.
Monsieur Beaucaire. Tarkington, B.
M. Poirier's son-in-law. See Augier, E. and Sandeau, J. Le gendre de M. Poirier
Le mont sauvage; ou, Le solitaire. Pixérécourt, R. See Payne, J. Mount Savage
La montana de las brujas. See Sánchez Gardel, J. The witches' mountain
Monte Cristo. Fechter, C.
Montezuma. Robertson, L.
Month in the country, A. Turgenev, I.
Moon. Heide, R.
Moon for the misbegotten, A. O'Neill, E.
Moon in the Yellow river, The. Johnston, D.
Moon is blue, The. Herbert, F.
Moon is down, The. Steinbeck, J.
Moon of the Caribbees, The. O'Neill, E.
Moon on a rainbow shawl. John, E.
Moonchildren. Weller, M.
Moonlight is silver. Ashton, W.
Moonshine. Hopkins, A.
Moor of Venice, The. See Shakespeare, W. Othello
Moral. Thoma, L.
Moral play of Albion, knight, A. Anonymous plays
Moral play of Everyman, The. See Anonymous plays. Everyman
Mörder, Hoffnung der Frauen. See Kokoschka, O. Murderer hope of woman-kind
More, Sir Thomas (An ill May-day). Anonymous plays
Moremi. Ladipo, D.
Morning's at seven. Osborn, P.
La mort de Seneque. See Hermite, l' T. The death of Seneca
La mort de Tintagiles. See Maeterlinck, M. The death of Tintagiles
La mort du grand Osman. See

Hermite, l' T. Osman
La morte in vacanze. See Casella, A. Death takes a holiday
Morts sans sépulture. See Sartre, J. The victors
Moses in the bulrushes. More, H.
Most beautiful eyes in the world, The. See Sarment, J. Les plus beaux yeux du monde
Most happy fella, The. Loesser, F.
Most likely to succeed. See Kanin, F. Goodbye, my fancy
Most pleasant comedie of Mucedorus the kings sonne of Valentia and Amadine, the kings daughter of Arragon, A. See Anonymous plays. Mucedorus
Mostellaria. See Plautus, T. The haunted house
Motel: a masque for three dolls. Van Itallie, C.
Motel. See also Van Itallie, J. America hurrah
Moth and the flame, The. Fitch, C.
Mother and child. Hughes, L.
Mother Bombie. Lyly, J.
Mother Courage. Brecht, B.
Mother Courage and her children. See Brecht, B. Mother Courage
Mother earth. Halbe, M.
Mother-in-law, The. Terentius Afer, P.
Motherly love. Strindberg, A.
Mother's a mother, A. See Filippo, E. Filumena Marturano
Motley assembly, The. Anonymous plays
Motomezuka. See Kanze Kiyotsugu Kan'ami. The sought-for grave
Mount Savage. Payne, J.
Mountain, The. Williams, N.
Mourners, The. See Aeschylus. Choephoroe
Mourning becomes Electra. O'Neill, E.
Mouse trap, The. Howells, W.
Mucedorus. Anonymous plays
Much ado about nothing. Shakespeare, W.
Muérete ¡y verás! Bretón de los Herreros, M.
Mulatto. Hughes, L.
Mulberry bush, The. Wilson, A.
Mulberry garden, The. Sedley, C.
Mullato's orgy. Hernández, L.
Mulligan guard ball, The. Harrigan, E.
Mundus et infans. See Anonymous plays. The world and the child
Murder in the cathedral. Eliot, T.
Murder mistaken. Green, J.
Murder of Abel, The (Wakefield). Anonymous plays
Murderer hope of womankind. Kokoschka, O.
Murderer the women's hope. See Kokoschka, O. Murderer hope of womankind
Mushrooms. Kvares, D.
Music crept by me upon the waters, The. MacLeish, A.
Musical chairs. Mackenzie, R.
Mu-tan t'ing. See T'ang Hsien-tsu. Peony pavilion
Mutter Courage und ihre kinder. See Brecht, B. Mother Courage
Mutter, Die. Brendle, T.
Mutter erde. See Halbe, M. Mother earth
Muzeeka. Guare, J.
My childhood. Humphrey, H. and Baldwin, J.
My client Curley. Corwin, N.
My fair lady. Lerner, A.
My heart's in the highlands. Saroyan, W.
My kinsman, Major Molineux. Lowell, R.
My lady dreams. Pillot, E.
My partner. Campbell, B.
My Poll and my partner Joe. Haines, J.

My poor nerves. See Vargas Tejada, L. Las convulsiones
My sister Eileen. Fields, J. and Chodorov, J.
My sister Eileen. See also Fields, J. and Chodorov, J. Wonderful town
My 3 angels. Spewack, S. and Spewack, B.
Myrrha. Alfieri, V.
Le mystère d'Adam. See Anonymous plays. Adam
Les mystères de l'amour. See Vitrac, R. The mysteries of love
Mysteries of love, The. Vitrac, R.
Mysterium resurrectionis. Anonymous plays
Mystery-bouffe (Second variant). Mayakóvsky, V.
Mystery of Adam, The. See Anonymous plays. Adam
Mystery of Mary Magdalene and the apostles, The. Anonymous plays
Mystery of the redemption, The. Anonymous plays
Mystery play of Elche, The. Anonymous plays
Mystery tour, The. Fischer, L.

N

N. Town plays. See Ludus Coventriae plays
Ña Catita. Segura, M.
Nachstück. See Hildesheimer, W. Nightpiece
Nagananda. Harsha, son of Hira
Nakamitsu. Seami, M.
Naked. Pirandello, L.
Naked island. Braddon, R.
Nanine. Voltaire, F.
Nannie's night out. O'Casey, S.
Napoleon crossing the Rockies. MacKaye, P.
Narukami. Danjuro, I.
Nat Turner. Peters, P.
Nathan der weise. See Lessing, G. Nathan the wise
Nathan Hale. Fitch, C.
Nathan the wise. Lessing, G.
National velvet. Bagnold, E.
Native son. Wright, R. and Green, P.
Nativity (The Chantilly play), The. Bourlet, Katherine
Nativity, The (Chester). Anonymous plays
Nativity, The. (Wakefield). See Anonymous plays. The second shepherds' play
Nativity, The (York). See Anonymous plays. The York nativity
Nativity play (Coventry). See Anonymous plays. The pageant of the shearmen and tailors
Natural man. Browne, T.
Natural son, The. See Kotzebue, A. Lovers' vows
Nature. Medwall, H.
Nature of the four elements, The. Anonymous plays
Naughty Anthony. Belasco, D.
Naval encounter. Goering, R.
Necklace, The. See Harsha, son of Hira. Retnavali
Nec-natama. Shiels, J.
Ned Kelly. Stewart, D.
Ned McCobb's daughter. Howard, S.
Nederlaget. See Grieg, N. The defeat
Needles and pins. Daly, A.
Nero. Anonymous plays
Nest, The. Geraldy, P.
Nest of another, The. See Benavente y Martínez, J. El nido ajeno
Never come Monday. Knight, E.
New Chautaqua, The. Gaines, F.
New custom. Anonymous plays
New gossoon, The. Shiels, G.
New house, The. Behan, B.
New men and old acres. Taylor, T.
New morality, The. Chapin, H.

New sin, The. Hastings, B.
New tenant, The. Ionesco, E.
New trick to cheat the divell. Davenport, R.
New way to pay old debts, A. Massinger, P.
New wing at Elsinore, The. See "Mr. Punch" (pseud.) A dramatic sequel to Hamlet
New Year's eve. Frank, W.
New York idea, The. Mitchell, L.
News item, The. Olmo, L.
News of the night; or, A trip to Niagara. Bird, R.
Next. McNally, T.
Next thing, The. Smith, M.
Next time I'll sing to you. Saunders, J.
Nice people. Crothers, R.
Nice wanton. Anonymous plays
El nido ajeno. Benavente y Martínez, J.
Nie wieder friede. See Toller, E. No more peace!
Niels Ebbesen. Munk, K.
Night and war in the Prado Museum. Alberti, R.
Night at an inn, A. Dunsany, E.
Night-cap. Anonymous plays
Night must fall. Williams, E.
Night of the iguana, The. Williams, T.
Night out, A. Pinter, H.
Night shelter, A. See Gorki, M. [pseud.] The lower depths
Night time stood still, The. See Mitson, R. Beyond the bourn
Night to make the angels weep, A. Terson, P.
Nightmare abbey. Sharp, A.
Nightpiece. Hildesheimer, W.
Night's lodging. See Gorki, M. [pseud.] The lower depths
Nihilist, The. Monson, W.
Nil carborundum. Livings, H.
Nishikigi. See Seami, M. The brocade tree
No 'count boy, The. Green, P.
No exit. See Sartre, J. Huis clos
No fumadores. See Benavente y Martínez, J. No smoking
No hay mal que por bien no venga (Don Domingo de Don Blas). Ruiz de Alarcón y Mendoza, J.
No more frontier. Jennings, T.
No more ladies. Thomas, A. E.
No more peace! Toller, E.
No mother to guide her. Mortimer, L.
No place to be somebody. Gordone, C.
No quarter. Bermange, B.
No room at the inn. Temple, J.
No siempre lo peor es cierto. Calderón de la Barca, P.
No smoking. Benavente y Martínez, J.
No song no supper. Hoare, P.
No strings attached. Moss, H.
No thoroughfare. Smee, L.
No time for comedy. Behrman, S.
No time for sergeants. Levin, I.
No trifling with love. See Musset, A. de. On ne badine pas avec l'amour
Noah. Obey, A.
Noah (Wakefield). Anonymous plays
Noah and his sons. See Anonymous plays. The deluge
Noah's ark. Holt, B.
Noah's deluge. See Anonymous plays. The deluge
Noah's flood. See Anonymous plays. The deluge
Noble souldier, The. Anonymous plays
Noch eppes vom Peter seim Handwerk. Miller, D.
Les noces d'argent. See Geraldy, P. The nest
Noche de guerra en el Museo del Prado. See Alberti, R. Night and war in the Prado

Museum
La noche de los asesinos. See Triana, J. The criminals
Noel Coward in two keys. Coward, N.
None beneath the king. See Rojas Zorrilla, F. Del rey abajo, ninguno
Nonomiya. See Anonymous plays. The shrine in the fields
Nooschens duhn viel. See Fink, E. Noshions duhn
Nora. See Ibsen, H. A doll's house
Norwich play of Adam and Eve. See Anonymous plays. Adam and Eve
Noshions duhn. Fink, E.
Not in the book. Watkyn, A.
Notes from a strange God. Drayton, R.
Notes on a love affair. Marcus, F.
Nothing but a man. Roemer, M.
Notorious Mrs. Ebbsmith, The. Pinero, A.
Le nouveau locataire. See Ionesco, E. The new tenant
Now there's just the three of us. Weller, M.
Nubes. See Aristophanes. The clouds
Numance, La. See Cervantes Saavedra, M. La Numancia
La Numancia. Cervantes Saavedra, M.
Nun and the barbarian, The. See Pérez Galdós, B. Electra
Nüremberg egg, The. Harlan, W.
Das Nürnburgisch ei. See Harlan, W. The Nüremberg egg

O

O mistress mine. Rattigan, T.
O pagador de promesas. See Gomes, A. Payment as pledged
Obasute. See Seami, M. The deserted crone
Oberon, the fairy prince. Jonson, B.
Oberufer plays. See Anonymous plays: The paradise play; The shepherds' play; The three kings' play
Object, The. Cooper, G.
Obstinacy. Benedix, R.
Occupe-toi d'Amélie! See Feydeau, G. Keep an eye on Amélie
Octavia. Seneca, L.
Octoroon, The; or, Life in Louisiana. Boucicault, D.
Odd couple, The. Simon, N.
Odna. See Alyoshin, S. Alone
Ododo. Walker, J.
L'odyssée d'Ulysse le palmipède. See Gilbert-Lecomte, R. The odyssey of Ulysses the palmiped
Odyssey of Runyon Jones, The. Corwin, N.
Odyssey of Ulysses the palmiped. Gilbert-Lecomte, R.
Oedipe. See Voltaire, F. Oedipus
Oedipus. Gide, A.
Oedipus. Seneca, L.
Oedipus. Voltaire, F.
Oedipus. See also Sophocles. Oedipus the king
Oedipus at Colonus. Sophocles
Oedipus coloneus. See Sophocles. Oedipus at Colonus
Oedipus, King of Thebes. See Sophocles. Oedipus the king
Oedipus rex. See Sophocles. Oedipus the king
Oedipus the king. Sophocles
Oedipus turannos. See Sophocles. Oedipus the king
Oedipus tyrannus. See Sophocles. Oedipus the king
L'Oeuf. See Marceau, F. The egg
Of mice and men. Steinbeck, J.
Of thee I sing. Kaufman, G. and Ryskind, M.
Off Nags Head. MacMillan, D.
Off the rails. Schlüter, K.

Offentliche anklager, Der. See Hŏchwalder, F. The public prosecutor
Offering of the magi, The (Wakefield). Anonymous plays
Oh, Amelia. See Feydeau, G. Keep an eye on Amélie
Oh dad, poor dad, mamma's hung you in the closet and I'm feelin' so sad. Kopit, A.
Oh, men! Oh, women! Chodorov, E.
Ohara gokō. See Seami, M. The imperial visit to Ohara
Oklahoma! Hammerstein, O.
Old folks at home. Harwood, H.
Old Fortunatus. Dekker, T.
Old glory. See Lowell, R. Beneto Cereno
Old Homestead, The. Thompson, O.
Old ladies, The. Ackland, R.
Old lady says "NO!", The. Johnston, D.
Old lady shows her medals, The. Barrie, J.
Old lady's visit, The. See Duerrenmatt, F. The visit
Old love letters. Howard, B.
Old maid, The. Akins, Z.
Old soak, The. Marquis, D.
Old tune, The. Pinget, R.
Old wives' tale, The. Peele, G.
Oliver Cromwell. Drinkwater, J.
Oliver Erwenter. See McEnroe, R. The silver whistle
Olives, The. Rueda, L.
Ollántay. Rojas, R.
Olympe's marriage. See Auguer, E. Le mariage d'Olympe
Omar and oh my! "Mr. Punch" [pseud.]
On Baile's strand. Yeats, W.
On being hit. Goss, C.
On borrowed time. Osborn, P.
On ne badine pas avec l'amour. Musset, A. de
On Owl Creek. Enrico, R.
On the corner of Cherry and elsewhere. Lee, J.
On the eve. Afinogenyev, A.
On trial. Rice, E.
Once in a lifetime. Kaufman, G. and Hart, M.
Once is enough. See Lonsdale, F. Let them eat cake
Ondine. Giraudoux, J.
One, The. Pitcher, O.
One bright day. Miller, S.
One day more. Conrad, J.
One day of the year, The. Seymour, A.
One of our girls. Howard, B.
One Sunday afternoon. Hagan, J.
One-third of a nation. Arent, A.
One way pendulum. Simpson, N.
Only jealousy of Emer, The. Yeats, W.
Ønsket. See Sigurjónsson, J. The wish
Op hoop van zegen. See Heijermans, H. The good hope
Open twenty-four hours. Cornish, R.
Opening sequence. Trumbo, D.
Opera of Flora, The; or, Hob in the well. See Dogget, T. Hob
Optimicheskaya tragediya. See Vishnevskii, V. An optimistic tragedy
Optimistic tragedy, An. Vishnevskii, V.
Orange souffle. Bellow, S.
Orchards of Polovchansk, The. Leonov, L.
Orchestra, The. Anouilh, J.
L'orchestre. See Anouilh, J. The orchestra
Oresteia (trilogy). See Aeschylus. Agamemnon; Choephoroe; Eumenides
Orestes. Euripides
Orientals, The. Grecco, S.
Origin of the feast of Purim, The; or, The destinies of Haman and Mordecai. Tyler, R.
Orléans sepulcher, The. Anonymous plays

Oroonoko. Southerne, T.
Oropaste; ou, Le faux Tonoxare. See Boyer, C. Oropastes
Oropastes. Boyer, C.
Orphan of Chao, The. Chi, C.
Orphans of the storm. See D'Ennery, A. and Cormon, E. The two orphans
Orphée. Cocteau, J.
Orpheus descending. Williams, T.
Osman. Hermite, l'T.
L'osteria della posta. See Goldoni, C. The post-inn
Othello, An. Marowitz, C.
Othello, the Moor of Venice. Shakespeare, W.
Other danger, The. Donnay, C.
Other player, The. Arno, O.
Other side of a saint, The. See Curel, F. de. L'envers d'une sainte
Other tomorrows. Palarca, J.
Otho the Great. Keats, J.
Ou les beaux jours. See Beckett, Samuel. Happy days
Our American cousin. Taylor, T.
Our betters. Maugham, W.
Our boarding house. Grover, L.
Our lan'. Ward, T.
Our little trip. Ferlinghetti, L.
Our lord of the ships. Pirandello, L.
Our pageant. Ouless, E.
Our power and our glory. Grieg, N.
Our town. Wilder, T.
Out of the crocodile. Cooper, G.
Outer edge of society, The. Dumas, A., fils
Outrageous fortune. Franken, R.
Outsider, The. Borchert, W.
Outward bound. Vane, S.
Over evne. See Bjørnson, B. Beyond our power
Over 21. Gordon, R.
Overtones. Gerstenberg, A.
Overture. Bolitho, W.
Owl and cave, The. Field C.
Owl answers, The. Kennedy, A.
Oxfordshire St. George play, The. Anonymous plays
Oyster and the pearl, The. Saroyan, W.

P

P.S. 193. Rayfiel, D.
Paachspel. See Anonymous plays. The Maastricht play
Paddle your own canoe. Diamant-Berger, M.
Paddle your own canoe. Regnier, M.
Pageant of shearmen and tailors, The (Coventry). Anonymous plays
Painted laugh, The. See Andreev, L. He who gets slapped
Painting, The. Ionesco, E.
Pair of drawers, A. See Sternheim, C. The underpants
Pair of spectacles, A. Grundy, S.
La paix du ménage. See Maupassant, G. de. The household peace
Pajama game, The. Abbott, G. and Bissell, R.
Pantagleize. Ghelderode, M.
Pantomime for Easter day, A. Anonymous plays
Paolo and Francesca. Phillips, S.
Papa is all. Greene, P.
Papa Juan: centenario. See Alvarez Quintero, S. and Alvarez Quintero, J. A hundred years old
Paphnutius. Hrotsvit
Papp. Cameron, K.
Le paquebot Tenacity. Vildrac, C.
Par un jour de pluie. Forest, L.
Paradise play (Oberufer), The. Anonymous plays
Paragon, The. Pertwee, R.

and Pertwee, M.
Le pardon. See Lemaître, J. The pardon
Pardon, The. Lemaître, J.
Pardoner and the friar, The. Heywood, J.
Las paredes oyen. Ruiz de Alarcón y Mendoza, J.
Les parents terribles. See Cocteau, J. Intimate relations
Paris and Helen. Schwartz, D.
Paris bound. Barry, P.
Paris Commune, A. play about the. See Grieg, N. The defeat
Parisian woman, The. See Becque, H. La Parisienne.
La Parisienne. Becque, H.
Parliament of bees, The. Anonymous plays
Parnassus plays (1598-1601). See Anonymous plays: The pilgrimage to Parnassus; The return from Parnassus
Parnell. Schauffler, E.
Parra kumpt, Der. Wieand, P.
Parson's wedding, The. Killigrew, T.
Partisans on the steppes of the Ukraine. See Korneichuk, A. Guerillas on the Ukrainian Steppes
Partizany v stepakh Ukrainy. See Korneichuk, A. Guerillas of the Ukrainian Steppes
Party, The. Arden, J.
Party spirit, The. Jones, P. and Jowett, J.
Paso de las olivas, El. See Rueda, L. The olives
Paso séptimo: de las aceitunas. See Rueda, L. The seventh farce
Passacaglia. Dey, J.
Passenger to Bali, A. St. Joseph, E.
Passer-by, The. Hsun, L.
Il Passero. See López, S. The sparrow
Passing of the magi, The. Zamacois, E.
Passing of the torch, The. See Hervieu, P. La course du flambeau
Passion flower, The. Benavente y Martínez, J.
Passion of Josef D., The. Chayefsky, P.
Passion play of Alsfeld, The. Anonymous plays
Passion, poison and petrifaction. Shaw, G.
Pasteur. Guitry, S.
Pastor song. See Bjørnson, B. Beyond our power
Los pastores. See Martínez Sierra, G. and Martínez Sierra, M. The two shepherds
Patate. See Achard, M. Rollo
Patchwork quilt, The. Field, R.
Le pâté et de la torte. See Anonymous plays. The chicken pie and the chocolate cake
Patelin, Pierre. See Anonymous plays. La farce de Maître Pierre Pathelin
Pathelin, Pierre. See Anonymous plays. La farce de Maître Pierre Pathelin
Patience; or, Bunthorne's bride. Gilbert W. and Sullivan A.
Patrician's daughter, The. Marston, J.
Patrick Pearse motel, The. Leonard, H.
Patrie! Sardou, V.
Patriot, The. Neumann, A. See Dukes, A. Such men are dangerous
Patriots, The. Kingsley, S.
Patriots, The. Munford, R.
Patroness, A. Gerstenberg, A.
Patter versus clatter. Mathews, C.
Patterns. Serling, R.
Les pattes de mouche. Sardou, V.
Paul Kauvar; or, Anarchy. MacKaye, S.
Pauvre Bitos; ou, Le diner

des têtes. See Anouilh, J. Poor Bitos
Pavane produced... See Van Itallie, J. Interview
Pax. See Aristophanes. Peace
Payment as pledged. Gomes, A.
Payment deferred. Dell, J.
Peace. Aristophanes
Peace comes to Peckham. Delderfield, R.
La pecadora. See Guimerá, A. Daniela
Le pêcheur d'ombres. Sarment, J.
Peculiar position, A. Scribe, E.
Pedro de Urdemalas. See Cervantes Saavedra, M. Pedro, the artful dodger
Pedro, the artful dodger. Cervantes Saavedra, M.
Peer and the peri, The. See Gilbert, W. and Sullivan, A. Iolanthe
Peer Gynt. Ibsen, H.
Peg o' my heart. Manners, J.
Peggy. Williamson, H.
Les pélican. See Radiguet, R. The pelicans
Pelicans, The. Radiguet, R.
Pelléas and Mélisande. See Maeterlinck, M. Pelléas et Mélisande
Pelléas et Mélisande. Maeterlinck, M.
Pen of my aunt, The. MacKintosh, E.
Penny for the poor, A. See Brecht, B. The three-penny opera
Penthesilea. Kleist, H.
Peony pavilion. T'ang Hsien-tsu
People in love. Reid, A.
People with light coming out of them, The. Saroyan, W.
People's lawyer, The. See Jones, J. S. Solon Shingle
Pepa la frescachona. Vega, R.
Le père de famille. Diderot, D.
Perhaps a poet. Josephson, R.
Peribanez and the commander of Ocana. See Vega Carpio, L. Peribáñez y el comendador de Ocaña
Peribáñez y el comendador de Ocaña. Vega Carpio, L.
La périchole. Offenbach, J.
Pericles, Prince of Tyre. Shakespeare, W.
Perikeiromene, The. See Menander. The shearing of Glycera
Period of adjustment. Williams, T.
Perkin Warbeck. See Ford, J. The chronicle history of Perkin Warbeck
Perrichon's voyage. See Labiche, E. and Martin, E. Le voyage de M. Perrichon
El perro del hortelano. See Vega Carpio, L. The dog in the manger
Persa, The. See Plautus, T. The girl from Persia
Persecution and assassination of Jean-Paul Marat as performed by the inmates of the Asylum of Charenton under the direction of the Marquis de Sade, The. Weiss, P.
Persecution and assassination of Marat..., The. See Weiss, P. The persecution and assassination of Jean-Paul Marat as performed by the inmates of the Asylum of Charenton under the direction of the Marquis de Sade
Persians, The. Aeschylus
Peter Quill's shenanigans. See Anonymous plays. La farce de Maître Pierre Pathelin
Der Peter soll en handwerk lernen. Miller, D.
Petit pauvre, Le. See Copeau, J. The little poor man
Les petits oiseaux. See Grundy, S. A pair of spectacles
Petrified forest, The. Sherwood, R.

Phaedra. Rexroth, K.
Phaedra. Seneca, L.
Phaedra. See Racine, J. Phèdre
Phantasms. Bracco, R.
Pharaoh (Wakefield). Anonymous plays
Pharaoh's daughter. Kotzebue, A.
Phèdre. Racine, J.
Phèdre et Hippolyte. See Racine, J. Phèdre
Philadelphia, here I come! Friel, B.
Philadelphia story, The. Barry, P.
Philanthropist, The. Hampton, C.
Philaster; or, Love lies a-bleeding. Beaumont, F. and Fletcher, J.
Philip Hotz's fury. See Frisch, M. The great fury of Philip Hotz
Philoctetes. Sophocles
Le philosophe dupé de l'amour. See Anonymous plays. The philosopher duped by love
Le philosophe sans le savoir. Sedaine, M.
Philosopher duped by love, The. Anonymous plays
Les philosophes. Palissot de Montenoy, C.
Phoenician maidens, The. See Euripides. The Phoenissae
Phoenician women, The. See Euripides. The Phoenissae
Phoenician women, The. Seneca, L.
Phoenissae, The. Euripides
Phoenissae. See Seneca, L. The Phoenician women
Phoenix too frequent, A. Fry, C.
Phormio. Terentius Afer, P.
Physician in spite of himself, The. See Molière, J. The doctor in spite of himself
Physicists, The. Duerrenmatt, F.
Die Physiker. See Duerrenmatt, F. The physicists
Pick-up girl. Shelley, E.
Picnic. Inge, W.
Picnic on the battlefield. Arrabal, F.
Picture, The. See Ionesco, E. The painting
La pie voleuse; ou, La servante de Palaisseau. Caigniez, L. and Baudouin, J. See Payne, J. Trial without jury
La pièce à l'étude. Duval, A. See Smith, R. Shakespeare in love
Pierre. Scott, D.
Pierre Patelin. See Anonymous plays. La farce de Maître Pierre Pathelin
Pierre Pathelin. See Anonymous plays. La farce de Maître Pierre Pathelin
Pierrot of the minute, The. Dowson, E.
Pigeon, The. Galsworthy, J.
Pigeons and people. Cohan, G.
Pigtail and sword. See Gutzkow, K. Sword and queue
Pilgrim and the book, The. MacKaye, P.
Pilgrimage. See Anonymous plays. The pilgrimage to Parnassus
Pilgrimage to Parnassus, The. Anonymous plays
Pilgrims, The (Wakefield). Anonymous plays
Pillars of salt. Scott, P.
Pillars of society. Ibsen, H.
Pinafore. See Gilbert, W. and Sullivan, A. H.M.S. Pinafore
Pinner of Wakefield, The. See Greene, R. George a Greene
Pioneers, The. Macmillan, M.
Pi-Pa-Ki. Kao, Tong Kia. See Howard, S. and Irwin, W. Lute song
Piper, The. Peabody, J.
Pippa passes. Browning, R.
Pique. Daly, A.
Pique-nique en campagne. See Arrabal, F. Picnic on the battlefield

La pire n'est pas toujours sûr. See Claudel, P. The satin slipper
La Place de l'Etoile. Desnos, R.
Place in the world, A. Sternheim, C.
Place where the mammals die, The. Díaz, J.
Il placere dell' onestà. See Pirandello, L. The pleasure of honesty
Les plaideurs. Racine, J.
Plain-dealer, The. Wycherley, W.
Plains of Chippewa, The. See Noah, M. She would be a soldier
Plaintiff in a pretty hat. Williams, H. and Williams, M.
Plane-tree, The. Farjeon, E.
Plant in the sun. Bengal, B.
Platon Krechet. Korneichuk, A.
Play about Joseph Smith, jr., A. Phelps, M.
Play in the castle, The. See Molnár, F. The play's the thing
Play of Adam, The. See Anonymous plays. Adam
Play of Robin and Marion, The. See Adam de la Halle. Le jeu de Robin et Marion
Play of St. George, The. See Anonymous plays. A Christmas mumming
Play of St. George, The. Version reconstructed from memory by Thomas Hardy. Anonymous plays
Play of Saint Nicholas, The. Bodel, J.
Play of the doctors, The (Wakefield). Anonymous plays
Play of the greensward, The. See Adam de la Halle. Le jeu de la feuillée
Play of the sacrament, The. Anonymous plays
Play of the wether, The. Heywood, J.
Play of wit and science, The. Redford, J.
Play with a tiger. Lessing, D.
Playboy of Seville, The. See Téllez, G. El burlador de Sevilla
Playboy of the western world, The. Synge, J.
Playe called the foure pp, The. See Heywood, J. The four pp
Playing with love. See Schnitzler, A. Light-o'-love
Play's the thing, The. Molnár, F.
Plaza suite. Simon, N.
Pleasant comedy of a gentle craft, A. See Dekker, T. The shoemaker's holiday
Pleasant comedy of Old Fortunatus, The. Dekker, T.
Pleasant conceited comedy of [George a Greene] the pinner of Wakefield, A. See Greene, R. George a Greene, the pinner of Wakefield
Pleasant history of the two angry women of Abington, The. Porter, H.
Pleasure garden, The. Mayor, B.
Pleasure of honesty, The. Pirandello, L.
Plot discover'd, A. See Otway, T. Venice preserv'd
Plots and playwrights. Massey, E.
Plough and the stars, The. O'Casey, S.
Plow and the stars, The. See O'Casey, S. The plough and the stars
Plumes. Johnson, G.
Les plus beaux yeux du monde. Sarment, J.
Plutus. Aristophanes
Po-ca-hon-tas. See Brougham, J. Pocahontas
Pocahontas; or, The gentle savage. Brougham, J.
Pocahontas; or, The settlers of Virginia. Custis, G.
Poenulus, The. See Plautus, T. The Carthaginian
Poet, The. Niccodemi, D.

Il poeta. See Niccodemi, D. The poet
Poet's papers, The. Starkweather, D.
Point of departure; or, Legend of lovers. See Anouilh, J. Eurydice
Point of no return. Osborn, P.
Point of view, The. Osborne, M.
Point Valaine. Coward, N.
Poker session, The. Leonard, H.
Police, The. Mrożek, S.
Policja. See Mrożek, S. The police
Polish Jew, The. See Lewis, L. The bells
Politician out-witted, The. Low, S.
Polly Honeycombe. Colman, G.
Polyeucte. Corneille, P.
Pompey the great. See Masefield, J. The tragedy of Pompey the great
Ponder heart, The. Fields, J. and Chodorov, J.
Il ponte. See Fratti, M. The bridge
Ponteach; or, The savages of America. Rogers, R.
Poor Aubrey. Kelly, G.
Poor Bitos. Anouilh, J.
Poor bride, The. Ostrovskiĭ, A.
Poor little watch girl, The. Williams, A.
Poor ostrich. Hemro
Porgy. Heyward, D. and Heyward, D.
La porta chiusa. See Praga, M. The closed door
Port-Royal. Montherland, H.
Portrait, The. Scala, F.
Portrait of a queen. Francis, W.
Portrait of the artist as Filipino, A. Joaquin, N.
Portsmouth defence, The. Lethbridge, N.
Post-inn, The. Goldoni, C.
Post office, The. Tagore, R.
El postrer duelo de España. Calderón de la Barca, P. See Payne, J. The last duel in Spain
Pot of gold, The. See Plautus, T. Aulularia
Pots of money. Labiche, E. and Delacour, A.
Potter's field. See Green, P. Roll sweet chariot
Potting shed, The. Greene, G.
La poudre aux yeux. Labiche, E. and Martin, E.
Pour Lucrece. See Giraudoux, J. Duel of angels
Power, a living newspaper. Arent, A.
Power of darkness, The; or, If a claw is caught the bird is lost. Tolstoĭ, L.
Prayer meeting. Caldwell, B.
La précaution inutile. See Beaumarchais, P. Le Barbier de Seville
Les précieuses ridicules. Molière, J.
Le préjué à la mode. La Chaussée, P.
Prenez garde à la peinture. See Fauchois, R. The late Christopher Bean
Presumptive evidence. See Boucicault, D. Mercy Dodd
Pretenders, The. Ibsen, H.
Pretentious ladies, The. See Molière, J. Les précieuses ridicules
Pretty interlude called Nice wanton, A. See Anonymous plays. Nice wanton
Price, The. Miller, A.
Price of wine, The. Anonymous plays
Pride and prejudice. Jerome, A.
Priest and the willow, The. Kanze Kojiro Nobumitsu
Prima pastorum (Wakefield). See Anonymous plays. The first shepherds' play (Wakefield)
Prince d'Aurec, The. Laveden, H.

Prince of court painters, The. Mackay, C.
Prince Frederick of Homburg. See Kleist, H. Prinz Friedrich von Homburg
Prince of Homburg, The. See Kleist, H. Prinz Friedrich von Homburg
Prince of Parthia, The. Godfrey, T.
Prince of peace, The. Debenham, A.
Princess Elizabeth. See Dowling, J. and Letton, F. The young Elizabeth
Princess Hollyhock. See Zenchiku, U. Aoi no Uye
El príncipe constante. See Calderón de la Barca. The constant prince
Printer's apprentice, The. Anonymous plays
Prinz Friedrich von Homburg. Kleist, H.
Prisoner of Second Avenue, The. Simon, N.
Prisoners of war. See Plautus, T. The captives
Private ear, The. Shaffer, P.
Private Hicks. Maltz, A.
Private life of the master race, The. Brecht, B.
Private lives. Coward, N.
Procession of the prophets, The (Wakefield). Anonymous plays
Processional. Lawson, J.
Processus Noe cum filiis (Wakefield). Anonymous plays
Prodigal, The. Richardson, J.
Prodigious snob, The. See Molière, J. The bourgeois gentilhomme
Professor Bernhardi. Schnitzler, A.
Professor Storitsyn. Andreev, L.
Professor Toranne. Adamov, A.
Prohibido suicidarse en primavera. See Rodríguez Alvarez, A. Suicide prohibited in springtime
Prologue to glory. Conkle, E.
Prometheus bound. Aeschylus
Prometheus desmotes. See Aeschylus. Prometheus bound
Prometheus unbound. Shelley, P.
Prometheus vinctus. See Aeschylus. Prometheus bound
Prophets, The (Chester). Anonymous plays
Proposal, The. See Chekhov, A. A marriage proposal
Der Protagonist. See Kaiser, G. The protagonist
Protagonist, The. Kaiser, G.
Provençal play, The. Anonymous plays
Provoked husband, The. Cibber, C.
Provoked husband, The. See Vanbrugh, J. A journey to London
Provok'd wife, The. Vanbrugh, J.
Prunella; or, Love in a Dutch garden. Housman, L. and Granville-Barker, H.
Psalms for two Davids. Schwartz, J.
Pseudolus. Plautus, T.
Public prosecutor, The. Hochwalder, F.
Pueblo de las mujeres. See Alvarez Quintero, S. and Alvarez Quintero, J. The women's town
Pullman car Hiawatha. Wilder, T.
Punished libertine, The; or, Don Giovanni. Ponte, L. Da
Puny little life show, The. McGough, R.
Puppet show, The. Blok, A.
Purgatory. Yeats, W.
Pure polemic. See Lamb, M. But what have you done for me lately?
Purification, The. See Williams, T. Dos ranchos
Purification of Mary, The (Wakefield). Anonymous plays
Purim. See Tyler, R. The origin of the feast of Purim;

or, The destinies of Haman and Mordecai
Puritan, The; or, The widow of Watling street. Anonymous plays
Puritan widow, The. See Anonymous plays. The puritan
Purlie victorious. Davis, O.
Purple dust. O'Casey, S.
Purple flower, The. Bonner, M.
Purple path to the poppy field. Meldon, M.
Puss in boots. See Tieck, J. Der gestiefelte kater
Pussycat and the expert plumber who was a man. Miller, A.
Pygmalion. Shaw, G.
Pygmalion. See also Lerner, A. My fair lady
Pygmalion and Galatea. Gilbert, W. and Sullivan, A.

Q

Quack doctor, The. Darthes, J.
Quare fellow, The. Behan, B.
Queen after death. See Montherlant, H. La reine morte
Queen and the rebels, The. Betti, U.
Queen and the Welshman, The. Sisson, R.
Queen Margaret of Norway. Kielland, T.
Queen mother of the West, The. Komparu-Zenchiku
Queen of hearts, The. Pakington, M.
Queen of Scots. MacKintosh, E.
Queen of camelias, The. See Dumas, A. fils. La dame aux camélias
Queen on tour, The. Abell, K.
Queen's enemies, The. Dunsany, E.
Queen's highland servant, The. Home, W.
Quem quaeritis, The (Trope). Anonymous plays
Querolus. Anonymous plays
Quest divine, The. Goold, M.
Quest of the Gorgon, The. Tharp, N.
Questa sera si recita a soggetto. See Pirandello, L. Tonight we improvise
Question of obedience, A. See Williamson, H. Teresa of Avila
Questioning the irrevocable. Schnitzler, A.
Quick nut bread to make your mouth water, A. Hoffman, W.
Quiet wedding. McCracken, E.

R

R. U. R. Čapek, K.
Rachel. Grimke, A.
Racket, The. Cormack, B.
Rackey. Culbertson, E.
Radio primer. Corwin, N.
Rafferty's chant. Dewhurst, K.
Raft of the Medusa, The. Kaiser, G.
Rags. Walter, N.
Raigne of King Edward the third, The. See Anonymous plays. The reign of King Edward the third
Rain. Colton, J. and Randolph, C.
Rain from heaven. Behrman, S.
Rain-killers, The. Hutchinson, A.
Rainmakers, The. Nash, R.
Raisin in the sun, A. Hansberry, L.
Raisin' the devil. Gard, R.
Raising the devil. Sachs, H.
Raising the wind. Kenney, J.
Ralph Roister Doister. Udall, N.
Rama's later history. See Bhavabhūti. The later story of Rama
Ranae. See Aristophanes. The

frogs
Ranchos, Dos; or, The purification. Williams, T.
Ranke viljer. See Weid, G. 2 x 2 = 5
Rasmus Montanus. Holberg, L.
Ratnavali. See Harsha, son of Hira. Retnavali
Rats, The. Hauptmann, G.
Rat's mass, A. Kennedy, A.
Rats of Norway, The. Winter, J.
Die ratten. See Hauptmann, G. The rats
Rattle of a simple man. Dyer, C.
Ravens, The. See Becque, H. Les corbeaux
Rawson's Y. See De Mille, H. and Barnard, C. The main line
Really, my dear... Morley, C.
Rebound. Stewart, D.
Rebound, The. See Picard, L. Les ricochets
Reckoning, The. See Schnitzler, A. Light-o'-love
Reclining figure. Kurnitz, H.
Reconciliation, The. See Hauptmann, G. Das friedensfest
Recruiting officer, The. Farquhar, G.
Red cross. Shepard, S.
Red detachment of women. Anonymous plays
Red gloves. See Sartre, J. Les mains sales
Red lantern. Ou-hung, W. and Chia, A.
Red night. Hodson, J.
Red robe, The. See Brieux, E. La robe rouge
Red roses for me. O'Casey, S.
Redemption, The. See Anonymous plays. The mystery of the redemption; Tolstoi, L. The live corpse
Reed cutter, The. Seami, M.
Refer to drawer. See Ross, G. Guilty party
Regina. See Hellman, L. The little foxes
Rehearsal, The. Anouilh, J.
Rehearsal, The. Baring, M.
Rehearsal, The. Buckingham, G.
Rehearsal. Morley, C.
Reigen. See Schnitzler, A. Round dance
Reign of King Edward the third, The. Anonymous plays
La reine morte. Montherlant, H.
El reino de Dios. See Martinez Sierra, G. and Martinez Sierra, M. The kingdom of God
Relapse, The; or, Virtue in danger. Vanbrugh, J.
Remains to be seen. Lindsay, H. and Crouse, R.
Remarkable Mr. Pennypacker, The. O'Brien, L.
Remorse. Coleridge, S.
Remote. See Afinogenyev, A. Far taiga
Renewal, The. See Green, P. and Green, E. Fixin's: The tragedy of a tenant farm woman
Rent-day, The. Jerrold, D.
Le repas du lion. Curel, F.
La répétition; ou, L'amour puni. See Anouilh, J. The rehearsal
Representative, The. See Hochhuth, R. The deputy
Requiem for Brother X. Mackey, W.
Requiem for a heavyweight. Serling, R.
Requiem for a nun. Ford, R. and Faulkner, W.
Residuary légatee, The. See Regnard, J. Le légataire universel
Resounding tinkle, A. Simpson, N.
Respublica. Anonymous plays
Restoration of Arnold Middleton, The. Storey, D.
Resurrection, The (York). Anonymous plays
Resurrection, The. Kimball, R.

Resurrection, The. Yeats, W.
Resurrection, harrowing of hell, and the last judgment. Anonymous plays
Resurrection of Christ, The (Wakefield). Anonymous plays
Retnavali; or, The necklace. Harsha, son of Hira
Return, The. Fratti, M.
Return from Parnassus, The; or, The scourge of Simony, pt. II. Anonymous plays
Return of Peter Grimm, The. Belasco, D.
Return of the prodigal, The. Hankin, St. J.
Reunion in Vienna. Sherwood, R.
Revenge of Bussy D'Ambois, The. Chapman, G.
Revengers' tragedy, The. Tourneur, C.
Reverend Griffith Davenport, The. Herne, J.
Revesby sword play, The. Anonymous plays
Revisor. See Gogol, N. The inspector
Los reyes pasan. See Zamacois, E. The passing of the Magi
Rhadamiste et Zénobie. Crébillon, P.
Rhadamistus and Zenobia. See Crébillon, P. Rhadamiste et Zénobie
Rhesus. Euripides
Rhinoceros. Ionesco, E.
Les rhinocéros. See Ionesco, E. Rhinoceros
Rhondda roundabout. Jones, J.
Rhythm of violence, The. Nkosi, L.
Richard of Bordeaux. Daviot, G. [pseud.]
Richard II. See Shakespeare, W. King Richard II
Richard III. See Shakespeare, W. King Richard III
Richelieu; or, The conspiracy. Bulwer-Lytton, E.
Les ricochets. Picard, L.
Rider of dreams, The. Torrence, F.
Riders to the sea. Synge, J.
Ridiculous précieuses, The. See Molière, J. Le précieuses ridicules
Rifle ball, The. See Wallach, L. Rosedale
Right you are! If you think so. Pirandello, L.
Ring around the moon. See Anouilh, J. Ring round the moon
Ring of General Macías, The. Niggli, J.
Ring round the moon. Anouilh, J.
Rip Van Winkle. Burke, C.
Rip Van Winkle, as played by Joseph Jefferson. Anonymous plays
Rising of the moon, The. Gregory, I.
Rites. Duffy, M.
Il ritorno. See Fratti, M. The return
Il rittrato. See Scala, F. The portrait
Rival queens, The; or, The death of Alexander the great. Lee, N.
Rivals, The. Sheridan, R.
River Niger, The. Walker, J.
Rivers and forests, The. Duras, M.
Road to Rome, The. Sherwood, R.
Roadside. Riggs, L.
La robe rouge. Brieux, E.
Robert Emmet. Boucicault, D.
Robin Hood and the friar. Anonymous plays
Robin Hood and the knight. Anonymous plays
Robin Hood and the potter. Anonymous plays
Robin Hood and the sheriff of Nottingham. Anonymous plays
Robust invalid, The. See Molière, J. Doctor's delight
Rock, The. Hamlin, M.
Rocket to the moon. Odets, C.

Rocking back and forth. Grass, G.
Rocking chairs. Kreymborg, A.
Rococo. Barcer, G.
Roger Bloomer. Lawson, J.
Rogue of Seville, The. See Téllez, G. El burlador de Sevilla
Roister Doister. See Udall, N. Ralph Roister Doister
Roll sweet chariot. Green, P.
Rollo. Achard, M.
Roman actor, The. Massinger, P.
Roman patriot, The. See Brown, D. Sertorius
Romance. Sheldon, E.
Romancers, The. Rostand, E.
Les romanesques. See Rostand, E. The romancers
Romantics, The. Rostand, E.
Romeo and Juliet. Shakespeare, W.
Romulus, the shepherd king. Payne, J.
La ronde. See Schnitzler, A. Round dance
Roots. Wesker, A.
Rope, The. O'Neill, E.
Rope, The. Plautus, T.
Rope dancers, The. Wishengrad, M.
Rosalie. Maurey, M.
Rose Michel. MacKaye, S.
Rose tattoo, The. Williams, T.
Rose without a thorn, The. Bax, C.
Rosedale; or, The rifle ball. Wallach, L.
Rosencrantz and Guilderstern are dead. Stoppard, T.
Rosmersholm. Ibsen, H.
Ross. Rattigan, T.
Rossum's universal robots. See Čapek, K. R.U.R.
Round dance. Schnitzler, A.
Royal family, The. Kaufman, G. and Ferber, E.
Royal hunt of the sun, The. Shaffer, P.
Royal slave, A. Bennett, C.
Royall master, The. Shirley, J.
Royster Doyster. See Udall, N. Ralph Roister Doister
Rudens, The. See Plautus, T. The rope
Rugged path, The. Sherwood, R.
Ruined family, The. Sundukiants, G.
Die Ruinerte familie. See Sundukiants, G. The ruined family
Rule a wife and have a wife. Fletcher, J.
Rumour, The. Munro, C.
Running dogs. Wexley, J.
Russian people, The. See Simonov, K. The Russians
Russians, The. Simonov, K.
Russkie lynde. See Simonov, K. The Russians
Rusty bugles. Elliott, S.
Rutherford and son. Sowerby, K.
Ruy Blas. Hugo, V.
Ruzzante returns from the wars. Beolco, A.

S

S. S. Tenacity. See Vildrac, C. Le paquebot Tenacity
Sabina. Montano, S.
Sabine woman, A. See Moody, W. The great divide
Sabrina fair. Taylor, S.
Sacking of Norman Banks, The. Ross, G.
Sacrifice of Isaac, The. See Anonymous plays. Abraham and Isaac; Anonymous plays. Abraham, Melchisedec and Isaac
Sad are the eyes of William Tell. Sastre, A.
Sad shepherd, The; or, A tale of Robin Hood. Jonson, B.
Safety match, The. Ginsbury, N.
La Sagra del signore della nave. See Pirandello, L. Our lord

of the ships
Sahdji, an African ballet. Bruce, R.
Sailor, beware! King, P. and Cary, F.
St. Claudia. Goold, M.
Saint Genesius. Rotrou, J.
Saint Genest. See Rotrou, J. Saint Genesius
St. George and the dragon. Anonymous plays
St. George play, Leicestershire. See Anonymous plays. Leicestershire St. George play
St. George play, The Oxfordshire. See Anonymous plays. The Oxfordshire St. George play
St. George plays. See Anonymous plays. Leicestershire St. George play; Anonymous plays. The Oxfordshire St. George play; Anonymous plays. The play of St. George, version reconstructed from memory by Thomas Hardy; Anonymous plays. St. George and the dragon
St. Helena. Sherriff, R. and De Casilis, J.
Saint Joan. Shaw, G.
Saint Joan of the stockyards. Brecht, B.
Saint John the evangelist. See Anonymous plays. John the evangelist
St. Louis woman. Bontemps, A. and Cullen, C.
Saint Nicholas and the image. See Hilarius. The miracle of Saint Nicholas and the image
Saint Nicholas and the schoolboys. See Anonymous plays. The miracle of Saint Nicholas and the schoolboys
Saint Nicholas and the three scholars. Anonymous plays
Saint Nicholas and the virgins. See Anonymous plays. The miracle of Saint Nicholas and the virgins
Saint of Bleecker Street, The. Menotti, G.
St. Patrick at Tara. Stephens, H.
Saint's day. Whiting, J.
Sakoontalā. See Kālidāsa. Shakuntalā
Sally Bowles. See Van Druten, J. I am a camera
Salome's head. Ortiz de Montellano, B.
Salutation and conception, The (Coventry). Anonymous plays
Salutation of Elizabeth, The (Wakefield). Anonymous plays
Salvation Nell; "Man's extremity is God's opportunity." Sheldon, E.
Salzburger grosse welttheater, Das. Hofmannsthal, H.
Sam average. MacKaye, P.
Same sky, The. Mitchell, Y.
Samfundets støtter. See Ibsen, H. Pillars of society
Samia. See Menander. The girl from Samos
Sam'l of Posen; or, The commercial drummer. Jessop, G.
Samson Agonistes. Milton, J.
Sandbox, The. Albee, E.
Sandcastle. Hite, B.
Sanibel and captiva. Terry, M.
Santos vega. Bayón Herrera, L.
Sappho. Grillparzer, F.
Sara und die Betz, Die. Wollenweber, L.
Satin slipper, The; or, The worst is not the worst. Claudel, P.
Satire of the three estates, The. Lindsay, D.
Saturday's children. Anderson, M.
Saul. Alfieri, V.
Saul. Du Ryer, P.
Saul le furieux. Taille, E.
Savages of America, The. See Rogers, R. Ponteach
Le savetier calbain. Anonymous plays
Savonarola. Nagle, U.

Say nothing. Hanley, J.
Scaevola. Du Ryer, P.
La scala. See Rosso di San Secondo, P. The stairs
Scapin. Molière, J.
Scarecrow, The. MacKaye, P.
Scenes from family life. Bermange, B.
Scenes from New York life and the Pacific railroad. See McCloskey, J. Across the continent
Scheme, The. Ogunyemi, W.
Le Schmürz. See Vian, B. The empire builders
School act, The. Anonymous plays
School for fathers, The. See Anouilh, J. Cecile
School for husbands. Molière, J.
School for pride, The. See Moreto y Cavaña, A. El desdén con el desdén
School for scandal, The. Sheridan, R.
Schrei aus der Strasse. See Lauckner, R. Cry in the street
Schubert's last serenade. Bovasso, J.
Scourge of Simony, The. See Anonymous plays. The return from Parnassus, pt. II
Scourging, The (Wakefield). Anonymous plays
Scrap of paper, A. See Sardou, V. Les pattes de mouche
Screens, The. Genêt, J.
Scuba Duba. Friedman, B.
Scyklon Z: But what have you done for me lately? or, Pure polemic. Lamb, M.
Sea fight. See Goering, R. Naval encounter
Sea-gull, The. Chekhov, A.
Seagulls over Sorrento. Hastings, H.
Sea horse, The. Moore, E.
Searching satyrs. Sophocles
Searching wind, The. Hellman, L.
Season in the sun. Gibbs, W.
Second lie, The. Mackay, I.
Second man, The. Behrman, S.
Second Mrs. Tanqueray, The. Pinero, A.
Second part of the return from Parnassus, The. See Anonymous plays. The return from Parnassus
Second play of the shepherds, The. See Anonymous plays. The second shepherds' play
Second shepherds' pageant, The. See Anonymous plays. The second shepherds' play (Wakefield)
Second shepherds' play, The (Wakefield). Anonymous plays
Second threshold. Barry, P.
Le secret. Bernstein, H.
Secret d'Arvers, Le. Bernard, J.
Secret service. Gillette, W.
Secretary bird, The. Home, W.
Secular masque, The. Dryden, J.
Secunda pastorum. See Anonymous plays. The second shepherds' play (Wakefield)
See Naples and die. Rice, E.
Seeker, The. McCauley, C.
Seeschlacht. See Goering, R. Naval encounter
Sei personaggi in cerca d'autore. See Pirandello, L. Six characters in search of an author
La seinte resureccion. Anonymous plays
Seiōbo. See Komparu-Zenchiku. The queen mother of the West
Sejanus, his fall. Jonson, B.
Sekidera Komachi. See Seami, M. Komachi at Sekidera
Self. Batemen, S.
Self avenger, The. See Terentius Afer, P. Heautontimorumenos
Self-tormentors, The. See

Terentius Afer, P. Heautontimorumenos
Selskabsrejsen. See Fischer, L. The mystery tour
Semimaru. Seami, M.
Sentinels, The; or, The two sergeants. Smith, R.
Separate tables. Rattigan, T.
Septem contra Thebas. See Aeschylus. The seven against Thebes
September lemonade. Denney, R.
Serenade, The. Jullien, J.
Serious charge. King, P.
Serjeant Musgrave's dance. Arden, J.
Serpent: a ceremony, The. Van Itallie, J.
Serpeinte, La. Moock Bousquet, A.
Sertorius; or, The Roman patriot. Brown, D.
Servant of two masters, The. Goldoni, C.
La servante de Palaisseau. Caigniez, L. and Baudouin, J. See Payne, J. Trial without jury
Service. Smith, D.
Il servitore di due padroni. See Goldoni, C. The servant of two masters
Settlers of Virginia, The. See Custis, G. Pocahontas
Seven against Thebes, The. Aeschylus
7-1/2 cents. See Abbott, G. and Bissell, R. The pajama game
Seven deadly sins of the lower middle classes, The. Brecht, B.
Seven keys to Baldpate. Cohan, G.
Seven year itch, The. Axelrod, G.
1776. Stone, P. and Edwards, S.
Seventh farce, The. Rueda, L.
Seventh seal, The. Bergman, I.
Severed head, A. Murdock, I. and Priestley, J.
Sganarelle. Molière, J.
Schachiapang. Anonymous plays
Shadow, The. Shvarts, E.
Shadow and substance. Carroll, P.
Shadow fisher, The. See Sarment, J. Le pêcheur d'ombres
Shadow of a gunman, The. O'Casey, S.
Shadow of doubt, The. King, N.
Shadow of heroes. See Ardrey, R. Stone and star
Shadow of suspicion. Hailey, A.
The shadow of the glen. Synge, J.
Shakespeare armoureux; ou, La pièce à l'étude. Duval, A. See Smith, R. Shakespeare in love
Shakespeare in love. Smith, R.
Shakuntalā. Kālidāsa
Shakuntalā and the ring of recognition. See Kālidāsa. Shakuntalā
Shakuntalā recognized by a ring-token. See Kālidāsa. Shakuntalā
Shall we join the ladies? Barrie, J.
Sham. Tompkins, F.
Sham doctor, The. See Ravenscroft, E. and Motteux, P. The anatomist
Sharon's grave. Keane, J.
Shaughraun, The. Boucicault, D.
She loves me. Masteroff, J.
She stoops to conquer; or, The mistakes of a night. Goldsmith, O.
She who was shorn. See Menander. The shearing of Glycera
She would be a soldier; or, The plains of Chippewa. Noah, M.
She would if she could. Etherege, G.
Shearing of Glycera, The. Menander
Sheep well, The. See Vega

Carpio, L. Fuente ovejuna
Shelter, The. Serling, R.
Shelter area. Boretz, N.
Shenandoah. Howard, B.
Shenandoah. Schwartz, D.
Shepherds, The. Goold, M.
Shepherds, The. See Anonymous plays. The second shepherds' play (Wakefield)
Shepherd's chameleon, The. See Ionesco, E. Improvisation
Shepherds' play, The (Coventry). Anonymous plays
Sheppey. Maugham, W.
Sherlock Holmes. Gillette, W.
Shetland sword dance. Anonymous plays
Shewing up of Blanco Posnet, The. Shaw, G.
Shifting heart, The. Beynon, R.
Shih wu kuan. See Anonymous plays. Fifteen strings of cash
Shining hour, The. Winter, J.
Shoemaker's holiday, The; or, The gentle craft. Dekker, T.
Shoemaker's prodigious wife, The. García Lorca, F.
Shōkun. Anonymous plays
Shoptalk. Turque, M.
Shore acres. Herne, J.
Short eyes. Piñero, M.
Show-off, The. Kelly, G.
Shred of evidence, A. Sherriff, R.
Shrike, The. Kramm, J.
Shrine in the fields, The. Anonymous plays
El sí de las niñas. Moratín, L.
Sicilian limes. Pirandello, L.
Die sieben todsunden der kleinbürger. See Brecht, B. The seven deadly sins of the lower middle classes
Siege, The. Clements, C.
Siege of Numantia, The. See Cervantes Saavedra, M. La Numancia
Siege of Rhodes, The. D'Avenant, W.
Siegfried. Giraudoux, J.
Siegfried's death. Hebbel, C.
No siempre lo peor es cierto. Calderón de la Barca, P.
Sign in Sidney Brustein's window, The. Hansberry, L.
Signet ring of Rakshasa, The. Vishakadatta
Signor Marc. Wilkins, J.
S'il vous plaît. See Breton, A. and Soupault, P. If you please
Silent knight, The. Wolfe, H.
Silent night, lonely night. Anderson, R.
Silent woman, The. See Jonson, B. Epicoene
Silver box, The. Galsworthy, J.
Silver cord, The. Howard, S.
Silver king, The. Jones, H.
Silver tassie, The. O'Casey, S.
Silver weddings. See Geraldy, P. The nest
Silver whistle, The. McEnroe, R.
Simon. Hines, L.
Simon and Laura. Melville, A.
Simon the leper. Anonymous plays
Simoom. See Lenormand, H. Le simoun
Le simoun. Lenormand, H.
Simple life, A. Ingham, R.
Simple spymen. Chapman, J.
Simply heaven. Hughes, L.
Singer, The. Pearse, P.
Singing birds. See Offenbach, J. La périchole
Singing valley. Niggli, J.
Sinner, The. See Guimerá, A. Daniela
Sinner beloved, A. Osgood, P.
Sir Courtley Nice; or, It cannot be. Crowne, J.
Sir Fopling Flutter. See Etherege, G. The man of mode
Sir Gyles Goosecappe. Anonymous plays
Sir John Oldcastle, pt. I. Anonymous plays
Sir Thomas More (An ill May-

day). Anonymous plays
Sister Cecilia. See Hastings, C. Bonaventure
Sisters, The. Chorell, W.
Sister's tragedy, The. Hughes, R.
Sit on the earth. Campbell, M. and Athas, D.
Siwan. Lewis, S.
Six characters in search of an author. Pirandello, L.
Six cylinder love. McGuire, W.
Six degrees of crime, The. Hill, F.
Six men of Dorset. Malleson, M. and Brooks, H.
Six of Calais, The. Shaw, G.
6 rms riv vu. Randall, B.
Sixteen. Stuart, A.
Sixty thousand nights. May, V.
Skin game, The. Galsworthy, J.
Skin of our teeth, The. Wilder, T.
Skipper next to God. Hartog, J.
Sky is green, The. Gear, B.
Skylark. Raphaelson, S.
Skyvers. Reckord, B.
Slander. See Echegaray y Eizaguirre, J. El gran Galeoto
Slaughter of the innocents, The. See Anonymous plays. The magi, Herod and the slaughter of the innocents
Slaughterhouse. Yankowitz, S.
Slave, The. Jones, L.
Slave with two faces, The. Davies, M.
Slaying of the innocents, The. Anonymous plays
Sleep of prisoners, A. Fry, C.
Sleuth. Shaffer, A.
Slight ache, A. Pinter, H.
Slipknot, The. See Plautus. Rudens
Slow dance on the killing ground. Hanley, W.
Small craft warnings. Williams, T.
Small hotel. Frost, R.
Smoke of the fatherland. Tur, L.; Tur, P. and Sheinen, L.
Der snob. See Sternheim, C. A place in the world
Snob, The. See Sternheim, C. A place in the world
Snow goose, The. Gallico, P.
Snow in mid-summer. Han-ching, K.
So ist das leben. See Wedekind, F. Such is life
Social success, A. Beerbohm, M.
Socialites, The. Jupp, K.
Society. Robertson, T.
Socrates. Bax, C.
Socrates. Voltaire, F.
Socrates wounded. Levinson, A.
Sodom and Gomorrah. Giraudoux, J.
Il sogno di Scipione. See Metastasio, P. The dream of Scipio
Soldier from the wars returning. Campton, D.
Soldier, soldier. Arden, J.
Soldier's fortune, The. See Lessing, G. Minna von Barnhelm
Soldier's wife. Franken, R.
Los soles truncos. See Marqués, R. The fanlights
Solid gold cadillac, The. Teichmann, H. and Kaufman, G.
Le solitaire. Pixérécourt, R. See Payne, J. Mount Savage
Solness, the master builder. See Ibsen, H. The master builder
Solon Shingle. Jones, J.
Somebody knows. Van Druten, J.
Something unspoken. Williams, T.
Sometimes even now. Chetham-Strode, W.
Son-in-law of M. Poirier, The. See Augier, E. and Sandeau, J. Le gendre de M. Poirier
Son, come home, A. Bullins, E.
Söndags promenaden. See

Forssell, L. The Sunday promenade
Song at twilight, A. Coward, N.
Song of a goat. Clark, J.
Song of songs. Giraudoux, J.
Song of songs which is Solomon's, The. Francis, A.
Song of the anvil. MacMahon, B.
Sons of Baldur, The. Scheffauer, H.
Sophonisaba. Mairet, J.
Sorrows of Han, The. Anonymous plays
Sorry, wrong number. Fletcher, L.
Søskende. See Branner, H. The judge
Sotoba Komachi. Kanze Kiyotsugu Kan'ami
Sought-for grave, The. Kanze Kiyotsugu Kan'ami
Soul gone home. Hughes, L.
Soul of Ch'ien-nu leaves her body, The. Chêng, T.
Souls and testamentary executors. Anonymous plays
Soul's revenge, The. See T'ang Hsien-tsu. Peony pavilion
Le soulier de satin: ou, La pire n'est pas toujours sûr. See Claudel, P. The satin slipper
Sound of murder, The. Fairchild, W.
Sounding shell, The. Krog, H.
South. Green, J.
South Pacific. Hammerstein, II, O.
Space fan, The. Schevill, J.
Spanish fryar, The; or, The double discovery. Dryden, J.
Spanish gipsie, The. Middleton, T. and Rowley, W.
Spanish husband, The; or, First and last love. Payne, J.
Spanish play, The. See Anonymous plays. The Wisemen
Spanish student, The. Longfellow, H.
Spanish tragedy, The; or, Hieronimo is mad again. Kyd, T.
Sparrow, The. Lopez, S.
Sparrow falls, A. Williams, H. and Williams, M.
Special providence. See Williams, H. and Williams, M. By accident
Speed the plough. Morton, T.
Das spiel vom deutschen bettelmann. Wiechert, E.
Spirochete. Sundgaard, A.
Spithead. Hale, J.
Spleen, The. See Payne, J. The black man
Splendid outcasts, The. Sisson, R.
Spogelses-sonaten. See Strindberg, A. The ghost sonata
Spook sonata, The. See Strindberg, A. The ghost sonata
Sport of my mad mother, The. Jellicoe, A.
Spreading the news. Gregory, I.
Spring for sure. McDonald, C. and Mason, W.
Springtime for Henry. Levy, B.
Spurt of blood, The. See Artaud, A. The jet of blood
Spy, The. Clinch, C.
Square of flowers, The. Ilyenkov, V.
Squaring the circle. Kataev, V.
Squaw man, The. Royle, E.
Squire Blue Boll. Barlach, E.
Squire of Alsatia, The. Shadwell, T.
Ssu fan. See Anonymous plays. Longing for worldly pleasures
Ssu Lang t'an mu. See Anonymous plays. Ssu Lang visits his mother
Ssu Lang visits his mother. Anonymous plays
Stable and the grove, The. Geddes, V.
Stage door. Kaufman, G. and Ferber, E.
Staircase. Dyer, C.
Stairs, The. Rosso di San Secondo, P.

Star, The (Bilsen play). Anonymous plays
Star of Seville, The. See Vega Carpio, L. La estrella de Sevilla
Star of the morning. Mitchell, L.
Starke mitteln. Rosen, J. See Daly, A. Needles and pins
Starter, The. Spence, E.
Star-wagon, The. Anderson, M.
State of the union. Lindsay, H. and Crouse, R.
Statue of Saint Nicholas, The. Hilarius
Steambath. Friedman, B.
Steamer Tenacity, The. See Vildrac, C. Le paquebot Tenacity
Steamship Tenacity, The. See Vildrac, C. Le paquebot Tenacity
Stella. Goethe, J.
Der Stellvertreter. See Hochhuth, R. The deputy
Stephen D. Leonard, H.
Step-in-the-hollow. MacDonagh, D.
Stichus. Plautus, T.
Sticks and bones. Rabe, D.
Still life. Molnár, F.
Stone and star. Ardrey, R.
Stone guest, The. Pushkin, A.
Stone guest, The. See also Molière, J. Don Juan
Stop him who can! See Reynolds, F. The dramatist
Stop it, whoever you are. Livings, H.
Stop the world--I want to get off. Bricusse, L. and Newley, A.
Stops. Auletta, R.
Stora landsvägen. See Strindberg, A. The great highway
Storm, The. See Ostrovskii, A. The thunderstorm
Storm operation. Anderson, M.
Storm within, The. See Cocteau, J. Intimate relations
Story of Louis Pasteur, The. Gibney, M. and Collings, P.
Story of Mary Surratt, The. Patrick, J.
Strange case of Dr. Jekyll and Mr. Hyde. Sieveking, L.
Straight and the Jew, The. Anonymous plays
Strange interlude. O'Neill, E.
Strange orchestra. Ackland, R.
Stranger, The. Kotzebue, A.
Strangler, The. Powell, A.
Stranglers of Paris, The. Belasco, D.
Stratagem of interlocking rings. Anonymous plays
Strayed reveler, The. Arnold, M.
Street scene. Rice, E.
Street singer, The. Echegaray y Eizaguirre, J.
Streetcar named desire, A. Williams, T.
Strictly dishonorable. Sturges, P.
Strictly matrimony. Hill, E.
Strife. Galsworthy, J.
Strings, my Lord, are false, The. Carroll, P.
Strong are lonely, The. Hochwalder, F.
Strongbox, The. Sternheim, C.
Stronger, The. See Strindberg, A. The stronger woman
Stronger are lonely, The. Hochenwälder, F.
Stronger woman, The. Strindberg, A.
Styopic and Manya. Evreinov, N.
Subject of scandal and concern, A. Osborne, J.
Subject was roses, The. Gilroy, F.
Submerged. See Gorki, M. [pseud.] The lower depths
Subscription list, The. Namiki Gohei III.
Subscription scroll, The. See Namiki Gohei III. The subscription list

Success. Milne, A.
Success story. Lawson, J.
Successful life of three, The. Fornés, M.
Such is life. Pirandello, L.
Such is life. Wedekind, F.
Such men are dangerous. Dukes, A.
Such stuff as dreams are made of. See Calderón de la Barca, P. La vida es sueño
Sud. See Green, J. South
Suddenly last summer. Williams, T.
Sugar cane. Wilson, F.
Suicide, The. Fratti, M.
Suicide, The. Freeman, C.
Suicide prohibited in springtime. Rodríguez Alvarez, A.
Il suicidio. See Fratti, M. The suicide
Suitors, The. See Racine, J. Les plaideurs
Summer and smoke. Williams, T.
Summer of the 17th doll. Lawler, R.
Summer ghost, A. Fredericks, C.
Summertime. Cowen, R.
Summoning of Everyman, The. See Anonymous plays. Everyman
Sun. Kennedy, A.
Sunday morning in the south. Jackson, G.
Sunday promenade, The. Forssell, L.
Sunken bell, The. Hauptmann, G.
Sunny morning, A. See Alvarez Quintero, S. and Alvarez Quintero, J. A bright morning
Sunshine boys, The. Simon, N.
Sunshine follows rain. See Girardin, D. La joie fait peur
Sunshine through the clouds. See Girardin, D. La joie fait peur
Sun-up. Vollmer, L.
Superstition. Barker, J.
Supper for the dead. Green, P.
Supper of pranks, The. See Benelli, S. The jest
Suppliant maidens, The. See Aeschylus. The suppliants
Suppliant women, The. See Euripides. The suppliants
Suppliants, The. Aeschylus
Suppliants, The. Euripides
Supposes. Gascoigne, G.
Suppositi, I. Ariosto. See Gascoigne, G. Supposes
Survey of the sciences, A. Davenport, R.
Susan and God. Crothers, R.
Suspecting truth, The. See Ruiz de Alarcón y Mendoza, J. La verdad sospechosa
Suspicious husband, The. Hoadly, B.
Svadba. See Chekhov, A. A wedding
Den svåra stunden, I-III. See Lagerkvist, P. The difficult hour, I-III
Swan, The. Molnár, F.
Swan song, The. Chekhov, A.
Swedenhielms, The. Bergman, H.
Sweeney Agonistes. Eliot, T.
Sweet bird of youth. Williams, T.
Sweet eros. McNally, T.
Sweethearts. Gilbert, W. and Sullivan, A.
Sword and queue. Gutzkow, K.
Sword of the Samurai, The. Mygatt, T.
Systrarna. See Chorell, W. The sisters

T

Table number seven. Rattigan, T.
Le tableau. See Ionesco, E. The painting
Tails up. Roberts, C.
Take a giant step. Peterson, L.
Taking Tiger Mountain by

strategy. Anonymous plays
Tale of mystery, A. Holcroft, T.
Tale of Robin Hood, A. See Jonson, B. The sad shepherd
Talents, The (Wakefield). Anonymous plays
Tales of Hoffman, The. Levine, M.; McNamee, G.; and Greenberg, D.
Talk to me like the rain and let me listen. Williams, T.
Tamburlaine the great. Marlowe, C.
Taming of the shrew, The. Shakespeare, W.
Tancred and Gismund; or, Gismond of Salerne. Wilmot, R.
Tancred King of Sicily; or, The archives of Palermo. Stone, J.
Tango. Slawomir, M.
Tango palace. Fornés, M.
Tanikō. See Anonymous plays. The valley rite
Tantris the fool. See Hardt, E. Tristram the jester
Tarnish. Pottle, E.
Tartuffe. See Molière, J. Le Tartuffe
Le Tartuffe; ou, L'imposteur. Molière, J.
Taste of honey, A. Delaney, S.
Taxes. Tolstoi, L.
Ta'ziya. See Anonymous plays. The martyrdom of Ali
Tchin-Tchin. Michaels, S.
Tes and sympathy. Anderson, R.
Tea for three. Locher, J.
Teahouse of the August moon, The. Patrick, J.
Tegue O. Divelly, The Irish priest. See Shadwell, T. The Lancashire witches and Tegue O. Divelly, the Irish priest
La tejedora de sueños. See Vallejo, A. The dream weaver
Telescope, The. Sherriff, R.
Temp. See Pogodin, N. Tempo
Temperance town, A. Hoyt, C.
Tempest, The. Shakespeare, W.
Tempest, The; or, The enchanted island. D'Avenant, W. and Dryden, J.
Tempo. Pogodin, N.
Le temps est un songe. See Lenormand, H. Time is a dream
Ten-minute alibi. Willis, A.
Ten nights in a bar-room. Pratt, W.
Tender trap, The. Shulman, M. and Smith, R.
Tenor, The. See Wedekind, F. Der kammersänger
Tenth man, The. Chayefsky, P.
Teresa of Avila. Williamson, H.
Test of fire, The. See Kleist, H. Kaethchen of Heilbronn; or, The test of fire
Tête-à-tête. Fulda, L.
Des Teufels General. See Zuckmayer, C. The devil's general
Texas steer, A; or, "Money makes the mare go." Hoyt, C.
Textiles. Anderson, S.
Thank you, Miss Victoria. Hoffman, W.
That champion season. Miller, J.
Theatre of the soul, The. Evreinov, N.
Their very own and golden city. Wesker, A.
Then... Campton, D.
Then and now. Chekhov, A.
There are crimes and crimes. Strindberg, A.
There shall be no night. Sherwood, R.
There's a girl in my soup. Frisby, T.
There's always Juliet. Van Druten, J.

There's no room for you here for a start. Livings, H.
Thérèse Raquin. Zola, E.
Thérèse, the orphan of Geneva. Payne, J.
Thersites. Anonymous plays
These cornfields. Courteline, G.
They came by night. Lyndon, B.
They came to the city. Priestley, J.
They fly through the air. Corwin, N.
They knew what they wanted. Howard, S.
They shall not die. Wexley, J.
They that sit in darkness. Burrill, M.
Thieves' carnival. Anouilh, J.
Thing itself, The. Sainer, A.
Third person. Rosenthal, A.
Thirteenth chair, The. Veiller, B.
37 sous of M. Montaudoin, The. See Labiche, E. and Martin, E. Les trente-sept sous de M. Montaudoin
Thirty years; or, The gambler's fate. Dunlap, W.
This bondage. Popplewell, O.
This bored world. See Pailleron, E. Le monde où l'on s'ennuie
This bull ate nutmeg. Niggli, J.
This earth is ours. Kozlenko, W.
This gentle ghost. See Patrick, J. The story of Mary Surratt
This year, next year. Ronder, J.
Thistle and the rose, The. Horne, W.
Thomas Cranmer of Canterbury. Williams, C.
Thomas Jefferson. See Kingsley, S. The patriots
Thomas, Lord Cromwell. Anonymous plays
Thomas Muskerry. Colum, P.
Thomas of India (Wakefield). Anonymous plays
Thomas of Woodstock. See Anonymous plays. Woodstock
Thompson's vacation. Lardner, R.
Those familiar spirits. See Miller, A. The crucible
Those golden gates fall down. Watson, H.
Thousand clowns, A. Gardner, H.
Three beach plays. Vodāhovic, S.
Three cuckolds, The. Anonymous plays
Three daughters of M. Dupont, The. See Brieux, E. Les trois filles de M. Dupont
3 filosofers in a firetower. Collins, M.
Three-fold path, The. Rye, E.
Three kings' play (Oberufer), The. Anonymous plays
Three Maries, The. Anonymous plays
Three men on a horse. Holm, J. and Abbott, G.
Three miles to Poley. Lynch, H.
Three months gone. Howarth, D.
Three penny day, The. Plautus, T.
Three pieces of money, The. See Plautus, T. The three penny day
Three sisters. See Chekhov, A. The three sisters
Three sisters, The. Chekhov, A.
Three top hats. Mihura, M.
Three weddings of a hunchback. Borsook, H.
Three X love. Zuber, R.
Three penny opera, The. Brecht, B.
Thrice promised bride, The. Hsiung, C.
Thunder. See Ostrovskiǐ, A. The thunder storm
Thunder-bolt, The. Pinero, A.
Thunder on Sycamore Street. Rose, R.

Thunder rock. Ardrey, R.
Thunderstorm, The. Ostrovskiĭ, A.
Thurber carnival, A. Thurber, J.
Thursday evening. Morley, C.
Thy will be done. Gallarati-Scotti, T.
Thyestes. Seneca, L.
Ticket-of-leave man, The. Taylor, T.
Ticklish acrobat, The. Hivnor, R.
Tide tarrieth no man, The. Wapull, G.
Tidings brought to Mary, The. See Claudel, P. L'annonce faite à Marie
Tidy passions, or kill kaleidoscope, kill. Koutoukas, H.
Tiger at the gates. Giraudoux, J.
Till the day I die. Odets, C.
Time and again. See Duerrenmatt, F. The visit
Time is a dream. Lenormand, H.
Time limit. Denker, H. and Berkey, R.
Time of the cuckoo, The. Laurents, A.
Time of your life, The. Saroyan, W.
Timocrate. See Corneille, T. Timocrates
Timocrates. Corneille, T.
Timon of Athens. Shakespeare, W.
Tinker, The. Dobie, L. and Sloman, R.
Tinker's curse. Corlett, W.
Tiny Alice. Albee, E.
Tiridate. Campistron, J.
'Tis a pity she's a whore. Ford, J.
'Tis all a notion. See Bird, R. 'Twas all for the best
Titus Andronicus. Shakespeare, W.
To Damascus, part 1. Strindberg, A.
To Dorothy, a son. MacDougall, R.
To love and to cherish. Egan, M.
To see ourselves. De La Pasture, E.
To the ladies! Kaufman, G. and Connelly, M.
To traade. See Soya, C. Two threads
Tobacco road. Kirkland, J. and Caldwell, E.
Tobias and Sara. Claudel, P.
Tobias and the angel. Mavor, O.
Die tochter Pharaonis. See Kotzebue, A. Pharaoh's daughter
Der tod des Tizian. See Hofmannsthal, H. von. The death of Titian
Toe jam. Jackson, E.
Toiler's trials, The. See Steele, S. The crock of gold
Toilet, The. Jones, L.
Tom Cobb. Gilbert, W.
Tom Thumb the great. See Fielding, H. The tragedy of tragedies
Tom Tyler and his wife. Anonymous plays
Tomb beneath the Arc de Triomphe, The. See Raynal, P. Le tombeau sous l'Arc de triomphe
Le tombeau sous l'Arc de triomphe. Raynal, P.
Tomorrow and tomorrow. Barry, P.
Tomorrow the world. Gow, J. and D'Usseau, A.
Tonight we improvise. Pirandello, L.
Too late to call backe yesterday. Davenport, R.
Top of the ladder. Guthrie, T.
Der tor und der tod. Hofmannsthal, H. von
Torch race, The. See Hervieu, P. La course du flambeau
Torioibune. See Kongō Yagorō. The bird-scaring boat
Torquato Tasso. Goethe, J.
Tortesa, the usurer. Willis, N.

Totentanz. Anonymous plays
Tottenham Court. Nabbes, T.
Touch it light. Storey, R.
Touch of the poet, A. O'Neill, E.
Touch wood. Smith, D. G.
Tour. McNally, T.
Tous contre tous. See Adamov, A. All against all
Tovarich. Deval, J.
Tower, The. Porter, H.
Tower, The. Weiss, P.
Tower of Babel, The. Goodman, P.
Town of Titipu, The. See Gilbert, W. and Sullivan, A. The mikado
Towneley play, The. Anonymous plays
Toy cart, The. See Shudraka. The little clay cart
Toys in the attic. Hellman, L.
Trachiniae, The. Sophocles
Tragedy of a tenant farm woman. See Green, P. and Green, E. Fixin's: The tragedy of a tenant farm woman
Tragedy of Antony and Cleopatra, The. See Shakespeare, W. Antony and Cleopatra
Tragedy of Hamlet, Prince of Denmark, The. See Shakespeare, W. Hamlet
Tragedy of Jane Shore, The. Rowe, N.
Tragedy of King Lear, The. See Shakespeare, W. King Lear
Tragedy of King Richard II, The. See Shakespeare, W. King Richard II
Tragedy of King Richard III, The. See Shakespeare, W. King Richard III
Tragedy of love, The. Heiberg, G.
Tragedy of Macbeth, The. See Shakespeare, W. Macbeth
Tragedy of Mustapha, the son of Solyman the magnificent. Orrery, R.
Tragedy of Nero. Anonymous plays
Tragedy of Othello, The. See Shakespeare, W. Othello, The Moor of Venice
Tragedy of Pompey the great, The. Masefield, J.
Tragedy of the Duchess of Malfi. See Webster, J. The Duchess of Malfi
Tragedy of tragedies, The; or, The life and death of Tom Thumb the great. Fielding, H.
Tragedy or interlude manifesting the chief promises of God unto man, A. See Bale, J. God's promises
Tragedy rehearsed, A. See Sheridan, R. The critic
Tragi-comedy of Calisto and Melibea, The. See Rojas, F. Celestina
Tragical history of the life and death of Doctor Faustus, The. See Marlowe, C. The tragical history of Doctor Faustus
Tragical history of Doctor Faustus, The. Marlowe, C.
Tragicomedia de Calixto y Melibea. See Rojas, F. Celestina
Tragidie of [Gorboduc; or of] Ferrex and Porrex, The. See Sackville, T. and Norton, T. Gorboduc
Trail of the torch, The. See Hervieu, P. La course du flambeau
Train to H... Bellido, J.
Traitor, The. Shirley, J.
Traitor, The. Wilde, P.
Transcending. Cregan, D.
Transfiguration. Toller, E.
Transformation. See Toller, E. Transfiguration
Translation of John Snaith, The. Cooke, B.
Trapolin's vagaries. See Tate, N. A duke and no duke
Trappolin suppos'd a prince. Cokain, A. See Tate, N. A duke and no duke

Traum ein leben, Der. Grillparzer, F.
Li tre becchi. See Anonymous plays. The three cuckolds
Tre maa man vaere. See Locher, J. Tea for three
Tread the green grass. Green, P.
Trelawny. Woods, A. and Rowell, G.
Trelawny of the "Wells." Pinero, A.
Tren a F... See Bellido, J. Train to H...
Trente ans; ou, La vie d'un joueur. Goubaux, P. and Ducange, V. See Dunlap, W. Thirty years
Les trente-sept sous de M. Montaudoin. Labiche, E. and Martin, E.
Tres clerici. See Anonymous plays. Saint Nicholas and the three scholars
Tres sombreros de copa. See Mihura, M. Three top hats
Trespassers. Reid, L.
Trial and error. Horne, K.
Trial horse no. 1: Many loves. Williams, W.
Trial of Atticus before Judge Beau, for a rape, The. Anonymous plays
Trial of Christ, The (Coventry). Anonymous plays
Trial of the Catonsville nine, The. Berrigan, D.
Trial of treasure, The. Anonymous plays
Trial without jury; or, The magpie and the maid. Payne, J.
Trick to catch the old one, A. Middleton, T.
Trickster, The. See Plautus. Pseudolus
Trickster of Seville, The. See Téllez, G. El burlador de Sevilla
Trickster of Seville and his guest of stone, The. See Téllez, G. El burlador de Sevilla
Trifles. Glaspell, S.
Trigon, The. Lynne, J.
Trinummus. See Plautus, T. The three penny day
Trip abroad, A. See Labiche, E. and Martin, E. Le voyage de Monsieur Perrichon
Trip to Chinatown, A; or, Idyl of San Francisco. Hoyt, C.
Trip to Niagara; or, Travellers in America, A. Dunlap, W.
Trip to Niagara, A. See also Bird, R. News of the night
Triple-A plowed under. Staff of the Living Newspaper
Tristram the jester. Hardt, E.
Triumph at Plattsburg, The. Smith, R.
Triumph of Bohemia, The. Stirling, G.
Triumph of prejudice, The. See Mérimée, P. Ines Mendo
Troades. See Euripides. The Trojan women; Seneca, L. The Trojan women
Troilus and Cressida. Shakespeare, W.
Les trois filles de M. Dupont. Brieux, E.
Trojan horse, The. MacLeish, A.
Trojan women, The. Euripides
Trojan women, The. Seneca, L.
Trouble in mind. Childress, A.
Trouble in the works. Pinter, H.
Trouble with reason, The. Griboîedov, A.
Troublesome reign and lamentable death of Edward the second, The. Marlowe, C.
Truculentus. Plautus, T.
True and honorable historie of the life of Sir John Oldcastle, the good Lord Cobham, The. See Anonymous plays. Sir John Oldcastle, pt. I
True chronicle history of the whole life and death of Thomas Lord Cromwell, The.

See Anonymous plays. Thomas Lord Cromwell
Truth, The. Fitch, C.
Truth about Blayds, The. Milne, A.
Truth suspected, The. See Ruiz de Alarcón y Mendoza, J. La verdad sospechosa
Try! Try! O'Hara, F.
Tryall of chevalry, The. Anonymous plays
Trysting-place, The. Tarkington, B.
Tsar Fyodor Ivánovitch. Tolstoĭ, A.
Tumult and the shouting, The. Pawley, T.
Turandot. Gozzi, C.
Turcaret. Le Sage, A.
Der Turm. See Weiss, P. The tower
'Twas all for the best; or, 'Tis all a notion. Bird, R.
Twelfth night; or, What you will. Shakespeare, W.
Twelve angry men. Rose, R.
Twelve months. Marshak, S.
Twelve-pound look, The. Barrie, J.
Twenty-fourth of February, The. See Werner, F. Der vierundzwanzigste Februar
27 wagons full of cotton. Williams, T.
Twilight crane. Konoshita, J.
Twin brothers, The. See Plautus, T. The Menaechmi
Twin Menaechmi, The. See Plautus, T. The Menaechmi
Twisting of the rope, The. Hyde, D.
Two angry women of Abington, The. See Porter, H. The pleasant history of the two angry women of Abington
Two bacchides, The. Plautus, T.
Two blind mice. Spewack, S.
Two bouquets, The. Farjeon, E. and Farjeon, H.
Two crooks and a lady. Pillot, E.
Two for the see-saw. Gibson, W.
Two gentlemen of Verona, The. Shakespeare, W.
Two noble kinsmen, The. Fletcher, J. and Shakespeare, W.
Two orphans, The. D'Ennery, A. and Cormon, E.
Two roses. Albery, J.
Two sergeants, The. See Smith, R. The sentinels
Two shepherds, The. Martínez Sierra, G. and Martínez Sierra, M.
Two sides of the door. Cropper, M.
Two sons-in-law, The. Payne, J.
Two thieves, The. Bates, E.
Two threads. Soya, C.
2 x 2 = 5. Wied, G.
Typists, The. Schisgal, M.
Tyranny of love, The. See Porto-Riche, G. Amoureuse
Tyranny of tears, The. Chambers, C.
Tzu forwitsich. Wieand, P.

U

Ubu Roi. See Jarry, A. King Ubu
Ubu the king. See Jarry, J., King Ubu
Ugly duckling, The. Milne, A.
Uh, uh, but how do it free us? Sánchez, S.
Ultimo. Moser, G. von. See Daly, A. The big bonanza
Ulysses in Nighttown. Barkentin, M.
Umbrian play, The. Anonymous plays
Un geste pour un autre. See Tardieu, J. One way for another
Unaccompanied cello. Harrison, J.
Uncertain joy. Hastings, C.
Unchastened woman, The. Anspacher, L.
Uncle Harry. Job, T.

Uncle Tom's cabin. Aiken, G.
Uncle Vanya. Chekhov, A.
Uncle's been dreaming. Vollmöller, K.
Under cover. Megrue, R.
Under milk wood. Thomas, D.
Under the gaslight. Daly, A.
Under the sycamore tree. Spewack, S.
Underpants, The. Sternheim, C.
Undertow. Spence, E.
Unexpected guests, The. Howells, W.
Uniform of flesh. See Coxe, L. and Chapman, R. Billy Budd
United family, A. Prévert, J.
Unknown Chinaman, The. Bernard, K.
Unknown soldier and his wife, The. Ustinov, P.
Unknown warrior, The. See Raynal, P. Le tombeau sous l'Arc de triomphe
Unman, Wittering and Zigo. Cooper, G.
Unter vier augen. See Fulda, L. Tête-à-tête
Until the monkey comes. Herndon, V.
Unto such glory. Green, P.
Upper room, The. Benson, R.
Urvashi won by valour. See Kālidāsa. Vikramorvacie
Usurper, The; or, Americans in Tripoli. Jones, J.

V

Vagabond King, The. See McCarthy, J. If I were king
Vale of content, The. Sudermann, H.
Valiant, The. Hall, H. and Middlemass, R.
Valley Forge. Anderson, M.
Valley rite, The. Anonymous plays
La valse de toréadors. See Anouilh, J. The waltz of the toreadors
Vasco. Schéhadé, G.
Venceslas. See Rotrou, J. Wenceshaus
La venda en los ojos. See López Rubio, J. The blindfold
Venetian, The. Bax, C.
Venice preserv'd; or, A plot discover'd. Otway, T.
Il ventaglio. See Goldoni, C. The fan
Venus and Adonis. Obey, A.
Venus observed. Fry, C.
La verdad sospechosa. Ruiz de Alarcón y Mendoza, J.
Die Verfolgung und Ermordung Jean Paul Marats dargestellt durch die Schauspielgruppe des Hospizes zu Charenton unter anleitung des Herrn de Sade. See Weiss, P. The persecution and assassination of Jean-Paul Marat as performed by the inmates of the Asylum of Charenton under the direction of the Marquis de Sade
Verhor des Lukullus, Das. Brecht, B.
Le véritable Saint Genest. See Rotrou, J. Saint Genesius
Le verre d'eau. Scribe, A.
Verrechelte rechler, Die. Barba, P.
Die versunkene glocke. See Hauptmann, G. The sunken bell
Very special baby, A. Aurthur, R.
Vespae. See Aristophanes. The wasps
Vested interests. See Benavente y Martínez, J. The bonds of interest
Vestire gl'ignudi. See Pirandello, L. Naked
Viceroy Sarah. Ginsbury, N.
Victoria Regina. Housman, L.
Victors, The. Sartre, J.
La vida es sueño. Calderón de la Barca, P.
La vie d'un joueur. Goubaux, P. and Ducange, V. See Dunlap, W. Thirty years

El viejo celoso. See Cervantes Saavedra, M. The jealous old man
Das vierte gebot. Anzengruber, L.
Der vierundzwanzigste Februar. Werner, F.
View from the bridge, A. Miller, A.
Vigilant sentinel, The. Cervantes Saavedra, M.
Vikramorvacie; or, The hero and the nymph. Kālidāsa
Vikramorvashiya. See Kālidāsa Vikramorvacie
Vildanden. See Ibsen, H. The wild duck
Violin maker of Cremona, The. Coppée, F.
Virgin goddess, The. Besier, R.
Virginian, The. Campbell, B.
Virginius. Knowles, J.
Virtue in danger. See Vanbrugh, J. The relapse
Vision of delight, The. Jonson, B.
Vision of the twelve goddesses, The. Daniel, S.
Vision of Vāsavadatta, The. Bhāsa.
Visionary forms, The. Eberhart, R.
Visions of sugar plums. Pritchard, B.
Visit, The. Duerrenmatt, F.
Visit to a small planet. Vidal, G.
La visite de la vieille dame. See Duerrenmatt, F. The visit
Visiting house, The. Molloy, M.
Visitor from Forest Hills. See Simon, H. Plaza suite
Visitor from Hollywood. See Simon, N. Plaza suite
Visitor from Mamaroneck. See Simon, N. Plaza suite
La vita che ti diedi. See Pirandello, L. Such is life
Vittoria Corombona. See Webster, J. The white devil
Vivat! Vivat! Regina. Bolt, R.
Le voeu. See Buchanan, G. Jephté; ou, Le voeu
Voice of the turtle, The. Van Druten, J.
Volpone. Zweig, S.
Volpone; or, The fox. Jonson, B.
Von morgens bis mitternachts. See Kaiser, G. From morn to midnight
Vortex, The. Coward, N.
Vortigern. Ireland, W.
Le voyage de M. Perrichon. Labiche, E. and Martin, E.
Voysey inheritance, The. Granville-Barker, H.
Vultures, The. See Becque, H. Les corbeaux

W

Wages for wives. See Bolton, G. Chicken feed
Wagon-lits. Morley, C.
Waiting for Gillian. Miller, R.
Waiting for Godot. Beckett, S.
Waiting for Lefty. Odets, C.
Waiting Room, The. Bowen, J.
Wakefield nativity. See Anonymous plays. The second shepherds' play
Wakefield plays. See Anonymous plays. Abraham; The annunciation; The ascension of the Lord; The betrayal; The buffeting; Caesar Augustus; Coliphazacio; The conspiracy; The creation; The crucifixion; The deliverance of souls; The deluge; The first shepherds' play; The flight into Egypt; The hanging of Judas; The harrowing of Hell; Herod the great; Isaac; Jacob; John the Baptist; The judgment; The killing of Abel; Lazarus; Magnus Herodes; Noah; The offering of the Magi; Pharaoh; The pilgrims; The play of the doctors; The procession of the prophets;

Processus noe cum filiis; The purification of Mary; The resurrection of Christ; The salutation of Elizabeth; The scourging; The second shepherds' play; The talents; Thomas of India
Wakefield second nativity play, The. See Anonymous plays. The second shepherds' play
Walk hard. Hill, A.
Walking through seaweed. Finley, I.
Wallenstein. See Schiller, J. The camp of Wallenstein; Schiller, J. The death of Wallenstein
Wallensteins lager. See Schiller, J. The camp of Wallenstein
Wallensteins tod. See Schiller, J. The death of Wallenstein
Walls of Jericho, The. Sutro, A.
Waltz of the toreadors, The. Anouilh, J.
Wandering Jew, The. Hutchins, M.
Wandering scholar and exorcist, The. See Sachs, H. Raising the devil
Wandering scholar from Paradise, The. Sachs, H.
Wandlung. See Toller, E. Transfiguration
War, a Te Deum. Hauptmann, C.
Warning--a theme for Linda, The. Milner, R.
Warrens of Virginia, The. De Mille, W.
Washington Square. See Goetz, R. and Goetz, A. The heiress
Washtub, The. Anonymous plays
Wasps, The. Aristophanes
Waste. Granville-Barker, H.
Waste disposal unit, The. Brophy, B.
Watch it, sailor! King, P. and Cary, F.
Watch on the Rhine. Hellman, L.
Watchmaker and the hen. See Kocherga, I. Masters of time
Water upon fire. Morselli, E.
Waters of the moon. Hunter, N.
Wax museum, The. Hawkes, J.
Way of the world, The. Congreve, W.
Way to keep him, The. Murphy, A.
Ways and means. Coward, N.
We are besieged. Acheson, S.
We find the bunyip. Mathew, R.
We hold these truths. Corwin, N.
We own the night. Garrett, J.
We righteous bombers. Bass, K.
We, the people. Rice, E.
Wealth. See Aristophanes. Plutus
Wealth and health. Anonymous plays
Weather breeder, The. Denison, M.
Weavers, The. Hauptmann, G.
Die weber. See Hauptmann, G. The weavers
Wedding, A. Chekhov, A.
Wedding, The. See Barry, P. Paris bound
Wedding, The. Shirley, J.
Wedding bells. Field, E.
Wedding day. See Ronder, J. This year, next year
Wedding march, The. See Labiche, E. and Michel, M. An Italian straw hat
Wedding on the Eiffel Tower, The. See Cocteau, J. Les mariés de la Tour Eiffel
Wednesday's child. Atlas, L.
Weekend in May. See Gow, R. The Edwardians
Weevil, The. See Plautus, T. Curculio
Der weisse heiland. See Hauptmann, G. The white saviour
Well, The. McKinney, J.
Well of the saints, The. Synge, W.

Well-remembered voice, A. Barrie, J.
Wenceshaus. Rotrou, J.
Wept of the wish-ton-wish, The. Anonymous plays
West chamber, The. Wang Shih-fu
West Indian, The. Cumberland, R.
What a life. Goldsmith, C.
What every woman knows. Barrie, J.
What if it had turned up heads? Gaines, J.
What men live by. Church, V.
What price glory? Anderson, M. and Stallings, L.
What the butler saw. Orton, J.
What you will. See Shakespeare, W. Twelfth night
Whelks and the cromium, The. Sanford, J.
When a girl says yes. See Moratín, L. El sí de las niñas
When ladies meet. Crothers, R.
When roses bloom again. Marquina, E.
When we dead awaken. See Ibsen, H. Ghosts
When you comin' back, Red Ryder? Medoff, M.
Where has Tommy Flowers gone? McNally, T.
Where is de queen? Van Itallie, J.
Where the cross is made. O'Neill, E.
Where the dear antelope play. Rogers, J.
White château, The. Berkeley, R.
White devil, The; or, Vittoria Corombona. Webster, J.
White dresses. Green, P.
White haired girl, The. Yi, T. and Ching-chih, H.
White House murder case, The. Feiffer, J.
White liars. See Shaffer, P. White lies
White lies. Shaffer, P.
White redeemer, The. See Hauptmann, G. The white saviour
White saviour, The. Hauptmann, G.
White slave, The. Campbell, B.
White steed, The. Carroll, P.
White whore and the bit player, The. Eyen, T.
Whiteheaded boy, The. Robinson, L.
Whither goest thou? Currie, C.
Who goes there! Dighton, J.
"Who ride on white horses," the story of Edmund Campion. Breen, R. and Schnibbe, H.
Whole truth, The. Mackie, P.
Who's afraid of Virginia Woolf? Albee, E.
Who's got his own. Milner, R.
Who's happy now. Hailey, O.
Why marry? Williams, J.
Why not? Williams, J.
Wicked cooks, The. Grass, G.
Widow of Watling street, The. See Anonymous plays. The puritan
Widowers' houses. Shaw, G.
Wife, The. Belasco, D. and De Mille, H.
Wife at a venture, A. Smith, R.
Wild birds. Totheroh, D.
Wild Decembers. Ashton, W.
Wild duck, The. Ibsen, H.
Wild-goose chase, The. Fletcher, J.
Wild horse of Tartary, The. See Payne, J. Mazeppa
Wilhelm Tell. See Schiller, J. William Tell
Will and no will, A. Macklin, C.
Will, The. Barrie, J.
Will this earth hold? Buck, P.
William Penn. Smith, R.
William Tell. Schiller, J.
William Tell has sad eyes. See Sastre, A. Sad are the eyes of William Tell

William the defeated. Jameson, S.
Willie Rough. Bryden, B.
Willie the germ. Mednick, M.
Wind and the rain, The. Hodge, M.
Window, The. Marcus, F.
Wine in the wilderness. Childress, A.
Winged victory. Hart, M.
Wingless victory, The. Anderson, M.
Wings of the dove, The. Taylor, C.
Wings over Europe. Nichols, R. and Browne, M.
Winslow boy, The. Rattigan, T.
Winter journey, A. See Odets, C. Country wife
Winter soldiers. James, D.
Winter's tale, The. Shakespeare, W.
Winterset. Anderson, M.
Wisdom of Dr. Dodypoll, The. Anonymous plays
Wisdom; or, Mind, will, and understanding. See Anonymous plays. Mind, will, and understanding
Wisdom tooth, The. Connelly, M.
Wise virgins and the foolish virgins, The. Anonymous plays
Wisemen [The Spanish play], The. Anonymous plays
Wish, The. Sigurjónsson, J.
Wish you were here. Kobler, A. and Logan, J.
Wisteria trees, The. Logan, J.
Wit and science. See Anonymous plays. The marriage of wit and science; Redford, J. The play of wit and science
Wit and wisdom. See Anonymous plays. The contract of marriage between wit and wisdom
Wit works woe. Griboîedov, A.
Witch of Edmonton, The. Ford, J., Dekker, T., and Rowley, W.
Witches' mountain, The. Sánchez Gardel, J.
Witches' sabbath, The. Benavente y Martínez, J.
Witching hour, The. Thomas, A.
With intent. Williams, H. and Williams, M.
With malice aforethought. Stranack, J.
Within an inch of his life. Herne, J.
Within the law. Veiller, B.
Witness for the prosecution. Christie, A.
Wits, The. D'Avenant, W.
Wives metamorphos'd, The. See Jevon, T.; Coffey, C.; Mottley, J. and Cibber, T. The devil to pay
Woe from wit. See Griboîedov, A. Wit works woe
Wolf-hunt, The. Verga, G.
Die Wölff. See Brust, A. The wolves
Wolves, The. Brust, A.
Woman and the walnut tree, The. Box, S.
Woman is a weathercock. Field, N.
Woman killed with kindness, A. Heywood, T.
Woman of Andros, The. Terentius Afer, P.
Woman of no importance, A. Wilde, O.
Woman of Paris, The. See Becque, H. La Parisienne
Woman of Samos. See Menander. The girl from Samos
Woman taken in adultery, The. (N. town). Anonymous plays
Woman too many, A. Sønderby, K.
Woman's craze for titles. Dancourt, F.
Woman's revenge. Payne, J.
Women, The. Boothe, C.
Women, beware women. Middleton, T.

Women celebrating the Thesmophoria, The. See Aristophanes. Thesmophoriazusae
Women have their way, The. See Alvarez Quintero, S. and Alvarez Quintero, J. The women's town
Women of Trachis, The. See Sophocles. The Trachiniae
Women's representative, The. Yu, S.
Women's town, The. Alvarez Quintero, S. and Alvarez Quintero, J.
Won at last. MacKaye, S.
Wonder-working magician, The. Calderón de la Barca, P.
Wonderful town. Fields, J. and Chodorov, J.
Wood demon, The. See Chekhov, A. Uncle Vanya
Woodstock. Anonymous plays
Words upon the window-pane, The. Yeats, W.
Workhouse ward, The. Gregory, I.
World a mask, The. Boker, G.
World and his wife, The. See Echegaray y Eizaguirre, J. El gran Galeoto
World and the child, The. Anonymous plays
World of boredom, The. See Pailleron, E. Le monde où l'on s'ennuie
World tipped over, and laying on its side, The. Feldhaus-Weber, M.
World we live in, The. See Čapek, K. and Čapek, J. And so ad infinitum
World we make, The. Kingsley, S.
World well lost, The. See Dryden, J. All for love
World's own, The. See Howe, J. Leonora
Worm's eye view. Delderfield, R.
Worst is not the worst, The. See Claudel, P. The satin slipper
Worst not always true, The. See Calderón de la Barca, P. No siempre lo peor es cierto
Would-be gentleman, The. See Molière, J. The cit turned gentleman
Would-be invalid, The. See Molière, J. Doctor's delight
Woyzeck. Büchner, G.
Wozzeck. See Büchner, G. Woyzeck
Wunder um Verdun. See Chlumberg, H. The miracle at Verdun
Wyt and science. See Anonymous plays. The marriage of wit and science; Redford, J. The play of wit and science

X

Xmas in Las Vegas. Richardson, J.
X
X X
X X
X. Hoffman, W.

Y

Y nos dijeron que éramos inmortales. See Dragún, O. And they told us that we were immortal
Yahoo. Longford, E.
Years ago. Gordon, R.
Years between, The. See Bernard, J. Glamour
Yegor Bulichov and others. Gorki, M. [pseud.]
Yellow jack. Howard, S. and De Kruif, P.
Yellow jacket, The. Hazelton, G. and Benrimo, J.
Yerma. García Lorca, F.
Yes, and after. Hastings, M.
Yes, my darling daughter. Reed, M.

Yesterday. Pau-hua, C.
Yo también hablo de la rosa. See Carballido, E. I too speak of roses
Yoke, The. Guinon, A. and Marnière, J.
Yōkihi. Komparu-Zenchiku
York crucifixion, The. See Anonymous plays. The crucifixion (York)
York nativity, The. Anonymous plays
York plays. See Anonymous plays. The birth of Jesus; The creation and the fall of Lucifer; The creation of Adam and Eve; The crucifixion; The fall of man; The judgment day; The York nativity; Resurrection
Yorkshire tragedy, A. Anonymous plays
You and I. Barry, P.
You can't take it with you. Kaufman, G. and Hart, M.
You know I can't hear you when the water's running. Anderson, R.
You must stay to tea. Block, T.
Young Elizabeth, The. Dowling, J. and Letton, Francis
Young hopeful, The. Fonvízin, D.
Young idea, The. Coward, N.
Young wives' tale. Jeans, R.
Young Woodley. Van Druten, J.
Youngest, The. Barry, P.
Your own thing. Driver, D.
You're a good man, Charlie Brown. Gesner, C.
You're human like the rest of them. Johnson, B.
Youth. Anonymous plays
Youth at the helm. Vulpius, P.
Youth must be served. Ford, H.
Youthful adventures of El Cid, The. See Castro y Bellvis, G. de. Las mocedades del Cid
Youth's the season...? Manning, M.
Yugyō yanagi. See Kanze Kojirō Nobumitsu. The priest and the willow
Yûzuru. See Kinoshita, J. Twilight crane

Z

Zaire. Voltaire, F.
La zapatera prodigiosa. See García Lorca, F. The shoemaker's prodigious wife
Zeal of thy house, The. Sayers, D.
Der zerbrochene krug. Kleist, H.
Ze zivota honyzu. See Čapek, K. and Čapek, J. And so ad infinitum
Zen substitute, The. Shiko, O.
Zoo in Silesia. Pollock, R.
Zoo story, The. Albee, E.
Zopf und schwert. See Gutzkow, K. Sword and queue
Zwischenspiel. See Schnitzler, A. Intermezzo